MIKHAIL GORBA
MEMOIRS

MIKHAIL GORBACHEV

MEMOIRS

BANTAM BOOKS

LONDON · NEW YORK · TORONTO · SYDNEY · AUCKLAND

MEMOIRS
A BANTAM BOOK : 0553 50636 6

First published in Germany by Wolf Jobst Siedler Verlag GmbH, Berlin 1995

Originally published in Great Britain by Doubleday,
a division of Transworld Publishers Ltd

PRINTING HISTORY
Doubleday edition published 1996
Bantam edition published 1997

This edition based on the translation by Georges Peronansky and Tatjana Varsavsky

Set in 11/12pt Times New Roman by
Phoenix Typesetting, Ilkley, West Yorkshire

Bantam Books are published by Transworld Publishers Ltd,
61−63 Uxbridge Road, London, W5 5SA,
in Australia by Transworld Publishers (Australia) Pty Ltd,
15–25 Helles Avenue, Moorebank, NSW 2170,
and in New Zealand by Transworld Publishers (NZ) Ltd,
3 William Pickering Drive, Albany, Auckland.

Reproduced, printed and bound in Great Britain by
Cox & Wyman Ltd, Reading, Berks.

CONTENTS

FOREWORD
by Martin McCauley

TO UNDERSTAND THE PROBLEMS MIKHAIL GORBACHEV FACED
when he took supreme office in the Soviet Union in 1985, the
situation he inherited in the country, his achievements and his
failures, the Western reader unfamiliar with Soviet politics may
need some assistance. For this reason the editors of this book have
added copious footnotes, a glossary, a chronology of the main
events during the period, and brief 'biographies' of the principal
characters in the story. In addition, this Foreword attempts to
provide the reader with the essential background to the political
struggles Gorbachev describes, beginning with an outline of
Soviet history. In particular, the Foreword describes the workings
of the Soviet state and shows how the functions of its components
changed over time. Gorbachev himself provides some further
background on pp. 139ff.

The October Revolution in 1917 gave birth to the Soviet state.
It took place in an underdeveloped country, and this had a significant impact on the nature of the state which emerged. The
majority of the population supported revolution in 1917, but what
type of revolution was it to be? The Bolsheviks, who had
launched the successful bid for power, were quite clear in their
own minds. It was to be a socialist revolution. Lenin, their leader,
was convinced that Karl Marx had arrived at a definitive analysis
of world history and that, by following his writings, the
Bolsheviks would succeed in building a new society in Russia.
This would be true not only of the Soviet state; the whole world

would eventually become Marxist socialist. A major disadvantage of Marx's writings was that they declared the inevitability of socialism but did not provide a blueprint on how to get there. To Marx, capitalism would inevitably collapse and socialism take over. Hence Lenin and the Bolsheviks used Marx as an inspiration but had to find their own route to the promised land.

Given the fact that imperial Russia was an autocratic state, only just beginning the process of industrialization and the move to representative institutions and democracy, it was almost inevitable that the new Bolshevik state would borrow heavily from the old regime. Russia, an empire, was a strong, centralized state, or aspired to be one. There was considerable debate among the Bolsheviks about the direction of the new state: should it be weak or strong? In October 1917 Lenin proclaimed that a new state had come into being, one ruled by soviets; hence it was called Soviet Russia and, from 1922, the Soviet Union. In October 1917 the Bolsheviks set up their own government, the Council of People's Commissars (Sovnarkom), and the division of responsibilities within it mirrored very closely that of the last imperial government. There was a people's commissariat for internal affairs, another for foreign affairs, one for finance and so on. To Lenin the key question was not administrative, it was who the official in the commissariat was. If he was a Bolshevik, everything would be fine. Lenin chose to be head of the new government and remained so until his death in 1924.

If the government was to exercise executive power, what was to be the role of the Communist Party (the name adopted for the Party in 1918)? Would it be consultative and restrict itself to providing ideological inspiration for the new government and state? There was certain to be tension between the government and the Party; how was conflict to be resolved? One of the striking features about the Soviet Union was that the relationship between the government and the Party was never defined. Which should be more important? This problem was never resolved.

The experience of the Bolsheviks during their first four years in power shaped the Soviet Union. One of the first problems facing Lenin's government was how to end the war with

Germany and its allies. This issue split the Bolsheviks; Lenin wanted peace at any price, Bukharin wanted revolutionary war, and Trotsky proposed neither peace nor war. Lenin eventually had his way when the Treaty of Brest-Litovsk was signed in March 1918. However, it had to be ratified. In a free vote, there was not a majority for ratification in the Congress of Soviets, the parliament, so Lenin insisted that Bolshevik members should vote to ratify the treaty not according to their consciences but according to the decision of the Bolshevik Party. This was democratic centralism in action, and discipline held. The Treaty was ratified. But it nevertheless underlined one of the problems of the rule of soviets: they would not necessarily do Lenin's bidding. Bolsheviks were often in the minority in the soviets. The onset of the civil war in the summer of 1918 brought to a head the problem of the relationship between the soviets and the Bolshevik Party. The soviets were directly elected and thus enjoyed a certain legitimacy. To the Bolsheviks their primary function was to implement central policy, but the soviets wanted to rule their localities. The situation became so desperate that the Bolsheviks became more and more dictatorial in order to survive. The first Soviet government was all Bolshevik, but in December 1917 Lenin bowed to pressure from within his own party to fashion a coalition socialist government which failed to survive the conflict over the signing of the Treaty of Brest-Litovsk. Hence from the spring of 1918 the Bolsheviks, a minority in the country, formed the government.

Lenin had not given much thought to the role of the Communist Party after the revolution, but the conflict over Brest-Litovsk and the onset of civil war drove the Bolsheviks in on themselves. Democracy within the Party was restricted because of the desperate struggle to survive, and democracy outside the Party, in the soviets, suffered the same fate. All the leading Bolsheviks in the government were also members of the Party Central Committee. The Central Committee became too large for effective decision-making, and so a Politburo came into being in 1919, consisting of the top Bolsheviks, most of whom occupied key government posts. Gradually it emerged that the Politburo was more important than Sovnarkom. Given a choice, a minister would miss a Sovnarkom meeting but not a Politburo meeting. Lenin hastened this process by allowing ministers outvoted in Sovnarkom to appeal to the Politburo. By 1921, at the end of the civil war, a pecking order had emerged: first, the Politburo, then Sovnarkom, then the soviets.

The Bolsheviks won the civil war because they were ruthless in pursuing their objective – victory. However, Lenin came to the conclusion that the Bolsheviks would not stay in power if they continued with the policies which had won the civil war. The most important problem was agriculture (about 80 per cent of the population lived in the countryside); the peasants wanted relief from forced requisitioning. In March 1921, at the Xth Party Congress, Lenin proclaimed the New Economic Policy (NEP), a retreat from full-scale socialism and the return of a rural market economy. He also forced through a resolution on Party unity which stated that decisions of higher Party bodies were binding on lower bodies. If a comrade opposed the decisions of the Party leadership he was guilty of factionalism and could be expelled from the Party. This also applied to members of the Central Committee; if there was a two-thirds majority in favour, the offending member could be expelled. This ban on factionalism was perceived by Lenin to be only temporary, but it remained until the Gorbachev era. It had a formative influence on the Party because it prevented debate and democracy developing. It also stifled initiative and the introduction of new ideas, which under this regime could emerge only from the top. This also meant that debates within the government on economic and social policy could be decided only by the Politburo. At the Xth Party Congress, Lenin introduced the doctrine of the infallibility of the Politburo. Inadvertently, he was shaping the power struggle which would take place after his demise. To dominate the country, one had to secure a majority in the Politburo. Since the Central Committee elected the Politburo, the necessary stepping stone was a majority there. If one had a two-thirds majority in the Central Committee, one could expel one's political opponents. Lenin had, without knowing it, put in place mechanisms which Stalin could skilfully use later, to the detriment of the Party and the country.

The Bolsheviks did not control the country before the onset of the civil war, but in 1921 they could expand into every part of the Soviet Union. Many officials were sent from the capital to rule in Moscow's name. They were called first Party secretaries and were responsible for everything in their region. Their main responsibility was to ensure that Party control in their territory was effective. In this they were aided by the political police, called Cheka in December 1917, and then under various names, the most well-known being the KGB, from 1922 onwards. The Cheka had proved itself during the civil war as the ruthless defender of Party power. During the New Economic Policy period, only the commanding heights of the economy (energy, communications, transport, heavy industry etc.) were in state hands, and light industry, trade and agriculture were in private hands. The mixed economy saw democracy develop in the country, but the Bolshevik goal remained a socialist economy. The struggle to succeed Lenin began before he died in 1924 and went through various stages until the late 1920s, when Stalin became the principal leader.

But the lack of unity in the Party leadership during the 1920s enabled Sovnarkom to play an important role, headed by one of Stalin's rivals. Stalin's power base was the Party apparatus; he had been made General Secretary in 1922. This ensured that there would be tension between the Party and government apparatuses during the 1920s. Should an aspiring young man or woman join the Party or state apparatus? It was not clear in the 1920s, but when Stalin became leader it became likely that he would give preference to Party rather than state institutions.

One of Lenin's tenets in introducing the NEP was that peasants could not be coerced into socialism; they had to join co-operatives voluntarily. The main reason for introducing the NEP had been the fear that the peasants would cease feeding the cities. What made it possible to end the NEP in the late 1920s was the victory of Stalin over his rivals in the fierce struggle to succeed Lenin and his imposition of firm central rule.

Stalin became head of government in 1941 and remained so until his death in 1953. His concept of government was to view it as the mechanism for implementing decisions taken by him and his associates. Who was to supervise the implementation of the plans? That function fell to the Party apparatus. Who supervised the Party apparatus and everyone else? The political police. Hence there were competing elites, all being juggled by Stalin to ensure that a coalition did not form which could topple him. Planning favoured the emergence of large enterprises and each one tried to become a monopoly. A ministry in Moscow was responsible for all the enterprises in its sector. A major problem for Stalin was to discover each plant's reserves and its true potential since each had a vested interest in concealing both in order to ensure a 'soft' plan. One of the tasks of the Party official was to collect such information and also to ensure that the enterprise fulfilled its plan. If it did not, both he and the enterprise would be punished. This system produced tension between the Party and the government apparatuses. Ministries enhanced their power during the Great Patriotic War (1941–5), when about a third of Soviet industry was moved from European Russia to the east. Local enterprises collaborated for their mutual benefit and Party officials had a vital role to play, ensuring that bottlenecks were eliminated. After the war, ministries consolidated their position as the economy expanded and the Cold War got under way. The latter increased secrecy and made it easier for ministries and enterprises to conceal information.

The massive task of introducing a planned economy in a country undergoing rapid industrialization and enforced collectivization of agriculture could not have been achieved by democratic means. The population would not willingly have voted to undergo the sacrifices of the 1930s. Stalinism ruthlessly mobilized the population in the pursuit of one goal, to make the Soviet Union a modern state and a leading world power. Coercion was endemic and millions of lives were sacrificed. The system was effective in channelling human and physical resources towards certain goals. Heavy industry had priority and light industry was neglected. The successful official was someone who got things done, irrespective of the obstacles. Mutual suspicion reigned. Citizens were encouraged to denounce others. Party officials, known as the nomenklatura, wished to become local Stalins, subservient to the master in the Kremlin, of course. If they reported success, they could prosper. There was the Party nomenklatura and the state nomenklatura and they were competitors. Stalin's sytem was effective but very wasteful. Since the decisions of the Party could not be criticized, conformity became the rule. If there was not an order to do something, initiative was inadvisable. Stalinism was very hierarchical and as the economy became more complex Moscow's ability to regulate it declined. Moscow attempted to ensure implementation of its plans by taking every decision and depriving localities of decision-making. For instance, the hotel menu in Tbilisi, Georgia, was set in Moscow.

Stalin left a flawed legacy. However, under him the Soviet Union was modernized, defeated Germany and thus became the leading power in Europe in 1945. By the 1970s it was a superpower, in direct competition with the United States. One can speak of Stalin being absolute ruler from 1934 onwards. He acted like a Russian tsar (ironic given that he was not Russian but a Georgian) by imposing autocratic rule. Stalinism is an amalgam of Imperial Russian and Soviet political and economic cultures. Stalin did not achieve total control, never being able to take over the private sphere, but he came nearer than any other Soviet ruler to achieving his goal. His concept of the state can be compared to a wheel, with the spokes being the efforts of the population to achieve the goals set by the master. The Communist Party withered under his leadership. After 1934 neither the Politburo nor the Central Committee met regularly. There was no Party Congress between 1939 and 1952. Stalin liked to use military metaphors. He talked of the leadership being the General Staff, Party cadres being the officers; the rest were the foot soldiers. His power structure was based on three institutions: the Party, the government, and the political police. Policy-making was concentrated in Stalin's inner circle and the dictator normally took counsel not in large groups, but in small functional groups. Ideology was simplified and to be learnt by rote. There was one correct view.

Khrushchev attempted to break the Stalinist mould but insisted that the Party should retain the monopoly of power. He also rejected any market-oriented solutions to Soviet economic problems, believing that full-blown communism (to each according to his needs, from each according to his abilities) could begin in 1980. After Stalin's death in 1953, Malenkov tried to reassert the importance of the government. Khrushchev's power base was the Party and eventually he defeated Malenkov and the other government-based opponents. His victory in 1957 over those who opposed his radical innovations, the Anti-Party Group, enhanced the role of the Party by according it the dominant role in the economy. Khrushchev came to realize that Party officials were a brake on attempts to improve economic efficiency; cadres were more concerned to increase their privileges than to increase economic efficiency. He split the Party into industrial and non-industrial wings and in 1962 introduced restrictions on how long an official could occupy his office. However, the nomenklatura, the Party and state elites, eventually rebelled and deposed Khrushchev in 1964. The main reason why this was possible was that Khrushchev abjured the use of force to resolve problems. His removal demonstrated the influence of the nomenklatura and under Brezhnev it grew in self-confidence. Brezhnev prided himself that his expertise consisted of keeping cadres happy. This was fine as long as the Soviet economy was growing but was fatally flawed when things began to go wrong. Also Brezhnev's own health declined from the mid-1970s, when he became increasingly dependent on sleeping drugs. The Brezhnev era was the golden period of nomenklatura. There was stability of cadres, in other words, posts were usually for life; this led to the rise of a gerontocracy. By the early 1980s most Politburo and government members were past normal retirement age. The Politburo was called the Presidium between 1952 and 1966.

If Party officials had become very conservative and resented change, the government was in the same position. In a non-market environment, the state being the customer who ordered and who bought the product, no company went bankrupt. Each Party official sought to attract as much investment to his region as possible and the enterprises and government ministries also wanted more investment and subsidies. The most powerful regions were those associated with the military-industrial complex, since they were immune to criticism, except from the Party leader himself. Various policy areas were no-go zones in the Politburo: defence, security, the military-industrial complex and foreign trade. The greater the secrecy, the greater the opportunity for those involved to run their own domains. In these circumstances privileged ministries and enterprises paid no attention to the interests of others and were, literally, a law unto themselves.

When Mikhail Gorbachev became General Secretary in 1985 he inherited a conservative Party, a conservative government and a nomenklatura which was not addressing the pressing economic and social problems of the moment. Kosygin had been frustrated by his inability to introduce significant economic reforms, and the same problems surfaced under Gorbachev. So many institutions had to be consulted in order to introduce change that the whole process had become cumbersome and lengthy. This style had developed under Brezhnev in order to ensure that decisions were implemented. Gorbachev introduced radical reforms and this disturbed the consensus at the top.

In order to comprehend the world in which Gorbachev operated, it is necessary to consider three institutions, the Party, the government and the soviets. According to the statutes of the Party, the supreme policy-making body was the Congress, which convened every four or five years (in the early post-revolutionary period, annually). A Congress was normally meticulously planned, with every speech checked and rechecked. It was like a play which unfolded before the audience, who were also participants. Between Congresses, the Central Committee was the highest policy-making body and it was an assembly which Party leaders usually took seriously. However, whereas under Khrushchev it met quite often, under Brezhnev and Gorbachev it convened only twice or three times a year, indicating that it was not the institution which ran the country on a month-to-month or day-to-day basis. That role fell to the Central Committee Secretariat. Its apparatus consisted of departments, most of which, by design, paralleled government ministries. Each department had a head, and each Secretary of the Central Committee supervised groups of departments covering his (rarely her) area of responsibility. Some Central Committee Secretaries were also members of the Politburo, and this marked them out as powerful men and potential future Party leaders. The relationship between the Central Committee Secretary and the corresponding minister changed over time. After 1957 the Central Committee Secretary was normally superior to the minister. The top Secretary was called the General Secretary, responsible for all the other Secretaries, and indeed the Party. Stalin was General Secretary from 1922 to 1934, but this post did not confer on him primacy in the Party and the state. He had to outmanoeuvre his competitors in order to become dictator. From 1934 to his death in 1953 he was referred to as merely a Secretary of the Central Committee, but this deceived no-one. Stalin was boss.

When Stalin died there was uncertainty about which institution was dominant, the Party or the government. Malenkov chose to be head of the government but Khrushchev, given the title of First Secretary in 1953 (this was retained until 1966, when Brezhnev reverted to General Secretary), eventually proved the victor. After his defeat in 1957 of the Anti-Party Group, the primary position in the state became the head of the Communist Party. This remained the case until Gorbachev was elected President of the USSR in 1990.

The supreme policy-making body in the post-Stalin period was the Politburo, consisting of the elite of the Party, government, security and armed forces. Until 1957 a majority of full members held government posts; after 1957 the majority was always made up of Party officials. In 1990 Gorbachev reformed the Politburo, with all those performing governmental functions leaving. The last Politburo consisted entirely of the Party elite. The Politburo was elected at each Congress and a comrade was, as a rule, first elected as a candidate member (he could attend and speak, but not vote) and then promoted to full membership. Gorbachev, in a hurry, advanced several supporters to full membership without going through the preliminary phase of candidate member.

There were twenty departments of the Central Committee Secretariat in the autumn of 1988 before Gorbachev began pruning it back in line with the decision to remove the Secretariat from involvement in the economy. He reduced the number to nine. There are several departments which appear often in these memoirs because of their significance in the management of the

Party and state. The general department worked closest with the General Secretary, preparing the agenda for Politburo meetings and providing background papers. The organizational department was responsible for cadres. The administrative organs department supervised the Ministry of Civil Aviation, the Ministry of Defence, the KGB, the Ministry of Internal Affairs, the Ministry of Justice, the Prokuratura, the Supreme Court and the civil defence apparatus.

Although the Communist Party of the Soviet Union was, in outward appearance, a federal party, each republic except the Russian Federation having its own Communist Party, in reality it was highly centralized, with republican parties expected to go through Moscow in order to discuss policy with another Communist Party. This rigid centralism began to break down under Brezhnev and did not apply under Gorbachev. Gorbachev was ready to accept a genuinely federal Communist Party, with each republican party autonomous and Moscow co-ordinating but not running affairs. The republican Communist Parties were headed by a bureau (except in Ukraine, where it was also called the Politburo), elected by a Central Committee at a Congress. Each also had a Secretariat and Central Committee Secretaries. The top Party boss was the first secretary. Meetings of the Central Committee between Congresses were called plenums, as at the all-Union level. Republics were divided administratively into oblasts and krais, with the latter containing within its territory an autonomous oblast, in which lived a non-Slav nationality. Hence Stavropol krai included a non-Slav ethnic territory. Oblasts and krais and cities were divided into raions. The Party leader was the first secretary. In these memoirs the first Party secretary in an oblast, krai, raion and city is referred to as the first secretary of the obkom, kraikom, raikom and gorkom. The backbone of the Party was the obkom and kraikom first secretaries, most of whom were elected to the Central Committee. Every Party leader after 1953 had occupied one of these posts. Gorbachev's decision to take the Party out of economic management in 1988 was a bitter blow to this elite, who previously had run their localities as their fiefdoms. In this sense Soviet politics was like Italian politics, where personal relations take precedence over law and state.

The Komsomol (the Communist Party for youth) mirrored the Communist Party organization, and it was normal for officials to begin in the Komsomol, prove themselves and then be promoted to Party work. Patronage was very important in the Komsomol and Communist Party. Rising officials gathered around themselves reliable and effective men and a few women, so that when they rose, their faithful retinue rose as well. Gorbachev's patrons were Kulakov, Suslov and Andropov. When Gorbachev became General Secretary he brought a large number of officials from Stavropol krai to work with him in Moscow.

State institutions consisted of the government, the executive, and elected agencies, the local soviets. The constitution stated that the supreme power in the state rested with the USSR Supreme Soviet, which elected the government and passed all the main legislation. In reality, the Party Politburo was the supreme policy-making body, the prime minister always being a member of it. It is quite clear from Gorbachev's memoirs that the General Secretary took precedence over the prime minister. Until the reforms of 1989, there was almost always only one candidate in elections to the soviets at all levels. The USSR Supreme Soviet met only twice a year, for a week in all, and rubber-stamped decisions taken elsewhere. Local soviets (all soviets below the level of the republic) were responsible for running local government but were subordinate to the Party organization. If the Party secretary thought the soviets were not fulfilling their functions he could take decisions for them and order their implementation.

The USSR Council of Ministers was the Soviet government, and each republic and autonomous republic had its own Council of Ministers. Some ministries were all-Union, in other words, responsible for the whole of the Soviet Union. All the key ministries were all-Union: the Ministry of Defence, the Ministry of Foreign Affairs, the Ministry for Medium Machine-Building (which produced atomic weapons for the military) etc. Many ministries – for example, the Ministry of Agriculture – were Union-republican, in other words, there was a USSR ministry and a ministry in each republic, all subordinate to the Union ministry. Economic ministries were powerful as they and the enterprises subordinate to them attempted to become monopolies. It became very difficult to reform them, as there was no market and all the high-technology ministries were connected with the military-industrial complex. They defeated Khrushchev's attempts to make them more accountable to the Party leadership, and under prime minister Kosygin (1964–80) there were no radical reforms. The overall plan was drafted by Gosplan, the State Planning Committee, which found it extremely difficult to promote innovation and risk-taking. Throughout the Soviet period, quantitative plan fulfilment was more important than qualitative. Under Brezhnev, the Party boss usually developed a close relationship with the KGB boss and also with enterprise directors, and this led to increasing corruption; republics such as Kazakhstan slipped out of the effective control of Moscow. Radical economic reform could not be carried through successfully if the government, industry and agriculture opposed it.

The most radical reforms of the Soviet political system since 1917 were implemented in 1989 and 1990. The essence of these was the transfer of power from the Party apparatus to the government and the soviets. The Party was no longer the manager of the country. Elected representatives became accountable, not only to those above them, but also to those below them, the electors. Competitive elections were introduced, first and foremost to the USSR Congress of People's Deputies (it is true, however, that 750 of the 2,250 places were reserved for social organizations such as the Party, which had 100 places – the so-called 'Red Hundred'). This was a super-parliament. The Congress, in turn, elected from among its members a USSR Supreme Soviet. It was expected to meet for about forty weeks a year. Like the previous body, it was bicameral: the Soviet of the Union and the Soviet of Nationalities. These institutions became genuine debating bodies and were parliaments in the Western sense.

Gorbachev came to the conclusion that an executive presidency was needed. The Soviet version, unique in Russian and Soviet history, was based on the French and American presidencies. The chairman of the Presidium of the USSR Supreme Soviet had been head of state and was sometimes referred to as President. Now the word *Prezident* was introduced to the Constitution. Under the President were two new institutions, the Presidential Council and the Council of the Federation. They were both consultative. The President nominated his Council, and the Council of the Federation brought together the top representatives of the fifteen republics. The latter was important in keeping the Union together and drafting the treaty for a Union of Sovereign States which would succeed the USSR. The USSR Security Council, dominated by the power ministries (Internal Affairs, Defence and the KGB), came into being. The Politburo began to meet less frequently and in July 1990 was completely remodelled, thereafter consisting only of Party officials from the Secretariat and leaders of the republican parties. The executive presidency was also accompanied by a radical shake-up of government. The USSR Council of Ministers was, according to the Constitution, subordinate to the USSR Supreme Soviet. Gorbachev wanted a government which was subordinate to the President. The result was a Cabinet of Ministers and a prime minister, a *Premier Ministr*. Gorbachev needed a body which could perform the function of manager of the state. It would be responsible for ensuring the implementation of reform. This was the USSR State Council.

The republics elected their own parliaments in 1990 and only Russia chose to have the dual system of a Congress and a Supreme Soviet. All the others made do with a Supreme Soviet. One of the consequences of these elections was that the new parliaments could claim legitimacy and spoke for the people. In Russia this led to the election of Boris Yeltsin as President, and in the Baltic republics the parliaments, led by Lithuania, made it clear that they wanted independence and therefore wished to leave the Soviet Union. This led to a system which can be called dual power, with the Soviet parliament passing legislation and it being annulled in some republican parliaments. More and more republics passed laws on sovereignty in defiance of Moscow. The key to the future of the Soviet Union was Russia, and Yeltsin's decision to go for independence destroyed Gorbachev's hope of a federal state to succeed the USSR. In hindsight, had Gorbachev succeeded in fashioning a Union of Sovereign States (the Baltic states would never have joined), the former Soviet Union would probably be better off today.

The attempted coup in August 1991 was timed to prevent the signing of the agreement establishing the Union of Sovereign States. It achieved the opposite of what it intended: the banning of the Communist Party, the emergence of President Yeltsin as a hero and, in consequence, the break-up of the Soviet Union. Many republics rushed to escape from the USSR lest another coup succeed. Gorbachev's adoption of an executive presidency and a government subordinate to the President has stood the test of time and has functioned in Russia and other states since 1991.

The USSR was sometimes described as a Party-government state. The main features of the relationship between the Party and the government are shown in the following table. The approximate equivalence of Party and governmental bodies is given at each territorial level.

Party	Government
Politburo (Presidium between 1952 and 1966)	Presidium of the USSR Council of Ministers
Central Committee (CC)	USSR Council of Ministers
CPSU Congress	Presidium of the USSR Supreme Soviet USSR Supreme Soviet
Republican (e.g. Ukrainian) Party Secretariat	Republican Council of Ministers
Republican Central Committee	Presidium of Republican Supreme Soviet
Republican Party Congress	Republican Supreme Soviet
Regional (krai, oblast) Party committee	City, krai or oblast soviet

Party	Government
Regional Party conference	No equivalent
District (raion, etc.) Party bodies	Raion-village soviet
District Party Conference	No equivalent
Primary Party Organizations (enterprises, collective farms, etc.)	No equivalent
Rank-and-file Party members	Voters

A NOTE ON RUSSIAN NAMES

Russian names consist of a first name, a patronymic (father's name) and a surname. Hence Mikhail Sergeyevich Gorbachev or Mikhail, the son of Sergei Gorbachev. A sister would have been called Anna Sergeyevna (the daughter of Sergei) Gorbacheva. Gorbachev's wife is Raisa Maksimovna, Raisa, the daughter of Maksim, née Titorenko. (Titorenko is a Ukrainian name, hence does not end in the feminine a.) Another Russian name is Rimashevsky (masculine) and Rimashevskaya (feminine). The latter denotes both the daughter and the wife.

Many Russian names end in *ov* and *ev*. This is the genitive plural. Gorbachev (pronounced Gorbachoff) has an *ev* ending because it follows *ch*. The stress is at the end, on the *ev*. He would have been addressed formally as Mikhail Sergeyevich, because the title *gospodin* (mister or lord) had been dropped in 1917 (it is now again in use in Russia). He could also be addressed as *Tovarishch* (Comrade) Gorbachev.

Most Russian names have a diminutive: Sasha for Aleksandr, Volodya for Vladimir, Kolya for Nikolai, Seryozha for Sergei, Misha for Mikhail, Nadya for Nadezhda, Tanya for Tatyana, Raya for Raisa, and so on. Children, animals and close friends are addressed with the diminutive. There is also Ivan Ivanovich Ivanov: Ivan (John), the son of Ivan Johnson. Donald MacDonald – Donald, the son of Donald – would be Donald Donaldovich Donaldov in Russian.

Ukrainian names sometimes end in *a*: e.g. Kuchma, but this is both masculine and feminine. As mentioned above, Titorenko is masculine and feminine. Some names end in *o*: e.g. Chernenko. This would be Chernenkov in Russian. There are also names ending in *enko, chenko, lenko*, denoting the diminutive: e.g. Kirilenko, little Kiril or Cyril; Mikhailichenko, little Mikhail or little Michael. A common Armenian surname ending is *yan*: e.g. Mikoyan (the stress is always at the end). Common Georgian surname endings are *vili, adze, elli*: e.g. Dzhugashvili (or Djugashvili); Shevardnadze; Tseretelli; Chekhidze. Muslim surnames adopt the Russian ending *ov* or *ev*: e.g. Aliyev, Kunayev, Rakhmanov, Nazarbayev.

Martin McCauley
Senior Lecturer in Politics
School of Slavonic and East European Studies
University of London
April 1996

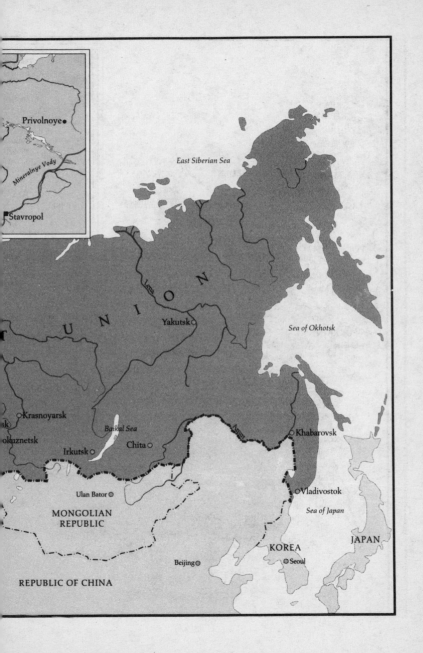

Privolnoye •

Mineralnye Vody

Stavropol

East Siberian Sea

U N I O N

Lena

Yakutsk ○

Sea of Okhotsk

Krasnoyarsk

Baikal Sea

okuznetsk

Irkutsk ○

Chita ○

Amur

Khabarovsk ○

Ulan Bator ◎

MONGOLIAN
REPUBLIC

Vladivostok ○

Sea of Japan

KOREA

JAPAN

Beijing ◎

○ Seoul

REPUBLIC OF CHINA

TO THE READER

IN OUR TIMES OF TURMOIL THE PEOPLES OF RUSSIA AND OF THE former Soviet states as well as people throughout the world ask themselves many questions. What has been happening to us in recent years? Was the development of our society bound to lead to this upheaval, or was it the result of the will of the people – good-will, according to some, or ill-will, according to others? What are the underlying causes of the events that, for the second time in our century, have dramatically changed the life of our country and have had worldwide implications? What does the future hold in store for us?

From 1985 until the end of 1991 I was at the centre of events. Now, freed from the burden of my duties as head of state, I believe it is right to tell everything I know and to present my views on the issues which are of such grave concern to my contemporaries. Needless to say, my comments will primarily relate to political matters, power structures, the new thinking, the reforms we initiated and the subsequent changes on the international political scene. Yet there is more to it than that. I am often questioned about my private life, the origins of perestroika, how, where and when the intention took shape to put an end to the totalitarian system in our country. I shall also turn to these problems.

However, this book will be not so much about myself but rather about the times and circumstances that shaped our generation, about the men and women who helped me gain insight into the 'mysteries of life and politics' and influenced both my character and my beliefs. Ever since my student years, I have had the opportunity of meeting many remarkable people. My almost seven years spent at the helm of state power were particularly enriching, and I am forever indebted to all those who actively assisted me in my work or provided moral support. I shall elucidate the role they played.

Obviously, there were adversaries. I harbour no grudge against them – certainly not against those who openly defended their beliefs and threw down the gauntlet, unlike the sycophants who eventually betrayed me and stabbed me in the back. Let history be our judge.

I have read and heard many divergent opinions about me personally, my convictions and my work. Fair descriptions of past events are interspersed with conjecture, speculation and even outright lies, which fall on fertile ground. However, there is no need to respond to slander.

In my early days as General Secretary, I wanted my plans to be understood. In these memoirs I write about myself and my efforts to explain my decisions and to describe the difficulties involved in implementing radical change during perestroika.

I want to avoid any kind of exaggeration or bias in my writing. I hope I have succeeded in this endeavour; such at least was my intent.

I do not necessarily justify all my decisions or actions. Neither do I shrink from the responsibility for the reforms I began, for I still firmly believe that they were vital for my country, with beneficial effects on the rest of the world.

As I worked on my memoirs, I was steadily encouraged and supported by my wife, Raisa Maksimovna. Her inquisitive mind and female intuition, as well as the fact that she was my partner in all the vicissitudes of life, were of vital importance in writing this book.

My warm thanks to all those who helped me in this work. I am especially grateful to those friends and allies who supported me during the years of perestroika and to my colleagues at the Gorbachev Foundation: A. S. Chernyaev, V. A. Medvedev, G. Kh. Shakhnazarov, V. T. Loginov, G. S. Ostroumov, V. V. Zagladin, A. B. Veber, and V. B. Kuvaldin.

I am sincerely grateful to T. P. Mokacheva and I. G. Vaghina,

my long-time assistants. Important work was accomplished by
L. N. Puchkova, G. K. Prozorova, O. I. Dubrovina,
S. L. Kuznetsov, and V. N. Mironova.

* * *

The idea of writing an 'account' of my life and the reforms had
been lingering in the back of my mind for some time. Towards
the end of 1991 this idea developed into an urgent need.

During those last dramatic days, events took a completely
unpredictable turn, with far-reaching implications for the country
and for me personally. One of the most powerful states in the
world, the Soviet Union, collapsed before our very eyes. The
people seemed almost to welcome the event! The Supreme
Soviets of the Republics rejected the Treaty on the Union of
Sovereign States, drafted by the USSR State Council under the
guidance of the country's President, and swallowed the poisoned
fruit of the Belovezh scheme[1] instead. The intelligentsia remained
silent. The media were thrown into disarray. My appeals to the
deputies of the Supreme Soviet and to the people, my warning that
the disintegration of the Soviet Union was fraught with dire consequences, went unheeded – society was bewildered and unable
to appraise the crisis. Destructive forces in the country exploited
the confusion, usurping the people's right to decide their own
future. It was what I had feared most of all.

Many of the issues hotly debated in 1990 and 1991 appear
clearer today. The promised unity of a common economic, political, defensive and, in particular, 'civil' space within the borders
of the Commonwealth of Independent States (CIS) has failed to
materialize. The present state of the former Soviet republics is a
cause of anguish to me: a crumbling economy, armed conflicts,
aggression, crime and a patent violation of citizens' and minorities' rights. This is the price to be paid for the reckless policy of
ambitious politicians who drove society and the state from the
course of reforms to the road of 'great upheavals'.

[1] The agreement by the Presidents of Russia, Ukraine and Belarus in December 1991
to dissolve the USSR and establish the CIS.

Time is a merciless judge. Eventually things will be seen in their proper perspective. The glamour of yesterday's idols has already faded, the acclamation of the crowds has turned to curses. It seems that there is a fledgling awareness of the dangers involved in falling prey to illusions; this is the premise for our recovery and the realization of our hopes. I am still firmly convinced that the reforms conceived and initiated in 1985 were generated by historic necessity. Once the period of trials and tribulations is over, our countrymen will learn to make proper use of the main achievements of perestroika – liberty, democracy and civil rights. Russia and the other former Soviet republics will find a way to restore their Union – not in its past unitary and imperial form, but as a democratic community of states.

Moreover, I contend that once the period of discord and disarray resulting from the end of the old bipolar system becomes history, the international community will be able to build a new world order and, by joining forces, avert the ever-looming dangers of war, environmental pollution, etc. The progress made in striving towards a nuclear-free world and global security by former antagonists will undoubtedly be sustained.

With these convictions and aspirations I invite the reader to accompany me on this journey.

Mikhail Gorbachev

IN PLACE OF A PREFACE

A transcript of the televised 'Address to the Soviet Citizens' by the President of the USSR on 25 December 1991

Dear fellow countrymen! Compatriots!

Given the current situation and the formation of the Commonwealth of Independent States, I am ceasing my activities as President of the USSR. I have arrived at this decision for reasons of principle.

I have always spoken out firmly in favour of autonomy and the independence of nations and sovereignty of the republics. But at the same time, I support the preservation of a Union state and the integrity of the country.

Events have taken a different course. A trend towards dismembering the country and the disintegration of the state has prevailed, which I cannot accept.

My position on this issue has not changed after the Alma Ata meeting[1] and the decisions made there.

Furthermore, I am convinced that decisions of such importance should have been made by popular will.

However, I will do everything within my power to ensure that the Alma Ata agreements bring real unity to our society and

---

[1] On 21–22 December 1991, when eleven of the fifteen former Soviet republics confirmed the decisions effectively abolishing the USSR.

pave the way out of the crisis, facilitating a sustained reform process.

Addressing you for the last time as President of the USSR, I find it necessary to state my position with regard to the path we have embarked upon since 1985 – especially since controversial, superficial and biased judgements abound.

Fate had decided that, when I became head of state, it was already obvious that there was something wrong in this country. We had plenty of everything: land, oil, gas and other natural resources, and God has also endowed us with intellect and talent– yet we lived much worse than people in other industrialized countries and the gap was constantly widening.

The reason was apparent even then – our society was stifled in the grip of a bureaucratic command system. Doomed to serve ideology and bear the heavy burden of the arms race, it was strained to the utmost.

All attempts at implementing half-hearted reforms – and there have been many – failed, one after the other. The country was losing hope. We could not go on living like this. We had to change everything radically.

For this reason, I never regretted that I did not use my position as General Secretary merely to 'reign' for a few years. This would have been irresponsible and immoral.

I understood that initiating reforms on such a large scale in a society like ours was a most difficult and risky undertaking. But even now, I am convinced that the democratic reforms started in the spring of 1985 were historically justified.

The process of renovating this country and bringing about fundamental changes in the international community proved to be much more complex than originally anticipated. However, let us acknowledge what has been achieved so far.

Society has acquired freedom; it has been freed politically and spiritually. And this is the most important achievement, which we have not fully come to grips with, in part because we still have not learned how to use our freedom. However, a historic task has been accomplished:

- The totalitarian system, which prevented this country from becoming wealthy and prosperous a long time ago, has been dismantled.
- A breakthrough has been made on the road to democratic reforms. Free elections, freedom of the press, freedom of worship, representative legislatures, and a multi-party system have all become realities.
- We have set out to introduce a pluralistic economy, and the equality of all forms of ownership is being established. In the course of the land reform, the peasantry is reviving, individual farmers have appeared and millions of hectares of land have been allocated to the urban and rural population. Laws were passed on the economic freedom of producers, and free enterprise, shareholding and privatization are under way.
- Shifting the course of our economy towards a free market, we must not forget that this is being done for the benefit of the individual. In these times of hardship, everything must be done to ensure the social protection of the individual – particularly old people and children.

We live in a new world:

- An end has been put to the 'Cold War', the arms race and the insane militarization of our country, which crippled our economy, distorted our thinking and undermined our morals. The threat of a world war is no more.

Once again, I should like to stress that I have done everything in my power during the transition period to ensure safe control over nuclear weapons.

- We opened ourselves up to the rest of the world, renounced interference in the affairs of others and the use of troops beyond our borders. In response, we have gained trust, solidarity and respect.
- We have become a major stronghold for the reorganization of

modern civilization on the basis of peaceful, democratic principles.

- The peoples and nations of this country have acquired genuine freedom to choose their own way towards self-determination. The quest for a democratic reform of our multinational state has led us to the point where we were about to sign a new Union treaty.

All these changes demanded utmost exertion and were carried through under conditions of an unrelenting struggle against the growing resistance from the old, obsolete and reactionary forces – the former Party and state structures and the economic management apparatus – as well as our patterns, our ideological prejudices, our egalitarian and parasitic psychology. The change ran up against our intolerance, a low level of political culture and a fear of change. That is why we have wasted so much time. The old system tumbled down before the new one could begin functioning. And our society slid into an even deeper crisis.

I am aware of the dissatisfaction with today's grave situation, the harsh criticisms of the authorities at all levels and of my personal role. But I would like to stress once again: in so vast a country, given its heritage, fundamental changes cannot be carried out without difficulties and pain.

The August coup brought the overall crisis to a breaking point. The most disastrous aspect of this crisis is the collapse of statehood. And today I watch apprehensively the loss of the citizenship of a great country by our citizens – the consequences of this could be grave, for all of us.

I consider it vitally important to sustain the democratic achievements of the last few years. We have earned them through the suffering of our entire history and our tragic experience. We must not abandon them under any circumstances, under any pretext. Otherwise, all our hopes for a better future will be buried.

I am speaking of this frankly and honestly. It is my moral duty.

Today I want to express my gratitude to all those citizens who have given their support to the policy of renovating this country and who participated in the democratic reforms.

I am thankful to statesmen, political and public leaders and millions of ordinary people in other countries – to all those who understood our objectives and gave us their support, meeting us halfway and offering genuine co-operation.

I leave my post with concern – but also with hope, with faith in you, your wisdom and spiritual strength. We are the heirs of a great civilization, and its revival and transformation to a modern and dignified life depend on all and everyone.

I would like to express my heartfelt thanks to those who stood by my side, defending the right and good cause over all these years. We certainly could have avoided certain errors and done better in many ways. But I am convinced that, sooner or later, our common efforts will bear fruit and our peoples will live in a prosperous and democratic society.

I wish all the best to everyone.

PART I

ROOTS

1

27 NOVEMBER 1978

THIS DATE IS WRITTEN ON THE COVER OF A NOTEBOOK I discovered in my personal archives. It is a momentous date in my political career. On Monday, the 27th of November 1978, I was elected a Secretary of the CPSU Central Committee at its plenum.[1] I had arrived in Moscow from Stavropol on the 25th. At noon on the following day, a Sunday, I was invited to a birthday party for Marat Gramov, an old Komsomol[2] friend and colleague from Stavropol. It was his fiftieth birthday and an ideal occasion for a reunion of friends. A small group of people, mostly from Stavropol, gathered in his apartment on the fourth floor of a new building on Malaya Filevskaya Street. Our Russian style of celebration on such occasions is well known: lavish parties, plenty of food, hearty conversation, jokes and songs. Moreover, this time it was a meeting of old friends. We started dinner with the traditional toasts. Everyone was in high spirits, including the host: what's fifty years? Nothing! Not even a halfway mark!

The toasts were followed by general conversation. Speculations ranged around the choice of successor to the late Fedor Kulakov as Central Committee secretary for agriculture. As a rule, we regional secretaries and members of the Central Committee knew who was 'coming up', as we used to say. Sometimes we were even consulted in these matters. Contrary to

[1] Meeting of the Party Central Committee between Congresses. There had to be at least two plenums per year.
[2] Communist League of Youth.

3

my expectations, there were no preliminary consultations this time.

We spent some hours feasting and by the end of the day we learned that Chernenko's office had been trying desperately to contact me all day. It turned out that Leonid Ilyich Brezhnev wanted to see me. Someone had telephoned the garage of the Central Committee's administrative department and was told that Gorbachev had called for a car and the driver had taken him to Gramov's home. When the telephone rang at midday at Gramov's apartment, nobody paid any attention to it. Gramov's son took the call, and, asked to call Gorbachev to the phone, simply answered: 'Wrong number' . . .

Hours later, a few minutes before six p.m., another friend from Stavropol joined the company and told us the entire hotel was in turmoil: they were looking for Gorbachev.

I dialled the phone number he gave me. It was Chernenko's office. 'The General Secretary wants to see you. We'll lose our jobs . . .'

'OK,' I replied, 'I'll be right over.' This seemed to reassure my interlocutor.

It should be pointed out that in those days it was customary to drink liquor quite frequently on various occasions. However, having never had a propensity for alcohol, I was in a fairly normal state when I arrived at Chernenko's office. Yet a certain, well, awkwardness was obvious, and I explained it away: 'A gathering of countrymen, you see, we got together for a while and had a chat.' Konstantin Ustinovich was not up to the joke. And he burst forth suddenly, without any preliminary niceties: 'At tomorrow's plenum Leonid Ilyich intends to propose you for election as a secretary of the Central Committee. That's what he wanted to see you about.'

A MEANINGFUL SUGGESTION

I was on fairly good terms with Konstantin Ustinovich at that time: in my function as first secretary of a krai committee, I maintained regular contact with him on issues important to us. I was looking forward to a frank conversation. But this discussion turned out to be unlike any other before.

We knew Chernenko to be rather uncommunicative; some called him 'the silent one'. This sort of person is often thought to be discreet and even modest, while men of a different character and temperament like myself may appear over-ambitious by comparison. Still, I prefer to deal with open people. I am always on my guard with the Chernenko-type 'quiet ones': their ostensible modesty may conceal the most unexpected traits.

I expressed doubts as to whether the decision about my election had been thoroughly considered. I added that although I was familiar with the situation in agriculture, I was not sure I would be able to do what was needed today for the rural areas. Chernenko listened to me attentively and made a peculiar remark: 'Leonid Ilyich assumes that you are on his side, that you are loyal to him. He appreciates that.'

My relations with Brezhnev were business-like and even-handed, but far from intimate.

I was going to continue the conversation but Chernenko interrupted me: 'If Leonid Ilyich arrived at this conclusion, there can be no further discussion.'

I saw that Chernenko had no intention of prolonging our talk, and I had to know when to stop. I asked whether Leonid Ilyich intended to speak to me before the opening of the plenum.

'I don't know. We didn't talk about that. He only asked me to convey to you what I have told you already.'

Chernenko was in a hurry.

I still needed to know whether I was expected to speak at the plenum.

'I don't think a speech by you at the plenum will be needed. Leonid Ilyich will propose your nomination himself, and the Central Committee will therefore back it straight away . . . Besides, you made a speech not that long ago,' Chernenko added sarcastically. This was the end of our conversation.

WHAT MADE THEM CHOOSE ME?

When in Moscow, I used to stay at the Rossiya Hotel. I have stayed at the Moskva Hotel only two or three times. I have often been asked why, as my rank 'entitled' me to stay at the Moskva. But somehow I got used to the Rossiya. My room was No. 98 on the tenth floor, with windows overlooking the Kremlin. Returning late at night, exhausted from the day's hustle, it was pleasant to find a quiet room, remote from street noise, away from loud drunkards and midnight brawls at the entrance of the hotel restaurant. The Kremlin was directly opposite. At night, especially when it was illuminated, it was more than just a beautiful sight: it evoked a very special feeling. Even years later, when the Kremlin became my permanent residence, I never became indifferent to its cathedrals and squares, its gardens and its park. I used to go for walks with my family around the area. We would sometimes drive to the Kremlin on state holidays to watch the fireworks.

I spent a sleepless night. I pushed the armchair to the window without turning on the light: before me the domes of St Basil's Cathedral were outlined against the night sky and the majestic silhouette of the Kremlin . . . God knows, I had not expected such an important appointment!

After graduating from university, I had worked for almost a quarter of a century in Stavropol, including nearly nine years as first secretary of the Stavropol krai committee of the CPSU. During this time I was able to do and to understand a great deal, but many problems remained unresolved. And it was not altogether my fault – more often than not the solutions were blocked by the existing order of things.

Once, in the early 1970s, P. N. Demichev had asked me how I would feel about directing the Central Committee Propaganda Department. F. D. Kulakov hinted at the post of USSR Minister of Agriculture. Apparently I had also been considered for the post of Procurator General of the USSR. Rudenko's state of health had seriously deteriorated and a suitable successor had to be found, which was an extremely difficult task, considering the criteria which were involved at the time in this kind of decision-making.

N. I. Savinkin, head of the Central Committee administrative department, later told me that A. P. Kirilenko had opposed my nomination because they had 'found an axe under the bench': in Savinkin's interpretation, this meant that they had other plans for me.

I declined all such offers. Obviously it was not merely a question of my sentiments. The members of the Politburo[1] had divergent views about me. From confidential conversations with some Central Committee officials I gathered that some people did not particularly approve of the independently minded secretary from Stavropol. As my friend Nikolai Karpovich Kirichenko, first secretary of the Crimea oblast committee (obkom),[2] used to say: 'Don't stick your nose out, or else you'll get smacked in the mug.' So nothing went any further than exchanges of views. My personal wishes mattered little in those times, anyway. The decisive factor, I think, was the view shared by the whole leadership.

Furthermore, the unfailing yardstick of one's status was foreign travel. Departments of the Central Committee occasionally invited me to visit this or that country as a member or head of a delegation. I usually agreed, but at the last minute someone would object. The explanation would usually be: 'You know, the leadership thinks that your krai is vast, hence, it isn't advisable at this time to pull you out of your work.' I was not unduly upset about it; I would just ask, tongue in cheek: 'Do those who travel abroad have so little work, or are they inveterate loafers?' Everybody laughed and that was the end of that.

But never mind the trips abroad, there were other more important issues to worry about. In all the years as secretary of a krai committee, from early 1970 until November 1978, that is, eight and a half years, I was given the floor only once during the Central Committee plenum debates and once during a session of the Supreme Soviet of the USSR, whereas many of my colleagues were given far more opportunities to expound their views. I found

[1] Leading body of the Communist Party.

[2] The Party organization in the Crimea was an oblast committee (obkom), responsible for everything in the Crimea and part of the Communist Party of Ukraine, which was, in turn, subordinate to the Communist Party Secretariat in Moscow.

ways of expressing my views publicly, namely through articles in national and regional newspapers and journals. I also had extensive discussions with secretaries of the Central Committee and with members of the Union and Russian governments.

In spite of our mutual good feelings my arguments with F. D. Kulakov were becoming increasingly frequent and heated. I remember particularly a discussion in the late autumn of 1977. It probably was engraved in my memory because this time we didn't leave it at an exchange of opinions. Ostensibly, it started with a specific issue – credits and guaranteed wages for the farmers.

'How do we grant credits?' I said. 'If a farm is inefficient and operating at a loss, then it'll get more: whereas if it's a well-run farm, it will receive neither credits nor building materials, only to be told "You have to look after yourself." Those with a potential for growth are deprived of our support. And what's happening now? Instead of letting the rural workers and the kolkhoz[1] or sovkhoz[2] either earn money or go bankrupt, we introduce guaranteed wages that make everyone equal. The rural population is losing its incentive to work.'

'A know-it-all, aren't you?' replied Kulakov. 'You sit around in your provincial Stavropol and you don't see further than the tip of your nose. Here in Central Russia, woods are encroaching on the farmland more and more. We have to offer the people a minimum to prevent the last ones from deserting the land.'

The comment about 'the tip of my nose' really got me going...

'If you consider the issue as an "urgent measure", you're right that we must help. But how long can we continue to "take measures", "save", "fight" for the harvest, for the cattle, for heads and tails? In the central belt, where precipitation and other climatic conditions are normal, the farms show the same poor results and the land perishes. Whereas in the past the farmer used to live, work and feed the country ... This simply means that we have to change our policy. You take pride in the 1965 March

[1] Collective farm.
[2] State farm.

plenum.[1] Yes, we should be proud of it: it was a major step forward to a political solution of agricultural problems, that is from the point of view of relationship with agriculture and farmers in general. And look what is happening now? The March plenum is a dead letter: the normal, mutually beneficial terms of trade between industry and agriculture have been disrupted. Hence, the farmer reasons: "If you don't pay me adequately for production, I couldn't care less about anything." Especially since the wages are guaranteed. There's no way out for you, you'll provide the credits and he won't pay them back because you are the debtor and not the farmer . . . Everything's been turned upside down . . .'

Kulakov responded emotionally. One could understand him from a purely human point of view: both in Stavropol and during his tenure as agriculture secretary of the Central Committee, he had been defending the countryside with all his clout, working hard to get tractors, combines, cars, spare parts and fertilizers for the farmers. And now to have to listen to such words, coming from someone like Gorbachcv! Without trying to control his wounded ego, he informed me that the next Central Committee plenum on agriculture was in the offing, but that A. N. Kosygin had been unexpectedly appointed to be the head of the Preparatory Commission instead of Kulakov, although Kulakov was a member of the Politburo and Central Committee secretary responsible for precisely these matters. He wasn't even included in the commission as a regular member.

I was taken aback. For it was Kosygin who in the late 1960s was responsible for the deteriorating terms of trade between the city and the countryside.[2]

'Why don't you write down what you have just said?' suggested Kulakov with a cunning smile. He was sure I would refuse to do so. But I agreed. 'OK, when do you want it?'

'Before the first of January.'

I worked thoroughly on the memorandum: it grew to

[1] Meeting of the Party Central Committee which took important decisions on Soviet agriculture.
[2] This meant that agricultural prices lagged behind industrial prices, so that those in the countryside paid more for their city purchases.

seventy-two pages. I finished editing the final version at 3 p.m. on 31 December and sent it right away to Kulakov. Kulakov studied it, showed it to Brezhnev's aide Golikov, and telephoned me some two or three months later:

'Listen, Mikhail, how about sending your memorandum to all the members of the Politburo commission?'

I replied that I had written it personally for him and that it would have to be revised for the commission. He agreed, asking me to do it as quickly as possible. A week later an abridged version of the memorandum was submitted to the Central Committee. It contained all the main arguments of the original. This version was then sent to the Politburo commission.

I remember that July Central Committee plenum well. On 3 July Brezhnev spoke on 'Further development of agriculture in the USSR', and then the floor was open to debate. On the second day of the meeting, 4 July, the USSR Minister of Agriculture, V. K. Mesyats, and the first secretary of the Central Committee of the Belorussian Communist Party, P. M. Masherov, took the floor. My turn came after the first secretary of the Amur oblast committee. It was my first statement at a plenum of the Central Committee, in my ninth year as secretary of a krai committee. I was determined to present in condensed form the topics drawn from the memorandum . . .

The atmosphere in the conference hall was usually business-like. Even when a speech didn't arouse the interest of the participants, they would still keep quiet, sometimes even too quiet. However, there was usually some background noise, whispering and the rustle of newspapers.

I went up to the rostrum. As I elaborated my arguments, an uneasy silence fell upon the conference hall. After an initial hush, I overheard comments in the presidium behind me.

I finished my speech and returned to my seat. L. Yu. Florentiev, Minister of Agriculture of the Russian Federation, an old friend of mine and a very wise man, whispered to me:

'All in all, not bad. But you should have listened to me: I warned you to keep mum about certain issues. They have become pretty edgy in the presidium.'

Why then did they choose me to succeed Kulakov only a year

later? What had happened? Chernenko's remark came to my mind: 'Leonid Ilyich assumes that you are on his side.' Did this imply that there was another side, and if so where was it, what was it like, and who was on that 'other side'?

I knew of the existence of different opinions on certain problems and disagreements among the country's leadership: but I considered it a normal way of trying to find the optimal solutions through discussions. Only after starting work in the Central Committee did I realize that it was more than just a divergence of opinions: it was due to the existence of different groups in the leadership and their infighting. Yet it was not a struggle between 'reformers' and 'conservatives'. No, they were all people of the same 'faith', loyal to the system. The rival factions were fighting for power. And Brezhnev was looking for support. Initially there were Grechko and Kirilenko, then Gromyko and Ustinov on his side, joined later by Andropov and Kulakov. Subsequently, backing came from Shcherbitsky, followed by Kunayev, Rashidov and Aliyev . . .

I am not mentioning the others who held lower positions in the hierarchy and who also supported Brezhnev. It seems to me now that the consolidation of the Politburo around the person of the General Secretary had in the long run a more negative than positive effect, with nascent new forms of Stalinism and curbs on democracy. Thus, the suppression of one faction by another was not as innocuous as it might have seemed.

After the death of Kulakov in July 1978, Brezhnev started looking for a substitute. First and foremost, he needed someone who would not upset the precarious balance attained at 'the top'. At the time I understood this but wasn't aware of a lot of things I was to learn later. Today, I can fully imagine the extent of discussion involved to recommend me to the plenum. There was the fear of making a mistake: the agriculture secretary holds a key post in the Central Committee structure, maintaining permanent contact with the entire country, with the first secretaries of the Central Committees of the republics, the krais and the oblasts. And the body of first secretaries represents the fief and the mainstay of the General Secretary. Thus Brezhnev had the last word in the choice of a candidate for this post.

THE 'ANDROPOV FACTOR'

In August 1978 Yury Vladimirovich Andropov, then head of the KGB, telephoned me in Stavropol.

'How are things going?'

'We're expecting a good harvest; it's a good year for the crops. And the general situation in our krai is not too bad.'

'When do you intend to go on holiday?'

'This year I thought of leaving earlier than usual.'

'Great! Then we'll meet in Kislovodsk.'

I didn't attach special importance to this telephone call. I considered it a confirmation by Andropov of our good relations, nothing more. Today, I recall that we met more often than usual during our holidays in Kislovodsk that year, talking less about Stavropol and more about the general situation in the country. Yury Vladimirovich was generous in sharing information and his views on many issues of foreign policy. I recall his comments on the decisive role of the 'Brezhnev factor' in maintaining unity in the leadership, and consolidation of the country and of the socialist states. Now I realize that Andropov's 'educational talks' with me were not without a purpose: obviously people at the top were already 'prying into my affairs', and he was briefing me accordingly. But to me at the time these conversations seemed to be just a continuation of a debate we had started long before, when I had openly confided my doubts to him.

This is how it had happened. During a discussion back in 1975, I made a blunt remark:

'Are you or aren't you thinking of the good of the country?'

'What a crazy question!' Yury Vladimirovich was taken aback, although he was used to my 'outbursts'.

'In the coming three, four, five years the majority of the members of the Politburo will be no more. They'll just die. They practically have one foot in the grave . . .'

It is noteworthy that the issue of the ageing of the Politburo had by then become critical: the average age of individual Politburo members had reached something like seventy. People were sick of the fact that many leaders, not excelling in any respect, had been in power for twenty or thirty years and were now, for obvious reasons, unable to attend to their duties. And nevertheless they all remained in the leadership.

Andropov laughed: 'Well, that's a harsh statement . . .'

'I don't mean you personally,' I said, 'but it is a real problem. Just look at many of the regional secretaries.'

Andropov argued that older men were promoted because they had experience and lacked ambition: they would do their jobs without pursuing careerist aims. Whereas the young think only of their career and how to get ahead . . . In short, the general idea was that 'an old horse can be depended upon'.

'That's something new in Lenin's teaching about cadres,'[1] I replied, half-jokingly. 'Up to now I've imagined that placing young cadres alongside the experienced ones is always a necessity: that this particular practice provides a synthesis, creates a felicitous blend. The older colleagues put you on guard against recklessness, while the younger ones watch out for stagnation and conservatism.'

Andropov dismissed my argument. 'This is all in theory; life is different.'

'Nevertheless, I agree with Lenin on this issue.' I was pushing on heatedly.

'I, too, agree with Lenin,' replied Yury Vladimirovich ironically.

'OK, forget Lenin . . . Remember the saying: "There's no trees without saplings."'

Andropov never forgot this remark about saplings or the whole conversation. But the country refused to accept the 'council of the elders'. Obviously, information about the public mood reached the 'higher echelons', both overtly and in another, more 'classic' form – anonymous letters and jokes. I remember one of them, which circulated later, after the XXVIth Party Congress. It began with the question 'How will the XXVIIth Party Congress be opened?' The answer: 'The delegates will be asked to stand up while the members of the Politburo are carried in.'

In short, those 'signals' reached both the Politburo and the General Secretary, and it bothered them. Thus, Kulakov's

[1] Personnel, staff.

13

replacement had to be relatively young. I suspect that Andropov 'had a hand' in my nomination, although he never so much as dropped a hint about it.

Another episode marked that autumn. On 19 September Brezhnev left Moscow by train for celebrations to mark the awarding of the Order of Lenin to Baku, the capital of Azerbaijan. He was accompanied by Chernenko. At each stop the local leaders came to welcome them. In Donetsk, Leonid Ilyich met the first secretary of the oblast committee, B. Kachura; in Rostov it was Bondarenko; at the Kavkazskaya station in Krasnodar he was received by Medunov.

Later that same evening the special train arrived at the Mineralnye Vody station. I, Andropov and the chairman of the Stavropol krai executive committee, I. T. Taranov, were there to greet them. The night was warm and very dark. The mountains were outlined against the sky. The lights of the city glittered in the distance. The sky was studded with those enormous bright stars which are only visible in the south. The silence was occasionally broken by the aeroplanes landing at the Mineralnye Vody airport. The train came slowly to a halt. Brezhnev emerged from the car, followed by Chernenko in a track suit. Taranov walked away after greeting the General Secretary. The four of us, Brezhnev, Andropov, Chernenko and I, strolled up and down the empty station platform . . .

Much was written later about this meeting. It became the subject of a lot of idle talk . . . It was indeed a rare sight: four men who in the near future were to succeed each other as General Secretaries of the Party!

Andropov and I had travelled up in the same ZIL car[1] from Kislovodsk to greet Brezhnev. We were talking as usual. Yury Vladimirovich dropped a seemingly casual remark:

'Listen, you're the host over here, so you should take the initiative conducting the conversation . . .'

But the conversation was strained: having exchanged greetings and the standard questions about health and my and Andropov's holiday, we all fell silent. It was almost as if the General Secretary

[1] Cars produced by the ZIL car company, Moscow, for Party and state use.

was not quite there and didn't notice us as we walked alongside him. The silence was becoming oppressive . . .

I had often met Brezhnev; I had been to his office to discuss our local problems on various occasions. He invariably showed genuine interest in my concerns and lent me his support. Therefore I was not surprised when he suddenly asked after this long pause:

'Well, Mikhail Sergeyevich, how are things going in your sheep empire?'

The Stavropol krai accounted for 27 per cent of all the fine wool produced in the Russian Federation. In early summer, after lambing, thousands of flocks grazed in the steppes: a total of ten million sheep. An impressive sight, I can tell you: truly a 'sheep empire'. I briefed him about our achievements. That year we had had a very rich harvest: over five million tonnes of grain, two tonnes per inhabitant of the Stavropol region.

Another question followed:

'How is the canal getting on? It seems to be taking so long! Are you planning to make it the longest in the world?'

I tried to explain what was holding things up. But Brezhnev fell silent again. Yury Vladimirovich was looking at me expectantly, while Chernenko was as dumb as a fish: he appeared to be some sort of 'walking silent recording machine'.

'And what about your vacation, Leonid Ilyich? Won't it work out?' I asked, trying at least to keep the conversation going. He shook his head.

'Yes, indeed, I should . . .'

Andropov joined in. They exchanged comments about Brezhnev's programme in Baku. Then there was another silence. It was obvious that the General Secretary was not inclined to continue the conversation. It was time to board the train. We went up to the carriage. Standing on the platform and holding on to the handrail, he suddenly turned to Yury Vladimirovich:

'How's my speech?'

'Good, good, Leonid Ilyich,' Andropov answered quickly.

In the car on the way back, I asked which speech the General Secretary had in mind. Andropov explained that I had misunderstood – Leonid Ilyich was having increasing trouble with speaking. This may have accounted for his silence, although he was by nature a sociable person. The meeting left me with an uneasy impression, while Andropov seemed pleased.

Another 'study' of me was made after the meeting with Brezhnev at the Mineralnye Vody station, when A. P. Kirilenko unexpectedly visited Stavropol krai. He was spending his vacation in Sochi and arrived by helicopter. We spent twenty-four hours together driving around the krai, visiting the observatory of the USSR Academy of Sciences in Zelenchuk and some rural communities. I told him about our problems. I was put off by his manner of picking constantly on every detail, whether it was relevant or not . . .

Seeing an agricultural machinery store, he burst into an angry diatribe:

'How many idle vehicles do you have there? You've grabbed too much machinery . . . Or do you intend to scrap them? You're getting too spoiled over here . . .'

He was in charge of the machine-building industry in the Politburo, and considered the requests made by the agricultural sector outrageous. His overbearing, hectoring tone got on one's nerves, while his inarticulate speech turned every conversation into an ordeal: it was impossible to understand what he was trying to say.

We disliked each other from the start, and this never changed. Kirilenko proved to be a power-hungry and malevolent man. Our relations deteriorated, reaching the stage of antagonism, and later led to a political confrontation.

But in spite of it all they chose me. Brezhnev was clearly afraid of making a mistake and hesitated up to the very last moment. This was the reason why our meeting had not taken place earlier. Brezhnev was very cautious in selecting his candidates for the leadership, it took him a long time to decide. However, once he made up his mind he never reversed his decision.

*　　　*　　　*

And so I spent that night at my hotel window, recalling many past events and experiences. Morning came, and it was time to go to the plenum. I thought it over once more and decided that if I were requested to speak, I would definitely mention both the situation of the people living in the country and the need for changes in the government's agricultural policy.

I left the hotel early to avoid meeting anyone. I didn't feel like having to explain anything.

The plenum opened at ten o'clock. The seats in the Kremlin's Sverdlov assembly hall were not reserved in advance, but everyone knew his place: some people had occupied the same seats for decades.

Everything happened as Chernenko had predicted. The meeting opened with a discussion of organizational matters. Brezhnev proposed first to elect the Secretary of the Central Committee for Agriculture, mentioned my name and referred to me. I stood up. There were no questions. The nomination was approved unanimously, impassively, without any display of emotion.

The plenum voted equally dispassionately to promote Politburo candidate member Chernenko to full membership, while Tikhonov and Shevardnadze became candidate members. Mazurov, a Politburo member, was relieved of his post, 'for health reasons and at his own request'. The entire procedure took no more than a few minutes: no-one took the floor, no-one asked a question, no-one voted against.

During a break in the plenum, colleagues, ministers and acquaintances surrounded me in the hallway to congratulate me on my appointment. After a little while I was invited to the presidium office, where the members and candidate members of the Politburo and the secretaries of the Central Committee had gathered.

I stepped into the office. Everybody was already there. Andropov stood closest to me. He smiled and made a step in my direction, saying 'Congratulations, sapling.' Kosygin came up to me and said quite warmly: 'Congratulations on your election. I am glad to see you here with us.' I went over to talk to Brezhnev. He was drinking tea and only nodded in reply. After the closing of the plenum I returned to the hotel, where I was already expected: 'A ZIL car is at your disposal and we have already installed a high-frequency telephone in your room. A

17

duty officer will take all your orders . . .' I could see for myself the efficiency of the services of the KGB and the administrative department of the Central Committee.

A CONVERSATION WITH BREZHNEV

I telephoned Raisa Maksimovna at home, telling her to listen to the evening news. The next morning, without invitation and not having requested an appointment in advance, I went to the Kremlin and asked to see Brezhnev. I really needed an audience with the General Secretary. I wanted to share my ideas with him, since I thought it impossible to begin my work without having done so. I do not know whether he wanted to see me or not, but I was ushered into his office at once. Leonid Ilyich was alone, sitting at a huge conference table. I sat down next to him and could not help noticing that he was in low spirits. This did not change throughout our conversation.

'I don't know how I will manage,' I concluded, 'but I can assure you that I will do my best. And knowing your concern for agriculture, I hope for your support.'

On my way to the Kremlin, I had intended to tell Brezhnev about some changes in the agricultural policy I considered necessary – but now I realized, or rather sensed, that this would be useless. Not only did he not take up the conversation, but he showed no response at all, neither to my words nor to myself. I had the impression that he was, at this moment, completely indifferent to my presence. The only sentence he uttered was: 'It's a pity about Kulakov, he was a good man . . .'

I was taken aback. After the meeting with Brezhnev, it dawned on me that 'It's really sink or swim for me now'. My heart was heavy.

I went from the Kremlin to Staraya Ploshchad ('Old Square').[1] Pavlov, the Central Committee's chief of administration, was already expecting me. My predecessor Kulakov had had an office on the fourth floor in the old building – not far from Brezhnev's

[1] The Party Central Committee building was situated here.

office on the fifth floor. The office assigned to me was a little further away, in the new building.

Pavlov gave me a detailed report of the 'perks' a Central Committee secretary was entitled to – 800 rubles a month ('same as Leonid Ilyich'), a special food allocation allowing me to order 200 rubles worth of food products (Politburo members got 400 rubles). Food and entertainment expenses incurred during my work would also be paid for by the administrative department.

'Suggestions concerning an apartment and a dacha as well as the personnel assigned to you will be ready when you return from Stavropol,' Pavlov concluded.

I decided to pay courtesy calls on the Central Committee secretaries – to have a chat and establish contacts, as we would have to work together, after all. I called on Dolgikh, Kapitonov, Zimyanin, Ryabov and Rusakov. Ponomarev started at once advising me on matters of agriculture when I visited him. Incidentally, he continued doing so until his retirement. Boris Nikolaevich was an 'amateur agriculturist': driving from his dacha in Uspenskoe he noted everything he saw on the way . . .

'Yesterday I saw a field along the road. The crops are ripe. It's time to harvest, but nothing's being done. Why?'

'Yesterday I went for a walk near my dacha and came across some ravines: the grass is waist-high . . . Why doesn't anyone mow it? What are they thinking about?'

This is the way it was – an expert in international relations did not shrink from giving expert advice on agriculture.

But what struck me most during my visits to the Central Committee secretaries was the attitude of the employees, assistants, consultants and legal advisers. I knew many of them fairly well. On my trips to Moscow we had chatted and joked dozens of times – perfectly normal relations, or so it seemed to me then. And now, all of a sudden . . . In every anteroom, I had the impression that I was meeting strangers. A certain 'distance' was maintained by everyone. The 'apparatchik' staff was drilled and disciplined, and respect for rank was an established standard in the Communist Party.

I convened the agricultural department staff, my new co-workers. The same thing happened . . . Only the day before they had been giving me advice and instructions and interfering in our Stavropol affairs. And everyone would add significantly: 'There is a view that . . .', without ever mentioning whose view it was. But now they all had a guarded look (watching 'the new chief'), full of anxiety ('a new broom sweeps clean'). To make things clear and to ease the tension I said straight away: 'I don't intend to reshuffle the staff. Let's continue working as in the past.' Everyone calmed down and we had a business-like discussion.

THE RULES OF THE GAME

Next I called on Andropov. It had been his idea to have a meeting. I had nonetheless the impression that he had arranged our appointment . . . with Brezhnev's consent. He started somewhat hesitantly, and the entire conversation was very different from the numerous talks we had had in the past.

'Mikhail, I would like to outline the picture somewhat to you. You see, unity is now the most important thing. And its nerve centre is Brezhnev. Remember that. Among the leadership, there have been in the past . . . how should I say? I mean for example people like Shelest or Shelepin, or Podgorny for that matter. They pulled in different directions. Well, we don't have that any more, and we have to reinforce this achievement.'

It was not my way to beat around the bush when talking with Andropov and I said frankly:

'Yury Vladimirovich, you know me better than the others, my views and my opinions. And I do not intend to change them just to please anyone.'

Andropov smiled . . .

'Well, that's good. It's just that I have noticed that Aleksei Nikolaevich has already started to court you. Hold your ground.'

So that was it! During the break in the plenary meeting, while I was being congratulated in the presidium office, I noticed Andropov's watchful eye. Apparently, Kosygin's remark and his confidential tone hadn't escaped him.

'Yury Vladimirovich,' I asked, 'I beg your pardon . . . but until now I thought that we were friends. Has anything changed?'

'No, not at all,' he answered. 'It's true, we are friends.' And Andropov was a man of his word.

Next I rang up Suslov and he invited me to his office. I had known Mikhail Andreyevich for a long time; he had very strong ties with Stavropol. In 1939 he had been transferred from Rostov to the Stavropol krai committee as first secretary. In the Stavropol region, people link his name with the end of the brutal Stalinist repressions of the 1930s. He told me once that the situation had been extremely tense: the initial steps he took to correct the 'mistakes' were opposed by some of the cadres. The conference of the Kaganovich district in Stavropol had adopted a motion declaring the entire bureau of the krai committee, which Suslov headed, to be 'enemies of the people'. But fortunately there were no consequences.

Conversations with Suslov were always short. He hated talkative people and had a quick mind, grasping the heart of the matter immediately. He disliked displays of emotion and kept his interlocutors at a distance, treating everyone with the same official politeness, using only the polite, formal second-person plural form of 'you' in Russian (*vy*). He made an exception for very few people indeed.

This time, he had summoned me to discuss my successor as the Stavropol krai committee's first secretary. Two personal files were on his desk. He asked for my recommendation and I gave it.

'Good, that's agreed then,' Suslov concluded, standing up. 'Now go and carry out the decision. I'll send you all the necessary documents.'

Soon afterwards I boarded the plane to Stavropol.

2

STAVROPOL – MOSCOW – STAVROPOL

I OFTEN FLEW FROM STAVROPOL TO MOSCOW – TO ATTEND central Committee plenums, sessions of the USSR Supreme Soviet, conferences and seminars, and on business trips to the capital concerning regional issues . . .

Initially I had to fly from Mineralnye Vody airport. But then (not without my participation) Stavropol airport was finally built, with a runway large enough for big aeroplanes. The pace of life was such that I was constantly trying to save time, and I considered those who preferred to travel by train to be work-dodgers – in fact, arranging an additional official holiday.

The flights as such always evoked positive emotions. I enjoyed flying. When the aeroplane breaks through the clouds on a rainy day or during a snowstorm and you suddenly find yourself gazing into the sun, you get an ineffable sensation of freedom and expansiveness.

This time I flew to Stavropol on a personal plane from the special aircraft pool placed at the service of the country's leadership, which I had never done before. The escorting bodyguards sat down in the other compartment and I was left alone. I leaned over to the window, waiting for the sensation of freedom, of life, that flying usually gave me. Alas, I felt restless instead. It suddenly dawned on me that I would be leaving Stavropol for a long time, if not for good. I was forty-seven and I had lived for forty-two years in this land. During my university years I had come home for every summer vacation (I didn't have enough money for another trip in winter).

Here were my roots; this was my homeland. I was bound to its earth, its lifeblood ran in my veins. I loved the land of Stavropol.

ORIGINS

I often heard from Muscovites, especially during my university years: 'You, in your province, live in ignorance, in a sleepy land. All peace and quiet.' They were convinced that the entire history of mankind was made in capital cities alone. But I knew that this was not so. And the history of my homeland was an excellent example of it – instead of a 'sleepy land', a peripheral province, it was at the juncture of continents, the crossroads of different civilizations, cultures, religions, the meeting-place of many peoples, languages, traditions and ways of life.

In the first millennium B.C. the Stavropol region and North West Caucasus were inhabited by tribes known to the classical authors as Meos and Sindhs, who according to some scholars had founded a slave-owning state on the territory of the North Caucasus. Scythians coming from the Dniester and Crimea invaded the region in the eighth and seventh centuries B.C. Later the land fell into the sphere of influence of Greek colonization. The Alani arrived here at the beginning of our era. They founded their own state, which endured for centuries and was finally devastated by the Huns. Christianity arrived from the Byzantine Empire approximately in the ninth century. The first Rus appeared in the tenth century A.D., founding the principality of Tmutarakan, with close links to the Kievan state. The Tatar-Mongol invasion began in the thirteenth century.

As the Russian state formed, the peoples of the Caucasus sought salvation from invaders by establishing ties with it. In August 1555 the envoy of Ivan IV, 'the terrible', Andrei Shchepetov, returned to Moscow from a journey to the North Caucasus accompanied by a delegation of Adyge princes. Ivan IV proclaimed the kingdom of Pyatigorsk to have come forever under Russian rule. The building of frontier defences for the Russian state developed rapidly. During the reign of Catherine the Great the so-called Azov-Mozdok frontier defence line was erected, consisting of seven fortresses. Among them was Stavropol. The first guards were Khoper Cossacks from the Voronezh province and grenadiers of the Vladimir regiment from Vladimir province.

Russian troops started pouring in. Cossack *stanitsas* (fortified settlements) were established. Peasants fled south from the bondage of cruel landowners. Later peasants were forcibly moved to settle on this land, and this compulsory migration resulted in many victims. Both my father's and my mother's ancestors arrived here in this way, the Gorbachevs from the Voronezh province and the Gopkalos from Chernigov.

My great-grandfather, Moisei Gorbachev, together with his three sons, Aleksei, Grigory and Andrei, settled on the outskirts of the village Privolnoye. Initially they lived together, a big family of eighteen. Their neighbours were close and distant relatives, all of them bearing the family name of Gorbachev. And if you asked a villager on his way there where he was heading, he would answer 'To Gorbachevland'. The family rule was strict and clear: Great-grandfather was the boss, and his word was law. Later, huts were built for the sons and their families. My grandfather, Andrei Moiseyevich, who had in the meantime married my grandmother, Stepanida, started living on his own. In 1909 my grandmother gave birth to my father, Sergei Andreyevich Gorbachev.

THE PAST WITHIN ME

The past lived on in legends and oral traditions, was part of the surrounding life – and I constantly felt that I, too, was linked to all the events that had taken place in this Stavropol land in times of yore . . .

I was deeply moved by the fate of the insurgents of 1825 who were exiled to these parts. The Decembrists were high-born officers who nobly and courageously defied Tsarist autocracy. Eleven of them were sent to the Caucasus. Later their number rose to twenty-five. Many of them lost their lives in the innumerable skirmishes with native hill-people during the Caucasian wars.

Behind the Decembrist officers stood the common soldiers of the Chernigov and other regiments who had been drawn into the conspiracy by the 'Society of United Slavs'[1] – sentenced later by the Belotserkovskaya court martial and deported to Stavropol. In seventy-five days the six companies of the Chernigov regiment marched over 1200 versts.[2] They passed through the Stavropol steppe and the village of Letnitskoye, where I was baptized in the local church by my grandfather, Andrei, who changed the name given to me at birth, Viktor, to Mikhail. The Chernigov soldiers passed through Medvezhe, now called Krasnogvardeiskoye, our district centre. My native village, Privolnoye, lies exactly halfway between Letnitskoye and Medvezhe.

Hence I regarded the Chernigov soldiers as my countrymen too. There were the ruins of an old fortress right in the centre of Stavropol. The plain ramshackle one-storey building, which once housed the garrison service quarters, stood for a long time. Pushkin and Lermontov, Odoevsky and other Decembrist officers and soldiers had stayed there. Unfortunately the building and the old marketplace were later demolished by municipal decree to make room for the central square and a large building complex.

MY HOMELAND

When people jeer at 'local patriotism' they tend to consider this love for one's 'little homeland' almost as a sign of provincial narrow-mindedness. Conversely, I believe that the perception of your 'bigger homeland', seen through your own and your ancestors' eyes and emanating from the destiny of your own native land, represents patriotism in its true meaning, its roots entrenched in your native soil – rather than being an abstract concept.

[1] One of the secret Russian organizations which was behind the attempt to assassinate Nicholas I. Five of the 289 arrested Decembrists (mainly upper-class military officers) were executed, thirty-one were imprisoned, and most of the rest were banished to Siberia.

[2] A verst was equivalent to 1.06 kilometre.

An important aspect of our patriotism is that it was not formed in a 'mono-national' society, but under conditions of an extra-ordinary multilingual diversity and 'multinationalism'.

Just as after spring floods a river leaves big and small pools along its bank (we used to call them 'mochaki'), migrations and movements of peoples over millennia had left in Stavropol a great variety of different ethnic groups. Travelling along our roads, one comes occasionally across words like Antusta, Dzhalga, Takhta (in addition to the usual Russian names) – which were originally Mongolian, or Archikulak or Arzgir – most likely of Turkish origin.

When I became President of the USSR and had to face the national problems of our country, I was not a novice in these matters. Apart from the Russians, who comprised 83 per cent of the krai's population, there also lived in the Stavropol area Karachais, Circassians, Abazians, Nogais, Ossetians, Greeks, Armenians, Turkmen and other nationalities.

Life in this multi-ethnic society taught tolerance and consideration and respect towards others. To offend or insult a hill-dweller was tantamount to making him your mortal enemy, whereas showing respect for his dignity and his customs was a sure way to gain a loyal friend. I had many such friends; even then I had gradually learned that it was not enmity but tolerance and concord that assured peace among people.

Today these words sound somewhat trite. But it is not a hollow statement. Both the history of mankind and the history of my native land are eloquent illustrations of this principle. The innumerable aggressive wars of history as well as the interminable Caucasian wars of our recent past have taken a great many lives. The civil war also left a terrible trail of blood in our area.

To those who learned about the revolution and the civil war from films and popular pamphlets, it appeared as a kind of grand sports parade – the workers and peasants on one side, the bourgeois and landowners on the other, marching in orderly ranks under red and white banners. But I knew that it was not like that. Society was split down the middle not only along class, ethnic or religious lines – families were split too.

The struggle went on with extreme brutality. Some of the

Cossacks, together with the 'newcomers' from other regions, joined the Red Army. But a significant number of Cossacks joined the ranks of the White Movement. It was a life-and-death struggle. In May 1918 a rebellion took place on the River Don and General Krasnov established military rule with the help of German troops: about 45,000 Cossacks sympathetic to Soviet rule were either shot or hanged. But the Reds, too, were ruthless: a great deal has been written by now about the horrors of 'razkazachivanie', the dispossession of the Cossacks. I recall one episode. It was the celebration of the anniversary of Soviet power, and the usual meetings with veterans of the Revolution and civil war were organized. One of the veterans, General Vasily Ivanovich Kniga, who had also distinguished himself during the Great Patriotic War (his native village was named Knigino after him), was asked to share his reminiscences in a far-off village in the north of the region. He hesitated:

'Will you give me an armed escort?'

'An escort? What for?!'

'Well, it's an old story,' explained Vasily Ivanovich morosely. 'We massacred the entire village during the Civil War.'

'What do you mean by massacre?'

'Just like that, we slaughtered them, and that's it.'

'You killed everybody?'

'Well, maybe not everybody . . . and I keep thinking: maybe someone is still alive . . . who would remember?'

I was shaken by this conversation. One could understand the struggle of two enemy armies in wartime. But this was different. How many villages had been slaughtered, rooted out both by the Whites and the Reds? They were exterminating themselves, their own people. Vasily Ivanovich Kniga was a professional soldier; they obviously perceive death differently, yet he had no peace of mind. Something must have been tormenting him, if he remembered the massacre forty years later.

Then and now I often happen to read 'profound' arguments that violence is not only justified but even necessary in the transition to a new society. It goes without saying that during revolutions bloodshed is, indeed, often impossible to avoid. But to look upon violence as a panacea, to encourage it in the name of some allegedly 'higher' aims, that is, to accept the slaughter of entire families, villages, peoples? No, this is inadmissible.

MY FAMILY ROOTS

My grandfather, Pantelei Yefimovich Gopkalo, accepted the revolution unconditionally. He was thirteen – the eldest of five children – when he lost his father. It was a typical poor peasant family. In the First World War he had fought on the Turkish front. With the advent of Soviet rule he received land. It was a family saying: 'The Soviets gave us the land.' From *bednyaki* (poor, landless peasants), they acquired the status of *serednyaki* (middle-class farmers). In the 1920s Grandfather took part in founding a TOZ in our village, an Association for the Joint Cultivation of Land.[1] Both my grandmother, Vasilisa Lukyanovna (her maiden name was Litovchenko, her forebears too coming from Ukraine), and my mother, Maria Panteleyevna, then a young woman, worked at the TOZ.

In 1928 Grandfather joined the CPSU (B)[2] and became a communist.[3] He participated in organizing our kolkhoz, 'Khleborob',[4] and was its first chairman. Whenever I asked my grandmother to tell me about it she would reply facetiously: 'Your grandad would spend the whole night organizing, but in the morning everyone's run away.'

In the 1930s Grandfather was chairman of the 'Red October' kolkhoz in the neighbouring village, some twenty kilometres from Privolnoye. I lived mainly with my grandparents until I started going to school. I enjoyed absolute freedom. My grandparents made me feel like the most important member of the family. Try as they would to keep me with my parents, at least

---

[1] Peasants cultivated the land together, but equipment and animals remained the property of the individual peasants. This was one of the predecessors of the collective farm, in which everything was pooled.

[2] The Communist Party.

[3] Throughout these memoirs 'communist' means a member of the Party.

[4] This was the name of the collective farm.

for a while, they never succeeded. I was not the only one who was happy with this arrangement; my parents and my grandparents were happy about it, too.

As a child, I still found vestiges of the way of life that was typical for the Russian village before the Revolution and collectivization. Adobe huts with an earthen floor, and no beds at all: people slept either on planks fixed above the stove or on the *pech* (the Russian stove), with sheepskin coats or rags for a cover. In winter, the calf would be brought into the hut from the freezing cold. In spring, hens and often geese would be brought inside, there to expedite hatching. From a present-day point of view people lived in wretched poverty. The worst part was the back-breaking labour. When our contemporary advocates of peasants' happiness refer to the 'golden age' of the Russian countryside I honestly do not understand what they mean. Either these people do not know anything at all or they are deliberately misguiding others – or else their memory has totally failed them.

On a bookshelf knocked together in my grandfather Pantelei Yefimovich's house, I discovered a series of slim booklets: Marx, Engels and Lenin. There were also Stalin's *Principles of Leninism* and Kalinin's essays and speeches, while the other corner of the room was adorned by an icon with an icon-lamp: Grandmother was deeply religious. Under the icon, on a little home-made table, stood portraits of Lenin and Stalin. This 'peaceful co-existence' did not bother Grandfather in the least. He was not a believer himself, but he was endowed with admirable tolerance. He was immensely respected in the village. His favourite joke was 'The most important thing for a man are shoes that don't pinch his feet.' Actually, it wasn't just a joke.

THE PURGE OF 1937–8

It was then that I experienced my first real trauma – when they arrested my grandfather. They took him away in the middle of the night. Grandmother Vasilisa moved to my parents' house in Privolnoye.

I remember how after Grandfather's arrest our neighbours

began shunning our house as if it were plague-stricken. Only at night would some close relative venture to drop by. Even the boys from the neighbourhood avoided me. Now I understand that one cannot blame them: anyone who maintained contact or simply associated with the family of an 'enemy of the people' was also subject to arrest. All of this was a great shock to me and has remained engraved in my memory ever since.

Many years have passed since, but even in my time as secretary of the city, the krai and the Central Committee – when I could have gained access to the records of the proceedings against my grandfather – I never managed to cross the invisible mental barrier to ask for them. It was only after the August 1991 coup that I asked Vadim Bakatin to find the records for me.

To begin with, the chairman of the province's executive committee was arrested: he was accused of being the alleged leader of an 'underground right-wing Trotskyist counter-revolutionary organization'. He was tortured for a long time to extract from him the names of other members of the organization. The man broke down under the torture and named fifty-eight people, i.e. the entire leadership of the district, including my grandfather, who was at the time head of the district land department.

The following is the record of my grandfather Pantelei Yefimovich Gopkalo's interrogation:

'You have been arrested on the charge of being a member of a counter-revolutionary right-wing Trotskyist organi-zation. Do you plead guilty?'

'I do not plead guilty. I have never been a member of a counter-revolutionary organization.'

'You're not telling the truth. The prosecution has at its disposal precise information about your membership of a counter-revolutionary right-wing Trotskyist organization. Give us truthful evidence in the case.'

'I repeat, I have not been a member of a counter-revolutionary organization.'

'You are lying. A number of people charged in this case testified against you, corroborating your counter-

30

revolutionary activity. The prosecution insists on obtaining truthful evidence.'

'I deny the accusations categorically. I don't know of any counter-revolutionary organization.'

The report bears Grandfather's signature. I have also seen the indictment, in which Grandfather was accused of the following:

a) he impeded harvesting operations and thus created conditions for the loss of grain. Pursuing the destruction of the kolkhoz livestock he artificially reduced the fodder base by ploughing up meadows which resulted in kolkhoz cattle starving;

b) he obstructed the progress of the Stakhanovite movement in the kolkhoz by repressing Stakhanovites . . .

On the basis of the facts stated heretofore he is charged with anti-Soviet activities: being an enemy of the CPSU (B) and of the Soviet system and having established ties with the members of an abolished anti-Soviet right-wing Trotskyist organization, he carried out their instructions of subversive acts at the 'Red October' kolkhoz which were aimed at undermining the economic well-being of the kolkhoz . . .

Bakatin also sent me records of the proceedings against Raisa Maksimovna's grandfather, Petr Stepanovich Parada, also a peasant arrested in 1937 in the Altai region.

Thousands of kilometres lie between Stavropol and the Altai, but the questions and charges were an exact copy of my grandfather's case:

'The prosecution has at its disposal sufficient information corroborating the evidence that you were engaged in counter-revolutionary agitation at the kolkhoz which was directed against the implementation of all measures and against Soviet power . . .'

31

'I was never engaged in counter-revolutionary agitation at the kolkhoz and I plead not guilty.'

'Remaining in the kolkhoz after your exclusion from the kolkhoz, you systematically agitated both among the kolkhoz and the factory workers against the Soviet system, against collectivization, against the Stakhanovite movement, thereby trying to undermine the working discipline in the kolkhoz.'

'I have never spoken out against the Soviet regime as I have never spoken out or agitated against collectivization.'

These are excerpts from the interrogation record of P. S. Parada dated 3 August 1937. It's very similar, is it not? But the two cases had a different outcome. The prosecutor confirmed the indictment against the peasant Parada. In accordance with the decision of a special three-member committee, commonly known as a 'troika', Petr Stepanovich was executed. Raisa Maksimovna's family did not receive a certificate of his rehabilitation until January 1988.

The case of my grandfather Gopkalo fortunately had another ending. The proceedings against him lasted fourteen months. The indictment was sent to Stavropol in September 1938. Some bureaucrat from the prosecution scribbled 'I agree with the indictment' on the file. But the assistant krai prosecutor wrote that he could not find evidence to charge Grandfather under article 58, which in those times meant certain death. He proposed to apply article 109, the lesser charge of official misconduct. At the same time a purge of the secret police, NKVD,[1] was unleashed, the head of our regional department committed suicide, and in December 1938 Grandfather was released from prison. He returned to Privolnoye and was re-elected chairman of the kolkhoz in 1939.

I remember well the winter evening when Grandfather returned home. His closest relatives sat around the hand-planed rustic

---

[1] People's Commissariat of Internal Affairs; at that time the political police (later KGB) were merged with the commissariat.

table and Pantelei Yefimovich recounted all that had been done to him.

Trying to get him to confess, the investigator blinded him with a glaring lamp, beat him unmercifully, broke his arms by squeezing them in the door. When these 'standard' tortures proved futile, they invented a new one: they put a wet sheepskin coat on him and sat him on a hot stove. Pantelei Yefimovich endured this too, as well as much else.

Those who were imprisoned with him later told me that all the inmates of the prison cell tried to revive him after the inter-rogation sessions. Pantelei Yefimovich recounted all this just once – that very evening. Nobody ever heard him speak about it afterwards. He was convinced that Stalin did not know about the misdeeds of the NKVD and he never blamed the Soviet regime for his misfortunes. Grandfather did not live long. He died at the age of fifty-nine.

My other grandfather, Andrei Moiseyevich Gorbachev, had fought on the western front in the First World War, and there is a photograph of him from that time, wearing a beautiful service cap with a badge, handsomely astride a black horse. 'What kind of uniform is that?' I used to ask. But Grandfather, bent with age though still wiry and lean, only brushed me aside. In those times this kind of photograph was easily made: a screen showed a dashing cavalier upon his horse and there was a hole cut out for the head. You just had to stick your head through the hole.

Grandfather Andrei's fate was tragic, indeed, but at the same time characteristic of our peasantry. He left his father's home to start farming on his own. The family was growing: six children were born. As ill-luck would have it they had only two sons, and the village commune distributed the land only to males. They had to get as much as they could from their plot of farmland, and the entire family, young and old, would toil day and night on the farm. Grandfather Andrei was stern and unyielding at work, both towards himself and to family members. But the labour did not always produce the expected results, as drought often followed drought. *Bednyaki* to begin with, they gradually climbed to the social status of *serednyaki*.

In 1929 the eldest son, Sergei, my father, married the

neighbour's daughter Gopkalo. The young couple lived for a while at grandfather Andrei's house, but they soon went off on their own. The land had to be divided, too. Grandfather rejected the collectivization and remained on his own, an individual peasant.

In 1933 famine struck the Stavropol region. Historians still argue about its causes: was it deliberately planned in order to break the back of the peasantry or could it be attributed to climatic conditions? I do not know about other regions, but we suffered that year from drought. But this was not the only reason. Mass collectivization had undermined the old way of life, destroying the customary pattern of farming and sustenance in the countryside.

The famine was terrible. A third, if not half, of the population of Privolnoye died of hunger. Entire families were dying, and the half-ruined ownerless huts would remain deserted for years.

Three of Andrei's children died of hunger. And he was arrested in spring 1934 for not having fulfilled the sowing plan – established by the government for individual peasants. But no seeds were available to fulfil the plan. Grandfather Andrei was declared a 'saboteur' and sent to fell trees at a forced labour camp in the Irkutsk region. My grandmother Stepanida was left alone with two children, Anastasiya and Aleksandra. My father had to shoulder all the duties by himself, as the family were 'non-persons' of sorts. Grandfather Andrei worked well at the camp, and they released him two years later, in 1935, before the end of his term. He returned to Privolnoye bearing two letters of appreciation for his work and joined the kolkhoz immediately. He knew how to work hard: soon he was managing the kolkhoz pig farm, which always ranked first in the region. Grandfather started receiving honorary certificates again . . .

Shortly before the war life started to return to normal more or less. Both grandfathers were back home. The shops had calico and paraffin to sell. The kolkhoz began distributing grain as payment for the work-days.[1] Grandfather Pantelei replaced the

[1] Labour on the collective farm was measured in work-days. A tractor driver, for instance, received many more work-days for one day's work than an ordinary labourer. A collective farm did not offer a guaranteed wage but paid only at the end of the harvest; and if the farm had made a loss there were no wages.

thatched roof with tiles. Gramophones appeared in the shops. On rare occasions, 'silent' movies would be shown on portable film projectors. And the height of bliss for us children would be the ice cream brought to the village now and then. The families spent Sunday, their day off, in the woods. The men would sing languid Russian and Ukrainian songs, drink vodka and sometimes fight. The children played ball, the women exchanged news and watched over husbands and children.

On one of these Sundays, on the morning of 22 June 1941, we had terrifying news: the Germans had invaded. All the inhabitants of Privolnoye gathered at the village soviet council, where a radio had been installed, and listened with bated breath to Molotov's speech . . .

THE WAR

Wartime impressions and experiences remain engraved in my mind. I remember how the village was drained of its inhabitants within weeks – all the men had gone. My father's conscription, along with that of the other machine-operators, was deferred for the harvest season, but his call-up finally arrived in August. The order was delivered in the evening, and preparations were made during the night. In the morning we put his few possessions on a cart and set out for the district centre twenty kilometres away. Entire families would accompany their men, profusely shedding tears and voicing parting wishes all the way. We said goodbye at the district centre. Women, children and old men cried their hearts out, the weeping merging into one heart-rending wail of sorrow. My father bought me an ice cream for the last time, and a balalaika for a keepsake.

The mobilization was over by autumn. There remained in our village women, children, the old and those men too ill or disabled to go to war. Now the conscription papers were replaced by 'killed in battle' notices.

At home the only newspaper we received was *Pravda*. Father subscribed to it. I was reading it now. And I read it aloud in the evenings to the women, reporting the bad news to them. Town after town fell to the enemy. The first evacuees arrived in our parts. Before the war we boys had used to sing spunky songs, repeating enthusiastically 'We don't covet a single inch of foreign land, but we won't yield an inch of our own'. We believed that the Nazis would soon be defeated. But by autumn the enemy was nearing Moscow and Rostov.

The first wartime winter came early and was particularly severe. I've never experienced such a winter in my entire life. The first snow fell on 8 October – in our southern parts a most exceptional phenomenon. And what a snowfall it was! The village was snowbound, buried under a thick white layer. Some huts, including the outbuildings, the cattle and the fowl, were invisible under the snowdrifts. Those able to leave their house shovelled passages and tunnels to come to the rescue of their neighbours.

The snow did not melt until spring – a 'kingdom of snow', indeed. But it was very hard to survive in this kingdom. The heavy snowfalls disrupted communication. Post was seldom delivered. There were no radios in the village. The rare newspapers were read and re-read by everyone in turn. Late in the evening the women would gather at someone's home to spend time together, have a chat, discuss the news and read their husbands' letters. These encounters helped them to keep going. But often they would break out in a flood of tears – and one would feel unbearable terror.

I remember well our jubilation at hearing the news that Moscow had thwarted the enemy attacks and that the Germans had been driven back. Once a booklet called *Tanya* was included in an issue of *Pravda*. It was the story of the partisan girl Zoya Kosmodemyanskaya. I read it aloud to the gathering. The listeners were shaken to the core by the cruelty of the Germans and deeply impressed by the courage of the Komsomol girl.

Since Father had left for the front, I had to take care of a multitude of household chores. In the spring of 1942 I also worked in the vegetable patch which provided food for the family. Later my main duty consisted in stocking up on hay for the cow and on fuel for the house. Our way of life had changed completely. And we, the wartime children, skipped from childhood directly into adulthood.

Towards the end of summer 1942 a wave of refugees from Rostov passed through our region. The people dragged themselves along, some carrying knapsacks or kit-bags, others pushing prams or handcarts, exchanging their goods for food. Herds of cows and horses as well as flocks of sheep were driven back from the advancing Germans.

Grandmother Vasilisa and grandfather Pantelei packed up their belongings and left for an unknown destination. The fuel tanks at the rural oil base were drained; all the fuel poured out into the shallow River Egorlyk. The crops in the field were set on fire.

On 27 July 1942 our troops withdrew from Rostov. It was a hurried retreat. Tired, glum soldiers passed through, their faces marked by sorrow and guilt. The explosions, the roar of heavy guns and the sound of shooting were approaching – as if circumventing Privolnoye on both sides. Together with the neighbours we dug out a trench in the river embankment and for the first time I saw the volley of the Katyusha guns: fiery arrows crossing the skies with a frightening whistling sound . . .

Suddenly there was an uncanny silence. Two days of silence. Neither our troops nor the Germans were to be seen. And on the third day, coming from Rostov, German motorcyclists burst into the village. Soon German infantry marched into our village. Within three days the Germans had crowded Privolnoye. They started camouflaging themselves against the air raids and uprooted the orchards which had taken decades to cultivate.

Grandmother Vasilisa returned a few days later together with Grandfather. They had nearly reached Stavropol but had been outdone by the German tanks: the city was taken on 5 August 1942. Grandfather had decided to cross the front line while Grandmother returned home to us with her belongings – where else could she go?

The Germans advanced from Rostov to Nalchik without meeting any serious resistance. Our troops were in disarray. Special detachments operated past Nalchik, their task being to carry out Stalin's order 'not a step backward'. They acted resolutely, organizing the retreating troops into units which were sent right back to the front line. As a result of such extreme effort, the advancing German troops, which were desperately trying to

reach the Baku oil fields, were finally stopped at Ordzhonikidze
– for good, as it turned out.

When the German troops continued on their eastward push,
they left a small garrison in Privolnoye, which was later replaced
by some unit: I recall only insignia on their sleeves and that they
spoke Ukrainian. Thus began life under occupation.

The first thing that happened was that the deserters from the
Red Army who had hidden for months in cellars had resurfaced.
Many joined the Germans, usually the police force. Policemen
turned up unexpectedly after Grandmother's return. They
searched our place, turning everything upside down. I don't
know what they were looking for. Then they got into a horse-
drawn carriage, ordering Grandmother to follow them on foot to
the police station. They questioned her there. What could she
say? That her husband was a communist, chairman of the
kolkhoz, and that both her son and son-in-law were in the Red
Army. Everybody knew that anyway. Mother did not flinch
during the search and arrest. Her courage was due not only to
her character – she was a strong woman – but grew out of
despair at not knowing how all this would end . . . The family
was in danger. Coming home from a day's forced labour, she
would often tell us how some of the villagers openly threatened
her, saying, 'Wait, your turn will come . . . This is very different from the Reds.' Rumours of mass executions in the
neighbouring towns circulated, and of machines that poisoned
people with gas (all of this was confirmed after the liberation;
thousands of people, mostly Jews, were shot in the city of
Mineralnye Vody); also of an impending massacre of communist families. We knew that our family would be at the top of the
list. Grandmother and Mother hid me on a farm outside the village. The massacre was supposedly planned for 26 January
1943, but five days before that our troops liberated Privolnoye.

The German occupation lasted for four and a half months. The
Germans appointed the aged Savvaty Zaitsev, 'Grandad Savka',
as village elder. He firmly resisted the appointment but eventually the villagers persuaded him to accept it: at least he was one
of us. Everyone in the village knew that Zaitsev would do all he
could to protect the people. After the Germans were driven out

he was sentenced to ten years for 'high treason'. The villagers wrote scores of letters explaining that he had served the occupiers against his will and that many of us owed our survival to him, but nothing helped. Grandad Savka died in prison as an 'enemy of the people'.

Still, we were saved by the advance of the Red Army. We learned from the Germans themselves of the total defeat of the German troops at Stalingrad. Soon their armies, fearing another encirclement, retreated from North Caucasus. How jubilantly we welcomed the Red Army units!

The battle front passed once more through our area, this time moving westwards. Life had to be reorganized; we had to rebuild the kolkhoz. But how? Everything had been destroyed; no machines were left, no cattle, no seeds. Spring came. We ploughed the land by hitching cows from our individual households. The picture is still fresh in my memory, the women crying and the sad eyes of the cows.

In winter and spring 1944 famine broke out. We survived, thanks to Mother's efforts and to a stroke of luck. In early spring, when the roads were nearly impassable, she (then aged thirty-three) and a few other villagers hitched the two remaining bulls to a cart and set out for the Kuban region, where rumour had it there was a maize harvest. Mother took out Father's belongings from their peasant trunk, two pairs of new box-calf boots and a suit he had never worn, to exchange them for corn. It turned out that Father's clothes had a good exchange value and Mother got a sack of corn for them, three poods or about 109 pounds. We were truly saved!

Later, like God's gift and to everybody's delight, the rains came. And everything in the fields and in the vegetable gardens sprouted. Once again, the earth had saved us.

Practically no goods were delivered to our village. Neither machines, nor clothes, shoes, salt, soap, paraffin lamps nor matches . . .

First, we learned how to mend our footwear and clothing. When these patched and mended rags had completely disintegrated, we found another solution: we started growing hemp. We harvested it by hand, tied it into sheaves, retted it in the river, then dried and scutched it to get the rough thread. Old hand-operated looms would be brought down from the attics, and in nearly every hut people would weave and bleach the fabric. This was then used to make shirts, the collars embroidered with black thread for decoration. Such a shirt felt as if it was made of wood.

We washed and combed the sheep's wool, and spun the thread on spindles to weave a simple coarse cloth for outer garments. The fermented and depilated hides were dried, kneaded and impregnated with petroleum to make rudimentary footwear. Salt was obtained from the Salt Lake, fifty kilometres from Privolnoye. In some mysterious way people managed to get sal soda for making soap. Fire was produced by striking sparks from flint and kindling ash-impregnated cotton, and 'matches' with TNT from antitank bombs. For lighting we used lamps made out of shell cases. When paraffin appeared in the village, we started making new lamps. We had to learn everything from scratch and I became very good at it. Now I sometimes wonder whether I could go through it all over again.

In late summer 1944 a strange letter arrived from the battle front. We opened the envelope. It contained documents, family photographs Father had taken with him to the front, and a short notice saying that Sergeant-Major Sergei Gorbachev had fallen in battle in the Carpathians on the Magura Mountain . . .

By that time, my father already had much wartime experience. When I became President of the USSR, Defence Minister D. T. Yazov made me a unique present: a book on the history of the army units in which my father had served during the war. It was with great emotion that I read this wartime story, and it gave me a clearer and more profound insight into the arduous road to victory and the heavy price our people had paid for it.

I had learned a great deal about Father's wartime experiences from him, and now I had this document in front of me. His baptism of fire came as early as November–December 1941, during the Battle of Rostov, in a unit of the 56th Army of the Transcaucasian front. The losses of the brigade in which he served were terrible: 440 soldiers killed, 120 wounded, and 651 missing. Father survived. Until March 1942 they held the defence line along the River Myass. Again the casualties were very heavy. The brigade was sent to Michurinsk, where it was integrated into the 161st Rifle Division and sent to the Voronezh front to join the 60th Army.

He could have been killed dozens of times. The division participated in the Battle of Kursk, in the operations at Ostrogozhsk-Rossoshansk and Kharkov, in the forcing of the Dnieper in the region of Pereyaslav-Khemlnitsky and in the defence of the famous Bukrinsk bridgehead.

Father told us later how they crossed the Dnieper in small fishing boats, under relentless bombardments and gunfire, as well as by 'ingenious means' – home-made rafts and ferryboats. He commanded a pioneer unit charged with the transport of mortars on one of those ferryboats.

Father was awarded the Medal of Valour for the Dnieper operation, and he was very proud of it, although later other awards were conferred upon him, including two Orders of the Red Star. In November–December 1943 his division participated in the Kiev operation; in April 1944 in the Proskurov-Chernovitsy battle; in July–August in the Lvov-Sandomir operation and the liberation of the city of Stanislav. The division lost 461 men and over 1,500 wounded in the Carpathians. To survive such a bloody carnage and then meet death on this accursed Magura Mountain . . .

The family cried for three days. Then a letter arrived from Father saying he was alive and well.

Both letters were dated 27 August 1944. Maybe he had written a letter and then gone into battle and was killed? But four days later we received another letter from him, dated 31 August. Father was alive and beating the fascists! I wrote to him to express my indignation at the death notice sent to us. In his reply Father defended his comrades, saying 'Son, you are unjustly blaming the soldiers: anything may happen at the front.' I have remembered this all my life.

After the end of the war he told us what had happened. His unit was ambushed. The darkness saved them; none of the men was lost, it was like a miracle.

In the morning our infantry attacked, and some soldiers

discovered Father's bag on the mountain. Assuming that he had fallen during the assault on the Magura Mountain they mailed the documents and photographs to his family.

Nevertheless the war had marked Sergeant-Major Gorbachev for life. Once, after a difficult and dangerous raid at the enemy rear, during which they cleared mines and severed communications, the group was resting after many sleepless nights when a German aeroplane, fleeing our fighter planes, dropped all its bombs. One of the bombs exploded near my father, and an enormous splinter cut his leg.

This was in Czechoslovakia, near the city of Košice. For my father it was the end of his life as a front-line soldier. He was treated in a hospital in Cracow. Soon it would be 9 May 1945, Victory Day.

The war was a tragedy for the entire country. Everything that had been built up at such sacrifice had been destroyed. Hopes for a happy life were shattered. Entire families were torn apart: fatherless children, widows, girls without their fiancés.

The front-line soldiers endured great hardships and terrible trials. Mankind ought to be forever indebted to this generation of brave men and women. Until his death Father could not erase his wartime memories. He told many war stories about the unbelievable hardships they had to endure, particularly at the beginning. Near Taganrog, for example, Father fought in a hand-to-hand combat. It was hard for him to talk about it even years later.

Like everyone else, I experienced a lot during the war years. And yet whenever the subject is brought up one horrible image arises in my mind. In late February or early March 1943, when the snow had thawed, we children roamed through the countryside in search of trophies and came to a remote stretch of forest between Privolnoye and the neighbouring village, Belaya Glina. There we stumbled upon the remains of Red Army soldiers, who had fought their last battle there in summer 1942. It was an unspeakable horror: decaying corpses, partly devoured by animals, skulls in rusted helmets, bleached bones, rifles protruding from the sleeves of the rotting jackets. There was a light machine-gun, some hand grenades, heaps of empty cartridges. There they lay, in the thick mud of the trenches and craters, unburied, staring at us out of black, gaping eye-sockets. We came home in a state of shock.

These nameless soldiers were buried in a common grave. Today, in the centre of Privolnoye, a simple obelisk has engraved on it the names of those who never returned from the war, with an entire column of Gorbachevs among them.

I was fourteen when the war ended. Our generation is the generation of wartime children. It has burned us, leaving its mark both on our characters and on our view of the world.

RETURN TO SCHOOL

I returned to school in 1944, after a two-year interruption. I had no particular interest in studying. After all I had lived through, it seemed a waste of time.

The school of that time, its teachers and its pupils, defies unemotional description. As a matter of fact, it was not even a school. Aside from being housed in various village buildings built for completely different purposes, it possessed only a handful of textbooks, a few maps and visual aids and some chalk, an item not obtained without some effort. That was virtually all we had. The rest was up to the teachers and pupils. There were no copybooks and I used Father's handbooks on machine-operating instead. We made our ink ourselves. The school had to bring in firewood, and therefore it kept horses and a cart. I recall how the entire school would save the horses from starving in winter; they were so emaciated and exhausted that they could not stand up. We were getting fodder for them from every imaginable source! And it was difficult to find: the entire village was on the same quest, trying to save privately owned cattle − to say nothing of the kolkhoz cattle farm, where animal carcasses were carted away daily.

Our teachers, too, had a hard life during the war, what with the cold, the hunger, the anguish. But to do them justice: even then they tried (and one can only guess how hard it must have been) to do their job conscientiously, exerting every effort imaginable.

Thus the country was getting desperately needed specialists just a few years after the war.

Our village school had eight grades. It took nearly twenty years to build a modern secondary school in Privolnoye. For the ninth and tenth grades we had to attend the district secondary school some twenty kilometres away. With the other children from my village I rented a room in a flat at the district centre and once a week had to return to the village to get some food. Nobody supervised my studies. My parents considered me responsible enough to work on my own, without pressure. Only once in all these years was I able to convince my father to attend a parents' meeting. When I grew older and started going out to parties and on evening walks with the other youngsters, I recall my father remarking to Mother: 'Mikhail comes home pretty late these days . . .'

I studied zealously. My interest emanated from my inquisitive mind and the desire to get to the bottom of things. I enjoyed physics and mathematics. History fascinated me, while literature made me oblivious to anything else.

In those years everybody was keen to participate in amateur theatre, and loved athletics, although there were virtually no facilities for these activities. Not only did I take part in every performance and competition, but as Komsomol secretary I also organized them. Our music teams roamed villages and homesteads and all the places where villagers were at work. We staged our plays mostly in sports halls, but occasionally we also performed in hallways. What was the attraction of these amateur groups? I think it was mainly the desire to be with people of our own age – but also the wish to unfold our full potential and learn new things. At my school, theatre became such a craze that the drama group could not admit all the enthusiasts. New members had to be carefully selected! What kind of plays did we stage? Unlike professional companies, we never questioned our abilities. We performed classical and modern plays, but obviously preferred Russian playwrights. I suppose the results are easily imagined. But we must have enjoyed a certain success, because our performances attracted even adults. Once our drama group went on a tour of the district villages giving paid performances. The money we collected was used to buy thirty-five pairs of shoes for children who had nothing to wear to school.

Somehow news of our drama group reached Stavropol and the actors of the krai theatre paid us an unexpected visit on one of their tours. We performed Lermontov's *Masquerade* for them. They complimented us and gave us advice; some of it I still remember, other suggestions I promptly forgot. While paying tribute to our spirited rendition of the dialogue between the heroes of Lermontov's drama, Arbenin and Zvezdich, the professional actors suggested we should not try to grab each other's sleeves; in high society, this is not done, not even during heated debates.

BY FATHER'S SIDE

Meanwhile the realities of life made their relentless demands on everyone, including myself.

From 1946 I started operating the combine harvester each summer together with my father. In Privolnoye, the school was about two kilometres from our home, and after classes I would run over to grandfather Pantelei's, who lived in the village centre, change into my working outfit and rush to the MTS, the machine tractor station, to help my father get the combine harvester ready. In the evening we would walk home from work together.

Then came the harvest season. From the end of June to the end of August we worked away from home. Even when harvesting had to be interrupted because of rains, we stayed in the fields, taking care of the machinery and waiting for the weather to improve. Father and I had many discussions during these 'idle' days. We talked about a great variety of topics, work and life alike. Our simple father-son relationship had developed into a bond between two persons who shared a common cause and a common job. Father treated me with respect and we became true friends.

Father knew perfectly how to operate the combine, and he taught me. After a year or two I could adjust any mechanism. I was particularly proud of my ability to detect a fault in the combine immediately, just by the sound of it.

To say that work on the combine harvester was hard is an

understatement. It was back-breaking labour twenty hours a day, with no more than three or four hours of sleep. In dry weather, when the crops were ready to thresh, we would seize the opportunity and work without a break, replacing each other at the controls while the combine was still moving. Sometimes I could no longer stand it, and fell asleep at the controls. The first years I often suffered from nosebleeds, my teenage body reacting to the exhausting routine. Fifteen- or sixteen-year-olds usually put on weight and gain strength. I became strong, but during every harvest season I lost at least five kilos.

The peasant labour was very hard. Yet it did not bring prosperity to the farmers. The only hope was the private plot of land where everything was cultivated to make ends meet somehow. But every household was heavily taxed and had to deliver part of the home-grown produce to the state. It did not matter if you kept cattle or not, you still had to deliver 120 litres of milk, so much butter and so much meat. Annual taxes were imposed on fruit trees although they did not bear fruit every year. And the peasants had to cut down their orchards.

There was no escape: peasants were not issued passports.[1] And without a passport any policeman could stop you and nobody in town would give you a job. There was only one way out: to enlist via 'orgnabor', organized recruitment for some 'major construction project'. What difference was there between this life and serfdom?

Our family was somewhat better off than the others, since mechanics were paid both in money and in produce. But it was an extremely low salary just the same, and if clothes or household goods were needed some home-grown products had to be sold. The markets were miles away – in Rostov, Stalingrad or Shakhty. We were always short of everything.

Even in the fields, during the harvest, we would not have much to eat. But when you had threshed thirty hectares a day, the rules entitled you to a 'parcel': something cooked especially for you, butter dumplings or stewed meat or, even better, a pot of honey.

---

[1] Without internal passports, peasants could not leave their farm to work or live elsewhere. Peasants received internal passports only in the 1960s.

And the invariable vodka – two half-litre bottles. Although I did not really care for the vodka, such a meal would be the most delicious thing on earth. Not just a 'parcel', but a gift from God… A feast indeed!

Speaking about vodka, a wicked joke was played on me once in the harvesting team. It happened in 1946. The hard work was over and the mechanics decided to celebrate the end of the first post-war harvest with drinks: although it was not a bumper year, the job was done just the same. They bought a case of vodka and somewhere purchased medical alcohol. We gathered in the field wagon and sat around eating and drinking and telling all sorts of tall tales. The chaps in our team were all strong and young but experienced: most of them were war veterans. Father was thirty-seven then. I, at fifteen, was the youngest. I sat there eating and listening to their conversation.

The team-leader started pressing me:

'Why are you sitting around? The harvest is over. Come on, have a drink. It's time you became a real man.'

I looked at my father, who did not say anything and just laughed. They gave me a full mug. I thought it was vodka, but it turned out to be pure alcohol. There is a special 'technique' for drinking it: first you exhale and then down the alcohol at once, washing it down immediately with cold water without catching your breath. I simply downed it.

The state I was in! The mechanics were laughing their heads off, my father most of all. But the lesson served me well, indeed: after that experience I have never felt any pleasure in drinking vodka or spirits. The others agreed on the spot to avenge me and played a practical joke on the team-leader, the one behind the prank. They filled a mug with alcohol, and instead of water to wash it down they gave him another mug of alcohol. The team-leader exhaled, downed one mug and then the other. Everyone screamed with laughter. He just grunted. He was a tough character. In fact they were all good pals, one would say they were even friends. They helped each other in their hard life. And they knew how to work.

Years later, having become General Secretary of the Central Committee, I would meet the men from our team, the tractor and combine operators, on every home visit; by then they had grown older. We met informally, old pals who can talk to each other openly.

Incidentally, after field work, studying was no longer a burden – rather a source of enjoyment and pleasure.

You had to sweat for your bread in those days. 1946 was a lean year. Drought struck the grain-producing regions. According to official statistics, the entire grain harvest in the country amounted to 39.6 million tonnes (of this amount, the state took 17 million tonnes).[1] In 1940, by contrast, 95.7 million tonnes had been harvested (the state taking 36.4 million tonnes). The situation was clearly disastrous. Once again famine broke out in many regions.

The Stavropol land also yielded a bad harvest. In the spring of 1947, a wave of people from Stalingrad descended on our region, driven by hunger. They offered all their possessions for grain. We did not have anything to exchange. And yet people bartered.

1947 was a better year for the country. 65.9 million tonnes of grain were harvested (and 27.5 million tonnes were delivered to the state). Immediately after the end of the war the government promised that rationing of food and consumer goods would be repealed within a year, but the repeal had to be postponed for another year because of the drought in 1946. In December 1947 ration cards were finally abolished. It was a festive occasion, but we were not much elated since we had another bad harvest in Stavropol that year. We somehow managed to make it through the winter, with our hopes set on the 1948 harvest.

In early spring (April), dust storms, the terrible companions of drought, suddenly swept across the land. 'Bad luck again,' Father said, 'for the third year in a row.' But a warm rain followed shortly. It rained for one day, the next and then the third. And the crops started sprouting . . .

This was our first bumper harvest. We gathered an average of 22 centners per hectare[2] – an unprecedented result in those times, especially after the lean years. A decree of the Presidium of the

---

[1] The state procurement plan required that farms first supply their quota to the state, before disposing of any surplus. State procurement prices were lower than those the farms could get for their surplus produce.

[2] A centner was one tenth of a tonne. In Western terms, the yield was low.

USSR Supreme Soviet took effect in 1947: 10,000 centners of grain threshed with your combine earned you the title of Hero of Socialist Labour, and for 8,000 centners you were awarded the Order of Lenin. Father and I had threshed 8,888 centners. Father received the Order of Lenin and I the Order of the Red Banner of Labour. I was seventeen then, and this has been the most cherished of all my awards. The official communication came in the autumn. Students of all the grades gathered for a meeting. I was self-conscious but naturally very happy too. On that occasion I delivered my first speech at a meeting.

1948 was, if not a happy year, at least a lucky one for our family. It was also a good year for the country, the first post-war year without ration cards. In spite of the manifold price increases on food and consumer goods, life was slowly but steadily reverting to normal.

My brother was born on 7 September 1947, when I was sixteen years old. I remember my father waking me up at dawn and asking me to leave the room we all shared. I obeyed and then fell asleep again. When I woke up Father told me that I had a brother. I suggested naming him Aleksandr.

The country was rising from the ruins after the tragic war. A few years later, when I travelled to Moscow and back, I visited Rostov, Kharkov, Voronezh, Orel and Kursk – ruins everywhere, deep scars left by the war. A few times I went to Moscow via Stalingrad. I arranged my schedule so as to arrive there in the morning and leave for Moscow the same evening or night. I strolled through the city, went up the Mamai hill, which still bore the traces of shells, mines and bombs – seven or eight years after the Battle of Stalingrad. I visited the sites of the fiercest combats. And I remember vividly the new city gradually developing each year, slowly emerging from the devastation.

Life was hard for my country. In fact, it was not life, rather a struggle to survive. In wartime people knew that they had to save their motherland. And they believed that after the war and after victory, a decent life would be ahead for us. But nothing much changed after the war, especially during the initial post-war years. There was nothing but hard labour again, and the belief that once reconstruction was complete, we would finally be able to lead a normal life. Hope inspired the most laborious, humiliating work, instilling it with a meaning and helping us to endure all hardships.

When I think of my father or grandfather Pantelei, I am increasingly aware that their understanding of duty, their life and deeds, their attitude towards their work, their family and their country – all had a tremendous influence on me and served as a moral example. Nature had richly endowed my father, a simple country man, with discernment, acumen, intelligence, humanity, and many other virtues! These gifts made him stand out among the other villagers. People respected and trusted him. As an adult I was even more fascinated by my father. His inextinguishable interest in life impressed me deeply. He was concerned about the problems of his own country and of far-off lands alike. I always appreciated his thoughtfulness towards Mother. It was neither overt nor refined, rather reserved, simple and warm – not grandiloquent but heartfelt.

He would bring her presents from wherever he went. Father also immediately took my wife Raisa to his heart. He was always pleased to see her and was especially interested in her studies in philosophy. It seems that the word 'philosophy' was a magic spell for him. Father and Mother were delighted when their granddaughter Irina was born, and she spent many a summer with them. Irina greatly enjoyed riding on a two-wheel cart through the fields, mowing the grass and spending the night in the steppe.

My father, Sergei Andreyevich Gorbachev, died unexpectedly of a brain haemorrhage. We buried him on the Day of the Soviet Army, 23 February 1976. The earth of Privolnoye, where he was born, where he had ploughed, sowed and harvested from early childhood and which he had defended with his life, had finally taken him into its bosom.

3

MOSCOW STATE UNIVERSITY

I GRADUATED FROM SCHOOL IN 1950 WITH A SILVER MEDAL. I WAS nineteen years old, that is of conscription age, and I had to decide what to do. I well remember Father's words: 'After school you have to see for yourself. If you so decide, we can work together. If you decide to continue your studies, do it! I will try to help. But it is a serious question, and you have to decide it for yourself.'

I had already made up my mind. I wanted to continue studying. My schoolmates applied to the institutes of higher education in Stavropol, Krasnodar or Rostov. I, however, decided that I must apply to the most important, the Lomonosov Moscow State University, and I chose the law faculty.

I cannot say that it was a thoroughly thought-out plan. I had only a rather vague idea what jurisprudence and law were all about. But the position of a judge or prosecutor impressed me. I sent the application forms to the admissions office of the law faculty and waited for an answer. The days passed and there was no reaction at all. I sent a cable with a prepaid reply, and finally received an answer: 'Admitted with accommodation at the student hostel', i.e. a first-rate admission, without as much as an interview! Everything had apparently worked out in my favour: my 'worker and peasant' origin, my work record, the fact that I was already a candidate Party member and, obviously, the high state award I had received. In addition, my candidacy was welcome because it helped to 'balance' the social composition of the student body, an aim which was also achieved by admitting war veterans.

And so I became a student at Moscow University. For the first weeks and months I felt rather ill at ease. After all, compare the Privolnoye village I came from . . . and then Moscow. Too much of a difference and too sharp a break with the past.

Everything was new to me – Red Square, the Kremlin, the Bolshoi Theatre (my first opera, my first ballet), the Tretyakov Gallery, the Pushkin Museum of Fine Arts, my first boat trip on the Moskva River, excursions to the countryside around Moscow, my first October demonstration . . . And every time, I was over-whelmed by an incomparable sensation of novelty.

Obviously, to get to know old Moscow with its original 'Russianness', its maze of hundreds of side streets and lanes, you would need at least five, if not fifty, years. But all the streets and lanes around our university and all the islands of the students' archipelago around our residence (the Molot Cinema on Rusakov Street, the Rusakov Club, the unique charm of the old Preobrazhenskaya Square, the old public bath houses on Bukhvostovskaya, the park in Sokolniki) – all this remains engraved in my memory.

It was only later, in our fourth academic year, that we moved to the Lenin Hills, and shared a room for two, sometimes staying there for one or even two weeks at a time without leaving our 'home of the Gentry' to go to town. But on the Stromynka we first-years lived twenty-two to one room (in the second year it was eleven, and in the third year only six people to a room).

We had our own cafeteria where we could buy a cup of tea for a few kopeks, with unlimited amounts of bread available on the tables. There was a barber's shop and a laundry, although more often than not we washed our clothes ourselves, for lack of money or for want of a change of clothes. We also had our own poly-clinic.[1] This, too, was a novelty for me, since in our village we had only a first-aid station. The building also housed a library, with spacious reading rooms, and a club providing all kinds of cultural and sporting activities. A world of its own, it was

[1] Hospital.

a students' fellowship with its unwritten laws and rules.

Our student life was frugal. We had to make ends meet. Like all my friends, in the last week before the monthly grant was paid I would be desperately short of money, which forced me to subsist on 'dry rations' – a can of beans or anything that cost no more than one ruble. And yet we would not spend our last ruble on food – instead we would go to the cinema.

University studies captivated me from the start and they took up all my time. I studied eagerly and passionately. My Muscovite friends used to tease me about my 'ignorance': a great deal of what was new to me they had learned way back at school. Well, unlike them, I had only had a village school education.

CURIOSITY AND PRIDE

What was remarkable about our law faculty? First of all, it provided a comprehensive and wide-ranging curriculum. Its highlight was the course of historical sciences: the history and theory of statehood and law; the history of political ideas; the history of diplomacy; political economy, taught at almost the same level as in the economics faculty; the history of philosophy, dialectical and historical materialism; logic; Latin and German. And finally a broad range of legal topics: civil and criminal law, criminal statistics, forensic medicine and psychiatry, administrative, financial and kolkhoz law, marriage and family law, accounting. And, naturally, public and private international law, state system and law of bourgeois countries, etc. . . .

The underlying premise was that mastering purely juridical subjects required a fundamental knowledge of modern socioeconomic and political processes, and, therefore, had to be part of a comprehensive curriculum which included all the social sciences.

To me, the university was a temple of learning, the focal point of minds that were our national pride, a centre of youthful energy, passion and quest. Here one felt the influence of age-old Russian culture; here the democratic traditions of Russian universities lived on in spite of everything. Many famous scientists and academicians considered it an honour to teach at Moscow State University or to lecture there. Each represented a scientific school and had written dozens of books and textbooks. Their lectures revealed a new world, entire strata of human knowledge hitherto unknown to me, and introduced us to the logic of scientific thought. Even in the darkest years of Stalinism, the pulse of public life within the walls of the building on Mokhovaya Street was throbbing. Although to a large extent latent, the spirit of creative quest and sound criticism continued.

Naturally the true situation that reigned at the university should not be idealized. The first three years of my studies coincided with the so-called 'late Stalinist period' – a new round of repressions, the infamous campaign against 'rootless cosmopolitanism'[1] and so on. Stalin's *Short Course in the History of the CP (B)* was held up as a model of scientific thought. The teaching process seemed to aim at brainwashing young minds from the first weeks of their studies, shielding them from the temptations of independent thought, analysis and comparison. The grip of ideology was omnipresent in lectures and seminars as well as in discussions at student meetings.

At a meeting one day, I ventured a critical comment directed at one of our teachers – concerning his method of analysing a specific problem. My fellow-student Valery Shlapko, a war veteran and our course leader (he is today a professor and the author of many works), suggested that I should refrain from this kind of statement until after the exams. At the time I only laughed at his circumspection. And then the examination day came. I answered all the questions confidently. At one point, I referred to a book, somewhat distorting its title. The examiner feigned astonishment. I corrected myself immediately, but too late . . .

With a sarcastic smile, he jotted down something in his notebook. He did not even listen to the rest of my answer. He could barely disguise his malicious pleasure. When I had finished, he declared, 'Well, Gorbachev, that's a definite "four" for sure . . .' and entered the mark at once into my grade-book.

I did not repeat this exam, although I scored five for all other

[1] The campaign was used to attack Jewish scholars and writers.

subjects. It cost me my personal grant. It was a heavy blow to my self-esteem and, especially, to my budget.

I now realize that the university – both the professors and the student body – was under close surveillance. Apparently, there existed an effective system of generalized control over the state of our minds. The slightest deviation from the official line, any attempt to question anything, was fraught with consequences, culminating, at best, in a censure at the Komsomol or Party meeting.

Echoes reached us of a new wave of purges directed against the university professors. The absurdity of the charges was sometimes so obvious that the 'powers that be' would be forced to beat a retreat. There was the case of Professor S. V. Yuzhkov, an outstanding scholar who had devoted his life's work to the study of Kievan Russia, only to be suddenly accused of . . . 'rootless cosmopolitanism'!

Yuzhkov was torn to pieces at the academic council meeting. Completely shattered, he walked up to the rostrum, and instead of adducing some counter-arguments in his defence, he merely uttered one sentence: 'Look at me!' There he was, facing the audience in his Russian-style shirt belted with a cord and an old straw hat in his hand – a very incarnation of the old-fashioned respectable Russian intellectual. The audience burst out laughing. Instead of discussing vague pseudo-scientific charges, common sense prevailed, prompting the audience simply to ask themselves: 'Are we completely crazy to suspect this man of being a cosmopolite?' The inquiry into Yuzhkov's case was immediately stopped.

We loved Serafim Vladimirovich's lectures. As a matter of fact, they were more like conversation in a living room than lectures – fascinating tales of bygone times and of the lives of our forefathers. Yuzhkov was a master of his subject. But we would often play a kind of 'ideological prank' on him, such as asking why the dear professor avoided quotations from the classics of Marxism-Leninism in his lecture? Yuzhkov would frantically open his bulky and apparently capacious briefcase, fumble for one of his books, put on his spectacles and look for the pertinent passages.

I would be less than sincere if I claimed that the massive ideological brainwashing to which the university alumni were subjected did not affect our minds. We were children of our time. If some professors – as it appears to me today – were forced to follow the 'rules of the game', we, the students, took many of the professed theses for granted, sincerely convinced of their truth.

The entire educational system was designed to prevent us from developing a critical mind. Nevertheless, in our third academic year the very process of acquiring knowledge brought us to a stage where we would seriously begin to reflect on all the facts we had learned and assimilated.

Some of my modern readers (mainly my younger fellow-citizens) may scoff on learning that the first authors who sowed the seeds of doubt about the unquestionable 'ultimate truth' presented to us were Karl Marx, Friedrich Engels and Vladimir Lenin. But it is true. In spite of all their (sometimes excessive) polemical sharpness, these works contained a detailed criticism of their opponents' theses, a system of counter-arguments and theoretically sustained conclusions: all of this was in sharp contrast to Stalin's so-called methods of 'debating', which tended to supplant argument by sheer abuse or, at best, by spelling out unquestionable truths.

In 1952, I joined the Communist Party. A problem arose: what was I supposed to write on my application form concerning my two grandfathers, who had both been victims of repressions? Although grandfather Pantelei had not been convicted, he had still spent fourteen months in prison. And grandfather Andrei had been sent to Siberia without even a trial.

The question did not bother anyone when I became a candidate Party member, as the people in Stavropol knew everything about me. I wrote Father a letter, since I assumed that he would have had to answer the same questions when he joined the Party. But when we met in the summer, Father said: 'I didn't write anything. We didn't have any of this at the front. People were admitted to the Party before fighting. Death was waiting for us – that says it all.'

Well, I, his son, had to explain, by and large, the history of my forefathers before the Party committee and, later, at the Lenin district committee of the CPSU.

We were gradually maturing intellectually. The dogmatic attitude of some teachers – who regarded the students only as objects for ideological indoctrination – was becoming unbearable. There was something insulting about it that was degrading to human dignity.

I remember how in autumn 1952, when Stalin's work on the *Economic Problems of Socialism in the USSR* was published, one of our instructors could think of nothing better during his lecture than to read out to us page after page from this book. I ran out of patience and sent him a note pointing out, in essence, that we had already read the book, while its mechanical reading during a lecture was a sign of disrespect for the audience.

The reaction was immediate. The infuriated mentor's reply was basically that those bold spirits afraid to sign their name under a note were conceited to imagine that they had already absorbed 'all the richness of the theses and the conclusions in the work of comrade Stalin'.

I got up and said that I was the author of the note. News of this incident travelled through the Komsomol and Party organizations and reached the Moscow city committee. And I was, at that time, deputy secretary of the faculty Komsomol organization – responsible for ideology! (The secretary was Boris Spiridonov, the future secretary of the Moscow State University Party committee.) There was an investigation, but the scandal was finally quenched – it seems that my 'worker and peasant' origin had once more helped me.

Everyday reality intruded into our studies to introduce significant corrections to our abstract ideas both about 'the most just society' and 'the inviolable friendship of peoples'. One episode left a deep impression on my memory: it happened in the winter of 1952–3, when the public was stunned by the 'Doctors' Plot' which unleashed unbridled acts of anti-semitic provocation against the Jews, who were unjustly accused of treason.

Once, my friend Volodya Liberman (who had gone through great hardships at the front) failed to show up in time for the lecture. He arrived a few hours later. Never before had I seen him in such a despondent, depressed state. He looked terrible. 'What's happened?' I asked him. He could not retain his tears. It turned out that a hooting mob had showered him, a war veteran, with insults and abuse and pushed him off the tram. I was shocked.

Years later, during the difficult December days of 1991, I met one of my fellow students, the writer Belyaev. He said that in those years, I was considered little short of a 'dissident' (to use a modern expression) because of my radicalism. Obviously I was not a dissident at all, although I already 'felt' a burgeoning criticism of our reality.

In the summer of 1953, after the university term, I worked as a trainee at our district procuracy[1] in Stavropol. It was my first encounter with a rather typical example of regional leadership in those times. After this experience, I looked at my home district with very different eyes.

In her book *I Hope: Reminiscences and Reflections*, Raisa Maksimovna published an extract from one of my letters from those days:

> I am so depressed by the situation here. And I feel it especially keenly every time I receive a letter from you. It brings with it so much that is good, dear, close and understandable. And one feels all the more keenly how disgusting my surroundings are here. Especially the manner of life of the local bosses. The acceptance of convention, subordination, with everything predetermined, the open impudence of officials and the arrogance. When you look at one of the local leaders you see nothing outstanding apart from his belly. But what aplomb, what self-assurance and the condescending, patronizing tone!

[1] Legal authority, local branch of the USSR State Procuracy (Prokuratura).

STALIN'S DEATH

On the cold morning of 5 March 1953, total silence reigned in Hall 16, where the general lectures were usually held. The instructor came in and informed us with a tragic voice, tears veiling his eyes, of Stalin's untimely death, in the seventy-fourth year of his life.

Some students had relatives who were victims of the purges and some were more or less aware even then of the totalitarian nature of the regime. The overwhelming majority of the students were, however, deeply and sincerely moved by Stalin's death, perceiving it as a tragedy for the country. A similar feeling, and I won't deny it, welled up in me then.

The essay subject for my final school examination had been 'Stalin – our combat glory, Stalin – the elation of our youth'. I got the highest mark and my essay was held up to school graduates for some years as an example to be followed. And yet, did I not know the reality of Stalin's rule?

Some time ago, I read a letter by Academician Andrei Dmitrievich Sakharov, written in March 1953: 'I am deeply affected by the death of the Great Man. I ponder over his humanitarianism . . .' Apparently, I was not unique in my feelings. In those days, nothing seemed more important than paying our last respects to Stalin. I set out to do so with a group of fellow-students. We advanced slowly, all day, stopping for hours in one place. By taking side streets, we successfully avoided Trubnaya Square, where a terrible stampede had cost the lives of many participants in the mourning procession. We spent all night passing slowly through city blocks and finally reached the coffin.

I had never seen Stalin even from afar, although I obviously took part in festive demonstrations. Now, in the Hall of Columns, I saw him for the first time, dead, and at close range . . . A stony, waxen face, devoid of any signs of life. I searched for traces of his greatness, but there was something disturbing in his appearance that created mixed feelings.

THE 'THAW'

Signs of changes were soon to appear. Investigations of the 'Doctors' Plot' ceased. During the summer, which I was spending in the Stavropol area, I learned of Beria's arrest. *Pravda*, and, later, other newspapers too, started publishing articles about the 'personality cult' (as yet nameless) and its incompatibility with Marxism-Leninism. Some tokens of a thaw in the cultural life of the country were apparent, which had repercussions on our university life as well. The lectures were becoming more and more interesting and the seminars livelier. The same was true of the activities of student societies.

The atmosphere at the university underwent changes during my last two academic years. Doubts were expressed – warily at first, but gradually more outspoken – challenging the 'traditional' interpretation of various historical events and even some aspects of contemporary political life. It was, of course, still a long, long way from the manifestation of true pluralism, even within the framework of the 'socialist choice'. The Party leadership had loosened the ideological reins somewhat, but showed no intention of releasing them altogether.

RAISA

My student years at the university were very intense. Studies, lectures and seminars took up at least twelve or fourteen hours daily – practically seven days a week. I had to fill the gaps in my village school education, especially painful during the first academic years. And, speaking frankly, I never suffered from a lack of pride. I was quick to grasp unfamiliar issues, but to assimilate newly acquired knowledge required the reading of a wide range of additional literature. Incidentally, this was also the main difference between studies at our university and those at most other institutes of higher education.

Moscow University was not only a meeting point of different minds, different life experiences and different nationalities. It was a crossroads of human destinies – sometimes a brief encounter, often long years. There was a centre where this kind of meeting would usually take place – our student club on Stromynka Street. A plain low building (a former barracks, I think), it became for us the centre of true culture. Famous singers and actors would join us there – Lemeshev, Kozlovsky, Obukhova, Yanshin, Maretskaya, Mordvinov – the elite of Moscow's theatre world. The actors saw it as their duty to foster in the young the love of beauty. It was a wonderful pre-revolutionary tradition of the artistic intelligentsia, which has, alas, nearly vanished today. And such encounters would indeed initiate us, the students from 'many a town and hamlet', to true art.

The club provided for miscellaneous activities, from the art of housekeeping (where one could learn how to make scrambled eggs or to patch up an old skirt or a pair of trousers) to ballroom dancing, the dances being at the time all the rage. Dance parties were occasionally organized at the club. I rarely went there, preferring to stay with my books. I was reading one evening when two friends burst into my room.

'Misha,' they said, 'there's a wonderful girl! A new one, Let's go!'

'OK,' I said, 'you go ahead, I'll catch up with you later . . .'

The boys left and I tried to continue studying. But curiosity finally got the better of me and I went to the club. Little did I know that I went to meet my destiny.

From the entrance I noticed Yury Topilin, my roommate, tall and with his usual military stiffness, dancing with a girl I did not know. The music stopped. I went over to them and we were introduced. Raisa Titorenko was studying philosophy: the arts faculty was housed in the same university building as law, she lived in the same hostel on Stromynka Street, and I just cannot understand how I had not noticed her before.

From this day on, there began for me a period of torment and delight. My feeling at the time was that our first meeting had not impressed Raisa at all. She appeared calm and indifferent – judging by the look in her eyes. I tried to meet her again, and a friend once invited the girls from Raisa's room over to our room. We treated them to tea and spoke about everything with a certain exaltation, as always happens on such occasions. I wanted to 'impress' her. I think I made a terrible fool of myself. She was reserved and the first to suggest breaking up the gathering . . .

Time and again I tried to meet her and talk to her. But the weeks passed, a month, and then two months. It was only in December 1951 that an opportunity arose. One evening, having finished studying, I went over to the club. There was another meeting with artists, and the room was overcrowded. A short break was announced and I went down the aisle towards the stage, looking for some friends. I suddenly sensed rather than noticed that someone was looking at me. I greeted Raisa and said that I was looking for an empty seat.

'You can have mine, I am leaving,' she answered, getting up, 'it doesn't interest me that much.'

I had the impression that she did not feel well and offered to accompany her. She did not object. It was early yet for us students, about ten, and I suggested taking a walk into the city. Raisa agreed, and a few minutes later we went down Stromynka Street to the Rusakov Club.

We had a long walk, discussing many subjects, mostly the imminent exams and other student business. The next day we met again, and soon we were spending all our free time together. The rest of my life somehow faded into the background. I even neglected my studies, although I passed the tests and the exams.

But one winter day, something unexpected happened. We met as usual after lectures in the Moscow University courtyard on Mokhovaya Street. We decided to walk back to the hostel on Stromynka Street, but Raya kept silent most of the way and answered my questions reluctantly. I sensed that something was wrong and asked her outright what it was. She unexpectedly said: 'We shouldn't meet any more. I was happy all this time. I have come back to life. I broke with a man I trusted and it was a shattering blow to me. I am grateful to you. But I won't be able to get over anything like that should it happen again. Let's stop seeing each other now, before it's too late . . .'

We walked on for a while in silence. We were already close to the Stromynka when I told Raya that I just could not satisfy her wish, that it would spell disaster for me. I thus confessed my feelings for her.

We entered the hostel. I saw Raya to her room and said before leaving her that I would be waiting for her at the same place, the square at Moscow State University, two days from now.

'We shouldn't meet any more,' Raya insisted.

'I'll be waiting,' I replied.

Two days later we met again.

And again, we spent all our free time together. We strolled along the Moscow boulevards, exchanging our most intimate thoughts and discovering with wonder and joy all of the things about each other that drew us closer.

In June 1952, we spent another sleepless night talking until dawn in the garden of our Stromynka Street hostel. Probably it was on that June night that we realized – we could not and should not part. Life was to prove that our choice was right.

A year later, we decided to marry. The usual questions arose: where will we live, how will our parents react to this 'student marriage', and, most important, what will the newly-weds have to live on? Two meagre grants and the token assistance from home?

We could not hope for a separate room at the Stromynka hostel. But we were young and that was all that mattered. After the end of the third term I went home, informed my parents of our decision and spent the entire summer working as a mechanic at the machine and tractor station. I worked as never before and Father would joke: 'You've got a new work incentive.'

Before I left for Moscow, Father and I sold nine centners of grain and earned, together with our salary, nearly one thousand rubles – a substantial sum in those days. I had never had so much money in my hands before. The financial base for our family was thus established.

I returned to Moscow a few days earlier to meet Raya, who had spent the holiday with her parents. On one of our first walks we passed the register office at Sokolniki. 'Let's look in!' I suggested.

We went inside and found out what documents we needed to register our marriage. On 25 September 1953 we crossed the threshold of this honourable institution, and obtained certificate No. RV 047 489 stating that citizen Gorbachev, Mikhail Sergeyevich, born in 1931, and citizen Titorenko, Raisa Maksimovna, born in 1932, entered into lawful matrimony, duly signed and sealed. The whole ceremony was rather prosaic, but at least it was over quickly.

Raisa remembers to this day a dream she had in those days.

She and I are at the bottom of a very deep, dark well, a ray of light glimmering somewhere high up. We are climbing the wall, helping each other. Our hands are cut and bleeding. The pain is unbearable. Raya falls but I catch her, and we resume our slow upward climb. Finally, completely exhausted, we drag ourselves out of this black hole, and a straight, smooth, tree-lined alley opens before us. On the horizon we see an enormous bright sun, and the alley seems to flow into it, dissolving in its rays. We walk towards the sun. But suddenly out of nowhere terrifying black shadows loom over us on both sides of the road. What is that? And we hear 'enemies, enemies, foes'. Our hearts are filled with anguish . . . Holding hands, we continue walking on the road towards the horizon, towards the sun . . .

A STUDENT WEDDING

We celebrated our wedding somewhat later, on 7 November, the anniversary of the October Revolution. For this occasion and with the money earned that summer, a beautiful Italian crepe dress was made for Raya at a dressmaker's shop on Kirovskaya Street. She simply looked gorgeous in it. I bought the first suit of my life, made of an expensive fabric called 'Shock Worker'. We were thus dressed for the celebration. Alas, we did not have enough money to buy white shoes for the bride. She had to borrow a pair from a girlfriend.

The wedding was celebrated in the cafeteria on the same Stromynka Street. We invited our friends and fellow-students. There was typical student fare, consisting mainly of the omnipresent Russian salad. We drank champagne and Stolichnaya vodka. One toast followed another. My friend Zdenek Mlynar managed to adorn his elegant 'foreign' suit with a big oil stain. The party was loud and in high spirits and we danced a great deal.

Then began a somewhat 'unusual' period in our family life. We would spend all day together, and late in the evening we parted to go back to our crowded 'hole' on the Stromynka. It was only in the autumn that we were allotted individual rooms, when we moved to the student hostel on the Lenin Hills, where the science and senior humanities students were housed.

We failed to obtain a separate 'family' room. On the contrary: worried about our morals, the rector's office had worked out a unique accommodation plan. All the hostel buildings were divided into male and female quarters. Raya got a room in the 'G zone', and I got one in the 'V zone'. Access to the zones was regulated by a strict system of permits. It took me a great deal of effort to obtain the authorization for daily visits. And every time I had to carry my passport as a proof that our marriage was legal. But even this was of no avail: at eleven p.m. on the dot the telephone rang in Raya's room and the woman on duty would say 'an unauthorized person is in your room'.

But finally December 1953 arrived, and at the first university Komsomol conference since Stalin's death we – the student delegates – gave the rector's office staff a merciless dressing down for his prudery. Satirical posters at the conference represented certain aspects of university life. One of them, four or five metres long, depicted the rector's foot stamping on a marriage certificate.

Following the Komsomol's firm stand, everything changed. Students from each department were housed together and normal contacts resumed. Life got back to normal. We now had our family breakfasts, suppers, sometimes even lunches, and friends would come to visit us. On the whole, we were happy, and I felt like a real family man.

In summer 1954 Raisa and I travelled to the Stavropol region. I was convinced that my parents would be delighted with my choice. But parents have their own ideas about 'choices' (I realized this later, when I became a father myself). Father took Raisa to his heart, and so did grandmother Vasilisa, but Mother was wary and jealous. And the impression from this initial meeting remained forever. In other words, the 'sentimental journey' had clearly failed.

We visited grandfather Pantelei's grave. He had died in late summer 1953. On the day of his burial a cold autumn rain drizzled down, yet all the villagers came to attend Grandfather's funeral. I stood at his grave for a long time, thinking about his cruel fate, which he shared with thousands of men and women like him . . .

Our studies at the university were drawing to an end. I submitted my graduation paper on time and defended[1] it successfully, receiving the highest mark. A large part of my paper dealt with the demonstration of the advantages of socialist democracy over bourgeois democracy. Obviously, we were still very far from understanding the principles of democracy. Yet, the simplified black-and-white picture of the world as presented by our propaganda was even then considered rather sceptically by the students. Jawaharlal Nehru's visit to Moscow in June 1955 served as an unexpected stimulus for me in this respect. I attended the meeting with the teachers and students at the university assembly hall on the Lenin Hills. This amazing man, his noble bearing, his intelligent, keen eyes and warm and disarming smile, made a deep impression on me. I recall his kind words for our *alma mater* and the hope he expressed that the university would educate young men and women 'great of mind and of heart' who would become the 'bearers of peace and good-will'.

Our Indian guest linked the question of peace to the preservation and progress of human civilization, the application of the most advanced scientific and technological knowledge to serve humanity as a whole, and the elimination of all obstacles and barriers impeding the growth of our mental and spiritual faculties.

To people brought up in the spirit of a class approach to the events and phenomena of the past, present and future, those words sounded, to say the least, unusual. They awakened the mind. I recalled them many years later, in December 1986 – when I was putting my name next to that of Nehru's grandson, Indian Prime Minister Rajiv Gandhi, as we signed the Delhi declaration

---

[1] The graduation paper was examined orally, with the student fielding questions from the examination panel.

setting out the principles of a nuclear-weapon-free and non-violent world.

WHAT NEXT?

Five years of studies were finally over. For the graduates, it was the onset of a very unsettling period: the postgraduate job assignment. Its outcome could be decisive in shaping one's future.

Raisa Maksimovna had already gone through it. Having graduated the year before, she had taken up a postgraduate course and passed the examinations for the candidate degree.[1] She was now working on her thesis, and her future looked quite promising: an academic career in the capital.

I, too, was offered a postgraduate course at the department of collective farm law,[2] but I could not accept it on principle. My views on the so-called collective farm law were crystal-clear: I considered this discipline totally spurious.

I was not really worried about the future. As a secretary of a Komsomol organization I was a member of the commission charged with postgraduate assignments, and I knew that my fate had already been decided. Together with twelve other postgraduates (eleven of them war veterans) I was assigned to the Prokuratura of the USSR.[3]

The rehabilitation of the victims of Stalinist repressions had begun, and we were to be employed in the new departments charged with the prosecutor's legal control over the state security organs. Hence I pictured my future work as a struggle for the victory of justice, in accordance with my political and moral beliefs.

I passed my final exam on 30 June. On my return to the hostel, I found an official letter in the mailbox, inviting me to report to the Prokuratura of the USSR. I went there in high spirits. I expected a briefing on my future duties, and accordingly

---

[1] Roughly equivalent to the Doctor of Philosophy (PhD) degree.

[2] Legislation regulating the activities of collective farms.

[3] The USSR State Procuracy, responsible for the implementation of the law and prosecution of law-breakers.

formulated my own suggestions. But when – all smiles and excitement – I crossed the threshold of the office indicated in the letter, I was informed in a cool and formal manner by the official that 'It is considered impossible to employ you in the USSR prosecution agencies.'

Apparently, the government had issued a secret decree, categorically prohibiting the employment of law institute gradu- ates by central legal authorities. Supposedly, one of the many causes of the wave of massive repression in the 1930s was the great number of 'green' young people with neither professional nor life experience who had been deciding people's fates. And, paradoxical as it might seem, I thus became myself an innocent victim of the 'fight for the restoration of socialist justice', although my own family had been the subject of Stalinist repression.

This shattered all my plans. They disintegrated in a moment. Obviously, in order to stay in Moscow I could have found some cosy job at the university, and my friends were already reviewing similar options. But this was not my wish.

I was offered employment at the Prokuratura in Tomsk, Blagoveshchensk, at the Prokuratura of the Republic of Tadzhikistan, and, finally, the post of assistant city prosecutor – with accommodation – in Stupino, not far from the capital. Raisa Maksimovna and I did not waste much time considering these offers. What good was it going to some unknown place, trying one's luck in some strange republic? So we were heading home, back to Stavropol. We decided, first, to visit Raisa Maksimovna's parents, 'to pray for forgiveness of our sins'.

They met us accordingly – without being openly unfriendly, their ill-disguised resentment at being informed of our marriage *ex post facto* was obvious. Now that I am a father myself I can understand them perfectly well. And to add insult to injury, we had some more 'good tidings' for them – their daughter was abandoning her postgraduate studies in Moscow in order to follow me into the unknown, to some Stavropol backwater.

I left Raisa with her parents for a month and returned to Moscow. I spent the last days of July preparing for departure. All our belongings fitted into two suitcases. And for the heavy load –

our books – I purchased an enormous crate, filled it to the brim, took it to the railway station in a taxi and sent it to Stavropol as freight, which was less expensive.

My train was leaving that night. I returned to the hostel and took a shower. I lay down on my bed and closed my eyes, and for the first time I thought about a question which later I would often ask myself – what significance had Moscow University had in my life?

It was clear to me that in many ways the 'worker-peasant' lad who in the summer of 1950 had first crossed the threshold of the building on Mokhovaya Street and the graduate of Moscow State University who five years later was getting ready for his departure for Stavropol were different persons.

Of course, my family provided the most important moral stimulus for my formation as an individual and as a responsible citizen. Of course, school and the teachers played a major role in my subsequent development. I am also thankful to my older comrades, the mechanics, who taught me how to work and helped me understand the system of values of the working man. And yet it was Moscow University that gave me the comprehensive knowledge and the spiritual vigour that was decisive in the choices I made. One thing I am sure of: without these five years of studies, there would have been no 'Gorbachev the politician'. The intellectual standards set by the university freed me for a long time from self-conceit and over-confidence. They also helped me to endure the most difficult days in my later life, when my 'habitat', my social sphere, had drastically changed.

4

AN INITIAL TEST OF STRENGTH

THERE WAS NOBODY TO MEET ME IN STAVROPOL. I LEFT MY luggage at the railway station and went to look for a place to stay. I did not really know my way around the town, having been there only for a few short visits. I finally found a hotel called 'Elbrus'. I paid for a bed and then went for a stroll through the streets.

The city surprised me by its luxuriant vegetation and its classical provincial aspect. Tall buildings were rare; the houses were mostly of one or two storeys, with extensions and super-structures of that indefinable architecture characteristic of so many Russian provincial towns. Every roof had a chimney, witness to the absence of central heating. Later I learned that the city lacked both a central water supply and central sewerage.

The city centre lies on a hill. There are also the ruins of the old fortification walls. I was told that before the war there had been a magnificent old cathedral, blown up in 1942 in anticipation of German occupation. Until the 1960s, the major part of the old city was occupied by the central square and the upper market, where people from all over the krai and from neighbouring oblasts would come to sell their agricultural produce.

The square was surrounded by unique buildings, the local sights: the former lycée, where German Lopatin – a brilliant, outstanding man, the first to translate Marx's *Das Kapital* into Russian – had studied; the former institute for girls of noble families (today it houses the Pedagogical Institute); a low-slung, one-storey building, once the headquarters of the commander-in-chief of the Caucasus army; the building of the former nobles' assembly (the Officers' Club); a theatre (the first in the Caucasus); and the governor's residence, later the krai party committee offices. A seven-hundred-year-old oak tree, gnarled with age, grew on the slope leading to the ponds. According to a story handed down from generation to generation, this had been one of Lermontov's favourite spots.

Down from the city centre, a broad avenue stretched out eastward to the former fortress gates. People used to call them 'the Tbilisi gates'. The famous road to Tbilisi in Georgia . . .

The Elbrus Hotel was near the incredibly dirty lower market, where the fruit and vegetables were unbelievably cheap – you could buy a bundle of tomatoes for a few kopeks. But I was very careful with my money, saving it for something else: I had to rent a room before Raisa arrived.

My probationary period at the krai Prokuratura began on 5 August. In the evening, I walked the streets in search of lodgings. One day passed, then another in futile search. I called at dozens of houses. My colleagues finally suggested that I should contact an estate agent. The Prokuratura and the militia kept up a desperate battle with such people and therefore had records on many of them. I was given the address of an efficient agent, a woman who lived at 26 Ipatova Street (such 'important' information remains engraved upon one's mind). I went there, and, to do her justice, she understood immediately that I had come not to fight her but in search of help. She charged me fifty rubles and gave me three addresses. One of them, on Kazanskaya Street, became our home for the next few years.

The house was occupied by a pleasant, well-mannered couple, both retired teachers, and their daughter and son-in-law, Lyuba and Volodya. Later a grandson, Anatoly, was born. The landlords let me a room – eleven square metres, a third of it occupied by a stove. The three windows opened onto a wonderful old garden. Closing these windows was a difficult task; everything was warped with the passage of time. The furniture consisted of a long, narrow iron bed with wire netting that reached down nearly to the floor. The entire room seemed rather shabby, but considering my finances, I had no choice. I agreed with the landlords on a rent of 250 rubles a month. I had to take care of fuel and paraffin myself. In the middle of the room, I placed the plywood crate which had arrived (fortunately intact) from Moscow: it would have to serve both as table and as bookcase. I built a clothes-rack. And just before Raisa Maksimovna's arrival I bought two chairs to complete the furnishings.

A NEW START

The curtness of the officials at the USSR Prokuratura, the callousness towards my family situation, and the manner of my posting had raised serious doubts in my mind about whether to pursue a career in law. The Stavropol trial period did nothing to dispel them. I decided to quit.

I went to the Komsomol krai committee, where I met some old acquaintances. I told them about my plans. They seemed to be impressed by my Moscow University badge and the record of my political activities at the law faculty. A few days later I was invited for an interview with the first secretary of the Komsomol krai committee, Viktor Mironenko: we introduced ourselves, had a discussion, and I accepted his offer to transfer to the krai committee as deputy head of the agitation and propaganda department.[1]

Ostensibly, everything seemed to proceed smoothly, but only on the surface. As a young specialist I was supposed to turn up at the job and take over the work given to me. Now, I somehow had to settle matters at the Prokuratura. My situation was somewhat eased by the fact that Mironenko had consulted the Party krai committee about my transfer to the Komsomol. But I decided I should discuss it with the krai prosecutor and insisted on a meeting with him. Vasily Nikolaevich Petukhov was highly respected and enjoyed a reputation as an independent person and a man of integrity. Later I had many opportunities to see that this respect was entirely justified.

Some thirty years later, Vasily Nikolaevich sent me two of his

---

[1] A department whose main responsibility was to raise the socialist consciousness of the local youth and stimulate them to be model citizens and fulfil all plans.

books with dedications and the following letter: 'Today I think with great satisfaction that I did the right thing then in letting you choose your own way.' But this was much later; at the time, my conversation with Petukhov left an unpleasant aftertaste.

I tried to settle down in my new job at the krai committee as quickly as possible, grasp my new duties and visit the local organizations. Thus began my regular trips through the districts of the Stavropol region. To reach the remote settlements, I had to take the train or hitch a ride with a lorry going the same way, and I had to get around in the district mostly on foot. My first month's salary (I received 840 rubles net) went on a pair of sturdy boots – any other kind of footwear would not last on our bad roads.

Even more crucial for people on business trips was the question of where to find food. After spending the whole day on your feet, you would be as hungry as a wolf, but there was just nowhere to eat – no snack bars, cafés, dining-halls or even simple canteens – nothing of the sort. It was a stroke of luck if a colleague or a villager was moved by pity and offered you a glass of milk or a piece of bread at his place. An invitation to the home of a local leader would be tantamount to a feast.

An even greater problem was to find accommodation for the night. Most of the villages had no hotels or guest-houses: with luck the traveller might be put up overnight in a district centre. My Komsomol colleagues usually helped me out, finding lodgings with an 'Aunt Manya' or inviting me to their home.

On one of my first trips, I went to a village in the south-east of the krai, Gorkaya Balka in the Vorontsov-Aleksandrovsk district. I spent days on end in workshops, on farms and among work teams: the situation was appalling, sheer misery and complete devastation everywhere. In the evenings I stayed for hours at the kolkhoz office, discussing endless problems with the workers. I have forgotten most of them, it was so long ago. But one impression stands out in my memory. One day we decided with the secretary of the local Komsomol organization to travel to the remotest cattle farm and meet the young people who worked there. We advanced virtually step by step, dragging our feet through thick mud. At last, after working our way up a slope, we stopped and looked around.

The sight was indeed incredible. Down in the valley, on both sides of the River Gorkaya Balka, the village stretched out over some twenty kilometres. As far as the eye could see, scattered at random, low, smoke-belching huts, blackened dilapidated fences . . . Down there, in those miserable dwellings, people led some kind of life. But the streets (if you could call them streets) were deserted. As if the plague had ravaged the entire village, no contacts or ties existed between these shanty-town microcosms, just the everlasting barking of the dogs. And I told myself that this was the reason why the young fled from this god-forsaken village. They fled from desolation and horror, from the terror of being buried alive.

On the hillside I wondered: 'How is it possible, how can anyone live like that?'

People deserve a better life – that was always on my mind.

Meanwhile, life was going on. One trip followed another, both on Komsomol affairs and on Party business.

Whenever I arrived to deliver a talk people readily assembled and listened attentively – not just because of my oratory. Most of the villages had neither electricity nor radio, and they had never even heard of television. Newspapers arrived late and books were scarce. Therefore people would gather at the club as soon as the arrival of a lecturer from 'the centre' was announced. They were glad to socialize a bit; they settled down comfortably on the benches, the back rows would chew sunflower seeds, and everyone was willing to stay on and listen until the small hours of the morning.

But gradually the 'educational work' of the Komsomol was supplanted by a series of economic campaigns organized on the initiative of Nikita Khrushchev. It did not take me long to realize the pitfalls involved in working for the Party and Komsomol apparatus. It offered ready-made 'rules of the game' and forced people into a given rigid framework. The danger of slipping from public activities into a purely bureaucratic job like the one I had fled from at the Prokuratura was also present at the Komsomol.

In essence, this political youth organization was not independent at all: it was, in fact, acting as a sub-contractor for the CPSU. And what is more, any attempt on the part of the Komsomol to act independently at any level was regarded as not only undesirable, but even dangerous. Party organizations had taken over the direct management of the economy and were acting as economic administrators – and expecting the Komsomol to do likewise. Everything was assessed in the light of economic achievements: good results meant that both the Party organizations and the Komsomol were doing a good job. Poor economic results were simply attributed to inefficient political work.

During my trip to the village of Gorkaya Balka I had heard more than enough about economic disorganization, and the hopelessness of such a life. But the young people suffered most from a feeling of utter isolation from the rest of the world. Something had to be done. I decided to consult some specialists, mainly young professionals like myself. Everyone agreed: young people needed social contacts. We decided to organize discussion groups for political and other education – to fling open a window on the outside world, as we say. The first meetings were attended not only by the young, but also by older people. The audience expressed the wish to meet on a regular basis: the ice was broken. At the end of my assignment, I went to the district Party committee to see their first secretary, Dmitriev. I told him what I had seen in Gorkaya Balka and what I had done; then I repeated all the complaints I had heard, and returned to Stavropol.

A few days later I was summoned to the Party krai committee: they asked me what had happened.

'Nothing special,' I said, 'but my impressions were discouraging.'

'Well, we received word from the secretary of the district committee that a certain Gorbachev from the Komsomol krai committee had arrived and started organizing some kind of group, instead of restoring order, reinforcing work discipline and propagating advanced production methods.'

I was stunned. It took me a while to understand. Dmitriev had probably reasoned as follows: Gorbachev would tell the krai committee about the misery of life in the village and the lack of consideration for the villagers shown by the local Party apparatus.

Therefore Sergei Afanasievich Dmitriev had decided to make

75

a pre-emptive strike. He obviously never even mentioned the needs and problems of the farmers.

Relations were not always smooth with my Komsomol colleagues. My university education gave me some indisputable advantages, and I would immediately get involved in any debate on general issues (an old student habit) and spring unexpected arguments on my interlocutors, pulling the ground from under them. I did it, of course, solely to assert the truth and in the heat of the discussion.

At a conference of the krai committee Komsomol apparatus, I was once publicly blamed for taking unfair advantage of my university education. Later, in a more intimate circle, I was told: 'Tell you what, Misha, we love you, we respect you both for your knowledge and for your human qualities, but many fellows from the apparatus feel really hurt when, during a discussion, they emerge as ignoramuses or, even worse, fools. Is it their fault if they never went further than secondary night-school?'

I took this remark to heart. And, more important, I helped many of them to continue their studies at colleges of higher education.

THE XXTH COMMUNIST PARTY CONGRESS

Then came the spring of 1956. Khrushchev's secret speech at the XXth Party Congress[1] caused a political and psychological shock throughout the country.

At the Party krai committee I had the opportunity to read the Central Committee information bulletin, which was practically a verbatim report of Khrushchev's words. I fully supported Khrushchev's courageous step. I did not conceal my views and defended them publicly. But I noticed that the reaction of the apparatus to the report was mixed; some people even seemed confused.

One could understand their mixed feelings. For decades Party

[1] This speech, made in closed session, demolished the myth of Stalin's infallibility and attacked his record over the years 1934–53. It did not criticize forced collectivization and industrialization.

work and the organization of life in our country had been based on Stalin's authority, which alone had justified and consecrated everything. And now, the foundations were rocked. The spirit of iron discipline ingrained in every apparatchik demanded allegiance to the new course of the Central Committee, but many were simply unable to comprehend and accept it. A great number of them concealed their views, waiting for further developments and more guidance.

There was the question of how the Komsomol should react. We agreed that the most experienced Komsomol workers should explain the results of the XXth Party Congress to the young people. I was assigned to the Novo-Aleksandrovsky district. The situation there was typical. On my arrival I visited N. I. Veretennikov, secretary of the district Party committee for ideology, and on hearing about my mission he sympathized with me. I realized he thought I had been 'set up'. In any case, he was in a state of utter confusion and did not know what to do. 'I'll be frank with you,' he remarked, 'the people just refuse to accept the condemnation of the personality cult.'

But I already knew what was implied by 'the people': it usually meant 'members of the Party apparatus'. And I decided, therefore, that I had to find out for myself the general mood. I spent two weeks in the district, meeting daily with Komsomol members and talking to Communists. My impressions were rather contradictory. Some of the people to whom I talked – especially the younger and better-educated ones and those who themselves had in some way been victims of Stalinist repression – applauded the condemnation of the personality cult. Others refused to believe the facts stated in Khrushchev's report and rejected his assessment of Stalin's role and activities. A third, fairly large group did not doubt for a moment the veracity of the stated facts, but kept asking the same question: 'What for? What is the point of washing one's dirty linen in public, speaking publicly about these things and fuelling unrest among the people?'

There was another explanation of the purges that I found amazing. It had arisen in the minds of many ordinary people, and according to them, Stalin had punished those who had oppressed the people. 'They paid for our tears.' And this in a region that had gone through the bloody carnage of the terrible 1930s.

Those 'at the top' realized immediately – some by intuition, others consciously – that to criticize Stalin was tantamount to criticizing the system as a whole. This was a threat to its very survival, hence, a threat to the well-being of the 'powers that be'.

This threat was manifest at the first meeting held to discuss the XXth Party Congress decisions, when the leadership at every level was to be confronted with the question: 'And where were all of you at that time?'

Andropov, then the Soviet Ambassador to Hungary, told me later that soon after the XXth Party Congress the Hungarian leader Matyas Rakosi invited him to go hunting. When they were alone, Rakosi said in Russian (he clearly expected Moscow to be informed about their conversation): 'You can't act in this way. You shouldn't have hurried. What you have done at your congress is a disaster. And I don't know what will come out of it, either in your country or in mine.'

When I arrived in the district, I soon realized that what was needed were frank and friendly talks instead of public speeches. After my return to Stavropol, I shared my impressions and suggestions with the Party krai committee, where they aroused interest. It seemed that everything had gone relatively well – and yet I was not satisfied. I kept asking myself more questions than ever, without finding answers to many of them. It dawned on me that one of the main reasons for this lay in the report made by Khrushchev. It lacked an analytic or reasoned approach, and was rather a personal, emotional utterance. It aimed to strike the raw nerves of the people, rather than to be rational and convincing. It reduced the causes of a series of highly complicated political, socio-economic and socio-psychological processes to various evil traits in the character of the leader. What was needed was a more in-depth analysis. But alas . . .

In any case, the XXth Party Congress provided a strong impetus for Soviet society, initiating a process of reassessment of our domestic and foreign policies and a fresh analysis of the past. And yet the old forces refused to yield.

A GROWING BURDEN OF RESPONSIBILITY

It was a year since I had started working at the Komsomol krai committee. I had spent most of the time travelling on official business, but I had also established good relations with the Stavropol intelligentsia and students and knew about their problems. Yet – since I was somewhat of a newcomer in the city – I did not expect to be considered for the post of first secretary of the Stavropol Komsomol city committee.[1] Nevertheless, I was nominated and endorsed, and assumed my new duties in early September.

I spent a long time considering what to do first – there were scores of problems to be solved. It was hard to find work not only for school-leavers but also for graduates from higher education. A disorganized life it was, with people doomed to live in idleness and the concomitant negative phenomena – yes, we in Stavropol had to face these problems too. On the other hand, intellectual ferment was spreading in society since the XXth Party Congress, especially among the young people, who nurtured growing expectations.

I began by organizing a discussion club. Later, in the 1960s, clubs like this and 'talk programmes'[2] appeared in many cities and became, to a certain extent, the standard forum for ideological work. But when I and Larion Anisimovich Rudenko, faculty head at the college of education, decided to found such a club in our home town, it was considered (at least in our krai) an unheard-of novelty.

The topic of the first discussion seemed innocuous enough: 'Let's talk about taste'. But the way we defined it touched on the most acute problems. We invited everyone to participate in the debate, which was to take place in the House of Teachers.[3] The reaction was immediate: vigilant, well-meaning citizens started calling the secretary of the city Party committee to draw

---

[1] The Komsomol was organized on parallel lines to the Communist Party.

[2] These took place in the evenings and consisted of songs, political discussions, debates, satirical sketches and so on.

[3] A kind of civic centre for teachers.

his attention to the event '. . . taking place right in the centre – some kind of camouflage . . . an obvious provocation!'

The first discussion went fairly well. Arguments were lively, people were excited and did not spare their vocal cords. We organized a second, then a third meeting. The room was jammed to overflowing; people sat in hallways and on the steps. Those who could not leave their coats in the cloakroom clutched them in their laps. We had to find a larger place . . . the militia club!

I chaired all the club meetings. One of them I will remember all my life. The topic was culture in general and we discussed different aspects of the issue. A young man – apparently well-read and educated – spoke nervously about culture in a socialist society. He argued that 'culture' meant, first and foremost, 'Man and his age-old history', whereas we had reduced it to a single aspect, ideology: and the ideas drummed into our heads served only to distort the concept of culture.

Rudenko and I counter-attacked 'in defence of socialism'. We said that only socialism had inherited and assimilated all the richness of mankind's spiritual heritage, and only socialism made culture available to the masses. And we advanced a series of additional arguments in the sincere belief that they were true. Our 'ideological enemy' was patently inexperienced in public debate, and we scored an early victory. But this 'victory' left an unpleasant aftertaste. It was obvious that the chap was someone who reasoned about problems. At the time I was only worried lest our popular discussion club would be closed down.

Our club became a favourite meeting place in Stavropol for thinking young people. I knew very well that most of them were yearning for action rather than debate. Hence we organized the 'OKO' operative Komsomol unit. I do not know whether it was one of the first in our country; I had certainly not heard of anything similar at the time.

As I said before, many of Stavropol's young people found themselves idle, hanging around without jobs or any meaningful work. Consequently, alcoholism, hooliganism and crime were rampant. The militia tried to cure these problems by traditional methods, with little or no effect. Then suddenly a mobile operations unit appeared in our city: disciplined, courageous, decisive; moreover, it was a voluntary group of youngsters. The effect was astounding – OKO gained enormous credibility.

It seemed to be a perfect example for the advocates of 'forceful methods only' in dealing with all kinds of problem. Yet we were soon to realize that to rely only on force was nonsensical and dangerous. First, hooligans and thugs began acting under the guise of our operative unit. Second, a growing number of cases were reported when our own boys, taking a fancy to 'forceful methods', arrested and beat people up in open defiance of the law. Eventually we had to reinforce control over OKO and assign an experienced policeman to each group.

But we directed our attention mainly to providing jobs and organizing recreational activities for young people. Since it was proclaimed long ago that in our country unemployment had been eradicated once and for all, there was no government institution to help them. Hence the city committee had to assume the additional functions of an employment agency. All available jobs in the city were registered. We had endless arguments with enterprise managers. And I was more concerned with the number of jobs available to young men and women than with the number of OKO volunteers. The Komsomol enjoyed no formal rights, but I made use of the fact that I was a member of the Party city committee bureau. This allowed me to represent the interests of young people successfully at bureau meetings, plenary sessions and meetings of work collectives.

We also created 'satirical windows', borrowing the name from the repertoire of the 'Blue Blouses' and 'Light Cavalry' – satirical groups of the 1920s. Photographs displayed on stands in the city showed filthy factory yards and dirty streets, thieving vendors and drunk and unruly officials 'on the spree'. The stands were always crowded with people and had a tremendous effect. In short, we were always looking for and finding ways to make people aware of the Komsomol committees and the interests of youth.

THE BIRTH OF OUR DAUGHTER

Changes were also taking place in our private life. On 5 January 1957 Raisa Maksimovna celebrated her twenty-fifth birthday – and on 6 January she gave birth to our daughter Irina. We were very happy – we both wanted children – but it was a stressful period: the doctors told Raisa she should never have another child because she had suffered from a dangerous rheumatic disease in her student years. Our life became rather complicated. We were still living on Kazanskaya Street and both shops and market were far away in the centre of town. We had to fetch water from a pump; the toilet was outdoors, as was the coal and fuel storage. In those years a mother was entitled to only fifty-five days' maternity leave. We could not exist on one salary, and Raisa had to go back to work. We started looking for a nanny. It turned out to be a difficult task, but we finally found a short-term one. Poor Raisa Maksimovna really had a tough time. To nurse our daughter, she had to rush home during the day, and save some of her milk for later. Baby food was unavailable: we had to use our ingenuity. We lacked everything and led a frugal life indeed. We were still wearing the clothes our parents had bought for us in our student days.

Seeing our plight, my colleagues joined efforts to have an apartment assigned to us. Thus we moved into two rooms in a so-called administrative and residential building: the two upper floors had been designed for housing, while the lower floor was allocated to different institutions, or offices, as one would say today. But the city had an acute shortage of housing, and this floor was eventually also used to lodge people, becoming a vast communal apartment with nine rooms and a shared kitchen and toilet. We lived there for three years before moving into a separate two-room flat.

I remember those years very well. Our communal apartment was shared by a welder, a retired colonel, a mechanic working in a garment factory, and their families; an alcoholic bachelor with his mother; and four single women – a unique world where frustration and aggressiveness caused by the crowded and ill-equipped quarters co-existed with mutual heartfelt helpfulness. It was a peculiar form of collectivism, if you like: people made friends, quarrelled, made up, celebrated anniversaries and feast days together and played dominoes in the evenings.

Father would visit us and bring food from the village. We had long talks with him about village life, events in the krai and in the world. On rare occasions grandmother Vasilisa would arrive for major religious feasts (there was no church in Privolnoye). She would complain about her health and the lack of attention from family members and chide us for not having our daughter baptized – although she was never cross about it. She grew very fond of Raisa Maksimovna and Irina, and whenever she went to church, she repeated affectionately: 'I'll pray for the three of you. May God forgive your sins, you godless people.' We were to learn years later that Irina was secretly baptized during one of her stays at Privolnoye.

A NEW APPOINTMENT

On 25 April 1958 a plenum of the Stavropol Komsomol krai committee elected me second secretary, and in March 1961 I became first secretary of the Komsomol krai committee. Now, when I travelled to remote areas, I used a car – the famous jeep-like 'Gazik'. But where the car could not go, I went on foot, in my old sturdy boots.

These four years of my life were packed with bureaucratic routine, a situation that was symptomatic for the Komsomol in those days. One mass campaign followed another. My desk was piled high every day with innumerable instructions arriving from the Komsomol Central Committee. Those 'at the top' seemed to be firmly convinced that without their bureaucratic directives no grass would grow and no cow would calve – and that the economy could only function under a regime of 'permanent mobilization'.

Among other things, my new position introduced me to another circle, the 'upper spheres' of the local political elite, the secretaries of the Party krai committee. Every one of them personified in his own special way the times in which he lived.

Ivan Pavlovich Boitsov held the position of first secretary for ten years from 1946. During the war, he had been one of the leaders of the partisan movement in Kalinin oblast. This man had a most controversial reputation. He was restrained and austere, while enjoying enormous authority and influence. But his authority was based mainly on fear – a typical feature of Stalinist times. After the XXth Party Congress, Boitsov's position became shaky. The Central Committee blamed him for being slow in carrying out new directives. And all those who only yesterday had trembled when hearing his name made him pay for it today.

He was succeeded in March 1956 by Ivan Kononovich Lebedev, a man of unlimited energy who knew how to make everyone work. During the peak harvest season I believe he would have resurrected the dead to make them harvest the crops or bale hay. But if you were to ask him 'Why? What for?', Ivan Kononovich would have been at a loss for an answer.

In 1956 we were pressured by Moscow to introduce two-stage harvesting methods in Stavropol krai, mowing the crops first, then collecting and threshing during the second stage. It was a good way to harvest in a dry season, but that year we had a rainy summer. And yet, defying all common sense, the specialists and mechanics were forced to apply this method. Lebedev would not accept any arguments for a selective use of the new method and as a result many people lost their jobs. And yet no-one was held responsible for the consequences of this action, which resulted in hundreds of thousands of acres of crops rotting in the fields.

At first it seemed to me that Ivan Kononovich's character was highly original. But when Khrushchev came to Stavropol in October 1958 to award the krai the Order of Lenin, I understood that it was not so. For the first time I had a good look at Khrushchev. Watching him, I noticed his open and frank ways, his peculiar folksy manner and his desire to establish contact with everyone. Khrushchev's style created a kind of standard – and many leaders of lower rank tried to imitate him.

The problem was that this 'leadership style' – especially against the background of a vastly inadequate level of general culture – would often end up being vulgar. The spontaneity and folksiness occasionally turned into open boorishness, not to mention the foul language and heavy drinking.

Ivan Kononovich would unabashedly try to ingratiate himself with any senior official who arrived from Moscow. But the moment anyone tumbled down from the heights of power, Lebedev was ready to kick him. This happened with Bulganin. After the defeat of the 'Anti-Party Group' in 1957,[1] Bulganin was later dismissed from his post as Chairman of the USSR Council of Ministers and from membership of the Central Committee Presidium, and was 'exiled' to our region as chairman of the krai economic council. He received a warm welcome in Stavropol. In the mornings, when Bulganin arrived in his office at the economic council, a crowd – sometimes numbering several hundred people – would be waiting there for him. This only infuriated Lebedev.

'Playing up to retrograde sentiments, huh?' he would shout at Bulganin from the rostrum at party meetings. 'Why did you come here, to propagate democracy, or what?'

Lebedev virtually scorned Bulganin, collected bits and pieces of scandalous rumours about him, summoned him to the bureau for the slightest error, and finally tried to dismiss him from his post at the krai economic council and transfer him to be director of a minor factory. Bulganin avoided this 'transfer', thanks to Khrushchev's direct intervention. He eventually retired and left Stavropol for good.

The end of Lebedev's career was typical for those times. He carried out every decision taken by superiors without questioning it, and things seemed to proceed smoothly for him. In 1956 he received the Order of Lenin for 'successfully introducing the two-stage harvesting method'. The next year he received his second Order of Lenin on the occasion of his fiftieth birthday. In 1958 we had a bumper harvest and delivered over 100 million poods[2] of grain to the state: the krai was awarded the Order of Lenin and Lebedev received his third Order. Impressive, isn't it: three Orders of Lenin within three years? And only a year later he was ousted.

---

[1] This group, which included Molotov, Malenkov and Kaganovich, attempted to remove Khrushchev as First Party Secretary because of policy differences.

[2] A pood was equivalent to 16.38 kilograms.

It was Lebedev's over-zealousness that eventually destroyed him. At the end of 1958, when the euphoria of the first achievements in agriculture went to Khrushchev's head, he publicly proclaimed the goal of catching up with and overtaking the United States in *per-capita* production of meat and milk. Nikita Sergeyevich made it clear to Party leaders that he expected quick and impressive results. And, because the goal was simply impossible to achieve, he thus encouraged, irrespective of his intentions, blatant and large-scale deceit. Authorities used pressure to buy up cattle from the peasants' individual smallholdings and bought additional livestock from neighbouring regions. The Ryazan secretary Larionov distinguished himself particularly during this campaign; in one year, 1959, Ryazan oblast fulfilled the three-year plan for meat production, while Stavropol fulfilled the plan for two and a half years. But at what a cost! Flocks of sheep, oxen and horses were butchered, and the peasants' smallholdings completely devastated.

The press glorified the 'harbingers of spring' and called on others to emulate the example of the vanguard regions. However, the deception was soon uncovered. Larionov shot himself and Lebedev was dismissed in January 1960 'for health reasons'. But the deed was done: this 'meat campaign' dealt such a blow to the country's private agricultural sector that its consequences have continued to be felt until recently.

THE XXIIND PARTY CONGRESS

The XXIInd Party Congress (for me it was my first) in October 1961 reflected the contradictions of the time. I wrote down my impressions as diligently as I could, but even without those notes many events during the weeks of debates are still vivid in my memory. I recall particularly the episodes connected with the criticisms of Stalin's 'personality cult'. After the defeat of the 'anti-Party group', Khrushchev had succeeded in forcing many of the remaining leaders to state their views publicly on this issue in their speeches to the Congress.

Emotions reached their climax on 30 October when D. A. Lazurkina, an old Bolshevik, took the floor during the morning meeting. Her speech had a tinge of mysticism. She even provided factual evidence of supernatural communication with the hereafter. 'I always carry Lenin in my heart,' she said, 'and, comrades, I endured the greatest hardships in my life only thanks to the fact that Lenin was in my heart and that I took counsel with him. Yesterday, I consulted with Lenin, as if he were alive, standing before me, and he said: "I hate being together with Stalin, who has brought so many misfortunes upon the Party".' The Congress adopted unanimously a resolution to remove Stalin's coffin from the Mausoleum and bury it near the Kremlin wall.

In Stavropol, an openly hostile crowd gathered when in the middle of the night workers with tractors started removing an enormous statue of Stalin that stood in the city centre. But the worst was avoided and the job completed: the statue was removed and Stalin Avenue renamed Marx Avenue.

At the time, we viewed criticism of the personality cult as a confirmation and continuation of the reformist course established by the XXth Party Congress. But alarming signs became more and more common, as Khrushchev was praised to the skies. This was particularly conspicuous during discussion of the new Party programme. Personally, I was happy to see a document that addressed the needs of the people and proclaimed the necessity for peace and peaceful co-existence – but many passages were triumphalist in tone, and complex social issues had been dealt with too superficially.

And yet a number of delegates, all of them prominent Party members, virtually engaged in a singing contest with their odes to Khrushchev. One compared Nikita Sergeyevich's rather confused speech to the sound of 'a powerful symphony'. Another called Khrushchev 'an outstanding Leninist', who had 'great insight into the fundamental life processes, and an ardent fighter for peace'. What irritated me most was the fact that Khrushchev seemed to enjoy listening to these eulogies. It reminded me of something painfully familiar. And how did the delegates react? We applauded, although many of us felt ill at ease.

KHRUSHCHEV'S DRAMA

I am convinced that history will never forget Khrushchev's denunciation of Stalin's personality cult. It is, of course, true that his secret report to the XXth Party Congress contained scant analysis and was excessively subjective. To attribute the complex problem of totalitarianism simply to external factors and the evil character of a dictator was a simple and hard-hitting tactic – but it did not reveal the profound roots of this tragedy. Khrushchev's personal political aims were also transparent: by being the first to denounce the personality cult, he shrewdly isolated his closest rivals and antagonists, Molotov, Malenkov, Kaganovich and Voroshilov – who, together with Khrushchev, had been Stalin's closest associates.

True enough. But in terms of history and 'wider politics' the actual consequences of Khrushchev's political actions were crucial. The criticism of Stalin, who personified the regime, served not only to disclose the gravity of the situation in our society and the perverted character of the political struggle that was taking place within it – it also revealed a lack of basic legitimacy. The criticism morally discredited totalitarianism, arousing hopes for a reform of the system and serving as a strong impetus to new processes in the sphere of politics and economics as well as in the spiritual life of our country. Khrushchev and his supporters must be given full credit for this. Khrushchev must be given credit too for the rehabilitation of thousands of people, and the restoration of the good name of hundreds of thousands of innocent citizens who perished in Stalinist prisons and camps.

Khrushchev's denunciation of Stalin's crimes is a telling illustration of the controversial role he played in our history: on the one hand, his daring and resolute stand, his readiness to breast the current – and, on the other hand, a political vision hampered by stereotyped thinking and his inability or reluctance to reveal the underlying causes of the contentious phenomena he was facing.

To perceive the tragic events in Soviet history as the result of Stalin's 'evil' nature is a fundamental mistake. If that were the only reason, it would have been sufficient to replace a bad leader with a good one, and we would be spared from repeating previous errors. Khrushchev seemed to suggest exchanging one personality cult for another, without questioning the system's foundations.

Khrushchev had no intention of analysing systematically the roots of totalitarianism. He was probably not even capable of doing so. And for this very reason the criticism of the personality cult, though rhetorically harsh, was in essence incomplete and confined from the start to well-defined limits. The process of true democratization was nipped in the bud.

Khrushchev's foreign policy was characterized by the same inconsistencies. His active presence in the international political arena, his proposal of peaceful co-existence and his initial attempts at normalizing relations with the leading countries of the capitalist world; the newly defined relations with India, Egypt and other Third World states; and finally, his attempt to democratize ties with socialist allies – including his decision to mend matters with Yugoslavia – all this was well received both in our country and in the rest of the world and, undoubtedly, helped to improve the international situation.

But at the same time there was the brutal crushing of the Hungarian uprising in 1956; the adventurism that culminated in the Cuba crisis of 1962, when the world was on the brink of a nuclear disaster; and the quarrel with China, which resulted in a protracted period of antagonism and enmity.

All domestic and foreign policy decisions made at that time undoubtedly reflected not only Khrushchev's personal understanding of the problems and his moods, but also the different political forces that he had to consider. The pressure of Party and government structures was especially strong, forcing him to manoeuvre and to present this or that measure in a form acceptable to such influential groups.

I assume that Khrushchev could have pursued his ideas and objectives much further had it not been for the conditions under which he was forced to act. I cannot accept the view that he acted as a reformer only to defeat the 'Stalinist guard' and thus reinforce his own position, before carrying out his arbitrary and subjective views. In spite of his inner contradictions,

Khrushchev appears to me as someone more consistent in his actions.

Khrushchev, obviously, never challenged the leading role of the Party; his intention was simply to modernize it and to reduce its overall monopoly. But he met with bitter resistance that led to his eventual defeat. True, he won the first round in 1957. At the time, the Central Committee – i.e. principally the first secretaries of the republic, oblast and krai committees – successfully defended Khrushchev from his opponents. He had removed the old Party 'marshals', who treated the regional secretaries like pawns, and instead expanded the rights of republican and local powers. These measures were naturally approved by the 'generals' – the rank-and-file members of the Central Committee, who resolutely sided with Khrushchev against the 'anti-Party group'. The army, too, backed him at the time.

But Khrushchev's subsequent actions changed the situation. The break-up of the oblast organizations, the reshuffling of Party cadres, and the endless reassignments aimed at rejuvenating the latter, affected their own interests adversely and stirred unrest among the group of 'Party generals'. The decision to hold annual elections for the secretaries of grass-roots Party organizations – supposedly to improve the rotation of cadres and prevent their 'taking root' and remaining too long at the same posts – caused a negative reaction from the Party 'officer corps', which was carrying the brunt of the work in the workers' collectives.

And this was not all. Khrushchev's popularity with the common people was also dwindling rapidly. Suslov's fears, expressed on the eve of the October 1964 plenary meeting, that Khrushchev's removal might cause unrest among the population proved to be unfounded. The 1961 currency reform eventually affected the interests of the working masses. And Khrushchev's campaign against the peasants' smallholdings made him unpopular in the countryside. The poor harvest of 1963 aggravated the food situation and led to a 'temporary' increase in food prices. Khrushchev's relations with the army and with the scientific and artistic world rapidly deteriorated.

There were ample anti-Khrushchev arguments to justify the

palace revolution. But under the surface of lofty words about 'the good of the people' was first and foremost the desire of Party 'generals' and 'officers' to cling to power – and in October 1964 the Central Committee of the CPSU, which had supported Khrushchev in 1957, overthrew him.

5

LAUNCHING MY PARTY CAREER

KULAKOV'S ARRIVAL

IN JANUARY 1960, OUR FIRST SECRETARY, LEBEDEV, WAS replaced by N. I. Belyaev, former member of the CPSU Central Committee Presidium and first secretary of the Central Committee of the Communist Party of Kazakhstan. He came to our krai after the tragic events in Temirtau, where growing unrest among the workers had been crushed by army tanks. Belyaev was here in a sort of exile – he appeared to be completely lost, thrown off his path. He left Stravropol barely six months later, and Fedor Davydovich Kulakov became our krai committee first secretary.

Kulakov came from a peasant family in Kursk oblast and knew rural life quite well. He received a warm welcome in our krai; his arrival aroused many hopes. He was forty-two years old. He differed from his predecessors not only because of his youth, but also because of his enviably resolute and open nature. Such, at least, was the initial impression he made on me (and on many others).

I was re-elected first secretary of the Komsomol krai committee at the annual conference in January 1962. Fedor Davydovich summoned me a few weeks later and suggested that I should transfer from Komsomol to Party work. In March 1962, I took up the newly created post of krai committee representative for the Stavropol territorial department, which included three suburban agricultural districts. Selection for this post was extremely rigorous and involved an interview of all candidates at the CPSU Central Committee.

I was totally committed to my job. I spent days, and often nights, travelling around the districts, visiting farms and trying to develop new management structures. I was deeply convinced that we had embarked upon the right path and once the technocrats were free to do their job it would soon bear fruit. Being a candidate member of the krai Party committee bureau, I had frequent dealings with Kulakov. As in the past, he would entrust me with all kinds of tasks and invite me on trips through the krai.

In late November Kulakov invited me to his office and suggested (a bolt from the blue!) that I should join the agricultural krai committee as head of the Department of Party Organs. I took up my new duties on 1 January 1963.

The CPSU had, in fact, supplanted all functions – and taken over not only the country's leadership but also all other governing functions in our society. Hence the Department of Party Organs predominated over other departments. We had miscellaneous tasks to fulfil: organizational work in the krai Party organizations, 'supervision' of the soviets, trade unions and the Komsomol. But the department's actual importance lay in its responsibility for the 'selection, appointment and education' of the cadres, the famous 'nomenklatura' which included all positions of any importance – ranging from pure Party jobs to leading posts in enterprises and including sovkhoz and kolkhoz chairmen. This was the source of the krai committee's real power.

My work at the Department of Party Organs brought me closer to Kulakov. We met almost daily and gradually established a sound working relationship.

Kulakov had a strong and generous character. Having often accompanied him on his trips around the krai, I saw the ease with which he found a common language both with farmers and with specialists; he was himself an expert in the field. His intelligence was of a special kind – he was endowed with a kind of peasant cunning, I would say. When Kulakov was transferred to the Party Central Committee in October 1964, we parted as friends and maintained close relations throughout the subsequent years.

ANOTHER LEADER IN DISGRACE

Leonid Nikolaevich Yefremov's arrival as Kulakov's successor was totally unexpected. I later learned that Kulakov had taken an active part in the preparations for Khrushchev's removal: he was among the Secretaries summoned to Moscow on the eve of the October plenary meeting to carry out a special mission: they were to present their accusations should the members of the Central Committee Presidium[1] run out of convincing arguments in favour of Khrushchev's 'voluntary' retirement. Brezhnev appreciated Kulakov's willingness to support him. Immediately after the October plenum Fedor Davydovich was confirmed as head of the Central Committee agricultural department, and eleven months later, in September 1965, he was elected a secretary of the Central Committee.

Yefremov was renowned among Party members and throughout the country. He was an experienced man, having worked for years as second secretary and chairman of the Kuibyshev oblast Soviet executive committee, and later as first secretary of the Kursk and Gorky oblast Party committees. In 1962, he had become first deputy chairman of the Central Committee bureau for the Russian Federation. Khrushchev himself chaired the bureau, but all the routine work was done by his deputies, Yefremov and Kirilenko: they were both candidate members of the Central Committee Presidium, and they were supposedly of equal rank.

Yefremov was not involved in the plotting of the October palace revolution. He later told me that he had learned of the events while on a business trip to Ulan Ude. He had no prior information of the plenum and when he heard about it he rushed to the airport, where he was told that the plane needed repairs and the flight was delayed. Undoubtedly, this delay had been planned in advance.

Yefremov was known as a fervent Khrushchev supporter. Not long before these events, Khrushchev had visited a number of Russian oblasts – in the company of Yefremov. A documentary

[1] Politburo.

was made about this trip, and there was Leonid Nikolaevich right behind Nikita Khrushchev. These pictures were well remembered.

I heard from various sources that anyone visiting Yefremov's office on a business matter was immediately confronted with one of Khrushchev's books arranged neatly on his desk, which Yefremov would open to display an abundance of bookmarks and notes and start quoting from it. He used to conclude all conversations with the words: 'See, this is what Comrade Khrushchev has written on this issue. So you should start from there.'

According to Yefremov's own recollection, he joined the anti-Khrushchev campaign upon his return to Moscow – but like Mikoyan, he supported the view that Nikita Sergeyevich should stay in office.

This was probably the reason why the Central Committee Presidium decided to transfer Leonid Nikolaevich to Stavropol, while he retained his post as candidate member of the Presidium. In November 1964 the Central Committee plenum heard N. V. Podgorny's report and decided to reunite the industrial and agricultural oblast and krai Party organizations. And as of 1 December Yefremov was appointed head of the organizational bureau that was to implement this decision in Stavropol.

Weeks of hectic activity ensued. Barely two years had passed since the division of the krai committee into two separate units – but the alienation and rivalry between the two organizations had at times reached appalling proportions. Now that a single staff had to be recreated combining the cadres of both krai committees, a virtual battle was unleashed over the vacancies to be reassigned. As head of the Department of Party Organs of the former agricultural krai committee, I found myself in the eye of the storm. Everyone fought for himself, defending not only personal interests and jobs but also the social status and power that went with them. Many could not care less about things that really mattered.

The first two years of my work with Yefremov developed into a period of mutual adjustment, maybe even of drawing closer. Yefremov differed from his predecessor in his broad political horizon, his erudition and his general education and culture. He was, undoubtedly, an outstanding personality, while being at the same time a refined product of the system – an impressive representative of the CPSU cadre school. In this respect, the years I spent working together with him were a most instructive experience for me.

Yefremov greatly resented his transfer to the provinces. It was partly due to this that he had such a hard time dealing with the details of krai affairs. Apparently he still harboured the illusion that Brezhnev would call him back to Moscow. And he was initially much more interested in events in Moscow than in local Stavropol problems.

I used to telephone Yefremov before going to his office to discuss ideas or documents. But once I chanced into his office without prior notice. He was sitting at his desk, his chin resting on his fists, staring blankly at the wall. I approached him and sat down, but the embarrassing silence dragged on. Deep in his thoughts, he was not aware of my presence.

'Leonid Nikolaevich, are you all right?' I asked in an undertone. As if startled from a dream, but still absorbed in his thoughts, he started talking:

'How could this have happened? You see, I backed Kirilenko, I defended him, but he didn't say a word in my favour.'

'What are you talking about, Leonid Nikolaevich?' I could not grasp his meaning. He pulled himself together, waving the thoughts aside with a smile.

'Nothing . . . I was just remembering the Presidium sessions in October 1964 . . . Well, Mikhail, such is life.'

Yefremov was anxiously awaiting the XXIIIrd Party Congress. He still believed he would remain candidate member of the Central Committee Presidium. Whenever Brezhnev went to a seaside resort for his holiday, Leonid Nikolaevich went out of his way to get there too. They would meet, sometimes even in a family circle, and in his heart of hearts glimmered the hope that a successful speech by him at the Congress would help him return to Moscow. He never doubted that he would be given the floor.

At the end of March 1966 – on the eve of the Party Congress – I happened to be in Moscow on business. Yefremov asked me to stay on and help him with his speech. He was terribly nervous, and seeing his plight I wanted to lend him a hand. Every day while the Congress was in session I had to stay in his room at the Peking Hotel, working on his forthcoming speech and amending it in the light of the Congress debates. Leonid Nikolaevich used every break in the proceedings to telephone me at the hotel and outline additional remarks and introduce alternative views or new emphases which had eluded me.

As might have been expected, the miracle did not happen and Yefremov was not asked to take the floor. As krai committee secretary he remained a Central Committee member, but he could not hope for more. And, to give Leonid Nikolaevich his due, he became fully involved in Stavropol problems.

SECRETARY OF THE STAVROPOL GORKOM

On 26 September 1966 I was unanimously elected first secretary at the plenum of the Stavropol city committee. According to the nomenklatura scale (and, accordingly, the scale of wages), this position ranked lower than the one I held at the krai committee as head of the Department of Party Organs. But what attracted me was the greater independence I would enjoy in this job. The city committee officials received me well; many remembered me from my work at the Komsomol and I had maintained contact with the city's Party administration throughout the subsequent years. I knew most of the leading members of the academic and artistic communities and Party officials.

There were scores of problems to worry about. As I said, Stavropol was in those years an ordinary provincial town, so typical of our Russian hinterland. Until the mid-1960s the entire infrastructure of the city – health care, education, culture, consumer services, transport, water supply and heating systems, and, particularly, the sewage system – was in a miserable state. Sewage often poured into the open gutters lining the streets. Stavropol's industry consisted merely of a plant for wood-processing machines, a textile and a footwear factory, a liquor and vodka distillery, and several dairies.

The need for major changes was in the air, as the saying goes.

The city's unique landscape, with its hills, its ponds in the lowlands and the woods closing in on the suburban areas – all this offered wonderful opportunities for urban development. And in September 1966 – the month I was appointed secretary of the city committee – the city Soviet adopted a general development project for Stavropol to be implemented over the next twenty-five years.

The eternal question arose of where to get the necessary funds for reconstruction and building. In addition to meagre state funds from central financing institutions, we could obtain financial support only from the very few industrial enterprises in the city. The one-sided geographical distribution of industries in the country brought about over many years by Gosplan exacerbated this problem. Only the creation of local economic councils enabled us to build modern plants in the city, including an electrical appliances factory, a trailer factory, a chemical plant for the processing of reagents etc. Our urban development projects depended on the 'Kosygin reform' implemented throughout the country – expanding the financial and economic independence of individual enterprises, particularly their newly acquired right to dispose of a considerable part of their income at their discretion. The success of the reform depended to a large extent on its acceptance by cadres, engineers and technicians.

In April 1967 we called a city committee plenum to discuss the problems of implementing our reforms. Although we had tried to define our own role and had to the best of our abilities pushed ahead with the reforms, there was still no significant progress.

The key to changes was out of reach of Stavropol. It seemed that the central ministries and agencies were coping with separate individual problems, avoiding comprehensive decisions – and were not in the least interested in a genuine transition to a new system of work planning and incentives. The krai Party committee and the Central Committee alike were primarily concerned with the fulfilment of the plan.

Nonetheless, the Stavropol general development project gradually progressed. Buildings were covered with scaffolding. Virtually all of us, the workers of the city Party committee, turned into construction foremen. New industrial plants were being built and there was a growing need for qualified labour. In my time as secretary of the city Komsomol there had been an acute shortage of jobs for young people in the city, which drove them to other regions; but now we had to invite specialists from outside. We felt the need for a technical university. To begin with, we opened a branch of the Krasnodar polytechnic institute and expanded the existing institutes and technical schools.

Housing construction increased significantly, as new apartment blocks were built and new residential complexes created. A new plant was turning out prefabricated houses. The city streets were paved and a trolley line appeared. A circus, a swimming pool and a library were built.

There were also changes in our family. In 1967 Raisa Maksimovna successfully defended her dissertation in sociology and earned the academic title of candidate of philosophical sciences (PhD). She worked enthusiastically, lecturing and teaching, and carried out a number of sociological research projects in the krai districts. That same year, I graduated from the faculty of economics at the agricultural institute. Together with friends we celebrated my wife's successful defence of her dissertation and my graduation.

We led a life which to us was important and meaningful. We lived in harmony and helped each other whenever it was needed. Our living conditions improved with increased income. We were able to furnish the two-room flat we had received in 1960. We bought an Elektron television set.

Problems, of course, abounded. About this time a rift first appeared in my relations with Yefremov, with disagreements on numerous, often trivial matters. We talked less frequently, and I concentrated on my city job.

APPARATUS GAMES

'Major apparatus games' at the krai committee marked the summer of 1968, culminating in the reassignment of various officials. It happened because the First Secretary of the Karachai-Cherkess oblast committee, Luzhin, brazenly left his wife for another woman. Public opinion was indignant. Luzhin was dismissed from his post, and F. P. Burmistrov, who had previously worked as second secretary of the krai committee, was elected in his stead.

Yefremov's group was on the move. None of this concerned me at all – I had my own plans. I had made up my mind to turn to academic work. I passed the candidate exams, chose as a thesis topic the problems of specialization and geographical distribution of agricultural industries in the Stavropol region, and started to gather research material. When the fierce battle for the position of Second Secretary flared up, I took a holiday and booked places at a health resort in Sochi for me and Raisa Maksimovna.

But just before our departure, I received an unexpected telephone call from the head of the general department, Pavel Yudin. 'Mikhail, don't leave yet. Stay a while; it's Leonid Nikolaevich's instruction.'

A day passed, then another. I telephoned Yefremov.

'Leonid Nikolaevich, I received your request to stay. But I've made reservations at a health resort, and my family's waiting to leave. Would you please allow me to take my holiday?'

'Wait till the plenum,' insisted Yefremov.

'The plenum will do without me. I support your motion in advance.'

'I told you to wait. That's all.' And Yefremov hung up.

A few days passed. Finally Yefremov summoned me to his office – to discuss my possible candidacy.

'Leonid Nikolaevich,' I said, 'you don't want to work with me. Why force yourself? There are plenty of people who want the job, so why don't you let me take my vacation?'

'You're going to Moscow,' he replied with apparent resentment.

It turned out that my nomination for the post of Second Secretary had already been decided. Yefremov called a meeting of the krai committee bureau and my candidacy was supported unanimously. Everyone left after the meeting. I stayed, waiting for Yefremov. When it became obvious that he had no intention of inviting me to see him, I decided to call on him myself.

'Go to Moscow,' was all he said.

'Where to? To see whom? What do you recommend?'

'You know very well where to. To the Central Committee organization department. There are plenty of people there who support you.'

I have in front of me the minutes of the Stavropol krai committee plenum of 5 August 1968: 'Having thoroughly considered the question and having consulted the Central Committee, guided by the Leninist principle of combining young and old cadres, we nominate Comrade Mikhail Sergeyevich Gorbachev as second secretary of the krai committee.'

No questions were addressed to me. The election was unanimous. The minutes create the impression of a general felicitous unanimity, as if there were no passionate fights behind the nomination. But both I and the other krai committee members knew perfectly well that among the undivided and disciplined 'yes' votes there were also those that had firmly opposed the decision – among them Yefremov, who went on holiday to Kislovodsk immediately after my nomination, without even speaking to me.

After two or three months of mutual adjustment we gradually restored our former normal and friendly relations, which we sustained, notwithstanding all the disagreements we may have had.

THE DEFEAT OF THE REFORMERS

The spirit of reform kindled in the 1950s and 1960s was strong and dynamic; the need for changes in so many spheres of social life was only too obvious. Brezhnev was forced to manoeuvre skilfully between different Politburo factions and to disguise carefully his own conservative views. Both the March 1965 plenum on agriculture and the September plenum on economic incentives to increase industrial productivity were essentially progressive and aimed at reforming the existing system of economic management.

Yet the decisions taken at these meetings were never implemented. An ambiguous situation developed: while the press heatedly discussed all kinds of projects and published articles by economists and publicists, the resurrected ministries were 'quietly doing their job', tightening the screws of bureaucratic centralism. Local authorities viewed all innovations with scepticism: 'Up there in Moscow all they do is talk, while we have to do the job and fulfil the plan.' The so-called Barakov case was a striking illustration of this attitude. It happened in Stavropol, before my nomination as Second Secretary of the krai committee.

I knew Innokenty Barakov quite well. He was energetic, had an independent mind and was probably too impulsive. He was friendly with the reformist economist Lisichkin and an ardent exponent of the latter's ideas. Nobody objected as long as Barakov – whether in private or in public – spoke only of the need for 'easing' the state plan and expanding the rights of the kolkhozes to allow them to sell their produce freely. But things took a serious turn when he tried to implement these ideas in his Georgievsk district.

As head of the district agricultural department, Barakov stopped forcing the farms to fulfil rigid plans, leaving the initiative to them. In those days, the krai committee perceived this as an open assault upon the entire 'system'. Barakov was first summoned to a bureau meeting and warned, then on 21 January 1967 he was relieved of his duties.

I had not attended that meeting, but I learned that Barakov was accused of committing 'grave errors in a number of his pronouncements on fundamental political issues'. It was further pointed out that his 'insistent, confusing statements' about the right of the kolkhozes and sovkhozes to sell their produce on the free market and to strengthen their economies by any means and methods 'caused objective harm to the education of the cadres in the spirit of responsibility toward the implementation of Party and government decisions. Failing to fulfil the state plan for the sale of grain and other products, some kolkhozes had permitted the free marketing of their produce . . .'

Yefremov – who had a fine nose for sensing which way the wind was blowing – decided that it was high time for 'our organization to present its views nationally'. On 13 September 1967 the Central Committee agricultural newspaper, *Selskaya Zhizn*, published an article entitled 'Contrary to facts', signed by Yefremov and other krai party workers. The article attacked Gennady Lisichkin's essay 'After two years', which had appeared in the journal *Novy Mir* in February 1967.

Lisichkin was accused of 'making absurd, unrealistic suggestions, such as free trade in kolkhoz and sovkhoz produce, the abolition of planned state purchases of produce paid in kind ... disregarding the principle of socialist planning based on the maximum levels already achieved'. But the main charge was that by 'trying to substantiate his economic recommendations, which are both theoretically confused and not adapted to real life, Lisichkin distorts and juggles with facts drawn from the life and work of the kolkhozes and sovkhozes of Stavropol krai'.

Barakov's fate made the future appear rather ominous. That was the time when the decisions of the March 1965 Central Committee plcnum – which had spurred the quest for new solutions in agriculture – were supposed to be implemented. You might have expected that the 'Kosygin reforms' would serve as an additional impetus for this quest. Alas, as in industry, changes in agriculture were not to exceed the clearly defined limits. Barakov's and Lisichkin's suggestions went further – and, therefore, the 'Barakov case' demonstrated the urgent need for changes and bore testimony to the system's immediate sharp reaction to the mere possibility of such changes. It was a hard lesson for me.

In the early summer of 1967, I met Zdenek Mlynar, an old friend from Moscow University. He worked at the State and Law Institute of the Czechoslovak Academy of Sciences and had come to Moscow to discuss proposals for planned political reforms. His speech met a cool reception in Moscow academic circles. Subsequently he visited Georgia and came to Stavropol to spend a few days with us.

I have already mentioned that we lived in a two-room flat on the fourth floor. This was our first self-contained home and we liked it. Zdenek inspected it rather critically. Apparently, by Czechoslovak standards, it was rather modest for a Party committee secretary of a capital city. Zdenek asked me about the situation in our country and our krai and about our life. He described the latest developments in Czechoslovakia in detail, telling us how Novotny's[1] authority was dwindling. From what he said, I realized that Czechoslovakia was on the verge of major upheaval.

A few months later I read in a newspaper that Mlynar had been appointed to the Central Committee of the Czechoslovak Communist Party. He was one of the authors of the famous 'Action programme of the Czechoslovak CP' and an active participant in the 'Prague Spring'. I wrote him a letter, but waited in vain for an answer. From hints dropped by the head of the krai KGB, who was also a member of the krai committee bureau, I understood that my letter had landed in a different postbox.

We received only biased reports about the 1968 events in Prague. All information was under strict and total control, and this news, obviously, even more so. The events – I mean the entry of armed forces – started on 21 August, only days after I had been elected second secretary. Since Yefremov was away, I chaired the meetings of the krai committee bureau. Leonid Nikolaevich telephoned me before the meeting which had been called to discuss the Politburo communiqué on the invasion by Warsaw Pact troops. He informed me about the deliberations of the Central Committee and outlined his own suggestions. The bureau then adopted a resolution approving the 'decisive and timely measures taken in defence of socialist achievements in the CSSR' (Czechoslovakia). The krai committee expressed its support for the Central Committee, although, quite frankly, one had to wonder about the purpose of the invasion and whether it was excessive.

Guided by these and similar thoughts, I was trying to grasp the underlying causes of many grievous phenomena in our domestic and foreign policies. Patently reaction was on the move. After 21 August ideological 'streamlining' and the harsh suppression of the smallest display of dissent were the order of the day. The Central Committee demanded that local authorities should take decisive ideological measures – the struggle against dissent was intensified all over the country.

[1] First Secretary of the Communist Party of Czechoslovakia.

In early 1969 F. B. Sadykov, the acting head of the faculty of philosophy at the Stavropol agricultural institute, published a book with the krai publishing house under the title *Unity of the People and Contradictions of Socialism*. It had been written earlier – on the wave of hopes and expectations aroused by Khrushchev's and also Kosygin's reforms. The manuscript of the book was discussed at the faculty a year before its publication. Sadykov had brought it to Moscow – had even shown it to someone in the Central Committee apparatus and published an article in the journal *Voprosy Filosofii* (*Problems of Philosophy*).

Basically, Sadykov had formulated a number of ideas which began to be implemented during the period of perestroika. But that was still over fifteen years ahead. And by 1969 ideas half-heartedly accepted a few years earlier were considered 'subversive'.

Moscow sent word: 'Severe criticism necessary'. At the krai committee bureau meeting held on 13 May, we reviewed the 'grave errors contained in the book by F. B. Sadykov, assistant professor at the faculty of philosophy of the Stavropol agricultural institute'. We really tore him to pieces. Yes, this was a real execution. Our leading 'ideologist', Likhota, demanded Sadykov's expulsion from the Party. Yefremov did not support the motion. My speech was highly critical. Sadykov was severely reprimanded and dismissed as faculty head. Soon afterwards he left Stavropol for Ufa, if I remember correctly.

I was deeply affected by what had happened to Barakov and Sadykov. I knew both of them personally as intelligent, thoughtful people. I had qualms of conscience about the cruel and undeserved punishment meted out to them.

The reformist spirit was dying before our very eyes. The implementation of sensible, intelligent decisions taken at the 1965–7 Central Committee plenums came to a standstill. The 'Kosygin reform' was losing its impetus. Letters written by the specialists and scientists were carefully stored away in the archive cellars. The events in Czechoslovakia had practically put an end to all subsequent quests for ways and means to transform the existing system of economic management.

It was the beginning of 'the period of stagnation'.

6

THE CHALLENGE OF POWER

FIRST SECRETARIES – A SPECIAL PHENOMENON

FINALLY, IN THE SPRING OF 1970, YEFREMOV'S DESIRE WAS satisfied and he left for Moscow. I replaced him as first secretary of the Stavropol Kraikom (Territorial Committee).

The sweeping powers enjoyed by the first secretaries of the republican central committees, the obkoms (regional party committees) and the kraikoms were conditioned by the internal structure and mechanisms which shaped the prevailing system. First secretaries were the mainstay of the regime. They integrated the scattered and diverse departmental and administrative units of the apparatus into a single system within the state and the social structure. They made up the majority of the Party Central Committee, and their votes were decisive in the election of the General Secretary. Hence their clout. They had propelled Khrushchev to victory in the struggle against Molotov and Malenkov. His subsequent downfall was also engineered by them. The system hand-picked the most active and dynamic leaders from industry and agriculture, science and academia. They came from a wide variety of social groups and strata. However, once they joined the ranks of the nomenklatura each was assigned a certain place within the system and each had to play the rules of the game. Finally, having sifted the cadres through such a 'Party Separator' the system processed the 'butter' into 'cream'.

The prestige of a first secretary in his domain was comparable to that of a tsarist governor. First secretaries held the reins of power firmly in their hands. In their regions the entire management system, even including elective organizations, was under their control. No appointment escaped their attention, and even minor executive positions needed their approval. No enterprise or institution would make an appointment without the nod of the first secretary. The defence sector, being 'a state within a state', was perhaps the only exception to this rule. Yet even there the local Party leadership was consulted.

The first secretary was a key figure in the system. The special status he enjoyed and the enormous power he wielded were not built on the will of the people or the result of free elections, but were bestowed on him by the supreme establishment in Moscow: the Politburo, the Secretariat of the Central Committee, the General Secretary of the Communist Party. In fact, that was the weak point of a first secretary and reflected the duality of his situation. He could instantly lose his position and his power as soon as the powers that be changed their opinion of him.

The General Secretary had the last word on the appointment of a first secretary. Brezhnev chose them most carefully. The procedure required a far-reaching investigation of the candidate's background, which was usually carried out by I. V. Kapitonov and K. U. Chernenko. They drew their information from various sources. A preliminary judgement was made, based on the results of the investigation. Then the candidate met the Central Committee secretaries, and eventually was admitted to 'him in person', i.e. the General Secretary. I ran the entire gamut of the procedure. As soon as the problem of Yefremov's departure was raised, I was summoned to Moscow. I had appointments with Kapitonov, Kulakov and Suslov. It was a mandatory practice, to which all district, regional and republican first secretaries had to submit.

These interviews were strange and, I would say, absurd. We sat there opposite one another, smiling, engaged in casual but deliberate conversation. I knew perfectly well why I was there, but nothing was ever mentioned to that effect, for the decision was up to Brezhnev.

The last meeting, with the General Secretary, was quite a

different matter. Leonid Brezhnev knew how to create an amicable atmosphere; I realized that during my first meeting with him and in subsequent conversations. To begin with, he informed me that the Central Committee had recommended me for the post. 'Well,' he said, 'until now we've had outsiders doing this job – now we'll have a native.' Then, almost intimately, he began to reminisce about the war and the retreat to Novorossiisk through the region of the Don and the Kuban.

'The heat, the dust, the aridity . . . So hard to find a drop of water to quench our thirst! I observed people collecting rain-water on their roofs . . .'

Our conversation shifted easily to Stavropol and its problems. His artless intent was easily discerned: first he listened attentively, then made up his mind about his interlocutor's ability to analyse local and all-Union[1] problems.

Then our discussion turned to the state of the economy, the favourable outlook for the eighth Five Year Plan, and foreign policy issues. Détente was in the air, and the cadres worked more efficiently as a result of sustained stability in the country. All these matters were discussed by Brezhnev as if he were confiding his intimate thoughts to me. Our meeting in his office at Staraya Ploshchad lasted for several hours. Not in my wildest dreams could I have imagined that this office would be mine fifteen years later.

I have to note here that in the mid-1960s and the early 1970s Brezhnev was nothing like the cartoon figure that is made of him now.

GETTING DOWN TO BUSINESS

During my earliest days as first secretary of the krai committee I suggested developing a new policy to boost specialization, revamp industrial technology, and radically change the system of distribution of agricultural produce, which, in turn, should eventually improve the living standards of the local population. The

---

[1] Embracing the whole of the Soviet Union.

discussions led to the adoption of a long-term programme of agricultural development which was subsequently approved at the krai committee meeting in the autumn. Its key components included the appropriate location of agricultural enterprises, their specialization, the introduction of industrial technologies, the expansion of the irrigation network, the training of personnel and scientific research. Almost ten years of my life were devoted to the implementation of this programme aimed at stabilizing agricultural production.

The major task concerned the creation of a stable agriculture. According to the calculations of the Stavropol Zone Agricultural Research Institute, poor harvests were recorded in 75 of the 100 years between 1870 and 1970, and 52 of those years were afflicted by drought. Almost half of the territory is made up of dry or highly arid steppe. Disaster looms when dust storms from Astrakhan in the east whip over its southern region. They sweep over Stavropol heading westward. The crop yield was never certain until the grain was safely delivered to the silos.

Plans to build a water supply system dated back to the end of the nineteenth century. However, the initial work began in the 1930s, when the Terek-Kuma project was built and the Kuban-Egorlyk and Kuban-Kalaus canals were started. At the end of 1969 the two systems were renamed the Great Stavropol Canal. We arrived at the conclusion that, at the present pace of construction, neither we nor our children would benefit from the Great Stavropol Canal. The speeding up of the construction of the water supply system in the North Caucasus was discussed at the Central Committee plenum in May 1966 and again in July 1970. I decided that it was time to act. I drafted a memorandum to the Party Central Committee with a proposal to build a 480-kilometre-long canal stretching from the Prikuban area up to the Kuban and further on to the Kalmyk steppes.

While holidaying in Kislovodsk in the autumn of 1970, I met Yevgeny Yevgenevich Alekseyevsky, the USSR Minister of Land Reclamation and Water Management. I suggested he read my paper and set aside two or three days to visit the territory. Having complied with my request, the minister consulted experts and asked a great many questions. Subsequently he promised help. He suggested that instead of proposing a fifteen-year programme, we should plan for the next five years. An appointment with Brezhnev now became important.

At the time Baku was marking the fiftieth anniversary of Soviet power in Azerbaijan, and I was one of the guests from many republics who had gathered. Brezhnev was the guest of honour. I was standing next to him on the rostrum, and I asked him for an appointment. I explained the reason for my request and he agreed to see me. We met in December. Once again, I was facing an attentive listener. He studied the background information, asked many questions and finally requested that I leave the papers with him, including a table of droughts covering the last 100 years. Shortly afterwards a Politburo meeting was convened, to which I was not invited, and Brezhnev personally presented the plans for the canal system. I learned later that he had referred to 'new young leaders who address issues of national importance' and who 'deserve our support'.

On 7 January 1971 the Party Central Committee and the USSR Council of Ministers[1] adopted a resolution on the speeding up of the construction of the Great Stavropol Canal system and the water supply and irrigation project. To that end important funds were allocated. The project was proclaimed the 'All-Union Komsomol Project' and, consequently, thousands of young people flocked to our area and the necessary technical equipment was sent to us. The special task of building three tunnels was entrusted to the Metrostroi (Administration for the Construction of the Moscow Underground) organization.

Work proceeded speedily. By April 1974 the tunnel under the Crimea-Gireev Hills was complete, and in November the second section of the Great Stavropol Canal system was launched. However, the final completion of all six sections was still ahead of us. Other aspects of this programme had to be considered, in particular the choice of a relevant agricultural structure adapted to our specific needs. This problem was first raised in November 1970. At the time it seemed rather simple – the irrigated land would be used for wheat crops. Another proposal was to use this

---

[1] The Soviet government.

land for fodder crops such as alfalfa, which yields crops five times a season. Wheat was to be produced by applying the so-called dry-farming method, involving a series of technical measures based on the proper use of fallow soil. This method was recommended by the Stavropol Research Institute.

Nikolai Tereshchenko quietly went about implementing these pilot projects in his collective farm. As soon as the new irrigation system was extended and reached his collective farm's fields, he replanted alfalfa and maize in the irrigated area and transformed the fields which had become vacant into fallow land. The results were promising. In the arid years, when the harvest was scorched, Tereshchenko managed to attain about 20 centners per hectare from his collective farm. In better years, when other farms yielded 20 to 25 centners per hectare, Tereshchenko's farm produced at least 35.

Obviously, this practice should have been introduced elsewhere. Yet as soon as 'fallow lands' were mentioned, we were reminded that these were at variance with Central Committee policy. The Central Committee's resolution had designated the North Caucasus as an area where wheat was to be grown on irrigated lands. At the time, such a decision represented an insurmountable barrier, and no contrary arguments were acceptable. But, as the adage says, 'Every cloud has a silver lining'.

In 1975 and 1976 terrible droughts hit Stavropol. It was unusual for droughts to occur in two successive years. This disaster was intensified by severe frost and summer dust storms. In Stavropol such a combination had struck only once before in this century. 1976 was a harsh year. Total crop loss was observed on half of the fields; corn, pulses and grass were burned. In anticipation of the disaster the farmers left their houses and their land and moved to other areas or to neighbouring republics. We had to consider suspending work at every third collective farm in the krai, a total of 127.

On 29 May I set off from Stavropol on a small plane for the Arzgir region, where disaster had also struck and where I was to meet managers of collective and state farms. Flying at low altitude we saw nothing but burned fields. Small oases brightened the blackness only where scarce local water sources were available. My thoughts were gloomy – what consolation could I offer the people? True, the people of the steppe are known to be tough. After landing we headed to the House of Culture. As we entered, the audience looked up at us expectantly.

Earlier, I had had a stormy encounter with Kalinin, Russia's Deputy Minister of Agriculture. A native of our area, he had been in charge of the agricultural department before he was promoted to the ministerial post. I do not know what made him repeat insistently: 'We must slaughter the cattle immediately . . .' Perhaps he had panicked after inspecting the drought areas.

Georgy Starshikov, my friend and deputy chairman of krai-ispolkom, was present during that conversation. A taciturn but sensible and resolute man, he lost his cool: 'Take it easy, Yury Petrovich, will you? Are you here to help us or to scare us? We are in bad shape without you . . . Stop fussing . . . We'll assume our responsibility . . .'

Kalinin was miffed and left to report to the Central Committee. Next day Karlov, head of the Central Committee's department of agriculture, phoned me: 'Listen, Mikhail Sergeyevich, Kalinin is confused. He claims that you underestimate the situation. Kulakov seems to be there with him. You may expect a call from him shortly.'

He was right. The telephone rang soon afterwards. Kulakov was on the line.

'What are you up to, Mikhail?' The irritation in his voice was unmistakable. We had been working around the clock, and our nerves were stretched, to say the least. In order to control my temper I disregarded his tone and answered with deliberate calm:

'Nothing is being left to chance. We have considered our plans thoroughly. If we slaughtered the sheep and the cattle now it would take decades to restore the ruined farms. I'll do everything to prevent it.'

Kulakov fell silent and then added: 'If you are sure of what you are doing, go ahead. But watch out, the responsibility is yours.'

I do not know why Kulakov reacted so resentfully to my arguments. I suspected it was because in 1975, under similar circumstances, he had done what Kalinin was now suggesting – ordered the slaughter of millions of pigs throughout the country.

My opening words in Arzgir were as follows:

'You all know that we are facing disaster. We were born and raised on this land and we know how tricky and unpredictable the situation here may sometimes be. Therefore I shan't dwell on it. Our crops are lost on fifty per cent of the territory, but elsewhere the situation is normal. Now, let's get our heads together and see how we can save our cattle and our farms.'

An approving rumble went through the audience.

'I suggest you drive some of the meat cattle to the mountain pastures. Let the animals fatten up there and then they can be slaughtered. The whole population in the krai, everybody, without exception, must start immediately to prepare the fodder. We'll parcel out the fodder areas in the disaster-free zones to the steppe population. There is no other way. Anything else spells disaster. We're responsible for our krai, and I am sure that the country will help us.'

Fodder was collected in ditches and in forest strips, in gullies and in urban lawns. Even holiday-makers joined this all-out campaign.

I immediately took the plane to Moscow, informed Kulakov of my plans, and succeeded in getting to see Brezhnev. The centre extended its emergency aid by supplying 60,000 tonnes of concentrated fodder even before the new crop was harvested. Another crucial problem was the water shortage, which affected the people and the animals alike. The only possible solution was to bring water from other parts of the krai. As a result, water carriers and sprinkler vehicles disappeared from city streets for two months.

Then the rains came. Late fodder grass and maize were hurriedly sown. By the end of the year, 700,000 tonnes of grain forage had been distributed to the drought-afflicted areas. The krai was saved.

In the summer of 1976 I became convinced that the use of fallow land in farming was absolutely necessary. Once more, it was the experience of Tereshchenko and his followers which clearly confirmed this view. Their wheat harvest remained intact through the drought, although some yield was lost. In August I prepared a memorandum to the Politburo, pleading in favour of the dry-farming method best suited to our specific type of agriculture. I submitted my paper to Kulakov, aware of his adamant hostility to this method. I could not expect him to grasp the gravity of the situation, since he had spent most of his life in other regions. We had no intention of changing the grain procurement plans; it was just a matter of allowing farmers to decide on their own which farming method they would prefer. Once again Kulakov put the responsibility on me. 'If you don't mind the risk, discuss it with Leonid Ilyich,' he said. Brezhnev was then holidaying in the Crimea. Two days passed. On the third day the telephone rang at night from the krai committee headquarters. However, it was not the response I had been expecting. It was a message sent to all oblast and krai committee secretaries by a group of scientists at the Lenin All-Union Academy of Agricultural Sciences, recommending an *expansion* of winter crop surfaces due to favourable conditions. But I had sent off my memorandum to Brezhnev recommending a reduction! The paper prepared by the academics had probably been masterminded by Kulakov. Another two days passed before Brezhnev finally telephoned me.

'Mikhail Sergeyevich, I've read your paper. I've given it some thought and have consulted people. I remember Kazakhstan only too well. At that time, way back, Terenty Maltsev warned me that we wouldn't pull through without the use of fallow. Go ahead with your plan, I'll back you.'

I realized that his terse response came after much doubt. I later found out that Sergei Manyakin, secretary of the Omsk Party oblast committee, had been holidaying at the same time in the Crimea. He was a native of the Arzgir region in our krai. He often went for walks with the General Secretary's assistants and, when the issue of fallow came up, he responded, 'Gorbachev is right.' That is the way crucial problems were sometimes solved . . .

Once more I was on my way to Moscow. Together with Kulakov I drafted a decision of the Politburo and the government on the introduction of fallow methods in the agricultural area of our krai. The proposal was soon adopted. Attempts were immediately made to block the programme. The initial 'vigilance' signals originated with the apparatchiks at the Russian Council of Ministers. I was greatly put off by a Politburo resolution, soon after my plans were approved, recommending a further expansion of grain in all regions across the country! But I stood firm on my decision without yielding to pressure. I won. The following year, 1977, we had a bumper crop as a result of using fallow. The next year surprised us by an unheard-of yield – two tonnes *per capita* in Stavropol. The wounds inflicted by the drought were healing. People who had initially abandoned our area flocked back.

Stavropol was an important centre for fine-wooled sheep breeding. There, too, the time was ripe for changes. Extensive development was no longer possible. New, more efficient methods had to be devised.

When I became first secretary I had to handle this problem too. My colleagues and I had to lobby once more to make central funds available for the needs of the sheep-breeders. We walked many miles of corridors in the Moscow headquarters. Finally, a resolution was adopted by the Party Central Committee and the Council of Ministers, 'On the further development of the material and technical basis for fine-wool sheep breeding stocks in the Stavropol krai'. This resolution was followed by much pioneering work.

We had been advancing step by step over the years, experimenting to find the best and most efficient methods for sheep breeding. But, as soon as we transferred the breeding ewes from the pastures to mechanized sheep farms and sent the young stock to mechanized fattening farms, we knew that something was wrong. It turned out that there were limits to the number of sheep that can be crowded together, and that roaming freely on pastures most of the time was essential to their survival. We were taught a severe lesson, seeing our production drop. Fortunately, we realized our mistakes in time and corrected our plans. By the end of the 1970s our wool production was rapidly increasing and its quality showed a sustained improvement. The breeding project began to pay off. Several thousand breeding sheep were sold outside of the krai. Our pedigree animals were purchased by socialist countries and by Arab and Asian countries, including India.

115

The building of the Great Stavropol Canal was proceeding well. In August 1978 the Metrostroi Tunnel Department completed the seven-kilometre stretch of the tunnel near Aleksandrovsky village. The steppes east of Stavropol could now be supplied with water from the River Kuban. Villages, fields and farms would have access to water supplies. Even in drought periods the use of fallow provided a fairly stable yield. Five million tonnes were harvested to begin with, and subsequent yields were even higher. Fodder crops on irrigated land reached record levels for this kind of crop in Russia.

Meat production was another headache. Our krai supplied 75 per cent of the meat we produced to other areas. At the same time meat was becoming scarce in our food stores. On my travels to towns and rural areas I had to do a lot of explaining. At the Nevynnomysk chemical plant, workers accused me of toadying to the Central Committee and shipping local produce to areas outside the krai while disregarding the needs of the Stavropol population.

We had to act on our own. A project was set up to create, within eighteen months to two years, new poultry production plants, concentrated in twenty-eight major farms. That meant shifting part of the agricultural procurement plan to poultry, while the meat produced at private plots would be sold to the people in our krai.

By the time I left Stavropol for Moscow, poultry meat production had soared from a low 11,000 tonnes to 44,000 tonnes. Meanwhile, private subsidiary farming was encouraged, and horticultural and vegetable-growing co-operatives had been set up in suburban areas.

Stavropol was becoming a region of electronic, electro-technical, chemical and cement industries, as well as machine building. New power plants were built and old ones renovated, so that the krai no longer had a shortage of power, and, eventually, power supplies could be channelled to neighbouring areas. Another project involved the supply of gas to populated areas, as well as road construction connecting urban and regional centres and providing an integrated network for most rural areas. Light industries and food production were modernized.

Industrial construction aggravated social problems, although it also opened up new opportunities. Stavropol was virtually flooded with requests from ministries and departments to build new enterprises and expand existing ones, while we, in turn, imposed increasingly rigorous requirements, with an emphasis on social issues. Collective farms were invited to participate in decision-making. Target programmes had to be devised with the assistance of the research institutes in Stavropol. Unfortunately, Stavropol did not have a sufficient number of local scientists. Therefore, the next step involved contacts with research institutes in Moscow. As a result of these, our regional policy was put on a sound footing and many errors were avoided.

As I write all this, it occurs to me that the reader may weary of the details of harvests, droughts, irrigation, road networks, and so on. There were endless plans, developments, plenums, memoranda to the Central Committee, 'wheedling' the big bosses, clashes with the 'retrogrades'. Alas, I cannot change it – that is the field of activity of the krai committee first secretary. All of it required round-the-clock commitment, and I worked from early in the morning late into the night.

There were, of course, people in 'gubernatorial positions' who lived in grand style and assigned all the work to their subordinates. But to my knowledge the majority of those in the first rank toiled like slaves, which wore them out rapidly, the responsibility of the job taking its toll in stress and nervous tension.

Even then, I wondered about a system that was so dependent on the 'big boss', his resourcefulness and his ability to extricate himself from seemingly insoluble predicaments. How was it, I asked myself, that any initiative which patently served the interests of society was immediately viewed with suspicion and even with overt hostility? Why was our system so unresponsive to renewal and innovation?

Other rebellious thoughts crossed my mind. But I was much too busy to give them serious consideration.

In those years I had to face the system of decision-making under the demands of a command economy and a centralized state bureaucracy. Practically all issues had to be put before the State Planning Committee (Gosplan) and approved by a dozen ministries and departments, as well as by innumerable officials. Then there were the endless trips to the capital, the cajoling, and having to endure abusive language and rudeness from officials. All this taxed the nerves.

The things one had to do to humour the Moscow red-tapists! A country of wheeler-dealers and go-getters, although one would think that common sense ought to prevail within a planned system.

Was it really a planned system? The super-centralized attempt to control every single detail of life in an immense state sapped the vital energies of society. The slightest deviation from the established course was nipped in the bud.

Many people will remember the unfortunate outcome of an experiment in the early 1960s to pay piece-rate wages in the virgin lands of Kazakhstan.[1] Notwithstanding the efforts of *Komsomolskaya Pravda* journalists, and public opinion, some of the pioneers ended up in prison. For a long time no-one dared repeat that experiment. The experiment at the Shchekino Chemical Combine came to an end in a similar way. The ministry would not tolerate any enterprise, and stifled all nascent initiative.

These and other cases where the system suppressed new proposals seemed to me to reveal a lingering illness of our economy. Society was ready to accept changes. And at the top? Within the highest echelons of power, many people harboured similar thoughts but they preferred not to take risks.

The beginning of the second period of my work as first secretary of the Party krai committee was marked by my concern with these recurring problems. At first I was inclined to attribute the failure to achieve the expected results, despite tremendous investment, to the inefficiency and incompetence of the cadres, flaws in the management structure or gaps in legislation. Of course, there was plenty of evidence of these. But gradually I arrived at the conclusion that the roots of inefficiency lay much deeper.

By then the situation was taking a turn for the absurd: while the

---

[1] Wages were based on productivity and quickly resulted in a rapid increase in output. However, this was opposed by the bureaucrats because it permitted farmers to escape their supervision.

leaders proclaimed achievements, the real state of affairs was worsening. The centre expected positive reports from the field and rapid spectacular results. Well, whenever there is demand, there will be supply. At the beginning of each year the oblast Party committees would make unrealistic commitments, which were promptly forgotten. Manipulators were the heroes of the day. Those who worked diligently were looked upon with pity.

I have already mentioned the Great Stavropol Canal. Its initial 200 kilometres passed through a fertile zone which needed no irrigation. The Kuban water was eagerly awaited by the people of Stavropol's arid steppe. While this stretch of the canal was being built the Stavropol population was subjected to constant reproach: 'Money is being invested and where are the results?' 'The cost is too high' etc. The model to be followed was Shibayev's plan: he had launched large-scale irrigation projects in the Saratov region at a cost no higher than 500–1,000 rubles per hectare, instead of the 5,000 rubles spent by Stavropol. At the time I did not quite trust the Saratov figures, and my suspicions were eventually to be confirmed. Years later, when I was a secretary for agriculture of the Party Central Committee, the USSR Minister of Land Reclamation asked me for approval to write off the Saratov irrigated land. It was then that the Shibayev irrigation plan emerged as a patent swindle. Volga waters were channelled via temporary ducts to the fields – that was all. This was not a watering system, but simply a cheat, which ruined the soil, good soil at that. Conversely, in the left-bank area, where the irrigation system was not built according to Shibayev's plan but was based on sound projects, the people have brought to life thousands of hectares of arid land.

A similar situation prevailed in the development of animal husbandry complexes which were in fact nothing more than the erection of expensive buildings and equipment. The centre controlled the use of loans granted for construction projects, while the rest was beyond its field of vision. Even a layman could see that, unless such crucial needs as personnel, fodder, the selection of animals and the development of an infrastructure were dealt with, building projects were a waste of money. These scandalous practices went unheeded as long as the idea originated at the top. Should you come up with your own ideas – be prepared for trouble. You could even land in jail. It was actually impossible to do something sensible while complying with all the regulations and instructions. A popular adage hit the mark: 'All initiative is punishable.'

There was no room for initiative within a system under which all aspects, including minute details, were determined by the plan and the budget. At the same time the 'bosses' were dissatisfied with low returns, and tried to improve the situation by reshuffling the cadres or creating new managerial structures. Thus the heavy-handed system of management became even more cumbersome.

The more I learned about life, and the more deeply I reflected upon it, the more I looked for an answer to these problems. I continued to study publications on these subjects, but there was not much that was new in them. As a member of the Central Committee I had access to the works of Western politicians, political scientists and theorists issued by the Moscow 'Progress' publishing house. To this day, I keep some of the books on my shelves: there are two volumes of L. Aragon's *The Parallel History of the USSR,* Garaudy's *The French Model of Socialism,* G. Boffa's *History of the Soviet Union,* and the *History of Marxism,* as well as books on Togliatti, the famous journals of Gramsci etc. This broadened my horizons, as well as revealing modern processes in other countries on both sides of the ideological divide.

ANDROPOV, KOSYGIN, KULAKOV

My contacts with Andropov and Kosygin were very important to me. I met Andropov while I was second kraikom secretary. Apparently the events of August 1968 had kept him from taking his usual holiday, and he arrived unexpectedly in Zhelznovodsk in April 1969. Since Andropov tactfully declined Yefremov's 'courtesy visit', the latter asked me to replace him.

The chairman of the KGB was staying at the Dubovaya Roshcha Sanatorium in a three-room luxury suite. I arrived at the appointed time and he asked me to wait. Forty minutes elapsed.

Finally, he emerged, greeting me warmly and apologizing for the delay 'because of an important call from Moscow.'

'I have good news for you. At the plenum of the Czechoslovak Communist Party, Gustav Husák was elected First Secretary.' For Andropov, this was a sign of stabilization.

Later, Andropov and I met on numerous occasions. Twice we holidayed at the same time at the Krasnie Kamni Sanatorium. We made family excursions to the surroundings of Kislovodsk and went to the mountains. Sometimes we stayed late, cooked shashlik and sat around a bonfire. Like me, Andropov did not favour noisy parties. The southern night was magnificent, it was quiet and we talked openly.

A guards officer brought a tape recorder along. Some time later I found out that Yury Vladimirovich had a fine ear for music. But during his holidays he listened only to the 'bards of the 1960s'. He was particularly fond of Vladimir Vysotsky and Yury Visbor. He liked their songs, sang quite well himself, and so did his wife, Tatyana Filippovna. Once he challenged me to a competition of Cossack songs. I agreed, thoughtlessly, and was utterly defeated. Andropov's father was of Don Cossack origin and he himself spent his childhood among the Terek Cossacks.

Had we really been close? Yes, I think so. I say that with a pinch of salt, because I was to discover later that human feelings mean something quite different at the top level of power. Despite Andropov's restraint, I could sense that he was well disposed towards me. Yet he never opened up completely, and his trust and frankness did not exceed the established framework. More than anyone else, Andropov knew what was going on. But I would think that he reasoned like many others: deal with the cadres, introduce tighter discipline, and the rest will be all right.

My relationship with Kosygin was somewhat different. Undoubtedly he was a major figure in politics and an interesting personality. I was impressed by his memory; he had a plethora of figures and facts at his fingertips. He did not know much about agriculture, but whenever he was in Stavropol, he met the collective and state farm leaders and showed an interest in rural life. I had the impression that he was trying to understand why the agrarian sector was lagging behind.

He could not bear to be bothered by local authorities while travelling around, and he disliked formal meetings. He did not favour dinner parties, and frowned upon idle table talk. He liked meeting people, working on documents, reading and walking.

Aleksei Nikolaevich was always modest; I would even say that his asceticism reminded me of Suslov. During his holiday he never stayed at the dacha but in the common sanatorium building at Krasnie Kamni. This appeared to testify to his modesty – but only up to a point, since he and his staff occupied an entire floor.

Kosygin never shunned other holiday-makers; on the contrary, he could be sociable. Once I was invited to his birthday. The invitation was given to me on the telephone in a somewhat unusual manner.

'Why don't you come if you have time? We shall be pleased.'

He was holidaying in Kislovodsk. I went there. 'We' turned out to be his daughter Lyudmilla and her girl-friend; among the other guests there, if I'm not mistaken, were the wife of the chief Moscow architect, Posokhin, and the chief of his bodyguard, Colonel Yevgeny Karasev. We sat down at the table, congratulated him, all went its usual way, and he was in a good mood. And when he turned on music, he invited his daughter's friend for a dance and I invited Lyudmilla Alekseyevna.

Nevertheless, even when the two of us talked in private, he remained wrapped up in his shell even more than Andropov, and carefully kept his distance. His reserve and caution were understandable; he had been at the top too long; he had worked with Voznesensky and Kuznetsov, who had been executed during the 'Leningrad affair'.[1] Of this group of prominent figures, Kosygin was the only survivor. He avoided speaking about the Stalin era. However, I remember one conversation we had on this topic:

'Well, let me tell you – life was difficult. Primarily, morally and psychologically. After all, we were strictly supervised. Wherever I went,' he added with bitterness, 'I was never left on my own.' This was a man who was a member of the highest political leadership, one of Stalin's entourage.

---

[1] The leaders of the Leningrad Party organization were jailed and some of them executed in the late Stalinist period.

Kosygin was fond of walking. Whenever I came to visit him we would immediately set off, choosing a picturesque itinerary. It was during these outings that we discussed all kinds of subjects, more often than not of an economic nature.

A discussion that was to continue in subsequent years began during our early meetings. It evolved around the theme mentioned above – the functioning of the economy and mechanisms to create incentives for the individual.

'Here I am, a member of the Central Committee, a deputy of the Supreme Soviet, I carry a tremendous responsibility on my shoulders. Yet I have neither the right nor the financial means to make even the most ordinary decisions. With very few exceptions, all producer taxes and taxes paid by the population go directly to the centre. I cannot even change the personnel or the structure of the oblast Party committee and krai Soviet executive committee. I have no right to hire efficient staff and pay them good wages. Instead, I have to keep fifteen lowly paid employees who would never make up a good team.'

'It is like that everywhere; Moscow has put up rigid structures. In the final analysis it leads to the creation of an increasingly incompetent management apparatus,' I burst out somewhat heatedly.

Aleksei Nikolaevich listened silently, sometimes smiling at my fervour, but he was not prepared to become involved in this issue. On the whole, Kosygin's silence was very special. Although there was no response I realized that he agreed with me.

In July 1978 Kulakov died of heart failure. He was only sixty, and his death was a great loss. Strangely enough, neither Brezhnev nor the other members of the Politburo interrupted their holidays to pay their respects to their late colleague. I believe I realized then, for the first time, how incredibly remote these people at the top levels of power were from each other.

I felt it my human duty to attend Kulakov's funeral and to say a few words of farewell. The request was granted, but the Central Committee Secretary, Mikhail Zimyanin, asked me to submit a text of my speech to him beforehand, 'so as to avoid repetition and divergence of opinion with the other speakers'. The funeral took place on 19 July; Kulakov was buried at the Kremlin wall.

I went up to the Mausoleum for the first time, and I was deeply moved as I wished farewell to a man for whom I had nothing but warm feelings; at the same time I expressed my sincere condolences to his family.

A DRAMATIC CONFRONTATION

By 1973 crime had become a serious problem in Stavropol. A series of crime waves swept through urban and rural areas. After several cruel murders and rapes, the situation had to be taken in hand. People were frightened and began to question whether there was any effective authority in the krai. Harsh criticism of law enforcement agencies had no effect. The situation required immediate action. Dozens of commissions had produced no workable results, and eventually I enlisted the help of some experienced, reliable and independent-minded retired jurists. Surprisingly, the official data on crime revealed no particular upward trend. The commission I had set up revealed the grossest violations of the law inside the krai departments of internal affairs. Everything was brought to light – deception, concealment of crimes and official corruption.

The Minister of Internal Affairs, N. A. Shchelokov, an ambitious man who had Brezhnev's support, was anxious to 'prove himself'. This had induced him to 'correct' the crime statistics and become more lenient in enforcing the law. It was a deliberate gesture, aimed at creating an image of a politician with a broad horizon and a democrat. He liked to repeat the slogan: 'Prison has never reformed anyone yet'. Basically, this is true – but coming from him it was sheer demagoguery. Shchelokov succeeded in having a resolution adopted which replaced prison with other sentences in many types of case. This undermined the general effort to fight crime.

The conclusions of our commission led to the application of drastic measures: the generals in the local administration of the Ministry of Internal Affairs were sacked, departments such as the criminal investigation department came under close scrutiny, while the Party organization became more active. Now everything came into the open. The head of the criminal investigation department committed suicide – his conscience had been burdened by grave abuses. New police chiefs were appointed in one third of the cities and regions. It was an all-out operation to uphold legality, first and foremost in the law enforcement system. Workers' groups and the Komsomol became involved in defending law and order, and within a month life in populated areas had become safer. Meanwhile, the krai dropped from 11th to 67th place in Russia as regards reported crimes.

Shchelokov sent to the krai an Interior Ministry team headed by his deputy B. T. Shumilin. I considered Shumilin a decent person and was taken aback by his statement which was, basically, blackmail in disguise: 'How come, there is law and order all around but not here! People will wonder about your krai committee . . .'

My response was curt: 'Keep this in mind: I shall not retreat from my position. You can tell that to Shchelokov.' Shumilin was visibly ill at ease, but nevertheless continued to try to change my mind.

When the Prokuratura of the Russian Federation carried out a similar inspection in Sverdlovsk, worse crimes came to light, including even an attempt to conceal murder. I was told that the head of the Sverdlovsk department of internal affairs committed suicide. Subsequently, things began to fall into place . . . The era of massaged statistics had come to an end and the 'Shchelokov system' was crumbling. The dispute between us continued until he was ousted from his ministerial post. Later, when I was Chairman of the Supreme Soviet of the USSR and a commission of deputies looked into the allegations of the investigators Gdlyan and Ivanov, we learned among other things that during the Chernenko period Shchelokov had said of me to his associates: 'That man must be destroyed.'

LIFE IN OTHER COUNTRIES

My first trips abroad date from the period before my appointment as first kraikom Party secretary. In 1966 I visited the German

Democratic Republic, and three years later I travelled to Bulgaria and Czechoslovakia.

Party workers were sent to the GDR to study the implementation of reforms there. At the time the German comrades were testing new planning and economic management methods and were experimenting with an incentive policy which would provide enterprises with broad administrative independence. For two days we attended lectures; between them, by way of recreation, we went sightseeing in Berlin.

My visit to Berlin, even twenty years after the war, stirred me. Being in that city was a profound emotional experience. The ruined houses and monuments, heaps of debris on an abandoned plot, once the site of the Reich Chancellery, impressed me deeply. There was the Brandenburg Gate and, behind it, the Berlin Wall, put up five years earlier – a symbol of the divided post-war world. Beyond the Wall and to the west of the Brandenburg Gate loomed the gloomy skeleton of the Reichstag. At the time Berlin impressed me as a cold and forbidding place. Cottbus was altogether different. And so was Dresden. I was particularly impressed by the 'Saxon Switzerland', an area along the Elbe River on the Czech border. Wherever we went, whether sightseeing in cities, visiting industrial plants or strolling through rural areas, we met people in a pleasant atmosphere, although they seemed to lack warmth.

This was five years before Honecker replaced Ulbricht in 1971. At this time Honecker already displayed a noticeable self-assurance. At the end of our stay he received the delegation in a very friendly atmosphere.

We submitted a report on our trip to the Central Committee, concluding that the pilot reform in the GDR deserved our fullest attention. The report must have been one of many written at the time.

The trip to Bulgaria in 1969 was an outcome of the regional relationship between Stavropol and the Pazardzhik district. We had been invited to participate in the celebrations marking the twenty-fifth anniversary of Socialist Bulgaria. There were numerous meetings, assemblies, speeches: oceans of emotional outpourings and mutual protestations of eternal friendship.

In 1974 there was another trip to Bulgaria. I stayed in Sofia, travelling to Shipka, Plovdiv, and many new residential areas and private houses, enterprises, greenhouses and roads. Vineyards and vegetable fields were cultivated according to modern methods. It seemed an Eden of orchards and flowers. The country was changing before our very eyes. We decided that the Bulgarians were heading in the right direction. Little did we know then that the country was living beyond its means.

The most difficult mission, I would say, was to Czechoslovakia in 1969. The delegation included Ligachev, then first secretary of the Tomsk oblast committee, and Pastukhov, secretary of the Komsomol. We were to discuss the prospects for the youth movement in Czechoslovakia. At the time of our arrival seventeen youth organizations were active there, and none of them recognized the authority of the Communist Party of Czechoslovakia.

Countless meetings and heated discussions took place in Prague, Brno and Bratislava, all searching for ways to win the young people over. It was really quite impossible to divorce this problem from the general context of the situation in Czechoslovakia after the 1968 invasion. To say that we felt uneasy and downcast would be an understatement. We felt viscerally, deep down, that this action was indignantly rejected by the people.

Prague was in a state of torpor. Colleagues were unable to introduce us to workers' collectives and dared not approach them. We asked them: 'Why don't you speak to the people?' And their response was: 'First we'll have to analyse the situation, and then we can act...' Not only were they reluctant to contact the people, but they were patently afraid of them.

The eve of the Student Day was spent in Brno, where our hosts ventured to organize a visit to a large plant. When we arrived, people refused to talk to us and did not answer our greetings. It was very unpleasant. Most members of the plant's Party committee strongly condemned the action of the Soviet leadership. We learned that the plant workers had defended Dubcek's government in August 1968, and troops had occupied the plant in order to neutralize them. In August 1969 mass demonstrations were staged in Brno against the regime and the

Soviet intervention. The situation was at breaking-point, and our delegation was guarded around the clock.

In Bratislava we were struck by the city's appearance: there were bullet holes in practically every building in the centre of town and the walls were densely covered with anti-Soviet slogans. Our delegation was greeted by Slavik, first secretary of the Central Committee of the Communist Party of Slovakia. At first all went well, but when one of us reminded him that Lenin, while being an exponent of federalism in the state, resolutely rejected such an approach to the building of the Party, the first secretary got up and left. The following morning none of the local leaders appeared. Our face was saved by an acquaintance in the Central Committee apparatus. At noon we went up to the Devin Mountain, a cemetery for Red Army soldiers who had been killed during the liberation of Slovakia, where we stood in silence with bowed heads. It was a balmy day. Below us, we saw the glistening waters of the Danube and farther off the golden contours of Vienna. Our hearts were heavy as we left Bratislava.

At night we arrived in a rural settlement – its name escapes me. The local people greeted us with bread and salt, with wine and music. It took a load off our minds. We stayed until late into the night talking to our hosts. I remembered that somewhere in that area, near Košice, my father had been seriously wounded. The peasants told us they had been wary of Dubcek's liberalizing innovations. A year later, on another visit to Czechoslovakia, I found that the rural population had developed friendly ties with our soldiers. The peasants warmly appreciated the help they were getting from the Soviet Army and, although resentment against the Soviet Union persisted, it was no longer a primary concern.

How did the Soviet leaders justify their action on 21 August 1968? First of all, they argued that there was an external threat to the Warsaw Pact countries; and, secondly, they claimed that internal counter-revolution with Western backing was seeking to trample the socialist achievements of the workers. We saw, however, that the working people themselves resented this kind of defence of their interests. Was there really an external threat? The fact that, in mid-1968, articles were appearing in the Czechoslovak press hinting at the possible withdrawal of the country from the Warsaw Pact reflected the attitudes of Czechoslovak political forces. In other words, it resulted from developments inside the country.

During my visit I was informed that the Soviet leadership had originally welcomed the replacement of Novotny by Dubcek. Novotny's request for Soviet support against Dubcek had been rejected as an internal affair of the Communist Party of Czechoslovakia. The new Czechoslovak leadership had regarded this as a sign of the CPSU's approval to carry on with the reforms which had hitherto been shelved. However, the scope and dynamic development of the reform process in Czechoslovakia had frightened our leaders into scrapping their own timid attempts at economic reform and tightening the political and ideological screws.

I returned home weighed down by gloomy thoughts, as I realized that there was a direct link between our situation and the Czechoslovak events in August 1968. After my trip I talked to Yefremov. He listened carefully to what I had to say, but his response was cool and formal.

In the 1970s I travelled to Italy, France, Belgium and the Federal Republic of Germany. One trip was official, the others were undertaken at the invitation of the Communist Parties of those countries. These trips were longer and gave me a better chance to see a country and the way people lived there.

My travels abroad – whatever the occasion – were instructive for me, particularly because the information available to us about other countries was scanty and subject to thorough processing. The distribution of newspapers, journals, books and films was under strict control, and radio broadcasts were jammed. Those were the years when tourism was limited mostly to East European countries, and journeys to the West were possible only after an all-out investigation of a person's ideological reliability. Hence, the 'Iron Curtain' was not only a literary metaphor, although it existed 'on the other side' too. As a result, misinterpretation of life in the West and vice versa was commonplace, nurturing mutual fears and suspicion.

Yet, to my surprise, I did not observe any animosity towards the Soviet people in any of the countries which I visited. Of course endless questions were raised, but we raised them too. After all, neither walls nor curtains can divide people.

And – what was most important – there was a desire on both sides to talk openly and find out what was really happening. We were amazed by the open and relaxed attitude of the people we met and marvelled at their unrestrained judgement of everything, including the activity of their governments and their national and local politicians. They were often at variance in their views, whereas we behaved abroad as we did back home (excepting, of course, our discussions in the kitchen), displaying our constant solidarity and our unity of opinion on all subjects. And we talked cautiously lest our countrymen should get God-knows-what ideas about us.

At the same time much of what I observed was unacceptable to me. For example, my comparisons reinforced my opinion (which I have not changed to this day) that public education and medical services were organized more fairly in our country. And our emphasis on public transport was better than any other urban transport policy.

However, my previous belief in the superiority of socialist democracy over the bourgeois system was shaken as I observed the functioning of civic society and the different political systems. Finally, the most significant conclusion drawn from the journeys abroad: people there lived in better conditions and were better off than in our country. The question haunted me: why was the standard of living in our country lower than in other developed countries? It seemed that our aged leaders were not especially worried about our undeniably lower living standards, our unsatisfactory way of life, and our falling behind in the field of advanced technologies. Instead of seeking ways to catch up with other countries and prevent the country and the system from sinking deeper into a state of crisis, the leadership was primarily concerned with devising new artificial ideological concepts which would sanctify the existing realities and present them as historical achievements.

FAREWELL TO STAVROPOL

After my appointment as a secretary of the Central Committee, I returned to Stavropol to hand over affairs to my successor, Murakhovsky. I was aware of the anxiety felt by the district and city committee secretaries and in the ranks of the most active Party members. A change of first secretary usually involved a drastic reshuffling of the cadres. Murakhovsky and I therefore decided to emphasize in all our public appearances that current policies would be sustained. In order to ease the tension I told members of the plenum that Vsevolod Serafimovich Murakhovsky and I fully agreed on key matters concerning the cadres, and that I would be consulted on any problem which might arise in future.

And that is how it turned out. However, I tried to avoid any kind of patronizing attitude towards him, because people who assume responsibility should be free to act and use their own judgement.

I parted warmly from the members of the krai committee plenum. I gave up the idea of a farewell trip through the territory as an immodest gesture. Later I regretted this decision. I should have said goodbye to people with whom I had formed such close ties in the past.

At the age of forty-seven one is mature, and I understood that my departure from Stavropol put an end to a period of my life. I was sad to be leaving. Not only was I born and raised in Stavropol, but all my working life so far had been spent in that area.

Stavropol had also become home to my wife Raisa Maksimovna. After looking for a job for several years she had finally found work in her speciality, lecturing in the department of economics at the Stavropol Agricultural Institute. She taught undergraduate and postgraduate courses on aesthetics, philosophy and religious problems. As a participant in the research work of the faculty she started studying the sociological aspects of the life and attitudes of the population. She walked hundreds of kilometres, visiting villages and settlements, holding long open conversations with the people in an attempt to understand their problems and their concerns. Such activity leaves a deep impression on one's soul, and nurtures a sense of belonging to the life of the people. This particular period coincided with the revival of sociology in the Soviet Union. The results of Raisa's study of the social and psychological problems of modern peasantry stirred interest in Moscow. I too was interested in her studies, which helped me in making certain decisions.

After Raisa had completed her thesis she worked for several years as a lecturer, and eventually received an offer to head the department. But, at a family council, it was decided to reject the offer. We had to consider provincial circumstances (and not only provincial), under which this offer would be interpreted as favouritism due to my position. Frankly speaking, she was not anxious to be a 'boss'. Her independent scientific work and lecturing were a full-time job and gave her great moral satisfaction.

My work and Raisa Maksimovna's profession compelled us to make a great effort at 'self-improvement'. We used every opportunity to do so. Our hobby was reading and we collected a fine library. One of the privileges enjoyed by first secretaries allowed us to purchase books through the Central Committee, which provided a list of publications. We made ample use of this possibility. Every new order was thoroughly discussed in the family to consider the specific interests of each of its members.

Our family life was based on the active participation of all its members, but as the years went by my share in it dwindled. Raisa Maksimovna had to combine her professional activities, which required great devotion, with those of a housewife and mother. Her dedication was truly remarkable.

Irina, our only child, was a good pupil at school, graduating with a gold medal. I do not recall applying any special philosophy of education. We simply led an active, interesting and busy life. I was fully absorbed by my work and constantly on the road. Raisa Maksimovna was engaged at the Institute full-time. We trusted our daughter and she, in turn, used her independence well. At sixteen she had read all the Russian classics and all the foreign literature in our library. As an adult she confessed that most of her reading was done at night.

During the last year of our life in Stavropol a major event occurred in our family – Irina got married. The wedding of Irina and Anatoly was celebrated on 15 April 1978.

The young couple spent their honeymoon on a Volga excursion boat. They returned from that trip on the eve of our silver wedding anniversary, brimming over with impressions and happy.

I believe that for Irina and Anatoly it was easier to leave Stavropol than for us. Moscow was beckoning. Their whispering to each other and their impatient looks betrayed their eagerness to move to the capital.

On the day of our departure Raisa Maksimovna and I decided to take our leave of the city. We drove from the historic centre of town to a modern suburb where the sprawling city spilled over its original limits, reaching out to the nearby forest. We drove on to the Russky (Russian) forest, where every footpath was familiar. In times of crisis I sought out nature to restore my spirits. When nervous tension at work reached breaking-point, I would set out for the woods or the steppe. Nature never failed to allay my worries, to quell my irritation, to revive me and restore my equilibrium.

Even during the dark and tragic periods when merciless heat scorched the beautiful steppe, it was nature that gave me courage and self-discipline. As soon as the first rains poured down on this scorched area a miracle occurred. The steppe, which had seemed dead only a few days before, was suddenly restored to life. To observe this renewal filled man with hope.

Raisa Maksimovna shared my passionate love of nature. We walked together for miles and miles. We walked in winter and in summer, oblivious to the weather; we even roamed the country in a snowstorm. It could be dangerous; in our area people died in snow-drifts. Once we were caught in a heavy snowstorm and barely made it to safety; thank God, we came across a power line which helped us to orient ourselves.

We cherished our Stavropol steppe above all, especially at the end of June. The two of us would leave the city far behind, heading for the point where the undulating grain fields met the horizon. We found remote forest clearings where we could abandon ourselves to silence and beauty. At dusk the heat would abate and the fields became alive with quail song. And that was the ultimate unsurpassed bliss, a state of happiness about all that was there – the steppe, the grain, the smell of grass, the bird-song and the stars high in the sky. Simply the joy of being.

The oneness with nature was sometimes so strong that we seemed to inhabit a different world. No words can express that feeling. Probably a true believer experiences the same soaring of the spirit in church. But then, to me, nature is also a church – it has never represented an 'environment' or a 'recreation area' where townsfolk come to pick flowers. My close organic ties with nature – and this I can affirm – greatly influenced my development in addition to people and society. My character and my entire perception of the world were to a large extent shaped by nature, and by the awareness that not only do I exist in it, but that nature lives inside me. What are the origins of this? Probably it goes back to my roots. In the remote pre-war years, when my grandfather Pantelei became chairman of the Krasnaya Zvezda kolkhoz in another area, he left my parents a vegetable patch and a large orchard, about one hectare. That was my world.

Apparently, the layout of the orchard had been planned. Five or six apricot trees grew in the centre. They were at least thirty or forty years old and seemed gigantic to me. I also remember the sweetness of the apricot stones. Cherry-plum bushes grew between the trees on silky grass.

To one side of the apricots a young cherry orchard unfolded its beauty. The cherry trees were known as 'Spanish'. The fruit was either large and tart or smaller but very sweet. Not only do I remember the taste; who could ever forget the snow-white 'foam' of the cherry blossoms!

Different varieties of apple and pear trees were abundant. At the time I was not interested in their names. I just recall their taste and that they ripened at different times, so that there was always enough in the summer and autumn. In the wake of the apples and pears came the black and white plums. Gradually, the garden merged into a thicket of smooth-leaved elms; in front, there were the elm trees and, farther on, behind them, began the undergrowth. A real jungle, it occupied almost a third of the garden area. I had my hide-aways and, when I came across Thomas Mayne Reid's book *Afloat in the Forest*, I disappeared there for nearly three days. My mother went out of her mind. I re-appeared only after finishing the story. And you can imagine the 'disciplinary scrape' I got into afterwards!

The once deep ditch which surrounded the land had gradually become overgrown and looked like a broad shallow furrow. There were many cherry-plum trees (*alycha*) all along the length of the orchard, with a great variety of differently coloured fruit of varying taste and juiciness. Next to it grew the acacia trees, not the thorny variety used for fences but the delicate white-flowered one, the inspiration of poets.

I still see that garden before me, but, alas, it no longer exists. During the snowy winter of 1941 I crawled in my *valenki* (felt boots) on the frozen ice crust and cut off the tree tops protruding through the snow-drifts. Later, after the snow melted, it was the turn of the trees – after all, we had to survive and heat our house. Many gardens were destroyed during the brief stay of the Germans in Privolnoye in 1942.

Yet some vestiges of the orchards remained, and we used them in the post-war years. But what remained was cut down as a result of the Zverev tax (called after the Finance Minister Zverev) which levied every tree regardless of whether it yielded fruit or not. That was the end of our orchards.

During my university years in Moscow my parents built another hut, closer to where my father worked. There, I used to spend my holidays, and Raisa Maksimovna was introduced to my parents. The hut was sold. The new owners did not stay there long. Privolnoye was developing, houses were being built according to a new plan and the outskirts became deserted.

Once when I went back to Privolnoye, I went to the edge of the village. Now there are fields all over the place. Our old hut had disappeared along with the enchanted garden of my childhood. They live on only in my memory.

On the day of our departure, having crossed the city by car, we stopped at the edge of the forest beyond the city limits. It was 5 December. Raisa Maksimovna and I left the car and continued on foot. The forest was not as lovely as in autumn. It looked sad in the dusk, as if it, too, had to bid farewell to us. We felt a pang in our hearts.

The next day the aeroplane soared above Stavropol carrying us to Moscow.

7

AT STARAYA PLOSHCHAD

FOR SOME TIME WE HAD NO APARTMENT IN THE CITY. WE WERE
temporarily housed in a dacha outside Moscow. Irina and
Anatoly stayed behind in Stavropol, and to begin with we felt
lonely and disorientated. At the same time, we felt uneasy about
being 'kept in cotton wool'. The dacha was not large and no
auxiliary quarters were available, so that the service personnel
and the guards officer were always around. Raisa Maksimovna
and I could talk freely only when we were in the grounds outside
the house, at night during a walk after work.

Soon we were offered another dacha in Sosnovka, not far from
Krylatskoye and right across the Moskva River from
Serebryanny Bor. In the 1930s, Sergo Ordzhonikidze had lived
in that house and, before us, Chernenko. It was not what one
would call an architectural success, being an old, rather run-down
wooden building, but it was convenient. It had not been properly
taken care of, because it was due to be demolished to make way
for a new building. Gradually, it had been turned into a guest-
house of sorts to accommodate new electees. Raisa Maksimovna
returned to Stavropol to fetch the rest of the family, as well as our
belongings. Then she set about furnishing the place. We celebrated New Year 1979 in our family circle. At the stroke of
midnight we raised our glasses and wished each other luck.

As I rose up the Party hierarchy we moved on to different
lodgings. According to an established pattern, a member of the
Politburo was entitled to a more opulent home than a candidate
member of the Politburo or a Central Committee Secretary.

Notwithstanding the differences, all these buildings bore the stamp of sad, barrack-like structures. At first we could not rid ourselves of the feeling of being in a hotel, but thanks to the efforts of Raisa Maksimovna our familiar microcosm was finally restored.

Eventually we ended up on Shchusev Street, in a building which was known in Moscow as 'the Nest of the Gentry'.[1] Irina and her husband also moved in with us. But we kept the dacha; to settle down properly in our new home was a lengthy process.

I had come to Moscow fully aware of the commitments I was to assume. I plunged immediately into my work and, from the very first day of my arrival, toiled twelve to fifteen hours a day. I had worked as first secretary in Stavropol for almost ten years, at the cutting edge of politics. When I began my Party career, the thought of changing my profession occasionally crossed my mind. However, my job as kraikom secretary firmly convinced me that I had made the right choice. Politics had won the upper hand. I had acquired a taste for it, and was captivated by it.

As a member of the Central Committee and regional kraikom secretary I had been constantly in contact with the 'higher echelons'. Ostensibly, I should have been familiar with the customs of the 'tsar's court'. But it was only in the capital that I realized how much more complicated they were. It took time to catch on, to understand all the subtleties and nuances of relationships higher up. In the beginning, my active participation in the activities of the Central Committee Secretariat and my discussion of certain problems were met with misgivings by my colleagues. Some of them considered me an upstart. In every way possible I resisted being drawn into the machine, to become another victim of routine subordination, but it was easier said than done. As a kraikom secretary in Stavropol I had enjoyed much greater freedom than I did here, even though I had now joined the top ranks of power.

[1] An allusion to Turgenev's novel *Home of the Gentry*.

BACKGROUND INFORMATION

My account of my work in the Central Committee Secretariat and in the Politburo will be more convincing and comprehensible if I briefly describe the origins of these institutions. The term 'Politburo' was coined in 1917, when a political body to lead the uprising had to be created. It was only in March 1919 that the Politburo became the permanent leading structure. Originally all problems, including minor ones, had to be resolved by the Central Committee, which met more or less on a weekly basis, even at the height of revolutionary events.

As long as the Central Committee membership was only ten or twenty persons, this practice was realistic. However, as the Party membership grew, its Central Committee expanded and it was no longer possible to work as before. Consequently the Politburo and the Orgburo (Organization Bureau) were created to guide the Party during the intervals between Central Committee plenums. Gradually these organs assumed absolute power.

The Politburo was made up of the nucleus of the original Central Committee members. They were political figures known in the Party and in the country. Officially, there was no chairman; the authority of each member did not depend on the position he held but the position depended on real authority. The meetings were usually chaired by V. I. Lenin – his leadership was unchallenged. Yet the chair could be occupied by another person; sometimes it was Kamenev.

Substantial political problems were put before the Politburo, whereas everyday issues, or 'noodles', as they were called, were handled by the Orgburo. Two consistent trends emerged with regard to the Council of People's Commissars (Sovnarkom) and other state organs and establishments. On the one hand Lenin repeatedly stated that it was inadmissible to tread on the government's heels, while, on the other, the people's commissars were threatened with being 'dragged before the Politburo' whenever conflict arose. Eventually, when the top Party leader no longer headed the government, this trend became a dominant feature.

As the years went by, the composition and functions of the Secretariat changed. These changes reflected the dependence of the position and role of this body on the person in charge of it. In August 1917 Ya. M. Sverdlov headed the Secretariat, while occupying the post of chairman of the All-Union Central Executive Committee. Under his guidance, all the organizational and technical work, the so-called 'apparatus' activity, was markedly subordinate, directed solely at servicing the Central Committee.

After Sverdlov's death the Secretariat was expanded, since the organizational work was growing, and in 1919 M. N. Krestinsky, Ye. A. Preobrazhensky and L. P. Serebryakov joined its ranks. They were members of the Central Committee and the CC Organization Bureau. Krestinsky was the only one who was also a member of the Politburo. Occasionally he would be referred to as 'First Secretary', but apparently he was much more interested in the People's Commissariat of Finances, which he continued to direct at the same time. It is noteworthy that the old revolutionaries were somewhat contemptuous of 'secretarial' posts. A 'People's Commissar' carried more weight.

In 1921 all three secretaries joined the ranks of the opposition. They had in any case proved rather useless as 'apparatchiks'. Therefore, less prominent officials were chosen after the Xth Congress of the Russian Communist Party (Bolsheviks). These nominees were regarded as more suitable for the work of the 'apparatus'.

The Secretariat included V. M. Molotov, V. M. Mikhailov and Ye. M. Yaroslavsky. All were members of the Central Committee and its Organization Bureau. None were members of the Politburo.

It soon became obvious that the authority of the Secretariat needed a boost. There was a real need to put the Party's house in order. Stalin, a member of the Politburo, was proposed for a job in the Secretariat. He was the only one to be a People's Commissar twice over, that is, he was in charge of nationality affairs and the workers' and peasant inspection. In order not to slight him, the post was renamed, and he became not simply a Central Committee Secretary or a First Secretary but General Secretary of the Central Committee of the Russian Communist Party (Bolsheviks) at the plenum on 3 April 1922.

Nine months later, on 25 December 1922, Lenin wrote: 'Having become General Secretary, Comrade Stalin succeeded in consolidating immense power in his hands. I am not sure that he will always know how to use it judiciously . . .'

Stalin showed what it meant to rule over the apparatus, and first and foremost over the cadres and to fill all more or less important posts at the centre and in the provinces. He even exerted his influence on the Politburo agenda and its resolutions, inasmuch as the draft resolutions were prepared inside the Secretariat. Thus an auxiliary organ intended to provide organizational and technical support to the Politburo was gradually transformed into an executive organ of the political leadership.

The influence of the Politburo, chaired by the spineless Kamenev, and also that of the Council of People's Commissars under Rykov, was declining. On the other hand, the clout wielded by the Secretariat, being closely linked to the regional Party leadership, was growing stronger. Stalin succeeded in establishing relations with local cadres and in moving his own people into key positions and, with their help, crushing his rivals.

Eventually the Soviets assumed the role of defenders of local interests, whereas the people's commissariats represented the interests of various branches and industries. The Party had become an integrating force defending 'national interests'. Gradually, Party committees began influencing state organs at the centre as well as at local levels. At Bureau meetings and plenums in Moscow and in the regions not only political problems were on the agenda; purely economic issues were also raised.

It was not merely the power system that was undergoing a change, acquiring an increasingly totalitarian character. The Party and its functions were also changing. It was no longer an ordinary social and political organization but had turned into a mechanism to rule society, and it had become a key component in a command and bureaucratic system. Any attempt at changing that role was regarded as an attempt to 'undermine the foundations'.

A. N. Kosygin could certainly not be called naive. When powerful departments were being organized in the apparatus of the Central Committee under Brezhnev to handle all national economic problems, Kosygin tried to prevent it. However, he failed to halt the process. These departments were finally formed, and even a 'sector for organic silicon production' was included in the functions of the Central Committee. The departments and sectors were not directly accountable for the results of their work, but exercised rigid controls over the ministries and enterprises, interfering in their business. In response, the Council of Ministers set up various agencies of its own.

The Party and government apparatuses never ceased to compete with each other. Backbiting and intrigues flourished. As a result, a heavy-handed and unwieldy bureaucratic Party and state system of management was created.

In the spirit of the existing constitutions, the Party was to develop policy, the USSR Supreme Soviet enacted legislation, while the government should have been implementing this policy and complying with the laws. Such a system might seem quite democratic. But, insofar as the Party meddled in matters which involved the functions of the legislative and executive power, the system crumbled before one's eyes. There was a thorough muddle: on the one hand, a total lack of any system of power-sharing and control; on the other, a consolidation of unlimited power.

Brezhnev learned his lesson from Khrushchev's experience. He restored the rural district committees and the original role of regional Party committees. At the XXIIIrd Congress he revived and occupied the post of General Secretary. His main support came from the first oblast, krai and Central Committee secretaries in the republics. It was a well-tried Stalinist policy. Under Stalin it was sustained by a system of repression, whereas under Brezhnev it became a 'social contract' of sorts between the exponents of power.

That 'contract' was never spelled out; nor was it recorded or, obviously, ever mentioned. But it existed in reality. Its intent was to endow all first secretaries with almost unlimited power in their regions, and they in turn had to support the General Secretary, praising him as leader and chief. That was the substance of this gentlemen's agreement. It was strictly complied with. It is note-worthy that Leonid Ilyich kept in personal touch with the first secretaries even when he became seriously ill and could speak only with difficulty.

An analogous 'agreement' existed with the government. The government's right to manage the country's socio-economic affairs was recognized. But any problem which could be regarded as having even the slightest importance was subject to preliminary approval by the Party organization. Some leading ministries, such as the Ministries of Foreign Affairs, Defence, State Security and Internal Affairs, were in fact entirely in the hands of the Politburo and the Secretariat, while remaining within the budget and the structure of the Council of Ministers.

For decades, the leading and omnipresent role of the Party structure was not embodied in any legislation. In the Stalinist constitution, mention was made of the Party as a leading nucleus of all workers' organizations, including public and state bodies. However, this reference was somewhat lost in the text of the constitution, and was mentioned only in the articles on the rights and obligations of the citizens. Hence it was regarded as some sort of general declaration instead of a constitutional and legal standard. Finally, in Brezhnev's constitution, article 6 laid down the status of the Communist Party of the Soviet Union as the 'nucleus of the political system'. This reflected attempts to give a semblance of legitimacy to the reality in the country by constitutional provisions.

BREZHNEV'S RULE

Brezhnev had come to power in October 1964, as a result of a compromise between the groups which ousted Khrushchev. He was then regarded as a rather insignificant figure who could be easily manipulated. This was a miscalculation. By the use of simple tactics he succeeded in strengthening his position until he became practically invulnerable.

His forte consisted in his ability to split rivals, fanning mutual suspicion and subsequently acting as chief arbiter and peace-maker. In time I discerned another of Brezhnev's characteristics: vindictiveness. He never forgot the slightest disloyalty towards himself, but he was shrewd enough to wait for an appropriate moment to replace the offender. He never resorted to direct confrontation, proceeding cautiously, step by step, until he gained the upper hand.

The removal of Podgorny in 1977 and of Kosygin in 1980 finally sealed the personal power of Brezhnev. The irony was that this happened when his capacity for work was already ebbing. His grip on power had by then become ephemeral.

According to his doctor, Academician Chazov, the General Secretary's illness had been developing since the early 1970s. The main reasons were thought to be arteriosclerosis and overdoses of tranquillizers, which caused depression and slug-gishness. He was changing before our eyes. Before, he had been more dynamic and, moreover, more democratic, and he did not shun normal human contacts. He used to encourage discussion, occasionally even at meetings of the Politburo and the Secretariat. Now the situation changed radically. Discussion was excluded, and any kind of self-critical comments on his part were out of the question.

It may seem that Brezhnev's general state of physical and mental health would have brought up the issue of his retirement. Such a step would make sense from a human point of view, as well as being in the interests of the state. But neither Brezhnev himself nor his close entourage would dream of giving up their power. They convinced themselves, and tried to convince others, that Brezhnev's departure would upset the balance and under-mine stability. In short, he was 'irreplaceable', although more dead than alive. I remember a Politburo meeting where the chairman had a mental block and could not remember the subject of the discussion. All the other participants carried on as if nothing had happened. After the meeting I shared my feelings about it with Andropov.

'Look, Mikhail,' he said, and repeated almost word for word what he had told me before, 'we must do everything possible to support Leonid Ilyich, even in his present state. It is a matter of stability within the Party and the state as well as an issue of international stability.'

Andropov was not the only one who did not want Brezhnev to leave. This view was shared by the majority of the Politburo members. An ailing General Secretary suited the kraikom and obkom first secretaries, as well as the Prime Minister and the ministers, since it gave them free rein in their 'dioceses'.

The precarious balance was sustained by a carefully preserved pattern of subordination. Each and every one had to know his place, stay on his 'patch' and not claim anything more than was accorded to him. This table of rank sometimes created absurd situations, and it influenced virtually everything, even the seating order in the Politburo meeting hall. I am not joking. It might seem that all ceremony should be cast aside when colleagues and comrades gather. But no, each member had an assigned place. On the right of Brezhnev was Suslov, on the left Kosygin or, after his retirement, Tikhonov. Next to Suslov sat Kirilenko, then Pelshe, Solomentsev, Ponomarev and Demichev. Across from the table and next to Kosygin was Grishin, and after him Gromyko, Andropov, Ustinov, Chernenko and, finally, Gorbachev. It was a long table, and when Leonid Ilyich consulted with someone on one side of the table, Suslov for example, those of us sitting at the end of the table on the other side could not hear what was being said.

Sitting next to Konstantin Chernenko also had its inconveniences. He was constantly jumping up from his seat and dashing towards Leonid Ilyich, shuffling his papers. 'We have decided that one already,' he would say, or: 'That has been removed from the agenda.'

It was a sad sight. All this was done without any visible embarrassment. I was ashamed, and sometimes assumed that the others must have similar feelings. Whether right or wrong, they sat there without batting an eyelid.

As a witness to these 'court games', I realized that the only way to avoid sinking into this quagmire of intrigue was my work, to which I was committed and for which I had assumed responsibility. Consequently I tried to spend my time primarily in the analysis and reappraisal of agrarian policy.

A CLASH WITH KOSYGIN

Considerably less grain was harvested in 1979 than in the previous year. I came to the sad conclusion that the state procurement plan would not be fulfilled, and that the shortfall would need to be made up by grain purchases from abroad. I prepared a tentative forecast and, after the return from holiday of the chief members of the leadership, I sent a note to Politburo members. But something occurred before the matter was discussed officially.

On 7 September the cosmonauts V. A. Lyakhov and V. V. Rumin were to receive awards at the Kremlin for what was at that time the longest ever space flight, 175 days. All the leadership then in Moscow went there to take part in the ceremony. We stood at the entrance of the Catherine Hall talking together, and Leonid Ilyich as usual was interested in the grain harvest. I said that we should urgently send extra lorries to Kazakhstan to transport grain, and also to the central regions for the beet harvest. At this point Kosygin broke in rather sharply: 'What has happened here is that the agriculture department has sent a memorandum to members of the Politburo, and Gorbachev has signed it. He and his Department have yielded to parochial considerations, but we have no more hard currency to buy grain. We should not be so liberal, but should be firmer in demanding that the state procurement plan be fulfilled.'

I had been sure that the Council of Ministers (Sovmin)[1] bureaucracy would try to put Kosygin in a negative mood, but I never expected such a reaction. Since the accusations were rather serious, I could not contain myself. I said that if the Chairman of the Council of Ministers considered that I and my department had failed in some way, why did he not instruct his own organization to produce the grain and implement such requisitioning?

There was a deathly silence. Some way had to be found to avoid this scandal from developing. An official came to the rescue. 'Leonid Ilyich,' he said in a loud voice, 'everything is ready. It is time to go.' We all filed into the Catherine Hall behind Brezhnev.

[1] The Soviet government.

The awards were duly made to the cosmonauts, and I returned to my office. I was in a depressed mood, not least because the conflict was with Kosygin, whom I greatly respected. At such times, I always tried to remain calm and consider soberly whether I had not made some mistake. We had taken a hard line on grain procurement, but I considered that there were limits beyond which one simply should not go. To go to the limit was, of course, always possible, and the Party had more than enough experience to do that in such cases. But this would not have been honest with the farmers, and would be against the national interest. We should not use coercion, but should seek a wise solution.

Fifteen minutes later Brezhnev telephoned. 'Are you upset?' he asked. I said that I was, but that something else was bothering me – I did not agree that my position was contrary to the interests of the state. 'You behaved correctly, don't worry. We should indeed see that the government occupies itself more with agriculture.' At that, the conversation finished.

Two hours later I received another telephone call. As if nothing had happened, it was Kosygin:

'I want to continue the conversation we started.'

'Aleksei Nikolaevich . . .' I answered, now feeling no nervousness or offence, '. . . maybe you would agree to carry the initiative forward yourself at this concluding phase. This is the first campaign for me, and also it is a difficult year.'

Kosygin remained silent, and then he said: 'I read your memorandum again. Send your proposals to the Politburo.' He said this without any irritation, without lecturing me, but also not apologizing.

Incidentally, I can say in retrospect that the state procurement targets were never fulfilled.

The affair with Aleksei Nikolaevich had a very unexpected result for me. Some in the leadership seemed to regard it as evidence of my tough stand against Kosygin. I thought so when one day in late autumn Suslov telephoned me: 'We had a discussion. A plenum is coming. It is intended to strengthen your position. There has been a proposal to make you a Politburo member. But I voiced opposition and I want you to know about it. I shall recommend you as a candidate member[1] to the Politburo. That will be better. You will have secretaries working with you with five, ten, fifteen years' experience. Why create needless strains?'

He was right.

THE AFGHANISTAN WAR AND THE FOOD PROGRAMME

After our forces were sent to Afghanistan, the USA and other nations took a number of measures against us. The Americans, in particular, stopped shipping even those consignments of grain that they had already contracted to send. The embargo resulted in our not receiving about 17 million tonnes.

In January 1980 Brezhnev invited Gromyko, Ustinov and me to see him. For the first time, I was present at the small group which in effect took all the major decisions affecting the fate of the country. Gromyko and Ustinov began first by giving their optimistic views of the situation in Afghanistan. It was left to me to speak about the alarming grain shortage.

What I said disturbed everyone present. I was ordered to prepare an analysis of the minimum necessary for the normal sustenance of the population, and the directives that needed to be given about this to the Foreign Ministry and the Ministry of Foreign Trade. Then, for the first time, I raised the problem of preparing a plan to free us from the necessity of importing grain. I was not yet calling it 'the food programme', but that was what we were discussing.

The idea of this programme was not conceived on the spur of the moment. For over a year I had been trying to get to the root of the food problem. A disastrous picture unfolded before my eyes. The land, our sustenance, as we call it, showed itself to be worn out, untended or simply abandoned. And I became increasingly aware that this vandalism was the consequence of a policy which had been implemented over the last decades. A rampant

---

[1] A candidate member could attend, speak but not vote at meetings.

technocracy suppressed all moral principles. The land had been totally disregarded for many years in favour of raw-material production such as coal-mining and the oil and gas industries. Millions of hectares were lost to farming and used for road and railway construction. For the sake of hydroelectric power plants, fourteen million hectares of fertile river terraces, which could have produced first-class vegetables and high-quality animal fodder, had been flooded by artificial lakes. Tens of millions of hectares were set aside for army bases and for frontier protection zones which were off-limits to farmers. Obviously land had to be allotted for these purposes, but the way it was done, without any consideration for standards and needs, without any control, was wrong. The sole criterion had been that 'It costs nothing'.

And how was land used for agricultural purposes? Metaphorically speaking, a plough had been dragged right across the country, covering areas varying from fertile black soil to deserts. As a result, the wind blew off the top soil, and millions of hectares were ruined. More millions of hectares were 'consumed' by ravines and deserts. To reclaim these lands would require many decades or even centuries.

I had come across this situation while still in Stavropol. I knew that a different mode of soil cultivation should be applied in each climate zone, depending on the type of soil. Keeping the soil fertile requires all kinds of know-how.

I also learned that millions of hectares were unsuitable for agriculture simply because the reclamation systems failed to provide for drainage. All that in order to save money! Without a drainage system, salts are carried into the arable land and cause damaging, so-called secondary soil salination.

Herbicides were widely used. Were they needed, one wonders? Yes, to kill weeds. The farmers lost 30 per cent of their crops for that reason. But no arrangements had been made for a balanced application of chemicals, so that vast areas of land, rivers and lakes were polluted, while irrevocable damage was inflicted on the fauna and flora.

Studying these phenomena, I tried to understand why we were unable to produce a good yield of soya, which we badly needed, in the Blagoveshchensk region of the Amur oblast. It finally turned out that only one thing was missing, soil desalination. This is another example of negligent attitudes towards the soil. At the same time, the soils in the Baltic Republics and in Belorussia were treated repeatedly with lime, which lowered their acidity and resulted in higher yields. When Masherov was the leader in Belorussia and Snieckus in Lithuania, the living standards in the countryside improved, and so did the mood of the rural population. But in nearby Latvia, where the focus was on industrialization, the rural areas were sapped of life.

The fate of some regions in the country was truly tragic. Barbarous oil and gas production methods in the north inflicted monstrous damage on the unique tundra zone, where nature is particularly susceptible and where its balance had been established over millions of years. Then there are the Caspian and the Aral seas, and all of Central Asia, where the careless expansion of cotton fields and the non-observance of crop rotation led to diseases of both the soil and the people.

The traditional concept of the peasant as a second-class citizen had a further negative effect. While statistics on the overall growth in power production looked encouraging, the countryside, with its 100 million people, received only 10 per cent of this electric power. Despite the enormous growth in coal-mining, the rural population was forced to use all sorts of devious ways to get fuel, because only one third of their needs was met through official channels. I was shown a map of gas pipelines criss-crossing the country in every possible direction. A gas network was introduced in urban areas but the farmers were deprived of it, and there were no plans in prospect to make gas available to them.

Rural areas were badly off for roads, schools, medical services, public utilities, newspaper and magazine supplies, cinemas and cultural entertainment. The situation was particularly unfavourable in the *nechernozemie* (non-black earth) areas, which comprised 30 oblasts in Russia. Errors in planning the distribution of production forces resulted in a super-concentration of industries, while the rural areas had fallen into oblivion. Peasants abandoned their villages, lured by

150

the bright lights of the cities, where working hours were fixed, salaries higher and streets paved, and where, in general, life was more comfortable. There was a similar situation in other parts of the country. The farmer abandoned his land, and in his footsteps came people without roots in the countryside. Seasonal workers harvested and stored the grain, worked on the farms and in the repair shops, some of them under the guise of so-called 'volunteer' help, others under contract. It is beyond human understanding how the relationship between man and his land could have been allowed to reach such a state. The village had been drained of the farmers.

The desolation of the countryside became so acute in the *nech- ernozemie* areas that it was considered useless to invest in them. I have to admit that even I, looking at things from my 'Stavropol perspective', felt that investments would be more useful where they would give quick profits. Later, giving the problem serious thought, I came to the conclusion that neither purely economic nor immediate short-term considerations were appropriate. This was an issue touching the very core of the Russian nation.

When it became clear that the population could not be kept in the countryside unless improvements were made, some scholars and politicians advocated enlarging the villages and the farms by combining them, so as to supply them with electricity, fuel, schools, medical services and road and transport networks, because it would have been impossible to do so for each hamlet or village separately. But, when the enlargement project was launched, it turned out that there was another difficulty: the invisible ties which bound the peasant to his land would be severed to an even greater extent. After all, land is not only the site where wheat or potatoes are grown. It is one's home, one's Motherland.

To begin with, I wanted to clarify the possibilities. When the Zonal Research Institute analysed the work of 500 model farms, selected from all over the country to reflect differing geographical and natural climatic zones, we saw that if the ordinary collective and state farms ever attained their full capacity, we would not know what to do with the milk and meat surplus, while the grain crops would mount to at least 260 million tonnes.

The next step was to measure the supply of energy, the amounts of fertilizer per hectare of arable land, and the land surface cultivated by each agricultural worker. The results were compared with ordinary collective and state farms, and they were predictable: the productivity of the farm was directly proportional to the investment in it. This suggested a simple conclusion: the current system would function well were the necessary equipment, fertilizers and organizational methods to be provided.

However, the very comparison of model farm production with the production of collective and state farms was faulty. These experimental farms employ selective methods, advanced technologies and highly competent people. They cultivate and sell high-quality grain and pedigree cattle, which fetch prices two or three times higher than the regular farms receive. Moreover, the experimental farms enjoy greater independence in producing and selling; collective and state farms have no such privileges. A basic question came to the fore, namely that of the government subsidy system versus the encouragement of initiative, with consequent more efficient operations and better income. Most of the country's farms lacked the economic facilities to foster the more effective management which would have made farming more profitable to the peasants.

The decisions of the 1965 March Central Committee plenum, convened to discuss the problems of procurement prices, had been overtaken by events. Moreover, the price gap continued to widen as the supply of still inefficient but more expensive machinery to rural areas increased. The debts of collective and state farms were now nearing 200 billion rubles. However, instead of transforming economic relationships in the rural areas, the simplest solution was applied: the loan was first extended and then, eventually, written off. Whenever there was a crisis in the production of a given crop, higher procurement prices were set. As a result of this method, cotton prices increased, followed by grape and tobacco prices.

For a while these measures were helpful, but within two or three years the benefits were outweighed by further increases in the prices of machines, fuel, fertilizers and construction materials. Sixty per cent of expenditure on agricultural production was attributed to industrial supplies to the rural areas.

I have already mentioned that a 'theory' had been proposed for the purpose of reducing expenditure allocated to rural areas. This 'theory' claimed that agriculture consumed more national income than it produced. Briefly, agriculture was regarded as a hopeless liability on the national economy, a sort of bottomless pit absorbing immense resources. The idea was widespread among not only industrialists, planners and financiers, but also among the Secretaries of the Central Committee. Hence the logical proposition that the country had no need of a large-scale food programme, but rather should introduce some kind of order to agricultural production. 'Introducing order' was the phrase on everyone's lips, then and later, when nobody knew what to do.

For better or worse, the only way to launch a realistic food programme was to start by refuting such faulty 'theoretical' assumptions. I studied the methodology of computing our national income, assuming that it was there that 'the dog lies buried'. As usual, I was assisted by experts, particularly Vladimir Aleksandrovich Tikhonov. I made public the results of the study in *Kommunist*, the official journal of the Central Committee. The article stated that 'a substantial share of national income is being created in agriculture, namely 28 per cent (including turnover tax as a share of the net profit achieved from the sales of industrial productions). Over two thirds of the products sold retail in the system of state and co-operative trade consist of agricultural goods and merchandise produced from agricultural raw materials . . .'

Statements claiming that agriculture was 'unprofitable' were found to be wrong. All data pointed to the fact that much more was siphoned off from agriculture than invested in it. And, of course, the nation's economic development had been achieved largely at the expense of the countryside.

After publication of this data none of my opponents ventured to describe the agrarian sector as a 'bottomless pit'. This again provided an opportunity to raise the question of equitable purchase prices for agricultural production. The problem was at whose expense should this be done? At the time, any noticeable increase in retail food prices was resolutely rejected. The problem was totally divorced from economic considerations, and regarded as a purely political issue. The alternative was to increase subsidies from the state budget. However, by the early 1980s these already amounted to about 40 billion rubles, and showed a sustained tendency to increase further.

This problem dominated our debates. All agreed that the collective and state farms could no longer subsist on a starvation diet. Yet the Finance Ministry flatly refused new investment projects. 'The State has no money,' V. F. Garbuzov, the minister, repeated, countering all my arguments. He knew the real state of the budget. Its mainstay was such sources of income as covert price increases, increases in the rate of vodka production, and, finally, petro-dollars. But even these could no longer make ends meet. The yawning deficit was covered by State Bank loans at the expense of citizens' savings.

N. K. Baibakov, Chairman of the State Planning Committee of the Council of Ministers, was the first to hint to me at the possibility of cutting the defence budget. The growth in military expenditure was far ahead of the growth in national income. Yet no attempt had ever been made to analyse that budget rationally, with a view to an optimal redistribution of means and resources. Once, when we were alone after a meeting, Baibakov asked me point-blank: 'Would you be willing to raise this question?'

'No, I wouldn't,' I answered.

'You see, I wouldn't do it either,' he added regretfully. We both knew perfectly well that even a mention of this subject would mean immediate dismissal. It was the General Secretary's turf.

LIFE IN THE CAPITAL

Central Committee work left me little time for my family or for rest. But we wanted to participate in the life of the capital and to make new contacts. Naturally we wanted to understand the atmosphere of the city where the families of my new colleagues lived, and also simply to become acquainted with them. Alas, it was not all as I had imagined.

Meeting people and visiting their homes was not encouraged.

Brezhnev himself invited only a strictly limited circle – Gromyko, Ustinov, less often Andropov and Kirilenko. There were, it is true, exceptions. In the early summer of 1979, Suslov invited our family for the day. We agreed to go for a walk in the grounds of one of the deserted dachas formerly belonging to Stalin. He brought his daughter, grandchildren and son-in-law. We spent nearly the whole day there, walking and talking. We did not have lunch, but there was tea. This was a meeting between those from the same region; an old inhabitant of Moscow was, as it were, paying some attention to a young colleague from Stavropol.

Even with Andropov, despite our cordial relations, we never visited each other's home. Once I tried to take the initiative, and with some discomfort I remember to this day what came of it. It was towards the end of 1980, after I had become a member of the Politburo. Our dachas were next door to each other, and one day in the summer I telephoned Andropov. 'Today, we are arranging a meal in Stavropol style and, as in the good old days, we invite you and Tatyana Filippovna to dinner.'

'Yes, those were the days, but I have to decline your invitation, Mikhail,' Andropov answered in a calm, quiet voice.

'Why?' I asked.

'Because, tomorrow, there would be all kinds of loose talk – who, where, why, what was said?'

'What are you saying, Yury Vladimirovich?' I tried, quite sincerely, to suggest that it was not so.

'No, that's the way it really is. While we were still on our way to you, Leonid Ilyich would hear about it. I say this, Mikhail, first and foremost for your sake.'

After this incident we no longer had any wish to invite anyone or to be invited. We continued to meet old acquaintances and made new ones, we invited them to come to us and we went as guests to them. But we never did this with colleagues on the Politburo or in the Secretariat.

Raisa Maksimovna also found it difficult to adjust to the new kind of relationships. She was never quite comfortable among the 'Kremlin wives'. She never became close to any of them. After attending a number of meetings of such wives, Raisa

Maksimovna was astonished at the atmosphere, full of arrogance, suspicion, sycophancy, and tactlessness.

The world of these wives was a mirror image of the leadership hierarchy, with the addition of some feminine subtleties. For example, on 8 March 1979 there was a traditional state reception. All the wives of the leaders gathered at the entrance to the hall, so as to welcome the foreign and local guests. Raisa Maksimovna stood where there was room, little thinking that a pecking order was in operation. One of the 'principal' ladies, Kirilenko's wife, turned to her and, without any embarrassment, pointed, saying 'This is your place – at the end!' Raisa Maksimovna often remarked: 'What kind of people are these?'

Outside the 'select circle' everything was easier. Irina and Anatoly were quickly accepted into their new student environment and made new friends. A few years later they delighted us by producing our first grandchild, a girl, who was named Kseniya.

Raisa Maksimovna renewed her academic contacts, her old acquaintances and colleagues at Moscow University, and at the Philosophy Institute, and she soon entered into her familiar world of academic discussions, symposiums, conferences and simple friendly get-togethers. She studied English.

After our arrival in the capital, as soon as we found some free time we took the car to see the sights of Moscow. Our first itineraries took in the old places dear to our hearts: Mokhovaya Street, the 'Red Gate', Krasnoselskaya, Sokolniki, with its familiar fire observation tower, the Rusakov Club, Stromynka... Once we drove to the Yauza River. Crossing the bridge, we came to Preobrazhenskaya Square – and did not recognize it! The old square was there no longer; it was painfully sad.

We felt much the same at Krasnaya Presnya, where in 1951, as a student and deputy leader of a political-agitation group (*agitkollektiv*)[1] I took part in a get-out-the-vote campaign.[2] I rushed around among the small, old, half tumbled-down houses in the Bolshaya Gruzinskaya and Malaya Gruzinskaya Streets. I tried to make the voters happy by petitioning for repairs to their

---

[1] Concerned with mobilizing support to implement economic plans.
[2] Ensuring that voters participated in elections to soviets.

stairways and roofs, to their plumbing and switches, their doors and locks, knowing that, on the eve of voting, any old lady could say: 'You do all that, my dear, or I won't vote!'

But that was the Moscow of the 1950s. Now, in place of the little old houses, there were towering multi-storey buildings. There had also been changes in the landscape around the Lenin Hills where, in my time, the University itself and the ski-jump by the Moskva River used to be seen, solitary and somehow lonely, against a background of empty land and small buildings. Where the former village of Cheremyshki used to be, where construction workers lived, and where we used to go to receive parcels sent by our relatives, a great modern district with all amenities had appeared.

What I saw filled me with contradictory feelings. On the one hand, it was not possible to go on living in those small, old and decrepit houses. But there had been a special warmth there, a closeness to nature, a special way of life, difficult to part with. Then for the first time, I realized what a human drama must have occurred for thousands of Muscovites when they said farewell to the Old Arbat. When the complex of high-rise buildings was built on the Kalinin Prospect, the Muscovites called it the 'false teeth' of Moscow. Even now I feel nostalgic about the old Moscow, the city of my youth.

At first we chose the route for our drives around Moscow rather arbitrarily. We got into the car, drove off, and then stopped somewhere to get out and walk. The surroundings somehow entered into our souls, invoking reminiscences from some far corners of our memories. But we did not only wish to know that modern Moscow where we had been fated to live. As time passed, the idea grew of excursions based around Moscow's different periods of development: first Moscow of the fourteenth–sixteenth centuries, then the seventeenth and eighteenth centuries, and so on. We were usually joined by some experts on the history of old Moscow, acquaintances of Raisa Maksimovna.

Still later we drove out to Podmoskovie, the Moscow suburbs and surroundings. We went to Arkhangelskoe. We particularly liked the lovely landscapes along the Moskva River banks. We had heard previously of Kolomenskoye, but what we actually saw cast a spell over us: the Ascension Church reaching upwards to the sky – to God.

We made use of our new situation to indulge our old passion for the theatre. Even on our short visits to Moscow, we had always tried to see the most interesting productions. We often went to the Moscow Arts Theatre (MKhAT) or the Maly Theatre, our old favourites. We fell in love with the Vakhtangov Theatre, the Theatre of Satire, the Sovremennik Theatre. I particularly recall *Ten Days that Shook the World* and *The Anti-Worlds* at the Taganka, and a marvellous, enthralling performance of *Spartacus*[1] at the Bolshoi, with Vasiliev, Maksimova and Liepa.

When we had settled down in Moscow, we began to go to the theatre again, as it were to check our memories of former years. As before, we preferred the Vakhtangov Theatre, but we also liked the Moscow Arts, the Sovremennik and the Mayakovsky and Mossovet Theatres. We frequented the Bolshoi. Of course, we also visited the Tretyakov Gallery, the Pushkin Museum of Fine Arts, and the Great Hall of the Conservatory.

Reading these words over again, I am surprised. Memory works in mysterious ways: it retains mainly the best of what happened in life – even when there was not much of it.

PALACE GAMES

Suslov died on 25 January 1982. His death aggravated the in-fighting among the political leadership. Suslov had never aspired to the post of General Secretary and was totally loyal to Brezhnev, although he ventured to contradict him at times. In the leadership entourage he played a stabilizing role, and to a certain extent moderated the contending forces.

But now he was no more. The first question was who would replace him. Actually, it was a matter of who would be Brezhnev's successor, a 'second' secretary who, according to tradition, would eventually become 'first' and, under the incumbent General Secretary, gradually take over the levers of

---

[1] A ballet with music by Aram Khachaturyan, first performed in 1953.

power and assume leadership. Obviously the candidate would have to be acceptable to Brezhnev.

However, such was the state of health of Leonid Ilyich that his judgement of people and ideas had become inadequate. To a large extent it depended on Chernenko, who never left the General Secretary's side all day long except during his siesta. Every Thursday, after the Politburo meeting, Brezhnev left with Chernenko for Zavidovo, the hunting lodge managed by the military. Occasionally, when unfinished business at the Politburo required Chernenko's presence, he stayed over on Friday, but the weekend was invariably spent at Zavidovo.

Chernenko's influence stemmed not only from having co-operated with Brezhnev for many years, but also from his activity as the foremost image-builder. A group of people around Chernenko guided the mass media, the ideological Party structures and Party Committees accordingly. Clichés such as 'the universally recognized leader', 'the foremost theorist', 'the indisputable authority', and the 'outstanding fighter for peace and progress' became widespread. Considering that, in his later years, Leonid Ilyich was able to work – or rather to be present at work – only a few hours a day, it was quite a job to create some semblance of an active life. Each public appearance and each trip of the General Secretary was carefully orchestrated; ghost-writers worked on his articles, memoirs, and collected works. Brezhnev enjoyed it all.

Having gained the General Secretary's confidence, almost in the role of his executor, Chernenko was undeniably a contender for the post of the 'second person'. This situation also nurtured the exorbitant ambitions of his 'group', apparatchiks without any political credibility. In a way, Chernenko himself was being manipulated by them.

Any analysis of the political balance after Suslov's death would have to include some Politburo members, primarily the leaders of major republican organizations[1] such as Kunayev or Shcherbitsky. One of Brezhnev's assistants told me the following

---

[1] First Party secretaries of Union republics, such as Kazakhstan and Ukraine.

story. Shcherbitsky was visiting Brezhnev for a regular talk and dwelled at length on achievements in Ukraine. As they were saying goodbye, Brezhnev, who was pleased with the information, responded with feeling, pointing to his armchair: 'Volodya, this is your place after I am gone.'

It was 1978. Shcherbitsky was sixty years old. It was neither a joke nor a moment of weakness. Leonid Ilyich had really been attached to him for a long time. As soon as he had come to power he pulled Shcherbitsky out of Dnepropetrovsk, where he had been sent by Khrushchev, and succeeded in having him appointed Chairman of the Council of Ministers of Ukraine, and subsequently elected to the Politburo. He had already decided to replace Shelest, his predecessor. Although Shcherbitsky's personality was not extraordinary, he commanded prestige as someone who 'led' his republic firmly. Even more important, he was, in his own words, a steadfast follower of Bogdan Khmelnitsky: a symbol of Ukraine's unity with Russia.

Suslov's death must have put ideas into the heads of a few people. Andropov, for instance, received an unexpected call from his old friend Gromyko, who quite openly explored the ground for his possible move to the post of second-in-command. He understood perfectly well what it meant to occupy this position, and who would take over Brezhnev's powers. A man of experience, he was used to calculating his moves well ahead. After all, he succeeded in keeping his post as Minister of Foreign Affairs under every regime for twenty-eight years.

Andropov told me about this telephone conversation, which left him wondering and baffled, though he responded coolly to his interlocutor: 'Andrei, it's up to the General Secretary.'

Incidentally, Andropov's reaction to this call betrayed his own intentions. Yury Vladimirovich was also a pretender to the post, and I was absolutely certain that he would get it. Ustinov shared this view. He was on very close terms with Andropov.

We often discussed the possibility of Yury Vladimirovich's return to the Central Committee staff during our meetings. Back in Kislovodsk, during one of his holidays there, I told him: 'You have worked enough for State Security. It's time you returned to the home you left.'[1]

He pretended to take it as a joke, and only smiled in response.

Yury Vladimirovich told me later that, soon after Suslov's death, the General Secretary conferred with him about the possibility of his heading the Secretariat and managing the international department. He then added: 'I have no idea, though, what the final decision is going to be.'

Andropov was still not sure to what extent Chernenko's counter-measures could block that decision. Chernenko's influence increased whenever Brezhnev's health deteriorated, but the General Secretary was capable of taking a firm stand and defending it as soon as his condition improved. Finally, on 24 May 1982, the plenary sessions elected Andropov Secretary of the Central Committee.

I believe Brezhnev made his choice some time in the middle of March. Andropov told me at the time that he was to make a speech on the anniversary of Lenin's birth. According to 'Kremlinology' criteria, this reflected Brezhnev's ultimate decision. The speech was a success. What was supposed to be a routine address had given rise, for the first time in many years, to serious thoughts about the real problem of the state of society. It was then that Andropov said that we had a poor knowledge of the society in which we live.

It may well be that the election of Yury Vladimirovich could have been due to another, less well-known factor. By transferring Yury Vladimirovich to Party work, Brezhnev replaced him at State Security (KGB) by Fedorchuk, who was totally devoted to him. Andropov had a negative view of Fedorchuk, and had his own candidate for the post, namely Chebrikov. However, when Leonid Ilyich asked him point-blank about a potential successor, he was elusive: 'It's up to the General Secretary,' he answered.

When Brezhnev mentioned Fedorchuk, Yury Vladimirovich put forward no objections.

To me another matter was of the essence: the emphasis on

---

[1] Andropov had previously worked in the Party Central Committee Secretariat.

'palace games' distracted attention from the food programme, even though it was in its decisive phase.

The vulnerable aspect of the programme was the source of finance. I was able to make provision for modernizing agricultural machine building but the problem of increased purchasing prices remained unsolved and looked ever more hopeless. Where would the money come from? This idea haunted me constantly. I therefore studied what happened to agricultural credits. I have already mentioned the disparity in economic terms between the urban and rural areas. But the destructive practice of selling equipment, building materials and fuel at high prices, whereas grain and other agricultural commodities were cheap, had to generate some sort of compensatory mechanism, lest the entire agricultural sector went bankrupt. State credits represented one such compensatory mechanism.

Farms were granted such loans on an annual basis but no-one ever intended to pay them back in full. The argument went something like: 'Since you maintain low procurement prices which keep us from leading a normal life and work, you will always have to give us loans and subsequently write off the debts. There is no other way; you have to feed the country, whatever happens.'

It goes without saying that, under such conditions, there was no need to try to be more efficient and tackle real cost considerations, such as whether a new machine was needed or not. If you can snatch something, just go for it. Payment will be made out of the loans, which are never repaid.

I scanned the nationwide figures: even a rough estimate amounted to fifteen to seventeen billion rubles. Hence, unrepaid loans were tantamount to direct financing of state and collective farms. Why then could we not allocate such sums to boost purchase prices? With equitable prices, the farms would be encouraged to think of increasing output and consider real costs and possible savings. It seemed to me a solution, but I refrained from mentioning it without further detailed study.

A key element of the food programme was the social development plan for the countryside. In co-ordination with the government we completed the plan. Using all available sources, the cost would be 140 billion rubles.

Finally, the discussions in the commissions were finished, and the main elements of the food programme defined, developed and co-ordinated. I dropped in on Chernenko and told him that it was time to set up a meeting with Leonid Ilyich, since the Central Committee plenary session was only one month away.

The choice of who should present the main report, which is usually settled well ahead of time, turned out to be a thorny problem. It was taken for granted from the beginning that I should present it. But I sensed something like jealousy, particularly on the part of N. A. Tikhonov, but also from other members of the Politburo. I told Brezhnev that I would, of course, be willing to present the report, but considering its impact, and because this large-scale programme was being adopted for the first time in the country, it might be preferable for the General Secretary to do so.

Brezhnev hesitated. I was aware of the inner struggle that overwhelmed him. He had had enormous difficulties at the recent Party Congress even reading his report. But the temptation overrode all objections and, at the next Politburo meeting, Leonid Ilyich gave his consent. Then the time came to brief him about the programme.

Brezhnev was undergoing a regular check-up at the hospital in Granovsky Street. Next to his hospital room was a reception room for visitors. It was comfortable, and tea was served. Chernenko, Tikhonov, Andropov and I gathered there.

Leonid Ilyich welcomed us warmly. I was under the impression that he wanted to appear healthy and in high spirits. He did not look like someone who was seriously ill. Instead of hospital garb, he wore stylish slacks and a brown sports jacket with a zipper. Only those who remembered his old vigour would notice a certain sluggishness in his behaviour.

We greeted him, sat down around the table and discussed current affairs, health and general topics. Then Leonid Ilyich asked: 'What's happening there with the plenum?' All heads turned towards me. 'We are in the final stages of preparation,' I said. 'We have worked out a package of resolutions relevant to the programme. As to the planned performance figures, they are realistic. All that is left to do is to co-ordinate our positions on the sources of financing.'

Brezhnev responded instantly: 'We have to hold this plenum. However, there is one thing: you talked me into being the speaker, but what about financing? Do you expect me to go to the rostrum with an empty pocket?'

'Don't worry, Leonid Ilyich.' Chernenko jumped up from his seat. 'You'll see, everything will be all right, we'll come to terms.' Tikhonov assented, not sounding very sincere.

This meeting reminded me of the year 1978, and the station platform in Mineralnye Vody. There were the same faces: Brezhnev, Chernenko, Andropov, Gorbachev, and now Tikhonov. And the same mood of alarm in anticipation of the forthcoming changes.

Andropov sat without opening his mouth but keenly observing the course of the discussion. He was already aware of his forthcoming election as Central Committee secretary at the plenum, and of his consequent position as second-in-command. Tikhonov was equally aware of it, and therefore anxiously kept an eye on Yury Vladimirovich. Chernenko looked terribly nervous: he still did not know who would be nominated but guessed that it was not to be him, since Leonid Ilyich had made no such hint.

In the meantime, the talk continued. In order to ease Brezhnev's appearance at the plenum, we agreed to distribute the text of the food programme and the whole package of government resolutions to the members of the Central Committee and guests before the opening of the plenum. All the General Secretary would have to do was to present these documents and read a brief report. This being agreed, we all left.

The time came for a crucial discussion with Tikhonov. This did not promise to be pleasant, but without his participation the project was jeopardized.

We met in the Kremlin and talked for four hours. I presented extensive information on the entire range of problems, as well as ostensibly 'unbeatable' arguments. But, as soon as the figure of sixteen billion rubles was mentioned, Tikhonov stopped listening.

'Nikolai Aleksandrovich, you're an economic executive, you know what life is like. You know very well that, without that sum, the entire programme turns into a dead letter.'

'Mikhail Sergeyevich, no and no again,' insisted Tikhonov. 'I don't have that kind of money.'

At this point I brought up the subject of soft loans.

'Just take a look at the statistics: in the past five years, the collective and state farms have been taking up loans of seventeen billion rubles a year, and this sum has never been repaid.' I spread out the relevant papers in front of Tikhonov.

'What's that got to do with it?' he asked.

'The system of soft loans is also a method of financing, but certainly the worst possible one. Loans are simply taken and never repaid. This creates a grab-what-you-can mentality in rural areas; you yourself have mentioned it. As long as this system prevails things will not get better.'

Tea was served. Tikhonov's expression was impassive, and it was difficult to guess what lay behind it. The discussion resumed. All my economic arguments were rebounding like a rubber ball, and finally they were exhausted. Tikhonov was impervious to every one of them and, what was worse, he was silent. Try to argue with that one! Then, remembering our joint visit to the General Secretary, I shifted from persuasion to a tougher stand:

'Look at this memorandum which I prepared for the Politburo after our meeting with Leonid Ilyich. I want both of us to sign it: you, as the Chairman of the government, me as the person entrusted with this matter. We should submit it jointly to the Politburo.'

Silence on the part of Tikhonov.

'Well, if you don't sign it, I shall do so on my own, and table it before the Politburo. Let them decide. In Leonid Ilyich's office I warned that the problem of financing was still pending, but both you and Chernenko assured the General Secretary that it would be agreed upon.'

Tikhonov listened silently, thinking it over. More tea was served. There was another pause.

'I'm sure the Politburo will back me up,' I urged. 'Judging by the meeting I convened, this view is widespread within the Party and in the country. Let's work together. I'd hate us to part on that note.'

Finally Tikhonov said: 'Let me see the papers.'

He took the memorandum, the background information and the calculations and leafed through them silently, a decision developing in his mind.

'I'll take all this along and study it once more, but let us delete right away the issue of the State Agro-Industrial Committee. I don't mind them being in the regions, but not at the centre. Otherwise we would have a second government, wouldn't we?'

'Well, well,' I thought to myself. Tikhonov had been sitting there for four long hours and keeping silent about the main issue gnawing at his innermost thoughts. And I took such pains adducing economic evidence, searching for well-founded arguments to convince him . . . Not long before, Karlov had told me that rumours in the Central Committee apparatus and the Council of Ministers had it that Gorbachev was setting up the Agro-Industrial Committee 'for himself' to 'grab' half of the country's economy, or, even worse, 'to disguise Gorbachev's far-reaching ambition to become Chairman of the Council of Ministers . . .'

At the time this rumour did not bother me, and I regarded it as the usual gossip in the apparatus, no more than that. But some people took it very seriously indeed.

'No objection,' I affirmed. And I deleted every reference to the proposed committee from the memorandum addressed to the Politburo. A deep sigh of relief came from Nikolai Aleksandrovich, who visibly perked up. The deal was concluded.

The shock was general. Nobody had believed that Tikhonov would give in. My 'well-wishers' had been simply convinced that I couldn't manage Tikhonov. But I paid no attention to all this chatter. The long and exhausting marathon was over.

On 24 May 1982 the Central Committee plenum heard Brezhnev's report 'On the Food Programme of the USSR to 1990 and measures for its implementation'. Both the programme and the package of six resolutions on the individual questions related to the functioning of the Agro-Industrial Complex were approved.

The reader, our Russian reader in particular, will ask: what good did this programme do? The food situation was bad and it continued to be so. In fact, it became even worse. And why does the author go into all the stratagems and the struggles between the advocates and the enemies of the programme? Wouldn't it be more honest to admit that it was another utopia and represented renewed promises which were subsequently forgotten?

I have my own view on this matter. First, I wanted to describe my involvement in the decision-making process. Second, developing a programme of such scope was a kind of desperate attempt to make the system work in such a major area as food production. And, after all, something came out of it. Compared with the average production rate of previous years, the grain yield increased by 26.6 million tonnes, meat by 2.5 million tonnes, and milk by over 10 million tonnes during the 12th Five Year Plan, whereas the number of loss-making farms was reduced from 25,000 to 4,000, amounting to less than 10 per cent.

Third, the work of implementing the programme revealed that stabilizing the food market affected not only agriculture, but also depended on the general financial situation in the country and, primarily, on a balance between the growth of the people's incomes and their expenditures.

I remember how, in my Stavropol days as second kraikom secretary (1968–69), I had to deal with the problem of what to do with all the meat and butter produced, because people 'refused' to buy them. Meanwhile, *per-capita* consumption amounted to a mere 42 kilos of meat, and almost 100 kilos less milk than the 1990 level.

In fact, there is no need to look at the past. Now, practically all foodstuffs are available, but in 1992 alone, consumption dropped by 28 per cent on the previous year. What kind of trick is that? There is no trick; people's income is 'eaten away' by inflation, and they have no money to buy what they want. Nonetheless, the authorities claim that they have solved the food problem.

THE ANDROPOV–CHERNENKO TUG OF WAR

Meanwhile, the tug of war between Chernenko and Andropov, and their contest over who could exert the greatest influence on Brezhnev, continued. Chernenko attempted to isolate Brezhnev from any direct contact. He was prepared to stoop to anything in order to strengthen his position.

Although Yury Vladimirovich Andropov was given Suslov's office, he was not officially appointed to head the Central Committee Secretariat. I am not sure whether this was a deliberate policy or not, but Chernenko and, occasionally, Kirilenko took advantage of the situation and continued to chair the meetings of the Secretariat. This situation prevailed until July 1982. Then an incident took place which served to put things in order. Usually the secretaries met before the meeting in a room known as 'the dressing room'. When I arrived, Andropov was already there. He waited for a few minutes, then got up abruptly from his armchair and said:

'Let's go, are you ready? It's time to start.'

Yury Vladimirovich was the first one in the meeting hall and made straight for the chair. At the sight of Andropov in the chairman's seat Chernenko seemed to slump and he collapsed into the armchair across the table from me. He almost disappeared from view. An internal *coup d'état* had taken place before our eyes, reminiscent of a scene from Gogol.

Andropov chaired this session resolutely and confidently, in contrast to Chernenko's tedious manner. That night I telephoned him: 'Congratulations, it seems to have been an important event. I realized that you were under stress and totally withdrawn before the Secretariat meeting.'

'Thanks, Mikhail,' answered Andropov, 'I had good reason to be tense. Leonid Ilyich rang me up and asked: "Why do you think I took you from the KGB and transferred you to the Central Committee apparatus? So that you would merely be in attendance? I put you there to lead the Secretariat and deal with the cadres. Why don't you act?" That got me moving.'

Knowing Brezhnev's state of health, his ebbing willpower and his unwillingness to quarrel with Chernenko, I was certain that he would have been incapable of calling Andropov on his own. Someone had, as we say, 'put the heat on him'. It could not have been anyone else but Ustinov. Considering his influence over Brezhnev and his ability to act directly and bluntly, as well as his long friendship with Andropov, I could be quite sure of it.

That is how the new 'stability' came about. Now discussions were often brisk and business-like. Departments were called to order about their efficiency. Adopted resolutions were terse and to the point. A rigorous and tough policy was in effect. As to the officials' personal responsibility, Yury Vladimirovich evoked such dread in those who incurred his wrath that one could not but sympathize with the victims, even when they were guilty.

I detected a change in Andropov which I had not noticed before. It may well be that it was due to Brezhnev's faltering health and the rampant intrigues in his entourage, which threatened to escalate into total anarchy. Apparently Andropov had decided to undertake decisive measures to bolster the authority of the central power and to show that, regardless of the General Secretary's infirmity, the levers of power were still held firmly. First and foremost, this was targeted at the Politburo members.

An in-depth analysis of Yury Vladimirovich's measures shows that they were sporadic and were largely meant to demonstrate his resolve. The stifling atmosphere of stagnation had by then become so close that even the slightest whiff of air created the illusion of freshness. Unfortunately, so many problems had accumulated in the Brezhnev years that such disjointed measures were inadequate to overcome them.

The established pattern of disseminating information to the leadership of the country failed to provide objective data to manage the life of the society. The State Committee of Statistics (Goskomstat), the State Planning Commission, the Ministry of Finance, and the research centres often used non-comparable data and calculation methods, and they tried, as a rule, to supply only general and well-known information, which was inadequate for any analysis, reflection or the formulation of alternative estimates and judgements. The consequences might have been somewhat moderated by an appropriate system of control, but the head of the state no longer had the strength or the desire to apply it. Any attempt to provide a realistic appraisal of the situation in his presence was nipped in the bud. Whenever abuses and mismanagement were mentioned to him, tears would well up in his eyes and he would ask, bewilderment in his voice: 'Is it really that bad?'

After all, he was firmly convinced that he had brought happiness to the country and to the world. During these critical moments his 'guardian angel' Chernenko would emerge muttering: 'What's all this? What's the matter? Why this mood? Who let him in?'

Since the General Secretary was incapable of displaying initiative, the other Politburo members were discouraged from doing so, in order not to highlight the disparity between them and their chief. Brezhnev was no longer able to travel across the country. Consequently, all travel by others had to be curtailed even when it would have been effective.

Brezhnev's entourage was confronted with another challenge, namely to create the illusion of a busy and efficient General Secretary. Since he no longer generated fresh ideas and could not write and speak in public, trusted persons, aides and advisers acted on his behalf. Doggedly and adroitly, they put together reports and memoranda, sent letters and dispatched telegrams. Each 'historic' performance was orchestrated to elicit a broad response. All departments of the Central Committee participated in the preparation of such a 'response', which was supposed to reflect the enthusiasm with which Brezhnev's speech had been received.

Incidentally, an inside knowledge of the mechanism of power occasionally helped to push through reasonable decisions. Brezhnev's entourage was singularly bereft of any ideas and, whenever a 'memorandum' contained a decision-making proposal on any major problem on behalf of the General Secretary, the opportunity was immediately seized.

As already mentioned, this 'stability' under the ailing General Secretary was welcomed by many members of the leadership, since it gave them free rein to do as they liked in their regions and departments. It also suited Brezhnev's immediate entourage, inasmuch as this arrangement ensured their well-being. Everyone knew that a new General Secretary would inevitably make changes in the cadres.

Thus the reins of power and administrative activity gradually slipped into the bureaucratic apparatus. Not only were the last vestiges of democracy within the Party reduced to nil; the decay encouraged widespread bureaucratic intrigue, which often played a decisive role in the decision-making process, particularly with respect to the appointment of cadres.

By then, the General Secretary's alleged position no longer reflected his personal point of view, which should have been the outcome of independent analysis and a comparison of different ideas. It merely expressed the view of a group of people who at some given moment had succeeded in exerting pressure on Brezhnev.

In the last years of Brezhnev's reign, the Politburo was in total disarray. Some Politburo meetings lasted no longer than fifteen or twenty minutes, so as not to weary Leonid Ilyich. In fact, getting together took more time than the actual work accomplished at a meeting. Chernenko would arrange beforehand for someone to remark 'It's all quite clear' as soon as an agenda item had been introduced. The invited participants had to leave having barely crossed the threshold. Subsequently the problem in question was deemed to have been 'examined' by the Politburo.

Whenever a crucial issue concerning the life of the country was placed on the agenda, all hopes were pinned on its consideration by the government. But even in such important cases the debate at the Politburo was never substantive. Another ready-made phrase was then used: 'The comrades have worked, a preliminary exchange of views has taken place, and experts have been consulted. Any comments?' And if anyone ventured a comment, Chernenko would look daggers at him.

Even when he felt somewhat better, Brezhnev was still unable to follow a discussion or to summarize it. Therefore, whenever a key problem came up, he would be the first one to take the floor and read out a prepared text. Thereafter, it was considered improper to launch any discussion and the response was the same: 'Let us agree with Leonid Ilyich's opinion ... Let us approve ...' Sometimes Brezhnev would point out some omissions in a given project, or would suggest that a certain aspect should be emphasized. Such a suggestion would set off a joyous chorus of approval, and the meeting then stood adjourned.

The only exception to this state of affairs was the debates at the Politburo meetings when annual plans and budgets were discussed at length and heatedly, since they concerned the interests of those in charge of the various sectors or regions. At these meetings, too, the General Secretary opened the debate. To begin with, he read out the introductory remarks rather confusedly, and then opened the debate.

The parlance never varied. Shcherbitsky always pointed to the need for upgrading the Donbass industrial plant[1] 'or else problems in metallurgy and the mines would bring about a crisis in power supply, and that not only in our republic but nationwide.' Kunayev fretted over the state of virgin lands and the development of the Ekibastuz Energy Production Centre, requesting more funds. Grishin rambled as usual, and also asked for more money for Moscow. Rashidov's themes never varied: the one-sided development of the Central Asian region, employment problems and the need to create jobs and, last but not least, irrigation. Notwithstanding the importance and complexity of all these problems, they never triggered off any discussion, exchange of opinions or controversy. And, of course, no draft plan or budget was ever challenged and returned for further study.

Eventually, more than twenty permanent and ad hoc commissions were set up to examine the specific issues and present their conclusions, while the Politburo simply approved them. There was a Commission on China, a Commission on Poland, a Commission on Afghanistan, and an array of commissions on internal and external problems. All the commissions met in the Central Committee and never gathered elsewhere, so as to allow Chernenko to control their activity. In fact, these commissions gradually became a substitute for the Politburo and the Secretariat. In the meantime the impact of the Politburo sessions was withering away.

Yet those were the times when it would have been possible to halt many harmful processes in the life of the country and to begin reforming society. Alas, time was running out. Under the impact of achievements in science and technology, immense transformations were taking place in the world, involving production, communications, and everyday life. These processes required

[1] In Ukraine.

fundamental changes. Other countries made painful readjustments and then rose to the challenge of the times, whereas our system, supposedly built on scientific premises and a planned systematic approach, as well as scientific management methods, spurned innovation and moved against the general tide of progress.

Leonid Ilyich gave priority to two sectors, agriculture and the military, in that order, it seemed to me. I remember a conversation about the need once again to send troops to help with the harvest, which was brought up in the Walnut Room before the Politburo meeting. Ustinov complained that at each harvest time a substantial part of the pool of lorries was unavailable for army use. He implied the need for replenishing the army car pool, with a view to squeezing funds from the State Planning Commission.

Commenting on the situation, Dmitry Fedorovich remarked casually that he was fully aware that 'defence and bread' were the key issues. I corrected this statement: to me 'bread and defence' was the right order of priorities. Brezhnev remarked with a smile: 'I think Gorbachev is right.'

But Ustinov persisted: 'Leonid Ilyich, you are the one to know that defence means life.'

'What about bread?' chuckled Brezhnev. 'Isn't that life, too?'

But was it indeed 'bread and defence'? Alas, that was not how it worked. The military-industrial complex strengthened its position year by year. This was not due to Brezhnev's personal preference, or to the propensities of Ustinov and other Politburo members. It was due to the hard logic of a world split down the middle, and the lethal and costly armaments race. In order to match the competition, increasing funds and material resources were needed. In virtually all branches of the national economy, military expenditure sapped the vital juices.

Whenever I had an opportunity to visit factories that produced both military hardware and agricultural machinery I was always taken aback. It sufficed to drop in on a workshop that was equipped with the latest machinery and which, for example, produced the most advanced tanks, and then proceed to another where obsolete tractors were being assembled on ancient production lines, to conclude that agricultural machinery making was banned to the backyard, and played the role of a sort of step-child. Not to speak of the little antediluvian food-processing factories, many of which enjoyed the dubious honour of having beaten all world records for longevity!

At some point, the General Secretary ought to have reflected on the soundness of continuing the military build-up and the arms race with the United States.

In the last Five Year Plans, military expenditure rose twice as fast as the GNP. This Moloch devoured the fruits of hard labour and mercilessly exploited the industrial plant, which was ageing and in dire need of modernization, particularly the machine-tool and mining industry sectors. Worst of all, the problem could not even be analysed. All statistics concerning the military-industrial complex were top secret, inaccessible even to members of the Politburo. A mere allusion to the inadequate operation of a defence enterprise and Ustinov would pounce upon the 'immature fault-finder'. No-one in the Politburo dared to stand up to him.

BREZHNEV'S DEATH

Leonid Ilyich died unexpectedly. Thanks to the mass media, the entire country had known for some months about his physical condition and followed the clinical progress of the General Secretary on television. However, his illness lingered on for so long that people got used to it, and his probable demise did not enter their minds.

On 7 November 1982, the anniversary of the October celebration, Brezhnev reviewed the military parade in his capacity as General Secretary of the Central Committee, Chairman of the Presidium of the Supreme Soviet, Commander-in-Chief and Chairman of the Defence Council. A formal reception followed, where he read out his greeting to the guests. There was nothing unusual.

On 10 November I received a Slovak delegation. We were engaged in animated talk when we were interrupted by an assistant bringing me a message from the Secretariat: 'Andropov wants you urgently. He knows that you are busy with a delegation, but please apologize to them, suggest a break and go to his office right away.'

I understood that something serious must have happened. When I entered Andropov's office, his face betrayed no emotion whatsoever, but his calm countenance belied his tremendous inner tension. He seemed unruffled when he told me that Viktoria Petrovna, Brezhnev's wife, had sent him an urgent message announcing her husband's death and asking him to come to the dacha in Zareche. He was the only person she wanted to see. Andropov had already been there and talked to Dr Chazov and members of the bodyguard. Brezhnev had died in his sleep several hours before the ambulance arrived.

We sat silently. Then I said:

'Well, this is a decisive moment for Staraya Ploshchad. A decision has to be taken and I think that it will directly concern you.'

Andropov, who seemed absorbed in his thoughts, did not answer. Our relationship made it possible for me to talk openly with him instead of beating about the bush. 'Have you met the inner circle?' I asked.

He nodded. Yes, they had met and agreed that Andropov should be nominated. He mentioned Ustinov, Gromyko and Tikhonov. Nothing was said about Chernenko, and I am not sure that he participated in that meeting.

'Whatever happens you cannot dodge the responsibility,' I said. 'I shall strongly support your candidacy.'

A Politburo meeting was convened the same day. A committee was set up under Andropov to organize the funeral. Decisions had to be made about the arrangements to bid a last farewell to the state and Party leader. It was decided to convene a special session of the Central Committee plenum and Tikhonov's proposal to approve Yury Vladimirovich's candidacy for the post of General Secretary was unanimously backed. Chernenko was to report it to the plenum on behalf of the Politburo.

Frankly speaking, Brezhnev's death, although it came unexpectedly, had not shaken or upset anyone. Neither was it regarded as a grievous loss by the people, notwithstanding all the propaganda efforts, maybe even because of them. During those

175

days all of us were, of course, thinking about the future, the state of the country and the perspectives ahead of us. The prevailing mood was the expectation of far-reaching changes.

Much has been written about the eighteen-year period of stagnation under Brezhnev. I suggest that this description needs analysis and in-depth interpretation; all the more because in recent times conservative and fundamentalist forces have attempted to rehabilitate Brezhnevism. The purpose is obvious – to prove that the process of perestroika was needless and to shift the blame for the present crisis in the country onto its initiators.

In a political sense, Brezhnevism was nothing but a conservative reaction against Khrushchev's attempt at reforming the authoritarian model of his time.

There was a lot of talk about democracy under Brezhnev, and the new constitution was adopted with tremendous pomp. Meanwhile, an unprecedented struggle against dissidents was launched; some were imprisoned, others whisked away to psychiatric wards, and still others exiled.

Just as many urgent pleas were made about the need to practise cost-cutting, to intensify production, expedite scientific and technical progress and expand the independence of enterprises. However, even a very modest Kosygin reform in 1965 encountered fierce resistance, and was eventually derailed. The planned plenum on scientific and technical progress was never convened. The economy was carried further and further down a spendthrift path, which would inevitably lead to bankruptcy.

The arms race continued, gaining momentum even after achieving military and strategic parity with the United States of America. The Prague Spring was crushed mercilessly. For the first time since the Second World War our armed forces were engaged in a hopeless military adventure in Afghanistan.

But the most important thing about Brezhnevism was its failure to meet the challenges of the time. Through its blind adherence to old dogmas and obsolete ideas the leadership overlooked the far-reaching changes that were taking place in science and technology, and in the life and activity of the people, and they ignored the transformations that were occurring in other countries. A solid barrier was set up against any kind of change; the country had thus been driven into an impasse, and was doomed to lag far behind.

Following Brezhnev's death the question was: Will the status quo be maintained and the downward course of our society continue, or will far-reaching changes occur, involving the priority issue of renewing the political leadership?

Two tendencies emerged among our leading personalities in those days. On the part of some, there was an inclination to make Brezhnev into another 'classic figure' and 'icon', thus preserving the former entourage while constraining the new leadership within a rigid framework. Others, however, thought it necessary to display a certain reserve when judging the Brezhnev era, so keeping the door open to the possibility of radical change.

As usual, these tendencies were not manifest in public debate and overt clashes, but only in subtle nuances.

The funeral ceremony organized by Chernenko was marked by ostentatious pomp. Chernenko's speech before the 12 November plenum was in the same vein. He painstakingly read out the text prepared by his aides, including grandiloquent praise for Brezhnev as 'the most consistent successor of Lenin's cause' and 'an outstanding theorist', endowed with every conceivable talent and virtue.

The stagnation of the cadres and the all too obvious ageing of the country's leadership were glorified as an achievement of Leonid Ilyich, who had created such a wise, competent and consolidated collective of political leaders. Chernenko's assertion that Andropov was the foremost exponent of Brezhnev's style of leadership, and of his concern for the cadres, was a two-edged compliment for Yury Vladimirovich. At the same time, the expression of confidence that Andropov would pursue Brezhnev's policy of 'collective leadership' sent an unmistakable message: 'Let us command together.'

The general mood permeating society was, as I have said, an awareness that changes were impending. Against that background these eulogies were patent bombast. In those days I spent a lot of time with Andropov, and I realized that he was aware of the need to dissociate himself from many aspects of the Brezhnev era. In this respect he was worried how his initial steps would be received. His speech on the occasion of his election as General Secretary at the 12 November plenum was rather reserved. All the proper words on Brezhnev's demise were said, but no more than that. His speech had a depressing effect on Chernenko, although it is noteworthy that, at the personal level, Yury Vladimirovich was invariably tolerant towards him.

The regular Central Committee plenum had been planned long beforehand for 15 November, and its agenda contained a draft state plan and budget for the coming year. Andropov realized that he would have to go beyond the draft agenda and at least briefly outline his future policy. It was agreed to defer the plenum for a week.

8

ON THE EVE

THE NEW GENERAL SECRETARY AT WORK

THE DAYS WERE HEAVY WITH TENSION. ANDROPOV CONTACTED people by telephone and in person. First of all, a decision had to be made on how to handle the report prepared for Brezhnev. It would, of course, be reworked, but Andropov did not want to give the impression that, after barely a week in office, he claimed to have all the answers.

I ventured to suggest to him: 'Undoubtedly, you won't be able to develop an entire programme within a week. However, it would be quite possible to put things in perspective and emphasize the key issues so that people would understand what you have in mind.'

The plenum opened on 22 November, and Andropov's presentation went well. Notwithstanding all the usual clichés and tired statements, a new approach was obvious. Yury Vladimirovich referred to serious economic shortcomings and the failure to fulfil the two preceding Five Year Plans, the need to improve economic management and the administrative and planning systems, the need to strengthen the independence of enterprises, to stimulate productivity and greater initiative. At the time this sounded rather novel and was met with applause. The applause resounded even more vigorously when Andropov spoke of the need to be more demanding and tighten discipline and control over the implementation of decisions. People were fed up with widespread laxity.

179

It goes without saying that many crucial problems were presented merely by way of declarations in the text of the report, but even that made an impression. During the drafting of the report a general agreement was reached about the need to adopt a totally new approach to the economy. At the time, we did not know what such an approach might be. And it was then that Andropov entered a handwritten comment stating that he could not offer a ready-made recipe for each and every possible case. It was an invitation to the Party and to society to initiate a common quest for the necessary solutions.

As a condition for holding the plenum, Yury Vladimirovich insisted that the heads of those ministries whose performance was especially poor should be mentioned in his report. Thus the text contained sharp criticism of the transport system and the state of the metallurgy and construction industries, which year in, year out had failed to satisfy the needs of the national economy. Soon afterwards the heads of the relevant ministries – Pavlovsky, Kazanets and Novikov – were dismissed.

Andropov worked in detail on the foreign policy section of his speech in consultation with Arbatov, Bovin and Aleksandrov. He showed me that section after the basic draft had been completed.

Noting that the Western press was concerned about Soviet foreign policy after Brezhnev's death, and was speculating about a possible turn for the worse, Andropov commented sarcastically that the same press had been unmercifully flaying this very policy not long before. I should mention that Yury Vladimirovich had personally participated in the shaping of foreign policy in the preceding years, and that he was an advocate of détente. He emphasized that it was not merely an episode in the history of mankind but a path which still lay ahead of us. Since a world without arms was a socialist ideal according to Lenin, a divergence over ideas should never turn into a confrontation between states and nations.

Andropov stated that he had no intention of focusing on the current differences of opinion in the disarmament talks, as was often done by our Western partners. To us, arms negotiations were a method of consolidating the efforts of different states in order to achieve results that would benefit all the parties involved.

Andropov also mentioned the need to halt the arms race and freeze the arsenals, but definitely not on a unilateral basis. Furthermore, he spoke of the need to improve our relations with China, which meant 'overcoming the inertia of prejudice'. These words were greeted with applause.

The first days and weeks had been spent in carefully observing the practical steps undertaken by Andropov. The General Secretary decided to start changing personnel at the plenum.

At the time of Brezhnev's summer holiday in 1982 I had drafted a memorandum on economic policy. I suggested creating a Politburo commission on economic policy issues. Before forwarding the text to the Crimea, where Brezhnev was staying, I showed it to Yury Vladimirovich. He made some amendments and promised to support my proposals. I then discussed the matter with Chernenko and Brezhnev's assistants. They took my memorandum, but there was no follow-up. I soon learned from hearsay that my proposal was seen in some circles as an attempt by Gorbachev to expand his power through the proposed commission.

Such suspiciousness could drive one crazy. Nobody cared about the tasks in hand; everybody was immediately suspected of ulterior motives. Nevertheless, I was determined to push through my proposal, and I redid my paper, turning it into a draft memorandum on behalf of the General Secretary. Only then was it forwarded to Leonid Ilyich. He telephoned me from the Crimea:

'I've got your memo. Everything is fine, but the ending is all wrong – it's another commission. I can't stand commissions, it's just a lot of jabbering. There are already too many of them. Well, here's my proposal – let's create an economic department in the Central Committee. Think who should be in charge. It's important to have an intelligent person to head the section, who would give it all his time.'

I could not have anticipated a better outcome for my initiative.

Now, discussing candidates for the post with Yury Vladimirovich, I insisted upon appointing someone new, and Nikolai Ivanovich Ryzhkov, who was First Deputy Chairman of Gosplan, was chosen. I felt that, although he had a certain tendency towards technocratic solutions, he would be able to look beyond the immediate horizon and would be receptive to new ideas. At the plenum of 22 November 1982, Ryzhkov was elected a Secretary of the Central Committee.

Ryzhkov and Andropov developed a good rapport. Nikolai Ivanovich revered Yury Vladimirovich and took every discussion with him to heart. After Ryzhkov joined the Central Committee Secretariat our co-operation became close and constant. Andropov wanted an entourage that would not only share his views but would work together on a friendly basis, and he kept a careful eye on the situation.

Andropov also announced his decision to shake up the ideological units of the Central Committee. At first I assumed that he intended to introduce far-reaching changes there. In the past, he had repeatedly stated that ideological problems required serious consideration. He had drafted a paper on this subject which he personally handed to Leonid Ilyich. Eventually Andropov showed me the memorandum and, to be frank, I was greatly disappointed. It contained no fresh ideas. The text argued for change in the general style of propaganda, renouncing obsolete stereotypes. But not a word was said about the need for an in-depth analysis of the changing situation. Moreover, having been drafted in the depths of the KGB apparatus, the paper to some extent reflected its spirit. Emphasis was primarily placed on 'imposing order' and a strengthening of an 'assertive position' in the sphere of ideology.

The removal of N. A. Shchelokov, USSR Minister of Internal Affairs, in December 1982 resounded throughout the country as something of a shock. Yury Vladimirovich had repeatedly stated that the Ministry of Internal Affairs was corrupt, that there were signs that it had links with mafia structures, and that in its present form it was unable to combat rising crime. But he had been unable to touch Shchelokov, who enjoyed the protection of Brezhnev.

He was also dissatisfied with the new KGB chairman, Fedorchuk. When I had asked Yury Vladimirovich about the work of his successor, he answered casually: 'You know, I talk to him only when he rings me up. But that's very rare. Rumour has it that he questioned some organizational changes I made in the Committee. In brief, he is showing off his independence, although I am told that he takes his cue from the Ukrainian leadership. But I stay away from it.'

Now Andropov completed two tasks with one stroke: he removed Shchelokov and sent him into retirement, replacing him with Fedorchuk. Andropov's former first deputy, Viktor Mikhailovich Chebrikov, was approved KGB chairman, and a year later he was elected candidate member of the Politburo.

On 22 November 1982 Kirilenko, Central Committee Secretary and member of the Politburo, was relieved of his duties. His health – or, to put it bluntly, his senility – had reached a stage where it could no longer be concealed. Profound cerebral changes accelerated the deterioration of his mind.

In March 1981, when at the XXVIth Party Congress he was asked to make a proposal on a new composition of the Central Committee, he managed to distort the names of a number of candidates even though they had been submitted to him in extra large print. The audience reacted with bewilderment, to say the least. Such incidents are not easily forgotten.

Nevertheless, for the sake of their old friendship, Brezhnev had included Kirilenko in the membership of the new Politburo. His state of health continued to deteriorate. He would lose the thread of a conversation before one's eyes, and failed to recognize acquaintances. Finally, Brezhnev asked Andropov to talk to Kirilenko and persuade him to hand in his resignation.

Yury Vladimirovich later told me about the conversation. Entering Kirilenko's office and trying not to offend him while speaking firmly, he said:

'Andrei, you understand – we are old comrades. I speak for all those who have always respected you and still do so. We have all come to the conclusion that your health has begun to affect your work. You are seriously ill and need treatment. It's time to decide.'

Overcome by emotion, Kirilenko burst into tears. It was no easy task to talk to him, yet Andropov continued:

'Please understand, Andrei, we must now make a decision in principle. Take a month or two's holiday, or as long as you want. You will keep everything, your car, your dacha, your medical benefits. We are talking to each other now like friends, but it is up to you to take the initial step. Remember, Kosygin was in a much better shape and yet he wrote . . .'

'It's all right, Yury,' said Kirilenko finally. 'If it has to be, so be it . . . But you must help me to write the request, I won't manage it on my own.'

Andropov quickly jotted down a short request for resignation. With great difficulty Andrei Pavlovich copied it in his own hand. The business was finished.

The decision was not confirmed at the plenum until after Brezhnev's death. At the same plenum Geidar Aliyev was elected to the Politburo. Subsequently, when I asked Andropov what had made him pick this particular candidate, Yury Vladimirovich answered reluctantly that the matter had been predetermined by Brezhnev and he was not inclined to change that decision.

Aliyev is, undoubtedly, an outstanding politician – astute, strong-willed and calculating. Observing his activity in Azerbaijan, I was at first impressed by his strong opposition to corruption and the black economy. However, as I delved deeper, I came gradually to realize that there were some rather ambiguous motives behind the ongoing changes. There is a widespread view that, in politics, inner motives are irrelevant in the assessment of the objective results. Not true. I know from experience that motives, particularly those that are improper, invariably affect the results. The original clan that had proliferated like a malignant growth, invading all the ruling structures of the republic and ousted by Aliyev for corruption and inefficiency, was supplanted by another clan, the so-called Nakhichevan group. As in the past, nepotism was rampant. Having thus created a powerful backing based on the clan principle, Aliyev reigned supreme. A variety of councils, assemblies, manifestations, press conferences, meetings with the populace and other democratic paraphernalia were merely a façade.

It is, however, noteworthy that many of the above practices were widespread in other republics too. Nepotism, hero worship and eulogizing the local 'leaders' – all this, accompanied by pompous ceremonies and ostentatious gifts, was common. Whenever a feast honoured the presence of 'guests from Moscow', and especially 'our dear Leonid Ilyich', the displays of loyalty, the flattery and the presents – nothing was too grand. The manifest extravagance and excess were disguised by references to national traditions and customs.

In April 1970 I was a member of a Russian delegation sent to the celebrations marking the fiftieth anniversary of the Azerbaijani Republic. Standing on the sidelines we could see that, whenever Brezhnev temporarily left the central rostrum, the procession would stop and fall silent. As soon as he reappeared, the marching, the songs and the dancing resumed. And, over all this, Aliyev virtually reigned. All he had to do was to cast a glance at a subordinate, who would immediately take it as an order. Though he would normally behave in a natural way, on such occasions Aliyev would put on a carefully cultivated mask of grandeur, which slipped off only during his contacts with Brezhnev, his immediate entourage and his Party colleagues.

This person now became a member of the Politburo. And it was not at all due to a promise given by Brezhnev. Aliyev had been working in the KGB for a long time; Andropov was his former boss. Thus, Aliyev's appearance in the Politburo bolstered Yury Vladimirovich's position. That was all there was to it.

Yury Vladimirovich was also perfectly aware that Grigory Vasilievich Romanov was a narrow-minded and insidious man, with dictatorial ways, and he recognized that at Politburo meetings Romanov rarely came up with a sound proposal or idea. Nevertheless, in June 1983 he transferred him to Moscow and recommended his election as a Secretary of the Central Committee.

By that time all defence matters were concentrated in Ustinov's hands. Yury Vladimirovich believed that in such an important sphere a concentration of power was dangerous. But a solution to that problem would have to be accepted by Ustinov himself. Andropov assumed that Ustinov would not object to Romanov. That is exactly what happened.

There were other changes in the Politburo. In 1983 Vitaly Ivanovich Vorotnikov arrived in Moscow from Krasnodar to replace M. S. Solomentsev, chairman of the Russian Federation's Council of Ministers. Solomentsev, in turn, was made chairman of the Committee of Party Control of the Central Committee.

Chernenko's disaffection, which he did not bother to conceal, was quite understandable. Formally he was second-in-command, but *de facto* many crucial questions were solved without him. Tikhonov, Shcherbitsky and Dolgikh were also on edge.

Dolgikh was an outstanding representative of our 'directorial corps' – a serious, hard-working, knowledgeable specialist. He worked with great zeal. Having become a Central Committee Secretary in 1972, he was in charge of heavy industry and liked to emphasize that his sphere was of the highest importance.

Apparently he nursed ambitions that went quite far. He was willing to tackle any job as long as it held the promise of political recognition and promotion. Once he was elected a candidate member of the Politburo in May 1982 he bore this title with tremendous pride, remembering his rank even in informal contacts.

When the creation of a Central Committee economic department was being considered Vladimir Ivanovich had no doubt that he would become its head. But Ryzhkov got the appointment. Dolgikh considered it a personal blow.

Andropov's relationship with Shcherbitsky was a difficult one. Shcherbitsky was greatly respected in Ukraine. Morally, he was one of the decent people. He was endowed with a technocrat's mind and he consistently implemented policies in the republic which he considered to be right. He resented nationalism; his internationalism would have been praiseworthy had it not gone to extremes. A truly outstanding figure, he was overpowering to people around him. Under him Ukraine produced no political leader of stature. He even looked like an immovable boulder, although it was that very appearance that earned him respect.

Brezhnev's remark that he saw his successor in the person of Vladimir Vasilievich apparently disturbed Shcherbitsky's mental balance. Shortly before Leonid Ilyich's death he unleashed a burst of frenetic activity, attempting to be at the centre of all major events at the top, telephoning and meeting with Fedorchuk.

After Andropov was elected General Secretary, their relationship seemed quite normal on the surface. But there was a hidden rivalry between the two, and both bore mutual grudges. Neither wanted to take a step towards the other. Throughout Andropov's term as General Secretary, Shcherbitsky never crossed the threshold of his office. Not once. I saw how agonizing even an infrequent telephone call was to both sides.

As to Tikhonov, he decided for no reason at all that Andropov owed his election to him. Hence his behaviour was unceremonious, and sometimes even gross.

'Let's do it this way,' he said to Yury Vladimirovich at the time, 'you know the administrative organs, ideology and foreign policy well. But I'll take care of the economy for you.'

When Andropov charged Ryzhkov, Dolgikh and me with drawing up a list of priority measures for improving economic management, Tikhonov became seriously worried. In order to ease the atmosphere, Yury Vladimirovich declared his trust and support for Tikhonov.

I understood that Yury Vladimirovich feared that Tikhonov might form a bloc with Chernenko. Andropov had to gain control over the situation. Having drawn Aliyev, Vorotnikov, Chebrikov, Ryzhkov and Ligachev into the leadership ranks, he strengthened his position. At the same time, he tried to avoid straining relations and creating ill feeling among Chernenko, Tikhonov, Grishin and Shcherbitsky.

'WHEN YOU GET TO MY AGE, YOU'LL UNDERSTAND'

Andropov and I were drawn even closer together in our work during his early months as General Secretary. I sensed his trust in me and his support. At the very end of 1982 he suggested meaningfully: 'You know what, Mikhail, don't limit your work to the agrarian sector. Try to look at other aspects.'

He fell silent and then added: 'In general terms, act as if you had to shoulder all the responsibility one day. I mean it.'

The first question we had to grapple with after Andropov's election concerned a decision which had been taken by the Politburo when Brezhnev was still alive, to increase prices for bread and cotton fabrics. Andropov asked Ryzhkov and me to examine the matter once more and to report our conclusions to him. Trying to understand the essence of the whole business, we asked for access to the budget, but Andropov simply laughed that off: 'Nothing doing! You're asking too much. The budget is off limits to you.'

I must say that many 'secrets' of the budget were so well kept that I found out about some of them only on the eve of my stepping down as President. Nonetheless, I knew the greatest 'secret', namely that our budget was full of holes. It was being continually replenished by the savings bank, in other words money was drawn from the savings of the citizens and by raising the internal debt. Meanwhile, it was officially proclaimed that the revenues always exceeded the expenditure and that all was very well balanced.

Ryzhkov and I arrived at the conclusion that an increase in bread and cotton prices, in and of itself, would not really work. Andropov's first reaction was to reject our arguments. He may have thought that such a step would demonstrate his courage and resolve. We nevertheless insisted on our opinion: a price increase of that kind was inappropriate for economic and political reasons. Having once more considered all the arguments for and against, the Politburo cancelled the decision it had earlier adopted.

The next priority was the question of purchasing grain from abroad. As usual, we were confronted with government opposition. The reasons were understandable: there was not enough money, yet there was no other visible solution. The General Secretary had to take a stance in that matter and, having listened to representatives of both sides, Andropov himself proposed the purchase.

The absence of 'quick' results led Yury Vladimirovich to take steps which struck me as, to say the least, of dubious value. I am referring to the manner in which the campaign for greater discipline and order was conducted, with people being 'caught loafing' during working hours in subways and shops, at hairdressers and in public baths and saunas. In waging this campaign, Andropov relied primarily on the state security and interior agencies, instead of engaging the help of civic organizations. To him this short-cut was easier.

I tried to argue to him that it was unseemly for people to be seized, in the name of Andropov, while they were taking turns to queue because they had no other time to do their shopping. I told him that these actions undermined his authority, and that jokes were already circulating.

Relying on the information supplied by Fedorchuk, Yury Vladimirovich sincerely believed that these measures would rally the ordinary people to his side. Brushing aside my objections, he would say: 'Just wait and see; when you get to my age, you'll understand.'

This 'understanding' of the people culminated in the sale of cheap vodka, which was immediately nicknamed 'Andropovka' or, according to the display of letters on the label, 'the crankshaft'. And, ironically, in some respects Yury Vladimirovich was right: as time has rushed by, much of what happened then has now fallen into oblivion or is scarcely remembered, but this episode of the 'struggle for discipline' still lingers on in the memory of many people.

REPORT ON LENIN

In March 1983 Andropov telephoned to tell me that he intended to propose to the Politburo that it should approve me as the speaker at the memorial meeting marking the 113th anniversary of V. I. Lenin's birth.

Throughout my life I have often resorted to Lenin's works. I assumed that the drafting of the report would not be difficult. However, my initial attempt failed. I then set about studying Lenin's writing anew, with a particular emphasis on the post-October period. Some volumes I re-read, others I just thumbed through.

Gradually I became so absorbed in the logic of events in the post-Revolutionary years that I sometimes had a sense of being a participant, and wondered what I would have done to try to solve the problems that had confronted Lenin. That was 'going too far' . . .

Yet all this reading was useful. I was interested in Lenin's later writings, especially those articles and speeches which evaluated a whole stage in the history of the Bolshevik power, and his blunt statement that the Bolsheviks 'had committed an error'. In my own time as General Secretary I was to draw on ideas generated by reading Lenin's works.

My speech in 1983 remained within the political and ideological framework of the time: there was no critical re-interpretation. Nevertheless, judged by our media as well as by the foreign press and radio, some of the points made in the report triggered off a lively reaction. However, the majority was more attentive to the fact that I had been chosen to present the report. People remembered that, after a similar speech the previous year, Andropov had become the second-in-command of the Party and the state.

A VISIT TO CANADA

In October 1981 the Canadian Secretary for Agriculture, Eugene Whelan, had paid us a visit. In return he invited me to Canada in May 1983.

Our ambassador, A. N. Yakovlev, had thoroughly planned my visit. Considering the then limited contact between our countries, the Canadian side, too, played up its significance. I also noticed a certain curiosity on their part towards a young Politburo member.

My trip turned out to be very informative. I met Prime Minister Pierre Trudeau. He wore his usual navy blue suit with a rose tucked into his side pocket, symbolizing his membership of the Liberal Party. He seemed somewhat aloof to begin with, but subsequently we engaged in a lively conversation, exceeding the time set by the protocol. Since that time I have kept in touch with Trudeau, and not just with him. Eventually Canadian newspapers were to claim that it was they who had really 'discovered' Gorbachev.

My main interest, however, was to see the country. In the vicinity of Ottawa we visited a state animal husbandry research centre, houses, farms, agricultural produce processing plants and a heavy dump-truck production plant near Windsor. In the province of Alberta, which is a major animal husbandry and grain area in Canada, we saw a large meat-cattle ranch near Calgary where the animals are left grazing in the open all year.

By meeting farmers I was trying to understand what 'made them tick' and achieve such good results. We saw a rather large farm in Alberta, with over 2,000 hectares of farmland. There was a herd of cows with a milk yield of 4,700 kg per cow, a set of various machines, repair tools in a shed, aluminium grain silos, two houses, cars: obviously, a wealthy farmer. We got talking.

'How many workers do you have?' I inquired.

'Two or three permanent hands. During the season, I hire more help.'

We talked and walked around, saw everything. Then it was time to leave. At the door I asked a parting question: 'Tell me, the year has just finished. Do you know now about your expenses and your income? And what does it total?'

The farmer looked at the minister, as if wondering: should he or should he not tell? But Whelan laughed: 'Tell him the truth.'

'To tell the truth,' answered the farmer, 'without subsidies and credit we wouldn't survive.'

He was taken aback by my questions about how he spent his vacation. 'Vacation, what's that? There are rural festivities, all sorts of competitions, with horses and bulls. We eke out a day or two and go there with the family, that's all. There's no-one to replace us at the farm.'

Some sort of voluntary 'slavery'!

'How come,' I asked Whelan, 'that you need subsidies with such crop and milk yields?'

'Mikhail,' answered the minister, 'the agrarian sector cannot exist at a modern level without state aid. We are spending dozens of billions on farm credits, and in the USA they are spending hundreds of billions of dollars. We try to compensate for these expenditures by grain exports.'

Upon my return to Moscow, I was asked to address the Academy of Social Sciences on 'The Pressing Problems of the Development of the Agro-Industrial Complex in our Country'. There was no time to write out a full text, and I went up to the rostrum carrying only my notes. But my Canadian travels served as a powerful impetus for thought, and I was greatly inspired in presenting my lecture. I spoke about the decline in economic incentives and the inefficient use of resources. Moreover, I mentioned the lack of an effective management mechanism, and the fragmented departmental character of administration. I also mentioned the inequitable terms of trade between agriculture and the industrial branches, and the need for state aid to collective, state and personal subsidiary farms. Finally, I contended that 'without a stable, highly-developed agrarian sector there cannot be a stable economy in our country.'

I didn't say much about Canada, to avoid distressing people. Each and everyone knew that the history, economic conditions and the very character of agricultural production were too different in our two countries. This was once more confirmed for me when I went to Kursk in early July to confer the Order of the Patriotic War, First Class, upon the city, on the occasion of the fortieth anniversary of the famous Battle of the Kursk Salient. I drove and walked across the fields where this great battle in the history of humanity was waged and where millions of people, armed with thousands of tanks, aircraft and artillery, had gathered to confront one another. I also visited the actual bend of the Kursk Bulge where my father had fought in 1943. Believing that the Russian soldiers were caught in a 'pocket', the Germans had dropped leaflets calling upon them to surrender. However, it ended in our victory, which turned the course of the Second World War.

After visiting the battlefields I gained a new awareness of the price paid for the Great Victory. There was no hamlet, no small town, in that area without a modest obelisk inscribed with hundreds and thousands of names of the dead or the missing. It was particularly terrifying seeing the lists of entire families or persons of different age-groups bearing the same name. It seemed as if fate had decided to annihilate entire clans, even unto the seventh generation. How many sons and daughters has this land sacrificed? And does it not deserve a happier lot?

BIDDING FAREWELL TO ANDROPOV

In the summer of 1983, it became manifest that hopes for the better were jeopardized by Andropov's health, which suddenly took a sharp turn for the worse. His illness was caused by a malfunctioning of the kidneys. Very few people knew about it. But as his illness progressed, even his looks changed: his face became unnaturally pale and his voice grew hoarse. Formerly, when he received a visitor in his office, Yury Vladimirovich would get up and greet him. Now he barely extended his hand, and did not get up from behind his desk.

At first weekly, then twice weekly, and eventually even more frequently, he had to undergo agonizing kidney dialysis treatment, connected to a special apparatus that purified his blood. It was no longer possible to conceal the marks visible on his arms, and everybody could see the bandages that began at his wrists. The rumour spread that 'Andropov has had it'. All those for whom Andropov's illness was a gift from heaven became active. At first there was whispering in the corners and, subsequently, some people no longer disguised their joy.

In September Andropov left for a holiday in the Crimea. We regularly talked over the telephone, and our conversations seemed to indicate that he was much better. Once, when I rang him up as usual, I was told that Yury Vladimirovich had left for the mountains. This was no surprise to me, since I had known from way back in Kislovodsk that he preferred mountains to the sea. Moreover, worried about the physical strain, the doctors had advised him against sea bathing.

About two hours later Yury Vladimirovich returned my call. From the way he talked I could sense that he was in high spirits. Apparently the mountain air had a beneficial effect on his health. We discussed the impending harvest and exchanged some other bits of news, I do not recollect the details. Engraved in my memory was that excellent mood of his. Little did I realize that it was never to happen again.

Two or three days later we learned that his health had taken a sharp turn for the worse. First, Andropov was transferred to his dacha and then, urgently, by plane to Moscow, directly to the

Central Clinical Hospital. An agonizing phase, complicated in every respect, set in . . .

Yury Vladimirovich suffered terribly. We exchanged telephone calls, and whenever the doctors permitted it I went to the hospital. In fact, everybody had been visiting him – some less often, others more frequently; some to support him, others to check on his condition once more. October and November passed. The suffering induced by his illness was aggravated by another worry: he sensed the intrigue.

Because of the General Secretary's illness, Politburo and Secretariat meetings were chaired by Chernenko. Rarely did he entrust me with the Secretariat. I believe that Tikhonov made an abortive attempt at taking over the chairmanship of the Politburo. Meanwhile, Yury Vladimirovich, seriously ill as he was, had not lost his lucidity.

Meanwhile, the manoeuvrings and whisperings among some members of the Politburo were becoming unseemly. It looked almost as if a division of power was under way, and a man was being buried alive. Andropov's aides, obviously sensitive to this kind of talk, were perhaps even overstating this. All this triggered off Andropov's outburst.

One day in December I had hardly crossed the threshold of my office when Ryzhkov rushed in: 'Yury Vladimirovich has just telephoned. He is in a terrible state. He was asking whether we had decided to replace him. I tried to tell him that this was out of the question, but he was not reassured.'

I immediately contacted his doctors and they agreed to let me see Andropov the following day. When I entered his room he was sitting in an armchair and made a weak attempt to smile. We greeted each other and embraced. The change since my last meeting with him was striking. I saw a totally different person in front of me. He was puffy-faced and haggard; his skin was sallow. His eyes were dim, he barely looked up, and sitting was obviously difficult. I exerted every effort to glance away, to somehow disguise my shock. It was the last time I saw Yury Vladimirovich.

Andropov's aides visited him almost daily. I believe Laptev and Volsky were the most frequent visitors. Just before the plenum he received Ligachev, who was to be elected a Central

Committee Secretary. Apparently, it was the aides' idea to draft Andropov's address and have it read out at the plenum. That is what happened. I learned about the background story of the text years later, after the publication of Volksky's memoirs. Earlier, only vague rumours were circulating. The essence of the matter was as follows: at the conclusion of the address there was to be a statement to the effect that in connection with his serious illness, considering state interests and with a view to safeguarding the continuity of the Party and national leadership, the General Secretary proposed that I should chair the Politburo meetings.

When Yury Vladimirovich's text was distributed to the Politburo members on the eve of the plenum, and subsequently, bound in a red cover, to the Central Committee members, that statement was missing. Rumour had it that something had been distorted or deleted. Personally I can neither corroborate nor disprove this version. Neither Andropov, nor Chernenko, nor Volksky himself ever talked to me about it.

The plenum met on the threshold of 1984. Baibakov's and Garbuzov's reports were presented. The participants behaved as if nothing unusual were happening. In reality, of course, it was clear to everyone that Andropov was dying.

I was profoundly affected by Yury Vladimirovich's death. Among the leaders of the country, there was no-one else with whom I had such close and old ties, and to whom I owed so much. Over many years I had shared my thoughts and my doubts with him. I had always been aware of his unfailing good feelings towards me. He was never condescending. It was not that he fully opened up to me, sharing his innermost feelings. Some hidden recesses in his life remained inaccessible – maybe because he himself was not too happy about their existence. Or maybe it was because he did not want to burden anyone with this information.

Raisa Maksimovna was shocked by the funeral ceremony in the Hall of Columns – genuine grief, tears and a show of respect by some people were in sharp contrast to the unconcealed joy, even triumph, you could see in other people's faces. A number of Central Committee secretaries were in high spirits and did not hide it, as if eager to tell her 'Your time is over.'

In trying to characterize Andropov's work, two aspects should be clearly distinguished: first, Andropov viewed as a practitioner of Realpolitik, and second, the Andropov phenomenon. Without such an approach, confusion, exaggerations and serious distortion could hardly be avoided. What was this Andropov phenomenon? There had been at first a general atmosphere of expectation and hope that the arrival of a new leader would generate beneficial changes. It was – if you like – a repudiation of all that was associated with Brezhnevism in the minds of the people, along with the conviction that reform was imperative and inevitable.

Andropov did not betray these hopes. First and foremost, he was a brilliant and large personality, generously endowed with gifts by nature, and a true intellectual. He resolutely denounced all the features commonly associated with Brezhnevism, that is, protectionism, in-fighting and intrigues, corruption, moral turpitude, bureaucracy, disorganization and laxity. Andropov's tough, and sometimes exaggerated, attitude to these problems instilled hope that an end would at last be put to all the outrageous practices, that those who had alienated themselves from the people would be held responsible. Consequently his actions, though they were sometimes excessive, created hope and were considered the harbingers of general and deeper changes. And here is the crux of the matter – would Andropov have gone any further and embarked upon the path of far-reaching transformations had his fate turned out differently? I do not believe so. Some of those who were not close to Yury Vladimirovich asserted that he had been nurturing ideas of reforming the system long before becoming General Secretary. I do not believe it. He realized the need for changes, yet Andropov always remained a man of his time, and was one of those who were unable to break through the barrier of old ideas and values.

The thought often occurs to me: he knew Stalin's crimes better than anyone else. Yet he never mentioned them. He witnessed Brezhnev's attempts to revive both Stalin's image and his model of organizing society. Nonetheless, he did not even attempt to counteract it. And what about his role in the events in Hungary and Czechoslovakia, in the Afghan War, and in the struggle against those who thought differently, the 'dissidents'?

Apparently the years spent in KGB work had left an imprint on his attitudes and perceptions, making him a suspicious man condemned to serve the system.

No. Just like Khrushchev, Andropov would not have initiated drastic changes. Who knows, maybe it was his fate that he died before he came face to face with the problems which would have inevitably frustrated him, dispelling people's illusions about him.

But such speculation will remain tentative and incomplete until the crucial fifteen-year period of his life as KGB chairman is studied. Much remained hidden behind the heavy walls of Lubyanka, even for me. Without such knowledge it is difficult to tell what would eventually have happened.

Andropov's stay at the peak of power was short-lived, but it instilled hope in people. All that bound us to each other with Yury Vladimirovich is indelibly engraved in my memory. How can I ever forget the southern night near Kislovodsk, the star-studded sky, the bright flame of the bonfire – and Yury Vladimirovich gazing at the fire in a dreamy serene mood? And the tape-recorder playing Yury Visbor's mischievous song, Andropov's favourite:

'Who needs it? No-one needs it.'

A SICK MAN AT THE HELM

I considered D. F. Ustinov, despite his seventy-five years, as Andropov's most suitable successor. Why? They had been close friends, and to me Ustinov would have been the only one capable of continuing Andropov's policies. Moreover, he enjoyed great prestige in the Party and the country.

I 'pressed' the claim of Dmitry Fedorovich, since I saw no other alternative. Some of the other candidates could no longer assume the responsible functions of a General Secretary, others were not up to it yet. Meanwhile Ustinov could have prepared the new generation of leaders.

Later, I learned that the possibility of my own nomination was not excluded. This information reached me from two sources. On the second or third day after Yury Vladimirovich's funeral, Raisa

197

Maksimovna paid a visit to his wife in order to give her some moral support. Sick and agitated, Tatyana Filippovna got up from her bed, lamenting: 'Why did they elect Chernenko? Why did they do it? Yura wanted it to be Mikhail Sergeyevich . . .'

Raisa Maksimovna soothed her and tried to change the subject.

To some extent this story corroborates the rumours mentioned above, concerning amendments introduced by the General Department to Andropov's speech at the December plenum.

Moreover, one of my colleagues, with whom I have worked for many years, told me about his conversation with G. M. Kornienko, who was then First Deputy of the USSR Minister of Foreign Affairs. According to him, immediately after Andropov's death, Gromyko, Ustinov, Tikhonov and Chernenko met, but failed to reach an agreement on a new candidate for the post of General Secretary. Allegedly, Ustinov stated that it would be up to the Politburo to make the choice and, as far as he was concerned, he would nominate me.

These consultations took place in the office of the deputy head of the Central Committee General Department. After the conversation Chernenko stayed behind in the office while Gromyko, Ustinov and Tikhonov went into the corridor. There they were eagerly awaited by their aides and bodyguards, whose nostrils were virtually quivering with curiosity. Luckily for them, Tikhonov was somewhat hard of hearing and he spoke louder than the others. According to eye-witnesses, Nikolai Aleksandrovich suddenly burst out, loudly enough to make heads turn in the corridor: 'I think we did the right thing. Mikhail is still young. And who knows how he would have behaved? Kostya is what we need.'

Let me repeat that I cannot vouch for this story. But that both Andropov and Ustinov had put their stakes on me I learned later directly from Dmitry Fedorovich. Why it turned out differently, he did not explain. Of course I, in turn, never questioned him about it.

Whatever happened, the election of the new General Secretary was extremely simple and, I would say, even routine. It was decided by Tikhonov's aggressive tactics. Chernenko had barely opened the proceedings when Nikolai Aleksandrovich asked for the floor to speak 'on a point of order'. To foil any possible surprises on Ustinov's part and skipping any niceties, he proposed to elect Konstantin Ustinovich as the next General Secretary. It may well be that Dmitry Fedorovich expected a refusal, a rejection of the nomination by Chernenko, who knew best the state of his health and ought to have admitted that the leadership of the country was, as we say, 'too big a piece of the pie to swallow'. But nothing happened. Raising one's voice 'against' was not in the tradition of that Politburo. Tikhonov's proposal was unanimously accepted by everyone, including myself. And the justification was ready: 'first and foremost to avoid a schism'. But for our society, the emergence of Chernenko as the leader of a great power was a shock.

After the Politburo meeting and in the day that followed, Ustinov, who had always been known for his cheerful disposition, appeared depressed, taciturn and withdrawn. But at the plenum I saw other faces: those cheered by the hope that their times were coming back, the tranquil, 'stable' times, in other words Brezhnevism.

Whom did we acquire in the post of General Secretary? Not merely a seriously sick and physically weak person but, in fact, an invalid. It was common knowledge, and immediately visible with the naked eye. It was impossible to disguise his infirmity and the shortness of breath caused by emphysema. The doctor who accompanied Margaret Thatcher to Andropov's funeral soon afterwards published a prognosis on Chernenko's life-span and erred by only a few weeks.

Chernenko had always been at Brezhnev's side, anticipating all his wishes, his confidant, that is to say, his shadow. A powerful weapon in his hands was the omnipotent Party apparatus. Still, it is difficult to understand how such ambitious plans were conceived in the mind of such a man, a quiet, withdrawn and typical red-tapist. I believe he was urged on by people who had their own ambitions. His first public address, at the commemorative meeting on the occasion of Andropov's funeral on 14 February 1984, left a sad and painful impression on all of us, on the country as a whole, and on our foreign guests. Chernenko was bound to evoke such feelings.

It did not take long to realize that society did not take him seriously, although the Central Committee ideological service exerted tremendous efforts to propagate the 'image of the General Secretary'. His mediocre personality, his lack of independent experience in the sphere of political and state activities, his superficial knowledge of the real life of the country and a weak strain in his character – all this was only too obvious. In April 1984, as if following in Andropov's footsteps, Chernenko visited the Moscow Serp i Molot (Sickle and Hammer) metallurgical plant to meet the workers. However, there was no real contact; on the contrary, the meeting merely served to pour oil on the fire. Chernenko had difficulties in communicating with people. And witnessing all this was simply unbearable for us.

Andropov's death and Chernenko's election as General Secretary instilled fresh hope in the foes of all reform. The schemers got a new lease of life, grew bolder and, I would even say, more impertinent. Quite openly they intensified their pressure on Chernenko in an attempt to bring Andropov's projects to an end. The first to be affected were Yury Vladimirovich's supporters, including myself. It was no surprise to me. Back in 1983, when Andropov's health was rapidly deteriorating, I was told that these people were busy searching for facts that would compromise Gorbachev. This 'hunt' involved even administrative organs. When I became General Secretary I found out about it in every detail.

Hence I was psychologically prepared for this kind of intrigue and aware of the long-standing plan to get rid of me. It was also reflected in the mood of 'the leading protagonists' at the very first meeting of the Politburo during discussions about the allocation of duties in the Politburo and in the Secretariat.

As I expected, Tikhonov launched the attack.

'I don't understand why we have to give the chairmanship of the Secretariat to Gorbachev,' he stated rather cuttingly. 'As far as we know, Mikhail Sergeyevich deals with agrarian matters. I am afraid that the Secretariat would be transformed into a body considering agrarian issues and used by him to exert pressure. Distortions would be inevitable.'

I sat there listening. And kept silent.

Ustinov retorted that Gorbachev had already been in charge of the Secretariat and no such 'distortions' had been noted. Thus the initial attempt to dismiss me failed. Then Grishin and Gromyko resorted to delaying tactics, essentially supporting Tikhonov. However, the main obstacle – Ustinov – was not surmounted. Chernenko tried to overrule something, made some sort of a statement, but was tedious, spiritless and wearisome. I was under the impression that the roles in that performance had been assigned beforehand.

Although a formal decision to that effect had not been taken, *de facto* I continued to head the Secretariat, while keeping the new General Secretary continuously informed. Regular meetings were convened, where problems concerning the Party, the economy and ideology were discussed. Meanwhile, the more efficient the functioning of the Secretariat and the more stringent the requirements made of the cadres, the greater the dissatisfaction, not only on the part of Tikhonov but also of the Ministry of Foreign Affairs, especially in the General Secretary's retinue. Tikhonov, consistently and with an enviable persistence, was implementing a policy designed to weaken the Secretariat. Meanwhile he made unsuccessful advances to Ligachev. As for Dolgikh, Tikhonov used a foolproof method to win him over to his side – somewhere in his presence he alluded to Dolgikh as his future successor. Henceforth Dolgikh spent most of his time in the Prime Minister's 'diocese', attending endless meetings and discussions.

Whatever happened – within less than three months the Secretariat had made itself felt, in the Party and, in particular, at the centre, in Moscow. Some people made efforts to attend the meetings, others were afraid to participate. Tikhonov was enraged, gave vent to his dissatisfaction and tried to cast aspersions on our work.

In these tough times for me I felt Ustinov's support. Our relationship was growing closer. I have to emphasize the practical and moral support also given to me by Ligachev. (By then, our relationship had developed into one of respect and trust.) We worked a great deal and efficiently with Ryzhkov. Even with Zimyanin, the Central Committee Secretary for Ideology, who often came to see me, we were able to work together constructively.

In brief, I felt secure and adopted a philosophical attitude of sorts towards my surroundings. I no longer raised the issue of official Politburo approval for my role in the Secretariat. I followed my age-old principle – things will sort themselves out in the end.

AT HOME AND ABROAD

On 30 April I was suddenly summoned by Chernenko. I entered his office assuming that we would discuss the First of May celebrations. However, from the outset the dialogue seemed to acquire a nervous undertone. He did not open the discussion very coherently, muddling his words, saying that he was under pressure, that a split was starting, the work was being disrupted, etc.

'Konstantin Ustinovich, what are you talking about? What is the question?'

'It concerns the chairmanship of the Secretariat.'

'You mustn't worry. Let's decide this problem at the Politburo, since it is a question of confidence. Moreover, I should like to find out from those colleagues who are made wiser by experience where my shortcomings and failures are. I hope that the issue does not concern my membership of the Politburo.'

'No, no, not at all,' mumbled Chernenko awkwardly.

And that was when I could no longer restrain my emotions, bursting out in a stormy monologue: 'If that's so, I am entitled to know what my colleagues and my opponents expect of me and to hear their critical comments. We would have to assess the work of the Central Committee Secretariat. Some people seem not very happy that after a certain period it is gaining momentum. As the General Secretary you have to consider everything and take a stand. I see a tug-of-war in the making that is fraught with consequences. Hence I am all for solving the problem, but only on the basis of principle. The situation in the leadership is complicated and a discussion is imperative. It has come to a head and we must not dodge it.'

Chernenko asked me to reiterate my arguments and took some notes. We agreed to convene a Politburo meeting on 3 May, congratulated each other on the forthcoming holiday and parted. There was resentment in my heart when I left. I had a feeling that, considering the General Secretary's wavering and amorphous attitude, anything might happen.

At the end of the day Ustinov telephoned me. I briefed him on my conversation with Chernenko. Dmitry Fedorovich sounded alarmed. He told me I had done the right thing, suggesting that I stand firm and take heart, because he believed the scheme against me was doomed to failure.

At the Politburo meeting on 3 May all the items on the agenda were discussed. However, the item raised in my talk with the General Secretary was never brought up. It turned out that Ustinov had urged Chernenko not to be led by Tikhonov and company. Two or three days later Konstantin Ustinovich told me: 'I have thought the matter over and decided against presenting it. Continue working as before . . .'

Tikhonov sent me a repentant letter in 1989. It contained an offer of his services in assisting the economic reforms. But in those earlier days the pressure exerted upon me through Chernenko had been unremitting. The situation was extremely nerve-racking, and whenever I had a chance to escape from Moscow and travel through the country I was happy to do so.

Scheming, petty intrigue and gossip continued to affect the general atmosphere at Staraya Ploshchad. Chernenko's illness grew progressively worse, the situation in the Politburo was increasingly aggravated, and in-fighting steadily increased. I shall not go into all the details. Anyway, it would be superfluous – by then everything was clear to everybody.

On 12 June 1984, when I participated in the economic meeting of the Council for Mutual Economic Assistance as a member of the official USSR delegation, the sad news of the death of Enrico Berlinguer, the leader of the Italian Communists, was received in Moscow. He had died unexpectedly during a political rally.

It was decided that I should head the CPSU delegation to the funeral. I did not know Berlinguer personally, but I well remembered hearing him speak at our Party Congresses. Berlinguer had spoken calmly, almost impassively, in a manner that is atypical for an Italian, but he always took the bull by the horns, as it were. Initially, our people were at a loss to know how to react to his speech. We had all heard something about 'Eurocommunism' and knew that we had a difficult relationship with the Italian Communist Party: the exchange of 'civilities' between our Parties occasionally surged up in the pages of our press.[1] However, to Party Congress delegates, reacting to Berlinguer was no problem: they simply watched the Presidium and followed its example.

Our departure for Rome to attend the funeral was so hasty that the Politburo had no time to issue any special instructions, although the wish had been expressed to discuss the relations between our Parties in a general context. What we witnessed there left an indelible impression in our hearts. The mourning was nationwide. Hundreds of thousands of people flocked to the funeral. Paglietta[2] stood next to me on the balcony of the Party building. Greetings to the CPSU delegation resounded from the passing ranks. I was asked then: 'What are your feelings and thoughts when you see how the Italians send Berlinguer on his last journey?'

The answer did not come easily. At least, not at the time.

The whole of Italy was bidding farewell to Berlinguer, including the leaders of all political parties. Pertini, the Italian President, bowed his head over the coffin of the leader of the opposition party on behalf of the nation. All this bore witness to a mentality different from our own. I had read the policy document of the Italian Communists, the famous 'Togliatti memorandum' that had appeared soon after the XXth CPSU Congress, some time before. I had also thoroughly studied Gramsci's *Prison Journals*. But a thought-provoking lesson about a different political culture was taught me at Berlinguer's funeral.

---

[1] The Italian Communist Party (PCI) was a leader in Eurocommunism, which rejected Stalinism and promoted democracy and human rights. It was also willing to enter into a government coalition.

[2] Leading Italian communist.

That same evening, on 13 June, we met leading members of the Italian Communist Party in the mansion of our embassy. The conversation was frank but seemed to be turning in circles. Finally, it was too much for me, and I said: 'Well, then, you have said a million times that you are free, independent, do not accept any orders from any centre. Whereas we have reiterated two million times that you are free, independent and that there is, indeed, no centre. And where do we go from there?'

Our Italian friends looked at me in bewilderment.

'Maybe we should start meeting,' I continued, 'to analyse the new world situation, to think it over together and exchange ideas.'

The conversation lasted all night, and in the small hours of the morning, as we were parting, there seemed to be signs of a mutual understanding.

The following day, on 14 June, I was received by the President of the Italian Republic. He greatly impressed me by his democratic ways, his sincere goodwill towards our people, and the respect he showed for the service rendered by the Soviet Union in the victory over fascism. Pertini himself had been in the resistance movement. I liked his easy-going manner and his straightforward judgements. He said that he favoured co-operation with Communists and Socialists. It was an interesting talk and when we parted our friendly embraces were sincere.

The same day we left for Moscow. Two Italian comrades accompanied us to the airport. Sitting there at a table with the roaring of the jet planes behind the huge glass windows, we resolved that we must develop comradely relations between our two parties, we must co-operate, we must interact. My report to the Politburo followed the same line.

The year 1984 finished with my visit to Great Britain. I arrived in London on 15 December as head of our parliamentary delegation. Fifteen years had passed since a similar delegation had visited England, although the relations between our countries had been rather strained in those years and such visits would have been helpful. Visits by parliamentary groups were then regarded as a formality, a matter of pure protocol. The Ministry of Foreign Affairs clearly did not attach much significance to our mission.

But this one turned out to be very different indeed . . .

On the second day of our stay in England we met the Prime Minister of Great Britain, Mrs Margaret Thatcher. Raisa Maksimovna and I went to Chequers, where the Prime Minister, in the company of her husband Denis and several ministers, welcomed us. Reporters were waiting for us at the entrance, and the famous photograph of the four of us, with Mrs Thatcher courteously pointing out where and how we should stand, was taken on that occasion. Funnily enough, many people later interpreted that photograph in a different way – Margaret Thatcher was supposed to have carefully scrutinized Raisa Maksimovna's clothes.

The meeting started with a lunch. Margaret Thatcher and I sat on one side of the table, Denis and Raisa Maksimovna on the other. Everything looked rather formal and proper. But even at luncheon our conversation took a rather polemic tone.

Mrs Thatcher is a confident and, I would say, a self-confident woman, the gentle charm and feminine façade disguising a rather tough and pragmatic politician. Her nickname the 'Iron Lady' is very apt. I told Mrs Thatcher: 'I know you are a person of staunch beliefs, someone who adheres to certain principles and values. This commands respect. But please consider that next to you is a person of your own ilk. And I can assure you that I am not under instructions from the Politburo to persuade you to join the Communist Party.'

After that statement she burst into a hearty laugh, and the stiff, polite and somewhat acerbic conversation flowed naturally into more interesting talk, which continued after lunch. The subject turned to disarmament problems. We started by using our prepared notes, but eventually I put mine aside while Mrs Thatcher stuffed hers into her handbag. I unfolded a large diagram representing all nuclear arsenals, grouped into a thousand little squares.

'Each of these squares,' I told Mrs Thatcher, 'suffices to eradicate all life on earth. Consequently, the available nuclear arsenals have a capacity to wipe out all life a thousand times.'

Her reaction was very eloquent and emotional. I believe she was quite sincere. Anyway, this conversation was a turning-point towards a major political dialogue between our countries.

According to protocol, Raisa Maksimovna was not present during that conversation. She was left to be 'devoured' by three or four government ministers and, to their utter surprise, engaged them in a conversation about English literature and philosophy, which had always been one of her major interests. On the following day, the London press, contrary to the usual prejudice against 'Kremlin wives', published long and favourable reports of that episode.

My speech before the British Parliament on 18 December went well. There too an initial attempt was made to lead a dialogue in a confrontational spirit. But I cut it short, saying: 'If you wish to engage in that kind of discussion, I can produce all the documents and papers I carry with me and start making an inventory of all the actions against the Soviet Union and against the establishment of normal relations. But what good would it do?'

Following this remark the talk shifted onto a more constructive and even friendly basis. It was then and there that all the ideas that I had been developing over recent years concerning foreign policy issues and the world order were brought before the British parliamentarians.

The text of my speech was published in our country and abroad, so I shall only sum up the highlights: the nuclear age demands 'new political thinking'; the Cold War is an abnormal form of international relations, fraught with military risks; in a nuclear war there can be no winner; no country can assure its security at the expense of the security of others; in limiting and reducing weapons, particularly nuclear arms, we are prepared to match whatever our Western negotiating partners would do. These remarks evoked the most lively reaction in the world press. The words 'Whatever is dividing us, we live on the same planet and Europe is our common home – a home, not a theatre of military operations' were much quoted.

Later there were meetings with ministers, leaders of political parties and representatives of the business community. We visited the Austin-Rover plant, the head office of the John Brown company, a research and development centre, the Chamber of Commerce, the British Museum and the Marx Memorial Library.

It so happened that I was unable to join the part of our

delegation that visited the grave of Karl Marx. What speculation that stirred up! Later, during the perestroika years, something similar happened when our 'free press' spread the 'news' about the 'Gold Card' – a credit card to which I was allegedly entitled abroad as a member of the Politburo! It was a disgrace to read all this nonsense, shaming to the 'intelligentsia' who had written it. And it was a particular disgrace to read this lie in Yeltsin's memoirs.

In our country, the London visit was virtually hushed up – for political reasons. Dobrynin, who had been our ambassador in the United States of America since 1962, told me that it had aroused a lot of interest among the American public and in political circles. Subsequently, he sent two telegrams to the Ministry of Foreign Affairs with a detailed account of the articles carried by major newspapers on that occasion. As a rule, such information was distributed to the members of the leadership. Not so in this case. When Anatoly Fedorovich went back to Moscow he got a dressing down from Gromyko: 'You, a most experienced politician, a wise diplomat and a mature person – you are sending two telegrams on a visit by a parliamentary delegation! What significance does it have?'

THE DÉNOUEMENT IS APPROACHING

Sad news reached me while I was in London – Ustinov had died. I interrupted my stay and returned to Moscow. Ustinov's death was a grave loss, particularly painful in those troubled times. The leadership of the country was in a deplorable state. Problems arose even with the weekly Politburo meetings. Quite often Konstantin Ustinovich was unable to attend scheduled meetings – fifteen or thirty minutes before the beginning there would be a telephone call and I would be instructed to take the chair. The reaction of the Politburo members to my assumption of the chairman's role was equivocal. Some were unperturbed, considering that it was a natural development, but others showed bewilderment and even ill-disguised irritation. Tikhonov repeatedly asked rather tactlessly: 'Did he instruct you to preside over the Politburo?'

I answered: 'Nikolai Aleksandrovich, do you really think I would come and open the meeting just like that, on my own? You've got the wrong idea about me.'

By the end of the year the problem had acquired dramatic proportions, inasmuch as Chernenko had dropped out altogether. Yet no decision was made about mandating anyone, whether Gorbachev, Tikhonov or someone else, to chair the meetings on a regular basis.

I know for a fact that some comrades had suggested to Chernenko that I should be entrusted 'temporarily' with the chairmanship of the Politburo. Meanwhile the immediate entourage of the General Secretary recommended that he retain this function. And every time I was in a quandary. But it was not a question of me personally; the situation affected the work of the Politburo and the Central Committee apparatus. In these circumstances the schemers got a free hand, whereas it was a disaster so far as business was concerned.

Thinking it over I decided to follow some rules. First, to deal with the work calmly, to bring up problems firmly and make no concessions to the 'retainers', whatever their rank. Second, to be loyal to the General Secretary and consult him on all major issues. Third, to work for unity in the Politburo and prevent a collapse of central authority. And fourth, to keep the secretaries of the republic, oblast and krai committees of the Party informed of what was going on. They would have to be aware of the gravity of the situation and understand the circumstances in which we had to function.

I believe that, overall, this policy proved itself. Working closely with my colleagues, I tried to keep things under control, taking decisions on current affairs and sometimes on more important issues. The renewal of cadres continued, despite the difficulties involved. Two major plenums were held – in spring on school reform and in October on a long-term land reclamation programme, with a report by Tikhonov.

Moreover, that winter was particularly severe. The centre was swamped with telegrams from various areas soliciting help. In the Urals, blizzards caused such huge snow-drifts that all traffic stopped. Hundreds, not dozens, of trains were abandoned. The national economy was threatened with total standstill.

It was even more difficult to work when Konstantin Ustinovich was taken to hospital. Everybody tried to argue his point by referring to a conversation with Chernenko. More often than not, one person would say one thing and the other quite the contrary, though both had referred to the General Secretary. In the leadership and the apparatus, factions were being formed. Some people tried to make my work more difficult, to confuse me. Others, and their number was growing, openly took the line of backing Gorbachev.

Looking at Chernenko, who was not only unable to work but had difficulties in speaking and breathing, I often wondered what had kept him from retiring and taking care of his health. What made him commit himself to the heavy burden of the leadership of the country?

The answer is not easily found on the surface.

It goes without saying that anyone dismissed from power – and no-one ever retired willingly in our country – felt, to put it mildly, rather uncomfortable, like any ousted person. But the main problem was that we had no normal democratic process by which power could change hands. The system existed according to its own laws, and a hopelessly sick, even senile person could sit at the top of the pyramid.

On 10 March 1985, I had barely returned home after work when the telephone rang and Chazov informed me of Chernenko's death. After that call I immediately contacted Gromyko, Tikhonov and Bogolyubov and convened a Politburo meeting for eleven p.m. that night.

I arranged to meet Gromyko twenty minutes before the scheduled meeting. I quote our conversation from memory:

'Andrei Andreyevich, we have to consolidate our effort, the moment is crucial.'

'I believe everything is clear.'

'I will proceed from the assumption that we now have to work together.'

Other Politburo and Central Committee Secretariat members began arriving.

At the start of the meeting I announced the news. We got up and there was a moment of silence. We listened to Chazov, who had been invited to the meeting. He briefed us on the circumstances of Chernenko's death. Having repeated my condolences on Konstantin Ustinovich's demise, I stated that documents would have to be prepared and a Central Committee plenum convened.

It was so decided. Ligachev, Bogolyubov and Sokolov were assigned the task of organizing the speedy arrival of Central Committee members in Moscow, with the assistance of the Ministry of Railways and the Air Force.

A funeral commission was set up, including all the Politburo members. When the issue of the commission chairman arose there was a slight hitch. As a rule, the future General Secretary was elected to head the commission on the funeral arrangements for a late General Secretary. Suddenly Grishin spoke up: 'Why the hesitation about the chairman? Everything is clear. Let's appoint Mikhail Sergeyevich.'

I suggested not rushing and scheduled a plenum for five p.m. the following day, with a Politburo meeting beforehand at two p.m. There was enough time for everybody to consider the problems and reflect upon them – a whole night and half a day. The decision would be made at the Politburo, and subsequently submitted to the plenum. Soon the urgently summoned members of the Central Committee staff began assembling. Working groups were set up to draft documents. I discussed with Medvedev, Yakovlev and Boldin the main themes of the speech I was to deliver at the plenum next day.

WE CAN'T GO ON LIVING LIKE THIS

It was about four o'clock in the morning when I returned home. Raisa Maksimovna was waiting up for me. We went out in the garden. From the very beginning of our life in Moscow we never carried on serious conversations in the apartment or at the dacha, one never knew . . . We walked the garden paths for a long time discussing the events and their possible implications.

It is difficult now to reproduce the details of our talk. However, my last words that night stand out in my memory: 'You see, I have come here with hope and the belief that I shall be able to accomplish something, but so far there was not much I could have done. Therefore if I really want to change something I would have to accept the nomination – if it is made, of course. *We can't go on living like this.*'

It was almost morning. The dawn of a new and fateful day was descending upon us.

I had a telephone call from Ligachev in the morning who said that he was virtually assailed by the first secretaries, one after another, inquiring about the Politburo's stance on the choice of a new General Secretary. I went to the Central Committee. The Politburo meeting and the plenary were to be held that day.

Many different rumours are still buzzing concerning those meetings. They can be summed up as follows: allegedly, a regular fight broke out and several candidates were proposed for the post of General Secretary, so the Politburo proceeded to the plenum without reaching agreement. Nothing like that happened. And the participants in those events, many of whom are still in good health, know this well.

The problems of a successor had indeed been discussed, in view of the sharp decline in Chernenko's health. Central Committee officials talked about nothing else. There were some who did not want me. Shortly before the General Secretary's demise, Chebrikov, then head of the KGB, told me about a talk with Tikhonov, who had tried to convince him that my election to the post of General Secretary was inadmissible. Chebrikov was amazed that Tikhonov never mentioned any other name except mine.

'Did he really expect to get the job?' Chebrikov wondered.

Meanwhile, my ill-wishers must have known the mood among the people, and the feeling of the regional first secretaries, who were increasingly determined not to let the Politburo juggle another old, sick or weak person into the top position again.

Several groups of oblast Party first secretaries came to see me. They appealed to me to take a firm stand and assume the tasks of the General Secretary. One of these groups declared that they had created an organizational nucleus and had no intention of allowing the Politburo to decide this kind of problem without taking their views into account.

Ustinov, on whose support one could have counted, was no longer there. Gromyko's attitude towards me was now tinged with jealousy, particularly after my visit to Great Britain. It was Andropov who had promoted Andrei Andreyevich to first deputy chairman of the Council of Ministers as a tribute to a friend and partner, and to placate him. Gromyko then occupied an office in the Kremlin, while retaining his residence at Smolenskaya Square. In Andropov's entourage rumours sprang up as to Andrei Andreyevich's lust for power and his vanity.

It is noteworthy that in drafting foreign policy documents and statements two trends were clearly discernible. One originated with the Central Committee international department and reached Chernenko through A. M. Aleksandrov; the other was that of the Ministry of Foreign Affairs. The former contained an invitation to negotiate, seek agreements, liberalize and upgrade relationships. The latter was more rigid and, one may say, locked in concrete. Gromyko overtly exerted pressure on Chernenko, and in their talks with foreign delegations he often interrupted or corrected him. He clearly monopolized the foreign policy sphere.

When I was *de facto* in charge of the Politburo and Secretariat I was determined to establish control over the activities of the Ministry of Foreign Affairs.

On that day – 10 March – I knew by intuition that throughout the night and half the day things would be developing in the right direction: it was corroborated by the information received by the Central Committee. Ligachev was in touch with the Party cadres and Ryzhkov with the ministers.

I should like to emphasize that I had not pronounced a definite 'yes' or 'no', not even to Ligachev and Ryzhkov. Why was that? I had to have a clear mandate. After all, I understood what was at stake. Should I get a mere 50 per cent plus one vote or something like that, I would be unable to solve the current problems. Frankly speaking, had there been any opposition to my candidacy in the Politburo or the Central Committee I would have withdrawn.

At two p.m. I took over the chair – in recent times it had been my regular seat – and opened the proceedings, stating that on behalf of the Politburo we had to submit a proposal on the post of General Secretary to the Central Committee plenum. Gromyko rose immediately and proposed my nomination. The floor was then taken by Tikhonov, who supported Gromyko's proposal 'without reservation'. Grishin followed, then the others. There was unanimous backing.

The Central Committee plenum was to follow. My comrades, who had taken soundings among its members, argued that they were so much in favour of my candidacy that no debate was necessary there and no other candidacy conceivable.

The plenum opened at five p.m. I sensed from the beginning an atmosphere of full support, which was further solidified by Gromyko's speech proposing my candidacy for the post of General Secretary on behalf of the Politburo. He spoke without a written text, apparently extempore and therefore especially sincere, and charged with potent emotion. It was a well-prepared and well-thought-out address, its effect on the listeners all the greater because it echoed the mood of the audience.

I was stirred – never before did I have a chance to hear such words about myself and such great appreciation.

The atmosphere at the plenum and the thunderous applause after my name was mentioned, the unanimity of the Central Committee members in electing me General Secretary, all this showed that my closest associates and I had made the right choice when we decided that right there, in my speech at the plenum, I should set forth our positions and goals. We were aware that everybody was waiting for the new Soviet leader to speak up.

Sensing this, I decided that I had to state my fundamental principles in my very first statements, even as I was bidding farewell to Chernenko. I stressed that the strategic policy developed at the XXVIth Congress and at subsequent Central Committee plenums would remain intact. It was a policy of accelerating the social and economic development of the country and seeking improvement in all aspects of the life of our society.

I must confess, however, that in this statement I deliberately ventured to stretch the point slightly. A reference to the XXVIth Congress was necessary insofar as the rules of the game had to be observed. Nevertheless, developed socialism was not mentioned, being replaced by a reference to accelerated social and economic progress in the light of new ideas. I emphasized that accelerating our progress was possible only if we shifted the national economy onto the path of intensive development, rapidly achieved leading positions in science and technology, and a world-class level of labour productivity. All this required perseverance in upgrading the economic mechanism and the system of management in its entirety.

In conjunction with the economic tasks, mention was made of the need to focus our attention on social policy, the improvement and development of democracy, and the formation of a social consciousness. Other issues concerned order, discipline, and legality. I emphasized the need for transparency (*glasnost*) in the work of Party, Soviet, state and public organizations.

With regard to foreign policy: continuity in the efforts to implement the policy of peace and progress. Our positions were expounded with utmost clarity: 'We want to stop and not to continue the arms race and, consequently, propose to freeze nuclear arsenals and stop further deployment of missiles; we want a genuine and large-scale reduction of accumulated armaments and not the creation of new arms systems.'

Referring to the CPSU I noted that the Party was a force capable of uniting society, thereby facilitating the enormous changes that were simply imperative. In conclusion, I expressed my firm conviction that we would be able to unfold the creative forces of socialism on a larger scale.

This was our declaration of intent. The ideas it contained had not crept up unexpectedly. Many of them were already present in earlier speeches. Now the emphasis was stronger, the problems raised more pointedly than before. The main objective was to reach the public consciousness and to stress the need for profound changes – and to show that our intentions were of the most resolute nature.

As to foreign policy matters, I did not go beyond the positions we had been maintaining in recent times. But there was a different tone to them – peace and an invitation to dialogue were in the air. This too was a deliberate move.

The reader may wonder: what was so special about Gorbachev's speech in those March 1985 days? Obviously, from today's position, it may seem shop-worn. However, those are today's positions. The speech should be measured against the realization that all subsequent events had their beginnings there and then.

I hoped for a positive response to all that I proposed. The positions on domestic policy issues as well as the speech in its entirety were supported by the plenum. People were quite open about it. For the first time in years, there was an atmosphere of genuine enthusiasm.

The foreign policy section also elicited a response. When the foreign delegations who had come to attend Chernenko's funeral were briefly introduced, according to tradition, I sensed, from the brief remarks during the handshakes, that my words had been heard and understood.

It was then that the important meetings with the 'leading protagonists' took place. I decided to invite the Foreign Minister to join me in these encounters. The meetings were interesting and there were many – with Bush, Kohl, Mitterrand, and Thatcher. An interesting talk took place with Nakasone.

There was a sense, an intuition, that an era was coming to a close. In less than three years, three General Secretaries, three leaders of the country, had died. So had many of the prominent Politburo leaders. Kosygin died at the end of 1980. In January 1982, it was Suslov's turn. In November, Brezhnev. In May 1983, Pelshe. In February 1984, Andropov. In December, Ustinov. In March 1985, Chernenko.

All this was fraught with symbolic meaning. The very system was dying away; its sluggish senile blood no longer contained any vital juices.

I realized the weight of responsibility I had to shoulder.

PART II

IN THE KREMLIN

9

GENERAL SECRETARY

ON TAKING OFFICE AS GENERAL SECRETARY IN 1985 I WAS
immediately faced with an avalanche of problems. It was vital to
change our relationship with the West, particularly the United
States, and to bring the costly and dangerous arms race to an end.
We needed to withdraw from the damaging and costly war in
Afghanistan. The Soviet Union faced tremendous internal problems. The process of reform required new leadership and
courage. Long-term problems needed to be addressed as soon as
possible.

My notebooks of the period have helped me to reconstruct the
events and facts that defined perestroika. I talked to residents of
Moscow and Leningrad, had meetings with leaders of industry
and agriculture, scientists and experts, and members of the
Politburo and government. Some of these conversations were
short, and some more detailed.

I quickly began to fear that general policy would be shunted
into the background while I would spend my days and nights
listening to requests and making running decisions – where to
build a metro, how to accomplish land reclamation in some
region, where to obtain computer equipment, and so forth. A
programme that would stop the country's slide towards crisis
and prepare to meet the challenge of the future was urgently
needed.

FIRST STEPS

By tradition, the General Secretary was supposed to submit his evaluations and proposals for discussion to the central agencies of the Party and the Party organizations. First, it was necessary to decide what to do with the CPSU Programme, which was laughably outdated. Work on the draft plan for a new programme had been carried out under both Andropov and Chernenko. However, all that had been done to date consisted of the same old Marxist dogma (really pseudo-Marxist) presented in slightly updated language.

Of course at that stage neither I nor anyone else was ready to formulate a truly realistic evaluation of our situation, or to advance major new ideas. But a Party Congress was necessary to consolidate our new political course and to resolve personnel matters.

From the very beginning of my work as General Secretary I made it a rule not to limit the discussion of important decisions to Party structures. The Politburo in 1984, like the one fifteen years earlier, had postponed the Central Committee plenum on Matters of Scientific and Technical Progress. Because of the complexity of the problem and the need for a free exchange of opinion we decided not to call a plenum, but rather to convene an all-Union conference, which required thorough preparation. The first step was a meeting in the Central Committee with economists, academics and Party leaders. The conversation was quite frank. This authoritative forum recognized the country's technological inferiority and the need to modify the economic mechanism in order to offer greater autonomy to enterprises. One of the participants said, speaking in favour of such changes: 'A private business owner under our conditions, where everything is prescribed from above, would give up after a couple of days.'

I felt that we would not succeed in implementing reforms in the economy if we did not bring about fundamental restructuring of management structures and decentralization of management functions. Everyone enthusiastically agreed: without these no reforms would last. It is interesting that even some inveterate bureaucrats spoke in this spirit – apparently they thought that this would not affect them, or perhaps they did not believe that it would really happen.

At the conference it was recalled how Andropov had set about instilling discipline and order in the country. Everyone agreed that much could be achieved by taking a more demanding line and with better organization, but these were merely stop-gap solutions that could not make up for the lack of work incentives and flaws in the economic mechanism. We thus went beyond the narrow view of discipline, linking it more to improved industrial standards.

After the March plenum, I wanted to go 'outside the Party apparatus', to meet the people. In mid-April I visited the Likhachev Car Company and talked to the workers there. I said frankly that since the early 1970s we had been lagging further and further behind the advanced nations. We could no longer count on new labour and natural resources. We needed to increase productivity and to introduce energy-efficient and less wasteful technologies.

The car workers responded positively to my analysis. I felt they showed something more than just the traditional readiness to show respect to a 'very important person'.

THE APRIL PLENUM

As a rule at plenums the main item was discussed first, then the organizational questions. But this time we decided to break with tradition and begin with a little jolt. After opening the plenum on 23 April, I proposed that Ligachev, Ryzhkov and Chebrikov should be elected Politburo members and Nikonov a Central Committee Secretary. As always, the vote was unanimous. After congratulating the successful candidates, I asked the Politburo members to come up and join the Presidium and sat Ligachev next to myself to chair the meeting. 'So, Yegor Kuzmich, give me the floor,' I said. I did this on purpose so that the new line-up in the Kremlin would be clear from the start.

The April 1985 plenum is often seen as the starting point in the history of perestroika. The new policy was officially presented in the report 'On convening the XXVIIth CPSU Congress and the tasks connected with its preparation and conduct'. Reading this report today, I can see how difficult it was for us to part with ideological rhetoric and how painful it was to overcome deep-seated dogma and prejudice. As in March, I began by confirming the continuation of the course set by the XXVIth Party Congress – at that time such vows and assurances could not be avoided. But then I noted: 'In the Leninist interpretation, "continuity" means unflagging forward motion, the identification and resolution of new problems, the elimination of everything that interferes with development. We must keep strictly to this Leninist tradition while enriching and developing our party policy and our general line towards perfecting a society of developed socialism.'

Two principles were combined, as it were, in a single sentence: one, the 'unflagging forward motion, the identification and resolution of new problems'; and the other, 'perfecting a society of developed socialism.' Those who are fond of dissertations full of quotations and are masters at juggling phrases that have been torn from their historical context would say that Gorbachev took an oath to 'developed socialism', and then 'betrayed' it. However, for me and for those who began perestroika, the key point was 'the elimination of everything that interferes with development'. I remained true to this principle in spite of all of the difficulties that we met during perestroika.

'Contradictions' of this kind can also easily be found in other places in my report. It contains the theme generally recognized at that time, that 'by relying on the advantages of socialism, the country has in a short historical period reached the heights of historical and social progress.' But only two paragraphs later there is a reference to 'the need for further changes and transformations, for the achievement of a new qualitative state of society in the broadest sense of the word. This first of all means the scientific and technological renewal of industry and the achievement of labour productivity that is equal to that of the developed capitalist states . . . This means sweeping changes in the area of labour and the material and spiritual conditions of life. This means energizing the entire system of political and social

222

institutions, a deepening of socialist democratic principles, and self-government for the people.'

Ever since the revolution there had been countless discussions, at Party congresses and plenums and Supreme Soviet sessions, on the unwieldiness and inefficiency of our management apparatus and its rampant bureaucracy. Decisions had been adopted – but the bureaucracy continued to grow, since attempts to solve the problem simply resulted in the creation of new management structures. It was therefore necessary to change the very system of economic management, keeping only social, economic and scientific-technological strategies under central direction and leaving everything else to the discretion of the industrial collectives.

The idea was to link the solution of social questions to the modernization of the economy, to expand local rights, to over-come the idea that wages should be levelled, and to block off sources of unearned income. Looking ahead even then to the development of the social programme for the XXVIIth Party Congress, we wondered whether it was possible simultaneously to modernize industry and to implement important measures in the social sphere. We concluded that this could be done if there was priority development of the production sphere. In other words, our thinking was still in thrall to conventional formulae.

Among the problems at the April plenum defined as 'urgent and vitally important' were housing, food, reform of public education and the development of a better-equipped health care system. In short, we defined the main directions for the development of society and the economy.

Although the April plenum was without question a break-through to the future, it still bore the imprint of the past. We still relied on the CPSU and the strengthening of its 'leadership role'. The issue of democracy was reduced to the declaration that 'complex and far-reaching problems can be solved only by relying on the creative work of the people.' We had attacked the historical problem of the renewal of our society, but of course we could not free our minds from previous shackles and blink-ers in a single stroke. I do not think this is a subject for sarcastic comments or cynical laughter. This is why I am not particularly bothered when some people attempt to malign me by saying: 'Look what Gorbachev said in 1985, in 1986, in 1987, and what he said in 1991 or 1994.'

THROUGH TOWNS AND VILLAGES

Perestroika – the process of change in our country – started from above. It could not have been otherwise in a totalitarian state. But past experience showed that if the spark of reform was not caught by the masses, it was doomed. We had to awaken society from its lethargy and indifference as quickly as possible and involve the people in the process of change. I looked on this as a guarantee of the success of perestroika and spoke about it at the April plenum; this was the purpose of my trips through the country.

One cannot say that there was anything extraordinary in the fact that I went on these trips. Excursions around the country explaining the decisions of congresses and plenums were normal in party practice. Members of the Politburo and the Central Committee Secretariat participated in such campaigns and gave speeches and reports to the '*aktiv*', i.e., gatherings of the Party, government and military leadership on a republic, oblast and city level. Outstanding workers and key figures of the local intelligentsia were also included. The idea was that the decisions of the 'centre' would be discussed at these forums, but in fact they were solemnly accepted without any questioning. At the very most, someone would complain to the visitor about his bosses and risk the whip after the guest's departure, like the merchants in Gogol's *The Inspector General* who dared to complain about the city governor.

In short, communication went primarily in one direction, from the top down. Hence one had first to learn how to listen to the people, to sense their attitude to our plans and intentions – whether we were gaining broad-based support or whether we were like a 'voice crying in the wilderness'.

On 15 May I went to Leningrad. By tradition I visited the monuments and laid flowers at the graves in the Piskarevo

Cemetery. I visited major enterprises – Elektrosila, Kirovsky Zavod, Svetlana, Bolshevichka – met teachers and students from the Polytechnical Institute, and visited the 'Intensifikatsiya-90' exhibition. I ended my visit with a major political meeting at Smolny.[1]

The people in Leningrad were not simply courteous and hospitable. They knew of the decisions of the April plenum and listened closely to my explanations, asked questions, gave advice and encouragement. When someone shouted 'Keep it up!', this was indeed heartening.

The press both here and abroad began to note the style of the new General Secretary: 'Gorbachev loves to meet the people.' In fact, I had always felt the need for this kind of direct communication and not at all for the sake of popularity. Short talks and mini-interviews in a factory workshop, on the kolkhoz fields, in a college auditorium, and most of all on the streets, were for me more important than sociological surveys.

Of course, it was difficult at first to get people to talk. They were a little afraid and held back. I could sense that most did not have very much faith in the seriousness of our intentions. They had heard assurances and promises so many times, but afterwards very little had changed in their lives.

At the end of June I went to Ukraine. I met the Kiev aviation workers who had designed the famous Ruslan cargo plane. I visited the Paton Institute of Electrowelding which was run by Boris Yevgenevich Paton – one of our most important scientists as well as an outstanding political figure, who supported me through all of the years of perestroika. From Kiev I flew to Dnepropetrovsk, with the idea that if we were to begin a critical re-evaluation of the Brezhnev period it would be appropriate to announce this in Brezhnev's homeland. Speaking on 26 June at the Dnepropetrovsk Metallurgical Plant, I asked directly: 'Maybe some of you are wondering: are we turning around too abruptly? What do you think?' The audience answered: 'This is right, and necessary!' I asked: 'What do we have here, just a few talking or

---

[1] Headquarters of the first Bolshevik government, 1917–18; then taken over by the Leningrad Party.

is this everyone's opinion?' The answer came in unison: 'Everyone's!'

At the end of the trip I met the members of the Ukrainian Central Committee, the first secretaries of the obkoms and key workers of the republican organs – those people who held the real power in Ukraine and on whom implementation of the ideas of the April plenum largely depended. Although Shcherbitsky and I had been together throughout my trip, I saw that he was nervous. I myself was not completely at ease. I had to find the proper tone of voice for the Ukrainian leadership: I had to say things plainly that were not so very pleasant to hear.

Ukraine and its citizens deserved recognition for their contribution to the affairs of the Soviet Union. But many of those at the meeting were shocked by the news that the growth rates for agricultural production in this republic had fallen so far that grain was having to be imported to the region. After all, the powers that be were present in the auditorium and this was the fruit of their activity – the republic with the most favourable conditions for agriculture was not able to feed itself. Then I showed with facts and figures the unenviable state of the leading industries which had always been a subject of pride in the republic – coal-mining, metallurgy, machine-building. On the whole, the leaders of Ukraine found themselves in an unusual situation at this meeting. Up to then no-one had spoken to them like this. Ukraine and its problems had always been the domain of Brezhnev, but because of his special attachment to it he had closed his eyes to what was happening.

How was I able to have an open, frank discussion with the Ukrainians at the very first meeting? There was nothing unfair in my talk. I pointed out with a clean conscience the many successes that these same cadres had achieved in the past. And, finally, I let them know that if they would start really working, they would have my full support.

As I write this, I remember how at that time I was still under the illusion that we could successfully solve new problems and produce radical reforms while keeping the same leaders. They included many talented and gifted people, fine organizers and specialists, not just red-tape experts and unprincipled wheeler-

226

dealers. But it was also a fact that they carried out their mission according to the methods of the command system and, along with it, had exhausted their potential and had begun to rest on their laurels. These laurels were wilting before their very eyes, like dried leaves. It took me too long to understand this, and no wonder: I myself had come from this environment and had suffered its diseases. However, at that time I was satisfied with the results of my trip to Ukraine.

My first trips through the country helped me to understand that I could not count on agitprop or on my associates to explain the policy of perestroika – no matter how little time I had, I would have to continue direct communication with the people, to see with my own eyes what was happening and to understand what was on the minds of both big chiefs and little chiefs.

Without losing any time, I began to prepare for a trip to West Siberia. I wanted to make an on-the-spot examination of the oil and gas industry and to see how people were living – there had already been much dissatisfaction voiced in letters to the Party Central Committee. Dolgikh, Yeltsin, Baibakov, the Minister of the Gas Industry, V. S. Chernomyrdin, and I arrived in Tyumen oblast on 4 September. I began with Nizhnevartovsk, the capital of the oil country. Then we went to Urengoi on the Arctic Circle, where large-scale work on extraction and transportation of gas was under way. We visited an electric power plant under construction and the building sites of new housing developments in Surgut.

The talks with the oil and gas workers were unusually sharp. The problems they had to deal with every day went beyond local interests: any increase of the state's economic power depended on developing this raw, distant, inhospitable land. There had been major miscalculations from the very start, and their effects had already begun to show. It is a commonplace truth: if one intends to develop major industry in unpopulated or underpopulated regions one must take care to develop the infrastructure ahead of time – to provide roads, housing, light and heat, not to mention schools, hospitals, libraries, stadiums – in brief, everything that is necessary for normal human life!

Even today I can see the meeting in Urengoi: all of the city's residents were out on the streets. The people were happy that the 'chief' had finally come to visit them – the talk was direct and unsparing. 'How is it that we live in slums or old railway carriages? There is a shortage of everything. Here, beyond the Arctic Circle, we cannot get regular flights to the capital or other cities! The Soviet Union and Europe need gas, but it turns out that no-one needs us.'

They informed me that suppliers were sending the 'pioneers of Siberia' old stock that could not be sold in other cities. There was a shortage of electric power in the region, even though this problem could easily have been solved if someone would only give the order to continue the construction of new generation capacity at the Surgut Regional Power Plant. Even the local dairy was short of power.

On this trip I encountered absurdities. It turned out that the machine factories were mostly sending machines and oilfield equipment to the north in individual parts rather than assembling them in the factories before delivery. As a result, entire assembly plants had to be built, which required workers and therefore additional housing and everything else.

I was impressed with the fact that people who came to Siberia did not think of themselves as temporary workers. They were outraged at the way the organization of work was ruthlessly destroying the forest, rivers and soil. There was no concern for efficient use of natural resources; from the very beginning, reliance was placed on spouting oil. Thousands of plumes blazed day and night. The oil-refining rate here was 58 per cent, while the world level was close to 80 per cent. Half as much product was produced from a cubic metre of wood than the average for the rest of the Soviet Union and several times less than in the developed Western countries. Plans for resource management were compiled regularly but never carried out. The world's richest country in natural resources was beginning to feel an increasing shortage of fuel, energy and even timber.

In Tyumen, where the oilfield workers of this enormous oblast had convened, I sensed from the reaction in the auditorium that people were tired of empty declarations and were waiting for real help.

On my return from this trip the Politburo made some immediate decisions. Pipe, cement, building materials and other equipment were dispatched to West Siberia. The quality of suppliers was improved. Improvements were made to the construction plans for new housing services and utilities. The decline in the extraction of oil was stopped, and production even increased slightly. Alas, political passions swept through the country soon afterwards and insufficient attention was given to this deep-seated problem. The oil and gas workers are right when they say that what had been begun was not completed.

Major miscalculations of economic policy were evident in other regions as well, as my trip to Kazakhstan confirmed. The main thing here was not so much to get acquainted with the work of collective and state farms and the research institutions in the virgin lands region – I had been there before – as to talk with representatives of Kazakhstan, Siberia and the Urals about how the Food Programme was being implemented. Three years had passed since its adoption. Agricultural production had on the whole increased, there were fewer unprofitable farms, the rural workers were beginning to get more equipment and to build roads and housing, but the food supply had essentially not improved. So where was the way out? The root causes lay in the general state of the economy. Moreover, standing in the foreground was the need to establish a reasonable balance between the civilian and military sectors.

'EVERYTHING DEPENDS ON CADRES'

I cannot say that the preparations for the XXVIIth Congress were different from those for earlier ones. It is true that once in a while there were timid signs of a nascent emancipation of consciousness. Party members, despite the efforts of the apparatchiks, began to reject the leaders that had been imposed on them and to elect people more to their liking. The workers began to speak out more boldly. But basically everything followed in the same old rut. The Party used the old methods and followed the written and unwritten rules that had been established over the decades.

229

It would have been childish to think that there would be changes in society without changes at the top. For some of the Politburo members the April plenum belonged to a different and new age, one in which they had no part. A sense of self-preservation prompted them to speak in favour of the new direction, but we could not count on them to carry out the new tasks. This compelled the replacement of Tikhonov by Ryzhkov as Chairman of the USSR Council of Ministers. Baibakov, the chairman of Gosplan, was replaced by Talyzin: Nuriev, who was responsible for the agro-industrial complex, was replaced by Murakhovsky; and Smirnov, who was in charge of the defence complex, was replaced by Maslyukov. Fedorchuk, head of the Ministry of Internal Affairs, was replaced by Vlasov, who had been the first secretary of the Rostov Party obkom.

After the April plenum some Politburo members had suggested combining the posts of General Secretary and Chairman of the Presidium of the USSR Supreme Soviet, as was the case under Brezhnev, Andropov and Chernenko.[1]

I disagreed. First, I felt that the public's perception of this would be negative. Second, I did not want additional duties that might divert my attention, time and effort during such sweeping and important changes. Finally, at that point it was essential to replace the Minister of Foreign Affairs and I could not see any way out other than to promote Gromyko to the chairmanship of the Presidium of the USSR Supreme Soviet. Gromyko was an important politician and diplomat, a man wise in experience. He emphasized his readiness for loyal co-operation with me. Of course Gromyko counted on keeping control of foreign policy, but he soon saw that I would not accept this and reacted calmly. You could not take away his ability to adapt to the situation: this was the secret of his survival.

Why was it necessary to replace the Minister of Foreign Affairs? Our foreign policy had to be radically reformed and it was clear that this would affect our many partners in foreign

[1] Brezhnev became the Chairman of the Presidium of the USSR Supreme Soviet, head of state, in 1977, and both Andropov and Chernenko followed this example. In July 1985 Gromyko became head of state and Gorbachev succeeded him in 1988. In 1990 he became USSR President.

affairs, allies, neutrals and adversaries, with whom it would be necessary to find a formula for reconciliation. A sharp change of direction in this area would be impossible if foreign policy remained in the same hands. Such a task was already beyond Gromyko's capacities.

Incidentally, Andrei Andreyevich regarded my offer as an honour, a proper reward for his services to the country. I did not in any way isolate him in the discussion of foreign policy issues or internal problems: just the reverse, I valued the opportunity to draw on his memory and experience.

After lengthy reflection, I decided that Gromyko's replacement would be Shevardnadze. I had met him at the XIIth Komsomol Congress. At that time he was not completely fluent in Russian. He was not, as is said, a 'live wire', or an outstanding orator. He did not fit the common idea of a 'typical Georgian'. Rather, he was very reserved and self-disciplined. But he had something in him that attracted one and made one want to talk to him. We had met more recently when we were both secretaries: he of the Central Committee of the Georgian Communist Party and I of the krai committee and later of the CPSU Central Committee. There had long been active ties between the people of Stavropol krai and Georgia; Shevardnadze and I promoted them in every way possible. Of course, neither he nor I imagined then where these contacts might lead years later.

With time we developed a sense of trust that allowed us to speak frankly about anything. I found that we had a common approach to many key problems, including foreign affairs. After I had become General Secretary and was reflecting on personnel, it came to me that just such a person as Shevardnadze, someone capable of deliberation and persuasion, graced with Eastern affability, could cope with the new tasks in the field of foreign policy.

Several days after my talk with Gromyko we met again to discuss the matter of his successor. He thought that one of the diplomats should be advanced to this post. He mentioned Kornienko, then mentioned and rejected Vorontsov, who was ambassador to France at that time. He also mentioned Dobrynin, although he did not like him, evidently realizing that in many ways Dobrynin was his equal and perhaps even his superior.

When I mentioned Shevardnadze, Gromyko's first reaction was close to shock. However, he quickly pulled himself together and began to weigh the pros and cons.

'I see that you do not favour Shevardnadze,' I said. 'Well, let's think who would be better.'

He quickly said: 'No, no, I see that you have thought this over carefully.'

'OK, let's think a little more and then continue our conversation later.'

The next time Chebrikov and Ligachev were present. I remarked that at the present time we would be unable to replace Gromyko with a man equal to him in experience and concluded: 'In reflecting on the future minister, I always arrive at the conclusion that he must be a major political figure, and because of this I lean towards Shevardnadze.'

Following a discussion, everyone agreed. I telephoned Shevardnadze in Tbilisi and said that he was being offered the post of USSR Minister of Foreign Affairs. There was a long silence, and then he said: 'I might have expected anything except this. I have to think. And you must think further. I am not a professional . . . I'm a Georgian . . . People may start asking questions. What does Gromyko say?'

I told him that Gromyko, Ligachev and Chebrikov supported his candidacy and I asked him to come to Moscow. The next day we had another conversation. Then I called on the Politburo members and the question was decided. At the Central Committee plenum on 1 July Shevardnadze was elected a member of the Politburo, and at a session of the Supreme Soviet on the following day he was designated Minister of Foreign Affairs. Gromyko was elected Chairman of the Presidium of the USSR Supreme Soviet at this same session.

Both here and abroad people were extremely puzzled by Shevardnadze's appointment. Many thought that only a Russian should hold such an important Soviet state function. But experienced people quickly guessed my thinking: 'He accorded Gromyko what was due to him and at the same time assured himself a free hand in foreign policy by bringing in a close friend and associate.'

At the July plenum Romanov was relieved of his duties as member of the Politburo and Secretary of the Central Committee. Yeltsin and Zaikov were elected Secretaries of the Central Committee, Aleksandr Yakovlev was confirmed as the head of the Department of Propaganda, and Anatoly Lukyanov was confirmed as the head of the General Department.

When I met Romanov, I let him know quite bluntly that there was no place for him in the leadership. He did not like this, but there was nothing he could say to change things. I told him that I should prefer not to bring the matter to a discussion in the Politburo and that it would be best to decide everything on a voluntary basis. Romanov 'shed a tear', but in the end accepted this suggestion. The question of his future was decided quietly at the plenum and he remained a member of the Central Committee.

The question of Tikhonov's retirement was not so simply solved. Everything seemed clear: here was a man almost eighty years old, whereas the head of government – especially the head of a government embarking on the path of reform – had to be a political figure who possessed a reserve of strength and time, one who was capable of looking into the future. Tikhonov was a figure not even of yesterday, but of the day before yesterday, from Stalinist times. However, he had his own opinion on this. He was sure that we could not do without his services and in our first conversation pronounced his readiness to 'work in the new and interesting circumstances'.

I politely declined his offer and, stressing the difficulty of the forthcoming transformations and the need to be concerned about the health of veterans who had served the country, let him understand that he had to retire. It turned out that Tikhonov was in fact prepared for such an outcome. He was anxious about his situation in retirement, and I promised that he could keep all of the perks that he enjoyed at that time. At the end of September he was released from his duties as head of government, and in October he left the Politburo at a Central Committee plenum.

Tikhonov's replacement as Chairman of the USSR Council of Ministers was Ryzhkov. We had collaborated fruitfully under Andropov and in many cases had found that our views on the economy and on the acute need for its radical restructuring were similar. We also agreed on political positions – at least, I do not remember any major disagreements. I was impressed by Nikolai Ivanovich's human qualities: clarity, sometimes sharpness of opinions, which never turned to rudeness, and a grasp of business that had been nurtured over years of practical activity in industry.

Our relations were not always unclouded. As events developed, we were both faced with situations that could not have been predicted. Our opinions underwent a kind of evolution, and there were moments of misunderstanding, hurt feelings and even exasperation. But I still believe that my choice was right. Ryzhkov was my chief ally in the business of reform; at that time we pursued the same goals, and no matter what happened later I remain grateful to him for this comradeship.

The next important cadre problem was the replacement of Grishin, the first secretary of the Moscow city committee, who was commonly known as the 'governor of Moscow'. It was clear to everyone that the capital's leadership had played itself out, and it would be foolish to count on its ability to work in the new style. Moscow, which they had ceremoniously promised to turn into a 'model communist city', was suffering from serious problems of housing and supply, and both its economy and its intellectual standing were in decline. Of course, the capital at that time could be considered a model city by comparison with what our democrats made of it later, in their four years of control. However, everything is relative. At that time almost no-one doubted the need to replace Grishin, although he thought differently and even hoped for higher positions. An extremely cocksure and power-loving person, he could not tolerate bright, independent thinkers around himself. Hence it was not surprising that there was no-one in the Moscow city committee suitable to replace Grishin – we had to look for such a person outside the city committee. Yeltsin's political career begins at this point, at least its Moscow stage. I recall his appointment as head of the Central Committee's construction department. Candidates for such positions were usually sought among the Secretaries, and the choice of Boris Nikolaevich was not an accident. He met all the formal requirements: he had managed a construction conglomerate for several years, had worked as the head of the construction department of the oblast committee, and since 1976 had been the first secretary of the obkom in Sverdlovsk (now Ekaterinburg).

I personally knew little about him, but what I knew put me on my guard. In my time as a Secretary of the Central Committee, a commission had been appointed to examine the work of the Sverdlovsk Party organization in animal husbandry. In its report the commission criticized the activity of the Sverdlovsk obkom. Yeltsin telephoned me and asked me not to submit the report to the Central Committee but rather to send it to the Sverdlovsk obkom so that it could be discussed and acted on there. At that time I supervised the Secretariat of the Central Committee and decided to meet the wish of the Sverdlovsk obkom: let them work things out for themselves; after all the intention was not to give them a dressing down. However, when he brought up the report for discussion at the obkom, Yeltsin not only did not consider it necessary to acquaint the participants of the obkom plenum with its contents but he essentially repudiated the basic findings of the commission. The Central Committee representative at the plenum, Ivan Kapustyan, a direct and steadfast person, took the floor, read the commission's report, and then offered an unflattering evaluation of the behaviour of the obkom's first secretary. At that time I noted for myself that Yeltsin did not adequately react to the criticisms directed towards him. Moreover, once in the heat of discussion at a session of the Supreme Soviet Yeltsin unexpectedly left the hall leaning on someone's arm. Many were worried about him – what had happened? His 'well-wishers' tried to calm people down: 'Nothing serious, just a little rise in the blood pressure.' People from Sverdlovsk just smiled: 'It happens with our first secretary; sometimes he has a little too much to drink.'

Because these things kept popping up in my mind, I decided to have a talk with Ryzhkov, since he had been a member of the Sverdlovsk obkom when he was the manager of Uralmash.[1]

'You'll have trouble with him,' answered Nikolai Ivanovich. 'I know him and I would not recommend him.'

[1] The Urals Machine-Building Production Association, one of the largest in the Soviet Union, of which Nikolai Ryzhkov was managing director, 1971–5.

This intensified my doubts. Ligachev, who was in charge of cadres, suggested: 'Let me go to Sverdlovsk and see for myself . . .'

After a few days he telephoned. 'I have asked around here and the opinion is that Yeltsin is the man we need. He has everything – knowledge, character. He can do things on a big scale and will be able to manage.'

'Are you sure, Yegor Kuzmich?'

'Yes, without a doubt.'

Thus Yeltsin started working at the Central Committee. We had a brief interview in connection with his appointment, but I do not recall what was said. He began to work actively, and compared with his predecessor he looked good. About that time I was always looking for people who were active, decisive and open to new ideas. There were not so many of them in the upper echelons. Yeltsin impressed me, and at the July plenum I proposed that he be elected Secretary of the Central Committee. Frankly, I was already 'measuring' him for the Moscow post when I did this.

On 22 December the Politburo made the decision to recommend Yeltsin for the position of first secretary of the Moscow City Committee. At the city conference he spoke with a clear ring of reform. I supported the critical message of his speech. It is true that we were worried how the secret ballot would go, since the Moscow party activists were more than a little upset that we had not found a worthy candidate in the capital's Party organization and had brought in an outsider. But the election went without a hitch. Here too, Yeltsin energetically set about his work. The Muscovites liked his insistence on high standards from bureaucrats of every rank. I considered our choice for the secretary of the capital's city committee to be a success.

THE XXVIIth PARTY CONGRESS

At the end of 1985 and the beginning of 1986 I was wholly engaged in preparation for the XXVIIth Party Congress. The breakthrough that had been made in March and April and the subsequent foreign policy initiatives were receiving support from the public. My trips throughout the country, my meetings with the leaders of the Warsaw Pact nations, my visit to France, and my talks with Reagan and other foreign leaders, all put many new tasks on the agenda. Now there had to be a systematic exposition and consolidation of the political course towards perestroika, and the practical guidelines had to be made specific. And, of course, it was necessary to adopt the new party programme; work on it had been finished in October and, after discussion at the Central Committee plenum, the draft was published for discussion.

By tradition the General Secretary gave a report at the Party congress. This time we decided to call it a political report, which distinguished it from a routine analysis of the work that had been done and allowed us to concentrate on strategic questions. The material for the report had been prepared by the end of December, and on the eve of the New Year I went to Pitsunda for a holiday. At that time of year the cold and restless sea has its own severe beauty – waves crashing on rocks, the sea spray, foam . . . The air is so saturated with ions that it seems palpable, weighty, like a tonic. It is wonderful to work in such an atmosphere.

I invited Aleksandr Yakovlev and Valery Boldin to come to Pitsunda immediately after the New Year holiday. In addition to the material of the working group, they brought me ideas for solutions to various specific problems that had been submitted at my request by academic institutes. In a cottage on the coast we reread, considered and discussed all the points of the report. The first attempts to advance to new evaluations and conclusions were made.

Of fundamental importance in the report was its stress on the interconnectedness, interdependence and integrity of the world, which had an enormous effect on our own and on world politics. Indeed, if this view is accepted as valid, the division of the world into opposing blocs must be seen as absurd. Thus the report contains the following statements: 'The policy of all-out struggle and military confrontation does not have a future.' 'The arms race, like nuclear war itself, cannot be won.' 'We must follow a path of co-operation to create a comprehensive system of international security.' Therefore 'security is a political problem, and it can be solved only by political means.'

We linked the transformation of society to the course of accelerated social and economic development that had been adopted at the April plenum. What we had in mind was not a revolution but a specific improvement of the system, which we then believed was possible. We longed for freedom so much that we thought that if we just gave society a breath of fresh air it would revive. We understood freedom in a broad sense, to include actual, not just rhetorical, control of the land by farmers, and of factories by workers, freedom of enterprise, changes in our investment and structural policies and an emphasis on social development. We were aware – although we did not formulate this idea very specifically – of the need for democratization of society and the state, and for the development of people's self-government.

It was almost a year after the April turnaround. It was obvious that the policy of perestroika was seen by many as just another campaign, which would soon run out of steam. We had to eliminate doubts of this kind and convince people of the need for the new course, and so the theme of glasnost – 'transparency' – came up in the report. 'Democracy does not and cannot exist without glasnost.' 'Glasnost must be made unfailing. It is necessary at the centre, but no less and perhaps even more in the provinces, where people live and work.' Today such incantations may sound trite, but at the time these were fundamental political precepts that played an enormous role in awakening public opinion and activity.

The first attempts to reach an understanding of the place of the Party in perestroika were made in the preparation of this speech. Some statements would be developed further at the January 1987 plenum and in particular at the XIXth CPSU Conference: 'The Party exercises political leadership, determines the general prospect of development . . . regarding ways and methods of solving specific economic and socio-cultural questions, broad freedom of choice is granted to each management organ, labour collective and to economic personnel . . . The Party decisively opposes mixing the functions of Party committees with the functions of state and public organs.' Of course, no-one saw a call to political reform in such statements then, even though objectively speaking that was exactly the role that they played.

Towards mid-January I submitted the draft of my speech to the Politburo. During the discussion I sensed for the first time how strong the grip of ideological stereotypes still was. Even members that I had promoted – people who, it would seem, could be called reformers in many respects – were extremely cautious. They simply raced to demonstrate their political orthodoxy.

After the discussion of the draft Raisa Maksimovna and I went to Zavidovo. Medvedev, Yakovlev and Boldin arrived a day later and the final stage of work on the report began. The problems remained, but the structure and exposition of the material were significantly altered. Raisa Maksimovna was there practically the whole time, listening to our discussions and participating in them. Her experience in social research, her work with university youth, and simply her knowledge of everyday life and female intuition proved to be useful. She chided us for ignoring the subject of the position of the family and women in society in the report and suggested ways to improve it. It is true – all through our history we loudly proclaimed slogans about the equality of women and their participation in the government of the country, but in practice we were behind not only Western countries, but also the Eastern countries in this matter. Today I regret that there were no women in the Gorbachev leadership. There are none in Yeltsin's either.

When the work on the report was completed, we found that there was a large gap between it and the new draft of the CPSU Programme; by comparison the latter looked 'pale' in every way – ideas, depth of analysis, clarity of argument in favour of the new political course. Corrections had to be made quickly in order to remove at least the most striking differences between the two documents. These amendments were proposed at a meeting of the Programme commission on 17 February 1986, and on the next day the Central Committee plenum approved the political report, the drafts of the new edition of the CPSU Programme and Statute and also the report on the basic directions of economic and social development of the USSR for the upcoming years.

The date on which the Congress began (25 February),

randomly selected, coincided with the thirtieth anniversary of the XXth Congress, which was somewhat symbolic. I got the impression that the delegates liked the political report, but in the discussion the inertia of the past was predominant. The delegates 'from the provinces', including Kunayev and Shcherbitsky, who spoke at the beginning, presented detailed but tedious accounts of their work. Some people could not avoid tributes to the General Secretary, even though one would have thought that the time for these had passed forever. When this theme was heard in the speeches by Lev Kulidzhanov and Eduard Shevardnadze, I broke into the discussion and asked them to 'Cut down on the pathos' and 'Stop invoking Mikhail Sergeyevich'. The Congress's reaction was surprising: the delegates laughed and burst into applause. You might think this was a trivial thing, but it reflected the prevailing mood. The discussion became more substantial and on the whole took on the imprint of the nascent transition from one state of society to another. Some of the delegates who had been very critical about the situation in the country raised the question of the responsibility of the former Party leadership. Yeltsin stood out among speakers voicing this attitude. Others gave a favourable verdict on what had been done by previous generations and called for continuity in politics. As I remember, Gromyko expressed this view the most strongly. However, there was no open clash at the Congress.

This 'accord' achieved at the XXVIIth Congress set up something of a trap for the new leadership. The process of perestroika was bound to move beyond the decisions of the Congress very quickly. The reformers would then be accused of 'revisionism', with predictable consequences. There was one way of avoiding this threat: to employ the authority of the Central Committee. According to Party tradition the Central Committee was the real centre of power and could make any decision while making only formal references to the guidelines of the last congress.

The Congress closed on 6 March. I immediately invited the Central Committee Secretaries and government members for a talk about the business in hand. First was the problem of the decentralization of the economy, which was already provoking a hostile reaction from the bureaucratic apparatus. I spotted signs of misunderstanding and dissatisfaction even in the upper echelons of the Party and government leadership. However, I was encouraged by the attitudes of the leaders of economic organizations and enterprises.

After the Congress I met newspaper editors and the heads of television and arts organizations, contacts that became a regular thing. But I was most interested in what was happening in the labour collectives, how the people were taking the decisions of the Congress and what actions the cadres were taking. In early April I left for Kuibyshev, which is today called Samara. I went there because major industry is concentrated in this region: aviation, chemical and metallurgical, together with large-scale agriculture and food industry. And, of course, at Togliatti, the famous VAZ,[1] flagship of the Soviet motor industry.

The visit lasted three days. My first sensation was that a time machine had taken me back exactly a year. The secretaries of the oblast and city committees glared all the time at their subordinates, defining the 'permissible' measure of communication between the General Secretary and the people. They would hold up a hand to stop people who were eager for a frank talk, or they broke off conversations that in their view were 'unnecessary'. My desire to learn the true state of affairs clearly did not suit the local bosses. My talking directly to the people so upset some of them that they tactlessly tried to break in. I had to publicly put them in their places and say that just then I was not interested in talking to them. Their faces would turn red with indignation.

I was glad to see the desire of the workers at the auto plant to master the new methods of economic management – it seemed that they succeeded in this better than others. At that time, the programme of modernization was being successfully implemented by the local metallurgy plant. The time for fast-moving and enterprising people had come.

Yet such successes were few and far between. Nor was I receiving encouraging reports from colleagues visiting other regions of the country. The general feeling was that everything was slowed by inertia; the policy of perestroika was making no

[1] Volga Car Company.

impact on the life of cities and enterprises. There was a stream of letters to the Central Committee, most of them filled with alarm at the lack of action of local officials. A man from Stavropol bitterly reported that when he approached the director of a state farm with plans for improving production, the director had turned him out of his office telling him not to pry – 'It is none of your business.' 'So this is the way it is,' the man concluded his letter, 'even after the Congress it's still none of my business.' I also got a letter from Gorky, from Vasily Mishin, a former fellow-student at Moscow State University and now a doctor of philosophy and head of department: 'Keep in mind, Mikhail, nothing is happening in Gorky, not a thing!'

At the 24 April Politburo meeting we discussed the reasons why perestroika was stuck. The feeling was that it had run up against the gigantic Party and state apparatus, which stood like a dam in the path of reforms. In my 1985 statement I had said that we would give everyone the opportunity to shape up, but recent events had convinced me of the need for a tougher approach to the cadres, for the question was no longer one of lack of understanding or inability, but rather direct sabotage. I called attention to a line from a newspaper article that had something in common with our conversation: 'The apparatus broke Khrushchev's neck and the same thing will happen now.'

Two days later we suffered a blow that put all of our plans into the background for a long time.

CHERNOBYL

The accident at the Chernobyl nuclear power station was graphic evidence, not only of how obsolete our technology was, but also of the failure of the old system. At the same time, and such is the irony of history, it severely affected our reforms by literally knocking the country off its tracks.

Today we know how great this tragedy really was and how much is still to be done for those who lost health and home.

It happened on Saturday, 26 April, at 1.25 a.m., when the only people on duty were a standby crew and people conducting an experiment on the turbogenerator during a scheduled shutdown of the fourth reactor. News of the accident reached Moscow on the morning of the 26th. It went via the Ministry of Medium Machine-Building, which was responsible for the 'nuclear complex', to Ryzhkov, who reported it to me.

I immediately called a meeting of the Politburo, where Dolgikh, who dealt with these matters, explained the situation. His information was quite vague and failed to give an idea of the scale of the disaster. It was decided to send to the site immediately a government commission headed by Boris Yevdokimovich Shcherbina, Deputy Chairman of the USSR Council of Ministers. The commission, which included specialists on nuclear power stations, doctors and radiologists, reached Chernobyl that same evening. Scientists from the USSR Academy of Sciences and the Ukrainian Academy of Sciences were also rushed in.

The commission began to send back reports the next day. These consisted mainly of preliminary fact-finding, with all kinds of cautious remarks but without any conclusions at all. The commission reported that there had been an explosion, two people had died, there was mass hospitalization for radiological observation, steps were being taken to localize the fire, the remaining three units had been shut down etc. It also reported that the explosion had released radioactive material.

On 28 April Ryzhkov reported the first results of the commission's work to the Politburo. Based on that information, the public was informed on television that evening and in the newspapers next day, after which there were regular reports as new information came in. I absolutely reject the accusation that the Soviet leadership intentionally held back the truth about Chernobyl. We simply did not know the whole truth yet.

Because of the extraordinary nature of the accident, we immediately set up a Politburo Operations Group, headed by Ryzhkov. Beginning on 29 April, it operated around the clock. The minutes of its work and its reports have been published.

During these days, we felt intuitively, since we still did not have complete information, that this was a very dramatic situation with potentially serious consequences. We needed first-hand information. On 2 May Ryzhkov and Ligachev flew to Chernobyl and, joined by Shcherbitsky, travelled around the area, heard the commission's report and talked with local residents.

The scale of the disaster became clearer every day. We began to see better what had to be done. The first thing was to make sure that the people in the area were safe. Literally everything available was put to use for continuous medical observation. A medical aid network was set up covering almost a million people, including more than 200,000 children. The commission decided that people in the city of Pripyat should be resettled. As soon as the initial survey of radioactive contamination had been completed and the scientists had concluded that it was impossible to continue living there, evacuation began, first from a ten-kilometre zone and then from a thirty-kilometre zone. This was extremely difficult: many people did not want to leave and had to be evicted by force. In the first few days of May approximately 135,000 people were resettled and the entire region was placed under strict control.

The damaged reactor unit was a very difficult engineering and scientific problem – there was a danger that it would collapse. Academician Velikhov told journalists at the beginning of May: 'The heart of the reactor – the hot radioactive core – is in suspension, as it were. It has been covered by a layer of sand, lead, boron and clay, and this puts an additional load on the structure. Can it hold up or will it sink into the ground? No-one has ever been in such a difficult position.'

Steps were taken to keep radioactive substances from migrating through the soil to the Dnieper River. Chemical defence troops were sent in, the necessary equipment was procured, and decontamination work was begun. The members of the government commission worked without stopping, and then switched to a one-week rotating schedule. Shcherbina, Silayev, Voronin, Maslyukov, Gusev, Vedernikov, and then Shcherbina again, in turn chaired the commission. Scientific institutes in Moscow, Leningrad, Kiev and other cities were working around the clock to solve dozens of unusual problems. Practically the entire country was involved. The best qualities of our people were seen in those anxious days of 1986: selflessness, humanity, high moral virtues. Many asked to be sent to

Chernobyl and offered help without thought for their own safety.

Eliminating the effects of the explosion cost initially 14 billion rubles, and then swallowed up several more billions. The organized efforts succeeded in limiting the number of victims and localizing the consequences of the accident. By July the idea of the 'sarcophagus' had been worked out and then this unique protective cover for the damaged reactor, with a permanent monitoring system, was built within a short time. The International Atomic Energy Authority (IAEA) observers were satisfied that everything possible and necessary was being done.

Nevertheless, it is necessary to say with all honesty that in the first days we just did not have a clear understanding that what had happened was not just a national catastrophe, but one that affected the whole world. We realized this as information came in. Both then and now there has been criticism of the actions of the leadership of Ukraine, Belorussia and the Soviet Union. Based on what I know, I would never suspect any of these individuals of having an irresponsible attitude towards the fate of people. If something was not done in a timely manner, it was mainly because of a lack of information. Neither the politicians, nor even the scientists and specialists, were prepared to fully grasp what had happened.

The closed nature and secrecy of the nuclear power industry, which was burdened by bureaucracy and monopolism in science, had an extremely bad effect. I spoke of this at a meeting of the Politburo on 3 July 1986: 'For thirty years you scientists, specialists and ministers have been telling us that everything was safe. And you think that we will look on you as gods. But now we have ended up with a fiasco. The ministers and scientific centres have been working outside of any controls. Throughout the entire system there has reigned a spirit of servility, fawning, clannishness and persecution of independent thinkers, window dressing, and personal and clan ties between leaders.'

The Cold War and the mutual secrecy of the two military alliances had also been a factor. There had been 151 significant radiation leaks at nuclear power stations throughout the world, but almost nothing was known about them or their consequences. Academician V. A. Legasov said that the likelihood of nuclear accidents was believed to be very small, and that science and technology throughout the world were not particularly prepared for them. Complacency and even flippancy ruled. I still recall what Academician A. P. Aleksandrov and Ye. P. Slavsky told the Politburo immediately after the accident. These men had stood at the heart of our nuclear power industry and were its creators – people who were honoured and respected. But what we heard from them were arguments like this: 'Nothing terrible has occurred. These things happen at nuclear reactors. Just drink a little vodka, have a bite to eat, have a good night's sleep – forget it.'

Departmentalism did more than just practical damage. Because of it, the moral principle without which knowledge can become a source of mortal danger had 'worn thin'. The fear of showing initiative, the dread of authority and the desire to avoid responsibility had an extremely adverse effect. The decision-making mechanism had failed the test.

Gradually, we began to see all the consequences of the accident clearly. At first the fate of Kiev and the Dnieper River was the greatest worry. But it turned out that Belorussia, especially Mogilev, was hit the hardest, because of wind patterns. Later contamination was detected in the Bryansk oblast and even further away, near Tula.

In mid-May I spoke on television. I expressed my sympathy to the victims, discussed the steps that were being taken and praised the bravery of the people who were dealing with the disaster. I also thanked everyone in other countries who had responded to our misfortune and who had extended a helping hand. First among these were the American doctors Robert Gale and P. Tarasaki and the IAEA President, Hans Blix. Government and public organizations, companies and private citizens from many countries had sent firefighting equipment, machinery and pharmaceuticals. This was an unprecedented display of solidarity. At the same time, some foreign propaganda centres, in a stream of accusations, showed that they were less interested in the tragedy itself than in using it to discredit our new policy. Even in our country there were a few who tried to treat Chernobyl as a subject for political speculation. In this connection I want to turn to the matter of how our people and the world were kept informed about this disaster.

There were two opinions in the Politburo. One was that information should be given out gradually so as not to cause a panic and even greater harm. Even today we see attempts to hold back or even suppress information about problems at nuclear power stations. Nevertheless, a different point of view prevailed in the Politburo – information should be released completely, as it arrived, without limitation, so long as it was reliable. This was my view. Ryzhkov, Ligachev, Yakovlev, Medvedev and Shevardnadze supported me. Chernobyl became a difficult test for glasnost, democracy and openness.

Telegrams containing exhaustive and up-to-date information were sent to the leaders of other countries. On 6 and 9 May Shcherbina and members of his commission held press conferences in Moscow. In mid-May representatives of the press, including the foreign press, travelled to Ukraine and were allowed to see for themselves whether Kiev was a 'dead city' and whether 'thousands of people' had died, as had been reported by the mass media in the West. A delegation headed by Academician Legasov was sent to Vienna. The reports presented there impressed the IAEA by their quality, precision and openness.

The government commission made its report to the Politburo on 3 July, in a meeting at which representatives of the republics were present. The first wide-ranging discussion of the reasons for the Chernobyl accident was held and the question of the future of the nuclear power industry was raised. The prospects of the 'peaceful atom' had now become the subject of wide-ranging public debate – in particular because of the problems of outdated nuclear power plants and the construction of new plants, especially in seismically unstable areas like Armenia or the Crimea.

After much reflection and listening to the findings of the nuclear proponents and opponents, including many world authorities, I concluded that we could not do without nuclear power for the present. Academician Sakharov said: 'It appears that in the future nuclear energy will have to play an increasingly important role, but of course, it must be made safe.' I. V. Kurchatov[1] had warned of this: 'You have to treat a nuclear reactor with the utmost caution – it won't forgive mistakes, and accidents will happen when people forget this.'

Later a long-term programme for eliminating the effects of the Chernobyl accident, based on proposals from Ukraine, Belorussia and the Russian Federation, was developed by the government and approved by the USSR Supreme Soviet. Evaluations of nuclear power station technology were commissioned, and proposals were made to join efforts to improve nuclear safety throughout the world and to increase participation in IAEA activity. I called for an end to nuclear testing and announced that the Soviet Union would extend its own moratorium on such tests.

Chernobyl was a bell calling mankind to understand what kind of age we live in. It made people recognize the danger of careless or even criminally negligent attitudes towards the environment. Public opinion now focused on the acute problems that the environmental movement had been pointing out.

Chernobyl shed light on many of the sicknesses of our system as a whole. Everything that had built up over the years converged in this drama: the concealing or hushing up of accidents and other bad news, irresponsibility and carelessness, slipshod work, wholesale drunkenness. This was one more convincing argument in favour of radical reforms.

AFTER THE CONGRESS

Chernobyl made me and my colleagues rethink a great many things. We saw the need to strengthen discipline and order, first of all in the nuclear power industry. But as I pondered these matters I became ever more convinced that the problem could not be solved merely by administrative pressure, punishment, stringent measures, Party penalties and reprimands. We had to move perestroika forward.

[1] The Soviet physicist who was the 'father of the Soviet atomic bomb'.

Mostly I feared that this time, as had happened in the past, everything would be drowned in propaganda. The first signs of this were slogans appearing in public places – 'Implement the decisions of the XXVIIth Congress' – and newspaper reports about the unanimous approval of these decisions. A quiet burial of the planned transformations was being prepared. To prevent an ignominious end to our ideas we first had to take control of the drafting of the new Five Year Plan covering the years 1986–90.

A Central Committee plenum was held on 16 June after numerous discussions of the 12th Five Year Plan in the government and Politburo. In my report I outlined the transformations that were planned to ensure stable growth rates for the national income. This was the first notice that in the next five year plan all branches of the economy were to be converted to new methods of economic management.

The plenum's decision made the new economic course fairly specific. But I could see that many of those who took part in the discussions were uneasy. People who for decades had held high positions were clearly worried that innovations would catapult them from their armchairs. With the leadership cadres in this frame of mind it was difficult to expect success.

Because of this, I held a meeting with the secretaries and heads of the Central Committee departments a week later. I shared my impressions of the plenum and noted that the Party organizations and leadership cadres were adjusting too slowly: if we did not have a 'minor revolution' in the Party we would not succeed. Many Party committees were engaging in very little reform and were just trying to sit things out. This was unacceptable and dangerous. The public had been awakened, and people were waiting for change. The Central Committee Secretariat could not just stand aside and watch.

One can see from the notes of the many discussions and conversations how deeply worried we were by the cadre problem then. Just before my trip to the Far East at the end of July 1986, at a meeting with local newspaper editors, I reproached them for indecisiveness and 'silence'. They answered bitterly: 'Mikhail Sergeyevich, tell all of this to the secretaries of the Party raikoms, gorkoms and obkoms. Our newspapers are, after all, their mouthpieces, and they do not want glasnost.'

My trip to Vladivostok, Komsomolsk-on-Amur and Khabarovsk convinced me that these editors were right. I could not have imagined such incompetence and indifference to the everyday lives of ordinary people as I found there. Openness and glasnost, of course, were the last things that the local bosses needed. No, they were absolutely not interested in airing dirty linen in public.

The Far East, a region of exceptional importance for the country, lacked attention and concern from the Centre. Problems that came up here were solved hugger-mugger, usually in great haste, when a catastrophe was imminent. My talks with officials, scientists, specialists and local residents provided me with much valuable material that was later used in decisions about the development of this area. This trip also helped me to understand what was happening away from Moscow and how perestroika was being received there. The answers were not comforting: the Party and administrative structures were not responding to the people's hopes for change – the 'bureaucratic nobility', instinctively or intentionally, was sabotaging perestroika and did not wish to decide even the simplest issues.

For example, I understood that you could not solve the housing problems of fishery workers in Vladivostok all at once: time and substantial investment were needed. But it was hard to figure out why the city officials of Komsomolsk-on-Amur and the local defence enterprises (which after all were able to build modern submarines and aircraft), knowing that their cargo planes flew goods to Tashkent almost every day, could not be bothered to arrange for them to bring back fruit and vegetables on the return trip. Why, in the heat of the summer, could not ice cream be made for the kids? Why were the residents of the city forced to travel to distant republics, to Central Asia, to buy furniture, when all that was needed was to expand local production?

The thing I heard the most during the trip was: 'Mikhail Sergeyevich, you have to let us choose our own leaders and to put intelligent, honest, hard-working people into office. Then things will get better.'

On 20 August I left for Nizhnyaya Oreanda in the Crimea, but I was unable to get any rest. I could not adjust to the idea of a holiday: I was filled with concern and anxiety and had a heavy heart. At the coast I continued to think over the situation, make notes and give instructions. Although I was certain that a radical renewal of the cadres and a new system for their selection and placement were needed, I reflected more and more often that the problem lay not only in the people, but also in the fact that they were operating within the strict framework of a system that left little room for initiative in economics or politics. Hence there would have to be some reform of the system itself.

Confidential information sent to me in the Crimea, press material and telephone talks with Ligachev (he had stayed in Moscow to 'mind the shop') and Central Committee and Party oblast committee secretaries reinforced my impression that the reforms were slipping. Without finishing my holiday, I left for Krasnodar and Stavropol. I wanted to be in places that I knew well and to talk with people and test my ideas.

No miracle had happened. Both in Krasnodar and in Stavropol I once again saw that things were changing only very slowly. Popular support for perestroika had not abated and had even become stronger, but the Party and administrative structures were immovable. It was as if no-one was against perestroika, everyone was 'for it', but nothing was changing. Was this a misunderstanding of what was happening, an inability to act in a new way, or was the instinct for self-preservation warning that what is 'new' carries significant danger?

Much later, in November 1991, I met Ed Hewitt, an economist and aide to the President of the USA. He told me: 'Beginning in 1985 I flew to Moscow three years in a row, immersing myself in the atmosphere of the capital, and met politicians, journalists, artists and writers. What were my impressions? Perestroika was going at full speed – a real tidal wave! Then I travelled from the capital into the countryside. Go some hundred or two hundred kilometres away and things were completely different – all quiet, no change.'

REORGANIZING THE CADRES

A discussion of the cadre problem was needed. Preparation for the plenum had begun in early autumn. The work on my report proved slow, and the plenum, which had been planned for autumn, had to be put off twice. At a Politburo meeting on 1 December, I mentioned my last meeting with the oblast committee secretaries and noted that many of them were still practising old methods: 'I am convinced that the main reason for stagnation is the fossilization of leading officials. If we wish to right things, the cadres and cadre policy must be changed. This is a question of our moral right to lead. People simply do not believe those who have soiled their hands.'

Each of the Politburo members had his own slant on things. Gromyko insisted on an 'optimistic direction in the report'. Shevardnadze wanted a more critical appraisal of the situation in the Party and the decline in its credibility. Solomentsev proposed that the report should speak more strongly about the 'exploitation of socialism by loafers and greedy people'. But in spite of all of those differences in emphasis the basic ideas of the report were supported by the Politburo.

Shortly before the end of the year I summoned the directors of Central Committee departments, who were objects of much dissatisfaction. I said: 'I know that there is discontent in the Party apparatus. After all, playing up to the higher authorities doesn't work today; competence, conscientiousness and responsibility are what count now. Many lack these qualities. The position that the Party staff and other officials held for many years is not acceptable to the leadership of the Central Committee. The situation in the country has become more and more difficult, decisions have been sidetracked, but the staff have kept quiet, or, at most, wrote memos.

'This position must be condemned and discarded. There are also some staff workers who count on the collapse of reforms and who secretly rejoice at each failure.

'The secretary of one of the Moscow district committees recently said: "Let's wait, in a couple of years things will settle down." He is convinced that perestroika will be buried. There

252

must be no place in the Party staff for such people. The nomenklatura approach to cadre policy must be rejected. We will not change the situation or implement perestroika if we do not democratize the Party and society.'

In this way I tested, one by one, the ideas for my report. Each meeting gave food for thought and for the formulation of tasks and at the same time gave us a real sense of what they call in mechanics 'the resistance of material'. (I recall that in a Politburo meeting Ryzhkov said that of sixty ministers not a single one had asked to retire, although the age for retirement for many of them had long passed.)

There was a moment in Zavidovo when the discussion of the structure and problems of the report became so heated that I nearly got into a quarrel with my closest aides. Even the presence of Raisa Maksimovna could not restrain our emotions and we stopped our work until the next day. In the final account this incident proved to be useful because, when passions died down, we quickly agreed on the disputed issues. All in all, the report was quite unlike previous ones and was a significant step towards understanding the past and choosing the right path for the future. Even though I had conferred with the Politburo members about many of its fundamental themes, nevertheless I was a little uneasy as we began the discussion of the report on 19 January 1987. I knew from preliminary conversations that I could count on the solidarity of Ryzhkov and the energetic, even emotional, support of Shevardnadze. I sensed, from a private conversation with him, that Vorotnikov was cautious, but what about the others? Would they support the basic ideas of democratization? After all, this essentially meant the end of the nomenklatura approach.

'The reality surpassed all expectation', as the saying goes. Essentially everyone supported the draft report and the critical issues raised in it helped to create an atmosphere of frankness that was unusual in that company. Possibly, feelings were awakened that had for many years been dormant somewhere in the depth of their souls. The tone was set by Gromyko: 'The draft is very profound . . . there are cadres who have not yet shown themselves, and there are those who won't be able to cope . . . The question is: is the socialist state to be or not to be?'

Ryzhkov noted that the 'criticism is severe, but does not convey a sense of hopelessness.' He spoke unequivocally in favour of the section on democratization and linked this theme to the problems of the economy. He proposed that term limitation be introduced for government offices, including ministers, and that there should be secret elections for Party committee secretaries.

Ligachev must have noticed that the report contained practically nothing of the routine material which he had approved and which had been prepared by the Central Committee's department. However, he praised the draft report. He supported the need for reform of the political system. 'Something must be done to keep us from going through periodic crises, which inflict incalculable harm. I am certain: the key is democratization.'

This theme was taken up by Shevardnadze. Recalling the Afghan war, he noted that formerly the principle of collective leadership had often been violated and decisions were made by a narrow group, bypassing even the Politburo, not to mention the CPSU Central Committee and higher state organs. Now 'an entire system of measures that guarantee against repetition of these errors is being developed. This is a moral revolution.'

Since Yeltsin had not volunteered to speak, I turned to him and asked if he would like to say something. He began by saying that he 'supported most of the points made in the report', shared the critical evaluation of the past, but considered it necessary to give a precise evaluation of the perestroika period. He also said that the members of past Politburos and Central Committees were responsible for the country's stagnation and sluggish development, and each of them should therefore be mentioned and criticized by name.

In summing up this long discussion, I noted that the plenum's main task was to bring to light the deep-seated factors that had led to today's situation and to provide support for perestroika, which was encountering serious difficulties. I spoke against reducing the analysis of the past merely to an evaluation of members of the leadership and of past Central Committees. Our priority was to draw political conclusions and lessons to be learned for the future. Perestroika was progressing too slowly, and the report noted that much of the blame lay with the cadre policy and with the methods of working of our administrative structures. We had to seek fresh forces, but the persecution of cadres and ruining their futures under the guise of increased insistence on high standards could not be allowed. Perestroika was begun in the name of establishing democratic principles in society and the Party, and these goals could not be achieved by undemocratic methods. I promised that, as far as possible, all of the most relevant comments would be integrated into the report.

When I finished speaking, Yeltsin appeared embarrassed and dejected: at that time many people in Moscow were complaining about his rudeness, lack of objectivity and even cruelty. I realized that it was not easy to work in Moscow and that Yeltsin, perhaps more acutely than others, was feeling the resistance of the Moscow Party and economic nomenklatura to perestroika. Nevertheless, I felt that such an attitude was unacceptable. 'I've learned my lesson,' Yeltsin suddenly said, 'and I think that it was not too soon.'

Ligachev's concluding remark was: 'The most difficult thing is to get used to the idea that you too may be slammed . . .'

THE JANUARY PLENUM

Ligachev was right when he said at a Politburo meeting: 'The XXVIIth Congress answered the question of what had happened, but the January plenum answered the question of why.' Indeed, the January plenum was the beginning of a probing analysis of every aspect of the nation's past and the first step on our road towards democracy.

At the plenum, thirty-four members of the Central Committee, of the seventy-seven who signed up to speak, took the floor. Every single one criticized the bureaucracy; every one had his hand raised in support of democratization.

Still, this plenum, which differed sharply from preceding ones in the uninhibited discussion, kept to old positions on the main issue; no-one dared to question the legitimacy of the Party's monopoly in appointing cadres. How to combine free elections with the nomenklatura mechanism was a subject that the speakers preferred to side-step.

The January 1987 plenum was also the first time that opposition to glasnost surfaced.

I was surprised to hear Valentina Golubeva, a weaver and twice a Hero of Socialist Labour say: 'I believe that the time for criticism for the sake of criticism and inspections just for the sake of identifying problems has dragged on too long. We must firmly and clearly distinguish concerned, constructive criticism from idle criticism and sometimes just plain malicious carping... People are savouring the shortcomings and seeing very little of what is positive. There should be a sense of proportion in everything. There is the danger of going to the opposite extreme . . .'

There were warning signs that the Party elite would not quietly accept the loss of their privileged position. Glasnost, as was expected, became the first skirmish in the battle for freedom.

The plenum approved the report, agreeing with our evaluations of the causes of the crisis in the late 1970s and early 1980s and supported the idea of democratization and the proposal to hold an all-Union Party conference.

At the same time, it became clear that many members of the Central Committee were not ready for the unexpected turn that the report implied. If that was the case, what reaction could we expect from Party officials and from all of the vast nomenklatura?

Historians will probably see 1986–7 as the first serious crisis of perestroika, and they will be right. We were feeling 'underground tremors', even though society was expecting happy and swift changes and did not yet sense what cataclysms lay in store, what difficulties and grief the stubborn resistance of retrogradists and the aggressiveness of radicals would bring.

The atmosphere was changing, as if someone had thrown open a window in a stuffy room and let in fresh air. This feeling was reflected even in songs. Two songs appeared with the same title, 'Fresh Breeze'.

THE ISSYK-KUL FORUM

An event that was to play an important role in the years of perestroika took place in October 1986. This was the gathering of leading artists and intellectuals at Issyk-Kul: Arthur Miller, Alexander King, Alvin Toffler, Peter Ustinov, Omer Livanelli, Federico Mayor, Afevork Tekle. The initiator of the forum was our writer Aitmatov. The purpose of the meeting was to discuss the nuclear threat, environmental pollution and the lack of morality, especially in politics.

I met the participants on 20 October, a week after the Reykjavik summit with President Reagan. We spent several hours in free-flowing conversation. I reminded them of Lenin's notion of 'the priority of the interests of social development over the interests of classes'. I said that this principle was of particular importance in the age of nuclear missiles and that we wanted it to be understood and recognized throughout the world.

This conversation, where Lenin's notion was re-interpreted in the light of today's realities, was reported in *Kommunist*.[1] It made an impact both in our country and abroad, especially the theme of universal human values. For the advocates of orthodox thinking, it was as if a bomb had gone off. Imagine the heated discussions and puzzled questions that came up at subsequent meetings of our Party activists!

'We don't reject universal human values,' Ligachev said to me, 'but you just can't throw out class interests.'

'Yes, but I am speaking about the priority of universal human values. This doesn't mean that we are negating class, group, national and other interests. However, it is clear that they will become meaningless if we fail to join together to prevent nuclear war. What importance will interests be in this case, or even classes? Everything will go up in smoke . . .'

We already had differing views of the changed world and new realities. At that time I suddenly realized how difficult it would be to make our way through the wall of hardened dogma! It

---

[1] Party theoretical journal.

seemed obvious: the nuclear threat, the ecological crisis, the division of the world – it was folly to move further in these directions. But now suspicions began to arise: 'There is a smell of anti-Marxist heresy here . . . Gorbachev has shown his hand – he has a hidden agenda.'

10

MORE LIGHT

MY TRIP TO LENINGRAD IN MAY 1985, IN WHICH THERE WAS unusual contact between leader and people, can be considered as 'the first event of glasnost'. My speech, given without any notes or preliminary consultations with my colleagues, created a real problem for the Politburo. Much of what was in the unpublished material of the March and April Central Committee plenums, what had been discussed 'in secret' in the upper echelons of the Party, was 'spilled out' for the first time for everyone to hear.

But what happened next?

As I was saying farewell to Zaikov at the airport, he gave me a videocassette of my speech at a meeting in Smolny with the activists of the city's Party organization. On Sunday at my dacha I decided to watch it with my family. Everyone was excited: 'I think everybody should hear this.' I thought: perhaps I should send copies to the obkoms? Let them hear the speech in its entirety, rather than just sound-bites on television and radio! It was hard to decide, because this might look like self-promotion. I telephoned Ligachev and said: 'Yegor Kuzmich, take a look at the video of my speech and tell me what you think. Do you think it would be a good idea to send it to the obkoms?'

A little later he phoned me back: 'I think that except for perhaps a few sentences this should be shown in its entirety on television. Zimyanin feels the same way.' Once I heard this from Ligachev (then my right-hand man) and Zimyanin (the chief ideologist), I agreed. Anyone who followed events at that time will remember what a lively response this speech produced in the country.

259

People began to hope that indeed something would begin to change.

The first step towards glasnost had been made, but there was still a long journey ahead. True, the head of the Department of Propaganda had been replaced in the summer of 1985, but for the entire enormous ideological machine of the Party – the apparatchiks, the press, Party schools, the Academy of Social Sciences and so forth – it was business as usual. The system could be altered only by opening up 'windows', one by one, in this system of total secrecy, and only the General Secretary had the means of doing this.

My interview for the American magazine *Time* in early September and the interview I gave to three French television correspondents in October were among those breakthroughs towards openness. As usual, the editors of *Time* who had requested an interview were asked to submit their questions in advance. The answers were prepared in writing, but when the Americans came for them on the appointed day we got into a lively discussion, which was published in its entirety in *Pravda* and met with great interest in our country and in the world. My meeting with French journalists on the eve of my visit to Paris had a similar result. It was a live broadcast and the journalists were quite aggressive, at times even rude, asking blunt questions. But I do not think I lost that battle.

For me these two interviews meant a new experience, a kind of personal achievement. I had the feeling that I had crossed a line. It is one thing to speak from a rostrum to a favourably minded, 'disciplined' auditorium, and another thing to speak face to face, when you may be interrupted at any moment with objections. I did not feel at ease immediately; at first I spoke cautiously, but gradually I warmed up, and stopped thinking about whether I was being recorded or whether this was a live transmission.

My new style of dealing with the media provided an example for other Party leaders. It came into general use and began to seem normal and everyday, although at first it was perceived as something unusual – delighting some and provoking censure in others.

The next step on our road toward glasnost was the encouragement of media criticism of those failings and abuses which in the past could not be mentioned aloud. Society had grown so tired of all kinds of restrictions and bans that one had only to give journalists a little 'oxygen' and they were seized by the criticism fever. They immediately ran into resistance from the nomenklatura, even persecution, which was particularly ferocious in the provinces.

I myself began to see that some of them were going too far: criticism began to be insulting and vicious; frankly libellous materials based on the distortion of facts were being published. Nearly every week 'daring' publications such as *Ogonek*, *Moskovskiye Novosti* and *Argumenty i fakty* would test the level of openness permitted at that moment. There was grumbling about this at the Central Committee plenums and among the Party staff and leadership. I had the growing conviction that it was vital to protect glasnost against encroachment, although the mass media should also be accountable. Both of these aims could be achieved by adopting a law on the press, rather than by yelling at the editors. I began to think about this some time in 1986, but quite a while passed before it could be realized.

Thanks to glasnost, perestroika began to find an increasingly broad social base. It is difficult to overestimate the importance of this. And it could only be done by truly committed people at the newspapers and television and radio stations, who day in, day out would describe and explain these new ideas. Without this we could hardly hope for practical results from the policy of perestroika.

I placed particular value on glasnost when I realized that the initiatives coming from the top were more and more often obstructed in the vertical structures of the Party apparatus and administrative organs. Freedom of speech made it possible to go over the heads of the apparatchiks and turn directly to the people, to give them the incentive to act and to win their support. The feedback that resulted also had the effect of stimulating the initiators of the reforms.

CLOSED ZONES

Soon we were faced with the question of what to do about 'zones that are closed to criticism'. Brezhnev preferred to spare his comrades-in-arms in the 'upper echelons', on whom he was dependent in one way or another. Was criticism of Kunayev, Shcherbitsky, Rashidov or Aliyev or of 'Grishin's Moscow' ever to be permitted? It was simply unthinkable.

The issue became broader. One could criticize almost everyone in the Soviet district government, even the chairman of the district executive committee, but not the district first party secretary, unless he were removed by higher-ups. This was an iron rule and, as Party workers of higher and higher rank found that they were no longer in the 'zone off limits to criticism', their reactions were very intense. There were scores of telephone calls to editors, to the Central Committee, people complaining about television and newspapers that were so 'bold' as to expose these 'princes' in their fiefdoms! Many complained about V. Afanasiev, the editor of *Pravda*. The oblast Party organizations kept records of how many times *Pravda*, the central Party organ, had mentioned them in a positive way and how many times it had criticized them, and they literally demanded that a 'balance' be kept 'so as not to offend the communists and workers of the oblast'. A great deal of lobbying was done via the Central Committee.

Taboo areas included everything to do with actual military expenditure, the situation in the army in general, the state of scientific research in the military-industrial complex, and data on how efficiently financial and material resources for defence were being used. Not even the Politburo members knew the full picture. They often authorized decisions on top-secret matters without the right to question or discuss them. When Ustinov was in charge of the defence industry, he essentially had monopoly control over these affairs. Besides Brezhnev, none of the Politburo members dared even to appear interested in this area, let alone demanding any information about it. Incidentally, the practice of soldiers persecuting new recruits had gone on for a long time, but had always been hushed up.

Foreign trade was another taboo area, especially the area of weapons deliveries, their amounts, types, destinations, payment, etc. Almost the same secrecy extended to trade in grain, oil, gas and metals. Detailed information about these was published in all foreign reference sources, but here it was guarded from the public as an important state secret.

The KGB was entirely off-limits. The most that ever came from the KGB were cryptic reports about the exile of a spy or connections between dissidents and some 'imperialist intelligence service'.

Almost all statistics were kept under a tight lid of censorship. Data on the economy, social questions, culture and demography were published exclusively by special resolution of the Central Committee, with great amounts of material either removed or 'cleaned up', especially anything to do with the standard of living. Information about crime and medical statistics was kept under lock and key.

It was not just the military budget, but the real state budget was also a secret. The budget deficit was kept from the public. Millions of depositors did not suspect that the deficit was being covered by illegal borrowing from their savings banks. Moreover, no-one knew that the growth rate of expenditure on defence in many years was one and one-half or two times greater than the planned and actual increases of national income!

The draft budget was submitted to the deputies of the USSR Supreme Soviet in 'perfect order'. It contained the item 'other expenses', which involved 100–120 billion rubles, but none of the representatives of the people risked the question: 'Just what are these "other expenses"?' After all, they were not just a minor item – they amounted to one fifth of the entire budget.

What was the usual reaction to any isolated attempt to obtain information on a 'sensitive matter'? It was either simply ignored or we were told that higher state interests did not permit disclosure of this information.

It was unbelievably difficult to open such 'closed zones'. Every attempt ran up against fierce resistance from the various agencies, growling from the keepers of the secrets and moaning from the ideologists. This was understandable. After all, the removal of the curtain of secrecy was tantamount to a death sentence for some organizations – their uselessness would be exposed. And the ideologists, who stood watch over the system, assumed, and rightly so, that truth would undermine faith in our system. Not just the emperor but the entire 'court' would be found to have no clothes.

GLASNOST AND THE ENVIRONMENT

Glasnost dramatically opened up to the public the subject of the environment, although it had not been completely banned before. Even under Stalin the newspapers had reported the losses of forest land and the importance of the protective forest strips created at the behest of the 'great helmsman'. Under Khrushchev a fashionable subject was the battle against swamps and marshes and the salination of the soil. And under Brezhnev the press would sometimes write about certain acute ecological problems – in Lake Baikal, the Aral Sea, Lake Ladoga, the Caspian Sea, the Sea of Azov.

Nonetheless, there was a strict boundary that absolutely could not be crossed. Only scraps of information reached the public. No-one even imagined the extent of our ecological disaster, how far we were behind the developed nations as a result of our barbaric attitude towards nature. Glasnost for the first time allowed the people to obtain not just isolated, carefully filtered crumbs of information, but rather the whole truth about what was happening to our land, our forests and our water, about the poor air quality in the cities. This gave a powerful impetus to the 'green' movement. People began to object to plans for the construction of major industrial works – especially nuclear power stations, chemical and metallurgical plants and airfields.

I recall how the people of Volgograd fought against the expansion of an agricultural chemicals plant, even though the planners guaranteed its ecological safety. It was the same elsewhere, even when the proposed factories were to produce pharmaceuticals or detergents, which were in short supply. Strong popular opposition forced the abandonment of a plan for diverting northern rivers, which threatened unpredictable cataclysms. Well-known writers stood up in defence of specific areas in the battle for the environment.

Glasnost revealed what an extravagant mindset we had: deluding ourselves that our natural resources would last for eternity. How unskilfully we extracted, or more precisely did not extract, oil! We trampled over the delicate plant cover of the tundra. We destroyed invaluable fish species when we built strings of electric power plants on the Volga River. In ninety cities – almost all of the major industrial cities of the Soviet Union – harmful substances in the atmosphere were found to be much higher than permissible norms. A wave of bitterness and anger rolled through the country when it came out that the genetic pool of our peoples had been threatened.

Even at that time 1,300 enterprises had to be shut down. Of course, this was hard for the economy and greatly complicated perestroika, but in spite of the objections of economic agencies and local authorities we supported public opinion in these matters. Enterprises whose products were needed for everyday life had to take immediate steps to meet ecological standards.

However, it was also necessary to speak out against overkill. For example, it was obvious that over-exploitation of the land could not be tolerated, but some fanatics demanded that we abandon land reclamation altogether. Some members of the leadership and economic managers used these excessive demands to argue that the green movement would ruin our economy. The reaction of the intelligentsia to environmental problems began to turn to generalizations. To some, these problems were only additional evidence of the 'original sins' of our system, while to others they were the result of short-sightedness, irresponsibility and mismanagement by the Party and state leadership. An all-out attack was launched against the government. Ryzhkov simply lost self-control at times. Once he exploded at a Politburo meeting in response to an extremely malicious television attack: 'I will not allow myself or my family to be insulted!'

CHILDREN OF THE ARBAT AND OTHER BREACHES IN THE WALL

Glasnost also meant the return of banned films that had been locked away in secret archives, the publication of highly critical works, including practically all 'dissident' and émigré works.

Rybakov's novel *Children of the Arbat* was an acid test of sorts for glasnost. Anatoly Rybakov sent me a letter and his manuscript, which Raisa Maksimovna and I read. From the artistic standpoint, it did not make a great impression on us, but it recreated the atmosphere of Stalinist times. The manuscript was read by dozens of people, who began to flood the Central Committee with letters and reviews calling the book 'the novel of the century'. It became a social phenomenon even before it was published. Rybakov had made himself a name with his books *Yekaterina Voronina* and *Heavy Sand*. I felt that the book had to be published and I was supported by Ligachev. The publication of Rybakov's novel helped to conquer the fear that many people still had of the consequences of unmasking totalitarianism.

Another test of this kind was the leadership's reaction to Tengiz Abuladze's film *Repentance*. It had been produced under the personal 'protection' of Shevardnadze and had been given a private screening at the House of Film and then shown in a few other closed halls. The film was a real bombshell; it became both an artistic and a political phenomenon. The ideologists wanted a discussion in the Politburo about whether or not to release it for general viewing. I objected, saying that this matter should be resolved by the cinematographers' and artists' unions, who had been waiting for this signal. Thus a precedent was set and soon censored works began to spill out. Publishers began to issue new works by Aitmatov, Astafiev, Rasputin, Mozhaev and other writers who had gone beyond the conventions of socialist realism and who were striving to restore the great traditions of Russian literature based on critical realism. Works by Karamzin, S. Soloviev, Klyuchevsky, Kostomarov and other historians began to be published in large editions. They were followed by books from the Russian émigré classics: Bunin, Merezhkovsky, Nabokov, Zamyatin and Aldanov. And then there came the 'homecoming' for a constellation of great thinkers who had been ostracized after the revolution: V. Soloviev, Feodorov, Berdiaev, Florensky, Ilyin.

I will not try to name them all. I mention only those whose works I got to know, even superficially. In those days I often thought: how sad that I could not have read all of this back in my student days! Yes, our generation was spiritually cheated, given meagre intellectual rations consisting of ideology alone and deprived of the chance to compare different schools of philosophical thought for ourselves and to make our own choices.

BRAKES ON GLASNOST

Glasnost was a powerful weapon, and people soon realized it. Instead of fairy tales of faked triumphs, Moscow was now receiving more information about the real state of affairs. The top echelons either had to adapt to the new situation or fight it; and many did the latter.

At a conference of regional and local press editors in Moscow there was wailing and gnashing of teeth. 'The authorities are strangling us,' they complained. 'They are trying to oust us from our jobs, they are setting up investigations and sullying the reputations of journalists who dare to air our dirty linen.' But different howls could be heard from the 'authorities': 'They're undermining our foundations, they are encroaching on socialism, the socialist edifice is being destroyed!' Our local bosses, whether managers of enterprises, collective farms, districts or oblasts, were used to criticism from above and suffered it in silence. But for just anyone, even subordinates, to be free to judge their work was something that had never happened and it was seen as a shaking of the foundations. Complaints poured into the Kremlin.

At the editors' conference mentioned above we learned much that indicated that the bureaucracy was maintaining a strong defence, and not letting the press out from under its strict control. The press was not always in a fighting mood; more often than not it was still easily intimidated. We began to encourage the central press organs to publish articles in support of the regional press.

Reviews of the most interesting material from local newspapers were printed, and correspondents who were being persecuted for their criticism were protected.

It was not just the nomenklatura that put the brakes on the progress of glasnost. The roots extended into the very system of mass media control that had been inherited from Stalin's time. The centre retained total control over this sphere, 'from Moscow to the hinterlands'. No matter what the newspaper – Party, trade union, Komsomol newspapers, the writers' union newspapers, hunters' and fishermen's organizations or veterans' newspapers – Agitprop[1] watched over everyone. All editors had to be approved by the Party. Once or twice a month there were meetings at the Central Committee Department of Propaganda with chief editors, sometimes involving deputy chairmen of the Council of Ministers or actual ministers. Publications were praised or censured and instructions were given about what and how to write. Any change concerning newspapers or magazines – their frequency, volume, number of pages – had to be sanctioned by the Central Committee Secretariat. The Party apparatus was constantly 'watching' what was being published; officials reported their observations and evaluations to the leadership; conformists were rewarded and bothersome critics were severely punished.

Censorship played an enormous role in protecting the regime. Officially, the relevant organ was innocuously called Glavlit and it was supposed to ensure only that state secrets were not revealed in print. In fact, though, it was a kind of ideological KGB before which editors and publishers literally trembled. Glavlit's tasks included close supervision of the periodical press and, especially, libraries and archives. Its reports were the basis for the approval of lists of banned literature and decisions about what should be kept in special secret depositories, what was 'secret', 'top secret', or 'for official use only'.

This practice was abolished in 1988, another victory of glasnost. Glavlit remained, but lost its former functions. Gradually the special depositories emptied. The list of books

[1] Department of Agitation and Propaganda.

subject to a ban or partial ban was reviewed several times, until all of the books had been returned to open shelves. A. I. Solzhenitsyn's books were among these.

THE PRESS GETS OUT OF CONTROL

Meanwhile, readers began to see the difference between the official publications which had to strictly maintain the Party line and the less fettered press.

Independently minded publications began to appear. One of these was *Moskovskiye Novosti* (*Moscow News*), whose bold articles caused a commotion in some departments. I had to take the editor, Yegor Yakovlev, under my protection more than once, even though he was also giving me plenty of trouble.

Kommunist, the theoretical and political organ of the CPSU Central Committee, had spoken out against the new ideas from the very beginning of perestroika. This was not surprising: it was run by Kosolapov, a conceited 'philosopher' and fanatical adherent of the dogma of 'developed socialism'. For the first few months I somehow put up with this, because I did not want to look like a leader who would 'settle accounts' with his predecessors' protégés. However, people began to wonder about such tolerance, and finally I had to 'consolidate', as the phrase went, the leading Party publication. Ivan Timofeyevich Frolov was proposed as a replacement. He was a corresponding member of the USSR Academy of Sciences and had distinguished himself by his courageous opposition to the 'theories' of Lysenko.[1] He had successfully run the journal *Voprosi filosofii*, but had been removed by the notorious reactionary Trapeznikov, head of the Central Committee Department of Science. Frolov had also worked at the Communist and Workers' Party journal *Problemy mira i sotsializma* (*World Marxist Review*) in Prague. In short, he was the perfect candidate for the post of chief editor of *Kommunist*. Very soon the journal greatly improved, developing

[1] Lysenko was a biologist, supported by Stalin and Khrushchev. His theories proved to be incorrect, and their application in agriculture was disastrous.

and spreading the ideas of perestroika. I came to know Ivan Timofeyevich more closely and to value his independence of judgement, and eventually I decided to appoint him as an aide for ideological problems. We worked together through the most important stages of our quest, analysing the past and working on the theoretical elaboration of important aspects of perestroika.

Pravda played an active catalytic role in the criticism of the legacy of the period of stagnation. At first it set the tone in the 'clean-up' work, and other publications emulated it. Its criticisms were aimed at ever more powerful officials, and it raised important issues about the economic changes.

However, there was a paradox: the farther glasnost reached and the more boldly the editors of other newspapers spoke out, the dryer, duller and more orthodox the materials published by *Pravda*, the Party's central organ, became. *Pravda* went from being the leader to bringing up the rear; from reformist views it slid to conservative ones. Its popularity declined and its circulation rate fell, in spite of the fact that the Party committees in one way or another promoted its distribution.

Pravda was becoming increasingly unpopular. Moreover, the newspaper staff openly complained about their chief editor, Viktor Afanasiev. People were angry at his indifference and undisguised disregard of his colleagues, not to mention the fact that he was always busy writing another book, to the detriment of the paper. We had to find a new editor. Primakov, Boldin, Nenashev, even Kapto, were mentioned. Finally, I again chose Frolov. For this important position I wanted someone who was not only a professional in this field (an academician and an experienced editor), but also someone who could be trusted.

POLARIZATION OF PUBLIC OPINION

The gradual liberation of the press from the dictates of Agitprop revealed growing disagreements about the reforms that were being carried out. Two opposing camps eventually formed. One consisted of the reformers, which at that time was still supported by a radical destructive wing, while the other consisted of moderate conservatives, from which again the openly revanchist group had not yet separated.

Of course, this analysis is oversimplified. The range of opinions and positions was vast, with many 'intermediate' centrist views within both groups. The newspapers and magazines were entrenched as spokesmen for specific social aspirations and political trends. A fierce battle developed, with harsh accusations, attacks, invective and slander, and skeletons dragged out of cupboards for everyone to see. The clash of opinions frequently turned into unprincipled squabbling, behind which lay the selfish interests of certain groups or the new bosses of the mass media. I would meet with the press in order to cool passions and remind the journalists of their responsibility to the people. For a time I was able to calm the opposing sides down, but then the polemic would escalate and heat up, with everyone making his own 'original contribution' to this scuffle.

Glasnost broke out of the limits that we had initially tried to frame and became a process that was beyond anybody's control. From the standpoint of democratization the positive aspects are obvious. On the other side of the coin, the unprincipled wrangling in the mass media sowed hatred, animosity and intolerance in society.

This was the case with the evaluation of the nation's history after the October 1917 Revolution. Perhaps none of the trends of glasnost had such a strong effect or produced such a psychological shock as the restoration of a reliable, rather than a mythological, idealized and romanticized history of the Soviet period, which included, along with many examples of heroism by the people and indisputable social achievements, the abominable onslaught of bureaucracy, mass repression and the totalitarian suppression of free thought. The people read publications that exposed these crimes hungrily. There was a second wave of debunking of Stalin (the first came after the XXth Party Congress). The verdict on Brezhnev was unsparing. Finally, it came to a re-evaluation of Lenin himself, Marxist ideology and the principles of socialism.

Much that was facile and sensational poured out for all to hear. The events of the past were frequently retold without serious analysis of the complex and contradictory nature of the processes that had occurred in the country. The mantle of lies and demagoguery that had covered many episodes in our history was lifted, but prejudice and bitterness more and more often led to attempts to replace 'Red' myths with 'White' ones and to paint an entirely negative picture of the great October Revolution.

I believed that catharsis through knowledge of one's own history was vital and that the people were entitled to know the full truth about the past. I felt that the bans should be lifted from the archives and all documents made accessible, and that it was only fair and honest to show the true picture of everything that we had lived through: our achievements and the price we paid for them, the losses we suffered, and what the 'building of socialism' had meant for several generations of Soviet citizens. Obviously, everything that had been connected with Stalinism and its throwbacks had to be thoroughly analysed and the tragic lessons of totalitarianism had to be learned forever. Nonetheless, we had to respect the memory of our fathers and grandfathers, who, in spite of their trials and tribulations, had continued to believe in the ideals of the October Revolution. Only then would we be able to understand the older generations who had lived through the Stalinist period, and who felt insulted and rejected by all the changes in society.

GLASNOST AND THE INTELLIGENTSIA

Under the ideological monopoly of the Party, cliques ruled the artists' unions, acting as intermediaries between the authorities and the intelligentsia. The scientific and artistic community – in the broad sense, the creative world – was firmly locked into the overall system of the distribution of roles, influence and the sharing of the 'government pie'. The Communist leaders realized perfectly the importance of the 'rulers of the mind', the 'engineers of the human soul', especially in Russia. While relentlessly making short work of opposition philosophers, artists, writers and musicians, Stalin had tried in every way to patronize those artists and writers who, either out of conviction or for their own survival, collaborated with the authorities. This was even more true under Khrushchev and Brezhnev. An enormous Party apparatus was set up to 'work' with the intelligentsia. 'Order' was maintained by a strict hierarchy in all areas of artistic activity. This had its own system of rewards and punishments and its own 'marshals' and 'generals' – Central Committee members, Supreme Soviet deputies, Heroes of Labour, who travelled around the world and who enjoyed the same privileges as the top levels of the Party apparatus. Their books were printed and reprinted in large editions, their pictures were regularly exhibited, their music was performed as if they were 'classics'.

It was clear from the outset that – spoiled and pampered as they were by the authorities – their primary concern was how to keep these privileges. Roughly speaking, one could distinguish three groups of people here. The first consisted of the conformists who were covered with medals and who were the cultural mainstay of the regime. The second consisted of those who, albeit trying to maintain some independence, were still not free from the temptation to beg a morsel from the 'master's table' – a bonus, a foreign trip, or an apartment. Finally, there was the third group – people of firm convictions who openly demonstrated their critical attitude towards what was going on in our society. To our ideological bosses and the leaders of the artists' unions these were a pain in the neck. They were subjected to restrictions, blackmail, and 'warnings'. Some gave in, but most withdrew into themselves and wrote 'for the bottom drawer'. In this group there were people with widely varying opinions and convictions, from 'pure Westernizers' to land-and-soil monarchists, from humanists and internationalists to fanatical nationalists.

By the time perestroika began, problems had accumulated in all spheres of culture. These had to be resolved not only within society as a whole, but also within the intellectual community itself, primarily in the artists' unions. This did not apply just to Moscow, even though all the leading art centres and most of the artistic world's luminaries were concentrated in the capital. The situation was similar in the republics, where strong national feelings were an additional factor. They were particularly obvious in

Georgia, but also manifested themselves in Belorussia and Ukraine.

Everywhere, culture and the arts were the preserve of ideological apparatchiks, whose principal task was to rally the intelligentsia 'around the Party' and to keep the dissidents 'under control'. Yet the root of all evil was not the unenlightened leadership, but the system.

Perestroika broke through one wall in the system after another. People began to speak their minds without fear and to attack the positions and privileges of the creative generals of the artistic world. The 'generals' ran to the authorities, crying: 'Protect us! After all, we have served you faithfully and truly!' But they soon realized that times had changed – they could not count solely on the favour of the bosses, who were no longer all-mighty, being themselves in a precarious position. All they could do was organize an all-round defence. The differences grew deeper and deeper, the polemics between writers' groups blazed even more fiercely and they joined ever closer into armies of like-minded thinkers. On the one side there were the journals *Nash Sovremennik, Molodaya gvardiya* and *Moskva*, and on the other *Znamya, Oktyabr* and *Novy Mir*. There were papers and journals in the middle, of course, but they were not setting the trend. Polarization spread to the popular press, flared up at congresses and plenums of artists' organizations, and drew all society into the battle. For some people the battle cry was: 'If the enemy does not surrender, destroy him!' No-one cared whether you were right or wrong, provided you were 'on our side'.

We were committed to giving people freedom – freedom of speech, thought and creativity – but how they used this freedom depended on the people themselves. It is with bitterness that I admit today that a significant number of the intelligentsia failed to make good use of this freedom for the benefit of society or even for themselves.

The conservative strongholds in the artists' unions were being destroyed by the advance of younger members. This bloodless revolution was triggered by the film-makers, who at their Vth Congress got rid of all of the former leaders of their union, electing E. Klimov as their new chairman. The writers, artists and architects soon followed suit. The 'die-hards' in the composers' union held out the longest; Tikhon Khrennikov, after all, was very influential and had for many decades led the Soviet musicians' organization. But in the end he too had to yield to 'new people'.

There was so much rejoicing at that time, so many excited speeches proclaiming the end of the dominance of red tape and incompetence and unheard-of opportunities opening for uncensored creativity. Indeed, a number of interesting stage productions, films and publications – mainly documentaries – appeared. But very soon the extreme radicalism of the reformers backlashed. Attempts to negate the artistic legacy of the Soviet period proved to be fruitless. After throwing out the former bosses and settling comfortably into their armchairs, the radicals were unable to create any major works, not to mention a normal creative atmosphere.

I did not have to agonize over the role of the artistic intelligentsia. From the start, I knew that they had an indispensable role to play in mobilizing people for perestroika. But first we had to make them part of perestroika, and that was not at all easy.

As perestroika continued and problems accumulated, the atmosphere at my meetings with the intellectuals changed. I did what I could to cool passions and ease bitterness, but was increasingly frustrated. Group interests ruled: battles for control of a journal, or of Litfond,[1] for seats on union secretariats or boards. Creative or common interests were put on the back burner. It is embarrassing to recall how some members of the intelligentsia behaved both at home and abroad, how much hysterical vilification one had to hear.

Maybe we should make some allowance for the deep spiritual crisis of our intelligentsia. After all, for decades the launch-pad for the creative process had been our specific social environment – its problems, conflicts and dramas – and this had been reflected in their creative works; now suddenly everything was 'not quite right', and needed to be revised. Thus many artists and writers found their work had been for naught and was not needed now by anyone.

[1] The writers' pension and social security fund.

Of course, I am convinced that opinions of this kind, extremely unjust and inaccurate in their one-sidedness, will some day be refuted. The superiority of true talent will eventually be rediscovered – it will not matter whether work was done from the standpoint of socialist realism or any other viewpoint. But will this belief really ease the suffering of the artist who today sees his works exposed to sneers and condemned to oblivion?

It is obvious that the revolution in thinking kindled by perestroika hit the intelligentsia hardest. For this reason I am not inclined to judge them severely, not to speak of denouncing them. The intelligentsia suffered the changes more sharply than anyone else. People whose very profession called for them to analyse and describe events were on the edge of a chasm. It was a serious crisis and not everyone could cope with it. Many became hysterical and viciously attacked both perestroika and me personally. Some sought vengeance for the destruction of their formerly comfortable lives. Others, intoxicated by freedom, tried to outdo one another in a show of courage.

11

THE FIRST ATTEMPT AT
ECONOMIC REFORM

AFTER A TRIP TO LATVIA AND ESTONIA IN FEBRUARY 1987 I TOOK a short holiday, leaving on 9 March for Pitsunda. Before my departure I raised the question of a plenum on economic reform in the Politburo. I asked Ryzhkov, Slyunkov and Medvedev to develop suggestions on this matter. I myself began reading material on the economy.

My thoughts kept going back to the early 1980s, when Andropov asked me and Ryzhkov, together with leading scholars and specialists, to attempt an objective analysis of the state of the national economy. The need for structural changes was clear even then, but there had to be many changes in the country before they could begin.

As I have mentioned before, only two or three people had access to data on the military-industrial complex. We were, of course, aware of how heavily our exorbitant military expenditure weighed on the economy, but I did not realize the true scale of the militarization of the country until I became General Secretary. Finally, although the leaders of the military-industrial complex opposed it, we published those data. It turned out that military expenditure was not 16 per cent of the state budget, as we had been told, but rather 40 per cent; and its production was not 6 per cent but 20 per cent of the gross national product. Of 25 billion rubles in total expenditure on science, 20 billion went to the military for technical research and development.

The economy continued to put more in and get less out. The costs of labour, fuel and raw material per unit of production were two to two and a half times higher than in the developed countries, while in agriculture they were ten times higher. We produced more coal, oil, metals, cement and other materials (except for synthetics) than the United States, but our end-product was at best half that of the USA.

In the 1960s and 1970s these negative trends were balanced by sharp increases in world oil and gas prices. We feverishly pumped oil from the fields of West Siberia without a thought for the future. But the rise in prices was followed by just as steep a fall and we were no better off than at the start. Economic growth had virtually stopped by the beginning of the 1980s and with it the improvement of the rather low living standard. The real *per-capita* income of the USSR was among the lowest of the socialist countries, not to speak of the developed Western nations.

We were faced with the prospect of social and economic decline. Finances were in disarray, and the economy was out of balance and in deficit. There was a shortage not only of foodstuffs and industrial goods, but also of metals, fuel and building materials, i.e. everything that was produced in enormous quantities. Latent, suppressed inflation began to make itself known through the black market. Speculation flourished. Economic ties were entangled in a dense network of 'unofficial relations' (extortions and gifts, bribery, exaggeration of results, embezzlement). State property began to be used for personal gain on a massive scale.

Production discipline was breaking down everywhere. There were mountains of uninstalled equipment, including imported goods. Cars and especially agricultural machines were being carelessly assembled and shipped with parts missing. There was pilferage *en route*, and on arrival they practically had to be assembled from the bottom up. Laxity had seized even the transport industry. Dozens of abandoned railway trucks loaded with goods stood in sidings and at line ends, subject to spoilage and pilferage.

Our analytical work in 1982–4 was more than just a statement of our economic woes. We tried to identify the underlying causes of the crisis and find ways to improve the economy. Here we were faced with a spectrum of opinions that would decide the practical activity of the leadership for years ahead.

There was perhaps only one thing about which no-one disagreed – the recognition of a general weakening of the management of the economy and its consequences – laxity and irresponsibility in production and at all levels of management. Andropov's policy of 'restoring order', which had received warm support at first, had its roots in this realization. But the one-sided emphasis on disciplinary measures immediately led to extremes that discredited the policy as a whole. It became clear that you could not go very far on discipline alone. A more fundamental approach was needed.

Opinions were divided on other issues. Independent specialists believed that the basic reason for the country's backwardness was that we had missed a new stage in the scientific and technological revolution, while the Western countries had moved far ahead both in restructuring their economies and in technological progress. The problem did not lie only in errors or in under-valuing science and technology, but rather in the archaic nature of our economic mechanisms, in the rigid centralization of administration, in over-reliance on planning and in the lack of genuine economic incentives. However, the recognition of the need to improve the economic mechanism did not go beyond the formula of 'more complete use of the potentialities of the socialist system'.

In the past blame was put on the economists in every critical analysis of problems and failures. Of course, they were responsible to some degree. Indeed, most economists had been broken of the habit of serious and unbiased research and were busy commenting on (or rather complimenting) Party decisions and the leaders' speeches and supporting the official ideological dogma. This was the pernicious result of the repression of our leading economists, the suppression of the progressive ideas developed by the exponents of mathematical economic theory, and periodic reprisals against our *tovarniks*.[1] Nevertheless, creative thinking in economics had not been choked off

[1] Those who advocated that supply and demand should influence prices.

completely, and critical and constructive work was still being produced. It played an invaluable role in the development of perestroika.

CHOOSING THE COURSE

In April 1985 we adopted a course towards 'acceleration of the social and economic development of the country'. This was the main topic at the June conference on problems of scientific and technological progress and it became the motto that the Party and its new leadership proclaimed both before and after the XXVIIth CPSU Congress. However, it was only in the spring of 1986 that the idea of 'acceleration' began to be used in combination with the notion of perestroika. This gave rise to the assertion that initially I had intended to increase industrial growth rates by applying the old methods, without attempting any serious reform of the system. How valid are these assertions?

I am not trying to idealize the economic policy of that time – its limitations and lack of depth became obvious soon enough. For some time we indeed hoped to overcome stagnation by relying on such 'advantages of Socialism' as planned mobilization of reserve capacities, organizational work, and evoking conscientiousness and a more active attitude from the workers.

The reader may say: you have just explained that even in 1984 you understood the need for structural reforms. Why then did you put them aside and continue to follow the old ways? The fact was that the extremely alarming economic situation that we had inherited required immediate measures. We felt that we could fix things, pull ourselves out of this hole by the old methods, and then begin significant reforms. This was probably a mistake that wasted time, but that was our thinking then.

Needless to say, the Party and state apparatus was interested in directing public expectations towards 'restoring order' without breaking up existing institutions. Ligachev, Solomentsev and, to some degree, Chebrikov and Vorotnikov approved this policy. Ryzhkov, Maslyukov and Talyzin emphasized scientific and technological progress, and we were backed by the economic managers – ministers and enterprise directors. Medvedev and Yakovlev advocated an immediate transformation in the economy.

While I was aware of the importance of economic reforms, I also believed that it was first necessary to try to modernize the economy – so as to set up conditions for radical economic reform by the early 1990s. This was the aim of the all-Union conference on scientific and technological progress. I note for clarity that these ideas were similar to Deng Xiaoping's reform methods in China.

The recommendations of the conference were translated into a programme for our machine-building[1] industry to be brought up to world standards by the early 1990s.

I placed particular hope on the 'target programmes of scientific and technological progress' for information science and computer technology, for the development of rotary and rotary-conveyor production lines, robotics, bio-technology, genetic engineering etc. These programmes, incidentally, called for significant restructuring of investment policy, extensive co-operation with the East European socialist countries, and the creation of joint ventures with Western firms, particularly in the Federal Republic of Germany. They were seen by the cadres as a marked change of direction – one that had been a long time coming. The speeches at the conference on scientific and technological progress revealed the prevailing mood. The time of glasnost was beginning. People loosened up and began to feel free.

Were we indulging in wishful thinking? To some degree. However, you cannot say that these plans were just idle schemes. The nation's potential should have made it possible, if not to surpass the developed nations of the West, at least to eliminate the enormous gap between us and the averages in the rest of the world.

Passions flared up around the machine-building programme when it came to finding resources for its implementation. I

---

[1] Broadly speaking, the engineering industry, to include machine tools and motor industries.

suggested a tried method – freeing resources by reducing capital investments in the branches that used the products of the machine-building industry. Since they wanted better machines and equipment, let them sacrifice a portion of their allocations.

My suggestion ran up against great resistance. I recall how fiercely Dolgikh fought for an increase in capital investment in the coal, oil and gas industries. He inundated me with memoranda. Looking at these branches of industry today, one may think that he was right. But today's situation, after all, resulted primarily from the outdated technological base. Increasing output without paying attention to resource-saving technologies and machines was the same as going up a blind alley.

An agreement was eventually reached, but not without pressure from me. Investment in the machine-building sector was to be increased 1.8 times. A number of organizational measures were adopted and a machine-building department of the USSR Council of Ministers was set up.

Nevertheless, as subsequent events showed, our decisions were one-sided and influenced by the outdated notion that one could achieve radical changes in the economy mostly by relying on resolute action.

In November 1985 the Politburo approved the resolution 'On further improvement of the management of the agro-industrial complex'. Agricultural management was concentrated in the hands of Gosagroprom – a super-agency created by merging a dozen or so ministries under the leadership of the First Deputy Chairman of the government. Similar agencies were set up in the republics and the provinces.

Unquestionably their work betrayed our traditional belief in the virtues of centralization. The negative results were soon to be seen. A bureaucratic leviathan that tried to determine and control everything loomed over the collective and state farms and the enterprises that processed agricultural commodities. A barrage of criticism, for the most part valid, soon fell on the agencies of Agroprom.

The bitter truth which has to be admitted is that we were moving too slowly. All too often the old administrative methods and inertia prevailed. Even the reformists, to say nothing of other members of the leadership, lacked clear vision and often wavered.

THE ANTI-ALCOHOL CAMPAIGN: A NOBLE CAUSE, A SAD END

The anti-alcohol programme adopted in May 1985 is to this day a subject of conjecture. Why, people ask, did we decide to begin with this measure at the risk of making reforms more difficult? How could we let such a good beginning backfire?

It is no secret that drunkenness has been a scourge in Russia since the Middle Ages. From time to time, the authorities set out on a crusade against alcoholism. 'Dry laws' were enacted in pre-revolutionary times and even during the first years of Soviet power. In 1958 Khrushchev had tried to root out this vice by raising prices for alcohol and limiting sales. However, the policy was soon dropped. Under Brezhnev the question was discussed several times in the Secretariat and a committee headed by A. Ya. Pelshe was set up, but when he died the commission was forgotten.

Alcoholism became an acute social problem that was shamefully hushed up for years. Drunkards were declared to be 'morally depraved', while Soviet propaganda asserted that in a socialist society there were no objective factors that could give rise to this phenomenon.

Meanwhile, the situation had become catastrophic. There were 5 million registered alcoholics alone. According to the Institute of Sociology of the USSR Academy of Sciences, the annual loss to the economy from drunkenness was an estimated 80 to 100 billion rubles. Life-expectancy was down, and the health of present and future generations was being undermined.

There were many causes for the widespread drunkenness: poor living conditions, the difficulty of everyday life, cultural backwardness. Many drank because of the impossibility of realizing their potential, of saying what they thought. The oppressive social atmosphere pushed weak natures to use alcohol to drown their feelings of inferiority and their fear of harsh reality. The example of the leaders, who paid lavish tribute to the 'green snake' of alcohol, also had a bad effect.

Society grew indifferent to drunkenness – it even became the subject of good-natured humour. The detention of drunks for fifteen days, their periods in drunk 'tanks', and time spent sweeping the streets became popular story-lines for jokes.

Perhaps the saddest thing was that although there was a severe shortage of consumer goods the authorities could not think of any way to maintain monetary circulation other than by selling alcohol to make people drunk. This sounds crazy, but it is the pure truth. The gap between the enormous money supply and the wretched supply of goods was filled with alcohol, and the manufacture of the cheap wine that people call 'bormotukha' increased steadily.

We were faced with this problem from the very beginning. Devastating reports on this national misfortune were presented to the Politburo. I recall how Gromyko, on reading the letters and other data on this issue, shared his outrage: 'Imagine, in this country people drink everywhere – at work and at home, in political and artists' organizations, in laboratories, school and universities, even kindergartens!' Andrei Andreyevich recalled one conversation with Brezhnev on the subject of drunkenness. They were driving back from Zavidovo with Brezhnev at the wheel. Gromyko complained to Brezhnev that drunkenness in the Soviet Union had reached a catastrophic scale and was affecting every aspect of life. After patiently listening to these arguments, Brezhnev kept silent for a while and then suddenly said: 'But you know, Andrei, a Russian cannot do without it . . .' Gromyko dropped the subject immediately.

There was strong public pressure on Party and governmental agencies, which were receiving a flood of letters, mainly from wives and mothers. These letters cited frightening examples of family tragedies, industrial accidents and crime due to drunkenness. Writers and doctors put their complaints in the starkest terms. Nevertheless, we did not impose a 'prohibition' – it was not even considered.

I disagree with those who believe that we did not plan how to compensate for the loss to the state budget resulting from reduced alcohol sales. Special economic calculations took into account the losses to industry due to drunkenness. The plan was to reduce alcohol sales gradually (I emphasize – gradually), as it was replaced by other goods in circulation and sources of budget revenue.

At first the general public (I am not speaking of inveterate drunkards) approved this decision, but the way it was implemented raised doubts, followed by growing dissatisfaction and even open animosity. What happened?

As is often the case, the idea and its implementation were miles apart. I would say that we were both realistic and responsible during the discussion and decision-making, but when the time came to carry out our decisions we began to do things helter-skelter and to allow excesses, and thus we ruined a useful and good initiative.

Ligachev and Solomentsev were entrusted with monitoring the implementation of the policy. They began with irrepressible zeal, but eventually they took everything to the point of absurdity. They demanded that Party leaders in the provinces and ministers and economic officials should carry out the plan of reducing the production of alcoholic beverages and replacing it with soft drinks. They arranged harsh denunciations of the 'laggards', even to the point of preventing them from working and excluding them from the Party. They called on everyone to emulate those who 'beat the schedule', even if it were at an enormous cost to the economy.

In our society people are more used to 'revolutionary leaps' than to diligent work over a long period of time. Alas, the anti-alcohol campaign became one more sad example of how faith in the omnipotence of command methods, extremism and administrative zeal can ruin a good idea. Soon drink shops and wine and vodka bottlers began to close, and in a few places even vineyards fell under the axe. Production of light wines was curtailed, which was certainly not our intention. Expensive brewing equipment bought in Czechoslovakia rusted and became useless. Home brewing became widespread. Sugar vanished from the shelves. Then cheap eau de Cologne vanished from the shelves – to be consumed in place of alcohol. The use of all kinds of 'substitutes' resulted in an increase in illnesses. Thus stretched the sinister chain. People became more and more frustrated by hours of queuing and the impossibility of buying a bottle of vodka or wine for some special occasion. They cursed the leadership, most of all the General Secretary, who was traditionally held responsible for everything. It was then that I got the nickname 'Mineral Water Secretary'.

It would be wrong to say that the anti-alcohol measures were absolutely useless or caused only bad feelings. There were decreases in accidents, fatalities, lost working time, hooliganism and divorces due to drunkenness and alcoholism. After all, the campaign did not consist simply of prohibitions. For the first time information was available on the manufacture and use of alcoholic beverages, along with statistical data that had previously been kept secret. However, the negative consequences of the anti-alcohol campaign greatly exceeded its positive aspects.

Well, I must admit that I bear a great share of the responsibility for this failure. I should not have entrusted the implementation of the policy entirely to others. In any case I should have become involved when the first signs of problems began to appear. But I was completely taken up with an avalanche of work – both foreign and domestic – and, to some degree, my own excessive reticence prevented me from stepping in.

Let me give one more argument in our defence: we were genuinely committed to getting rid of this scourge, but, frightened by the negative results of our campaign, we went to the other extreme and dropped it altogether. Today, the floodgates are open for a spate of drunkenness and look at the sad state we are in now! How much more difficult it will be to escape from today's predicament!

PREPARING FOR REFORM

We put considerable hopes into the economic experiment started in 1983 at enterprises under two Union and three republic ministries. This experiment involved expanding the rights of the enterprises and increasing their responsibility for their production. The results were satisfactory, and in July 1985 we decided that, beginning in 1986, we would extend this system to all enterprises and organizations in certain industries (machine-building, light industries, food, meat and dairy industries, fishing and local industries and services), and eventually, beginning in January 1987, to the whole of industry.

However, we very soon saw the limits of this kind of experiment. At the XXVIIth Party Congress we discussed the need for something more than partial improvements; we knew that we needed radical reform. First steps were taken in 1986. It was decided that the planning and evaluation of light industry should be based on orders placed through wholesale markets, while planning of trade and public food organizations would be based on their final profits. The industrial ministries were allowed to trade through their own firms. The basic criterion for evaluating the economic activity of industrial enterprises was to be 100-per-cent completion of their obligations to deliver products in accordance with signed contracts. Construction, road building and municipal service enterprises (as well as those of a number of non-manufacturing ministries) were tentatively converted to a system of procurement without allocation of quotas. A package of measures was adopted to improve product quality by introducing a state certification system. Proposals for new forms of industrial organization, such as collective contracting and leasing, were introduced. Finally, it was decided to implement a number of decisions that fundamentally changed the traditional approach to foreign economic activity: for the first time in many decades the right of direct export to the world market was granted to twenty ministries and seventy major associations and enterprises, and all enterprises and organizations were permitted to establish direct commercial relationships with partners from socialist countries.

I admit that this somewhat boring list may seem like an extract from a report to the Central Committee. I am also aware that today, when the economy of the country has changed radically, these first steps may seem extremely timid and deserving of the attention only of diligent historians and archivists. However, the reader should keep in mind that this, after all, was an essential part of my life and work. There were so many long and heated arguments over every detail, sleepless nights devoted to preparing documents, so many hopes and also disappointments!

It seemed that we had finally overcome inertia and got economic reform moving. Alas, that was all we had achieved! We had adopted an essentially piecemeal strategy that tackled isolated problems without providing a comprehensive solution. Moreover, some of these measures bore the stamp of traditional methods and eventually had to be abandoned. This applied first of all to the campaign to introduce a system of state quality certification. We wanted to improve product quality by any means and as quickly as possible, and we had a good example – the certification of products by military representatives at defence enterprises (a closer look later showed that even in this case the system was far from ideal). In spring 1986 we decided to introduce state certification for the most important products of the national economy by independent agencies set up for this purpose.

Even then a number of academics and experts expressed the view that we could hope at best for a short-term improvement, the only reliable quality controller being the consumer. However, for this to work we would have had to put an end to the shortages throughout the economy. The introduction of state certification, initially at 1,500 enterprises, produced a shock – many enterprises were compelled to reduce wages and stop bonuses. People began to blame state certification for disrupted production plans, and there was a flood of petitions to Party organs, Gosplan and the government asking us to relent. The more imaginative and enterprising managers rushed to set up 'contacts' ('You scratch my back and I'll scratch yours') with the newly appointed state inspectors, who, as a rule, had only yesterday been colleagues and subordinates.

After only two or three years state certification had vanished – one more clear signal that the solution lay not in administrative or organizational measures, but rather in the restructuring of the entire economic mechanism.

The conversion of enterprises to procurement via wholesale purchasing produced a curious situation. Those concerned complained that this meant abandoning guaranteed procurements.

Grievances and objections poured in from all sides. With great difficulty the USSR Academy of Sciences managed to preserve the old order, while others accepted the new situation but privately said that nothing would come of it. Alas, they turned out to be right! We even suspected that veteran planners and suppliers were counting on such an outcome. It was as if they were saying: 'You think you can do without us? Have your wholesale trade, the workers will not accept it and production will collapse.'

The history of the decisions about the personal land plots, collectively run orchards and gardens, and individual labour activity[1] that we planned to introduce is quite instructive. The planned reform was useful from all standpoints: it would have provided a source of additional income for many people, supplied the market with goods, developed the service sphere and provided work for pensioners and the disabled. The experience in this area in East Germany, Hungary, and other socialist countries had been favourable. In the Soviet Union cottage industries had always been seen as alien to socialism, even though they had a long history in this country. In Russia people always valued skilled workers who could build a fireplace, dig a well, renovate an apartment, or repair equipment. At the beginning of this century various associations and partnerships appeared, and a network of business co-operatives developed after the October Revolution, especially in the NEP period.

State control put a brutal end to these beginnings. Enterprising people were branded as harbouring secret desires to own private property. The thinking was: work should be for the sake of higher goals. To engage in individual labour and to earn a good living was considered shameful, but to while away the time in a large enterprise or in an institution was the normal order of things.

The absurd restrictions on orchard and garden associations were lifted first. According to these rules, stoves could not even be installed in the cottages, the sizes of structures were strictly regulated and 'violators' were punished, even to the point of tearing down the offending sheds. We put an end to this practice. Allocations of land for orchards and gardens were increased

[1] The right of individuals to work for themselves as self-employed persons.

sharply, along with sales of building materials to the general public. These measures were unanimously supported, but it proved to be much harder to get rid of prejudice towards individual labour and to change the attitude of Party and governmental structures, especially the local Soviets. It was then that the debate about private ownership and private enterprise began.

I once said to Finance Minister Gostev at a Politburo meeting: 'Are we going to stifle the people's initiative as in the past, or shall we let them live and work? Don't be afraid that someone might get rich by his own hard work!'

A tactic that was cleverly used by the opponents of change was to accompany decisions with instructions or 'explanations' from agencies or local authorities that emasculated or completely distorted their meaning. However, in most cases these decisions were simply ignored: a document would be received, filed away, and forgotten.

It must be said for the record that, in some cases, local authorities had a hard time trying to implement the often contradictory prescriptions coming from Moscow. And the watchful zealots of 'purity' were always on guard, ready to raise hell if something was just a little off. Hence our stop-go, back-and-forth progress.

Things were also beginning to get out of hand with the May 1986 decision to step up the battle with 'unearned income'.[1] These measures were supposed to be aimed at thieves, grafters, and extortionists, but in fact they more often affected those individual workers, craftsmen, mechanics and small 'middlemen' who were trying to make a little money.

To avoid further misunderstandings, we decided to prepare a new law on individual labour activity. After much serious debate, the draft was submitted to the USSR Supreme Soviet and passed on 19 November 1986. In spite of being imperfect and incomplete, it played a useful role in the transformation of economic relations.

The economic situation improved slightly in 1985–6. Industrial production increased by 4.4 per cent and agricultural production by 3 per cent. In two years almost 40 billion rubles more than

[1] Income from sources considered suspect, 'not earned from one's official job'.

proposed in the Five Year Plan had been invested in the social sphere.

This success was encouraging, but reality soon caught up with us. At the beginning of 1987 there was a serious drop in production: industrial output fell by 6 per cent compared with December 1986, mainly in machine-building and light industry. However, the metallurgical and chemical industries were also experiencing problems. The 1987 Plan was in danger of collapsing like a house of cards.

A heated discussion took place in the Politburo on 12 February. Talyzin and Voronin blamed the winter, the state certification system, the sluggishness of suppliers ('temporary delays with ball bearings and technical rubber products') etc. We eventually localized the problems and managed to keep the economy from slipping into crisis for another two years. But this was an unmistakable signal that the economy was unstable and that renewal processes were going badly. The ministries were making their last stand, refusing to share their prerogatives with production associations and enterprises. The programmes for the development of high-priority industries did not result in an acceleration of scientific and technological progress and the plans for modernization of machine-building were collapsing. Our intense efforts had largely foundered.

BIRTH PANGS

In March 1987 we came close to an understanding on the correct strategy for economic reform. We had learned from the bitter experience of earlier attempts, especially the Kosygin reform undertaken in the second half of the 1960s. It was considered rather bold for its time, especially in expanding the autonomy of enterprises and developing commodity-money relations between them. I well remember the hopes it raised in society and the positive effect it had on the Soviet economy in the 8th Five Year Plan, probably the most successful Five Year Plan of the postwar period.

However, that reform was essentially technocratic and lacked the proper political basis; moreover, it ran foul of the general trend of the country's development. That trend was not democratization but on the contrary a tightening of the screws, especially after the suppression of the 'Prague Spring' in 1968.

I believe too that the fact that Brezhnev and the 'partocracy' who supported him remained aloof from the development and implementation of the reform also contributed to its failure. They were not very heartened by its achievements and not particularly saddened by its failures, and at times would even deliberately throw a spanner into the works. There was no reason to doubt that we too would run up against this same kind of opposition and even open sabotage.

All the same, we had to begin with a Central Committee plenum; it was necessary to push a package of fundamental propositions through this supreme authority.

Some people still assert that our reforms were carried out hastily, were not sufficiently thought out, and were foisted on society. Nonsense! They were the result of truly collective efforts by reformers, science and society. In the nationwide discussion prior to the plenum, we obtained powerful support from labour collectives. We held a series of conferences in order to prepare society for the reforms. Only the most hard-headed members of the apparatus opposed them. And they were not implemented randomly, but rather at a pace dictated by society's readiness for change.

It is no exaggeration to say that for several months the preparation of the plenum kept the leadership of the country in a state of continuously growing tension. A number of important events, both domestic and international, occurred during this period. The process of preparing for the June Central Committee plenum unfolded like a play with an opening scene, several sub-plots, hidden action and open clashes of the characters, a culmination and a dénouement. Moreover, all of the participants were both authors and actors. Disagreements and contradictions were sometimes hidden from the public and sometimes reached public view to create a kind of sensation.

While earlier most of the discussion had raged between advocates of reform and adherents of command methods, now the dividing line was how deep the economic reforms should go. The main opposition to our ideas came from the heads of ministries and agencies, firstly the general economic agencies – Gosplan, Gossnab, Minfin[1] and the government apparatus. Later the opposition joined ranks with the Party bureaucracy. Needless to say, no-one was so bold as to speak out openly against reform; everyone was 'for' the reform process, but many offered half-hearted, ambiguous solutions that left many loopholes and sometimes even a direct opportunity for a roll back to the past.

Unfortunately I had clashes with Ryzhkov on a number of issues. I could see that he was under very strong pressure from his former fellow industrial managers, who were continuously planting an insidious idea: 'The government is required to ensure effective management of the economy and at the same time the dismantling of the plan system is robbing it of the means of control.' Nikolai Ivanovich would waver and vacillate and was sometimes inconsistent in his views. Added to this was his – albeit largely justified – extremely sharp reaction to the attempts of the Party Secretariat and Central Committee departments, especially Ligachev, to interfere in the functions of the government.

I tried to keep Ryzhkov on the path of reform, and I believe that, all in all, I succeeded. But it was then that people began to think of the Prime Minister as an advocate of conservative views.

The first clash of opinions occurred on 3 April, at the initial conference on preparation of the report for the plenum. This was an unhurried and informal, absolutely unfettered exchange of opinions, which lasted four hours. I cannot say that Ryzhkov's ideas were out of touch with the general mood, but certain under-tones put me on my guard. He insisted that we could not 'go beyond the framework of socialism'. I reacted: 'We will carry out reforms within the framework of socialism, but not within the framework that put chains on society and extinguished initiative and incentive.'

All of April and early May was filled with work on the

---

[1] Respectively, the State Planning Committee; the State Committee for Material and Technical Supply; and the Ministry of Finance.

discussion paper and speech for the plenum. I held regular consultations with the working group and tried not to lose sight of small, but important details; practically every day I went to Volynskoe, where the working group held sessions, or invited my colleagues to visit me. We would read section after section and argue about the necessary tone and precise wording. The speech had to be accessible, since it would be read by the entire country.

Work on the discussion paper was completed on 9 May, and this 40-page document was sent to the Politburo members. It painted a picture of the approaching economic crisis for the first time, although the word 'crisis' was not yet used. It also outlined the basic direction necessary for restructuring the management of the economy and creating a reliable mechanism to prevent inefficient spending.

We emphasized that perestroika was conceived within the framework of the socialist order. However, there were significant changes occurring in the very understanding of socialism, and we went on to ask just how closely the model of socialism that was developed in the 1930s corresponded with today's reality. We sharply criticized the excessive state control of public property, the under-valuation of co-operative and individual forms of labour, the equating of a plan system with centralism, and the infringement of democratic forms of government and self-government.

The paper explained and defined a new model of an economic enterprise (or association) as a 'socialist producer', which conducts its business completely independently. There was a radical change in the philosophy of planning: from planning by directive and decree, it was gradually to become planning by recommendation and forecasting. The key point in the reform was the transition to new principles of price formulation that essentially combined market mechanisms with state regulation. The basic directions for restructuring the bodies of economic management were presented in detail.

We had not yet dealt with such problems as the petty control the Party organs exercised over the economic activity of the enterprises. In his time Kosygin had suggested that the departments created in the Party Central Committee for the supervision of almost all branches of the economy be transferred to the government. Brezhnev and his entourage took this as an attempt to take the levers of management away from the Party leadership, leaving it with ideology alone. Hence the reaction was to do the opposite: these departments and sectors began to grow even faster. For this reason the paper contained only a general statement that Party committees should not interfere in the operational and economic activity of enterprises and that they should concentrate their efforts on helping to make economic management more democratic.

After the paper had been distributed to the Politburo members, I went down to Baikonur in Kazakhstan for a few days to inspect work on developing and launching the *Buran* space shuttle by a powerful rocket system. Once again I could see the enormous potential of our science and technology and the prospects that lay before us if they were supported with a strong economy.

On 14 May we discussed the paper at a Politburo meeting. There were no surprises and plenty of enthusiasm. Ryzhkov, Ligachev, Talyzin, Vorotnikov and others spoke as reviewers and critics. Since I was considered to be the author of the discussion paper, criticism was restrained and even disagreements on fundamental issues were presented as minor comments.

Ligachev, without going into questions of economic reform, suddenly launched into a sermon, preaching that perestroika should not be reduced to democratization, that democratization was only a lever of action of perestroika, and that our goal should be the strengthening of socialism. He also suggested that the critical evaluations of the past should be toned down.

Yeltsin noted the depth and novelty of the paper and suggested that we make the section about Party work stronger. He was after all the leader of the Moscow Party organization.

When I summed up the discussion, I stressed the need for a change in the Party's general attitude towards reform. We had set the ball rolling, but there was still a lot of resistance. I had seen this in my trip to Kazakhstan, when a voice had called to me from the crowd: 'When will perestroika finally reach us?' A hasty, cavalier approach would be wrong, but neither could we sit and wait.

CONTRADICTIONS BUILD UP

Meanwhile our work on a package of measures to be imple-mented by the government continued. At first a draft resolution on measures for the improvement of state statistics was submitted to the Politburo, followed by a resolution on reform of the financial and credit system and price formation. Ryzhkov's memorandum about the country's financial position, dealing, perhaps for the first time, with the problem of the budget deficit, was distributed to Politburo members.

Gostev reported that 21 billion rubles credit had been added to balance the budget. However, the total budget deficit amounted to 80 billion rubles, and it was not clear where the extra 60 billion rubles would come from. Today these questions are discussed at every turn, but then they were tantamount to a revelation, because nobody knew about the use of credit as an item of income in the budget. This, however, was the main source of the inflation in the economy.

The discussion turned to prices. The main trouble with the old system was that prices, as a rule, were set according to cost. As a result, we did not reward enterprises for economy in their use of resources; we actually punished them, thus encouraging depen-dence and reliance on state subsidies. But prices should reflect the socially necessary costs and product quality as well as supply and demand. Retail prices, too, had to be reviewed. Could it really be considered normal that subsidies for food products alone amounted to 56 billion rubles, i.e. more than 45 per cent of their total sales? At the same time, I categorically rejected any attempts to reduce the state budget deficit by raising prices. 'Everything that we receive in the future should be returned to the people through wages, with the possible exception of highly paid officials,' I said.

Tradition had a strong grip on our people. The Minister of Agricultural Machine-Building, A. A. Yezhevsky, complained that the order for combines was too low, that Gosagroprom had ordered 100,000 instead of the 108,000 stipulated by the plan. He therefore asked us to put pressure on the first secretaries so that they in turn would compel the oblasts, republics, collective and state farms to order equipment in the 'needed' amount. Needed by whom? I had long known Yezhevsky as a capable and concerned official, but I was surprised how deeply ingrained the old ways of thinking were in him!

Following a break, we discussed wholesale trade. The government argued that it had to be introduced gradually, as resources accumulated and shortages were overcome. It was a vicious circle indeed. The government saw wholesale trade as just another way of distributing equipment through Gossnab agencies.

Of course, everything had a simple explanation: no-one wanted to let go of power. Whoever determined targets and allotted resources was seen as tsar and god, potentate and benefactor. The system needed the shortages to be maintained, otherwise the monopoly, along with its fellow-travellers – bribes, graft, mutual favours and so forth – would simply collapse.

I was satisfied with the results of the discussion, but reaching the necessary decisions was like cutting one's way through jungle undergrowth. The system compelled people to fight for its preservation, since this served their interests, but I saw another side of things as well: routine and stereotyped thinking. Some people are simply stuck with stock phrases and clichés by which they run their lives. I once read about experiments by psychologists which showed that Soviet people, because of their dogmatic upbringing and education, have developed a unique property – the ability not to see, in the literal sense of the word, anything that does not correspond either to their ideas of what they are supposed to be seeing or to the slogan.

At Politburo meetings in May and June we continued the discussion of economic reform and draft resolutions. Differences became sharper. On 21 May an argument flared up in the discussion of draft resolutions on improving the work of the Council of Ministers and republican administrative organs and restructuring ministries and agencies. This time Ryzhkov did not hide his intention to uphold the interests of the top echelon of the state apparatus. When asked what functions the ministries would surrender under the new conditions, Nikolai Ivanovich snapped: 'None at all.'

On Saturday, 20 June, I asked Ryzhkov to come to Volynskoe

for final agreement on the positions that we would take. Yakovlev, Slyunkov and Medvedev were also present and participated in the discussion. Nikolai Ivanovich arrived with his aides. He seemed to be pleased with the invitation, but he was hesitant about whose side he should take – Gorbachev and the reform economists, or the powerful governmental, state planning and ministry structures.

I was aware of Ryzhkov's difficult position and did my best to be tactful. But there were more arguments over the same problems we had argued about for several months – the rights of the ministries, state orders, material and technical supply, and so forth. Finally, we agreed on a compromise.

On 8–9 July, I participated in a major conference of Party and state officials and economic managers at the Central Committee. Frankly, we called this conference not so much to clear up issues as to strengthen our own resolve, to 'gather courage' and to convince the people.

The final discussion of the report in the Politburo was relatively quiet. There were no objections to proposals which had earlier been the topic of sharp debate. Thus I was able to say: 'We are united both in principle and in the particulars.'

Alas, this conclusion was premature. Resistance to radical economic reform would not abate and the decisions we adopted would be torpedoed.

DEBATE AT THE PLENUM

On 25 July the Central Committee plenum heard the report 'On the tasks of the Party towards the radical restructuring of economic management'. Once again, I spoke of the need for democratization. The bureaucratic command system was holding us back.

I criticized the work not only of a number of central agencies, but also of the Politburo, Secretariat and the Council of Ministers. I even mentioned by name a number of top officials in ministries and agencies, republics, krais and oblasts who were responsible for serious oversights in their work. This was quite unusual for a Party forum and caused a hubbub in the hall.

I pointed to three problem areas – food, housing, and goods and services – and emphasized that these could be solved only by radical reform of our economy. What could we do to revive the spirit of responsibility, to maximize co-operation? How should we go about combining the interests of society, the collective and the worker? By raising these fundamental questions I wanted to draw the plenum participants away from narrow details and set the tone for a serious discussion.

Alas! In spite of the fact that the plenum participants had received the outline of the report and other papers in good time, in spite of the fact that we had carried out a thorough 'softening up' campaign, there was no serious discussion of reform at the plenum. The Party bosses, after duly swearing their allegiance to perestroika and casually touching on the problems mentioned in the report, went down their usual rut: what was going on in their republics and oblasts, what the problems were there, what help they expected from the Union agencies, and so forth.

In former times Politburo members discussed beforehand whether they should participate in debates. This practice was maintained for a while after I became General Secretary, but eventually it died out. I believed that each member of the leadership had the right to decide this for himself. Nevertheless, I was somewhat surprised by the fact that Ryzhkov remained silent at this plenum. It seemed to me that the head of the government ought to take the floor, if only to kill rumours about disagreements about the reforms.

On the whole, the plenum did not develop our ideas any further. Still, we had achieved a number of significant results. The participants confirmed the course towards democratization and we had defined the basic tasks and methods of conducting economic reform. Finally, we adopted the resolution to convene the XIXth Party Conference in the summer of 1988, which heralded the next stage of perestroika.

I used the plenum not only to advance the reform programme but also to regroup forces in the country's political leadership. Slyunkov and Yakovlev were promoted from candidate membership to full membership in the Politburo, Sokolov was 'relieved of his responsibilities' as a candidate member and Yazov was elected a candidate member in his stead. The reshuffle went off smoothly.

The transfer of Sokolov to the general inspectorate group of the Ministry of Defence (the so-called 'paradise' group created under Brezhnev for retired senior military leaders) was the result of an emergency – the escapade of the young German, Mathias Rust, who flew in and landed in Red Square in a light aircraft. This was a slap in the face to the country and its armed forces. More important, it was a signal of trouble in the country's security system and of irresponsibility in the higher military command. The sensational news of Rust's flight reached me at the meeting of the Warsaw Pact's political consultative committee conference in Berlin (Gromyko, Ryzhkov, Shevardnadze, Sokolov and Medvedev were also present at this meeting). The reader can easily imagine my amazement on receiving the news. I informed the conference participants about the incident, adding that this was no reason to doubt the efficiency of our technology or the reliability of our defence, although, to be frank, I was utterly shaken and completely at a loss as to how this could have happened: technically, our anti-aircraft defence systems offered a 100-per-cent guarantee against air-space violations even in incomparably more complicated circumstances. The real problem was the organization or, more precisely, lack of it in the armed forces.

We returned to Moscow in two aeroplanes – it was the custom that the whole leadership should not fly together. The conversation kept coming back to Rust's flight. My companions called for stern measures towards the guilty parties, especially the leadership of the Ministry of Defence. Sokolov must go, all the more so since there had already been signs of trouble in the armed forces.

At the Politburo meeting everyone was in favour of retiring the Minister of Defence and the Air Defence chief Koldunov, conducting a thorough investigation of the incident and making the responsible parties answer for what had happened. I concluded the discussion by characterizing this event as a blow to our entire policy that undermined confidence in the armed forces.

After a break a proposal was made to appoint Yazov as the next

Minister of Defence. There were no objections, although for many this was unexpected. Yazov was not well known and had not previously occupied any prestigious position – such as head of the general staff, commander of the western army group or of the Moscow military district. However, he was my choice. We had come to know each other in the Far East, where he commanded a district that was very complicated, scattered over thousands of kilometres, with a multitude of serious problems, especially those involving living conditions in the army, which caused discontent among the troops. He operated there with great assurance, calm and skill. He bridged the gap between the officers and the men and improved morale. His experience helped him in this; as a young officer he had taken part in the Second World War, and after the war he had served in many military districts as he climbed each rung on the ladder of his military career. He knew army life from top to bottom. As Deputy Defence Minister for cadres, Yazov had shown himself a capable leader. He worked to renew and revitalize the staff of generals and the officer corps, with 1,200 generals being retired.

The new minister had to cope with unusual problems in developing our positions for disarmament talks. Sometimes specialists from the Ministry of Foreign Affairs, the Ministry of Defence, the military-industrial complex, and the KGB were deadlocked. Although Yazov supported his representatives, he showed flexibility and common sense whenever it came to making political decisions. Together with Akhromeyev, he helped us to find a way out: how far we could go today, and what line we could not cross for now, what our main strategies should be and what our fallback position should be.

I write about Yazov in such detail because his behaviour in August 1991 was the hardest for me to understand. He was the last person I would have suspected of treachery.

THE POSITIONAL FIGHT ON THE ISSUE OF REFORM

The plenum's documents were a compromise. Many of them, especially from the vantage-point of today, may even appear naive. But for our society and the level of public awareness at that time these were radical, even revolutionary decisions. It was important to begin real progress along the planned course, to get started, and to let life and the logic of the reforms show the direction the changes needed to go.

Much, if not everything, depended on the government and the central economic authorities. Unfortunately, their actions did not change. They saw the plenum's decisions as an excessive concession to the reformers, as the last line of retreat from a planned centralized system of control.

In September, in order to see how the decisions of the Central Committee plenum were being implemented, the Politburo heard reports on the development of economic standards from Sitaryan and the drafting of the reform of prices from Pavlov. By that time, various enterprises had informed the Central Committee that central agencies were wilfully ignoring the plenum's decisions.

Even before the June plenum Ryzhkov argued that if we allowed enterprises to plan their own work and gave them autonomy in financial matters, the Five Year Plan would become meaningless. He insisted on the economic targets of the Five Year Plan, although it was clear from the results of 1986 and 1987 that they would not be met.

The management nomenklatura put up the most stubborn resistance to organizational restructuring. An attempt was even made to re-establish the system of bureaucratic departments subordinate to ministries, with inflated bureaucracies. Again, we had to discuss at a Politburo meeting how to eliminate distortions in the implementation of reform.

In a nutshell, there was protracted tactical manoeuvring on the issue of reform. The further it progressed, the more it became mired in the mud of endless stipulation, dull talk, and 'instinctive' and intentional sabotage.

THE DISCUSSION OF PRICES

The problem of prices gave rise to particularly sharp clashes. In April 1988 the Politburo reviewed the proposals for the reform of prices presented by the government on the instructions of the June plenum, and submitted ten months later. This was a fat stack of verbose, but not particularly clear, documents that in a number of points were clearly at cross-purposes with the concept of reform.

In particular, the government proposed that reform be broken down into several stages. Wholesale prices and tariffs were to be introduced into industry and transport, while the introduction of new purchase and retail prices was to be postponed indefinitely. The documents analysed the issue of prices in isolation from other important elements of economic reform. The draft did not contain solutions to important issues such as bringing domestic prices closer to those of the world market, decentralization and liberalization of price formation and transition to contract prices.

The Politburo severely criticized these documents and demanded that the Council of Ministers should not delay the resolution of these problems, since it was obvious that, with time, the conditions for major price reform would only deteriorate. However, those in the government were afraid to tackle this highly sensitive issue. Thus we lost several months in senseless bureaucratic wrangling. Meanwhile, rumours of an attack on stable prices trickled through society and caused growing alarm. This issue was eventually picked up by populists and politicized. In spite of many assurances that the revenue from price increases would be returned to the people (primarily to low-paid workers through wage increases) and that the decision on prices would not be made without discussing it with the people, a noisy campaign against price reform being counter to the interests of the people was carried on in the press.

'Hands off prices!' was the first slogan of the emerging radical democratic opposition. They were not at all bothered by the fact that this attitude blocked economic reform and that they themselves could not avoid taking this action if they came into power. As in many other instances, the interests of the nation were sacrificed to the desire to win cheap popularity. Radical newspapers published letters and wrathful diatribes, and in only a few weeks public opinion changed to total rejection of price reform. Almost all leading economists fell under the influence of this

303

attitude, even those who had been involved in developing the concept of economic reform. Succumbing to the general mood, they began to speak out in the press with warnings against undue haste. To be fair, there was a real basis for public concern. Disruptions in the consumer market and in monetary circulation began to show up even in 1988.

Under populist pressure, a decision was taken to abolish wage controls – an action that was clearly premature and which caused incomes to rise unduly. Co-operatives converted large amounts of money into ready cash. A number of unrealistic social programmes were adopted. Too much money was printed, which destabilized the consumer market. Various consumer goods began to vanish from the shelves: sugar, tobacco goods, soap and washing powder. Unfounded price increases for essential goods became common, which caused justified consumer concern.

I was seriously worried about the price situation. While on holiday in August, I pointed out the developing situation to Ryzhkov and Slyunkov. Aganbegyan sent a detailed memorandum in which he suggested a number of specific measures and highlighted the need to explain the situation to the public.

On 29 October 1988, at the suggestion of the Central Committee departments, the Politburo adopted a resolution on retail prices and tariffs for public services that condemned the practice of unjustified price increases. However, this measure failed to improve the public mood. In addition, the economists Zaslavskaya, Shatalin, Abalkin, Popov, Shmelev and others began to speak out in the press against price reforms 'in the next few years', saying that price rises would 'kill perestroika', arousing society against it.

What about the Council of Ministers, Gosplan and the State Price Committee? While mouthing their concern about the irresponsibility of the journalists and the apostasy of the economists, they were slow to act, lacking the will to get in the line of fire and accept responsibility for unpopular measures.

At a Politburo meeting in early November Ryzhkov raised the question of articles by Abalkin and Shatalin about the price issue. Everyone feigned indignation – and that was it! We should have raised the alarm by rallying the press, going on television and radio and speaking directly to the workers. We needed to make the public understand the simple truth that a radical reform of prices was an inseparable part of economic reform. No matter how undesirable a review of retail prices might be, we could not avoid it if we wanted a healthy economy and a sustained improvement in the standard of living.

In evaluating my role in the dramatic fate of the 'first attempt' at economic reform, I have to admit that we underestimated the odds against us. We were too long under the illusion that the problem was simply the difficulty of winning support for perestroika. We allowed the time-frame for structural transformations to be dragged out for three or four years and thus missed the most economically and politically favourable time for them in 1987–8. This was a strategic miscalculation. As a result, the situation in the country rapidly worsened and conditions became less and less favourable for successful reform. We therefore needed different, more radical approaches to reform.

12

THE DECISIVE STEP

HISTORIANS, WHO LIKE EVERYTHING TO BE IN NEAT ORDER, HAVE been arguing whether perestroika and reforms began in March 1985 or at some later date. Well, in the first three years we made serious efforts to bring the country out of stagnation and to achieve renewal in all aspects of life. We made our first attempt at radical reform of the economy.

However, the real turning-point, when perestroika became irreversible, was the XIXth All-Union Party Conference. This decisive step was prompted by the obvious failure of economic reform to get going and the radicalization of public opinion.

At that time, I decided to write a book about perestroika – to take stock and to set down my thoughts for the future. I could already see the overall plan of the book and its sections, and had kept notes on various subjects. I decided to share this idea with my associates.

I have to say that it was not warmly supported. Frolov advised me to prepare a series of lectures instead. Dobrynin and Yakovlev thought I should limit myself to publishing a collection of my articles. However, articles written on specific subjects could not replace a complete account of what my colleagues and I had discussed, what had been the subject of my talks with foreign politicians, and especially what remained unknown to the general public – how the idea of perestroika was born.

I also believed that it was important to provide a first-hand explanation of our intentions to the world. In spite of the fact that there were changes for the better in international affairs, conservative circles in the West had begun to show alarm and irritation. Our new policy undermined the psychology of confrontation that had developed during the Cold War years, and affected the interests of those who fed on it. Proposed reductions in military production meant a reduction in allocations, subsidies and jobs. In America even Reagan began to be attacked, although he had not yet embraced real disarmament.

This is why it was necessary to present our beliefs clearly. The rest of the world had to understand why it was not just the USSR that needed the reforms, but that in the final account perestroika was in the interests of other countries too.

This line of argument resulted in a more accurate title for the book: the word 'perestroika' was supplemented by another key idea, the 'new thinking'. Since then these two ideas have been inseparably linked, with reforms in our country designated as 'perestroika', their international aspect and the related foreign policy as 'new thinking'.

I sent the manuscript, if memory serves, to Ligachev, Ryzhkov, Yakovlev, Medvedev, Shevardnadze and Frolov, and asked them to read it and make comments. Medvedev sent the most substantive comments, most of which I accepted. The others sent only praise.

My first book was a success: almost five million copies were sold in 160 countries and 80 languages. The royalties totalled about three million dollars and approximately one million rubles. After payment of taxes and other deductions, these royalties were used for charitable purposes, including the Fund for Aid to Earthquake Victims in Armenia and Tajikistan. I might add that I donated both my Nobel Prize and the Fiuggi Prize – a total of more than a million dollars – to the same purposes. Significant sums were donated to public health, including hospitals where Chernobyl victims were being treated.

The reaction to this book was a kind of litmus test. We saw that the world was waiting for a change. And even though a few foreign reviewers criticized it for 'sloppiness' in the presentation of the material and reticence on certain subjects, it was well received in principle. Of course, it was not treated like an ordinary book; it was viewed as the manifesto of the initiator of perestroika.

MY SPEECH ON THE SEVENTIETH ANNIVERSARY OF THE OCTOBER REVOLUTION

In January 1987 we began discussing preparations for the celebration of the seventieth anniversary of the October Revolution. Tradition required that the General Secretary should provide his evaluations of fundamental issues on such an occasion.

At the time, discussions of the reforms were in full swing in the Party, in scholarly circles and among the general public. None of our leading historians, philosophers or economists came out in open opposition to socialism, but the question of the nature of our society and of just what socialism meant was being raised. The book *There's No Other Choice*, most of whose authors were radical democrats and which was published before the XIXth Party Conference, attracted attention.

I have often noted that until I fully grasp the internal logic of a subject, I cannot discuss it, speak about it or write about it. By nature I am inclined to a systematic approach and, when I began work on the speech, I felt the need to begin with the beginning – to return to the first years of Soviet power in order to gain a deeper understanding of the trends that began then. I once again re-read Lenin's writings from that period.

As is well known, the 'Immediate Tasks of Soviet Power' was written in the short interval of peacetime immediately after the Revolution. From this pamphlet one can judge what Lenin thought the movement to the new society would be like, what was the logic of the transformations, and the methods he intended to follow. In Lenin's subsequent works one can sense the atmosphere of the civil war, and the splitting of the country into opposing camps. Then come the articles of 1922–3, in which there is increasing alarm about the fate of the revolution. Lenin was worried that the methods used in the revolutionary upheaval and the irreconcilable war against counter-revolution had become too deep-rooted. Indeed, the 'state of emergency' and the emphasis on force had become the rule for the 'proletarian bureaucracy' and an inseparable element of the new order.

The need for a 'new understanding of socialism' was linked to a rejection of the legacy of the civil war as it applied to management of the country. The basis of this understanding lay in rejection of 'revolutionarism' and faith in the omnipotence of violent methods, and reliance on democracy and reform instead – plus the use of traditional ways that the people knew and understood, while gradually renewing them and filling them with socialist content.

Illness kept Lenin from completing this fundamental re-evaluation, which could have resulted in a completely different idea of socialist development from the one adopted by Stalin. The leader of October managed with his last determined effort only to make the Party accept NEP, the New Economic Policy, i.e. radical economic reforms. However, the party bureaucracy did not tolerate it for long. The seeds of the marketplace, of free enterprise, of ideological and political pluralism, were nipped in the bud. State or 'barracks' socialism ruled.

How does one explain the failure of NEP, in spite of its obvious advantages? I believe that it was due to the inability of the Bolsheviks to change their ways. New methods, new policies were needed, but the Bolsheviks continued to act like wartime commissars. Forced industrialization, which demanded investment, currency and imported equipment, resulted in a hard line towards the peasantry: forcible confiscation of production, forced collectivization. A kind of serfdom was created to 'feed' the bureaucracy, to create military might and to meet social needs, albeit at a low level. Command methods, suppression of heterodoxy and repression, which at first were said to be due to the peculiar conditions of capitalist encirclement, became an integral part of the system. A totalitarian regime developed, which relied on total state ownership, monopoly ideology and one-party rule.

Work on my speech for the seventieth anniversary of the October Revolution began on 29 April 1987 at a meeting with my inner circle. For some reason its participants best remember these words that I spoke then jokingly: 'You know, I think the fate of today's leadership is to die or advance perestroika.'

In the past, when we celebrated anniversaries of this kind, the speech would be simply an inventory of victories, along with one or two pseudo-critical paragraphs. In this speech the stress was to fall elsewhere: the anniversary had to be used to prompt an analysis moving through several stages in the development of social consciousness and understanding in the society in which we lived and to answer the question: 'What is to be done?'

The discussion was quite frank; ideas that were very bold for that time were considered, and, if they were not all included in the speech, it was only because we thought that the time for them had not yet arrived. We felt that it was necessary to give a more complete and precise evaluation of the tragic episodes in our history and of those Party activists who had been accused of being 'enemies of the people'. This meant Bukharin in particular.

I was able to catch the mood of the leadership on the eve of the October anniversary at the Politburo meeting on 28 September, immediately after my return from holiday. My thoughts on my book and the forthcoming speech, along with comment in the press and information from the provinces, necessitated a frank and thorough discussion. Foreign gossip about the state of my health, about disagreements between Ligachev and me, between Ligachev and Yakovlev, between Ryzhkov and somebody else etc., all fuelled the fire. My long absence, during which I had not had any direct contact with anyone except by telephone, demanded that I should quickly grab the wheel with both hands, as the saying goes.

The meeting lasted until 7.30 in the evening. A continuing theme was analysis of the progress of perestroika. I concluded that we had reached a critical stage. We had at our disposal the decisions of the January and June Central Committee plenums, and their implementation should push democratic processes far ahead. The rising tension in society was evidence of the people's worries about perestroika.

Indeed the 1987 results had proved to be much worse than the 1986 results. What made them worse still was the confusion caused by the haphazard transition of industry to a system of cost accounting, self-financing and self-management. Those who feared change began to capitalize on troubles. The cries became ever louder: 'Just look at your democracy (or cost accounting, or the contract systems, or co-operatives etc.)!' It was difficult to distinguish which of these cries reflected the genuine worries of the people and which were just the malicious intrigues of demagogues.

It was probably at this time that alienation began to develop between the central and local Party organs. For the most part the local Party organizations were not prepared to work in the atmosphere produced by democratization and glasnost and by the transition to new economic methods. At meetings you would always hear the same old thing: 'Tell us what to do, give us instructions.' These were ominous symptoms of crisis in a Party that had been formed for a completely different role in society. In the three years of perestroika, contested elections had resulted in significant changes in personnel. But even the new cadres were burdened by the weight of the past, and with rare exceptions acted in the same spirit and employed the same methods as before.

I sensed that society, in its impatient expectation of change, had left the Party behind, that there was a serious threat that the Party would 'miss the boat'. We had to find a way to overcome this danger.

At that same meeting the Politburo decided to create a commission to examine the repressions of the 1930s and subsequent years. This resumed the process of rehabilitating innocent people and restoring historical truth, which had been interrupted in Brezhnev's time.

By the middle of October we had prepared for discussion a rough draft of the anniversary speech – a solid composition of about 120 pages. Some of the comments were useful, but most of them amounted only to changes in the wording.

Yeltsin's comments were the most extensive. He felt that the emphasis in the speech had been shifted in favour of the February Revolution, to the detriment of the October Revolution; he said that the role of Lenin and his close associates was not prominent enough, the civil war period had been skipped, the parts devoted to industrialization and collectivization were out of proportion, the appraisals of important revolutionaries were premature (we should wait for the findings of the Politburo commission); and he judged that it would be better to circumvent the question of the phasing of perestroika and the preparation of a new constitution. Finally, he said that we must emphasize strongly the leading role of the Party in the development of Soviet society. As the reader can see, these were comments permeated by a spirit of great caution and conservatism. This was Yeltsin at that time.

On 2 November 1987 I spoke on the theme 'October and perestroika: the revolution continues' at a ceremony in the Kremlin. My speech was perceived as an important step in the lifting of myths from our history and restoration of truth. Needless to say, this speech was marked by certain constraints. We decided to be silent on some issues. We ourselves still had a great deal to grasp and many psychological barriers to overcome. There were still 'blank spots' that needed investigation. In such matters, as they say, a man can do no more than he can do.

My balanced and even cautious speech did not satisfy the extremists on either side. Some took the critical analysis of the past as 'slander' and 'lack of respect for our people', as a shaking of the foundations and the harbinger of a total re-examination of the history of the Soviet people. Others, for whom shallow magazine articles were enough to enable them to 'see clearly', said that they had expected more, that Gorbachev was marking time, that a complete break with the past was needed.

To some degree I had foreseen this kind of reaction. It was for this reason in particular that the speech was not definitive on a number of issues. When the retreat from the policies of the XXth Congress had begun in the 1960s, the 'cult of personality' was declared to be 'an issue that had been resolved by our Party long ago', so there was 'no need to reopen it'. On the contrary, my goal was not to close, but rather to open, the past to investigation. Even before this, our press had published many articles on historical subjects, but now we were being flooded with them. Of course, there were some shallow pieces, falsification of facts and bias, but as far as I can judge there was a real desire to reach an understanding of the difficult and twisted course of events following the October Revolution and to produce evaluations *sine ira et studio*.

People's attitudes towards our reforms could often be seen in discussions of the past. I noticed this at the Politburo meetings where we discussed the anniversary speech. Ligachev, for example, argued that Bukharin, Rykov and Tomsky had proposed a slower pace of industrialization, and that such a policy could have constrained the country's progress towards socialism. Didn't Yeltsin's later arguments about 'Gorbachev's indecision' argue a similar point? For Yeltsin, much as for Ligachev, 'decisiveness' was determined not so much by the depth and effectiveness of changes as by the time-frame . . .

This was our eternal and painful theme, recurring in almost all of the subsequent discussion about the pace of perestroika. History has decided this argument. The sad state of Russia today is directly due to the fact that at some point the evolutionary approach was abandoned, to be replaced by *Sturm und Drang* methods which tore apart our society, destroying people's lives.

THE YELTSIN AFFAIR

An incident involving Yeltsin occurred at a Central Committee plenum on 21 October during the discussion of the speech for the seventieth anniversary of the October Revolution. Usually anniversary speeches were not discussed at plenums. The general mood at this session indicated that there was no need for debate this time either. Ligachev, who was presiding, put the question to a vote. I think he saw Yeltsin's raised hand but decided not to pay any attention to him. I had to intervene and say: 'I believe Boris Nikolaevich Yeltsin wishes to say something.' Ligachev gave him the floor.

Yeltsin began by remarking that the speech for the seventieth anniversary had been discussed a number of times in the Politburo, that he had indeed made some suggestions, that some of them had been taken into consideration and that for this reason today he did not have any comments ('I support it completely,' he said). Then he went on to the 'current situation'. The logic of his arguments could be paraphrased as follows: 'Today we are discussing the drama and the tragedies that our society has suffered, and the outcome of these. They occurred largely because of a lack of democracy, as a result of the cult of personality and of everything connected with it. This cult developed gradually because of violations of the principle of collective leadership. All power ended up in the hands of one person, who was protected from criticism, and we ought to learn a lesson from this. Nothing like it is happening in the Politburo right now, but nevertheless the General Secretary is increasingly being glorified by certain comrades. This is unacceptable at a time when we are laying the foundation for democratic forms of comradeship in the Party. We must prevent the spread of this evil.'

Next Yeltsin mentioned the problems that perestroika was encountering. He questioned the goal of achieving an improvement in people's standard of living over the next two or three years. He said that such an alluring and absolutely baseless forecast could eventually give rise to disenchantment and bitterness. Finally, he made a sensational announcement: for various reasons he could not cope with his work in the Politburo, partly owing to his lack of experience, partly for other reasons, but the main factor was a lack of support, especially from Ligachev. For these reasons he asked to be released from his duties as a candidate member of the Politburo and from his position as first secretary of the Moscow gorkom.

What could one say? If Yeltsin had then raised the question of 'unhealthy tendencies' in the work of the Politburo and the Central Committee Secretariat, this would have been a subject of serious discussion, to the benefit of all. However, his remarks sounded like an ultimatum and caused a sharp reaction. Speakers mentioned his 'wounded pride' and 'excessive ambition'.

Indeed word had reached me that Yeltsin thought that I was keeping him, the first secretary of the Party organization of the capital, in the 'waiting room' as a candidate to full membership of the Politburo and that this was preventing him from operating with sufficient authority. Moreover, he said, this was happening while 'mastodons and dinosaurs' from the past were being kept in the Politburo; he had sent me a letter calling for their removal on 12 September, while I was on holiday in the Crimea.

I have said that I was initially well disposed towards Yeltsin. I was impressed by his straightforward manner, although even then

I fully understood that any kind of radicalism is good only when it is combined with balance and a capacity for self-analysis and self-control.

He had every right to raise the possibility of changing the composition of the Politburo, the issue of the poor work of the Secretariat, and to call attention to the 'glorification' of the General Secretary if he believed that these things were really happening. We could have discussed what perestroika had given to the people and the rate at which change should occur; passions had already flared up around this topic. All of this could, and should, have been argued in the search for truth; and if he had only been seeking truth we could have come to an agreement.

But it was wounded pride talking. Those who pointed to his overgrown ambition and lust for power were right. Time has only confirmed this evaluation.

There was also another factor that pushed Yeltsin to take this step. In Moscow he was faced with obstacles whose existence he had not even suspected in Sverdlovsk. He seemed to be under the impression that all he needed to do was to get settled in his new position of power, to strengthen it with loyal people and then just give a good shove – and everything would be OK.

But he was wrong. Nothing of the kind happened. After the January and June Central Committee plenums the nomenklatura sensed that its vital interests were at stake and put up ingenious resistance. It seems to me that Yeltsin happened to be in the eye of the storm, since it was in the capital that the interests of the city, republic and central institutions of the old system were most closely entwined. He tried to rally Moscow Party organizations and the Muscovites themselves against these structures, and in my opinion he was right in this attempt. However, from the very beginning he used populist methods to achieve his goal. He would suddenly appear at a factory, take the manager and lead him to the workers' cafeteria to give him a public dressing-down, acting as if he were the protector of the people and the manager a monster of cruelty. Sometimes he would get on a bus or a tram, or drop into a shop or hospital, and the next day all of Moscow would be filled with rumours of this. To the enraptured applause of Muscovites he promised that problems of housing, medical care and services would be resolved in record time. He displayed colourful drawings of meat processing plants and dairies being built around the capital to do away with the eternal shortage of sausage and buttermilk. All of this was trumpeted in the Moscow press, radio and television. His search for new forms of Party work was also meant mostly for effect. For example, meetings of the Moscow city committee began to be held at eleven or twelve at night.

The time came for him to give a report on the results of his work as first secretary of the Moscow city committee – but almost nothing had changed and there were only promises in the air. We tried to support him as best we could: the Politburo, government and Central Committee Secretariat granted aid to Moscow in the form of finance, food and cadres, but the situation in the capital changed little for the better.

Yeltsin got nervous. He panicked and tried to rule by adminis-trative fiat. Not knowing what to do, he resorted to endless tirades, completely forgetting his calls for democracy. Perhaps the main conclusion one should draw from this is that Yeltsin even then showed that he was not a real reformer. Everyday business and especially the difficult search for compromise were not for him. His human qualities were more suited to the era of *Sturm und Drang*. I do not know, perhaps this was due to his former profession – to the perpetual state of emergency in which our builders strove to complete one or another project at any price, often leaving new buildings full of defects or simply not finished. Or maybe it was a sense of helplessness, of growing disappointment that little had been achieved in Moscow, which knocked him off balance and led to his breakdown.

Incidentally, I reflected on all of this only later. And I have allowed myself this extensive digression so that it will be clear that Yeltsin cannot be categorized either as an inherently virtuous and upstanding political figure or as one who is by nature deficient and immoral. He chose his own path and followed it to the end. The October plenum was a watershed for him – the choice he made then largely determined his future.

I watched Yeltsin from the platform and I understood what was going on in his heart. On his face one could read a strange mixture

– bitterness, uncertainty, regret, in other words everything that is characteristic of an unbalanced nature. Those who took the floor – and there were quite a few who only the day before had curried favour with him – berated him fiercely and painfully, as our people know how to do. Things grew hotter. Some demanded that he be not only stripped of his position as a candidate member of the Politburo but also removed from the Central Committee immediately. At that point I insisted on giving him the opportunity to speak, arguing that if we were democratizing the Party, we should begin with the Central Committee. Yeltsin walked up to the rostrum, began to say something not particularly coherent and finally admitted his error. I threw him a life-belt by proposing that he should rethink his position and withdraw his resignation. However, he did not accept my support and, very nervously, said: 'No, I still request that I be released.'

The decision adopted by the plenum consisted of two points. The first was an evaluation of Yeltsin's speech. The second instructed the Politburo together with the City Committee to look into the situation and to decide on a new first secretary for the Moscow gorkom.

With that the Central Committee plenum closed. Ten days later, on 31 October, Yeltsin came to the Politburo session at which the final version of the speech for the seventieth anniversary of the October Revolution was being discussed. When he was offered the floor, he broke into a tirade, saying that in the initial stage of perestroika we had gathered speed, but now we had lost it; at that time the people's readiness for change was great, but we had promised too much and had missed the moment. According to him, since mid-1986 'we had again made significant progress, while I – and this is my chief mistake – because of ambition or pride avoided normal collaboration with Ligachev, Razumovsky and Yakovlev. However, my comrades in the Party gorkom have not turned away from me, even though they condemn my behaviour, and they ask me to stay,' he said.

It turned out that he had asked the secretaries of the Moscow gorkom to meet without him. The gorkom bureau had concluded that Yeltsin's behaviour and speech were erroneous but nevertheless reflected only his personal opinion; they complained that he had not discussed matters beforehand with his comrades and they recommended that he withdraw his resignation and continue working.

On 3 November, as if nothing had happened, he sent me a brief letter, in which he presented this opinion from the gorkom bureau and requested in this connection that he be allowed to continue work as the first secretary of the Moscow gorkom. It was simply impossible to understand his logic. No-one had the right to over-turn the decision of a Central Committee plenum. The situation was also complicated by the fact that the foreign press had published a fabricated text of Yeltsin's speech, and different versions of this started appearing in Moscow. Yeltsin himself did not refute the forgery. Obviously, he had begun to think of himself as a 'hero of the people'. Under these conditions his attempt to back out was at the least strange.

I gathered the Politburo members who were in town and told them about Yeltsin's letter; everyone present was in favour of implementing the plenum resolution. I telephoned Yeltsin and told him that the Politburo members had decided to take the question to the Party city committee, and I gave him a piece of my mind.

In the morning of 9 November, as I recall, I was informed of an emergency at the Moscow gorkom: Yeltsin had been found covered with blood. A team of doctors headed by Chazov was sent immediately. The mystery was soon resolved. Yeltsin, using office scissors, had simulated an attempt at suicide – there was no other way to interpret his action. The doctors said that the wound was not critical at all; the scissors, by slipping over his ribs, had left a bloody but superficial wound. Yeltsin was taken to hospital and the doctors did everything to prevent this unattractive story from becoming public. The rumour spread that he had been sitting at a table, had passed out, fallen against the table and accidentally cut himself with a pair of scissors which he had been holding. However, this tale did not suit Yeltsin and after a couple of years he came out with a different version, according to which he had been attacked on the street by two hooligans with sheath-knives; of course, he had 'tossed them about like kittens', but still he had received a knife wound.

Needless to say, this tale sounded much more heroic. By then, I had already discovered Yeltsin's talent for fiction.

Meanwhile, on 9 November, I had to call another urgent meeting of the Politburo. The doctors once again confirmed that the wound was not serious and that Yeltsin's condition had stabilized. We decided that the question of his future had to be resolved immediately. I myself talked to him by telephone. To spare him embarrassment I immediately said that I knew everything and I also knew how he must feel. Therefore, we had to set a date for a plenum of the Moscow gorkom.

The meeting was held on 12 November. I was accompanied by Ligachev and Zaikov. The mood was grave. Yeltsin was a great master at offending his colleagues and co-workers. He put people down meanly, painfully, often undeservedly, and he had to pay for it now. A number of the speeches were clearly motivated by revenge or malice. I recall a strident speech by Prokofiev, who gave a long account of how unjustly he had been treated. All of this left an unpleasant aftertaste. However, at the plenum Yeltsin showed self-control and, I would say, behaved like a man.

From the very beginning I tried not to turn the 'Yeltsin affair' into a scandal and attempted to resolve it in accord with the new atmosphere in the Central Committee, in the Party and in the country. Hence when the question of the publication of the speeches, including mine, at the Moscow gorkom plenum came up in the Politburo, I suggested that all of the personal statements about Yeltsin should be toned down, so as to avoid compromising his life and work.

I was supported: 'Yes, Yes! This is the way to do it.'

Yakovlev, Razumovsky and Boldin were asked to edit the press report that was being prepared in the city committee. However, later there were many rumours depicting the incident as the 'lynching' of the 'champion of the people'. One must assume that the rumours were started by Yeltsin himself, and by those who were already measuring him for the role of democratic leader.

Yeltsin was under treatment for some time after the Moscow gorkom plenum and then went on holiday. On 14 January 1988, he was named First Deputy Chairman of Gosstroi, with the rank of minister. He remained a candidate member of the Politburo and participated in several meetings until he was released from these duties at the February plenum. Later my colleagues reproached me more than once for not having brought the affair to an end: 'You should have driven him out of the Central Committee and sent him to a far-away place, to the ends of the earth, or, if you pity him that much, to some distant land as ambassador. There he would have faded away.' How many times I was told: 'Well, admit it, this was your biggest blunder!'

Such thoughts have never occurred to me. It is not in my nature to seek to get even with people. And this would contradict the spirit I strived to introduce into the Party. In deciding Yeltsin's new position, I proceeded from the conviction that everything should be built on comradeship. I did not have any hatred towards him and especially did not feel the need for revenge. Even when he began to shower me with accusations and insults of the lowest kind in the course of political struggles, he never succeeded in drawing me into that kind of an argument and I never lowered myself to his level of kitchen squabbling.

THE FEBRUARY PLENUM

The celebrations for the seventieth anniversary of the October Revolution, along with press articles on a wide range of sensitive issues, produced much excitement in the country. On 4–5 November we had an interesting discussion of the problems of historical development at a Kremlin meeting of public figures who had come for the anniversary ceremonies. There I first put forward the view that there could be more than one course of historical evolution and that the contradiction between two systems is not the determining factor. Moreover, the admission of the need to abandon the Party's monopoly on truth sounded quite 'mutinous', like a call to dissidence coming from the General Secretary.

The democratization of our society and radical economic reforms in the new stage of perestroika were discussed at a meeting of Party workers in late November and at a subsequent meeting with the leaders of the mass media, scholars and artists on 1 December. An article by Academician V. N. Kudryavtsev, who argued in favour of a state governed by law, published in the November issue of *Soviet State and Law*, was met with genuine interest. In general, the turn of the year from 1987 to 1988 was marked by deeper analysis in all social sciences. The archives and secret depositories were releasing the works of thinkers and artists whose names they had previously been afraid to say out loud. Intoxicated with freedom, historians, economists, philosophers, sociologists and literary scholars alike strove to cleanse their subject-areas of the distortions and delusions that had been engendered by Stalinism, and to make objective evaluations of the state of our society.

Even then, under an avalanche of new facts and data, we could see the deficiency and over-simplification of our former ideas of socialism and socialist values. If we indeed had the most advanced society, if we were really the bearers of the future, why then did we chronically lag behind other countries, both in standard of living and in labour productivity? If we were the most democratic country in the world, why were people deprived of spiritual freedom and why were they not permitted to participate in political processes and decision-making?

People now spoke openly about these and many other sensitive issues; the new generation, the young people, were not afraid of being accused of 'anti-Soviet agitation'. And, needless to say, the arguments of our ideologists regarding the 'creation of the basis of socialism', its 'complete and final victory' and, finally, 'the construction of a developed socialist society', which were purely apologetic and scholastic, could no longer satisfy anyone.

Meanwhile we were making gradual progress with the reform of the economy. On 1 January 1988 all enterprises were officially converted to a cost-accounting basis. Laws on their financial autonomy, the reforms of Gosbank and the creation of special credit institutions took effect. The Presidium of the USSR Supreme Soviet approved a decree on the administration of psychiatric services so as to prevent the abuses that had occurred in this area. In response to mass protests in many regions of the country, a decision was made to pay more attention to environmental protection. The public demanded that changes be made in the decisions taken after Brezhnev's death, and on 7 January former names were restored to a number of places: Naberezhnye Chelny, Cheremushki district in Moscow, Krasnogvardeiskaya Square in Leningrad. Moscow no longer had a Brezhnev Square. February began with a plenum of the USSR Supreme Court, which repealed the sentences of 1938 and ended legal proceedings against Bukharin, Rykov, Rakovsky and others who had been prosecuted for their alleged participation in an 'anti-Soviet right-wing Trotskyist bloc'.

On 9 February I announced specific steps for a political settlement in Afghanistan, including the withdrawal of our troops over a period of ten months. If one recalls how many lives this war cost us, how many young people were crippled for life, and the loss and sufferings of the Afghan people, one can understand the explosion of hope that came from the promise to end this conflict that had brought shame on our nation.

Yet my heart was not at peace. Democratization was giving rise to difficult contradictory processes in the spheres of ideology and inter-ethnic relations. More and more often, before the start of Politburo and secretariat meetings there were discussions of the harshest criticisms from the press, radio and television. Regardless of the agenda such conversations continued at the meetings themselves, sometimes pushing aside important questions that needed an immediate decision. Passions flared. Every time Politburo members, especially Yegor Ligachev, would repeat the very same thing: we have given in to the press and lost control over it. He laid the responsibility at Yakovlev's door. Of course, Yegor Kuzmich perfectly understood that this was a matter of policy, but since things had not yet reached the point of making direct attacks on the General Secretary, I was just told that I was too patient, and needed to do something to 'put an end to this'. As time went by, such comments came more and more frequently from Solomentsev, Chebrikov and Yazov, who were eventually joined by Ryzhkov.

Since glasnost had exposed many of the flaws of our reality, there were few who rejected the need for perestroika. But behind the apparent unity were different, sometimes directly opposing, views. The top levels of the Party and state apparatus seemed to believe that there was no need to replace the existing system – God forbid – it only needed a bit of fine tuning. When I tried to find out the nature of this 'fine tuning', I learned that it meant only purely cosmetic upkeep, similar to the painting of the façades on central streets that has been the practice for holidays here.

It is well known that extreme conservatism only feeds head-strong radicalism. Its advocates were yesterday's dissidents and some of the artistic intelligentsia, especially young academics, who, anxious to improve their social status and break into major politics, rushed headlong to expand the 'bounds of what is permitted'. Rejecting socialist values, these people, who only yesterday had been praising those same values in their disser-tations, demanded a complete and immediate dismantling of the previous system.

In a speech at the Central Committee plenum in February 1988, I warned against vulgar and simplistic analyses either of our past or of the society that we had created. I said that we must not see in our history merely a chain of bloody crimes. We must not mock the memories of our people. We must understand how our fathers and grandfathers lived, what they worked for, what millions of people believed in, how the great victories and defeats, successes and failures, revelations and mistakes, the bright and the tragic combined into a single whole.

I said that in this sense perestroika was both a result of our preceding development and a sort of 'negation of negation' phase, where we were beginning to free ourselves of what had become brakes to further progress. Thanks to the political and economic reforms, socialism was being freed of distortions, returned to its sources and at the same time was reaching new and historic frontiers of renewal.

When I re-read my speech today, I have mixed feelings. I was absolutely sincere in upholding the main lines of perestroika-glasnost, democratization, and economic reform. I spoke those words sincerely, like an incantation: 'everything that we are doing is aimed at revealing the potential of socialism'. It truly seemed to us then that the country's misfortunes were not in any way connected with any inherent properties of the system and that the contradictions that had built up in the economy, in politics and in the spiritual sphere could be resolved without going outside its original framework. In short, we were not yet aware of the scale of the impending changes, or that the crisis involved not just some aspects of the system, but rather all of it.

At the same time, even then I understood that the logic of reform required not simply an improvement in the system, but incursions into its very fundamentals. Although we used the same words, we spoke about different things.

I had already initiated discussion of the primacy of universal human values as the profound essence of a modern understanding of socialism. There would come a time when another lesson would become obvious to me: development of any kind is possible only if there is internal diversity. The achievement of an 'ideal' as a result of the complete victory of one trend inevitably leads the newly created system to internal crisis and ruin. Therefore it is scarcely valid or productive to strive towards a society with exclusively 'socialist' features. We must consider not only stages of development, but also the future of civilization: the criteria for creation of a new twenty-first-century society, a modern civilization. In any developed and dynamic society there are elements of conservatism and radicalism, individualism and collectivism, liberalism and socialist values, without which the very existence of the world community would be impossible (especially today, when we face the threat of nuclear and environmental destruction). It is the search for a synthesis of these elements and trends and their optimum interaction – and they are different in every historical era and for every people – that sustains movement towards a new civilization. From this standpoint we may speak of the socialist idea and of socialist values as a global phenomenon, as an organic component of mankind's intensive spiritual quest. This does not in any way belittle the importance of, say, liberal or purely democratic values.

Thus by radically changing the approach to the criteria of socialism, we arrive first at a myriad of ways of embodying the socialist ideal, and then at a new philosophy of history. I drew these conclusions only later. At the February plenum I said that it was man, his intellectual and political character, his mastery and capacity for creativity, his patriotism and internationalism that will be at the centre of existence and will in the final account determine the success of social transformations. Much of what I said was out of the ordinary. I proclaimed that the most important values were not the ones that we had been taught: the leading role of the Party, state property, planned economic development or, put more simply, tonnes of steel and wheat, kilometres of railroad and metres of cloth. When I stated that the leading role of the Party was 'not given by anyone from above or for all time', my colleagues immediately pricked up their ears. 'How can this be, what has happened to the leadership of the Party?' Had they been frank, their question would have been simpler: 'What about our power?' After all, the entire ideological balancing act was just a way of concealing the rule of the nomenklatura. This was also the reason why the administrative-command system suited them and why professional mourners for socialism and fierce defenders of Marxism-Leninism appeared.

The thrust of my speech at the February Central Committee plenum was once again to explain that perestroika would not happen without democratization, that without this there was no escape from the advancing crisis for our country.

After the February plenum, polarization became even stronger. Those who had felt the ground vanishing from under their feet since the beginning of democratization realized that the fate of the nation was connected with their own fate. I became increasingly convinced that behind their ruffled feelings and uncontrolled emotions and sometimes just plain bitterness was not so much concern for the people as fear of losing the positions they had held.

However, no-one would risk presenting the public with a self-serving programme. Private and group interests had to be camouflaged by supposedly disinterested service to high ideals and principles expressed in ultra-revolutionary phrases. And, when there is a 'public need' for some item of merchandise, it quickly appears on the market.

THE CREDO OF THE ANTI-PERESTROIKA FORCES

On 13 March I left for Yugoslavia on a state visit. On board the aircraft I was given the newspapers for that day as usual. Shakhnazarov, who had already looked through them, said that there was an article I ought to read. He meant Nina Andreyeva's anti-perestroika article 'I cannot go against my principles' in *Sovetskaya Rossiya*. It was a frontal assault on the reform process.

After my return from Yugoslavia, there was a discussion of this article in the Politburo. I pointed out that the publication of Nina Andreyeva's article was only made possible by perestroika and glasnost. But I strongly disagreed with the call from some of my colleagues to reprint this article in other papers. I doubted whether this material had been written by Andreyeva, who was a chemistry teacher at the technological institute. This article contained information known only to a relatively narrow circle.

There was a mixed reaction from other members of the Politburo who took the floor – and all of them did. Some of them, such as Vorotnikov and Ligachev, characterized the article as an understandable reaction to the negative view of our past. Others, including Yakovlev, Zaikov and Shevardnadze, agreed with me. 'The article is harmful,' Shevardnadze said. 'It is written by a narrow-minded person who is an enemy of perestroika and of renewal.'

Ryzhkov called for 'a balanced approach to ideology' and wondered why it needed more than one Politburo member – both Yakovlev and Ligachev – to deal with ideological work. Yazov complained that 'some things that you can see on television do not have a good effect on people.'

I concluded by saying that the conversation had been necessary. 'Our reaction to this article must be calm and serious,' I said.

That night I lay awake for a long time thinking over this discussion and its more remarkable episodes. Everyone had sworn their loyalty to perestroika and had taken an oath to unity. This, of course, was essential and would help us get through the next stage of reforms with fewer complications. On the other hand, the ephemeral nature of the solidarity of the leadership council had once again shown itself. Nostalgia for the past and internal disagreements with many of our innovations had slipped out in the arguments of some of my colleagues. Some were not in step, but were forcing themselves to tag along while suppressing their disagreement, simply so as not to lose power and the benefits it brought them. Of course, things could not go on like this forever. A split was inevitable. The question was, when?

EN ROUTE TO THE PARTY CONFERENCE

The idea of holding an All-Union Party Conference was first brought up at the January 1987 Central Committee plenum, and the formal decision to hold the conference was made by the June plenum that same year. In my concluding speech at that plenum I had said: 'For us Communists it will essentially be a political examination in the main subject of our life – perestroika. We must do all of our practical work so as to pass this exam with high marks and bring to the conference good practical experience and real results, so that we can draw lessons for the future.'

By spring 1988 it had become obvious that resistance to our reforms was growing. The forthcoming conference would be a test of strength between the reform and conservative wings of the Party – and of all society as well, since all of the politically active people in the country were in the Party. There was a lull before the storm. After the February plenum my opponents, sensing where the General Secretary was 'driving', were alarmed and began bustling about. Of course, where there is bustle, there are always mistakes, and so they 'exposed' themselves. Without knowing it, Nina Andreyeva actually helped us.

Pravda's editor, Afanasiev, and his colleagues wrote the initial draft of an editorial that was intended to be a response to the *Sovetskaya Rossiya* article. But it clearly was not 'up to snuff': it had neither breadth of view nor depth of conclusion. Yakovlev, Medvedev and my aides took up the task. The amended version was distributed to my closest associates, and I participated in the final stage of editing the text. *Pravda* published this article on 5 April. It seems that it was that very same day that Ligachev dropped in to see me. He was quite ill at ease. He denied that he was one of the authors of Andreyeva's article, and said that a check ought to be run. I stopped him: 'Calm down, there will be no need for any investigation. It would not do for us to create a split in the Central Committee and Politburo . . .'

I must remind the reader that the Central Committee could have called off the conference, since by its statutes this was its prerogative. If someone had started a 'mutiny', the reformers would be the worse off, since most Central Committee members were not on their side. Today I can talk about this openly. The reformers were Gorbachev, Yakovlev, Medvedev, Shevardnadze, Ryzhkov, Slyunkov. Who else? Zaikov, Razumovsky? – it is hard to say. However, the enormous respect that came with the position of General Secretary and the growing public support for perestroika helped to maintain our control over the situation. It was important to make use of this and so we rolled up our sleeves and began preparing for the conference, which was only two months away.

You can imagine how much I had to talk and listen to people then, to convince and sometimes to be convinced myself. At the all-Union congress of kolkhozniks,[1] at a meeting with representatives of the press and the arts intelligentsia, at a conference of heads of Central Committee departments (28 March) – everywhere I strived to carry out a dual task. On the one hand, I needed to have a better understanding of the state of mind and attitudes in various strata of society, and, on the other hand, I had to bring my ideas and my understanding of the prospects for the future to as broad an audience as possible, and to include the people in the shaping of policy in every way I could.

In the course of the preparation for the Party Conference I tested the idea of combining the positions of obkom first secretary and chairman of the oblast Soviet. Since we had only one ruling party, then we could at least put it under the control of the people in this way. My thought was that this would allow power to be transferred to the Soviets more smoothly and less painfully. On the other hand, the credibility of a Party leader would be tested in elections: if he obtained a mandate, then he would feel

[1] Meeting of collective-farm workers.

confident; if not, he would have to find work in a different field.

I have to say that this idea produced sharp debate, both in the Party and in society. Some argued that if these positions were combined the Soviets would again become run by the Party Secretaries. Others were afraid that this reform threatened to do away with the leading role of the Party. This argument came especially from those who feared, and not without reason, that the outcome of an election would be bad for them. I called on them to join in the election campaign so that this would not happen, but they were not enthusiastic. After all, up to that time they had been given positions or had positions taken away according to the rules of the nomenklatura and had been almighty in their 'private domains'. Why put all this to a vote? There had already been a few contested elections and even some who had considered their positions unshakable had been voted out as a result of secret ballots.

Some were particularly upset by the proposal to limit leadership positions to two terms. They asked: 'Starting when?' You could read on their faces their fear of losing the positions that many of them had only recently gained.

Although eventually a majority supported practically all the proposals that we prepared for the Conference, I could not help but feel that many Party secretaries were not ready for free elections and separation of powers.

At that time there was much talk about a serious shake-up of the cadres at the conference. However, I was against raising this issue at that moment. The cadre problem would unavoidably be the delegates' centre of attention and could push fundamental political decisions into the background or even threaten their passage. Moreover, it would have been a one-off operation. My idea was different; the Party conference was to open the way to political reform, so that the people could participate in solving these issues in the future as a result of free elections. Basically that was indeed what happened.

On 23 May a discussion paper was presented to a Central Committee plenum. Twenty of those present took the floor in the debates and endorsed the paper, which seemed a good omen. After useful suggestions were taken into account, the report was published in *Pravda* on 27 May, exactly one month before the start of the conference.

It would be no exaggeration to say that it was a bombshell. All of the mass media joined in the discussion; newspapers printed special sections. Before this, society had been still waiting to see where and when the 'top' would throw open the door. Now people began to believe that we were embarking on a fundamentally new course. There was freedom in the air.

Along with the discussion, people were closely following the elections of delegates to the conference. We made sure that the elections would not be the same as before, when almost all of the delegates were selected by the organizational department of the Central Committee. This time the Communists indeed held genuine elections, under the eye of a watchful press. After all, we did not have to re-invent the wheel – we simply had to demand strict observance of the CPSU statutes.

There was a latent anxiety of sorts in the preparation of my speech to the Conference – the lines drawn between positions in the leadership, in the Party and in society as a whole were making themselves felt. The reformers feared that the nomenklatura would again twist things in its favour and have its supporters elected as delegates, who would then bury the reforms.

THE XIXth PARTY CONFERENCE

The conference opened on 28 June in the Kremlin Palace of Congresses. My speech started off like Hamlet's famous soliloquy: 'How to deepen and make irreversible revolutionary perestroika, which on the initiative and under the leadership of the Party has been launched in our country – this is the fundamental question . . . Our answer to it will decide whether or not the Party is capable of acting as the political vanguard in the new stage of development of Soviet society.'

This statement was dictated by the realities of that time. The policy of perestroika was being taken up by the masses, people were emerging from a state of apathy and alienation, and the purification of the atmosphere in our society, that had been fouled by long years of stagnation, was gaining strength. But this was only part of the truth – otherwise there would have been no need to begin the speech in such a dramatic key. The other part of the truth was that the mechanisms of renewal were not yet fully operational and that the road to freedom was being blocked by the nomenklatura. The experience we had gained in perestroika, like the experience of preceding reformers, called for fundamental reforms to the political system.

I said that we had underestimated just how deeply distortions and stagnation had affected our society and that the situation had turned out to be far more critical than we had previously thought. I concentrated on analysing the results of the three years of perestroika. Though the situation was alarming, I said that salvation should be sought not in abandoning reforms or veering off the course that we had chosen, but rather in pushing ahead with the reform process.

I went on to formulate the basic tasks: implementation of radical economic reform, activation of the spiritual potential of society, reform of the political system, democratization of international relations. The Party Conference approved this approach, as could be seen from the decisions that were adopted. The delegates were so taken by the discussion that many set aside their prepared speeches and rushed to the rostrum with spontaneous speeches and remarks. The Party had not known such an open and lively debate since its first post-revolutionary congresses. In addition, it was broadcast live throughout the country. People were literally glued to their radios and televisions!

One might say that I had to assume the role of the captain of a ship riding out a storm. Indeed the conference 'ship' veered to port and to starboard, occasionally turning so sharply that I thought the wheel would be ripped from my hands. I admit that I felt proud at being able to keep control of the situation, without being driven off course.

The debate was opened by Bakatin. His speech was balanced and contained useful ideas on the democratization of the economy. He argued convincingly in support of the idea of combining the higher posts in the Party and Soviet organs. At some point the delegates engaged in a competition of sorts: who could take a better shot at higher-placed Party members. Melnikov, the first secretary of the Komi obkom, stopped just short of a call for a new witch hunt: 'Anyone who in former times actively carried out the policy of stagnation cannot hold a position in the central Party or Soviet organs today, in the period of perestroika,' he proclaimed. 'They must answer for everything, and answer personally.' One could have agreed with the idea, had it not been for its hysterical undertone. 'Any specific proposals?' I asked him. 'Otherwise we sit here without knowing whom you have in mind.' Melnikov replied that he was thinking of Solomentsev, Gromyko, Afanasiev (the editor of *Pravda*), Arbatov and others.

A note in defence of Gromyko was sent to the presidium: 'Andrei Andreyevich Gromyko is a respected man both among the people and in the Party. He has devoted his life and work to us. We the people, we Communists, have put this fresh burden upon him. And the principle "The hard worker gets the blame" has worked again. We have "run him into the ground". Today comrade Gromyko is behind the times. However, he has completed his work, the people will remember his good deeds, and we ought to refrain from these off-hand insults. He is respected and loved by the people.' The delegates applauded warmly when this note was read aloud.

There were many lively and emotional speeches. The actor Mikhail Ulyanov raised the issue of the freedom of the press, and I joined in the debate. I said that it was necessary to allow various points of view to be presented in the press so that the full spectrum of attitudes and problems would become clearer, and so that correct decisions could be made on this basis. We should not replace one monopoly with another or one half-truth with another half-truth. We needed the whole truth. Some newspapers and journals could easily, offhandedly, insult a person. Was this really acceptable? I said that this practice must be decisively condemned at the conference. At the same time, we needed to preserve glasnost through criticism and an active public opinion. We would not be able to solve our problems otherwise. The main trouble in the past was that the people had been excluded from public life and from the decision-making processes for too long.

The first signs of the fledgling right-wing conservative opposition could be seen at the conference. You could sense it in the aggressive speeches of a number of Party functionaries. However, the radically minded delegates, including Yeltsin, spoke out just as decisively. On the whole, Yeltsin supported perestroika in all specific aspects and, except for his criticism of the idea of combining the positions of first secretary and chairman of the Soviet, he tried to avoid confrontation. He paid particular attention to social justice, calling attention to 'privileges' and declaring that we must finally eliminate the special food 'perks' for the 'starving nomenklatura', and abolish both in substance and form the word 'Spets'[1] – special stores, special clinics, special health resorts, and so forth – since we did not have any special communists.

Later Yeltsin developed this 'down with privilege' theme and eventually made it his battle-cry. It is a paradox one can often encounter in the history of politics. While we exerted ourselves gradually to dismantle the system of unwarranted privileges and perquisites, braving the stubborn resistance of the nomenklatura, he somehow managed to get all the credit for it and to create for himself the image of the chief warrior against privilege. These unwarranted laurels opened his way to the top. However, having beaten his way to power, Yeltsin instantly forgot his wrathful speeches against abuses and allowed his associates to indulge in corruption and privileges such as the Communist nomenklatura had never dreamed of.

The drafts of documents were heatedly debated. Passions were high both in the committees and at the conference, especially on the matter of delimiting functions between Party and state organs. Many delegates realized that what we were in fact discussing was the transfer of real power to the Soviets. Indeed the plan was to change the structure of the Party apparatus and to abolish branch departments by the end of the year, to discuss the reorganization of the Soviets at the autumn session of the USSR Supreme Soviet and finally to recommend elections of the USSR people's deputies in April 1989 and elections to the Supreme Soviets of

[1] Special facilities for the nomenklatura.

the union republics and autonomous republics at the end of the year.

Many saw the proposal to combine posts by nominating the secretaries of Party committees for election as chairmen of Soviets as a slick move that would preserve the dominant role of the Party secretaries. I had to speak on this issue twice and I was able eventually to persuade most of the delegates that all we wanted was to assure a quiet and smooth transition from one political system to another. Many people still suspect Gorbachev of trying to save the Party nomenklatura. Sheer nonsense! My only intent was to promote political reform. I was greatly concerned about how the Party organizations would react. Time has shown that this worry was well founded. However, no-one could turn back the clock.

The discussion of the resolution 'on glasnost' produced many arguments about the status of *Pravda*. There were proposals to elect its editorial board and to make the members accountable at CPSU congresses, and that *Pravda* should be considered an organ of all the Party and not just the Central Committee. After weighing all the 'pros' and 'cons' – and this was a dangerous initiative, since at that critical moment a split was quite possible – the conference rejected the innovations.

A recurrent theme – the responsibility of the press for the publication of untrue or libellous material – was reflected in the resolution. At the same time, the resolution stated that critical press reports must not be constrained and that persecution for criticism would not be permitted. I supported the proposal to publish regular reports on all of the Party's finances.

As the conference progressed, there were frequent calls for more detailed coverage of the activity of higher Party organs. There were convincing arguments in favour of this: in order to prevent a return of a cult of personality, to keep 'wolves in sheep's clothing' from responsible positions, Communists should know what was happening in the Politburo, what the ambitions of individual members of the leadership were. In particular, the delegates asked for an explanation of how it could happen that Chernenko, a man who was terminally ill and unpopular in the Party, had been elected to the post of General Secretary.

The Party Conference made me aware of a growing rift in the CPSU and of an increasingly critical attitude towards perestroika. Later we ran up against what could be described as direct sabotage by a significant number of the Party secretaries and the Party apparatus. The results of the conference therefore became even more important with time. It authoritatively fixed the course of reforms and served as an official blessing of our ideas, sanctioning the timetable for transformation of the political system. It would be no exaggeration to say that the XIXth Party Conference served as the springboard for all our reforms.

The openness of the conference produced a shock, not only in the Soviet Union but also in the West. It showed that from then on the voice of the people would be heard and the will of the people would determine the choice of paths for the development and formation of state structures. It strengthened the spirit and improved the attitude of all true champions of democratic transformation.

The Party Conference was a personal landmark for me. It was a watershed, a clear line between 'before' and 'after'. In the 'before' I left behind the wavering, the fear of being torn from ideological propositions that had outlived their time but had still not lost their halo ('An idol cast down is still a god,' Lermontov wrote), the fear of sailing further with the danger of 'mutiny'. We had to put all our efforts in the 'after' so as to utilize fully the unique chance for real reform offered by the conference. Time was of the essence – we could not lose a day, or even an hour.

THE FOLLOW-UP

The implementation of the decisions of the Party Conference was discussed at two Politburo meetings on 4 July and 21 July. I opened the session by saying that we would be making a big mistake if we did not turn our attention to discontent with the progress of economic reform, the work of the ministries, the critical situation of both trade and transport and, in particular, of the food supply. Our propaganda had helped to produce great expectations that were not being fulfilled. And what a strain queues were causing among the people! The entire country was queuing: in shops, waiting for buses, in various offices, queuing for all kinds of permissions or certificates. People were wasting time just to solve the most simple problems. They were exhausted. And this was supposed to be perestroika!

We discussed agrarian policy at length. The reform attempts in 1965 and 1982 had not solved the agricultural problem. The organizational measures and the enormous amount of money invested in agriculture had failed to produce the expected results. I suggested a different approach to agrarian policy:

'We need radical transformation, and not only in neglected villages or unprofitable collective farms, but in all rural areas. Until we lift all restraints, nothing will happen. If a man wants to lease a farm, no-one has the right to say no. Any kind of production "target" is permissible only on a voluntary basis, when something is being offered in exchange – in other words when business is being conducted on a proper economic basis. Not by command, but rather by contract; and the bureaucrats should not be allowed near this. We must think of ways to promote leasing and individual labour more rapidly. Give people a chance to earn some money – in the non-black-earth region, in the Stavropol region, everywhere. Nikonov still thinks that the question can be resolved by orders from above, just by the allocation of finances and equipment. But we must create an atmosphere in which it will be possible to act on one's own initiative. Furthermore, we must mould public opinion, since even today a businessman here is considered to be a self-seeking money grabber. In China people were simply given land and told: do what you want, and in spite of all their poverty production has increased by 100 million tonnes of grain in only four years. We will achieve nothing if all we do is bawl: "You must, you must, you must!" The moment we get new economic relations going, products will appear – the peasants will be happy, and we shall need fewer people in agriculture. The plan that we have here will not do . . . Promising people that there will be sufficient food in ten or fifteen years! No, this won't do – we must change the forms of labour in agriculture over the next two or three years. Of course, agriculture and the food industry will need machines and fertilizers and resources. Money for these things must be found, even if it comes from the defence budget. We had heard the people's verdict on the XIXth Party Conference – no-one can ignore it. The shortage of food had come to affect our country's security.'

13

WORK AND REFLECTION

ON 1 AUGUST I WENT ON HOLIDAY, AS ALWAYS TO THE CRIMEA. This holiday differed little from others that I spent in my time as General Secretary. I prepared proposals for the reorganization of the Party apparatus and for plenums on nationalities policy and agrarian policy. I had also planned to do some theoretical reflection, as I always try to do on holiday, but the abundant stream of information distracted me from this.

I must admit that Ligachev's speeches on 5 August 1988 in Gorky and 31 August in Tula worried me. Much of what he said cast doubt on the results of the Party Conference and smacked of pre-perestroika dogmatism on the questions of the market, commodity-money relations and the nature of property ownership under socialism, and on the new thinking. 'We must assume the class character of international relations,' he said categorically. 'A different statement of the issue only brings confusion into the minds of Soviet people and our friends abroad.'

At first glance, this tirade appeared to be directed at the Minister of Foreign Affairs, but in fact Ligachev was aiming at the General Secretary. This is how it came about. At the end of July, literally on the eve of the plenum, Shevardnadze had made a speech at the Ministry of Foreign Affairs in which he said that, in light of the notion of the priority of human values, 'the philosophy of peaceful co-existence as a universal principle in international relations has a different content. The new thinking places it in the context of the realities of the nuclear age. We are right to refuse to see in it some specific form of the class struggle.'

Shevardnadze's speech was full of ideas that sounded radical for that time. His thesis that the antagonism between the two systems, capitalism versus socialism, could not be viewed as the leading trend of the modern era was true 'sedition' in the eyes of the official ideologues.

Ligachev was obviously reacting to this speech. Yakovlev did not keep out of the discussion, either. He spoke on 10 August in Riga and, although he did not mention Ligachev, he refuted Ligachev's arguments about the role of the market.

My fears of disagreements between members of the leadership were confirmed when Chebrikov, Lukyanov and Ryzhkov telephoned to discuss the speeches by Shevardnadze and Ligachev. Ligachev's 'pre-perestroika' positions did not go unnoticed in the West either. The US Ambassador, Jack Matlock, asked our specialists in international affairs what was the 'true meaning' of Ligachev's speech in Gorky.

On 14–15 August I continued dictating notes about the reorganization of the Party apparatus. I had to get this done quickly: elections in the lower rungs of the Party were about to begin.

Even at the VIIIth RCP(B)[1] Congress it had been said that the Party must implement its policy 'through the Soviets, ably, tactfully, not in such a way as to step on the toes of Sovnarkom or other institutions.' Indeed that was the origin of the tasks that we had to face in 1988. We were taking up anew, as it were, what had been interrupted for decades under the totalitarian regime.

I believed that all functions of direct management of the economy should be transferred from the Party to the government. However, we were forced to retreat in some matters – in particular, we decided to remain in a transitional stage until the Soviets and government organs had gathered enough strength. We decided to retain, for the time being, Central Committee departments of agrarian policy and defence. It was decided to create a special governmental department of law in order to ensure reliable control of the Ministry of Internal Affairs, the Ministry of Defence, and the Committee of State Security (KGB).

[1] 16–23 March 1919.

The economic situation was not good, there was growing dissatisfaction with the slow pace of transformation, and the radicals, who were gearing up for a run at power, had already begun to play on these moods. Sensing this threat, I felt that it was my duty to warn the people of the dangers of populism: often what comes in attractive packages and promises rapid changes is intended to achieve something completely different. Serious problems cannot be solved at one fell swoop by *fiat*. We know what this can lead to. During my August vacation I spoke with members of the leadership every day. I had several conversations with Aleksandr Yakovlev in connection with articles in the press on German-Soviet relations on the eve of the Second World War. In particular, we had a discussion about the article by Leonid Pochivalov, 'The Germans and Us', in *Literaturnaya Gazeta,* which had a great effect both here and abroad, especially in the GDR.[1]

I discussed the question of grain purchases with Ryzhkov; he complained about the one-sided approach of Ligachev and Nikonov towards problems of the agro-industrial complex. He seized the opportunity to state once again his view that the Central Committee should only have departments dealing with general policy. I agreed that we would come to this, but for now I felt that it would be risky to let defence and agrarian policy get out of Party control.

IMPRESSIONS OF KRASNOYARSK

My holiday slipped by quickly. On 5 September I returned to Moscow and on the 12th I left for Krasnoyarsk krai. It was a remarkable trip, one that left me with many memories! Everywhere, whether in the little village of Sizaya back in the Sayan foothills or in the world's largest non-ferrous metal smelting compound in polar Norilsk, I had very interesting meetings and uncommonly candid conversations.

I had barely touched down when I heard from the residents of

[1] German Democratic Republic (or East Germany).

Yemelyanovo settlement (during a short stop *en route* to Krasnoyarsk from the airport) the universal opinion of the residents of this krai: 'Unfortunately the bosses are doing a poor job of implementing perestroika and everything stays the same.' I was immediately in the firing-line – everything was shown on television, and not only here but also abroad the word was: 'The Siberians have shown Gorbachev a thing or two.'

Again there were planning problems, with the planners set on developing production capacities and leaving the social infrastructure 'for later'. But what could be achieved without people? In the past, much had been done by prisoners, but now there were significantly fewer of them – we were living in different times.

In the days when Kosygin was Chairman of the USSR Council of Ministers someone had the idea of building an industrial centre in the southern part of Krasnoyarsk krai, including power stations, electrical engineering works and aluminium factories. Concentrating more than a dozen large plants in such a small spot was a bad mistake. It required an enormous work-force from outside – after all, this was a sparsely populated region. Moreover, such a concentration of industry produced an enormous load on the environment. The all-powerful ministries acted like colonialists, disfiguring the landscape and the beauty that was there.

The natural habitat of the krai was almost completely destroyed around the giant Norilsk works. The construction trampled on the earth, but also the age-old foundations of life of the local people, and turned them into social outcasts. Where their fathers had lived was now a dead zone, as if in the aftermath of some terrible natural disaster. It is striking that out of the profit from the works, 1.1 billion rubles – which was a breathtaking figure for that time – the ministries did not set aside even ten million rubles to put the lives of these people back in order. One had to sympathize with the Evenkian writer Alitet Nemtushkin, who said at a workers' meeting: 'Leave us nature; without nature we cannot survive.'

It was more a headache than a visit, indeed. However, I did not lose my spirits – this would have been too great a luxury for the General Secretary. I tried to use all of my time in Krasnoyarsk talking to the people. At a meeting with workers of the Nadezhdinsk Metallurgical Works in Norilsk, I touched on the problem of the administrative apparatus. I noted that it consisted of 18 million people for a total of 125–127 million workers. Of these, 2.5 million were in ministries and agencies and the rest were in enterprises. Some of those present were decisively set against the bureaucrats. When I mentioned that I had received a letter suggesting that I give the command 'Fire on headquarters!', you could hear people shouting 'Absolutely right!'

'What do you mean, "Absolutely right"?' I asked. 'We are carrying out perestroika and we don't want to split the country into warring camps. Everyone knows what "Fire on headquarters" produced in China: it was fifteen years before they were able to come to grips with what had happened. We cannot solve today's problems by the methods of 1937. We must act through elections and take advantage of glasnost. Everyone wants the same thing: improvement as fast as possible. But we must not make a mess of things.'

The first and most general finding from my trip was that people were changing and their support of perestroika was becoming firmer. Moreover, they were showing their support openly. In Norilsk I was greeted by the entire city, a city of young people, frank people who were in an aggressive frame of mind. I realized then why people did not send letters to the kraikom, but rather to the Central Committee. People virtually camped out on the doorsteps of offices, but the bureaucrats would just drown them in red tape. Tin gods sat on the Party city committees and in the local organs of power. What could one expect people to feel when they saw all of this? Norilsk produced billions in profit for the state, but municipal services and public transport in the city were a disgrace.

What irritated people the most? The fact that most of the local cadres were still acting as they had done three, five, ten years ago. It was no accident that half of the secretaries of the Party organizations were replaced in the elections.

I heard much criticism about the food supply at that time. Older residents recalled apples from Minusinsk, melons, tomatoes and honey and Siberian breads. It is a historical fact that tariffs on Siberian grain imported to the central regions were higher, because the Siberian farmers were very competitive with the centre of Russia.

I had plenty to think about on my return from Krasnoyarsk. I could not get this question out of my mind: how were we running things if there was twice as much arable land per person in that krai as in the rest of the country, but *per-capita* agricultural production was only one third the average? Moreover, people were fleeing that area. We should be developing and settling this mighty Siberia! But first we had to increase the agricultural production there. The question was: why were we spending billions on industry, but only petty sums on the things necessary for a comfortable life?

REORGANIZATION OF THE CENTRAL COMMITTEE APPARATUS

My proposal for a reorganization of the Party apparatus was discussed by the Politburo prior to my trip to Siberia.

The Politburo members who were members of the government were in favour of completely releasing the Central Committee apparatus from 'non-Party' functions such as the 'supervision' of defence and foreign policy, while the secretaries (except perhaps for Yakovlev and Medvedev) tried to protect their 'allotments'. It was essentially a redistribution of power within the same 'command' circle. However, my plans went further – towards political reform.

I tactfully put the question of the distribution of forces in the leadership in the new situation and hinted that I was ready to introduce proposals for this. It was recorded that the General Secretary should think through the question of the placement of cadres in the Central Committee.

I believed that cadre changes had to begin by rejuvenating the leadership. After all, besides everything else, we had in recent years a true gerontocracy, with the average age of the members of the leadership over seventy. Even though many new faces had joined the Central Committee since I had taken over, people of an 'honourable age' still predominated.

Reshuffling cadres was a drama both for those being moved and for me as General Secretary, because of the human factor. I decided to speak personally to everyone affected. Almost everyone who was sent into retirement understood why, but all were rather concerned about their future, primarily their material situation.

Gromyko's age had begun to show – sometimes he would doze off at sessions and increasingly often he was not keeping up with what was happening; he would speak out quite inappropriately, which produced irritation or smirking from others. This even happened at sessions of the Presidium of the USSR Supreme Soviet.

The question of Demichev's retirement could no longer be avoided. In principle, it should have been resolved already by my predecessors, but for some reason he was automatically carried over from one team to the next. My talk with him was quite friendly: we had known each other for a long time.

There was still one more figure who had to be dealt with – Dolgikh. Because none of the issues before the Central Committee committees or the apparatus were ones that he had worked on earlier, I felt that he too should retire. While paying due respect to his professional qualities, I want to say that Dolgikh's position in the perestroika years was always that of a conformist and was more an attempt to adapt to the new conditions than any whole-hearted support for reform. Even moving him to a government position did not seem a good idea, and in fact there was no demand for him. He was a man unsuited to the new times, both in style and mentality.

Solomentsev's retirement made it possible to call Boris Karlovich Pugo from Latvia to Moscow to work as chairman of the Party control committee of the CPSU Central Committee. The Baltic republics were not represented in the leadership and, of the leaders in power at that time in the Baltic, he seemed to me the most appropriate. I had known him when he was secretary of the Central Committee of the Komsomol. In his republic he had climbed all the rungs in the Komsomol and in the Party, and even worked in state security. He was a man of integrity.

Vorotnikov was moved to the post of chairman of the Presidium of the Russian Federation Supreme Soviet on the basis of the decisions of the Party Conference.

There was no place left in the Central Committee Secretariat for Biryukova. For her time Aleksandra Pavlovna was a courageous, capable and active woman. Formerly a worker at the Trekhgorka factory, she had been well respected in the trade union movement. There had been proposals to recommend her for chairman of the VTsSPS,[1] but since there were no women in the Politburo it had been decided at the XXVIIth Congress to elect her a secretary of the Central Committee. Now Biryukova was proposed for the post of deputy chairman of the USSR Council of Ministers for social and cultural issues.

Lukyanov was to be elected first deputy chairman of the Presidium of the USSR Supreme Soviet in place of Demichev and released from his duties as a Central Committee secretary.

After Chebrikov was elected a Central Committee secretary, we had to find a successor for him. I have had to explain several times since how Kryuchkov came to the position of chairman of the KGB. After all, there were other candidates from both inside and outside the Committee for State Security. Nevertheless, I preferred him. Why? It was not just considerations of professionalism – there were other candidates probably more able than him. My decision was influenced by the fact that Kryuchkov had for many years been a close ally of Yury Andropov. Yury Vladimirovich's attitude towards him was the reason for my choice. The information I had at the time cast no doubt on his candidacy. My opinion of Kryuchkov was supported by Chebrikov and especially by Yakovlev; they were long-time acquaintances and at that time were particularly close.

Choices had to be made in the reorganization of the apparatus. For example, who should be in charge of the international department – Dobrynin, Yakovlev or Medvedev? At that time I preferred Yakovlev, who was closer to the new functions of the Party and, moreover, had been an ambassador and the head of

[1] All-Union Central Council of Trades Unions, the central organisation of all Soviet trade unions.

the leading academic institution in the field of foreign relations. I thought Medvedev should be given the leadership of the combined ideological department.

At a Central Committee plenum on 30 September, I read out Gromyko's request to retire from the position of chairman of the Presidium of the USSR Supreme Soviet and as a Politburo member. I spoke of him warmly and offered my best wishes. Andrei Andreyevich behaved fittingly. He noted that age is a stubborn thing and there is nothing you can do about it. In some way his bequest to the future lay in his statement that he always believed in the rightness of Marxism-Leninism and considered perestroika to be the only proper policy so long as it was supported by the ideological and political unity of the leadership. He was an outstanding man who maintained his integrity and faith in his time.

The plenum supported all of the cadre shifts that I proposed. Ligachev recommended me for the post of the chairman of the Presidium of the USSR Supreme Soviet and based his recommendation on the fact that 'both internally and internationally the General Secretary represents our state.' After receiving clamorous support by the Central Committee members it remained only for me to thank everyone and discuss my plans briefly.

On that same day, 30 September, the CPSU Central Control Committee released Kapitonov from his responsibilities as chairman.

A special session of the USSR Supreme Soviet was held on 1 October. Gromyko made a farewell speech. Zaikov presented the plenum's proposal for the chairmanship. It was decided 'to elect Comrade Gorbachev, Mikhail Sergeyevich, Chairman of the Presidium of the USSR Supreme Soviet'.

Both here and abroad, everyone wondered 'What could all these changes mean?' Ligachev was now the head of the committee for agrarian policy, aided by Nikonov. Yakovlev was moved to the international arena and Medvedev had switched to ideology. Of course, this was not simply a reshuffle. We had to respond to the section of public opinion that had been unwilling to accept Ligachev as the guardian of the ideological sphere. And we also had to respond to another group, especially in the Party,

During the war my father fought in the great battles for Rostov, the Kursk Salient, the crossing of the Dnieper and the Sandomierz bridgehead. He was seriously wounded during a battle near Košice, in the Carpathians. On Victory Day, he was in a military hospital in Cracow.

A family photograph. Sitting with me are Raisa Maksimovna, our granddaughter Kseniya, my mother, Maria Panteleyevna; standing: my sister-in-law Svetlana, our niece Lyudmila, my son-in-law Anatoly, our daughter Irina and my brother Aleksandr.

In 1953 Raisa and I were students at Moscow State University, she in the philosophy faculty, I in the law faculty.

Below: We celebrated our silver wedding anniversary in 1978 by making a trip with friends into the Caucasian mountains.

Right: *My favourite photograph of my wife.*

Below: *Early morning during a working visit to Siberia.*

Left: *With granddaughters Kseniya and Anastasiya during their first visit to the Kremlin.*

Right: *I am listening carefully here to the speeches of the deputies of the USSR Supreme Soviet.*

Below: *Return to Moscow after being freed from house-arrest during the 1991 attempted coup.*

Above: *In February 1991, on the anniversary of the withdrawal of Soviet troops from Afghanistan, I am presented with a painting entitled 'Spring in Kabul' from Afghan veterans.*

Below: *One of the first acts I issued during perestroika was the decree on the freedom of conscience and religious faith.*

Above: *Yury Andropov and I were always domino partners.*

Below: *The average age of Politburo members in 1980 was over seventy.*

During my first visit to Belorussia, I visited the place where the small village of Khatyn had once stood. Its inhabitants were murdered by the Nazis.

A meeting in Norilsk, north of the Arctic Circle. During one of the discussions there a worker demanded that I 'dismiss those officials' who were holding back reform. I replied: 'Everything must be done democratically.'

Above left: *During my visit to Cuba in April 1989 I had discussions several times a day with Fidel Castro.*

Above right: *Nikolai Ryzhkov and I in the Armenian city of Spital after the 1988 earthquake.*

Below: *During military manoeuvres in 1990 in Odessa military district. I visited the military to underline my support at a difficult time for them.*

that would not accept Yakovlev. Hence we had to make a manoeuvre that would defuse the situation.

Sometimes people ask: shouldn't we have got rid of Ligachev at that time? So soon after the recent Party Conference, such a decision might have unnecessarily aggravated the situation on the eve of political reform. It would also have been unfair to him and to those people whose attitudes he expressed. It is true that some of the public did not accept Ligachev and considered him to be the leader of the right wing, essentially a secret opponent of perestroika. However, no democratic party can demand 'uniformity'. I also had to bear in mind that ahead of us was the Party Congress, at which the future of various trends would be decided. To sum up, Ligachev had to be moved away from ideological work, but kept in the leadership. And so it was done.

The role of the Central Committee Secretariat, which had essentially acted as 'a small Sovnarkom'[1] before this, was reduced in the new Central Committee structure. Now it was left with deciding strictly intra-Party issues. I heard rumours that the change of role of the Secretariat was supposedly convenient for me in order to take power from Ligachev. This is not so; the important thing was to change the functions of this body, which duplicated the functions both of the Politburo and the government.

LAYING THE FOUNDATION

The time came to prepare for the plenum on political reform. Draft laws on amendments to the USSR Constitution and on procedures for elections were published on 22 and 23 October. A storm of criticism hit us from all sides. The ideological feebleness of the Party nomenklatura and its inability to carry on a dialogue with the people or an argument with its opponents became evident. Officials at city and district committees were simply afraid to show their faces in the streets and squares, where

[1] A small government; the Soviet government between 1917 and 1946 was known as Sovnarkom.

passions were high. They had grown up in a different atmosphere and had been nurtured in an incubator, and now they panicked at the thought of any public discussion or open political opposition. What a contrast between their helplessness and the propaganda campaign launched by the democrats! Indeed, two or three days after the draft laws had been published, the democrats started a protest campaign without really analysing the drafts. Their reactions were opinionated, not to say impudent.

Yury Afanasiev and his supporters considered the draft laws to be simply camouflage, since, they said, the Party remained the nucleus of the system, just as before. The idea of combining posts and of elections from public organizations was interpreted in this spirit. Dissatisfaction also appeared in the republics, especially in the Baltic. There the constitutional amendments were perceived as a further strengthening of the centre. Popular fronts arose, acting ever more aggressively, and separatist sentiment became stronger.

All of this provided ammunition for the opponents of reform. Needless to say, it really upset the Party nomenklatura. My appeals to them to learn to work under democracy, which I reiterated from plenum to plenum, went unheeded.

The speeches at the Politburo sessions were all filled with anxiety. Indeed, we were not adequately prepared for opposition, we did not understand how it worked. This was, after all, the first time there had been a real opposition, and a radical one at that. This seemed to be reason enough for panicking and calling for help. It turned out that, once we had opened the road to democracy, the unexpected gush of fresh air proved too much for many people.

In the discussion at the 28 November plenum after my speech 'On measures to implement political reform in state-building', some speakers sounded the alarm. Shcherbitsky noted that extremist nationalistic movements were becoming more and more organized. Foteyev, secretary of the Checheno-Ingush Party obkom, said that 'glasnost had produced naive enthusiasm' at first, but now bewilderment. Mendybaev, second secretary of the Central Committee of the Communist Party of Kazakhstan, spoke in favour of greater autonomy for the republics and declared that we could 'not let pass without notice' the anti-social statements and actions of some of the informal associations. Academician Logunov, the Rector of Moscow State University, reported that 'a radical faction had appeared at a Komsomol conference at the university, and, although its members' claims had been refuted, the delegates had forced the Komsomol Central Committee representative to leave the rostrum'. Mironenko, first secretary of the Central Committee of the Komsomol, suggested that it was time for all Party members to leave the trenches, for they were sitting things out, while life was passing them by. Vezirov, who had worked for six months as first secretary of the Central Committee of the Azerbaijan Communist Party, put the issue squarely: 'If we are talking about revolution, we must also be on the watch for counter-revolution.'

In short, there was plenty of alarm, much of it not unfounded. On the whole, however, the plenum was not panicked, but rather sounded a note of caution. The transformations that we had proposed got the go-ahead, essentially without amendments. Of course, this was partly due to the fact that they corresponded entirely to the decisions of the Party Conference.

In my closing speech I spoke of the need to be ready for work and for battle under the new conditions. I said that the forces coming into the political arena were very diverse and we should not consider everyone alike to be destructive. Our main goal was to defend perestroika – both from conservatives who would hold back the democratic process, and from extremists and demagogues. A new, democratic era was dawning in the country.

THOUGHTS, MY THOUGHTS

Another year of perestroika was coming to an end, a year saturated to the limit with work and events, both happy and sad. I remember seeing a large headline in a foreign newspaper: 'Gorbachev: Triumph and Pain'. The article was about my successful speech to the United Nations and the cruelly destructive earthquake in Armenia that happened on the same day, 7 December.

Unfortunately time was speeding along much faster than the reforms we had planned. I was genuinely concerned about the lack of results that we had counted on – what was holding us back, where were the reserves for accelerating the transformations?

Events were overtaking the Party. As a whole, society proved to be more receptive than the 'vanguard' to the new ideas. And the more the people's activity grew, the more perceptible this difference became. The CPSU, which I believed could be renewed, was retreating from its positions before one's very eyes. Besides bewilderment, the Party structures had already begun to show open dissatisfaction with the reformist centre.

We continually talked about the mechanism that was slowing things down, but without ever mentioning the Party. When I was alone, I began to realize that this mechanism was within the Party itself, which not only was falling behind but was even putting up resistance to the changes in the system. One had to bear in mind that the Party was the system's support structure. The brakes were being applied mainly through the apparatus – Party, state, economic. Of course, the non-Party members in the apparatus could be counted on the fingers of one hand. Having dared to encroach on the hitherto unshakable foundations of the 18-million-strong army of bureaucrats and having started to reduce its size, I realized what a hornet's nest I had stirred up. I knew they would show no mercy.

I had counted on the support of the people in the struggle with the command-administrative system, but here too there was cause for worry. I kept recalling a seemingly ordinary incident from my Krasnoyarsk trip. In Norilsk an elderly man had said to me on the street: 'Mikhail Sergeyevich, I really don't want to talk about small things – it's embarrassing, but unfortunately I have to. It is six years now since someone dumped slag containing metal filings around our home, and it is all still there. It cuts through your shoes and we're afraid to let the children out to play.'

You would think there was nothing special about this, that it was a typical situation. But that was the horror, that it was typical. That was the system, in all its ugliness! In order to get the land around his home cleaned up he had to complain to the General

Secretary – the highest leader in the country, no less! I was also struck by something else: the frustration and helplessness of that simple man when faced with the almighty bureaucrat. How much time would be needed for people to gain a sense of freedom and self-respect? Without this there could not be true perestroika.

I advised the man to 'give the authorities here a harder shake', for without people like him, ordinary citizens, I would never be able to rouse the bureaucrats out of their armchairs. But how long would it take for these people to become mature citizens? Had humble obedience settled in their souls forever? No, this could not be. I firmly believed that the process of democratization would awaken the people.

After the Party Conference we saw a build-up of political and social activity. This was visible in the appearance of hundreds and thousands of informal groups and movements devoted to various issues, including the specific concerns of different regions.

Meanwhile the opposition was becoming more and more consolidated. There was the conservative opposition, which had openly proclaimed itself in March; and the radical opposition, the constructive attitude of which I think we had somewhat over-estimated at the November plenum. As it happened, it was that autumn, when political tensions in the country were growing, that Yeltsin returned to active politics. After his November speech to the Higher Komsomol school, he gave many interviews and roundly criticized the draft laws on the Constitution and elections. He had already begun to see himself as the opposition leader and spokesman for the ideas of what later became the 'Democratic Russia' (DemRossiya) movement.

On 7 November I received a congratulatory telegram from him:

Dear Mikhail Sergeyevich

Accept my congratulations on our great holiday – the seventy-first anniversary of the October Revolution! Believing in the victory of perestroika, I wish for you, through the efforts of the Party that you lead and all of the people, complete implementation of Lenin's wishes and dreams in our country.

B. Yeltsin

Sometimes it seemed to me that the importance of perestroika was understood better abroad than in the USSR. That was confirmed by the unprecedented international solidarity for the victims of the Armenian earthquake. One got the impression that other nations were racing to help us. This was not simply out of human sympathy, but also a manifestation of political will.

Yet, even in times of doubt, I would immediately stop and rebuke myself for being unfair to my countrymen. Had all of my trips around the Soviet Union really not told me that our people were firmly behind reforms? Their dissatisfaction and the apathy that they had not yet overcome were due to irritation with the lack of serious change. It meant that we had to press on with our work.

I drove my associates hard and tried to employ every capability of the General Secretary, as both the Party and state leader, to spur on the Central Committee departments, the Supreme Soviet apparatus, the Council of Ministers, the press . . .

Nature had put a tragic stamp on the end of the outgoing year, but nevertheless I remained optimistic. Speaking to the Soviet people on the occasion of the new year (1989), I said, among other things: 'The up-coming year does not promise to be and will not be problem-free. There is much serious business ahead and much to do. We see that today we must act with greater decisiveness. We cannot outsmart life or sit things out at the side of the road. We do not expect and do not promise "manna from heaven"; we know that our road is difficult. However, the choice has been made and we have paved the way for perestroika.'

Eighty-five days remained until the first free elections of the USSR people's deputies.

MY FAMILY

With changes in my political career, it seemed to us at first that nothing really out of the ordinary had happened, that there was no need to disrupt our family routine. We talked about this at the very start and were all in agreement. Raisa Maksimovna has a sense of deep devotion to the family, to the internal world that binds us. 'My home,' she once said, 'is not simply my castle, it is my world, my galaxy.'

We never accepted the system of human relations prevalent in the upper circles of Moscow society when we returned to the capital in 1978. Our ideas were different. Our understanding of people's relationships was not weighed down by petty conventions or – if I may use this expression – 'Moscow provincialism'. I am, of course, speaking of the surroundings, the environment in which we were. We always valued sincerity, simplicity, mutual respect and the ability to understand others.

Raisa Maksimovna knew from her experience that co-workers value most of all your comradeship and your attitude towards work, how you 'pull your weight', how you fulfil your obligations. And if one of your colleagues needs support, you should be willing to help them out. These 'moral maxims' were conveyed to our daughter, Irina, who, along with her husband, agreed with them entirely. They had their own mission: to become professionals in their fields. No amount of 'protection' would help them in this. It is one thing to obtain a position or a promotion, and something completely different to become a highly qualified specialist. Their goals in life were right. We welcomed this attitude in every way; we also hoped that, no matter what, they would not interrupt their English lessons.

We all agreed that everything in our family should stay the same, that we should remain true to ourselves. Everything should stay the same? Real life does not always conform to one's plans.

We had been living in the dacha that we had moved into in 1981, after my election as a Politburo member. My election as General Secretary meant that we had to move. The dacha did not have enough room for the services connected with supporting the activity of the head of state, which *de facto* the General Secretary of the CPSU Central Committee was. The reader may ask: didn't Brezhnev, Andropov and, finally, Chernenko live and work in dachas? Why not move to one of them? Yes, these dachas had not gone anywhere, but by Politburo decision the families of the deceased General Secretaries continued to live in them. Chebrikov suggested that one of the dachas being built near the village of Razdory be adapted for the General

Secretary's residence. Changes were made to the plans, adding a guard building, a strategic communications building, a helicopter landing area and a building for transport vehicles and special equipment. Guest rooms, rooms for Politburo sessions or meetings when necessary, and a room for medical personnel were added to the main building. Our family moved to the new dacha a year later. This dacha is now the suburban residence of the President of the Russian Federation.

There was increased monitoring of the medical services and our food supply, of practically everything that came into the family and with which it was linked. In short, we began a life in a controlled environment. This was one aspect. On the other hand, there was increased attention from the press. This applied not just to me, but also to Raisa Maksimovna and indeed all the members of my family. Often we would gather late at night to have a brief talk about urgent matters or events or impressions. But it was not so easy to keep our home for ourselves, to open its doors only for friends and family, to keep the home fires burning.

Even during my first months as General Secretary, Irina and Anatoly began to be approached by all kinds of people – Muscovites, visitors from out of town, even from abroad. They complained about abuses by the local authorities, persecutions, prosecutions for criticism, they conveyed requests for pardons, help in obtaining treatment for serious diseases, and many other things. Wives, mothers and children whom I had allegedly 'abandoned' appeared. Strange people with obsessions and grand projects also showed up.

Of course, Irina and Anatoly could not resolve problems, but in order to respond to the appeals they advised people where to go, and in extreme cases, when things would not wait, they telephoned the general department of the Central Committee and helped these people get in contact with someone who might be able to do something.

We were also increasingly concerned about our ageing parents. My mother, who continued to live in Privolnoye, was continuously ill. The health of Raisa Maksimovna's parents, who lived in Krasnodar, had also begun to deteriorate. The years and the sufferings of their generation began to take their toll. In June 1986 a heavy sorrow befell us – Raisa Maksimovna's father died.

In March 1987 Irina gave birth to our second granddaughter. Irina had wanted a boy and intended to name him Mikhail, but she had another girl, Anastasiya – a wonderful little creature who brought us so much happiness. Our first granddaughter, Kseniya, started school in September of this year.

THE GENERAL SECRETARY'S WIFE

Raisa Maksimovna and I remained the same people in our opinions, in our relations with each other, and in our way of life. In 1985 we had been married for thirty-one years. Each of us had made our choices when we were students and everything had been determined by this. We were bound first of all by our marriage, but also by our common views on life. We both preached the principle of equality. We shared our common cares and helped each other always and in everything. Of course I did not give lectures in philosophy for Raisa Maksimovna, just as she did not do my work. But we knew how each other's affairs were going, and rejoiced at the successes and suffered the failures of the other, just as if they were our own.

However, the appearance of the General Secretary and his wife in public had an effect that was no less than that of the policy of perestroika. Really, nothing out of the ordinary happened, and we kept things simple. But in our society this was a shock for many people – both in the good and in the bad sense.

The Central Committee received many letters, the vast majority containing praise and support. However, some expressed bewilderment and even indignation at the appearance of Raisa Maksimovna at my side on various occasions, in particular during my trips: 'Who does she think she is, a member of the Politburo?!' The simplest answer would have been: 'No, she is my wife!' But how could I explain this to people who were reared in the traditions of *Domostroi*[1] and the 'battle against nepotism'[2]? Even some

[1] The ancient Russian code of rules for everyday life, which were rigidly patriarchal.
[2] An official's family should not share his power or be given top posts.

of my close colleagues felt uneasy, although they had to put up with it.

As soon as they smelled something cooking, the Western centres of psychological warfare pressed this point in order to discredit the Soviet leader. Political riff-raff in Moscow, the Urals and Siberia joined in this campaign of innuendo intended to ignite base emotions and produce hostility to changes and mistrust of the General Secretary and his reforms.

I could see that Raisa Maksimovna was upset by these non-sensical tales, but I advised her not to pay any attention. She bore it all with dignity and did a great deal to support me in these unbelievably difficult years. And she was neither an extra nor simply the President's shadow. No, whenever possible, she tactfully did things I did not have time for, and she did them in ways that I could not have done.

In my trips through the country I spent much time in meetings and conversations with the public. Raisa Maksimovna attended these meetings, but she used the remaining time for her own programme. She visited the families of workers and the homes of peasants, she went to new and old neighbourhoods and got to know how medical institutions, household services, shops operated, how the municipal and rural markets worked. This was due both to her natural curiosity and to her professional interest as a sociologist – she had always combined teaching in the university with research on people's living conditions.

Finally, Raisa Maksimovna greatly enjoyed meetings with the local intelligentsia, teachers and cultural figures. This was a familiar environment for her, and her impressions were always very valuable for me. It was easier for her to start up a candid conversation with people and to learn what was troubling them.

One subject that attracted Raisa Maksimovna's attention was the position of women in society. In Ukraine, in the Baltic republics, in Uzbekistan, in Murmansk and other cities, she had many meetings with women's committees and organizations, which often resulted in my giving assignments to various agencies to work on specific problems. Her professional training and practical experience allowed her to give me more than just a list of facts and impressions; she could share her thoughts and sometimes suggest specific policies.

A particular place in her public activity was given to the Soviet Cultural Foundation, which was started in the first years of perestroika. The idea for creating it came from Yakovlev. In supporting this proposal I advised him to try to enlist our most authoritative scholars, writers and artists and even suggested a few names. Yakovlev, however, believed that the Foundation would have a successful start if it was headed by Raisa Maksimovna. I promised to talk to her, but she firmly refused, while agreeing to work in the Foundation on a voluntary basis.

The choice of Academician Dmitry Likhachev as chairman of the Foundation and the participation of the General Secretary's wife as well as many famous cultural figures gave it high public status.

The Foundation began to gain strength and have a beneficial effect on the development of culture in the country and on the expanding relations with foreign cultural centres. Its slogan was: 'Preserve, develop, multiply – through culture, humanize human relationships'. Numerous programmes were developed under its aegis: 'Unique historical territories', 'The return of forgotten names', 'The great silk road', 'New names', 'Preservation and development of the culture of indigenous peoples', and, finally, 'Through culture to health and charity'.

Raisa Maksimovna was particularly enthusiastic about helping to set up the Roerikh Foundation in Moscow. At a meeting with Svyatoslav Nikolaevich Roerikh and his wife Devika, who was the niece of Rabindranath Tagore, we spoke about our countries and the similarity of our peoples, and discussed philosophical issues.

The Cultural Foundation has returned the notion of philanthropy to our lives. Raisa Maksimovna furthered this, giving particular attention to the Central Republican Children's Hospital, which was engaged in treating children with serious diseases from all regions of the country. After visiting Chernobyl and the contaminated regions of Belorussia, Raisa Maksimovna became a board member of 'Haematologists of the world for children', an association dedicated to the treatment of children suffering from leukaemia.

Later, after I had stepped down as President, Raisa Maksimovna and I continued our relations with those who had begun this enormously valuable humanitarian work. Through the Gorbachev Foundation we contacted people from many countries and asked them to give aid to the children. The public in the USA, Germany, Austria, Canada, the Netherlands and other countries responded. As a result, a bone marrow transplant unit opened in Moscow at the beginning of 1993, and 70 per cent of children treated there for leukaemia are cured.

While I was head of the Party and the state, Raisa Maksimovna spent much time on protocol matters such as welcoming foreign leaders. There was a need to bring our protocol up to date, since it still bore the stamp of the old traditions. Of course, this was the business of the Ministry of Foreign Affairs, but here too her observations proved useful. Raisa Maksimovna strove to represent her country with great responsibility as she accompanied me on official visits to various countries abroad. For her, as for me, the most important thing was to carry out with dignity the mission that fate had given us.

We were therefore amazed and even outraged by speculation about our relations, actions and ways of life. For some it was strange that we were together. But this was the way it was our entire lives. Our life, our activities and even our appearance aroused jealousy and envy in some. But nature had moulded us this way. It seemed to some that our life was almost a fairy tale, full of pleasure. But it was hard work – although it was joyous – for we were inspired by high ideals.

14

POLITICAL REFORM: POWER IS TRANSFERRED FROM STARAYA PLOSHCHAD TO THE KREMLIN

ELECTIONS

IF WE ATTEMPT TO CHARACTERIZE BRIEFLY THE POLITICAL reform as it was conceived and conducted, we may say that it was the transfer of power from the Communist Party into the hands of those to whom it should belong according to the Constitution – to the Soviets, through free elections. It is obvious that the success or failure of reform, especially in the early stages, was wholly dependent on the attitude of the CPSU itself, which in essence had to give up voluntarily its own dictatorship. This was an extremely complex political operation, one that was painful for millions of communists and especially difficult, one may say 'lethal', for the Party nomenklatura. 'Abdication of the throne' threatened the gradual loss of the privileges that the nomenklatura had enjoyed.

It was quite clear that the Party and state bureaucracy would not welcome these changes. Since at that time the bureaucrats still controlled the main levers of power, there were only two ways of assuring the success of reform: creating significant pressure on them from the majority of society, which was strongly in favour of radical change, and cutting off the most conservative elements of the nomenklatura, inducing all those who were capable of fresh thinking to participate in the transformation. Without political manoeuvring the mighty bureaucracy that had formed under the totalitarian system would never relinquish power.

I want to draw the reader's attention to the necessity for such manoeuvres on my part, because they were the subject of frequent and merciless criticism from the democrats, and not just from the democrats, but also from my closest associates. They reproached me because I, supposedly, was still a Party man at heart, unable to abandon my allegiance to the Party nomenklatura, and incapable of freeing myself from the mental stereotypes inherent in them. I myself see this differently. My caution stemmed from my desire to avoid open mutiny, which could have defeated political reform even before it got started.

All of this was perhaps the clearest in relation to the so-called 'Party Hundred'.[1] Now I am still convinced that it was right to put forward exactly 100 candidates for the 100 positions allocated to the Communist Party in the Congress of People's Deputies. We simply could not allow certain members of the Party leadership of that time to be voted down. This would have immediately made them secret or open opponents of change and could have seriously jeopardized the situation.

Our analysis showed that if the slate of candidates had contained, say, 103–105 names, Ligachev, Ulyanov and Yakovlev would have received the largest number of 'black' ballots. Enlarge the list by another ten candidates and most of the members of the Politburo – Slyunkov, Nikonov, Medvedev, Zaikov and Primakov, for example – would not have been elected, not to mention famous writers such as Chengiz Aitmatov or Daniil Granin. And, with a longer list of candidates, there was a chance of the General Secretary and the Chairman of the USSR Council of Ministers being thrown out.

It would not have been difficult for any of them to find a constituency where he would be certain of the goodwill of the voters. However, this would have gone against the concept that these 100 deputies elected on the Party slate should represent the Party as a public organization. I confess that at first I myself

---

[1] In the elections to the USSR Congress, 750 of the 2,250 seats were reserved for public organizations, with the Party receiving 100.

vacillated. But after thinking about it, I concluded that the General Secretary should go to parliament not in a personal capacity, but as the leader of the Party.

Finally, the January 1989 Central Committee plenum could still reject or vote out any of the candidates, so democratic principles were not at all flouted in this case.

Since I have already mentioned the 'Red Hundred', as it was maliciously christened in some democratic publications, I cannot avoid the question of direct representation of public organizations in the Parliament, the more so since it was the subject of much debate for quite a while. The criticism, which was at times quite harsh, originated in the fact that our opponents did not take the trouble to really think about the motives behind this decision. On my part I believed it necessary then and I remain firm in this opinion today.

Of course, from the formal standpoint, 'corporate representation' according to pre-allotted quotas is not flawless, since the deputies' mandates in this case do not pass the test of the people's will. But one should bear in mind that only a relatively small number of deputies – one third – received their mandates in this way – and from the very beginning the idea was to employ this method only once. The Constitution was later amended.

Many advocates of perestroika, especially those among the scientific and artistic intelligentsia, had little chance of being elected. Direct representation of social organizations put into the body of deputies a relatively small, but extremely important group of influential democratic activists elected on the slates of the trades unions, the Komsomol, women's organizations, artists' unions and scientific associations, who were extremely important for the make-up of the future Parliament. Let me cite one example. It is hardly necessary to mention the important role played by Academician Sakharov at the USSR Congresses of People's Deputies – he was elected from the scientific associations. Certain other prominent scientists who failed to be elected by the USSR Academy of Sciences received their deputies' mandates in the same way.

Besides this fundamental factor, the quotas for social organizations had yet another important meaning. In the absence of a multi-party system, this measure made it possible to make the future Parliament somewhat more structured. Of course, the groups of deputies from social organizations could not replace party factions, but at this initial stage they represented the voice, mood and will of different social strata. The seeds of future parties that would eventually compete with the CPSU began to germinate with the formation of the Inter-Regional Group.

The election campaign showed immediately that we were in completely unfamiliar territory. There was a tough battle for the mass media, in particular for television time. A fierce polemic, sometimes going beyond the bounds of decency, raged in the press and at meetings with voters. There was much bitterness, and many hitherto unknown facts were published by the press. All of this caused irritation and alarm, even panic, in some of the leadership. For my part, I was pleased that we were able to awaken society and to achieve what we had strived for during all the preceding years of perestroika – to include the people in politics. Free elections turned up many new and interesting people and shed light on the feelings and attitudes of various social groups – about which, as it turned out, we had quite false impressions.

The paradox was that 85 per cent of the newly elected deputies were members of the CPSU (in the old USSR Supreme Soviet, approximately half were CPSU members), even though the top leadership took the election results as a defeat for the Party. The fact that the voters were 'so bold' as to give preference to 'someone else', to vote down such public figures as, say, Yu. Soloviev, who was first secretary of the Leningrad obkom and a candidate member of the Politburo, put some of them in a state of shock. The ruling elite were so self-confident that they could not even imagine an unfavourable election result.

After the elections we called a Politburo meeting on 28 March 1989. Most of the members were depressed, and failure was in the air. I characterized the elections as a major step in the implementation of the political reform that we had launched by our decisions. The elections had brought society to a new plateau and were eliminating the gap between constitutional norms and political practice. The government was becoming completely legitimate, which was an enormous achievement by itself.

As I spoke, I could sense that quite a few of my colleagues disagreed with this analysis. I continued, noting that the elections had been more successful for the Party and there had been fewer losses where people could really see the fruits of perestroika. Indeed, in North Caucasus, Stavropol krai and the central black-earth districts, up to 90 per cent of the voters supported the candidates of the local Party organs. People's attitudes towards leaders also had an effect. Those who were respected for their attention to the people's needs, their freedom from bureaucratic attitudes and their intolerance of corruption and other negative phenomena were assured of election.

However, I said, the overall picture was not simple, and we needed to use the election results to evaluate the work of Party and economic cadres – especially in Moscow and Leningrad, where the people were dissatisfied with the progress of perestroika. This was a message to the government and to the Central Committee, not to speak of the municipal and district committees.

I said it would be wrong to repudiate the criticisms that had been levelled at the leadership during the election campaign. After all, they were valid in many ways. The difficult economic situation was to a certain extent the result of the enormous costs of dealing with the aftermath of the Chernobyl accident, the earthquake in Armenia and the military adventure in Afghanistan. But it was also the result of our inability to find the right economic policy, to stop the deterioration in the consumer market and the financial sphere, and the fact that only now were we beginning to get a grip on all of this. The people were not in a bad frame of mind because of the intrigues of *Ogonek* or *Moskovskiye Novosti*, or of Yeltsin. Many things might have looked different if the Party and government structures had in fact changed their ways and moved closer to the people and become more attentive to their needs.

The Party's position was not hopeless at that time. There was both opportunity and time enough to overcome the psychological shock that came from parting with its unshakable monopoly on power. I said that we could gain the support of the people not by repeated references to the October Revolution or the Great

Patriotic War, but rather by an effective policy that guaranteed democracy, civil rights and a high standard of living. I believed then that such a transformation of the CPSU was possible. And what about other members of the Party leadership?

One could already perceive a left and a right wing in the leadership at that time, although we were still far from open polemics or a split. Some saw the elections as the victory of democracy, while others saw only the defeat of the Party. The desire to advance reforms predominated among the former, while the latter became increasingly nostalgic for the old order. For some the critical articles in the press were the normal development of glasnost and the occasion for thinking over our mistakes, while for others they were unbearable wilfulness, a slanderous campaign by anti-Party and anti-Soviet elements.

Let me give a brief excerpt from my concluding words: 'The Party has built up its credibility through the policy of perestroika: not by threat and terror, but rather by going openly to the people and thus stirring up criticism of itself. Now we must win credibility in a new situation – when practical affairs are being tackled we won't win any respect by shutting people up. The elections have shown that perestroika needs to be defended. But one can defend perestroika only by making it deeper and by developing it. The main thing now is practical business. We must not become obsessed with self-analysis or give in to self-flagellation. We must let the people feel that we are responding to their criticisms and are ready to act with calm confidence. This is the message we should take to the Congress.'

THE VANGUARD TURNS INTO THE REARGUARD

More and more often one could hear the idea that the elections reflected new realities, that the CPSU was lagging behind the times, and that the Party nomenklatura was turning into a brake on reforms.

Indeed, on my trips around the country I increasingly sensed that the administrative and Party structures were applying the brakes. They saw the changes as threats and did everything they could to prevent them. This was their mistake: they should have changed their style and got down to business, working more closely with the people. Instead, they continued to reign, sitting out their time in their offices and storing up ill-will. I had said openly to the entire country (and even louder in closed sessions): 'Those who do not want to change, to get into step with progress, will be left behind. The elections have shown "for whom the bell tolls."'

I confess that I was upset that the Party's 'indisposition' had become an incurable disease. Although I was the instigator of perestroika and I saw my main duty as the democratization of our society, at the same time, as General Secretary of the CPSU, I sincerely wanted the Party to lead this process. I thought that much had been done to prepare the ground for this.

Since the XXVIIth Party Congress the composition of the district and city committees had been changed three times, and the personnel in the various Soviet agencies had been almost completely replaced. After the January 1987 Central Committee plenum the first secretaries had stood for contested elections and many of the 'old hands' had been retired. However, a second, third or even fourth crew took the helm, and thus things went on as before. This was how strong the old ways were: Marxist dogma in the simplistic Stalinist interpretation had been beaten into their heads.

The elections revealed that the authority of the CPSU had fallen as soon as people had stopped being afraid of it. From this moment on people trusted communists not as representatives of a mighty power structure, but rather as personalities. 'You are a good man, you are an honest and decent fellow, you know how to work – we will support you,' they would say. The Party masses began to separate from the Party bureaucracy. And this was the striking result: the local bosses had at their disposal practically all the newspapers, radio stations, television, transport, an army of agitators, offices, houses of culture, and so on, but more often than not they were defeated – and by people who had been unknowns only yesterday.

The question of a real renewal of the composition of the Central Committee became urgent. It was not long since the XXVIIth

Party Congress, but many Central Committee members were no longer active or had retired (eighty-four out of 303 Central Committee members and twenty-seven out of 157 candidate members had retired). On the other hand, many people who were not in the Central Committee had been advanced to leadership positions.

It seemed reasonable to bring in new members to the Central Committee by promoting candidate members and also by co-option. First I discussed the issue with former Politburo members (those who remained in the Central Committee) and then met all the members of the Central Committee who had retired. I presented the situation to them and tactfully advised them that it was necessary to give way to new Party leaders and activists. I have to say that the 'old hands' received this message with dignity; no-one complained. They themselves were aware that the time had come for them to retire. Moreover, we had no intention of depriving these people, who had done much for the country, of participation in public affairs. Some of them were to be included in commissions created in the Central Committee.

More than 100 retired altogether, and this opened the way for a large group of candidate members to become full members of the Central Committee. However, nothing came of co-option. Ligachev and others argued that it was unacceptable and that under conditions of developing democracy we must adhere strictly to principles, that this would be negatively perceived by the Communists, and so forth. I confess that I was also not quite sure whether we would make the right choices – there would undoubtedly be arguments in the Politburo and everyone would strive to advance his own protégés.

In short, we decided to reject co-option, and this, of course, was a mistake. At that time, we could and should have introduced into the Central Committee staunch advocates of deeper reforms. In that way we would have made a decisive step towards perestroika of the Party itself. In any case, it would have sharply changed the ratio of progressive and conservative forces in the supreme Party organ, and the atmosphere at the plenums would have been quite different.

Prior to the plenum we also discussed the possibility of the collective resignation of the Politburo, to be followed by election of a new leadership. Ryzhkov did not actually come forward with this proposal – he simply warned that the General Secretary should be prepared for the issue to be raised. However, I did not believe that the time was ripe for risky experiments. Considering the composition of the Central Committee at that time, it was likely that an even more conservative Politburo would be elected. It would not have included Yakovlev or Medvedev, most likely not Shevardnadze, and possibly not even me.

Resignation of the Politburo did not come up at the plenum, but the uneasiness of the Party nomenklatura was clear. The recent elections were the direct or indirect subject of many speeches. Some simply reflected disappointment with the results for the Party or for themselves personally. Others blamed the leadership, which had 'brought us to such a mess' by its experiments with democracy. Probably the harshest speech was that of Aleksandr Melnikov, who was the head of the Central Committee Construction Department. I had thought of him as a thinking and resolute man who was inclined towards innovation. He was one of a number of Party leaders who had seemed wildly innovative in the 1970s. For this reason Brezhnev and Kapitonov had preferred to 'send' them a little farther from Moscow, but with the arrival of Andropov and Gorbachev these 'disturbers of the peace' began to join the Party leadership. However, gradually we realized that their desire to innovate worked only within the system.

Even so, I was both amazed and vexed by Melnikov's speech. It is true that he had not yet had the nerve to accuse me and my associates of treachery – our fundamentalists would have a field day with this a little later. But he accused the leadership of bringing the Party to bankruptcy. The leadership, he said, was so isolated from the people and so busy building castles in the air that we did not know what was happening in the country. Incidentally, this meshed nicely with what Ligachev had said at the Politburo meeting – I think he may have helped in the preparation of Melnikov's speech.

Before the plenum, the Politburo had decided to give out more information about it than usual, although they stopped short of making the Central Committee sessions public. At this point I realized that I must reveal to the public the complete 'balance of forces' in the Party leadership: let the people know who was who. This was not a sudden impulse. I had long felt the need to raise the curtain of secrecy separating the authorities from the people. In this case the position of the retrogradists in the Central Committee pushed me to make the suggestion that the discussions at the plenum be published in full.

A few voiced their approval, but it was clear that most were not particularly enthusiastic. And this was not just because the secretaries who had spoken out aggressively did not particularly want their words to reach the democratic press. For many this was equivalent to abandoning one of the most important privileges of the upper echelons of the Party. However, nobody was bold enough to speak out against this proposal. It is true that someone suggested an amendment: we should publish the discussions with commentaries. 'No,' I objected. 'Let the people decide for themselves, and the press can make its own commentary.' I had calculated correctly: the people saw the real situation in the CPSU Central Committee and the conditions under which the General Secretary had to operate.

As was the custom, the results of the plenum were discussed at a Politburo meeting. Everyone approved of them, although it was evident that the leadership factions gave different, if not absolutely opposite, interpretations to their approval. I emphasized that the main issue for the Party at that time was to help in solving practical problems, to learn new methods, to 'go to the people', to political rallies, rather than sit in our offices, and to learn to work under democracy.

Having crossed this obstacle of the plenum, we had to move farther and to prepare for an outstanding event in the history of our country – the first USSR Congress of People's Deputies after the first free elections. Two days after the Politburo meeting, on 27 April, I called together the inner circle, in order to think through all the details once again. After all, things did not come down to simply writing speeches – we had to present the concepts for the formation of a new system. And it was not merely a matter of preparing a draft law that would, as in former times, be unanimously approved by 'disciplined deputies' without much ado. We already knew that from the very beginning it would be necessary to deal with an energetic opposition, inspired by its undoubted success in the elections and avid for battle. How most of the deputies would behave was not completely clear.

I no longer remember who was the first to say this, but everybody was in support: from that time on the Congresses of People's Deputies, and not the CPSU congresses, would become the main political forums that determined the life of the country. This was a real watershed, which would be followed by a gradual replacement of the old institutions of power and even its symbols.

THE BIRTH OF PARLIAMENT

25 May 1989, ten a.m. The Kremlin Palace of Congresses is packed. As always, there is an enormous panel with Lenin's portrait. There are many familiar faces in the front rows and in the boxes for diplomats and journalists. The television cameras are running, everything seems routine. But there is something new: the members of the Politburo are seated among other people's deputies, rather than in the presidium. Moreover, the Congress is opened, not by the General Secretary of the CPSU Central Committee, but by the Chairman of the Central Commission for the Election of People's Deputies, V. P. Orlov.

Still, not much had really changed yet. This impression was strengthened by Orlov's brief opening speech. The Chairman of the Central Electoral Commission spoke in the old style, using the standard 'elevated' expressions. 'We have never had a more powerful national referendum in favour of the Communist Party and its policy of renewal,' he said. I was sitting in the first row and from behind me, where the deputies from Moscow sat, I could hear whispers, mutterings, people clearly beginning to be upset; no-one had expected such an opening of the Congress. I reproached myself for not paying enough attention to this important detail, but I had not had time to give thought to it. Indeed, the opening of the Congress of People's Deputies had hardly been announced when it ceased to follow the prepared scenario. The

369

first unplanned speech came from V. F. Tolpezhnikov, a doctor from Riga, and the assembly stood up in honour of those who had died in Tbilisi.[1] This emotional scene immediately changed the atmosphere in the hall. Now suddenly everyone realized that our ship of state, which for many years had been tied to the same mooring, had just set sail on uncharted waters.

This was clear even in the discussion of the agenda. The opposition, in the person of its leader, Sakharov, demanded a change in the order for discussion of issues: first the report of the Chairman of the Presidium of the USSR Supreme Soviet, then discussion of the situation in the country, and only afterwards the election of the new head of state and new USSR Supreme Soviet. 'I have many times in my speeches supported the candidacy of Mikhail Sergeyevich Gorbachev,' Sakharov said. 'I maintain this position even now, since I do not see another person who can lead our country. I cannot see this today. My support is therefore conditional. I believe that we need a discussion and the reports of the candidates, because we must keep in mind the principle of alternative candidates for all elections at this Congress, including elections of the Chairman of the USSR Supreme Soviet. I say "candidates" although I believe that it is quite possible that there will not be any other candidates. Mikhail Sergeyevich Gorbachev, who was the initiator of perestroika, whose name has been linked to the beginning of the process of perestroika and the leadership of the country for the last four years, must report on what has happened in our country during these four years. He must speak about the achievements and errors and do so self-critically. Our position will also be dependent on this.'

A certain contradiction is evident: on the one hand, Sakharov recognized that there might not be other candidates under current conditions, while on the other hand he insisted that my report be heard and evaluated first. Initially I thought this was due to his desire to carry out the work of the legislative body using strong democratic procedures from the very start. However, when I considered the positions of our radicals, I concluded that another

---

[1] On 9 April 1989 troops clashed with demonstrators outside the main government building in Tbilisi, the capital of Georgia, killing 19 people.

motive was much more important – they wanted to impose their own programme of action.

They must have reasoned approximately as follows: 'He was good for the first lap, but that's all.' In any case they did not forgive me for rejecting the role of leader of the democratic party, and very soon I felt this in the severity and indecency of the attacks on me, on almost any pretext, sometimes none at all.

Meanwhile the problem, of course, was not the limited nature of my programme or the indecisiveness ascribed to me as a politician. I never for a minute thought that the transformations I had initiated, no matter how far-reaching, would result in the replacement of the rule of the 'reds' by that of the 'whites'. Indeed, I saw the entire meaning of the reforms in eliminating the very principle of class dictatorship and finally healing the seven-decade-old split in our society, pulling up the roots of the deep civil conflict and creating a constitutional mechanism by which relations between social groups and people were decided, not by head-butting and bloodshed, but rather by politics.

Besides, one should bear in mind that I was the General Secretary of the Central Committee of the Communist Party. Millions of people trusted me in this position and it would have been dishonourable, dishonest, and even criminal simply to defect to the other camp. Even then, as Chairman of the USSR Supreme Soviet and later when I was President, I considered it a matter of principle to promote reforms not by one part of society coercing another, but rather by consensus or, failing that, by compromise.

A spontaneous structuring of the Congress into factions had begun long before it opened, immediately after the elections. The radically-minded deputies from the intelligentsia, mainly from Moscow and Leningrad, grouped together on one side. The organizational embryo of this faction was 'Memorial', later called the 'Inter-Regional Deputies Group', from which grew 'DemRossiya'[1] (Democratic Russia). Initially Sakharov was the

[1] A coalition of democratic organizations which eventually played a key role in the election of Boris Yeltsin as President of the Russian Federation. It was strongly anti-communist.

371

recognized leader of this party and G. K. Popov its principal ideologue. In the early days of the Congress, the Inter-Regional Group gave evasive answers to the probing questions of journalists about their objectives; but soon, if I recall correctly, Popov publicly admitted that they saw themselves as the opposition. True, they did not declare specifically to whom they were opposed. But one did not have to guess, since the CPSU remained the ruling party.

The paradox was that a significant number of the deputies who were in the Inter-Regional Group or attracted to it, or who went to its meetings without officially declaring membership, were members of the CPSU. Except for Sakharov, almost all the leaders of the Inter-Regional Group were Party members: Gavriil Popov, Yury Afanasiev etc. The division between the ruling majority and the opposition in Parliament was very blurred, and this caused a great deal of problems. The Central Committee apparatus, and most of the leadership as well, did not immediately recognize that we would be operating under completely different conditions, that we had to learn to play by the new rules. Some still started from the traditional notion of the 'alliance of Communists and non-Party people'. They probably reasoned as follows: 'The overwhelming majority of the deputies are members of the CPSU. Hence all we have to do is establish strict Party discipline in order to implement any decisions of the Central Committee.' The departments, without thinking much, proposed that we should assemble the deputies who had come to Moscow, carefully instruct them and remind them that their Party duty was to vote according to the instructions of the Central Committee.

Far from it – even before the deputies had left for Moscow, attempts to instruct them in the republic central committees and Party oblast committees had met with failure. The CPSU members who had won the elections running against 'official candidates' simply did not respond to the invitations of the local Party bosses to 'compare notes' prior to the Congress. Similar steps at the Union level were more successful. On 3 May I met deputies from Moscow at the Moscow Soviet. I was accompanied by Zaikov, Ligachev, Vorotnikov, Yakovlev and Medvedev. The deputies asked me all kinds of questions.

However, the attempt to form a parliamentary faction of the CPSU proved to be completely unsuccessful. I have to admit that the idea was mistaken from the very start. After all, if we had called together the Party faction in parallel with the meeting of the Congress, the work of the supreme state organ would have become purely formal in nature and would have essentially come down to the approval of directives developed by the Central Committee and the Politburo.

Therefore, I began to put the brakes on this game. It is true that at that time we did not exclude the possibility that later we would be able to organize something like a club of Communist deputies. Such attempts were made, but they too failed. The truth was that our Party was never really a group sharing the same philosophy. At the very first winds of freedom brought by perestroika, different, including completely opposing, political trends began to proclaim their existence loudly, sometimes even in a bellicose tone.

However, the pivotal question in the battle developing at the Congress was not the opposition of the 'aggressively obedient majority' (as Yury Afanasiev christened four fifths of the deputies) to the democratic minority headed by the Inter-Regional Group. Most of the people's deputies were ready to follow whoever was able to convince them of the rightness of his ideas. Moreover, one should not forget that the Congress of People's Deputies did not have to legislate in the direct sense of this word. The Congress mainly decided issues of paramount political importance or of a constitutional nature. And it must be said that in nine out of ten cases the deputies responded to common-sense arguments and made optimum decisions while rejecting extremist positions on the right and the left. However, the Inter-Regional Group failed to see this and took all the other deputies to be retrogradists.

Sakharov's proposal concerning the agenda was countered by Ye. N. Meshalkin from Novosibirsk, the director of a research institute. Referring to the fact that Academician Sakharov and his colleagues did not see alternatives to Gorbachev's candidacy, he proposed that the Congress first hold elections for the Chairman of the Supreme Soviet and then hear his report. As soon as discussion of the candidates for this position got under way, the debate focused on the issue of combining the positions of General Secretary of the CPSU Central Committee and Chairman of the USSR Supreme Soviet. Today this may not seem like an issue of great relevance. At that time, however, it was a most serious matter. The country had barely rid itself of a totalitarian regime and literally everyone, with the exception of inveterate Stalinists, feared that power might again be concentrated in the hands of one person. Many said with good reason that, knowing Gorbachev, they did not expect surprises from him for the young democracy that he himself was nurturing. Nevertheless, they wanted to take out some insurance: who could tell who might become the leader tomorrow?

In short, V. A. Logunov, who was then deputy chief editor of the newspaper *Moskovskaya Pravda*, suggested that I should give up the duties of General Secretary. He reminded us that in the pre-election campaign there had been many articles and citizens' letters in favour of this decision. V. P. Khmel, a construction worker from Angarsk, opposed him and her speech was followed by many short speeches supporting the policy of perestroika and praising me, along with critical comments, advice and wishes. Later there was much talk about Chengiz Aitmatov's speech. Some of his colleagues from the creative intelligentsia saw it as just short of an attempt to revive the sadly memorable tradition of exalting the leadership. I think it was Mayakovsky who wrote: 'They were so afraid of being branded as toadies that they cursed the bosses.' That is the way it was here – everyone was so sick of singing the praises of Brezhnev that it now became a must to chide the leader. I tried not to pay attention to this.

I will permit myself to present one excerpt from Aitmatov's speech and, honestly, I am not doing this to flatter myself. It is simply that I believe that with his writer's gift Aitmatov was able to find the right words to describe what had happened. Reminding his listeners that the Supreme Soviet had from the very first days of its existence been 'under the irresistible pressure of authoritarian regimes that reduced the role of the supreme legislative body to a mere appendage of the Party apparatus,' he continued:

'But now comes a man who has stirred up the sleeping

kingdom. He did not come from outside, but arose within this very system, possibly as our chance of survival through renewal, for, from a historical standpoint, the period of stagnation, like a snowball, continued to accumulate the destructive power of inertia and conservatism, which is dangerous both for society from within and for the surrounding world. As fate has willed it, this man arrived in the leadership just in time. Of course, following in the steps of his predecessors, he did not have to trouble himself; he could have sat calmly in the presidiums, read aloud from the rostrum the texts written by his secretaries and everything would have rolled smoothly along. But he dared, it would seem, the impossible – a revolution of minds while preserving the socialist order of society . . . He dared to follow the path of social renewal and he stands on it in the sharp wind of perestroika.'

My nomination went smoothly; everybody voted in favour, with just four abstentions. No serious rivals were found. A. M. Obolensky's self-nomination was not taken seriously by most of the delegates. Needless to say, he would not have stuck his neck out without securing the promise of the Inter-Regional Group to vote for him. It must be said that this incident did not do the opposition any honour. It would have been understandable if they had put forward Sakharov or Yeltsin as an opponent, or even Popov or Afanasiev, who were popular at the time; at least these activists were well known. But to suggest an absolutely unknown person for election to the highest position in the state was extremely irresponsible, even shameful.

The opposition did not dare at that point to dispute the post of chairman, since this would obviously have been a losing battle. Even Yeltsin, who was nominated by Burbulis, refused to accept the nomination, following an insistent plea by A. Kraiko, a deputy from Moscow. Yeltsin's remarks, though, were ambiguous. He reminded the deputies of the decisions of the XIXth Party Conference about combining the positions of General Secretary and Chairman and about the May Central Committee plenum, which recommended Gorbachev for the position of Chairman of the Supreme Soviet. He also said that he had abstained when the vote for my candidacy came up. On the other hand, he indicated that he would conform to the decisions of the plenum, since he was 'for perestroika.' He concluded by saying that since yesterday he had been out of work and could, 'working seriously and recognizing perestroika, agree to some offer.'

The result of the vote was announced by the chairman of the vote-counting committee, Academician Yu. A. Osipyan: 2,123 for Gorbachev, 87 against. Thus I was elected Chairman of the Supreme Soviet with 95.6 per cent of the vote.

I expressed heartfelt thanks to the Congress and returned to my office at Staraya Ploshchad, where my aides were already waiting to discuss the draft of my speech. There were, of course, congratulations, but it was felt that no significant change in my status had occurred. I had been the Chairman of the Presidium of the USSR Supreme Soviet, now I was 'simply' the Chairman. However, I myself realized the true importance of what had happened.

There were no particular surprises in the USSR Supreme Soviet elections. On the whole the results were as good as we could have hoped for – in the new Supreme Soviet were many people who became professional parliamentarians and who were able to get the legislative work going. From this standpoint, the USSR Supreme Soviet was greatly superior to the Russian Supreme Soviet. It was they who laid the legislative groundwork for the radical transformations in our country.

The Congress rejected the candidacies of some deputies who had been counted among the 'foremen of perestroika', which produced a storm of indignation from the ranks of the Inter-Regional Group and rude attacks by the publications that they controlled. They saw in these the intrigues of the nomenklatura, the re-birth of the former practice of controlling the Soviets, and so forth. There was not a grain of truth in any of this. Even if the Party apparatus had tried to use the old methods, it could hardly have succeeded, since such methods no longer suited the mood of the deputies. And the fact that they had voted out the most 'loud-mouthed' representatives of the Inter-Regional Group was mainly because they did not accept the arrogance and open rudeness with which some of this group treated the deputies from the provinces and districts, from factories, or from rural regions.

However, what else could the provincials expect, when even the newly elected Chairman of the USSR Supreme Soviet came under fire? I was accused of 'manipulating the majority' because of my efforts to conduct the meetings in a way that allowed everyone an opportunity to speak, and to ensure that parliamentary polemics would not develop into a brawl.

The signal was sent by Afanasiev, who described the assembly as a 'Stalin-Brezhnev Supreme Soviet'. Popov and Adamovich spoke after him in the same spirit, and they were answered, no less fiercely, by a large group of outraged deputies. Serious and weighty arguments were presented by both sides, but all kinds of harsh words were added to them in the heat of the battle. I tried to reason with the angry orators and called on them to turn their attention to the substantive arguments advanced by the Inter-Regional Group. The reasons for their aggressive tone were best related by Meshalkin, who attributed Afanasiev's and Popov's speeches to dissatisfaction with their position in the Congress and to the fact that they were in the minority, whereas they had initially hoped that, 'as in meetings in the Luzhniki stadium, they could rally everyone and immediately sweep away everything that interfered with their becoming the leaders at the congress.'

Frankly, I considered that the election of Yeltsin to the USSR Supreme Soviet would be useful. At the May plenum he had said many things that I was ready to subscribe to, although I felt that his political programme made too many claims. Nevertheless, Yeltsin was voted down as a result of secret balloting. But then a deputy from Omsk, the lawyer Aleksei Kazannik, proposed that he should give up his place in the Supreme Soviet to Yeltsin. This started a lively discussion on the legal aspects of such an unusual step. Finally, this trade-off was allowed.

INNOVATIONS

In the hustle and bustle of the Congress it was impossible to hold Politburo meetings, but we met informally for brief periods during recesses. Tea and coffee were served in an adjoining room and there we could discuss matters on the run. Everyone sensed that a radical change was taking place in the normal order of things. Formerly, everybody would have a chat at tea and then follow the General Secretary onto the stage in single file. Now the chairman went onto the stage and everyone else went into the hall. Being disciplined people, my Politburo colleagues did not show that they were unhappy. Nevertheless, I sensed their bad mood. How could it be otherwise when it was already clear to everybody that the days of Party dictatorship were over?

This was also the pivotal idea in my speech on the basic directions for the domestic and foreign policy of the USSR. The first part was rather traditional: an analysis of the situation in the economy, in the social sphere, and so forth. In the other sections I tried to outline a programme of fundamental reforms.

Regarding the economy, I spoke of the need for a radical change in socialist property relations and the establishment of a real market. I suggested that enterprises, concerns, joint stock companies and co-operatives should become the principal entities in the economy:

'In order to resolve general problems and co-ordinate efforts, they will probably create, on a voluntary basis, organizations, unions and associations, to which the functions of economic management now performed by the ministries will pass ... This approach does not mean that the role of the state will be reduced, if, of course, one does not confuse the state with the ministries, or management with state control. The ministries will no longer have the function of direct interference in the operative management of economic entities and will concentrate on the creation of a common normative framework and conditions for the activity of these entities.'

I defined the essence of political reform as the implementation of the historic slogan 'Power to the Soviets!' The reconstruction of representative organs and the comprehensive expansion of their rights and powers, along with the unconditional subordination of the apparatus to them, was the first condition for returning the real levers of power and management to the Soviets.

These issues remain unresolved to this day. Moreover, in October 1993, claiming that the Soviet form of popular representation was inherently flawed and associated with the totali-tarian dictatorship of the Party, Yeltsin not only dismissed every Soviet throughout the country – from the Supreme Soviet to district and village Soviets – but, what was even worse, destroyed representative power as such or, in other words, nullified the sovereignty of the people. The constitution that he imposed provided for such wretched and reduced rights both for municipal bodies and the federal assemblies that it is, of course, a parody of democracy. It is not even a constitutional monarchy, but really an absolute monarchy that is being established in Russia, under the guise of a presidential republic. It does not take a leap of the imagination to predict that, at the end of the twentieth century, and given the level of political culture that we have achieved, such a system cannot long survive. It will inevitably produce growing resistance, until the people restore a normal democratic republic. And let us hope that this will be bloodless, as in February 1917.

In the matter of inter-ethnic relations, I must admit that at that time we were still not ready to put forward a real programme of reform that would have included the transformation of the unitary state into a truly federal state. Nonetheless, the general direction had been determined, pointing to a significant expansion in the rights of the republics and harmonizing relations between them and the union.

My discussion of foreign policy confirmed principles that flowed from the new political thinking: the goal of abolishing nuclear weapons, recognizing the inadmissibility of the use or threat of force, and reliance on dialogue and negotiations to establish a balance of interests as the only means of resolving international problems.

Many suggestions and amendments to the programme were proposed in the discussion following my speech. However, I must say that there were no fundamental objections. On the other hand, the deputies concentrated strong critical fire on the powers that be. They strongly urged that the pace of reform be increased.

The Congress reinforced this message to the executive power, to the Party, to the people and even to itself, in many resolutions. The Chairman of the USSR Council of Ministers (Ryzhkov) and the higher judicial officials were appointed, and a constitutional commission set up. It would seem that we had put together the necessary prerequisites to really push forward with perestroika and to end the negative flow of events. Why did this fail to happen?

I think the reason was that the processes of disintegration outran the formation of new institutions of power and administration, while the increasingly strong radical democratic opposition systematically undermined the foundations of power as it expanded its fight against the centre and centrism. I will return to this subject later.

TWO 'CLASSICS'

Leonid Maksimovich Leonov celebrated his ninetieth birthday in the tension-filled days of the first Congress, and I requested an invitation to visit him in his flat on Herzen Street. A small celebration was prepared and family and friends had gathered. This was my second meeting with Leonov.

He was in an active state of mind. I was amazed how attentively he followed everything at the Congress and the discussions that preceded it, even nuances that I had not noticed, because to do so one had to read every magazine and newspaper or sit continuously in front of the television. His opinions were well-grounded and philosophical.

'I always try to understand,' said Leonov, 'what the source of our problems is. And this is what I see. What you have started within the framework of perestroika is a movement towards new forms of society. It will determine the life of this country for the coming centuries. However, people live today and they have many acute problems. And it is this contradiction between far-reaching plans and today's reality that creates this atmosphere. There is nothing to be surprised at and there is no way of getting around it. One must not lose sight of the goal, but you won't get by with only promises of a bright future.'

I could tell Leonov with a clear conscience that I shared his fears, that I myself had thought much about this, and that we were trying not to lose touch with reality. Of course, it is a long way from philosophical chats to political practice.

Leonid Maksimovich spoke about how much glasnost meant for our culture. 'Of course,' he said, 'a lot of rubbish has appeared [I do not remember his exact words, but this is the sense of what he said], but one must hope that with time everything will become clearer and reason will prevail.' He was particularly critical of the so-called mass culture, the excesses of vulgarity and bad taste in the press and on television.

Some people were spreading rumours that Leonov, the recognized head of the Russian writers' school, was the moving spirit behind the 'Slavophile crowd', which preached extreme conservatism and anti-semitism. I got a completely different impression from our conversations. A man of such intelligence and culture could not lower himself to primitive nationalism; all of his opinions were permeated with humanism. However, in spite of this, he did not avoid sharp analyses of negative phenomena in life, in politics, and in literature.

Of course, there are those among the Slavophiles who curse perestroika and reject almost any kind of change. But not only did Leonov stake his authority on perestroika, he also helped me to understand the problems and contradictions that we were grappling with. The support of this classic writer inspired me.

I stayed for about an hour and a half and then went outside. People had gathered in the alley connecting Vorovsky and Herzen Streets. The conversation was friendly, with questions about the Congress and different opinions being expressed. Someone gave me this advice: 'Mikhail Sergeyevich, don't give in either to the right or to the left, because they will lead us into woe.'

I have already discussed the key episodes in the work of the first Congress and its place in political reform, but I cannot omit the final emotional scene at this forum. The story concerns the man who was unquestionably the most outstanding personality at the Congress – Academician Sakharov.

I had, of course, heard about this disgraced scientist, who had been a great patriot in his youth and then had 'slid' into dissidence and anti-Soviet activity. Along with everyone else, I was outraged that he had, as the newspapers reported, advised the Americans not to agree to our proposal to commit themselves to the non-use of nuclear weapons.[1] Our propaganda machine had ascribed many other such 'treacherous' actions to Sakharov by twisting various statements that he had made.

The newspapers were silent on the attempts to take away his title of Academician and his colleagues' opposition to this. People expressed their surprise at the patience shown by the leadership, which tolerated this rebellious academician's 'infamous' statements and had exiled him 'only' to Gorky (Nizhny Novgorod), instead of forcing him to emigrate. The indignant ones quietened down when they were reminded that Sakharov possessed secret information. It never occurred to them that if Sakharov had wanted to send this information to the West, he would have found a way.

I asked myself occasionally whether the whole problem was perhaps that the Central Committee officials who were 'in charge of science' had not found the proper approach, had not been able to explain the error of Sakharov's positions. After all, he was a major scientist and it was important that he should work for the country – we must fight for such scientists, just as in the first years after the October Revolution they fought for Pavlov, Sechenov, Timiryazev and other leading figures of Russian science.

However, these were obviously passing thoughts that I did not share with anybody – anyway, at that time nobody was interested in my opinion. I had my first serious conversation about Sakharov with Petr Leonidovich Kapitsa.[2] I met him on two or three occasions in the Ordzhonikidze Sanatorium in Kislovodsk, where he and his wife were spending their holidays. I genuinely enjoyed every meeting with him. Academician Kapitsa was an amazingly interesting conversationalist, always at ease and full of goodwill – in any case, that was the impression I had from our meetings.

One evening I paid a 'courtesy call' on Kapitsa and his wife.

---

[1] A Soviet proposal that Moscow and Washington should agree not to be the first to use nuclear weapons.

[2] A brilliant physicist who worked on nuclear energy in England under Rutherford at the Cavendish Laboratory, Cambridge, until 1934, when he returned to the Soviet Union. He was not permitted to travel abroad until after Stalin's death.

Sakharov came up in the conversation, since at that time he was much written about in the press. But now Kapitsa, a Nobel Prize winner and one of the most respected scientists in the world, surprised me with his opinion. 'All of this noise about Sakharov,' he said, 'is largely due to the inadequate response by the leadership. In the field of physics Sakharov is undoubtedly a talent, a major phenomenon, but he is unfamiliar with politics and is remote from life's realities. Moreover, people who are involved in secret research sometimes get a kind of inferiority complex – the perception that their talent, thoughts and opinions remain, as it were, unclaimed by society, "locked behind seven seals."'

Sakharov had written a letter to the leadership. But no-one paid any attention to the letter, and apparently it was simply handed down to the Central Committee Department of Science for consideration. 'And this,' argued Kapitsa, 'was the insult that artificially created the "Sakharov problem."'

I must say that while he spoke critically of the leadership that had behaved so negligently towards a prominent scientist, Petr Leonidovich also reproached Sakharov for his excessive ambition and vanity.

When I became General Secretary, I considered it an important task to rescue Academician Sakharov from exile. Our first meeting took place at the forum that produced the International Foundation for Survival and Development, which was headed by Ye. P. Velikhov and which, in 1991, became one of the founding institutions of the Gorbachev Foundation.

Velikhov and his colleagues sat at a round table in the Catherine Hall in the Kremlin. I shook hands with everyone and sat down. Sakharov, who sat nearby, seized the opportunity to repeat his demands in the presence of Western scientists. He called for an end to persecution of dissidents and the release of prisoners of conscience, handing me an appeal and a list of names. I took the papers and assured him that they would be considered in good faith. I also informed him that following our earlier telephone conversation I had already given instructions to Chebrikov to deal with this issue immediately.

After Sakharov's return to the capital, the president of the Academy of Sciences, A. Aleksandrov, tried, with my encouragement, not only to create conditions for Sakharov to continue his normal scientific activity, but also to provide him with a position in the scientific world that corresponded to his status. There was talk of bringing Andrei Dmitrievich into the Presidium of the USSR Academy of Sciences. However, this was not a simple matter. On the one hand, the scientists had kept him from being excluded from the Academy – mainly so as not to create a precedent. But, on the other hand, many of them condemned his political views and his speeches. They even tried to keep him from becoming a people's deputy. Eventually, however, he was elected.

I would describe Sakharov's position in our Parliament as mostly constructive. He also supported me personally, although, as he put it himself, 'conditionally' – so long as we continued with the reforms without yielding to the right. In spite of the fact that Sakharov was guided by the most noble intentions, he was a politician 'by inspiration', an idealist, and did not always accurately weigh the consequences of his actions. He proclaimed his allegiance to socialism and to the Soviet system cleansed of totalitarianism.

Sakharov's actions were to a certain extent influenced by his entourage, which, along with sincere admirers and followers, included people who were simply looking for patronage. There were attempts to use the authority of the recognized leader of the democrats to promote the interests of one or another group. However, I do not believe that he was a pawn in anybody's hands. Incidentally, that was the way he spoke about Yeltsin, whom he disliked, feeling nonetheless that without Yeltsin the democrats could not manage.

As far as Sakharov's role in the Congress is concerned, I would like to mention three key points. First and, perhaps, most important was his speech demanding a declaration that the Congress should take absolute power. The goal was to disavow all existing organs, above all Party organs, to 'pull the plug on them' and to take away their power and functions. One could clearly see that the intention was to settle accounts with the regime and to do away with the monopoly rule of the CPSU in a single stroke.

There was a certain theatrical air in his speech and I could not help but see a parallel with the IInd Congress of Soviets, which had adopted the famous 'Decree on Power'.[1] This may be what his advisers intended. However, I could hardly suspect Sakharov of having any intention of striking a 'historical pose'.

Sakharov's proposal did not stand a chance of being adopted from the very beginning. Moreover, it was illogical from a legal point of view. According to the amendments that had been made to the USSR Constitution, the USSR Congress of People's Deputies was already the supreme organ of power. So what was the point of proclaiming this again?

Although the demand to proclaim the 'taking of power by the Congress' did not pass, there was nothing wrong in the fact that it had been brought up. It reminded both the Party and society that we were on the threshold of a new era, when the norms of the Constitution would cease to ring hollow and Soviets at all levels would indeed have to undertake the administration of the country. However, Sakharov's continued activity at the Congress began to cause concern. It was sad to watch how he would, too often, rush up to the podium and indiscriminately squander the respect he commanded on idle issues. Sometimes I had the impression that someone was intentionally setting him up so as to diminish his standing.

I held Sakharov in the highest regard. It seemed to me that this was a 'new Sakharov', who was inseparably linked to Gorbachev and who together with him personified perestroika. However, if that was the case, any devaluation of his credibility devalued in some measure our policy of reform as well. Needless to say, I did not have to accept without reservation everything that originated in the 'democratic corner', but I also did not want to reject out of hand all the ideas coming from them. This could have made people think that I lacked objectivity and was leaning towards the retrograde camp. God knows, I wanted to demonstrate my unbiased attitude in every way possible, whereas Andrei Dmitrievich kept on 'popping up', and it became more and more difficult for me to calm down the furious delegates.

[1] The Congress, on 26 October (8 November) 1917, proclaimed the passing of power to the Soviets.

One day I worked long after the congressional session in my Kremlin office. We were talking over issues that needed to be discussed and the plan of action for the next day. As I was leaving my office around ten p.m., one of the guards told me that Sakharov was waiting for me in the meeting hall. Indeed right next to the stage, in half-shadow, since the chandeliers had been turned off, was the well-known stooping figure.

I do not remember all the details of our talk, but on the whole it was a fairly good conversation. We exchanged our impressions of the Congress's progress. I said that in spite of all the problems, things were moving along and decisions were being made. Questions of rules and procedures were gradually being settled. His assessment was more critical: the dominance of conservatives at the Congress reflected the state of society – still, the democrats were working actively and they would carry out their mission.

'I am worried by the danger that the nomenklatura will take revenge,' Sakharov continued. 'They are putting pressure on you too. They threaten to publish certain information unless you do as they wish.'

'What kind of information, what do you mean?'

'That you have taken bribes.'

'Well, what do you think yourself, do you believe this?'

'I, no, but they say . . .' and he looked at me with embarrassment.

This was all the influence of Yeltsin and Gdlyan – it was from this corner that such information was being fed. Sakharov did not want to believe it, but he was secretly anxious that it might be true. This was why he decided to wait and risk asking me directly, face to face. It was clearly his own idea, not something that someone had 'authorized' him to do.

In the following days I had contact with him a number of times for various reasons. I always tried to give him the opportunity to speak. It was embarrassing to see him queuing for the microphone – this grey-haired man, this outstanding scientist. I was under the impression that someone was directing him and constantly summoning him from the hall.

The third episode is connected with Sakharov's appearance on the podium at the close of the Congress.

Sakharov's remarks about the actions of our soldiers in Afghanistan had already irritated many in the audience. Sakharov's associates fed him 'cooked' facts and he used them, without bothering to check, in one of his interviews, which produced a sharp reaction in the Congress. Sakharov was clearly embarrassed. And even though his last speech was, I assume, an attempt to restore his standing, there was also, besides his personal motives, the political calculation of his entourage. Sakharov must close the Congress with his parting words – this was their ploy.

His desire to take the floor produced strong resistance from the deputies. Nevertheless, I insisted on giving him five minutes. Under my pressure the Congress agreed. He began to talk, obviously repeating what he had already said ten days ago. In the sixth or seventh minute I reminded him: 'Andrei Dmitrievich, time has run out.'

Sakharov did not listen and continued speaking. I again and again asked him to come to an end. Finally, when the microphone was turned off, Sakharov raised his hands to heaven like a victim of tyranny. This produced a hubbub in the hall, with some of the deputies and the public loudly hailing him and expressing their anger at the Chairman. It was a well played act that was intended to show the nation how impudently the powers that be treated a man of honour. What good could one expect from them after this?

Nevertheless, in spite of all of these incidents, which I attribute to the insidious influence of certain people from his entourage, I end this story as I began: Sakharov made a constructive contribution to the work of the first Congress and to the establishment of a parliamentary system in our country.

But this is not the only service Sakharov rendered to Russia by any means. He was one of the first to speak out for democracy and freedom, for renewal of socialism, and for true power to the Soviets. Such was the essence of the draft of the constitution that Andrei Dmitrievich sent to the constitutional commission. We intended to use much of his wording, which was written incidentally not by a jurist, but by a physicist.

Thus the first Congress is firmly linked in my memory to two outstanding countrymen: the writer Leonov and the scientist

Sakharov. They were quite different and represented, as it were, two roles, two faces of the Russian intelligentsia. It would be simplistic and plain wrong to put conventional labels on them: one a 'gosudarstvennik'[1] and the other a democrat. They were both classics in their own right. Sakharov and Leonov were democrats, humanists and patriots. But each in his own way had his own ruling idea, his own passion, his own point of view. And both deserve our respect and, first and foremost, our understanding.

THE PARTY IN DOUBT

Several days later, on 19 June, we discussed the results of the Congress in the Politburo.

One thing that was unusual in this meeting was that Ryzhkov and Ligachev moved closer together. Before this, they had argued sharply about the delimitation of their respective powers. The Prime Minister objected sharply to petty interference by the Central Committee apparatus in his domain and was angry that officials from Staraya Ploshchad were giving instructions to ministers. The Central Committee Secretary in turn cited Lenin: 'No question can be resolved without the advice of the Central Committee.' Since they had sat on my right and left hands, sometimes I would feel a kind of high-voltage arc between them and would have to urge my colleagues to calm down.

Once we set to implementing political reforms, their bickering gradually vanished. I noted in passing that my colleagues had stopped provoking each other, and I was glad to see it, not taking the trouble to see what was up. And then I suddenly realized that these former opponents were now speaking in unison. I eventually saw what was happening, although not immediately. The competition for leadership of the economy had been pushed into the background – political reform had unambiguously decided this matter in favour of the Prime Minister. On the other hand, the arguments between systemic reformers and 'preservationists' in

[1] Someone who emphasizes the need for a strong state, implicitly for a 'firm hand'.

the Party was becoming sharper and sharper. Ryzhkov was not a conservative at heart – I have already mentioned that he and I worked 'hand in hand' at the beginning. However, at some stage he wavered and grew timid. Moreover, powerful attacks against the government by the democrats and assaults by the press pushed him to the right. This was the reason for his rapprochement with his former rival. Together they railed at the press, the democrats and the separatists, and worried that the Party was losing power. Others echoed them.

I must admit that I too had the feeling of a certain 'duality'. On the one hand, I was reasonably certain that reform had finally got under way, that the new parliament which had been created was no mere manifestation of an omnipotent Party, but a genuine meeting of representatives elected by the people. On the other hand, I was put on my guard by the excessive claims of the radicals, their frenzied onslaughts, their desire to obtain everything all at once, first and foremost to throw the Party out of power. The strategic aim of eliminating the monopoly rule of the CPSU, more accurately, of the Party and state apparatus, was correct – but tactically it would have been better to transfer power to the Soviets not all at once, but smoothly, in a gradual process, so that the country would remain governable and the 'partocracy' would not have grounds to blame perestroika for everything.

I shared these thoughts with my colleagues on that day and called upon them to cast aside their worries about their own personal positions and to see what was happening from the broader standpoint of perestroika as a revolutionary process. Indeed, the first Congress of People's Deputies was undoubtedly a great success: supreme organs of power had been formed which had the capacity to function, and accord had been achieved on the priorities for the short term.

I suggested a meeting of the first secretaries to discuss the results of the Congress. This was essential in order to overcome resentment and avoid despair. The Congress meant a real transfer of power at the top level, and this process would progress further at the republic and local levels and would be no less painful. We had to resolve these problems quickly and help the Soviets get on their feet. A general analysis of the elections had to be prepared, and new election law proposals made. Our economic programme needed amendment and approval. Here as well we had to advance by means of reform – not to put a bridle on reform.

The conference of secretaries opened on 8 July 1989. We discussed all the issues around which passions raged in the country, including the events in Tbilisi, and the secret Molotov-Ribbentrop protocol to the Soviet-German Pact of 1939,[1] which had a dramatic effect on the fate of the Baltic republics. Nevertheless, the Party and its role in society and the state and its responsibility for the past had been the central subject of the Congress from the first day to the last, and one could not pretend that nothing had happened. Fundamental discussion was now needed on a large number of issues connected with restructuring of the Party's work. It was clear to everyone that the conference would be a watershed in the development of the CPSU and even society as such. The Party continued to have an enormous influence on the life of the country.

I presented the conference with a very critical speech, containing proposals for the activity of the Party in the new context.

'The Congress of People's Deputies was a major step on the road of perestroika,' I said. 'We prepared the grounds for a real transfer of all state power to the Soviets, for the creation of a new democratic model and for the inclusion of the people in managing the affairs of state. In this way, political reform of our society is moving from the field of ideas, projects and plans to the practical plane and is becoming a living reality.

'. . . The issue of the Party was the centre of the discussion at the Congress. This has its own logic, for perestroika of the political system and sovereignty of the Soviets are unthinkable without a change of the role of the Party in our society. Indeed, there can be no renewal of society without renewal of the Party itself. It is no accident that the Party has come under fire from critics. The elections of people's deputies showed that the trust won by the Party through the development of a revolutionary

---

[1] The Lithuanian group at the Congress of People's Deputies was demanding that the authenticity of the protocol should be acknowledged by the Soviet leadership.

platform of renewal does not guarantee endless credit. What are the reasons for the move in public opinion towards a sharply critical attitude to the Party? You often hear the opinion that this is connected with the wave of criticism, the one-sided reports by our press and the exposure of past mistakes and distortions. But this alone or even largely cannot explain the changes in public opinion.

'Here we come to what, in my view, is the crux of the matter. Perestroika in the Party lags substantially behind the progress of society along the path of democratization. This poses the real threat that the Party will lose its leading role in society.'

In conclusion, I spoke out in favour of bringing forward the date of the next CPSU congress, at which the Party programme could be revised, new statutes adopted and basic directions set for development for the next five-year plan period. I proposed that a general Party discussion be prepared regarding the role of the CPSU in the life of society. The time when the ability to work hard and a conscientious attitude to the tasks at hand were sufficient was about to be relegated to the past.

FIRST BATTLES IN THE USSR SUPREME SOVIET

The first USSR Congress of People's Deputies created a new USSR Supreme Soviet. These were the foundations in the formation of a parliamentary system, but, as is well known, one is supposed to build a house on foundations. And we still did not have either a precise plan or many 'structural details'. Rules, procedures, the structure of committees, rights and responsibilities of the Presidium, the role of the Chairman, the status of the deputies – all these had to be developed. A difficult and at times tedious task began, which was more organizational than political.

In spite of the fact that I had spent many hours at sessions of the Supreme Soviet, now, when we had created a new and, I dare say, genuine parliament, we had to start from scratch. The work began with the election of the Chairman. For the Soviet of the Union (one of the two houses of the USSR Supreme Soviet), Velikhov, speaking on behalf of the Council of Elders, proposed

Primakov. It is no secret that this had first been discussed in the Politburo – not simply because we had still not abandoned the established practice of first addressing every serious cadre appointment at the highest Party level. It was also due to the fact that, since Yevgeny Maksimovich was a candidate member of the Politburo, he obviously had to get its agreement to the new appointment. I invited him to the podium to answer questions. I would like to call the reader's attention to one passage from his brief introductory speech: 'The Supreme Soviet and our chamber must without question safeguard the interests of the Soviet people in the process of perestroika. It is essential that both chambers carry out real control over the activity of the executive organs. Of course, these were not the functions of the previous Supreme Soviet. Today we are creating a new Supreme Soviet, a new Parliament, which must also work in a new way.'

This was how we all understood the task of political reform at that time – assurance of genuine control of representative organs over the government.

Primakov was asked many questions, not so much concerning himself personally as the upcoming work of the Supreme Soviet – what laws should be adopted first, how committees and commissions would operate. He answered intelligently and confidently. Then several deputies praised him, welcoming the fact that an Academician was being elected Chairman (Speaker) of the House. As a result, he was elected almost unanimously, with only three abstentions, and took over the chairmanship. The delegates proceeded to discuss committees and commissions – how many there should be, how best to distribute the functions of control of various spheres of activity among them. A particularly lively discussion arose in connection with the need to intensify and give legal protection to glasnost. The very same question that in 1993 would become the subject of bitter fighting was raised on almost the first day of our union Parliament.

I wonder if A. A. Sobchak remembers the speech he made on that occasion. He said that 'right now it is especially the mass media that need close control from the deputies.' B. N. Nikolsky, chief editor of the Leningrad magazine *Neva*, recalled the proposal to make the appointment of the chief editor of *Izvestiya* and the chairman of USSR Gosteleradio (State Television and Radio) a prerogative of the Congress or the Supreme Soviet. Three years later, the attempts of the deputies to return control of *Izvestiya* to the Supreme Soviet and to regain some influence over the television through supervisory boards would receive a hostile reception and be called 'an attack on the freedom of speech'. Whereas the fact that the Russian President and his team have made the mass media the mouthpiece of his party and are squeezing opposition publications in every way – that is supposed to be normal, 'business as usual'.

On 6 June the delegates elected the Chairman (Speaker) of the Council of Nationalities. The candidacy of Rafik N. Nishanov, former first secretary of the Communist Party of Uzbekistan, who had been proposed by the Central Committee, was generally greeted favourably. However, he had to begin by giving an account of the conflict with the Meskhetian Turks[1] in Fergana, which as it happened had taken place on the eve of the session.

I liked Rafik Nishanovich. His unchanging composure, humour and a certain philosophical distance from the petty vagaries of life – in other words everything that was usually associated with the 'wisdom of the East' – appealed to me. His ability to get along well with people and to settle conflicts worked well for him in the position of Chairman of the Council of Nationalities. I would even say that Nishanov was a natural speaker, had it not been for one quality that he lacked. This was decisiveness, the ability to cut the Gordian knot at the proper time. The diplomat in him got the upper hand over the politician and sometimes sessions of our 'nationalities chamber' lasted for days, even discussions on procedural matters, while simultaneously ethnic conflicts flared up in several parts of the Union. The body of deputies could have (and should have!) actively assisted in calming them down. To be fair, some committees and individual deputies went to the 'hot spots' on their own initiative. However, the Council of Nationalities and its Chairman did not

---

[1] An ethnic group deported by Stalin from Georgia to Central Asia, where clashes with the local population occurred a few days before the Congress.

do justice to its position as the organ of supreme power responsible for this sphere.

Of course, I direct this criticism first of all towards myself as Chairman of the USSR Supreme Soviet.

Nishanov had to 'dance' perhaps a little more than Primakov did before the delegates approved his nomination. He was cross-examined in order to discover his views on equal rights for all nationalities, the possibility of using indigenous languages, and ways of regulating conflicts between nationalities. However, most of the questions were asked not so much to get answers as to present the questioner's own positions on the subject. Some deputies, who were ready for harsh polemics, were obviously not satisfied by the composed and balanced opinions of Rafik Nishanovich or his conciliatory tone. In the end, Nishanov was elected chairman of the chamber by a convincing majority.

The next day, at a joint session of the chambers, I read out the resignation of the USSR Council of Ministers. In and of itself this was a routine phenomenon, but under our conditions this act was an important element of political reform. It emphasized our intention to follow constitutional norms to the letter and, speaking to the essence of the matter, to put the government under the control of Parliament from the very beginning.

In my introduction I favourably characterized Ryzhkov as not just a statesman who was one of the initiators of perestroika, but I also warmly praised his moral qualities, his democratic nature and his leanings towards innovation. I spoke all of that from my heart. At that time I was convinced that Nikolai Ivanovich's creative potential was far from exhausted and that his reformist impulse had not been stifled under the pressure of the economic and social problems which were then coming to a head. These problems were mentioned in my speech in a very general form: 'Not everything has been done as planned; serious mistakes have been made,' I said.

When asked by one of the deputies to explain this remark, Nikolai Ivanovich preferred to deny the existence of fundamental errors. One would think that there was no direct disagreement here. But a disagreement was indeed developing. I have already mentioned our differences in the analysis of our economic transformations in connection with the June 1987 Central Committee plenum and the fate of its decisions. Ryzhkov had to recognize this. However, evidently the position of the head of government, his heightened pride and touchiness, which were characteristic of this outstanding leader, did not allow him to admit our errors. Meanwhile, decisions on all important matters had, after all, been made collectively in the Politburo. Decision-making had included ministers, prominent specialists, scientists, almost the entire economics division of the USSR Academy of Sciences. Moreover, they had initially met with enthusiasm from the public.

I do not say this to deny in any way the responsibility for errors that occurred in the first stage of economic reform. No, I simply believe that the old ways of thinking ingrained in all of us still kept us from foreseeing all of the effects of the new and original decisions that were being made. We were looking forward, but our field of view was limited.

Ryzhkov's confirmation as Chairman of the USSR Council of Ministers developed into a lengthy and substantive discussion of issues of economic strategy. The situation in the national economy was quite complicated, although, of course, it was still far from the economic crisis, more precisely the quagmire, that was produced by subsequent experiments in shock therapy or even shock surgery. The increasing demands coming from the provinces, from various social and professional groups at that time, were due not so much to a decline in living standards as to expectations of a rapid rise in the standard of living. The 'revolution of expectations' caused a kind of consumer rush. Everyone rushed to the authorities to stake claims that they simply had not dared to press before. But the authorities, of course, were unable to satisfy them. At that time, even the most sober-minded and cautious economists had not yet arrived at the sad conclusion that to carry out structural economic reforms and reach the level of the developed Western countries would take not just a year or two, but more like fifteen to twenty years.

Many of the deputies took part in the debate over Nikolai Ivanovich's speech; almost all of the republics and oblasts rushed to tell their woes and to put in an order for their share of the state pie. However, along with the traditional requests and wishes, which were familiar from the former Supreme Soviet, there were quite a few interesting new proposals. Economic reform had not yet brought in anything meaningful in practice, but it had begun to pay other dividends by pushing resourceful, thinking and inventive people to the fore.

Ryzhkov was named Chairman of the USSR Council of Ministers, with nine votes against and thirty-one abstentions.

G. V. Kolbin was nominated as Chairman of the Committee of People's Control in place of S. I. Manyakin. Then a funny thing happened. Deputy L. I. Sukhov asked if Yeltsin would not be appropriate for this position. At that time I had spoken with Boris Nikolaevich and suggested that he head the USSR Supreme Soviet Committee on Construction and Architecture. He promised to think it over, but apparently decided that he preferred to take on the role of the opposition leader in Parliament. In short, I did not have to go into details, since Yeltsin himself supported Kolbin's candidacy. Ye. S. Smolentsev was elected Chairman of the USSR Supreme Court, Yu. G. Matveev was elected Chief of the State Arbitration Court and A. Ya. Sukharev was elected Procurator General. They were asked rather biting questions, but on the whole answered them well.

Then came the elections of the chairmen of the committees and commissions and the presentation of procedures and regulations – and at the same time a marathon discussion of the members of the government. This continued from the end of June to the last days of August and, frankly speaking, wore us all out. Ryzhkov complained to the Politburo that it was impossible to get any work done, since he had to sit day after day at sessions of Parliament, where ('rarely on business, more often in order to be seen on television or swagger a bit') some excessively knowledgeable deputy would try to embarrass an experienced minister. On the other hand, many deputies complained that the leadership wanted to keep on playing with the 'old deck', and was stubbornly dragging through parliamentary hearings many high officials who were incapable of working in the new style.

There was a grain of truth on both sides. Perhaps we were not decisive enough in replacing cadres and promoting new people. On the other hand, the body of deputies was not really capable of making a sufficiently competent evaluation of the candidates. Though the procedure for approving almost all of the Council of Ministers took up a lot of time and touched a lot of nerves, I am still convinced that it was necessary. After all, for the first time in our country we were creating a government that was truly responsible to the Parliament and that had undergone a process of legitimization. The first and, maybe, the last – at least, in this segment of history.

MINERS AND POLITICS

After completing the formation of the government, the USSR Supreme Soviet adopted a plan of legislative work. First, a law about the changes and amendments to the USSR Constitution had to be prepared and adopted in order to create legal foundations for a number of important 'organic' laws and all other activities of the Parliament.

The next problem was to stabilize the economic situation in the country by implementing reforms. These included laws on lease-hold and leasing relations, on a uniform tax system throughout the USSR, and on republican and regional economic self-accounting. Writing a law on property and the revision of legislative acts on land and land use were the most complicated and large-scale tasks.

Of decisive importance in terms of its impact was a set of laws establishing new relationships between the citizen and the state and guaranteeing real political freedoms and civil rights, as well as ideological and political pluralism. Among others, these included laws on the press and other mass media, on the social organization of USSR citizens, on the rights of trades unions, on freedom of conscience and of religious organizations. On 14 July this list of legislative acts was supplemented by one more bill, introduced by the government and the VTsSPS, on procedures for resolving collective labour disputes. At the last moment events forced us to postpone all other concerns. Immediately, on an emergency basis, we had to prepare a law regulating strikes.

In Poland the old system began to stagger when the Silesian

miners supported the Gdansk dock-workers, and strikes, lock-outs and hunger strikes began. I think the same thing can be said about us – the rapid destruction of a social order that had existed for seventy years began with unrest among the miners – one of the largest and most militant groups of the working class, the class on which Soviet power in theory relied. However, there was a significant difference between the way events developed in Poland and in the Soviet Union. In Poland the miners rose up against the Party-state nomenklatura, which had not yet given a thought to reforms. In the Soviet Union miners' demonstrations[1] had become possible because of the changes that had been initiated from above, and a blow of enormous force had ricocheted back on the reformers themselves.

At the USSR Supreme Soviet session on 19 July 1989 Kazemiras Uoka, Chairman of the Workers' Union of Lithuania, sent me a note: 'Mikhail Sergeyevich, the Workers' Union of Lithuania also opposes destabilizing strikes, but this has happened because conditions permitted workers to organize; there was no other way of fighting the local mafia. If you allow workers to organize, there will be fewer strikes.'

I supported this idea. 'We must rely in all of our work on the leading and decisive force of our society – the working class, its organization, responsibility, and allegiance to socialism and to the policy that we are now implementing through perestroika. But we cannot ignore the fact that workers recently have been putting harsh questions . . . Maybe the time has come to set up commit-tees to support perestroika and to oppose the saboteurs of perestroika?'

In Kemerovo, West Siberia, where the strike movement was concentrated, the workers were behaving responsibly. Shops that sold alcoholic beverages had been closed on the orders of the strike committees. The working class was demonstrating its excellent organization and at the same time its insistence on high standards. It had every basis for this. The commissions sent by the Party Central Committee and the government to the coal regions reported that year in, year out, over decades, decisions on

[1] For improved working and social conditions and more pay.

house building and the supply of food and consumer goods had not been implemented.

Coal-mining technology, especially the shaft method of mining, was outdated and far behind world standards. Extremely heavy labour under always risky conditions was not being properly rewarded. Immediate steps had to be taken. In particular, I sent Slyunkov to the Kuzbass (Kuznetsk Coal Basin in West Siberia), to hold talks with the leaders of the miners. He came back with detailed proposals.

I well understood the factors that made the miners go to such extremes to defend their own interests, and I never reproached them for this. However, the dissatisfaction of the workers was being exploited by radicals in the struggle for power. They did not seem to be very concerned about the fact that the shutdowns of enormous coal regions for many months deprived the nation of millions of tonnes of a valuable source of energy and threatened the operation of related branches of industry, metallurgy above all. This had a ruinous effect on many people's lives. Emissaries of the Inter-Regional Group, which had in fact already become a party, spread out through the country and instigated strikes by railway workers and workers in other branches of industry. This was truly a stab in the back – one that was fatal for perestroika.

Yeltsin and his associates knew – they could not help but know – that the government did not have the resources to meet all of the demands, no matter how valid they might be, in the short periods indicated by the miners' ultimatums. In the winter of 1993–4, after the radicals had been in power for two years, strikes began again in coal regions, since almost none of the promises Yeltsin's people had made to the miners had been met. In the trade unions and strike committees they had not forgotten the lessons taught by Bella Denisenko[1] and other agitators. So one should not be surprised when economic demands are joined by political demands, such as the resignation of the government, and early elections for President. Truly, what ye sow, so shall ye reap.

However, let me return to 1989. On 24 July I informed the

[1] Economic demands should be followed by political demands.

USSR Supreme Soviet that a draft agreement had been signed by Slyunkov, the first deputy chairman of the USSR Council of Ministers, Voronin, and the chairman of the VTsSPS, Shalaev, and the chairman of the Kuzbass strike committee, Avaliani, and his deputies. The government was prepared to extend the agreements that had been reached to other coal-mining regions, first of all, of course, to the Donbass (Donetsk Coal Basin, Ukraine) and Vorkuta, in the Russian Arctic. We were slowly getting out of a most serious crisis, which had perhaps been the most severe test of all the four years of perestroika. The miners' strikes were the focus of attention in the USSR Supreme Soviet and the subject of heated debates. I will reproduce an excerpt from the appeal of the strike committee of the cities of Inta and Vorkuta: 'The miners' strikes are directly relevant to perestroika; they are a sign of the impending crisis of the administrative-command system, which is not capable of meeting the interests of working people. We feel that the miners' actions are in support of perestroika and a warning to those who want everything to remain as it was.'

Statements such as this were clear evidence that the working class had ceased to consider the existing system to be its own and was categorically rejecting it. This signal was sent firstly to the Party, which nevertheless continued to rule the country in the name of the working class. However, even today our fundamentalists are still unable to interpret it. They still marvel, childlike, at the fact that the workers proved indifferent to the fate of the CPSU – in the new political climate many of them vote not even for the new socialist and social-democratic parties, but rather for right-wing parties and movements.

Later in the appeal it was stated: 'We understand that, in seeking economic autonomy, we must remember that the economy of the country is in a deep crisis. Today it would be difficult for the state to find the means to meet all our demands. However, we must be granted economic independence . . . we are tired of waiting for solutions to urgent problems from Five Year Plan to Five Year Plan. It is this that has compelled us to take an extreme step – to strike. The time has come when decisions on all of our demands cannot be put off even for a second.'

I will now cite the demands of the miners in the Pechora

basin '(1) The genuine transfer of power to the Soviets, land to the peasants and factories to the workers. (2) Abolition of elections to the USSR Supreme Soviet from public organizations. (3) Repeal of the article in the USSR Constitution regarding the leading and guiding role of the Party. (4) Direct and secret contested elections of the Chairman of the USSR Supreme Soviet, the chairmen of local Soviets, the heads of municipal and district departments of the Ministry of Internal Affairs. (5) Abolition of the practice of denying deputies the right to speak at sessions of the USSR Congresses of People's Deputies by vote. Each deputy has the right to speak, regardless of the opinion of the majority.' These demands repeated the radicals' programme and were written at their dictation in Moscow.

THE SOVIETS

Once the radicals came to power in autumn 1991, they unleashed a powerful attack on the Soviets, declaring them citadels of the totalitarian system. Then, using the events of 3–4 October 1993,[1] they wiped the entire Soviet system off the face of the earth. Here and there Soviets resisted, but in the end they were forced to disband. Is the Soviet form of government indeed not suitable for democracy? This conclusion is refuted by the fact that up to a certain point the radicals did not have any grievances against the Soviets. On the contrary, Sakharov even retained this form of government in his draft constitution, and in the Ist USSR Congress of People's Deputies he proposed that we should pass a decree on the transfer of all power to the Soviets. More than that, it was specifically through the Soviets and because of them that Gavriil Popov was elected chairman of the Moscow Soviet, Anatoly Sobchak, chairman of the Leningrad Soviet and Boris Yeltsin chairman of the Supreme Soviet of Russia. At that time, no criticism of the Soviet form of democracy came from this camp. Moreover, what complaints could Yeltsin have against the

---

[1] The armed conflict between supporters of President Yeltsin and his opponents, ensconced in the Russian White House, which resulted in loss of life.

Supreme Soviet, if the deputies – without thinking about the consequences – obediently and even enthusiastically adopted the Declaration of Independence of Russia, which undermined the Soviet Union, ratified the Belovezh agreement, invested the President with additional powers to implement economic reforms and agreed that he would head the government and form it entirely according to his own judgement?

Cause for dissatisfaction arose when the deputies, at least most of them, began to express their disagreement with 'shock surgery', timidly at first but then with increasing boldness, after they had realized that it would have ruinous consequences for both the state and the people. It was then that conflict began between the executive power and the organs of popular representation, which ended in the complete devastation of the latter.

Can the Soviet principle be combined with the principle of the separation of powers, which is the mainstay of the parliamentary system? The answer has to be yes. At least the brief experience of our new Parliament confirmed the possibility of combining these two.

Its opponents usually argue that the ultimate authority of the Soviets is incompatible with the separation of powers. However, this is either a failure to understand or an intentional distortion of the essence of the matter. It may be due in no small measure to problems inherent in the notion itself. Supreme power cannot be divided in any way. It must be integral and whole, for to believe otherwise is tantamount to accepting the existence of dual power or triple power in one state, and possibly the simultaneous conduct of several political courses – in other words, everything that is characteristic of brief 'times of trouble' and that ends in the collapse of one system and the establishment of another.

There must always be a body that is recognized as supreme. The basic meaning of the bourgeois or democratic revolutions was that they took supreme power from the monarchs and gave it to legislative assemblies as organs of popular representation. It is the parliaments that are the bearers of supreme authority in democratic states. Naturally, this rule also extends to our Supreme Soviet.

However, the recognition of the supremacy of organs of

popular representation does not preclude the possibility of the separation of the functions of power. Parliament concentrates on the principal task of state administration – legislation. Day-to-day management is accomplished by the government. And the application of laws and resolution of disputes is the concern of the courts. Moreover, vitally important issues concerning the destiny of the state and the rights of citizens (declarations of war, the signing of peace treaties, budgets, taxes) are left to parliament.

Thus the sovereignty of the Soviets by no means interferes with the separation of the functions of power or, as is conventionally said, separation of powers. The radicals destroyed the Soviets simply because they could not find support for their policies among the deputies.

To what extent then is the criticism of the Soviet system justified? The Soviets, like any popular assembly, provide the opportunity for endless meetings, which complicates and sometimes paralyses the adoption and implementation of decisions. This disease is also inherent in parliaments, which Marxists scornfully dismissed as 'talking shops'.

However, I would say that it is a treatable disease. The antidote can be found in exact procedures and rules for the work of elective organs and, above all, in a body of deputies who exhibit high professionalism.

I also mentioned this in my concluding speech: 'We have tried to put maximum professionalism into the work of the USSR Supreme Soviet, but not to the detriment of communication with the masses. We tried not to discuss issues in the mode of a political rally. It seems to me that we have essentially succeeded in this. We have produced a permanent supreme legislative, executive and controlling organ of power. There are many shortcomings and weaknesses in its operation, but day in and day out, before the eyes of millions, it has gained speed, improved its competence and shown a serious approach to the resolution of problems.'

I noted that in its first session the USSR Supreme Soviet had taken foreign policy under parliamentary control, which was an important innovation. In the past there had never been even a hint of such a possibility. At first there was no time for foreign policy issues and the deputies were more engaged in domestic affairs. But soon the deputies began to make inquiries about foreign policy, and after discussion several international acts were ratified.

Let me reveal a secret. In the first stages of our disarmament talks with the United States, the Americans kept referring to problems in Congress. 'We in the administration,' they would say, 'are ready to accept this or that proposal, but the senators will not ratify it.' On this basis they demanded concessions from the Soviet side. Among our inner circle there were serious discussions: would it not be useful to present the Americans with a similar argument by organizing critical speeches in the Supreme Soviet against the accords that were being prepared? Later this idea was rejected, since nobody would have believed that it was not just a set-up. The main reason, though, was that we were afraid of presenting a bad example: we were afraid that the deputies might really start criticizing our foreign policy.

But when the Parliament had begun to take foreign policy under its control, a conservative reaction to the major foreign policy measures based on the new thinking quickly made itself known. More and more often the deputies called Shevardnadze to account, and he and I, half joking, half seriously, would say that we had 'brought democracy upon ourselves'.

Some political commentators and historians still blame me because in my final speech on the results of the first session I spoke negatively about the creation of the Inter-Regional Group:

'Essentially we are talking about an attempt to give some organizational form to natural differences in opinion and in approaches to problems of our society's development. Will not such an artificial demarcation lead to a confrontation on specific issues which our Supreme Soviet must resolve, and complicate the completion of the tasks that the voters and the Soviet society expect us to carry out? If we have a common cause, if we all believe it to be our highest duty to lead the country out of this crisis on the paths of perestroika and to raise the level of material and spiritual welfare of the people, to renew our socialist and social order, to reveal its rich potential – if we agree about this – then we can always work to reach an agreement.'

The deputies in the Inter-Regional Group had their own objectives which were different from those of the other deputies. Moreover, differentiation was beginning to be visible among the rest of the deputies. This was a natural reflection of the plurality of social interests in society, which had been suppressed under totalitarianism but was bound to appear after the dismantling of the totalitarian regime. The formation of movements or parties was the logical consequence of the appearance of group (or class) interests. Strictly speaking, the formation of the Inter-Regional Group was the first step in this direction.

I must note in self-justification that I did not have any inclination to ban or disperse the Inter-Regional Group, or try to destroy this group by any kind of intrigue. Moreover, I have maintained good relations with many of its members. It did not take us long to draw correct conclusions from the development of this nucleus of a party of radicals. We began to think that the efficiency of the new parliament would be improved not by fruitless attempts to achieve artificial unity between all deputies, but rather by the formation of groups or factions and practical interaction between them. Of course, we were not yet thinking in terms of having a party faction system in our parliament. However, the first steps in this direction were made in the very next session.

MAKING LAWS

The second session of the USSR Supreme Soviet, held from 25 September to 28 November 1989, focused on legislation work. In a period of two months the Supreme Soviet passed the law on leasing relations in the USSR and the law on procedures for resolving collective labour disputes/conflicts. It approved in a first reading or sent for nationwide discussion bills on property ownership, land and land relationships, pensions, general principles of local self-government and local economic management, on the press and other mass media, on the fundamentals of legislation, concerning the legal system, on languages and citizenship, and many others.

This list alone shows that the second session was not simply a patching up of the legislative fabric. Rather, it was comparable in importance to such landmarks in the history of Russia as the creation of the new code of criminal laws under Tsar Aleksei Mikhailovich, the legal reforms of Peter I and Alexander II, and the revision of the entire legal system after the October Revolution. For now I shall leave aside any analysis of motives and effects and write only about the scale of the work that was done. It touched all the key areas of social and government machinery. The foundation was laid for a radical reform of our law and, through it, of the entire system of social relations in the country.

Of course, measures on such a scale are not accomplished in a flash. The four preceding years of transformation or attempts at transformation had laid the groundwork. For almost every major issue we already had a clear idea of what to do. In the process we had also acquired some practical experience. That is the reason why many of the laws written at this time were adopted with only slight modifications by the republics.

THIS ACCURSED ARTICLE 6

Someone has said: 'Power corrupts and absolute power corrupts absolutely.' A basic characteristic of absolute power is the absence of competitors – when those standing at the helm of state can do whatever they want without even a glance towards a non-existent or smothered opposition. This formula applies equally to a political party that eliminates all competitors and strives to secure perpetual supremacy. No matter how valid the ideas that inspire a party, no matter how wise its programme, no matter how strong the initial support from the people, sooner or later there will be an inevitable degeneration of a revolutionary party into a conservative party. Incidentally, Lenin was warned of this – by Plekhanov, Rosa Luxemburg, Karl Kautsky and other figures in the workers' movement.

Lenin did not deny this danger. But he believed that the 'victorious proletariat' and its 'political vanguard' would be able to avoid it by involving the popular masses in government, by intra-Party democracy, criticism and self-criticism, and so forth. As it seems to me, Lenin based this thinking on the level of political culture that was characteristic of Lenin himself and his circle. However, doubts soon crept in. Even in his articles of 1921 and 1922 a major theme was alarm caused by the rapid bureaucratization of Party officials, which threatened to cut the Communists off from the people. But, alas, Lenin was unable to find and employ a sufficiently strong antidote to this disease.

Our own experience – like, I suggest, the experience of other Communist parties – has shown quite convincingly that no inventions or tricks, including tolerance for factionalism, can serve as a reliable guarantee against bureaucratization and ossification. Of course, this does not relate to rank-and-file members. We are talking about the ruling stratum, which very quickly acquires a taste for power and is ready to do anything so as not to part with it. Over seventy years this stratum produced several generations of a Party-state elite whose chief tenet was confidence in its own natural and inalienable right to be in power forever. In its time the nobility probably felt the same way. Some heirs of noble families believe to this day that the revolutions that removed this estate from power were illegal and unjust. And so today some former members of the Central Committee and secretaries of oblast committees cannot forgive Gorbachev for the fact that they lost their 'fiefs' as a result of perestroika.

But while I was certain that elimination of the CPSU monopoly on power would be beneficial for the people and the Communist Party itself, at least the millions of rank-and-file Communists, I did not and do not believe that this had to be done all at once, that the CPSU had to renounce the throne only to allow it to be seized by those lads who even in 1988 would go to meetings with banners saying: 'Party, give us the helm!'

In 1989, while the country was already being rocked by separatist movements, by the actions of popular fronts and by the attacks of DemRossiya on the Centre, *Literaturnaya Gazeta* published an article by two sociologists, Igor Klyamkin and Andranik Migranyan, which essentially said that radical economic reforms could be successful only if they were carried out under the reliable shield of a strong authoritarian power. For me and my circle this argument was no revelation. We were not so simple as not to recognize that no significant transformations could be carried out without a firm grip on the reins of power and without an ability to overcome the inevitable opposition to the proposed reforms. This issue had been discussed thoroughly even on the eve of the XIXth Party Conference. We hoped at that time that the reforms would be best 'shielded' by a gradual transfer of power from the hands of the Party leadership to an elected state leadership, figuratively speaking from Staraya Ploshchad to the Kremlin.

Besides, we realized that power is not an object that can be passed from hand to hand. It is important not to lose it along the way, somewhere near GUM or the Ministry of Finance.[1] The transfer of power is a highly complex social process that involves inevitable resistance from those who have to part with it and that requires a certain preparedness of the new forces to take on the responsibility for administration of the country. One could easily see that the Soviets were not yet ready to carry out the functions of supreme power. They lacked the necessary structure, sufficient professionally trained cadres, experience, and, above all, confidence that henceforth they would have the last word, that there would be no need to run to the district or oblast Party committee and beg for consent. We needed time for these to develop.

Of course, questions of that kind are solved differently in violent revolutions. No time is wasted on manoeuvring – the old government is driven out and the new one is in session the next day, even if it does not have the necessary skills or knowledge. But the fact was that we did not see perestroika as a violent revolution, but rather a peaceful process of reform, that precluded cataclysms and the related destruction of the productive forces of society, and the resulting disastrous suffering of the people. It takes great skill to find the right moment for the transfer of power – to do it only when there is absolute conviction that power will not be left hanging in the air or fall into the wrong hands, but

[1] The buildings of the Ministry of Finance and the GUM department store are located between the residence of the Union Parliament in the Kremlin and Staraya Ploshchad, where the CPSU Central Committee was housed.

408

will be used by freely elected representatives of the people to strengthen democracy and to continue reforms aimed at the creation of a law-based state, a socially oriented market economy, and so forth.

To my great regret, we were unable to conclude this decisive operation at the optimum time. At some point there was a vacuum of power, and this affected the whole subsequent course of reforms. It is not my intention to avoid responsibility for this outcome, but I must say that it was not due to the naiveté or imprudence of our initial plans. We clearly underestimated the speed at which a political opposition would form, the fierceness with which it would attack the Party. And, the main thing, we underestimated the degree of support that not only the intelligentsia but even the working class would offer the opposition because of their extreme disappointment with the Communist Party and the nomenklatura's inability to change.

The decision that the CPSU would abandon its monopoly position in principle, with all of the ensuing results (the multi-party system, tolerance of a political opposition and so on), was passed by the XIXth Party Conference. However, while it was assumed that other elements of political reform, first of all elections and the creation of a parliament, were to be carried out without delay, the transition to a multi-party system was 'planned' as the next stage of reform. There was no plan to procrastinate, but there was no intention to rush our fences either. We had spent many hours discussing this subject and everyone agreed that the Party must remain the guarantor of stability until the new political structure was operating efficiently. Needless to say, no schedules were set up, but it was assumed that it would take at least two or three years for Parliament to become strong enough to allow the formation of a multi-party system.

I should like to draw the reader's attention to the fact that at that time no-one had yet dared to challenge openly the Party's leadership of society. Even the most desperate 'rebels' argued for ideological and political pluralism with the obligatory stipulation about the 'vanguard role of the CPSU'. Thus the Party on its own initiative had renounced its sole grip on power and had announced its readiness to fight for it on equal terms with other political organizations and movements. It is hardly necessary to point out that this was truly a watershed, a moment that heralded a break with Bolshevism. Unfortunately, it proved impossible to maintain a more or less reasonable pace in this area of reform.

The campaign to repeal article 6 of the 1977 USSR Constitution, which enshrined the Communist Party of the Soviet Union as 'the ruling and guiding force of Soviet society, the core of its political system and state and social organizations', was the first major political act of the fledgling opposition. Through their control of much of the media, the radicals were successful in convincing the public that the repeal of article 6 was key to the progress of perestroika. Any opposition to this demand, no matter how well-founded, was proclaimed to be retrograde, a vain attempt by the Party bureaucrats to preserve their supremacy and to interfere with the democratization of the country. Of course, there was more than a grain of truth in this. However, the radical democrats' extreme aggressiveness and a desire to 'spur on' events threatened to divert the process from a path of controllable changes to direct confrontation. Needless to say, I could not sympathize with this.

I recall that we had a long and stormy discussion of this issue at a Politburo meeting on the eve of the June 1989 Central Committee plenum. Among other things the following question was debated: should we abolish article 6 or agree merely to amend it? No-one in our 'supreme council' at that time would risk taking a radical stand. We agreed on the need to make changes, but the debate over the wording of these amendments was quite sharp. The conservative group that was already taking shape (Ligachev, Nikonov, Shcherbitsky) was in favour of cosmetic corrections that did not alter the exclusive position of the CPSU in our political system. The active advocates of reform (Medvedev, Shevardnadze, Yakovlev) objected – not so much in principle, as by referring to the 'unpassability' of the proposed version. And those who could be called centrists in the Politburo (Ryzhkov, Vorotnikov, Slyunkov, Chebrikov) suggested wordings designed for 'passability', while preserving for the Party the notion of 'political vanguard'.

I must admit that the proposals made at that time were no more than palliative measures that would not have solved the problem.

This issue remained at the centre of the debate at practically all Party forums until the IIIrd USSR Congress of People's Deputies.

A Central Committee plenum held in March 1990 decided that proposals for articles 6 and 7 of the Constitution should be introduced as a legislative initiative at the Congress. The importance of this step was perhaps best expressed by Frolov in his speech: 'What we are discussing now is only formally designated as a change of articles 6 and 7 of the Constitution of the country. However, in fact – and this again is an argument in favour of why we had to do this in the final stages of political reform – this, comrades, is in the literal sense an upheaval, the completion, the final stroke in changing the political system.'

Our last proposal concerning article 6 was adopted along with the draft of the new CPSU statutes by the Central Committee plenum which took place, with two breaks, from 11 March 1990 onwards.

It was characteristic that there was no serious discussion of this issue either at the plenum or at the Extraordinary IIIrd Congress of People's Deputies. The amendment of article 6 that we proposed suited more or less everyone. It was finally adopted with the following wording: 'The Communist Party of the Soviet Union, other political parties, as well as trades unions, youth and other social organizations and mass movements, via the representatives elected to the Soviets of People's Deputies and in other forms, shall participate in the development of the policy of the Soviet state, in the administration of state and social affairs.'

As the reader can see, the legislation recognizes in an undertone the possibility of other political parties while still giving prominence to the Communist Party. This was a halfway solution, but nevertheless a revolutionary one.

THE FIRST PRESIDENT OF THE USSR

Of equal importance was the fact that joined with article 6 were other sections of the Constitution which contained provisions to establish the post of President. This was not, of course, a tactical manoeuvre designed to 'trick' the delegates into passing the compromise wording. The amendment to article 6 and the addition of article 127 to the basic law were organically related. The first meant that our state would cease to be a single-party, even in a certain sense a theocratic, state and that one of the main principles of democracy – ideological and political pluralism – would be introduced. The second meant the recognition of a no less important principle of this democracy, namely the separation of powers.

I have to admit that it took me some time to realize that it was necessary to crown our new political structure with the office of President. I rejected the arguments of some of my associates and specialists who advanced similar proposals. I argued that the basis of our political system, even after reform, would still be the Soviets, which would not fit with the post of President. Perhaps at some time in the future, I argued, we would come to this form of government, but for now the replacement of the Chairman of the Presidium of the Supreme Soviet by the Chairman of the Supreme Soviet was a sufficient innovation. In and of itself, this would expand the capabilities of the head of state and incidentally endow him with many purely presidential powers. At the same time, he would remain the head of the Supreme Soviet and would therefore work on laws together with the deputies which would heighten his awareness of his responsibility to the elected representatives of the people.

Alas, only a few months later, I realized that I had made a mistake. As I sat in the Chairman's seat in the first session of the Supreme Soviet and painstakingly delved into every detail of the procedures, regulations and the work of committees and commissions, I realized that it was simply impossible from the physical standpoint to combine the direct leadership of Parliament with other functions.

There was yet another aspect to the problem. Legislative and executive powers required different approaches. This does not at all mean that they must be permanently squabbling or even at war with each other, as has happened recently – they should monitor each other, but this possibility was excluded in the kind of government we had chosen. Thus we depreciated one of the advantages of the separation of powers.

Unfortunately another, perhaps principal, argument became clear to me too late. No matter how perfect the state structures created by theoreticians and politicians may seem at times, they will not work if they are not understood and supported in the political culture of society and the psychology of the people. Over many decades we had created a kind of cult of the Politburo and the General Secretary that required unquestioning obedience to the orders and instructions issuing from them. The fact that this authoritative source of power, which was both respected and feared, had 'dried up' was immediately reflected in state discipline. This was even more obvious after its functions passed to the Supreme Soviet, which in the past had been only a ceremonial, decorative body. To believe that this new parliament really ruled was far from easy, at least not immediately. Most citizens, who had not been schooled in political definitions, did not find it easy to perceive any real difference between the Chairman of the Presidium of the Supreme Soviet and simply the Chairman.

It was necessary to introduce the office of President for reasons of a purely psychological nature too. The proposal to create the Council of the Federation and the Presidential Council, which was, in a sense, the equivalent of the Politburo in the new political system, served to reinforce the authority of the supreme power.

At the extraordinary session of the Congress of People's Deputies, the Kazakhstan leader Nazarbayev was one of the first speakers in the debates: while he supported the establishment of the office of President and my candidacy, at the same time he spoke strongly in favour of using the same model in the republics, in order, as he put it, 'to eliminate contradictions between the notion of the presidency and the desire of the republics to broaden their autonomy'. In other words, the republics immediately realized that the central power was being strengthened and, not wishing to yield the independence that they had gained, decided

413

to seize the opportunity to secure themselves. Nazarbayev, an experienced and clever politician, was playing a no-lose game.

To be frank, the creation of the office of President in the union republics was not part of my plans, as this cut in half the gains we had expected from improving the authority of the central power. While agreeing to give Moscow additional prerogatives, the republics immediately demanded their share. But nothing could be done – any attempt to argue the wisdom of this approach could only arouse passions and produce a situation in which the changes to the Constitution would fail to achieve the required majority. Again, I could see for myself (for the umpteenth time!) that politics is 'the art of the possible'.

But, as could have been expected, the main attack came from the democratic camp. Its herald was the very same Rector of the Moscow State Historical Archive Institute, who had coined the phrase 'the aggressively obedient majority of the Congress', Yury Afanasiev. He began by stating, misleadingly, that the purpose of the presidency was 'to legalize the extraordinary power of a certain person, at this moment Mikhail Sergeyevich Gorbachev'. Having thus distorted the issue, he began to ask rhetorical questions: 'Do we need this at all, does perestroika need this, do the citizens of the Soviet Union need this, does the initiator of perestroika need this?' He went on to announce that the Inter-Regional Group had met and passed a resolution that opposed the introduction of the office of president.

A comparison often came to mind. In the French Revolution on the extreme left flank was the Hébert-Roux group, who were called *les enragés*. And now we too had such 'ultra-revolutionaries'. Afanasiev was the obvious leader, sometimes together with Yury Chernichenko. Maybe the secret lies in the fact that, being a specialist in the French Revolution, he was inspired by the image of the incorruptible Robespierre and subconsciously hoped for a similar role in perestroika. According to Freud, this kind of thing happens.

Afanasiev's arguments were rejected by many of the deputies. Perhaps Academician V. I. Goldansky was closest to the mark. 'Of course,' he said, 'it would be better to elect a president on the basis of a universal equal and direct suffrage, as is proposed for the future. But today we simply do not have time for this. Today we are talking about, if I may use medical terminology, the immediate need for resuscitation, and not sanatorium treatment. I completely reject the statement that the creation of the office of president is the result of Gorbachev's desire for absolute personal power. As a matter of fact, he obtained exactly such absolute power five years ago, when he became General Secretary of the CPSU Central Committee. It would be absurd to suggest that after he had devoted all of his activity during these five years to the dismantling of the administrative-bureaucratic system, Gorbachev would today decide to seize power in a new embodiment. This in spite of the existence of our body of deputies and the USSR Supreme Soviet, and when accepting the office of president would mean taking on a very heavy load and great responsibility to the country and the entire world.'

I beg the reader's forgiveness for so many quotations, but a very dramatic story developed at that session – one that had a bearing not only on me personally, but also on the future of perestroika and the fate of the country. Some of the statements of that time sound like an echo of what is happening today. For example, N. T. Dobezea, a Moldavian writer, said: 'Many of us are in this hall because of Gorbachev, and now it is our turn to help Mikhail Sergeyevich, to "protect" Gorbachev from Gorbachev. Concentrating enormous power in the hands of one person presents a danger for the process of democratization of our society, which is linked to the name of Gorbachev. We trust him, but who can be certain that in four years or nine years there won't come a person who will want to create socialism of a tsarist stamp in the USSR? This is what we must fear. Yes, times are difficult for the country. There is the danger of a return to dictatorship, discipline is falling sharply, we all live under constant stress, no-one listens to anyone. In other words, in order to mend things, we need a "tsar". He may have a different title – General Secretary, Party Chairman – that is not what is important, what is important is that we have suddenly recognized that we need a "father", to whom one can complain about the local policeman or deputies and who would dissolve the Duma, if necessary, and so forth.'

Really, could it sound more topical? It was clear from the rest of this speech that in the union republics they were afraid that the office of president would allow the centre to take from them the sovereignty that they had gained because of perestroika. For this reason, they were ready to support the office of president only under the condition that the Presidential Council would include fifteen vice-presidents, who would chair the meetings by turns. In other words, it was one of the first models of the Commonwealth.

The people's deputies elected from autonomous republics, autonomous oblasts and districts had their own, somewhat special point of view. They made a declaration to the Congress which emphasized the rights of nations to self-determination, independent determination by them of their own political status and protection of small indigenous peoples. The central political condition put forward by the autonomous republics was participation on an equal footing with the union republics in the Council of the Federation.

It became clear that the overwhelming majority of deputies supported the establishment of the office of president and the election of the first President at the Congress. After this, the discussion concentrated on whether the President should remain head of the Party. The approach to this issue was not formally judicial, but rather political. There were few who doubted that I would be elected first President and, therefore, the question whether or not this would be connected with my leaving the post of General Secretary of the Central Committee of the Communist Party of the Soviet Union became very important.

I have discussed this issue a number of times and presented my arguments, and for this reason I will not repeat myself. I will say only that at that time, in March 1990, my relinquishing the role of General Secretary would have been perhaps even less justified than earlier. The conservative anti-perestroika forces in the upper levels of the CPSU had become more active. If they held in their hands the leadership of the Party, with the enormous political influence that it still commanded, they could have returned the country to the former order.

There were more than enough arguments against the obligatory separation of the supreme state and Party posts. First of all, there was the reminder that other constitutions did not have such a requirement and that in practice the heads of many states retained the leadership of their political parties. But the main argument of the Inter-Regionalists was that the President would rule in the name of the Politburo and carry out its decisions.

In the end the amendment to article 127, which forbade the President from heading a political party, did not obtain the required majority and was turned down. Together the right and left wings had a total of 1,303 votes, but with 607 against, it was not enough to pass the amendment.[1] It was clear from the voting results that it had been supported both by the Inter-Regionalists and the Party fundamentalists, who had already shown their desire to replace the General Secretary.

Then attention switched to very important details of the proposed changes to the Constitution. The discussion concerned the exact wording of the power of the President to declare a state of emergency, who should have control of the 'nuclear button', the powers and composition of the newly created Council of the Federation and Presidential Council. After a thorough discussion of all these questions the amendments were passed, and the Congress proceeded to discuss candidates for the office of President.

Deputy V. A. Ivashko, who was at that time the first secretary of the Central Committee of the Communist Party of Ukraine and later was elected the deputy general secretary of the CPSU Central Committee, reported that I had been unanimously nominated for the office of President of the USSR at the Central Committee plenum held two days earlier. He added that the plenum had expressed a number of recommendations if I were elected.

But after these bouquets came the brickbats. Among the harshest was a speech by the well-known T. G. Avaliani, who at that time was deputy director of the Kiselevskugol coal-mining concern in the Kemerovo oblast. He accused me of indecisiveness and wavering and of setting 'one flank of the people against

---

[1] Two thirds of all deputies (1,500 out of 2,250) were required to pass a constitutional amendment.

417

the other'. Kutsenko and Shchelkanov (the 'rabid' right and the 'rabid' left) expressed opinions just as severe.

However, support for my candidacy predominated in the speeches. Ryzhkov and Bakatin, who had both been nominated, refused to accept the nominations. I disliked the idea of being the only candidate and, to be honest, I had counted on the Inter-Regional Group nominating, if not Yeltsin, then another of their chieftains, say Popov or Afanasiev. However, this did not happen. And it was not just because any competing candidate would have had no chance of winning. Under other circumstances this would not have kept the democrats from nominating a candidate in order to be able to promote their own policies and to reaffirm their commitment to the principle of not allowing single-candidate elections. This time, the reason was clear – the desire to diminish the legitimacy of my presidency in any way possible. They would say, not only was he elected by the Congress rather than by a popular vote, but it was not even a contested election. These people let it be known beforehand that they did not intend to reconcile themselves to the will of the majority and would continue their merciless battle for power.

There were 1,329 votes for and 495 against; as the newly elected President I immediately gave a short speech to the Congress in which I tried to respond to its concerns. I said that I would carry out the presidential mandate with the firm intention of continuing the policy of perestroika.

I told the deputies who feared that the presidency could give rise to usurpation of power that there was no basis for such fears: 'The guarantee is the Constitution itself, which now is being guarded by supreme representative organs of state power that are strong and have real rights – the Congress of People's Deputies and the USSR Supreme Soviet . . . The guarantee is also glasnost, which has become a reality here, and political pluralism.'

Looking back, I can say that these arguments had merit. The unsuccessful attempt to usurp power in August 1991 and then the successful attempt in December of the same year are evidence that the danger did not come from the broad powers of the President as spelt out in article 127 of the Constitution.

In the evening of that memorable day, after the Congress

418

session had ended, I spent two or three hours receiving the congratulations of deputies and listening to their requests, wishes and counsel. I also had to give several short interviews to Soviet and foreign correspondents. When the lights had already been put out in the meeting hall, I went up to my office, where Raisa Maksimovna was waiting, along with my aides Shakhnazarov and Ignatenko. We celebrated with champagne and then had a cup of coffee. I was wondering: has anything really changed in my status?

FLAWS OF THE NEW STRUCTURE

Imagine a commander surrounded by a staff, marshals and generals, but not having army units at his disposal. To some degree this was our situation after the IIIrd Congress. We had a President, a staff (the Council of the Federation and the Presidential Council), but there was no supporting groundwork. No-one directly disputed the prerogatives of the supreme central power, but its policies did not receive energetic reciprocal support. The Party organizations had already disconnected themselves from administrative affairs, while the Soviets had not yet really connected up. The real power lay somewhere in the middle, was poorly protected, and essentially neglected. It was quickly picked up by the republics, and a significant portion was grabbed or pocketed by various organizations, 'strong men', and the mafia, which was beginning to emerge as an organized force.

After making the proper decision to introduce the office of president, we failed to think the issues through to the end. The strengths of the presidential system, while substantial, could be revealed only if the appropriate mechanism were created. Here we wavered and acted inconsistently. Opinions were divided when changes were discussed, both in my own circle and, to an even greater degree, in the Politburo.

Theory is theory, but practice – real politics – always has the last word. And so it turned out this time too. The concern of our government for its powers was the major factor that worked against the consistent introduction of a presidential republic. Ryzhkov and his associates feared that the Council of Ministers would be downgraded, shoved into the background, transformed into a 'sovnarkhoz'.[1] They strongly objected, while at that time I did not have sufficient grounds or any intention to quarrel with Nikolai Ivanovich. I was hearing convincing arguments from my advisers that the President should not be saddled directly with the burden of management of the economy. Problems were accumulating and he would have to answer for every trifling detail.

In short, it was decided at that time that the functions of the Council of Ministers would not be re-examined. I subsequently realized that this was a major contradiction.

Another important shortcoming was that along with the institution of presidency we did not create a fairly powerful judicial authority. There were grounds to believe that the Constitutional Oversight Committee would fill this gap. However, months passed, while the committee remained silent. At best, decisions were made on unimportant issues, or ambiguous verdicts allowed conflicting interpretations. Wags joked that the decisions of the Constitutional Oversight Committee required Pythian priestesses to interpret their oracular utterances. The passivity of the committee was the source of many complaints, but I did not think I could interfere since I genuinely believed in the principle of separation of powers.

It goes without saying that the vacillation over the status of the government and problems with the judicial authority are not in any way to be compared with the principal reason for the poor efficiency of the presidential system. As I have already said, this was the parade of sovereignties that unfolded immediately after the Supreme Soviet of Russia adopted its declaration of independence.[2] This was followed by the so-called 'war of laws'. The republics agreed to recognize only those Union legislative acts

[1] Council of the National Economy (1957–65).

[2] The Russian Parliament adopted a law on sovereignty in 1990 which stated that Russian legislation took precedence over legislation passed by the Supreme Soviet of the USSR. One can see this as the beginning of the disintegration of the Soviet Union.

that were approved by their parliaments. The central power was being fatally undermined.

It was becoming obvious that we would not be successful if we limited ourselves to patching up the Constitution – we had to conclude a new Union treaty and to change the entire state structure accordingly. Thus, although we had hardly finished one radical restructuring, we were faced with the need to begin another.

15

NATIONALITIES POLICY:
A DIFFICULT SEARCH

DEEP ROOTS

TODAY, AS I WRITE THESE LINES, I AM UNBEARABLY SADDENED to see what is happening in my country. Conflicts between nationalities have developed into wars; hundreds of thousands of refugees have been forced to leave their land, their homes, the graves of their forefathers. Jaunty soldiers pose against the background of burning cities. And the most alarming thing is the indifference of most of the general public.

What have we become?

I am not looking for justification. The political leaders who took on the responsibility for the reforms had considerable experience of relations between nationalities and knew that at times conflicts could become intense. Any claims to ignorance would be frivolous. I had the same kind of experience. When I discussed my origins and roots in Stavropol I mentioned the special characteristics of this place, which became part of my life: people of different nationalities living side by side. As I came into contact with the culture, traditions and peculiarities of life and human relationships among the dozens of peoples dwelling in the Caucasus, I recognized the delicacy of this subject. Spontaneous flare-ups of nationalist passions were a real danger, particularly when strife among nationalities had been deliberately incited for the sake of selfish interests and ambitions.

After the Nazis had been driven from the Caucasus, the Kalmyks, Chechens, Ingushi and Balkars were forcibly resettled, sent into exile, to 'settlements in Siberia'. The Karachai were removed in only three days! Rumour had it that this was a reprisal for collaborating with the occupying forces – the Vlasov forces,[1] the followers of Bendera,[2] and the local policemen in the German army. There were collaborators in my village too. But what was the point of sending into exile children and old people? Upon returning from the war, front-line soldiers, among whom there had been many heroes, had to look in Kazakhstan, Central Asia and Siberia for their relatives, many of whom had perished *en route*, unable to survive after having been stripped of everything they had – the roofs over their heads, their property, and even their motherland.

When I was secretary of the Komsomol kraikom I helped with the return of the Kalmyks and Karachai to their native regions. The government and local authorities at that time made special decisions regarding the resettlement of the returning families, building homes and setting up new enterprises to give them the opportunity to find work. They were also resettled outside those areas where they had lived earlier. Quotas were established in the universities of the Stavropol region for the special admission of children from Karachai families. Assistance was provided to set up higher education institutions where they lived. Much was done to help these people return to a normal life and forget the past.

However, bitterness remained for many years. The smallest impingement in questions of representation in Soviets or Party organizations, or in deciding administrative positions, was keenly felt. Even unintentional neglect or oversimplification caused hurt and unrest; everyday clashes between peoples of different nationalities rapidly turned to sharp conflict.

The multitude of peoples and cultures means at the same time a multitude of religions: Muslims, Buddhists, Christians of all shades – from Old Believers to Baptists. Stavropol was among the regions that had been criticized for its shortcomings in

---

[1] Vlasov was a Red Army commander who defected to the Germans.
[2] Ukrainian nationalists who fought the Red Army on the German side.

combating the influence of religion.[1] The situation reached the point of absurdity. A Party official would die and official farewells would be arranged. A secular funeral procession would start out and suddenly meet a large group of people of the same nationality as the deceased, along with his friends and relatives, who would grab the coffin and carry it off to the hamlet where the official had been born. And if they did not 'hijack' the coffin, they would bury him in an Islamic cemetery following Islamic rites. It was a difficult situation indeed: to go or not to go to the funeral? Many held back. Some went, risking being accused of lacking principles or of encouraging such behaviour. In most cases we 'turned a blind eye', so long as these actions did not become too obvious. In such cases we were forced to react.

There were two different opinions concerning the construction of mosques and churches. Some said that this would encourage religion, while others argued that it was the banning that stimulated religious feelings. Prohibitions did not prevent the existence of semi-clandestine sects. Indeed the number of unregistered religious communities, especially Islamic, greatly exceeded the number of openly operating registered communities. They met in secret, forced into opposition to the established order.

Raisa Maksimovna collected interesting material in her study of kolkhoz life in rural areas, Cossack settlements and ethnic regions. A significant number of young and middle-aged people did not profess any faith, but rather showed their respect for their fathers and grandfathers by paying tribute to tradition. I could see this in my own family. Both of my grandmothers, Vasilisa and Stepanida, were religious. Grandfather Andrei was also a believer, and grandfather Pantelei, a Communist, considered it a personal obligation to respect believers. On the other hand, we the 'Party cadres' followed the instructions of the Party Central Committee and carried on high-pressure anti-religious propaganda, more often than not in violation of the constitutional guarantee of freedom of conscience. Just like religious orders who zealously convert 'heretics' to their own faith, our

---

[1] The Party always conducted a campaign against religious believers, but religious traditions continued to be observed, sometimes by Party members.

ideologues carried out a wholesale war on religion, thereby causing unnecessary dissatisfaction among ordinary people.

Our legacy is a difficult one. In the past, governments drew boundaries as they wished – cut a little off here, add a little there. They created dual republics, mixing peoples who were not related by blood or family – Chechens and Ingushi, Kabardins and Balkars. Even when the population consisted of a single people, as in Adygeya, the land was chopped up, so that conflicts were bound to happen. It was the old principle of Rome: divide and rule!

The republics and national autonomies[1] were rigidly bound to Russia. The second secretaries of Party committees were always Slavs. When national disputes or claims arose, Stalin considered them as a manifestation of anti-Soviet feelings and wasted no time in explanations or exhortations. And even so he could not cope with the problem of, say, Karabakh, which came up regularly every ten years. And Karabakh was not alone.

My experience nourished the conviction that there was only one possible way to handle this problem, through co-operation! Repression was useless, since the problems remained unsolved. This can be seen throughout the world – in the European countries, India, China, Canada, the United States. Force can drive contradictions arising on ethnic grounds underground, but at the very first opportunity they will rise up again.

The minefield of conflicts between the nationalities was laid decades, if not centuries, ago.

However, it is not enough to say that the roots of most conflicts reach into the past. We must also recognize that some of them did not develop until after the October Revolution. The nationalities policy conducted by the Party at various times brought many indisputable achievements but also did enormous harm. In this sphere, as in others, the legacy of Bolshevism is mixed.

Before the revolution, Lenin and the Bolsheviks approached the nationalities issue as orthodox Marxists. When the revolution of 1905 broke out, countries and peoples who had joined or had

---

[1] Autonomous republics, regions and districts: ethnic entities within, respectively, a Union republic, krai or oblast.

been attached to Russia did not raise the question of separation. They asked merely for autonomy. Only after the First World War and the October Revolution, when he had become convinced of the insurmountable longing of many of the peoples of the former Russian empire to acquire independence, did Lenin recognize the right of nations to self-determination, even to the point of secession.

This was the origin of the federation – the only possible way of preserving the integrity of the state. It was the result of the new internationalist policy of the revolutionary government.

Lenin's idea of a federation assumed the possibility of many ways and many levels of participating in it: from national states that retain a greater degree of independence (in today's terminology they might be called 'associated entities') down to oblast and district autonomies. In the first years after the October Revolution there were more than 5,000 national districts, which allowed even numerically insignificant national minorities to safeguard themselves, their languages, customs and cultures.

Stalin adopted a very different policy. He did not infringe the principle of federation, but he 'interpreted' it in his own way. As the Centre began to feel more and more secure, real powers were taken away from the republics – both the Union and the autonomous republics – and in the end their statehood was reduced to ordinary local self-government. At the most, opulent symbols were retained. In this way the 'leader of the peoples' transformed the Union into a supercentralized unitary state while remaining true to Lenin's behest in the eyes of the Party, which he considered to be very important. After all, the Party had preferred him to Trotsky because a majority considered that 'Stalin continued Lenin's cause.' Stalin and his colleagues drew boundaries, distributed natural resources and land, and positioned industries in a manner that created problems for the future. Russia had never before existed in the boundaries defined for the Russian Federation; Kazakhstan's boundaries were changed to include enormous areas populated mainly by Russians. The configuration of other republics, too – for example Georgia and Abkhazia, Armenia and Azerbaijan – was done so that they could not even think of themselves as being outside the Union.

Many of the ideas which formed the basis of our Union state were shown to have been correct. The unification of efforts made it possible for each nation and society as a whole to speed up its development. Today, now that the Union has broken up or, more accurately, has been 'quartered' by separatists, the idea of the Union has not died, for it expresses an objective social reality and need and remains the optimum choice for the peoples of the newly formed commonwealth.

Essentially, there were three stages in the evolution of our views of the nationality issue and practical action in this area of social relations.

At first we based our policy on decades-old practice. We were following this policy when the conflict developed in Alma Ata and other parts of Kazakhstan because of protests against the change of leadership of the republic.

TROUBLE COMES TO THE SURFACE

I do not think that Kazakhstan was suffering from serious nationality conflicts when trouble surfaced there in December 1986. Still, people were upset and dissatisfied because of the dominance of one of the local communities, the 'Dzhus clan'. Anyone could see the advantages extracted by the relatives, close and distant, of the 'top man', Kunayev. His position as autocrat of the republic was not subject to criticism.

One by one, the first secretaries of the oblast committees came to see me. They were followed by a group of secretaries of the Central Committee of the Communist Party of Kazakhstan, both Kazakhs and Russians. They told me that affairs in the republic were not in good order.

Kunayev himself complained about 'troublemakers' and requested a meeting. He argued that the situation in the Central Committee bureau was due to intrigues by the Prime Minister Nazarbayev, who was spoiling for power. Indeed, Kunayev painted an extremely negative picture of him, constantly repeating: 'This is a dangerous man. He must be stopped.'

Eventually Kunayev requested that I transfer Nazarbayev to a position in Moscow or appoint him to the USSR Ministry of Foreign Affairs and send him abroad.

I decided to speak openly with Kunayev. I told him that a group of his Central Committee secretaries had complained about his leadership. After outlining their criticisms, I suggested that we should continue our conversation at a Politburo meeting, inviting all of the members of the Bureau of the Central Committee of the Communist Party of Kazakhstan to attend.

'No, no, that's not necessary,' he answered hurriedly, 'I will resign.'

We discussed the question of a suitable successor. Kunayev, who wanted to stop Nazarbayev's advancement, said that his replacement should be a Russian.

After several discussions with Politburo members, we decided on G. V. Kolbin. His election was supported both in the Bureau and at the plenum of the Central Committee of the Communist Party of Kazakhstan. However, in the light of subsequent events I think we made a mistake. In spite of Kunayev's advice and the consent of the republic leadership, we should have realized that it would be difficult for Kazakhs to accept a Russian in this position. We were at the beginning of perestroika, but to some degree we were still following the old ways. The consequences of our decision were absolutely not what we expected.

Rioting broke out in Alma Ata on 17–18 December 1986. The riots began among students and then spread to other groups. At some point the situation became quite dramatic. Force was used.

On 25 December the Politburo adopted a very traditional resolution that was not so much an attempt to get a grip on what had occurred and learn a lesson from that, as to teach a lesson to Kazakhstan and the others.

In reacting to these events, we were ruled by obsolete stereotypes – that everything must take place in unity and friendship, and that the only danger lay in spontaneous outbreaks of nationalism. Moreover, these outbreaks were not attributed to the existence of real problems, but were rather considered to be caused by hangovers from the past and the influence of outside forces.

In mid-1987 we were faced with another nationality problem,

the origins of which went back to the Stalinist period. In the situation created by glasnost and perestroika the Crimean Tatars organized themselves into a strong movement. The reader may know that after the liberation of the Crimea in 1944 all the Tatar population living there was forcefully resettled to camps in the Urals, Siberia and Central Asia. As in similar cases, this was done with extreme brutality, and thousands of people perished.

In 1955 the Soviet authorities closed down the camps and in the early 1960s the Crimean Tatars began to organize demonstrations demanding their return to the Crimea. At the time, and later as well, their public protests were rebuffed.

In June 1987 they demonstrated continuously for three days outside the Kremlin, demanding complete restoration of their rights and return to the Crimea.

The leadership commissioned Gromyko and the USSR Minister of Internal Affairs to meet with a delegation of the Crimean Tatars. Gromyko informed them that he would lead a committee to study this question. In spite of the acute nature of the situation both sides were pursuing a political process. This made it possible to look for a solution that would be acceptable to everyone, even though the protests and demonstrations continued.

In early 1988 the commission, acting together with the Ukrainian authorities, reported the possibility of returning some of the Tatars to the Crimea. This decision met the demands of the Tatars halfway and at the same time took into account the fact that full restoration of an ethnic autonomous republic was impossible. By now the Crimea was populated mainly by Russians and Ukrainians. The population had increased severalfold by comparison with the pre-war level. Since the war people had put down roots in the Crimean Peninsula and had built a life there through their own efforts. In looking at the situation everyone had to take into account historical changes.

We had taken a valid, accommodating step, but the leaders of the national movement would not budge from their unrealistic demands. They created an atmosphere of hysteria among their countrymen, forcing many who had found a haven in Central Asia and had not been thinking of resettling to sell their homes and move to the Crimea. Several thousands gathered in Krasnodar krai. Their endless meetings resulted in protests from the local population. The local authorities took measures to maintain public order without resorting to arrests or force.

Then Gromyko announced that *all* Crimean Tatars would receive permission to return to the Crimea. However, the commission rejected the re-creation of the autonomous republic of the Crimean Tatars. It argued, among other things, that the administrative and territorial division of the Soviet Union had been made binding by the Constitution. Later, in the summer of 1989, the idea of autonomy reappeared, but in a different version. When this issue was discussed in the USSR Supreme Soviet, a number of deputies suggested that we look into the question of creating a Crimean autonomous oblast (that is, not ethnically based).

The problems of rehabilitation and restoration of the rights of repressed peoples – the Crimean Tatars, the Volga Germans, the Kabardins and Balkars, the Ingushi and others, required a thoroughly considered and balanced approach. Clearly, it would be impossible to find a stable solution to these problems without taking into account the changing demographics. We could not turn the clock back and change history. 'Sow the wind and reap the whirlwind' – I felt that this proverb could describe the result of unilateral action, haste and trying to use strong-arm tactics.

Signs of unrest appeared in the Baltic republics in 1987. National ferment had never died in this region; it was simply less apparent. The main reason was dissatisfaction with the Russification of the region, which threatened to make Latvians and Estonians national minorities in their own republics. New enterprises mushroomed and people from other regions were called to work in them. Just as in Siberia, the Urals or Central Asia, a work-force was assembled from all parts of the country. In a relatively short period, the ethnic balance of the population underwent a significant change. Local authorities furthered this by lobbying for additional investment in their areas. The Lithuanian leadership won significant funds for land reclamation and reconstruction of rural areas, the Latvians for development of industry, and Estonians for all of these projects.

As a result, the proportion of Estonians in Estonia fell to 60 per cent and of Latvians in Latvia to 50 per cent. People complained that they were being made to learn the Russian language, while Russians living there made practically no efforts to learn Latvian or Estonian. Leaving aside the question of coercion, I have to admit that there was indeed a human relations problem. Environmental problems connected with excessive pressure on the sea, rivers, land and air were also very acute in this region.

Added to this was the cover-up of the true history of the Baltic countries' joining the USSR. The anniversary of the signing of the 1939 Soviet-German Non-aggression Pact in August 1987 fuelled demands to publish the secret protocols that had determined the fate of these nations and to restore justice for the victims of mass deportations.

As always happens, the feeling of 'national oppression' was skilfully heated up by separatist circles. At that time no-one yet even hinted at separation from the Soviet Union, but the separatists had begun to prepare the ground well ahead of time. Nationalist publications appeared and anti-Russian sentiments were cultivated. 18 November – the day of the declaration of independence of Latvia in 1918 – was celebrated as a national holiday. On that day thousands of Latvians, ignoring the authorities' warnings, joined in a procession to lay flowers at the Monument of Freedom in Riga. The crowd was dispersed by the authorities; the organizers had evidently counted on this in order to stir up public opinion.

Similar events took place in Lithuania on 16 February 1988, in connection with the seventieth anniversary of independence. Public prayers and demonstrations were held. The authorities had learned a lesson from the events in Latvia, so that the organizers' plan was not completely successful. Something similar also occurred in Estonia.

THE KARABAKH EXPLOSION

In February 1988 the population of the Nagorno-Karabakh autonomous oblast (which was 85-per-cent Armenian) of the

Azerbaijan Soviet Socialist Republic demanded that it be made a part of the Armenian Soviet Socialist Republic. A resolution was passed by the oblast Soviet and immediately supported by thousands of people at demonstrations and meetings in Armenia. These demonstrations were carried out in an organized way, without excesses. The marchers carried large posters supporting perestroika and glasnost. Law-enforcement agencies only maintained order, without taking stronger measures – anyway, there was little they could have done against this sea of people.

This produced a sharp response in Azerbaijan, where mass meetings were likewise held, this time directed against Armenia.

In February the Politburo examined the Nagorno-Karabakh question. We received information about the positions of the leaders of the republics. The Azerbaijan leader, Bagirov, insisted that Moscow should guarantee the unchanged status of Nagorno-Karabakh. The Armenian leader, Denmirtchyan, suggested that the appeal of the Nagorno-Karabakh oblast Soviet should be considered in the Supreme Soviets of Azerbaijan, Armenia and the Soviet Union. It became clear that the argument between Baku and Yerevan over Stepanakert would have to be resolved by Moscow.

Ryzhkov said that we must 'act in accordance with the Constitution'. Chebrikov reported that these events were having a bad effect in other republics. In Estonia there was a growing sentiment in favour of leaving the Union. Tajikistan was debating its claim to Bukhara and Samarkand.

I believed that the problem had to be resolved by political means, that the Central Committee should declare any change of borders unacceptable, and that we needed to draft economic, social and cultural proposals aimed at improving the situation in Nagorno-Karabakh. We should let the Armenians and Azerbaijanis get together and decide the status of Nagorno-Karabakh for themselves, and we ought to accept any decision they made. I felt that the Russian intelligentsia and workers should join in their discussions. We decided to send Politburo representatives to both republics to lend assistance to the local leadership. Ligachev and Razumovsky flew to Baku, and Yakovlev and Dolgikh to Yerevan. Their mission was to establish contacts and reassure the people in those republics.

On 26 February I appealed to the peoples of Azerbaijan and Armenia, asking them to show understanding, responsibility and prudence. I said that we would not sidestep frank discussions of various proposals, but that this must be done calmly, within the framework of the democratic process and legality.

My speech contributed to some normalization. The continuous mass meetings in Yerevan stopped, and reassured people returned to their homes. I tried to get a dialogue going and explore ways of finding a compromise, which I was firmly convinced was the only way out of the situation.

The dispute over Karabakh goes into the distant past. From time immemorial two peoples have lived side by side on this fertile land. It passed from hand to hand; for centuries it was a part of Persia. But mainly it was populated by Armenians. Immediately after the revolution their ancient dream of reunification with the motherland almost came true. However, although the Azerbaijani leader of that time, Nariman Narimanov, initially gave his consent to this, he soon rescinded it. Afterwards, the question was raised many times, including after the war, but was never resolved. The result was that almost 500,000 Armenians lived in Azerbaijan, mainly in Karabakh, while 200,000 Azerbaijanis lived in Armenia. First of all, we had to address practical problems. Soon after the unrest started, a resolution was adopted to provide assistance to Nagorno-Karabakh, calling for 400 million rubles to be allotted for emergency needs there. Initially, this made a strong impression, but after two or three months we began to receive indications that the authorities in Azerbaijan were distributing the monies from the centre according to their own wishes, with only a small part reaching the intended recipients. We had to send commissions to verify these assertions. It appeared, however, that most of the needs of the local people had indeed been met.

If this had been done ten years earlier, if Aliyev had conducted a valid internationalist policy, a catastrophe could have been prevented. By 1988 it was already too late.

Events snowballed. Acts of violence broke out, the peak being the bloody pogrom on 27–29 February against Armenians in

Sumgait, where there was a large number of Azerbaijani refugees.

Troops were sent in. Unarmed soldiers tried to bring the brutal hooligans to their senses. Many young soldiers were wounded, some permanently disabled. However, I believe the consequences would have been even more severe if the soldiers had been armed.

We have often been reproached for 'showing weakness'. But when we were forced to bring in the militia and military units to avoid further bloodshed, we again fell under the fire of criticism, this time for using force. There is no doubt that the government had to act in the way they did. Extreme measures were due to extreme circumstances. The same thing would have been done in any democratic state.

The massacre in Sumgait produced universal outrage, everyone was shaken. At the same time, sympathy was shown in the Muslim republics for the people of their faith. Events threatened to get out of control.

The question of Nagorno-Karabakh was considered at an extraordinary Politburo meeting on 3 March, where I noted that the situation had reached a critical stage, that we had been late in dealing with Sumgait and had underestimated its implications.

'Protective measures may be required,' said I, 'in order to prevent loss of life, as occurred in Sumgait. The main thing is to use political methods. However, authority must always be authority. And when it must be used, it must be used in time. The law must rule.'

I demanded that those responsible should be swiftly brought to justice, and that steps must be taken so that chaos would not 'spill over' again. However, I also demanded that we avoid further attempts at a 'quick fix' in favour of working together patiently with our Armenian and Azerbaijani comrades.

Even before these tragic events I had a fairly complete picture of the sources of the conflict. Let us recall that the Armenians had suffered both from Persians and from Turks. Could they really erase from their memory the genocide of 1915, when the Turks slaughtered a million and a half Armenians and scattered two millions throughout the world? Eventually they turned to Russia, not out of love for the tsar, but in the hope of safety. They came to the Russian people for protection.

But the roots of the Azeris in Karabakh also went deep. Lenin had understood the complexity of this problem and commissioned Chicherin, the People's Commissar for Foreign Affairs, to look into the matter. Under Stalin those who were in charge of nationality affairs lacked subtlety. Problems and difficulties accumulated over the decades. The Azerbaijan leadership did not treat the Karabakh population in the spirit of the traditions of Lenin, and sometimes they simply acted in an inhumane way. Problems of language and culture arose, and serious mistakes were made in the cadre policy. All of this was brought to light under glasnost. Problems quickly came to a head.

In both republics many highly placed officials had soiled themselves by corruption. But when perestroika began and they sensed that the ground was shaking under them, it was these elements who tried to provoke ethnic conflicts. The national feelings of people became the object of merciless exploitation. In their hands Karabakh was a mine laid underneath perestroika.

We decided: (1) to publish our analysis of the situation in the press; (2) that the General Secretary should speak on television; (3) the question should be taken up in the Presidium of the USSR Supreme Soviet; (4) the report of the procurator's office on the investigation of the events in Sumgait should be published; (5) administrative agencies were to decide on the stationing of troops at flash points, but without imposing a curfew.

The Azerbaijan and Armenian leaders were again told to come to an understanding. This they were unable to do. Again the question was sent back to us for a decision.

At the Politburo session of 6 June 1988, I expressed the opinion that some people in the higher levels of power in the republics were fanning the flames and igniting passions. 'The one thing that we can never agree to is to support one people to the detriment of another,' I said. 'We must never be blackmailed into this. We will not permit, we must in no case allow the truth to be sought through blood!'

Under pressure from public opinion, the deputies of the Armenian Supreme Soviet resolved to agree to the transfer of

Nagorno-Karabakh to Armenia, and asked the USSR Supreme Soviet to consider this matter. Two days later the Azerbaijan Supreme Soviet declared this to be unacceptable, and announced measures to accelerate the social and economic development of Nagorno-Karabakh. On 25 June public meetings were held in Stepanakert. The people were angry that the local press had not reported the February resolution of the Nagorno-Karabakh Soviet concerning its exit from Azerbaijan.

Tension grew rapidly. Meetings and strikes in Stepanakert continued. Then, on 6 July, the airport in Yerevan was blockaded. The Nagorno-Karabakh oblast Soviet again passed a resolution 'on withdrawal', but in Baku it was again declared to be illegal.

What could we do? What was the way out of the situation? Gromyko suggested the usual solution: 'The army will appear on the street and order will be restored immediately.' Chebrikov objected. Yakovlev proposed that the administration of Nagorno-Karabakh should be transferred to Moscow. Shevardnadze was in favour of immediately giving Nagorno-Karabakh autonomous republic status. Ligachev tried to synthesize all of these ideas: 'There are already 20,000 refugees. People are homeless. If republic status for Nagorno-Karabakh does not help, we must bring in the troops, dismantle factories, dismiss the Party organizations and Soviet executive committees and establish order.'

I supported the proposal to set up an autonomous republic, but I felt that this matter had to be resolved by the conflicting sides themselves.

The Presidium of the USSR Supreme Soviet met on 18 July. All parties were invited to present their views. The session was broadcast on television, so that everyone's position would be clear to the general public. Our position – that of the central authorities – was supported by most people.

'How do you wish to solve this problem?' I asked. 'Victory at any price? Armenia wants to incorporate Nagorno-Karabakh. Azerbaijan does not intend to allow this and will not yield even a millimetre. This is all unrealistic! We must find a compromise that will suit everyone. Only a common victory will be a real victory. You cannot resolve issues while you are fighting one another. This is a political blind alley. Sumgait and other events concerning Nagorno-Karabakh have already made a deep imprint on the relations between the two peoples and it will take time for this to be smoothed over even a little. But even so, we must meet each other halfway and find a compromise.'

Suggestions were made at the meeting for strengthening the guarantees to the residents of Nagorno-Karabakh in order to prevent a repetition of the violence. In the past there had been many promises, but they had turned out to be hollow – essentially a fraud. I proposed that a special commission for consideration of all the proposals be set within the framework of the Council of Nationalities of the USSR Supreme Soviet. This commission was created and carried out useful work. Rasul Gamzatov's speech made a strong impression on me. He proposed that the administration of Nagorno-Karabakh be transferred temporarily to the Union's central agencies. Subsequently, the commission of the Council of Nationalities put forward the very same proposal.

On 20 July the resolution of the Presidium, reiterating that a change of boundaries was impossible, was published. On 26 July the Party Central Committee and the USSR Supreme Soviet Presidium passed a resolution to send an emissary, Arkady Volksky, to Nagorno-Karabakh. However, the situation did not normalize. On 21 September a state of emergency was declared and a curfew was put into effect in Stepanakert and the Agdam district.

After the autumn session of the USSR Supreme Soviet on 3 December I met with deputies from Azerbaijan and Armenia and the leaders of both republics and Nagorno-Karabakh. Ryzhkov, Slyunkov, Chebrikov, Lukyanov and Razumovsky were also present. 'We are on the brink of disaster,' I told them. 'You, the respected representatives of the two peoples, must sit down and together find a way out of this mess.'

When news of the earthquake in Armenia reached me I broke off my visit to the United States and immediately returned to Moscow and then flew to Yerevan. When I reached the earthquake region I was shaken by what I saw, but at the same time I felt a sense of admiration for what our people had done. I was told how on the first and most difficult night, when the city of Leninakan was cut off, the airport and roads destroyed and the railways unable to run, teams of physicians, construction workers, students and workers set out from Yerevan to provide aid. Such leaders as Mkrtchyan and Muradyan deserve special admiration: although they had lost their families, they stayed with the people day and night and found the strength to provide help.

The entire country responded heart and soul to the tragedy suffered by their Armenian brothers. Against the background of incipient conflicts between the nationalities, we saw the extraordinary resource that our Union possessed. Again, I became convinced of how important it was to preserve the interaction and support that had become a part of our life, and to protect everything that was good in our tradition.

Today I am even more convinced that the nationality issue can never be resolved by force. The tsars fought wars for decades in North Caucasus, creating a system of fortresses, Cossack settlements, punishing, threatening, destroying, and all to naught, for nothing good came from all this. The only positive results came from trade, co-operation among peoples, the establishment of an alliance with the ruling elite and tribal elders, which brought them closer to the tsar's court, honours and privileges. A kind of new association developed after the October Revolution. In spite of all the faults of this union, a certain balance of interests was preserved.

The peacemaking process was extremely complicated. It was even made more difficult by, among other things, the general atmosphere that had developed in the country, in the Supreme Soviets of the USSR and Russia. Essentially, there were two positions. One was that at the moment the conflict developed – especially after the events in Sumgait – it was necessary to strike decisively against the 'instigators' of the disturbances in Nagorno-Karabakh and nip the riots in the bud. The other position was to ask: since the people of Karabakh wished to reunite with their motherland, and we recognized the right of nations to self-determination, why not allow this? After all, the Nakhichevan autonomous republic is a part of Azerbaijan, even though separated from Azerbaijan by Armenian territory. The Nagorno-Karabakh question could be solved in exactly the same way.

At some point it seemed that a possible solution was to give Karabakh, like Nakhichevan, the status of autonomous republic, while keeping it as part of Azerbaijan. There was a time when this proposal was on the point of being implemented. However, it was just at this moment that the Supreme Soviet in Yerevan passed a resolution to incorporate Nagorno-Karabakh as part of Armenia and so everything fell apart. It fell apart because of internal antagonism, because the battle for power, for replacement of the ruling elite, was already in full swing there. It fell apart because the Armenian national movement, which was formed on the basis of the Karabakh committee, was in a hurry to seize power.

In this connection another possibility was mentioned at a Politburo meeting: the central authorities should use the armed forces to preserve the status quo. In other words, preserve the status quo in favour of Azerbaijan; at least this would be done not by Azeri extremists, but by the forces of legitimate power. I asked my colleagues: 'OK, so we introduce rule from the centre. Then what?' I did not get a clear answer.

Some members were very strongly in favour of 'imposing order'. Under such conditions it was not easy to defend my position. Nevertheless, I held to it from beginning to end, even though in extreme cases we were unable to avoid strictly limited harsh measures.

During this time, 1987–8, I strove to work out a uniform democratic approach to disputes between nationalities. The conflict over Nagorno-Karabakh did not at all push into the background other, seemingly more tranquil, but no less significant, processes which were gaining strength in the Baltic republics, Moldova and Georgia, and which have begun in Central Asia and in Ukraine. Issues such as the languages of indigenous peoples, economic sovereignty, and expanding rights were raised more and more frequently in various regions. To counter Russification, people often went to the other extreme, thus introducing a spirit of confrontation into the mass consciousness. However, in 1987 no-one raised the question of withdrawing from the Union except, perhaps, for extremist groups such as the Estonian independence association, J. Barkans's group in Latvia, and certain nationalist groups in Lithuania.

But if we were unable to achieve harmony of interests, where should the way out be sought? In patiently and persistently working for the achievement of a compromise, but mainly in changing the very conditions that produced the conflict. Indeed I believed that a lasting solution to the problems between nationalities could be found only in the general context of economic and political reform. By the end of my time as President I had no doubt that preservation and renewal of the Union could keep the peace.

A formula was put forward: 'A strong centre and strong republics.' Others expressed it differently: 'Strong republics and a strong centre.' Either way, it basically comes down to the same. After all, the new centre was to be formed on different foundations, to deal with issues such as security, co-ordination of the fundamentals of economic and social policy, co-ordination of foreign policy, maintaining order at borders, and so forth. And, of course, playing the role of arbiter when conflicts arose.

THE BALTIC REPUBLICS AND OTHERS

From the middle of 1988 up to 1990 nationality problems continued to mount, with the most vulnerable element of the Union – the Baltic republics – being in the vanguard.

The inaugural congress of the popular front of Estonia opened on 1 October 1988. The popular front of Latvia was formed a week later. That same month the inaugural congress of Sajudis was held in Lithuania. Initially the fronts were still supra-party associations. They included many fervent advocates of reform who were not at all disposed to secession. However, since the Party remained aloof and viewed every manifestation of nationalism with caution or hostility, these movements appeared to be an alternative to it. They confronted the questions that were troubling society, and for this reason the national fronts quickly became stronger in influence than the Party organizations.

They raised the question of making their native language the official language of the given republic, restoring the national anthems and flags of 1918, restricting immigration, and

440

achieving real independence for the republic. Incidentally, all of this was to be done in accordance with their constitutions and the USSR Constitution. On the whole, this all remained in keeping with the ideas of the XIXth Party Conference – without any demand for withdrawal from the Union.

The position of the Baltic republics in the Union had its own peculiar history. We had been taught that they had voluntarily joined the USSR in 1939. Glasnost revealed the truth. Although resolutions had been passed in favour of joining the Union by the parliaments of these nations at the time, the reality was that the incorporation took place on the basis of a secret agreement with Germany and under occupation by the Red Army. There is no question that the left-wing parties enthusiastically supported the link with the Union. But to assert that it was the result of popular will is debatable at the very least. For the entire half-century since the annexation, the Baltic states have had governments in exile. The West never recognized the legitimacy of their annexation.

These circumstances stimulated the desire to regain independence.

In August 1988 the Baltic authorities, taking a lesson from the preceding year, officially permitted public assemblies in connection with the forty-ninth anniversary of the Soviet-German pact. Mass demonstrations were held and nationalistic slogans were openly proclaimed.

The conflict took shape in the autumn. On 16 November the Estonian Supreme Soviet passed a law on amendments to the constitution of the republic and the Declaration of Sovereignty, both of which contradicted the USSR Constitution. The Presidium of the USSR Supreme Soviet on 18 November had to declare these decisions, which made Union laws dependent on approval by the republic, unconstitutional and invalid.

At that same meeting of the Presidium I tried to moderate passions – but I categorically declared the Estonian decisions to be unacceptable.

On my suggestion the following paragraph was added to the decree: 'It is appropriate in the present stage of political reform to develop, on the basis of constitutional norms, a system of measures and state-legal mechanisms – for safeguarding the political and socio-economic interests of the Union republics and expansion and protection of their sovereign rights in the USSR.'

At that time I assumed that we had to adhere strictly to the step-by-step plan of reform of the political system.

It goes without saying that the problem itself was far from simple, as we realized in the February 1988 discussion, in commissions of the USSR Supreme Soviet, of the 'General principles of restructuring the management of the economy and social sphere in the Union republics on the basis of an expansion of their sovereign rights, self-government and funding'. The debate became at times very heated.

The document prepared by the USSR Council of Ministers and approved by the CPSU Central Committee was submitted for discussion in the spring of 1989. It produced another outbreak of discontent in the Baltic republics. Again we had not explained beforehand that we were speaking only of the first stage of political reform. The people of the three republics received it as the final answer from the centre to their demands for sovereignty – just a palliative or half-refusal. Belated explanations went in one ear and out the other.

The pre-election manifesto of the popular front of Estonia was published in March 1989, demanding implementation of the resolution of the Supreme Soviet of the republic regarding sovereignty, significant changes in property ownership relations, and creation of new institutions of power on the basis of popular movements. The Party's position was especially important under these conditions. However, it was simply unable to operate under conditions of democracy. The Party leaders, who were accustomed to dealing with economic affairs, became confused when they had to engage in democratic politics.

From the very beginning the informal associations were declared to be opposition organizations. Instead of interacting with the opposition, valuable time was lost in the vain hope that the new organizations would just vanish, go away like a bad dream. If in the initial period there had been co-operation between the Party organizations and the informal associations, the elections of people's deputies in 1989 might have integrated the Party and the popular fronts into a common political process. But this did not happen. The popular fronts won the elections for USSR people's deputies in all of the Baltic republics.

Heartened by this example, similar organizations in other republics began to act decisively. The popular front of Georgia was created in June, the Birlik movement in Uzbekistan in May, and the Ukrainian Rukh in September. In Moldova and Yerevan informal movements held unauthorized meetings.

The activities of the popular fronts escalated, and separatist tendencies began to prevail more and more frequently. These tendencies were whipped up not only by events in the Baltic, but also by those in Tbilisi in April 1989. When I arrived back in Moscow from London, I was informed immediately at the airport that troops had been dispatched to Georgia for the protection of 'important facilities'. It was difficult to get details 'on the move', but sensing that something was about to happen, I instructed Shevardnadze and Razumovsky to fly to Tbilisi. However, this trip was put off, because the next day the Georgian leadership informed us that the situation was stabilizing. The storm broke on the night of 8–9 April.

How many times I have had to withstand 'searching glances', or listen to direct reproaches that 'the General Secretary must have known everything that was undertaken by the Georgian leadership'! In March 1994 Gavriil Popov declared in an article: 'I will never believe that Gorbachev did not know.' And yet the truth is: the decision to use force was taken without consulting me.

The echo of the events in Tbilisi, painfully felt in all regions, had an adverse effect on all of our attempts to bring harmony to relations between nationalities in our country for a long time.

THE OVERDUE PLENUM

At first, we planned to call a CPSU Central Committee plenum on this vitally important subject in June 1989. However, having analysed the materials we had received so far, we concluded that a more far-reaching document was needed. We had to entrust this to our working group and put off the debate until September.

This delay proved too long. The public was worked up and waiting for explanations. I decided to give a television address on the subject on 2 July. Speaking to our citizens, I called on them to recognize the danger, show responsibility and solve problems by democratic discussion and tolerance. 'The tranquillity and well-being of our people, the fate of perestroika and, if you wish, the fate and integrity of our nation, are dependent to a significant degree on finding a proper solution to the question of relations between nationalities.'

What did I see as the key to solving these problems? Above all else were human rights and the transformation of the Soviet federation. At the same time, I felt that it was necessary to warn against extremes. 'As we consider the restructuring of the federation, we must not fail to reckon with the realities that have developed over the centuries, especially during the Soviet period. Our peoples have gone down a long road of development and a unified national economic complex has been created. To break these ties means cutting apart a living organism. We must not, in search of something better, begin destroying what we have created.'

By August we finished work on the proposals which were the basis of the draft CPSU platform 'The nationalities policy of the Party under modern conditions', published on 17 August. It emphasized the continuing need for radical renewal of nationality policy, naming the following principal tasks: transformation within the Soviet federation, filling it with meaningful political and economic content; expanding the rights and opportunities of all forms and types of national autonomy; guarantees of equal rights for each people; the creation of conditions for the free development of national cultures and languages; and securing guarantees that precluded the infringement of the rights of citizens because of nationality.

We raised for the first time the question of preparing and signing a new Union Treaty. The role of Russia as the consolidating component in the Union was indicated in the draft, and it contained proposals to resolve the questions pertaining to the legal status of the RSFSR. With some slight modifications the platform was adopted by the September Central Committee plenum. I venture to say that this was an outstanding document, which presented a considered interpretation of important problems of national development and relations between nationalities and took into account Soviet and world experience.

But it is not for nothing that the common people say: 'An egg is dearest at Easter.' In spite of the value of decisions made at the plenum, they came much too late.

The start of 1990 was marked by fresh rifts in Armenian-Azerbaijani relations, which led to the Armenian pogroms in Baku and the exodus of Armenians from the city. In the evening of 13 January groups of thugs went on the rampage, resulting in loss of life. There were also dozens of wounded and houses were destroyed. Emergency measures were needed.

On 15 January the Central Committee Bureau of the Azerbaijan Communist Party discussed emergency measures to normalize the situation in Baku. It noted that criminal elements that had been working to destabilize the republic had now openly switched to practical realization of their schemes. Taking advantage of the sharp deterioration of the situation in Nagorno-Karabakh and adjacent regions, they had whipped up passions in Baku and pushed some refugees from Armenia into unlawful actions.

The authorities attempted to restore order. But they were too divided and paralysed to control the situation.

Ye. Primakov from the Presidential Council and A. Girenko from the CPSU Central Committee, who had been sent to Baku, passed on extremely alarming information about the development of the situation in Azerbaijan.

The Supreme Soviet, in the face of increasing moral terror, proved incapable of making adequate decisions.

On 19 January the CPSU Central Committee, the Presidium of the USSR Supreme Soviet and the Council of Ministers published an 'Appeal to the Peoples of Azerbaijan and Armenia'. On 20 January a state of emergency was declared in Baku and troops were sent there. The organizers of the riots refused to obey the decree on emergency measures, and that led to further casualties.

On 20 January I spoke on central television, giving an analysis

445

of the situation and an explanation of the leadership's decision to declare a state of emergency.

To this day, this action still receives mixed evaluations. Some feel that the state of emergency was declared too late, while others believe that it was not necessary at all. In answer to the former, I would say that the Union authorities could not go over the heads of the leaders of the republic to declare a state of emergency – the measure was introduced when the local authorities were paralysed. To the others, I say that we had to stop the escalation of violence.

The lesson I took from this tragic story is: authorities cannot avoid the use of force in extreme circumstances. Such action must be justified by absolute necessity and limited to a strictly considered degree. However, a true resolution of the problem is possible only by political means.

RUSSIA OPENS THE 'PARADE OF SOVEREIGNTIES'

After the elections to the Supreme Soviets of the republics in 1990, the question of sovereignty acquired a different dimension. The newly elected parliaments in the Baltic republics and the governments that they appointed were passing laws that meant a complete break with the Union.

We could not deny the right of nations to self-determination, even to the point of secession. It was provided for in our Constitution. Nevertheless, we had to do everything possible to show the people the catastrophic consequences of this step. And if it still proved inevitable, the process of 'divorce' had to be individualized so as to reduce potential damage to a minimum. A law defining the procedures and rules for secession was prepared and passed in a short period of time. First, secession was to occur on the basis of a referendum and, second, there was to be a transition period of four to five years. This was a principled and honourable position. In such a 'divorce process' there must be a transitional period, during which issues of all kinds were resolved – territorial, economic, defence, property, human rights issues – and future principles of relations and borders were defined.

What, then, was the deciding factor in the break-up of the USSR – which undermined all efforts to preserve a transformed Union?

The Baltic separatists, long before Yeltsin, had argued in favour of 'making Russia sovereign', and supported the idea of creating a Russian Communist Party. They understood that this was a key point: should Russia take this bait, it would mean an end to the Union. The supporters of an independent Ukraine also poured oil onto the fire.

In short, the separatists tried to 'jump-start Russian nation- alism'. No matter how they tried, they did not succeed – they ran up against the unshakable internationalist spirit of the people. The referendum of 17 March 1991[1] showed that the overwhelming majority of the citizens of Russia stood firmly behind the Union while agreeing to its transformation.

However, the separatists from the Baltic and other republics found like thinkers in Russia – DemRossiya, which openly set a course towards dismantling the Union state. DemRossiya managed to find a figure who agreed, for the sake of supreme power, to violate the will of his people. The Party nomenklatura of the Russian republic also shares responsibility for this sad outcome. Dissatisfied with the reformist wing and the policy of the CPSU leadership, unable to understand what they were being drawn into, Communist deputies in the Russian Supreme Soviet (with the exception of only three or four) voted for the Declaration of Sovereignty which drove the first nail in the coffin of the Union state. The same nomenklatura supported the coup in August 1991, which gave a strong push towards disintegration.

It must be said that the rebirth of national consciousness in Russia followed its own peculiar course. The question of restora- tion of justice for repressed peoples was raised in the first stage (1988–9). Autonomous regions demanded greater independence in resolving questions of economy, culture and language. The theme of equal rights for the subjects of the Russian Federation was eventually raised.

---

[1] Called by Gorbachev, voters were invited to vote for or against the renewal of the USSR as a federation.

The first reaction to the events in the Baltic republics, Moldova, and the Transcaucasian republics, was anger at the attempts to restrict the rights of the Russian and Russian-speaking citizens living there. The military feared the possibility of collapse of the ring of defences that had been built up with such effort. Patriotically minded representatives of the artistic and academic intelligentsia were deeply disheartened by the appearance of national egoism and anti-Russian statements coming from those who only yesterday had been their friends.

Russia and the Russians were held responsible for all the problems, past and present. The accusations were not only hurtful – they were also unjust. The command-administrative system had operated in the name of the Russian people, but it could not be equated with the Russian nation. Russians suffered from it no less, perhaps even more, than others.

At the USSR Congress of People's Deputies, in the Supreme Soviet of Russia, and in government circles, the idea of the rebirth of Russia had from the very first days smacked strongly of isolationism. A memorandum from a group of scholars asserting that there was a large flow of funds and resources from Russia to the republics through the Union budget was circulated widely among the public. The Union state was represented as a tool for redistribution that took from Russians what they produced, what was achieved by intensive exploitation of nature at the expense of future generations. The argument was that if Russia employed what it had for its own interest, in three or four years it would be among the most flourishing nations. This was the way Yeltsin formulated it too. It was the old song that not productivity, not technology, but redistribution of resources would 'save' Russia. Nevertheless, this argument proved far more powerful than all the others.

The reform of our enormous state indeed demanded decentralization and redistribution of powers between the centre and the regions. But the local elites tried to paint this need in the exaggerated colours of 'national survival'. It worked!

Did I understand the importance of the Russian problem at that time? Certainly. But interference in the course of the pre-election campaign and agitation against Yeltsin would have contradicted the nascent policy of democratization. We could have offered credible candidates to stand against him, but this was not done. The reason was simple: we underestimated the phenomenon of the election of Yeltsin in Moscow[1] and believed that this would not spread throughout Russia.

I spoke openly to the deputies of the first RSFSR Congress of People's Deputies and opposed the election of Yeltsin as Chairman of the Russian Supreme Soviet, since I foresaw that his arrival would increase confrontation between Russia and the Union. I already knew that this man was by nature a destroyer.

Some of the principles and provisions recorded in the declaration of state sovereignty of Russia could have formed the basis of a new Union Treaty. However, it also contained destructive ideas. The supreme bodies of government of the Russian Federation were, in fact, declaring their intention to act on their own without consulting the Union. The act, which was aimed firstly against the centre, was essentially an ultimatum, a show of disrespect for the remaining republics.

I am certain that, had it not been for this fatal step, the Union could have been preserved. The following episode, among other things, speaks in favour of this. In March 1990 the new leadership of Lithuania announced the independence of the republic. At the USSR Congress of People's Deputies this step was given a proper evaluation and the USSR President was instructed to consult with the authorities in Lithuania in order to clear up the entire range of issues arising. On their own initiative some Union enterprises had begun to break off ties with the republic and to restrict deliveries of fuel. The authorities in Vilnius sensed that not everything was going the way they had expected.

On 4 May Frolov conveyed to me the contents of a talk with a leading scholar from Vilnius University, who had been sent to Moscow by the leadership of the Central Committee of the Communist Party of Lithuania, at the request of Landsbergis. The Lithuanian leadership expressed its willingness to start a dialogue with the representatives of the centre, on the understanding that the decisions made by the Supreme Soviet of Lithuania after

---

[1] Yeltsin was elected in a landslide to the Russian Congress of People's Deputies.

March could be discussed and their action suspended; the declaration of independence of Lithuania could be viewed by the Union as an act that was largely symbolic; Lithuania would not object if we interpreted it to mean that the status of the republic would be that of an 'associate member of a renewed USSR'; at the same time, its specific implementation must be the result of a step-by-step process to be co-ordinated with the Union.

This was a suitable basis for seeking a mutually acceptable solution. The Baltic republics, because of their history and other characteristics, could enjoy special status in the Union.

However, the 'sovereignization' of Russia scuttled the search for a new formula for relations with the Baltic republics in a reformed Union. It caused a chain reaction, during which analogous enactments were passed by all of the Union republics and later autonomous republics. A 'parade of sovereignties' had begun. The only means of preventing the collapse of the Union was the preparation without delay of a new Union Treaty.

16

THE PARTY AND PERESTROIKA

IN THE TENDENTIOUS HISTORIOGRAPHY OF PERESTROIKA YOU will often find the assertion that the CPSU resisted the reforms from the beginning. The Party did indeed have its hard-core conservatives: the Party bureaucrats in particular, who felt their interests threatened, had a cautious attitude towards any changes. Nevertheless, most Communists recognized the need for a thorough change in the existing order – and it was the CPSU that acted as the initiator of reforms.

At the top level there was a group of people who were convinced of the vital need for reform and who were ready to accept enormous risks – undertaking not some kind of cosmetic maintenance job, but rather a complete overhaul of the extremely centralized, bureaucratized, ideology-ridden system, which had taken root over seven decades. The members of the Party leadership who began this undertaking with me were connected with various regions of the country, social strata, political trends and factions in the Party. They understood that attitudes in favour of renewal were strong, both in the CPSU and in the country as a whole. Hence the certainty that our programme would find support. Perestroika was more than just a one-day propaganda ploy or a clever slogan. The nation had come to it through much suffering.

One must also recognize that perestroika could succeed only if it originated within the Party itself. If any other official or unofficial organization had come out with an initiative like this, it would have been condemned to failure, rejected by the 'political core' of society, perceived as an attempt by dissidents to destroy the existing order.

By the mid-1980s our society resembled a steam boiler. There was only one alternative – either the Party itself would lead a process of change that would gradually embrace other strata of society, or it would preserve and protect the former system. In that case an explosion of colossal force would be inevitable. We also had to consider that only a force that held the reins of power could reform the system, that is, gradually reshape it. Moreover, the very idea of reform could not, at least at first, be a subject for public discussion. This would have immediately provoked rejection and irreparably damaged our work before we even began. It was important to get the 'engine of change' started and drive up to a point from which there was no turning back. All of the previous attempts to reform the system had taught us this lesson: I have in mind Khrushchev and Kosygin, not forgetting the *shestidesyatniki*,[1] or Sakharov and the dissident movement. All these could be seen as preparatory stages for the transformations that we began. They left their mark – if not on our political structures, then on our minds.

It has become fashionable to reproach me for slowness and to accuse me of vacillation – 'one step forward, two steps back.' However, if you carefully retrace the course of events, you will see that starting with the April 1985 plenum we never changed the course of our policy, always moving forward along the path of reform. Perhaps not always at the same rate, and sometimes there were interruptions – but we never retreated from the planned goal of democratic transformation.

We did not plough deep enough immediately – at first we only loosened the soil. But even then we considered issues of property ownership, commodity-money relations and new forms of economic management. Our destination took on increasingly distinct outlines as we gained experience and moved forward. Still, progress did not occur by itself and not by the will of the General Secretary alone, but rather on the basis of discussions

---

[1] Those writers, singers, poets and even politicians who became prominent during the Khrushchev thaw. Gorbachev was himself a *shestidesyatnik* (literally 'a 60s man').

and decisions made by official bodies of the ruling Communist Party.

If one were to scan these 'Party milestones', the history of perestroika would look approximately as follows. The first stage covered the period from April 1985 up to the XXVIIth CPSU Congress in 1986. The beginning is always the hard part. Gradually we freed ourselves of conventional ideological stereotypes and made our first attempts to understand the kind of society we had created, to what extent it matched Lenin's ideas, and the place it occupied in the world. We tried to see what our own history would look like in an undistorted mirror. We began a plan to renew society within the framework of socialist choice.

This, the philosophical stage, one may say, was followed by the organizational stage, when the programmes of economic, political and legal reform were being worked out and measures taken to put them into action. Here as well, every step forward was determined by the Party and by the decisions of its leading organs. I would like to remind the reader of the January 1987 plenum, which proclaimed the need to review outdated ideas of socialism and proposed a programme of radical measures for the democratization of society and the state; the June plenum of that same year, which criticized the command-administrative methods of managing the economy and came out in favour of radical economic reform; the February 1988 plenum, which bore the slogan: 'An ideology of renewal for revolutionary perestroika'; and finally, the XIXth All-Union CPSU Conference, whose decisions served as the basis for the transition from the philosophical conception of perestroika, and the first experimental attempts to put this into practice, to the full-scale and profound reform of all aspects of public life – beginning with the first free elections to parliament since 1917.

Thus any dispassionate researcher must recognize that even before the official repeal of article 6 of the USSR Constitution by the Congress of People's Deputies, the Party had agreed to abandon its monopoly position in our society.

After the Ist Congress of People's Deputies, power began to pass to the Soviets. The Party, as is proper in a democratic society, would no longer direct the nation's development and had to begin operating by political means. Nevertheless, it remained the sole powerful political force organized on an all-Union scale. But, having lost the command functions to which it was accustomed, it felt as if it had been knocked off balance.

Thus began the most difficult stage for the Party – in which it sought its place in a society that was renewing itself. The Communists were faced with a question that would truly determine the fate of the Party: was it capable of reforming itself? Was it capable of turning itself into a mass, democratically organized party of left-wing forces – from a structure that had become intergrown with the state and was largely bureaucratic? An all-Party discussion began spontaneously, which included a wave of criticism aimed at the leadership. The number of people leaving the Party ranks increased sharply. The unity of the CPSU was being gradually undermined and destroyed by separatist movements in the republics.

Even in this difficult time the CPSU continued to have an enormous influence on the course of events. Questions of implementation of the decisions of the XIXth Party Conference were discussed at the July 1988 plenum. The September plenum was concerned with improving the structure of the Party apparatus. In January 1989 the Central Committee approved the CPSU political platform for the elections. In March the Central Committee presented a new agrarian policy aimed mainly at reinstating the peasant as master of his land. A landmark event was the September plenum of that same year, which adopted the platform 'On the nationalities policy of the Party under modern conditions'. The platform of the CPSU Central Committee for the XXVIIIth Party Congress, 'Towards a humane democratic socialism', was approved at the plenum held on 5–7 February 1990.

I apologize to the reader for this Party chronology. By recounting the Party fora, I want to emphasize that political life in the Party had not died. When I was elected President of the USSR, I did not at all intend, as some claim today, 'to throw the Party to the winds of fate.' If that had indeed been my intention, it would have been simplest to accomplish it by relinquishing the post of General Secretary, which incidentally the democrats insistently demanded I do. But I recognized my continuing responsibility to the CPSU and to millions of Communists for the fate of the reforms. I considered it my duty to do everything possible to help the Party, once it had completed its internal democratization, to renew itself and occupy its proper place in the new political structure. The question of whether this task could be fulfilled or whether the conservative part of the apparatus would gain the upper hand was to be answered by the XXVIIIth CPSU Congress, which was convened ahead of schedule. The Ist Congress of the Russian Communist Party could be seen as an overture of sorts to this.

THE SECOND COMING OF THE RUSSIAN COMMUNIST PARTY

After the first free elections to the republic parliaments in spring 1990, the Party felt left behind by the developments in society and the state. Dissatisfaction with the reformers and the work of the CPSU Central Committee became stronger, and doubts arose about the policy of perestroika. Problems in the economy accumulated and interruptions in supply became more frequent. When Ryzhkov announced the forthcoming price increases, the conservative top echelon of the Party decided that the time had come for revenge. They disagreed only about the tactics to adopt. Which was more advantageous and had greater chance of success: to force the General Secretary to abandon the policy of perestroika and return everything to its former state, or to oust him? Needless to say, these schemes were not publicized. These experienced politicians did not want to be seen as retrograde, sensing that the people would not accept a return to the old ways. For this reason they justified their every step as the desire to carry on perestroika more actively and efficiently.

The radical democrats had used the slogan 'independence of Russia' in order to gain a large number of seats in the new Supreme Soviet of the republic and the election of their leader as Chairman of the Parliament. A number of Party leaders took this as a fine example to follow: 'If the democrats could play the Russian card, why shouldn't we do the same thing?'

First at Party meetings, and later at plenums of district and oblast committees and in the press, they asked: 'Why should all the republics have their own Communist parties and their own central committees, but not Russia?' They argued that this was unfair. After all, the CPSU Central Committee, engaged in the affairs of the entire Party, could not pay sufficient attention to republic concerns. The question soon turned into a demand from 'the Party masses' that sounded rather like an ultimatum.

I have no wish to say that the entire undertaking was a front. While its initiators saw this as a manoeuvre to create a strong counterbalance to the reformist centre, many rank-and-file Communists responded to the notion of an independent Russian Communist Party just as they did to the slogan of an independent Russian Federation. In short, the problem here was real, not imaginary.

I considered this whole issue in discussions with close colleagues, going back to the history of the question and Lenin's position on this matter. We all understood that the decision to create this kind of Party structure had not been spontaneous – there was obviously a reason for it. A separate independent ruling centre for the Communists in Russia (and this was two thirds of the Party) would create a constant threat of schism, whereas the Party was intended to be the most powerful unifying force in the USSR. Its internationalist ideology was seen as a guarantee against the country's break-up. This was the reason why Lenin, in creating the Union – in theory, a federal state – was categorically against the same solution for the Party.

We had to resolve this question anew. This time we could learn from our own history; not simply a unitary, but rather a super-centralized state had existed under the guise of a federation. Now we were talking about moving to a true federation. Objectively speaking, the creation of the Russian Communist Party (RCP) was therefore unavoidable. However, had the appropriate moment for this come? Shouldn't this problem be resolved after the transformation of the Soviet state on the basis of a new Union Treaty? Finally, we had to ask ourselves the most important question: would not the newly created RCP become a tool of anti-reform forces, a stronghold of sorts in the battle against the CPSU Central Committee, where at least the tone was set by the General Secretary and his allies, who were decisively in favour of deeper reforms?

By that time there was also a division in the Politburo. Discussion heated up over many issues. And, although common and consensus decisions were eventually made, this did not remove differences in opinions.

These differences could be seen almost immediately when the question of the Russian Communist Party was brought up. An energetic proponent was Ligachev, who noted that the idea of a separate Russian Party had already captured the imagination of many Communists. This was true to some degree, although, I repeat, I still cannot get away from the suspicion that the campaign in favour of the RCP was to a large degree instigated.

We all remembered the attempt to solve the 'Russian problem' undertaken when Khrushchev was in power. At that time the Bureau for the RSFSR of the CPSU Central Committee was created, with its own apparatus. It continued for several years until everyone recognized that it needlessly duplicated functions in the Party leadership. Nevertheless, for lack of a better idea, it was decided to use this experience – with the hope that under the new conditions it would turn out more successful. At the December 1989 plenum we set up the Russian Bureau of the CPSU Central Committee under the chairmanship of the General Secretary; the Bureau included Vorotnikov, Vlasov, Manayenkov, Prokofiev, Gidaspov and a number of other officials. However, it met infrequently and did not bring any particular benefit. To some degree, this was my fault – I was very busy with many other concerns.

However, the main problem was that the creation of the Bureau was met with open dissatisfaction from within the Party. It was taken as an attempt to make do with half-measures, to forestall the formation of a separate Russian Communist Party. Discontent grew steadily, with pressure on the leadership coming mainly from 'fundamentalist' circles. They were also moved by purely pragmatic interests – many members of the CPSU Central Committee who had been dislodged from their accustomed positions during perestroika and who had been incapable of adapting to the new conditions counted on using this opportunity for a come-back.

The issue was debated many times in the Politburo. Because of the increasing pressure from below we finally decided to agree to the formation of a separate Communist Party of Russia. Once this decision was made, we let the matter drift. The 'Russian movement' turned out to be led by the anti-reform faction of the Party leadership, which had formed by then. This could clearly be seen even at the joint session of the Russian Bureau of the Central Committee and the Preparatory Committee. In my introductory remarks I spoke in plain terms about the dangers connected with the formation of the RCP. Manayenkov spoke more cautiously about this. The speakers agreed that the newly created Russian Communist Party could not be allowed to become an organization of dogmatic positions in opposition to the CPSU. At the same time, speakers showed their unhappiness at the pressure on them as a result of national resentment and bitterness about the inferior position of Russian Party organizations compared with those of other republics. There were also suggestions that the RCP would defend socialist values – actually implying restoration of the monopoly rule of the Party.

In conclusion I emphasized that the Russian issue was the central problem of perestroika and everything else depended on it. It had not arisen out of nowhere, but rather because of real problems in the development of Russia, the mistakes that were made here, as well as the surge of national movements in other republics. However, certain people wanted to make use of it; both Kosolapov and Yeltsin were speculating on it. If we took the road of Russian isolationism, we would destroy both the Union and the Russian Federation.

To sum up, I felt uncomfortable with this undertaking from the very beginning and I had a bad feeling about how it might turn out. Still, since it was impossible to withstand the pressure for a separate Russian Communist Party, I began to consider how to reduce the negative consequences to a minimum.

The conference of Russian Communists opened on 19 June. Since it was held only two weeks before the XXVIIIth CPSU Congress, we decided after lengthy discussions not to hold separate elections, but to empower the delegates elected from the Party organizations of Russia. In this way we immediately elevated the status of the conference. Indeed, it acquired the importance of a dress rehearsal for the Party Congress. Since the Communists of Russia were a majority in the CPSU (62 per cent), to a certain degree the conference determined the outcome of the Congress.

Representatives of the government were invited to the presidium: Lukyanov and Ryzhkov from the leadership; Yeltsin and Silayev from the Union leadership. Formation of the organs of the conference went smoothly. True, when we began discussion of the agendas, Avaliani, the first secretary of the Kiselevsk Party gorkom, Kemerovo oblast, took the floor and proposed to change the status of the conference and transform it into the first Constituent Congress of the Russian Communist Party.

The proposal was not entirely unexpected – the question essentially had been predetermined. Following a brief exchange, the delegates decided to hear my report first and to agree afterwards on the subsequent agenda. At the same time, the delegates agreed to give the floor to representatives of both the Democratic and Marxist platforms in the CPSU. The open acknowledgement of such factions was evidence of how far democratization of the Party had progressed. The Party had seen nothing comparable since 1921, when it had put an end to all manifestations of dissent – organized and spontaneous.

The history of my report is interesting. Long before the conference we had set up a group to prepare material for it. Then we decided in the Politburo that the General Secretary should present the report. It was only in a council of representatives of the delegations that I learned of the existence of an alternative report. I was almost ready to agree to the proposal to distribute it among the delegates in written form. But something put me on my guard. I took the report home, read it, and saw that it was based on a completely different approach. I had to reject the idea of distributing it and said that I would use this material as a source in preparing my own report.

I considered it my duty to say approximately the same thing at the conference as at the CPSU Congress – that is, to clearly define my course. It was essential that the delegates should know my position, the more so since at that time some people in the press were complaining: 'Gorbachev,' they were saying, 'is manoeuvring, he prefers vague phrases, and even when he's talking about the opponents of perestroika he doesn't name names.' Unfortunately, this attitude is widespread in our country – and in the Party most of all: anyone who disagrees with you is your enemy and must be thrown out or, even better, hit over the head with a brick.

I began by saying that all of the preceding discussion had led to the conclusion that the formation of a Communist Party of the Russian Federation was necessary. However, I immediately emphasized that 'we should rule out any possibility of setting Russia against the USSR, and the Communist Party of the Russian Federation against the CPSU. All of our plans and actions must take into account historical reality and be extremely prudent. When we say the word "Rossiya" [Russia], we must always remember a word no less treasured – "Soyuz" [Union]. I feel that it is necessary to speak frankly about this at the very beginning of our Party conference . . . I absolutely disagree with those who seek Russia's salvation in isolation, seclusion and even withdrawal from the USSR. Perhaps some think that Russia will develop more successfully outside the Union. This is nothing but wishful thinking.'

The second principal theme of my speech was perestroika. 'At the XXth Party Congress we heard truths that shook our country, the socialist community and the world Communist movement. What we learned then about Stalinism was an insult to the ideals that inspired generations of our people, that aroused them to revolution, to great construction projects, to the defence of our homeland, and to the rebuilding of our destroyed nation. The shock was enormous. One would think that a natural result would have been profound social and political changes. And although we cannot say that nothing has changed since then, unfortunately the hopes for radical transformation were not realized. Even worse, crimes gradually began to be called mistakes, instead of reforms there was tinkering with that very same bureaucracy instead of striving for new ideas; we merely updated the old Stalinist textbooks. All of this caused festering wounds both in our society as a whole and in people's hearts; it poisoned ideological life, and aggravated international relations. Eventually, the logic of political struggle led from half-truths to the hushing up of the past, from condemnation of Stalin to backsliding – to the rehabilitation of Stalin in various forms. The inevitable result of all this was political impotence and stagnancy in all areas.'

I said that perestroika had been necessary and inevitable, and briefly described recent developments, without skipping over mistakes and delays in solving acute problems. The central question was the transition to a socially oriented market economy. 'Various opinions are being given in this matter, especially regarding the time-frame, formulas and tactics, and we must be open to any suggestion. However, one thing is unacceptable – a return to the command-administrative system. This would have dire consequences – it would be a blind alley for the nation.

'Since our past history and present-day transformations are directly linked to the work of the Party, it is easy to understand why it is at the focus of the discussions going on in society. Some are saying that the CPSU must repent and leave the political arena. It is obvious that these demands are intended to provoke us. Hence, the best thing that we Communists can do in response is to continue the reforms that were started on the Party's initiative. We must unequivocally declare that the CPSU, without any stipulations, reservations or compromises, rejects the ideology and practice of Stalinism that trampled the spiritual and moral ideals of socialism. The Party is decisively in favour of full power to the Soviets, and of government by the people; it renounces functions of government or economic management, rejects claims to monopoly, and any attempts to impose an ideology. The Party will strive for public support in realization of socialist values by persuasion, political work among the masses, participation in parliamentary discussion, and intends to act within the framework of the Constitution and laws.'

The debate was lively, with many memorable speeches. Vladimir Lysenko, who supported the Democratic platform, spoke out in favour of a renewed Party, which, he said, should

MEMOIRS

abandon all political privileges and win respect by its work among the people. Dogmatic and revanchist attitudes were expressed the most strongly in the statement from the so-called Initiative Congress. Valery Ivanovich Ladygin, a machinist from a locomotive depot of the Trans-Baikal railway, gave a fiery speech. I had the impression that experienced propagandists had thoroughly worked over his text. To the sound of applause, he proposed that the CPSU Central Committee should account for the failed five years of perestroika at the XXVIIIth Party Congress. ('Let historians deal with the past, we need an account for today's affairs.') In this context he brought up an idea that was subsequently supported at the XXVIIIth CPSU Congress – that the members of the Politburo should account personally to the Congress.

The interesting thing was that Ladygin had been instructed by his comrades to read the mandate of the XXVth Chita Party obkom, which, among other points, contained appeals to the Congress to throw aside personal and group ambitions, to show solidarity, to assist in mutual understanding, tolerance and friendship between peoples, to create a law-based, democratic society that guaranteed full development of human potential, respect for human rights and basic freedoms. Let me quote: 'Your duty is not to ignite passions but to seek ways of accord, rather than confrontation; not to blacken our history, but to understand and respect it in order to take the best from it.' Ladygin's speech ran directly contrary to his mandate.

The co-ordinated position of the first secretaries of the oblast committees was more than evident. Polozkov led the attack on behalf of the fundamentalists. Melnikov – the first secretary of the Kemerovo oblast committee and a protégé of Ligachev – was particularly harsh in his rejection of reform policies. His remarks were clearly intended to evoke an emotional reaction from the audience. 'Two weeks are left before the XXVIIIth Party Congress, the Party is seething, the country is on the brink of a social explosion, but the leadership of the Central Committee and the CPSU Central Committee Bureau for the Russian Federation, as we see, are living in a different world. With our connivance the Party is being blamed for every mistake, today's Communists

462

are being dragged through the mire for all of the sins and omissions of history and blamed for the faceless mafia and the corruption. With the deliberate assistance of the General Secretary's closest associates, we are bit by bit creeping into a new cult of individual personality, although perhaps in an unusual, democratic form. While I do not want to ignore the worldwide recognition of Mikhail Sergeyevich Gorbachev as the leader of the CPSU and the nation, and I do want to give proper respect to his personal merits, I am obliged, in the spirit of Party comradeship, to caution him and shield him in the name of our common cause and the great final purpose from this disease, which unfortunately is chronic for us.' Melnikov concluded by saying that on 1 June the Kuzbass Party conference had approved by an overwhelming majority of votes a resolution of no confidence in the Central Committee and the Politburo, and had demanded the resignation of all its members.

Some voices were heard in my support. Sklyar, secretary of the Obninsk Party gorkom of the Kaluga oblast, rebuked those who, in his words, wanted to 'write off all debts to Gorbachev's account'. 'There are many supporters of the General Secretary among our Communists,' he emphasized, 'and I am convinced that there are also many in other Party organizations.'

It goes without saying that the problem was not so much attitudes towards the General Secretary as the ability of the Party masses to understand the irreversibility of the changes and the need for radical reformation of the Party itself, without which it was likely to be left on the sidelines of politics. The composition of the delegates did not adequately reflect the attitudes prevailing in Party organizations at that time. Professional Party workers and other categories of the nomenklatura had ensured that they would have most of the seats of the Congress. However, in spite of all of these factors it was not easy for conservatives and retrogradists in the top Party leadership to impose their will on the conference or the Congress that followed it.

The first test of strength happened during the election of the leader of the Russian Communist Party. We had discussed this question in the Politburo and had consulted the secretaries of the regional Party committees. In spite of the fact that the attitudes towards the very idea of creating a Russian Communist Party were mixed, there was a general recognition that it ought to be headed by one of the leading figures of the CPSU. However, there was not a large choice. At a meeting of representatives of delegations who were supposed to come to an agreement on the nomination of a candidate for First Secretary, I first suggested Valentin Aleksandrovich Kuptsov, who at that time was the head of the department of public organizations and a member of the Central Committee CPSU Secretariat and the Russian Bureau. My impression of him was that he had clear convictions, was well-disposed towards democratic reforms, and sympathetic to innovation and acted accordingly.

I also mentioned O. Shenin, whom at that time I considered to be a sincere supporter of perestroika. Polozkov, Bakatin and certain others were also proposed as candidates. Polozkov withdrew his own nomination, but it was a rather peculiar withdrawal. He said that since he was not among the candidates mentioned by the General Secretary he could only refuse the nomination. You could tell that he was not simply offended; he hinted that he was a victim of a biased attitude towards him.

We agreed on Kuptsov's candidacy. I reported this to the delegates on the next day. Several other names were also nominated and discussions began. Kuptsov himself spoke quite well – calmly and modestly, although perhaps he lacked fire. O. I. Lobov, who was then secretary of the Central Committee of the Communist Party of Armenia, made a good impression. Shenin's speech was bland. Polozkov reappeared among the candidates, arguing that since the Party organization had shown confidence in him he felt that it was inadmissible to insist on withdrawing his nomination. The secretaries ensured that he won the election, albeit on the second round.

This was the first time that proposals emanating from the General Secretary and supported by representatives of the delegations had been rejected. Kuptsov was rejected even though it was hardly likely that anyone had any fundamental grievances against him. The nomenklatura had decided to put a man at the helm who would firmly defend its interests.

My worst fears were confirmed. The results of the Russian

Congress made a bad impression on the general public. Suddenly, there was a 'rejection reaction', especially from Party organizations in the areas of science and culture and among the engineering-technical communities. We received an avalanche of declarations of unwillingness to be a part of the RCP, resignations from the Party, refusals to pay members' dues. The RCP was called the Polozkov party. The conservative reputation of the RCP's leader carried over to the entire organization, destroying respect for it from the very start. 'Polozkov-dom' became a kind of common noun.

It was no secret to me who was pulling the strings in the upper echelon of the nomenklatura. Polozkov admitted to me that he had been advised by Ligachev 'that night' not to drop his candidacy. It was clear that I would have to deal with the same situation at the XXVIIIth Congress. Meanwhile, the question was raised in the Politburo whether the start of the Congress should not be delayed. Ligachev and Yakovlev agreed on this, and were supported by Ryzhkov. There were some who wanted additional time to consolidate support among the delegates for the decisions of the Russian Congress. Others were afraid of a repetition of what happened at the Russian Congress.

My preference was to hold the Congress as scheduled. It had been expected for a long time, the date had been moved forward at the request of Party organizations, and a delay would have been greatly upsetting. However, the main reason was that we could not prolong the state of uncertainty that threatened to turn into the spontaneous decomposition of the CPSU. Only a Congress could consolidate the Party on the basis of a new programme. Of course there was the risk that the Congress would end in a schism, but we had no choice. We decided to seek the views of the leaders of major Party organizations. The opinion was unanimous – the Congress could not be delayed.

THE EVE OF THE CONGRESS

The struggle between two trends in the Party – reformist and conservative – initially developed over the platform for the

XXVIIIth Congress. Debates on this issue continued within the Politburo up to the time the platform was approved.

The reaction to the CPSU platform in intellectual circles was rather cool – people were saying that although the document indicated a search for new approaches in theory and politics, it no longer met the spirit of the times.

In the course of preparing it for the Congress the platform was radically revised, with not a single paragraph from the initial text left intact. A completely different document was submitted to the Congress – naturally with a different title – and was viewed as the political programme of the Party forum.

Since the last Congress there had been sweeping changes in all aspects of the life of our society and, under their influence, in the surrounding world. Former theoretical notions were collapsing, and the entire ideological basis of the activity of the Party needed radical renewal.

My closest associates and I worked on my report for the Congress, striving to be objective in analysing key questions that had been raised in the course of our development. An atmosphere of intellectual freedom reigned. There were also clashes, when I had to 'pull apart' overheated opponents. But on the whole we worked amicably and, it seems to me, we were successful in producing a rather clear analysis of the state of society and in defining the new role of the Party.

Let me reproduce several excerpts from my report, which give an idea of my positions at a critical point, when the future of the CPSU was being determined.

'The question today is this,' I told the Congress: 'either Soviet society moves forward along the path of the profound transformations that have begun, in which case I am convinced that our great multinational state will have a worthy future. Or anti-perestroika forces will gain the upper hand, and then the nation and the people can expect – and we must look truth straight in the eye – dark times.

'The Stalinist model of socialism is being replaced by a civil society of free people. The political system is being radically transformed. True democracy with free elections, a multi-party system and human rights are being established and genuine government by the people is being reborn. Relations of production that alienated the workers from property and from the results of their work are being dismantled. Conditions are being created for free competition among socialist producers. We have begun the transformation of a highly centralized state to a truly Union state based on self-determination and the voluntary unity of peoples. Ideological dictatorship has been replaced by free thought and glasnost, openness of information in society. The new political thinking has helped us to see the surrounding world in a different way and to make a realistic analysis of it, and it has freed us of the confrontational approach in foreign policy. The USSR has become a nation open to the world and co-operation, one that does not evoke fear, but rather commands respect and solidarity.

' . . . We must do everything possible so that perestroika develops as a peaceful revolution by transforming the country, within the framework of socialist choice, to a qualitatively new state, without upheavals, which always affect the people first. We must create every democratic condition necessary so that those who come to power are truly talented people, who are devoted to perestroika, who express the spirit of the times and the mood of the masses and are capable of getting things done. More than ever before, we need the highest degree of accord in society. Now is not the time for ultimatums and conflicts or ill-considered actions, which divide people and make the situation even more difficult.'

I presented to the delegates an objective picture of the situation in the economy, with an honest admission of mistakes and miscalculations. I stated that in spite of the acute nature of the crisis a return to command-administrative methods should be precluded and that it was necessary to pursue fundamental changes in the economic system more decisively and at an increased pace. This meant the formation of a new economic model – a multi-structural model with various forms of property ownership and a modern market infrastructure, which would open vast opportunities for business activity and initiative and create strong motives for fruitful work.

In my report it was again pointed out that the concept of

perestroika was not the flash of inspiration of a certain group of people, but rather the completion of many years of searching that had begun after the XXth CPSU Congress. The April 1985 plenum gave a powerful impulse to theoretical quests and opened up opportunities for the free discussion of painful problems in the life of society. Thus was born the basic idea: while remaining within the framework of socialist choice, society would be thoroughly democratized and humanized and conditions worthy of human life would be created.

Perhaps the most important and fundamental innovation in the speech was the interpretation of the role of the CPSU in government and society. Without abandoning the notion of the 'vanguard party', I emphasized that this position could not be imposed and could be won only by actively striving for the interests of the workers and by practical deeds, by our entire political and moral character.

AN OPEN CLASH

I have already mentioned the importance of the XXVIIIth Congress. It was a battle between the reformist and orthodox-conservative currents in the Party. After almost ninety years of its existence, the Party at this Congress, without rejecting the positive aspects of its historical legacy, condemned totalitarianism and swore allegiance to democracy, freedom and humanism.

This was a break with Bolshevism, the first major step towards reforming the CPSU. But it was achieved only with great difficulty, and at several points everything hung by a thread. After the Congress we were left with the gnawing feeling that the progress achieved was very brittle. The CPSU stood with one leg on the new shore, but the other was still on the old.

For the first four or five days of the Congress, practically the entire discussion was dominated by conservatives. Their speeches castigated the leadership for the loss of monopoly rule by the CPSU. People complained – many sincerely – about the difficult problems in the economy, culture, relations between nationalities, without seeing any fault of their own and putting all of the responsibility on the 'zealous reformers', who were called 'destroyers'. In short, this was the extremely hostile reaction of the ruling elite to reforms that threatened to upset their power.

It was remarkable that in criticizing the leadership of the Party they were in fact cursing only its democratic wing. The names mentioned included that of the General Secretary, Yakovlev, Medvedev and Shevardnadze, sometimes Razumovsky – but not Vorotnikov, Kryuchkov, Yazov or other Politburo members and candidate members; as far as I can remember, Ligachev too was left out. Speakers ignored the fact that all our decisions had been made collectively by the Party leadership.

The dominance of conservative attitudes in the debates and their remoteness from the report was evidence of careful preparation, I would even say orchestration, conducted by the Central Committee organizational department. While we were making a serious attempt to understand what had happened and to draw the necessary conclusions for Party policy, retrogradists in the leadership and apparatus 'sat on the phones', and held all kinds of caucuses. This was, of course, the usual pre-conference practice, but this time it was employed in order to conduct the Congress according to the scenario set up by the anti-reform wing.

News reached me that the delegates were being instructed in a spirit that was far from the 'new thinking'. Ligachev, the deputy directors of the Central Committee's Organizational Department who shared his views, and O. Baklanov, the leader of the military-industrial complex, were especially busy. Of course, their views were no secret to me. Still, it seemed unthinkable that people who bore their own share of responsibility for every step towards perestroika were working behind the scenes with Congress delegates, inciting them to a kind of 'anti-perestroika mutiny'. I had obviously underestimated human flexibility.

The first secretaries of the Central Committees of the Communist Parties of Ukraine (S. Gurenko) and of Belorussia (Ye. Sokolov) and others helped organize the aggressive 'fundamentalist' majority at the Congress. They did this out of conviction. The possibilities of interfering with this – let me say straight out – subversive work were rather limited. After all, you just could not change the composition of the Politburo or the apparatus on the eve of the Congress.

I had a four-hour meeting with the secretaries of the district and city committees, which left me with the impression that they were struggling for survival, for preservation of their own power. This was the source of their attempt to take revenge, to return the Party to its old ways, eventually to bury the reforms.

At this point, I would like to say a few words about the other wing – the one that was more radical than the reformist leadership of the CPSU. My report provided its members with the opportunity to set the tone of the discussion and to develop their arguments, but they were unable to take advantage of it. Probably the leaders of the democratic platform were rather frightened by the fundamentalists.

This is not to say that reform ideas were not heard at all in the discussion. To be fair, I have to say that Yeltsin spoke in this spirit and moreover in blunt terms. He said that we had failed in our attempt to neutralize the conservative forces in the Party.

Regarding the future of the CPSU, he declared: 'either the Party apparatus, under the pressure of political reality, decides in favour of radical perestroika in the Party or it will cling to its old, doomed ways and remain in opposition to the people and in opposition to perestroika . . . We who have devoted dozens of years of our lives to the Party have thought it our duty to come here to try to say that there is a way out for the CPSU. It is difficult and arduous, but it is a way out: in a democratic state the transition to a multi-party system is inevitable. We must recognize the platforms that exist in the CPSU and give each Communist time for political self-determination. We must change the name of the Party. This should be a party of democratic socialism. The Party must free itself of any state functions.'

Let me say straight out that these ideas had much in common with the political report and were close to the positions of the reform wing. However, Yeltsin's goal was not reform of the Party, but rather its destruction.

This was also the aim of his statement that it was too early to discuss a platform and charter at the Congress. Essentially, Yeltsin did not want to join the reform wing or help save the Party by reorganizing it in a timely way. Moreover, I think this was not simply because he did not believe that it was possible. He no longer wanted to be a secondary player in the CPSU. He hungered for power and already saw himself as the boss of another party – his own.

Abalkin made a substantial speech. He warned that the economy was going downhill. He rightly noted that the priority for the Party was renewal of its ideological-theoretical foundation. 'Experience has shown that the model based on total state control of the economy, rejection of the variety of forms of property ownership and economic activity, and rejection of the market, is incapable of assuring good economic and social results,' he said.

As he argued in favour of a market economy, his speech was continuously interrupted. Nevertheless, Leonid Ivanovich refused to leave the podium, despite the increasingly heated atmosphere.

The question of personal accounts by Politburo members was raised in the course of approving the agenda for the XXVIIIth Congress. This was the main subject of the entire first part of the discussion. The battle between the conservative and reformist wings basically ended in a draw. The fundamentalists, who were burning with the desire to 'nail to the wall' those whom they saw as responsible for their loss of power, were successful in their demands for 'accounts' (but these were to be given mainly at section meetings). However, they did not succeed in obtaining public evaluations – a humiliating procedure, which would have resulted in a 'public flogging' of the reformist figures.

Both in the preliminary stages and at sessions of the Congress I openly said that none of this fuss made sense. The political report[1] was essentially the account of the entire Central Committee and the Politburo as collegiate bodies. Even though its members supervised different areas of Party activity, all fundamental issues were discussed and decided collectively.

Of course, in other circumstances there would have been nothing shameful in the proposal to hear each member of the

---

[1] Delivered by Gorbachev at the beginning of the Congress.

leadership so as to see once again 'who was who', or, as Peter the Great said, 'so that each man's foolishness is evident'. However, in such a frenzied political battle, this method of 'self-accounting' was clearly intended as a blow against me.

Eventually all of the members of the leadership gave their reports, with varying success. Some won in the first round, and were able to show their best sides thanks to skilfully prepared speeches. Others gained points by answering questions. Still others looked colourless. After the 'accounts' and the planned squall of criticism of the leadership's reform line, little was left of the opposition's 'prepared plays'. The plenary session, where the leaders of the sections gave their reports and some Politburo members answered questions, was carried out in a more constructive atmosphere.

There were all kinds of questions, both 'subversive' and constructive. My colleagues were able to find the right tone and present convincing arguments, so that the delegates were for the most part satisfied. As I perceived the change in the delegates' mood, I called for a vote on the proposal to stop hearing the 'accounts' of the Politburo members and candidates. The vote was 3,078 for and 1,113 against, with 50 abstentions. Compare this with the vote three days earlier: at that time 2,557 delegates were in favour of personal evaluations and 1,393 were opposed. This was how the Congress rocked back and forth. Gradually reason got the upper hand, and the effect of the pre-Congress pressure on the delegates abated.

I thought much and conferred with my colleagues over what in these circumstances my concluding speech should say about the discussion on the political report. I did not have a prepared and polished text and had to sit up most of the night working on my speech. In the morning of 10 July I took the floor and said:

'Our political course towards perestroika and renewal of society within the framework of socialist choice is being supported by the Congress. Most of the delegates recognize that it has been dictated by life itself. In spite of mistakes, errors, delays, in spite of the drama of today's situation in the country, the overall result of the changes that have been made is substantial and progressive.

'The principal achievement is that society has gained freedom. Perestroika has liberated the energy of the people, brought millions into the political process and allowed us to begin vitally important transformations. Without this we would not have the atmosphere in which this Congress is being conducted.

'It is true, however, that neither the Party nor the nation as a whole – the old or the newly formed movements, our new authorities – none of us has learned to use this newly acquired freedom. The roots of the crisis in the Party go back to our inability and unwillingness to recognize that we live and work in a new society – one with broad and essentially unbounded glasnost, with freedom unseen in all of our history. We need a different, renewed Party; without democratization and strengthening of our vital link to the people, without active work with the masses, we will be losing our positions.'

I spoke of how we should put the strategy of economic reform at the top of the agenda. 'Our history has shown the fruitlessness of attempts to escape the poverty in which both the state and the citizens find themselves by darning and patching the command-distribution system. If we continue down this road, we will lead the nation into bankruptcy. The advantages of a market economy have been shown on a worldwide scale and the question now is only whether we can, under market conditions, assure a high degree of social security and the other characteristics of a socialist system. Here is my answer: it is not only possible, but it is specifically a regulated market economy that will allow us to build social wealth that will improve the standard of living for everyone.

'Our declaration of intent to convert to a market economy has frightened the people. Today, the market means for them empty shelves at the stores and high prices. To begin with prices is not the right way, but without reform of the price system there can be no market . . .

'The ideology of socialism is not a textbook, where everything is spelled out, chapter and verse. It will develop along with socialism itself, as we help the country to become well fed, comfortable, civilized, spiritually rich, free and happy, as we relearn universal values – not as something alien, but rather as

473

what is normal for a normal person. These values developed over centuries and we see clearly what the neglect of them brought us. The ideology of socialism will develop as our country joins the overall progress of civilization. A broad framework for this is defined by the new thinking, which is already perceived throughout the world as our new internationalism, which unites the world, rather than splitting it into opposing camps.

'We inherited from Marx, Engels and Lenin a strong method-ology, the dialectic method of thinking, on which we shall rely in both our theory and our practice. But we must not allow every-thing created by the classics to become another 'short course'[1] which some people seem to regret. This will be fatal for pere-stroika and for society. This must not happen.'

Let me say frankly that I was heartened by the fact that these words were met with applause. This meant that the people were beginning to think for themselves, and to question previously indisputable dogma.

I also had to defend our foreign policy, which was being attacked by the fundamentalists, who blamed the leadership for the 'loss' of Eastern Europe (as if it were our colony!), the 'capitulation' to the West and the loss of Afghanistan. Incidentally, 'defence' is not exactly the word. I tried to show that only incorrigible 'hawks' could see anathema in a policy that did away with the hyper-militarization of the country, turned the world back from the nuclear precipice and created the basis for our integration into the economic and political structures of the world.

I ended my speech by touching on the subject of the Party and power. 'The Party will not be able to change its ways itself until we all understand that the CPSU monopoly on power and govern-ment has ended. Even if we succeed in winning a majority in the elections – and we can and should try to win a majority and preserve our position as the ruling party – even in that case it will be appropriate to collaborate with non-Party deputies and repre-sentatives of other legally recognized political movements that

---

[1] A reference to Stalin's *Short Course*, which provided the 'definitive' version of Party history and thinking.

are truly concerned with the fate of the country. We must put an end to sectarian attitudes and stamp them out of the consciousness of Party workers and all Communists forever.' With this thought I ended my speech.

A break was announced. I had hardly left the podium when I was surrounded by delegates. Some wanted to share impressions, some hastened to use this opportunity to raise an urgent question, and some simply wanted to remind me that they were there. These were all manifestations of human nature. Journalists requesting a brief interview also ran up. Once I got free, I went to a room where the entire Politburo was gathered around a large table. I was showered with congratulations – of varying degrees of sincerity. Even Ligachev joined in the choir of praises.

'Well, Mikhail Sergeyevich, today you were at your best,' he said.

We proceeded to prepare the resolutions. This was the first time at a Party Congress (except in Lenin's time, when, judging from the minutes, there were lively discussions of the drafts of even very short documents) that people took this procedure seriously. In any case, at the congresses in which I had participated everything was done purely formally, simplified even to the point of absurdity. At the XXIVth Congress they decided not to complicate things at all: 'Leonid Ilyich [Brezhnev] has given a wonderful speech, it contains everything necessary, let us approve a short resolution: to be guided by the contents of the report of the General Secretary.'

In this regard as well, the XXVIIIth Congress differed greatly from preceding ones. Pointed discussions began even over the formation of the commissions for the development of various documents. Usually the General Secretary, after being made the chairman of one or another commission, would pass authority for practical work to someone from his own close circle. This time, in spite of the dramatic debate at the plenary meeting and the need for my constant presence there, I also had to conduct several sessions of the statutes commission personally.

Thus I was continually shuttling between the Presidium of the Congress and the room where the commission was working. I met many interesting people and added some to the 'central slate', thus advancing them into the leadership organs of the CPSU.

I believe that what was written into the statutes at that time would have resulted in radical democratization of the Party, had its history not been broken off in August 1991. I am thinking firstly of the expansion of the rights of Communists and grass-roots organizations and the autonomy of the Communist parties of the republics. Decentralization of functions was ensured, and the inclusion of leaders of the Communist parties in the Politburo was a guarantee of unity.

I received daily reports on the work of the other commissions. In the commission on economic issues the reformers and conservatives lashed out at each other particularly fiercely. The battle over forms of property ownership was decided by agreeing on the wording 'work-related private property'. The orthodox group fought against the market from beginning to end. Eventually the commission reached positions that were consistent with those already approved by the general public and confirmed in the Supreme Soviet. At this time the government was already drafting urgent measures for the transition to a market economy.

It was an unyielding and stressful battle. Only in the thirteenth session, at which I gave a concluding speech on the report, was there a break in the flow of the Congress. Pitched battles over the election of a new leadership were still ahead, but we had achieved the main goal: the Party was not allowed to deviate from a course of reforms, and a foundation was laid for its own transformation.

A POLITICAL DRAMA IN THREE ACTS

Immediately after my concluding speech nominations for the position of General Secretary began. At the request of the 'Council of Representatives of Delegations', the floor was granted to Vladimir Andreyevich Koluta, a foreman of the Khimprom Production association from Kemerovo. He announced that four persons had been nominated: Gurenko, Ivashko, Lobov and Gorbachev. Gurenko and Ivashko withdrew their nominations, and Lobov called upon the delegates to vote for Gorbachev. The Council proposed that Mikhail Sergeyevich Gorbachev should be elected General Secretary.

As I listened to all this, I thought how much the situation in the Party had changed. The election of the General Secretary was contested, and no-one now was afraid that someone would twist his arms behind his back and ship him off who knows where. The thought flashed through my mind that it would have been a good sign if they had rejected my candidacy. Psychologically, I was ready for this and would have accepted it calmly, even with relief, since many were already trying to convince me to give up the leadership of the Party. However, the time was not yet ripe, as was shown by the debate that followed.

There were passionate speeches in favour of my re-election, and others asking me to withdraw my candidacy. Alternative candidates were mentioned, including people well known in the Party (Bakatin, Shevardnadze, Yakovlev) as well as young Communists, of whom no-one or few people had heard before the Congress. Golikov, the first secretary of the Usinsk gorkom, Komi ASSR, sarcastically proposed that we apply for an entry in the *Guinness Book of Records*: 'We are the only Party that does not want its leader to be President.'

Finally, two candidates remained on the slates; the outcome was 3,411 votes for Gorbachev and 501 for Avaliani. The voting was predictable, since 1,100 delegates (more or less) had taken a negative attitude towards the General Secretary from the beginning of the Congress. The reader may have guessed that most of this thousand or so consisted of Party and government nomenklatura.

Everything was consistent with democratic principles. We had thus been able to introduce them even into this preserve of the totalitarian system. Involuntarily I recalled that after Stalin's election as Secretary at the XVIth Party Congress in 1934, a little over 280 deputies who had voted against him were identified. In order 'not to be mistaken' they decided to triple this figure – and then they did away with almost the entire body of delegates.

The election of the General Secretary was followed by the election of his deputy. This position was particularly important, since I would henceforth have to devote more attention to my presidential duties, and day-to-day organizational work would fall on the shoulders of the deputy. Besides the functional side of work, there was also the political side. Did the Congress want the leadership to act as a unified team headed by the leader of the Party? Or, conversely, since the delegates had not risked replacing the General Secretary, who occupied the highest state position, would they intentionally give the second position in the CPSU to a figure who represented a different political constituency – as if to put a controller over Gorbachev?

Since the General Secretary was from Russia, it was natural to elect a representative of Ukraine as the deputy chairman. I chose V. A. Ivashko. He was an advocate of reforms, who maintained moderate political views, who did not have his head in the clouds, who gave preference to everyday common sense, and who was modest and simple in his dealings with people. I was impressed by his calm, assured way of conducting himself at the podium, and by his gentle Ukrainian humour.

Vladimir Antonovich's misfortune was that fate gave him a test that demanded strong will and the ability to take responsibility. This was not within his grasp. He vacillated, giving in to the influences of more forceful colleagues in the leadership, and finally 'went sour' in the fatal days of August 1991.

At that time, however, he was highly rated by the delegates. The Council nominees included Ligachev, Dyakov (first secretary of the Astrakhan obkom), Lobov, Bakatin, Yanayev, Yakovlev, Nazarbayev and others, a total of nine people. Most of them withdrew their nominations, leaving Ivashko and Ligachev to be considered by the Congress.

Bulatnikov, a worker at a petrochemical plant in Bashkiria, asked Ligachev to withdraw his candidacy. He reminded us how we Communists felt when General Secretary Chernenko had to be assisted to walk to the podium. Yusupov, the Rector of the Tashkent State University, declared: 'Mikhail Sergeyevich, you need a young, energetic, sober-minded assistant. Yegor Kuzmich is seventy years old, he has become irritable and is no longer self-critical, and therefore it is better to send him into retirement, with ceremony, honour and respect.'

There were proposals to refuse the withdrawals made by

Gurenko, Malofeyev, and others nominated earlier. I. T. Frolov and A. Rubiks were nominated, and A. S. Dudyrev, the Rector of the Leningrad Technological Institute, nominated himself, saying that he was forty-five years of age and ready to work for the same salary as he was then earning. In the end he, Ivashko and Ligachev remained on the ballot.

However, it turned out that we had violated the procedures by accepting self-withdrawals while failing to check whether there had been any challenges. This was a clear signal that many delegates were afraid that Ligachev would be elected and did not want him to remain on the slate. The debate heated up again and was dominated by speeches challenging Ligachev's nomination. The subject was clearly divisive. Eventually his name was left on the slate of candidates, but it was clear that his chances of being elected were nil.

Indeed the votes were Dudyrev: 150 for, 4,268 against; Ivashko: 3,109 for, 1,309 against; Ligachev: 776 for, 3,642 against. Even those delegates who always voted against Gorbachev and his supporters refused to support Ligachev. The right wing was defeated at the Congress, among other things, because it failed to find a sufficiently strong and credible leader. Probably this was no accident. What respect could be won in defence of a bankrupt system?

Ligachev's defeat meant a blow to the political line that he represented. At the same time this was a signal that from then on the fundamentalist forces in the Party intended to operate openly as a faction, in opposition to the reformist leadership. I admit, I underestimated this danger then. I especially cannot forgive myself for allowing a key position in the Politburo – supervising the Party organizational department – to be occupied by Shenin. Because of some strange aberration of vision I took him to be a sincere advocate of reform. Perhaps this was due to his ability to mimic, to skilfully play the part of a progressive, an innovator, while remaining an incorrigible retrogradist at heart? Shenin knew how to show fervent agreement, and he talked much of his plans for renewal of the cadres. In fact, all of this turned out to be bluff.

If the election of the General Secretary was the first act of the dramatic collision between fundamentalists and reformers that was developing at the Congress, and the election of the Deputy General Secretary was the second act, then the third act was the discussion of candidates and elections for a new Central Committee.

At first everything was conducted with proper decorum. Since the majority of future Central Committee members were nominated by delegations of the Communist Parties of the republics, the battle for these places had taken place some time before the Congress. And if echoes of the battle could still be heard before voting, the 'sorting out' was done within the delegations. By itself this system of proportional representation pointed to a new, nearly federal CPSU construction. In this sense the Party reform was in step (it had to be!) with the state reform.

The battle broke out around the so-called 'central slate'. There was general agreement that a certain 'quota' of Central Committee mandates should be allotted for Party members from the Union level – recognized members of the All-Party leadership, prominent CPSU ideologues, respected Communists engaged in Union government, major military leaders, intellectuals, artists, and so forth. Because I monitored the preparation of this slate, people unofficially called it the General Secretary's slate.

In question were 75 seats, for which 85 candidates were nominated. Among them were representatives of the new Russian leadership – Yeltsin, Silayev, Khasbulatov. Immediately after the slate had been made public, Yeltsin asked to speak. The gist of his announcement was that in connection with his election as Chairman of the Supreme Soviet of the RSFSR and the transition of society to a multi-party system, he would be unable to carry out only the decisions of the CPSU. Therefore, in accordance with the obligations that he had accepted in the pre-election period, he was leaving the CPSU. Yeltsin added that he had intended to make this declaration after the Congress, but his nomination to the Central Committee demanded that he should wait no longer.

I have no doubt that Yeltsin expected others to follow his lead and make similar declarations. However, this did not happen.

I, as chairman, decided to treat this question as a routine matter and said something to this effect: 'Since Yeltsin has declared his resignation from the Party, I think the Congress should ask the seating commission to introduce a proposal to cancel his mandate. As for the rest of it, this has been decided by comrade Yeltsin himself. You have heard his arguments and all we can do for now is to take note of them. In connection with this, the proposal to add his candidacy to the slate for election to the Central Committee is no longer applicable.'

From my seat in the presidium I was able to watch Yeltsin's ostentatious exit from the conference hall. He walked slowly, probably thinking that the delegates would applaud and someone would follow him. But the directors of this show did not get the effect they had hoped for.

Next followed what was perhaps the main battle at the Party forum. Orthodox delegates were demanding that thirteen names be eliminated from the General Secretary's slate. These were people who had enraged delegates because of their liberal views. This conservative reaction found fairly strong support from many delegates who took moderate positions on other questions. I fear that the traditional distrust of intellectuals also played a role here.

But at that time it was of fundamental importance to keep the 'thirteen' in the list. Several times I had to intervene in the discussion, which was at a high pitch, on the brink of hysteria. Eventually I was forced to make a declaration which some people later compared to Lenin's position in the debate on the Peace of Brest-Litovsk.[1] In fact, this was a turning-point in the course of the Congress, a kind of culmination, which led into a calmer finale. True, the central slate was 'weeded' pretty thoroughly during the voting. Nevertheless, I and my allies were successful in insisting on a number of Communists with firm democratic convictions being elected to the Central Committee.

In summary, the XXVIIIth Congress was a step forward for the Party, demonstrating as it did that, in spite of all the endeavours of the conservatives, most of its rank-and-file members had responded to the challenge of the new times.

[1] In agreeing to the German conditions for peace at Brest-Litovsk in 1918, Lenin went against the opinion of most of his colleagues.

17

HOW TO ENTER THE MARKET

THE XXVIIITH CPSU CONGRESS WIDENED THE GULF BETWEEN THE reformist and conservative forces in the Party. We had succeeded in defending perestroika and confirming our plans, including the movement towards market reforms. We had also made some progress in drawing a line between the functions of the Party and the state. However, at the same time the supporters of orthodoxy, who had gained a foothold in the Russian Communist Party leadership, were consolidating forces. And even among the Politburo members and secretaries of the CPSU Central Committee, there turned out to be many people with traditional conservative views.

The elections to the Supreme Soviets in Russia and the other republics held in spring 1990 greatly influenced the political situation in the country. The election of Yeltsin as Chairman of the Russian Supreme Soviet and the Supreme Soviet's adoption of the Law on Sovereignty initiated a sort of chain reaction. From then on, no major issue could be resolved outside the context of the relationship between the Union and the republics.

Economic reform again moved to the top of the agenda. However, now the battle was not between proponents and opponents of moving to a market economy – this issue seemed already resolved. No significant political force spoke out openly against it. Passions shifted to the ways and means of effecting the transition to the market. One of the most dramatic pages in the history of perestroika was the bitter polemic over the choice between the government's programme of transition to a market economy proposed by Ryzhkov and Abalkin and the 500-day programme drawn up by Shatalin and Yavlinsky.

Much has already been said and written about this. However, I believe that the truth has still not come out fully. Most of the opinions that have been heard come from special interests and are subjective and often tendentious. The proponents of the government programme argue that it would have allowed the country to enter the market smoothly, without shocks. Those who were for the Shatalin-Yavlinsky programme believe that it would have gained powerful support from democratic forces, making it possible to 'leap over' the crisis and create a fully operational market by one single mighty effort.

Both sides have criticized me: I supposedly betrayed Ryzhkov's government, or I backed out of arrangements with Yeltsin, or I first supported and then threw out the 500-day programme, and so forth. Today the distribution of forces is completely different: Gaidar and his team are the radicals, Shatalin and Abalkin caution against the extremes of monetarism, Yavlinsky is somewhere between these two poles, and government policy resembles a giant slalom course. The logic of the dispute and the arguments presented by both sides largely repeat the battles of 1990–91, which are therefore of more than just historical interest.

WHAT HAPPENED BEFORE THE 500-DAY PROGRAMME

The history of the government programme in the spring of 1990 can be traced back to the Ist USSR Congress of People's Deputies.

The 'Basic directions of domestic and foreign policy of the USSR' approved by the Congress set the task of moving to a new economic model that included the radical revision of property relations, the establishment of a fully operative socialist market, and the abandonment of direct state interference in the day-to-day management of economic entities. At that time it was decided to set up a state commission for economic reform, and Ryzhkov proposed that it should be chaired by Academician L. I. Abalkin. The Director of the Institute of Economics of the USSR Academy of Sciences had long been a proponent of the market, and because of this had had quite a few problems during Brezhnev's time. I approved this choice, since I was already acquainted with Leonid Ivanovich and valued both his high degree of professionalism and his firmness of character. I admit that he had irritated me by his sharply critical speech at the Ist Congress, but I very quickly recognized that he had evaluated the situation correctly.

There was another weighty argument in favour of naming him chairman. Even the first stage in the work on the programme of economic transformation (I have in mind the June 1987 Central Committee plenum) convinced me that we could not get things done without a close alliance between the authorities and the academic community.

The Academy of Sciences had earlier been involved in the development of various programmes. Memoranda were prepared in the institutes, projects were subjected to the Central Committee, the scholars themselves spent months with the apparatchiks in suburban dachas working on speeches for top officials. However, with very few exceptions, intellectuals were not admitted to the 'holy of holies' of the nomenklatura, the offices of the decision-makers.

Now we were getting ready to bring academics into the process of government decision-making. Ryzhkov often said with pride that in his government there were three or four members or corresponding members of the USSR Academy of Sciences and several dozen DSc's, and nearly every other person had a PhD. One may say sarcastically that academics did not save that government, but one can hardly dispute the idea of bringing gifted theoreticians into government alongside experienced practitioners. In a way Abalkin, when he became Deputy USSR Prime Minister, personified this alliance.

A plan and budget for 1990 were prepared in parallel with work on our programme. We had to put an immediate stop to the increasing discrepancy between people's incomes and the quantity of goods available. On Abalkin's proposal a progressive tax on wage increases exceeding 3 per cent was introduced for a fifteen-month period beginning 1 October 1989. Thus academics in the government were engaged in solving important practical problems. Nevertheless, the main concern of the commission was the reform programme. Three versions were proposed for discussion.

The first, the so-called evolutionary version, called for a gradual transformation of the forms of economic management and for moderate structural changes. Preference was given to administrative methods. There was no attempt, at least for the foreseeable future, at price reform.

The second, radical version called for simultaneous lifting of all restrictions on market mechanisms, complete abandonment of price and income controls, and a mass change-over to new forms of property ownership. In essence, this is the same programme that Gaidar's team began to implement under the slogan of 'shock therapy' in early 1992. Even then it was known that under our conditions this programme promised disorder in monetary circulation and galloping inflation, a sharp decline in production, massive unemployment, a significant fall in standards of living and a rise in inequality along with increased social tension. It is a picture clearly recognizable today.

Finally, there was the radical-moderate version that called for a complex of preliminary measures to create the initial conditions for the transition to a new economic mechanism; development of market relations, while maintaining the regulating role of the state; control of prices, income and inflation; and strong social security safety-nets, especially for low-income groups.

Abalkin's commission recommended the third version. In mid-November a conference attended by leading academics, economists and managers of economic agencies, together with members of the Politburo and the government, was held in the Hall of Columns of the House of Unions. Ryzhkov and I were also present. Abalkin's programme on the whole met with approval, and a revised version was presented by Ryzhkov in his speech to the IInd Congress of People's Deputies, where it was hotly debated. Yeltsin, Popov and other members of the Inter-Regional Group spoke against the Prime Minister's proposals. Academician Arbatov took the same position. People's deputy

Filshin demanded that we 'avail ourselves of our right of no-confidence in the government and that it avail itself of its right of resignation.' Someone proposed that Ryzhkov's speech be merely taken note of, without approving or rejecting it.

Eventually, the Congress expressed support for the government programme: 1,532 votes in favour, 419 against, with 44 abstentions. Regarding economic reform itself, one important factor was obvious. Neither the written report nor Ryzhkov's speech analysed the results of the preceding stage of economic reform or mentioned the fundamental decisions made in 1987. Who had been responsible for the failure to implement those reforms? If they had been insufficient or even erroneous, we ought to have recognized this and learned a lesson. If there were other reasons involved, they should have been considered. Instead we seemed to be starting again from square one.

You could make a case for Abalkin – he was new at the helm, although for the sake of accuracy it should be noted that as a scholar he had actively participated in the drafting of the 1987 programme. But the government's silence spoke more eloquently than anything else about the failure of the transformation outlined in 1987 and the responsibility of the Central Committee and the USSR Council of Ministers for this.

And where was the guarantee that this situation would not be repeated? This must have been in the minds of everyone, and caused distrust of Ryzhkov's government. I see my own culpability in that these questions were not identified and brought out into the open.

In many respects the reforms promoted in 1990 were no advance on those sketched out in 1987. Some were even a retreat. For example, the system of state orders was retained, though with certain stipulations. The price reform was being replaced by the development and introduction of wholesale and procurement prices, beginning in 1991, but retail prices were not mentioned. In place of a move from centralized distribution to wholesale trade in resources, it was proposed to increase the share of products sold by enterprises over and above state procurement at free or regulated prices.

In supporting this programme, the IInd Congress of People's

Deputies was in fact expressing a vote of confidence in the government, but it did not make a final decision: it called for the programme to be revised and 'the results presented to the USSR Supreme Soviet.' In this way we again lost time. At the end of 1989 and the beginning of 1990, the economic crisis in the country began to reach an acute phase. In December 1989 industrial production had declined, the collapse of the consumer market had accelerated, and the ruble had begun to lose value rapidly. It became clear that the economy was facing serious trouble.

In late January 1990 I had sent the Politburo members a memorandum from the Central Committee Department of Economic Policy suggesting that we should discuss measures for balancing finances and the consumer market. In the subsequent discussion, Ryzhkov's hour-long speech was vague. The Prime Minister did not hide his dissatisfaction with the memorandum and harshly criticized the newspapers, television and radio. After him, Slyunkov spoke with alarm about what was happening in the financial-monetary sphere and in the consumer market. He was supported by Medvedev, who emphasized that the situation demanded extraordinary measures. He said that we needed not partial but comprehensive reform of prices, to be implemented without further delay: reform of wholesale and procurement prices in mid-1990 and reform of retail prices in early 1991. Medvedev and Yakovlev also spoke out in defence of the mass media. Shevardnadze, Kryuchkov and Ligachev spoke of the government 'dragging its feet'.

How did the government react to the rapidly deteriorating situation and this harsh criticism in the Politburo? The battle continued between two basic trends, one may say, wings – between the traditional technocrats, and the economists, who gravitated towards market reform. This tug of war could not go on forever. A choice had to be made: either return to the former centralized system or move decisively to new market mechanisms. In fact, there was no choice; no-one was capable of bringing back the past. This was recognized first and foremost by Abalkin and by Maslyukov – a technocrat from the military-industrial complex, a thoughtful and decisive man.

Why did we not use the levers of influence that we had at that time to complete the debate in the USSR Supreme Soviet and approve a document that we could use as a basis of action as the situation demanded? This is not a simple question for me, or, I think, for others, but I do not want to give simplistic explanations or excuses.

I think that a principal cause was the vacillation that still existed, the lack of confidence that the decision expected from Parliament would produce a rapid recovery in the economy. Just imagine: practically every day you are button-holed by the leaders of various branches of industry and culture who caution you against hurried measures. The press is full of alarmist commentaries and predictions. With periodic strikes the workers let you know that they will not tolerate any drop in their already low standard of living. The radicals are sharpening their teeth, predicting the collapse of the Gorbachev reforms. And the government itself is passively awaiting the end of interminable debates in parliamentary committees, as if it were glad to prolong the pause so as to delay getting involved in such a risky enterprise.

Questions of the transition to a market economy were discussed twice, at joint sessions of the Presidential Council and the Council of the Federation, on 14 April and 22 May. Academicians and institute directors warned against underestimating the importance of centralized control. At that time the general public was filled with terror of an unknown monster – the free market. Advocates of a market economy could not resist the temptation of creating alibis for themselves, in case the reform collapsed and people began to assign blame.

Disputes within the government again focused on the revision of retail prices. I still find it difficult to explain why Ryzhkov decided to go on television and announce plans to raise prices more than six months before the increases were to be put into effect. Perhaps his nerve failed him. For an experienced politician and leader this was a serious miscalculation, one that produced great problems for the market programme and its implementation. Shelves in the shops were completely emptied. A wave of dissatisfaction rolled over the country, and it was only with great difficulty that we were able to calm public opinion.

In May Ryzhkov's report on the economic situation in the country and the transition to a regulated market economy was at last discussed. The marathon discussion continued for several days. However, the USSR Supreme Soviet again – for the umpteenth time – delayed a final decision and asked instead that a programme be submitted by 1 September 1990, recommending that the Supreme Soviets of the Union republics, autonomous republics and the local Soviets should discuss the plan.

The battle over the transition to a market economy was turning bitter.

ENTER YAVLINSKY

The problems of developing a market programme resulted not only from the extreme complexity of the problem itself, but also from the growing alienation between the government and the democratic opposition, supported by a section of the general public. Every step was subjected to derision from the press. Then a new factor appeared – the transition towards sovereignty in the republics, which had to be taken into account if we were to have successful economic transformation. Moreover, the new Russian leadership tried to seize the initiative in the race towards the market. A feverish search began for new ideas and new people. Yavlinsky's sudden rise to prominence took place in this atmosphere.

Where the initiative came from, who found whom, is hard for me to judge. The little-known young economist was recruited by Abalkin to the commission on economic reform of the USSR Council of Ministers and worked on the government's market transition programme. Yavlinsky produced his own drafts for the commission, which were more radical and emphasized monetarist methods. Some were approved by the commission, some rejected, mainly because they seemed unrealistic. However, noone thought of him as having a special position or being outside the framework of the working discussions.

But then Silayev invited Yavlinsky to join the Russian government as Deputy Prime Minister for Economic Reform. This appointment was made without reference to me. I did not even know Yavlinksy then. Later I was told that he conferred with Abalkin and Ryzhkov and received their consent. They thought this 'personal union' of economists would increase the opportunity for co-operation between the USSR and Russian governments. But that is not what happened. Yavlinsky proposed his own programme to the Russian leadership. This programme differed from that proposed by the USSR government; moreover the differences were artificially accentuated so as to emphasize the superiority of the Russian approach and its broad scope.

Under the new conditions it was impossible to accomplish any major social transformations without the active participation of the governments of Russia and the other republics. At the same time, transformations could not be accomplished within the framework of any single republic, even the Russian Federation. The basic levers of control of the single economic space remained in the hands of the centre. They understood this in the Russian White House[1] and wanted to force the USSR to speed up reforms. It was a no-lose situation. If the central powers gave in, the initiative and resolve of the Russian authorities would be demonstrated; if they resisted, the bankruptcy of the centre would be exposed.

After some time Yavlinsky asked to see me. I do not know if this was at Yeltsin's request or on his own initiative. More likely the former. I paid close attention to his arguments, and found much to agree with, especially his recognition of the need for a unified approach to reform in the Soviet Union.

Thus, on the one hand, the government's transition programme was supposed to be submitted to the USSR Supreme Soviet by the beginning of September. On the other hand, extensive work was being done on the Russian programme. There was thus a danger of confrontation between the centre and Russia. The position of the other republics was unclear: it was possible that they would support the Russian programme for political reasons.

It was then that the idea of combining efforts in the development of a market programme was born. Soon a document

---

[1] A popular name for the building in which the government of Russia is located.

appeared signed by Gorbachev, Yeltsin, Ryzhkov and Silayev, creating a working group that included Shatalin, Petrakov, Abalkin, Yavlinsky and other economists, as well as authorized representatives of the governments of the Soviet republics. The draft for a joint programme was to be ready no later than 1 September.

We signed the document creating the working group on 27 July. At first, Yeltsin proposed that just the two of us sign it. Silayev's signature meant nothing to him, and he found it difficult to accept the fact that Ryzhkov would be signing it. Ryzhkov's feathers were ruffled too, but eventually he yielded, citing his 'unwillingness to interfere with the improved co-operation between Gorbachev and Yeltsin.'

The first name on the list of members of the working group that was to draft the joint programme was Academician Shatalin. In late 1988 or the beginning of 1989 he had become my informal adviser on economics and other matters. I was impressed by his rigorous way of thinking and speaking out impartially on the most critical issues. In former times this habit had caused Shatalin a lot of trouble. He had been victimized as one of the leaders of the school of mathematical economics that was not acceptable to official circles.

Shatalin had not been directly involved in the development of Yavlinsky's programme. He was pulled into this work, as they say, on the run. He took to his new commission with great zeal, and thus it is quite right that the 500-day programme came to be called the Shatalin-Yavlinsky programme.

Thus the working group was set up. I went on holiday, maintaining communications with the working group through my aide Petrakov. But soon I began to receive contradictory and increasingly alarming signals from Moscow. The group was working at full steam and holding meetings with representatives of republican governments, but had failed to co-operate with the USSR Council of Ministers. Mutual hostilities grew. When, at my request, the working group met Ryzhkov, Abalkin and Silayev, they could not get along and took irreconcilable positions. The joint work on the programme never started. The Shatalin-Yavlinsky group continued to work on its own, separately from the Union government. Meanwhile, the Ryzhkov-Abalkin government worked on its own programme for transition to a market economy.

The controversy between them eventually leaked into the mass media. Some of the newspapers began baiting the Union government and its leader. As the situation was coming to a head, I decided to return to Moscow before the end of my holiday. On 30–31 August I called a joint session of the Presidential Council and the Council of the Federation in order to discuss the situation. Heads of economic agencies, academics, USSR and Russian people's deputies – a total of about 200 people – were invited to the conference hall of the USSR Supreme Soviet. The leaders of the republics, as expected, indicated that they favoured the Shatalin-Yavlinsky programme and emphasized that if the role of the republics were not taken into account, talk about economic reform would be just empty words. In this regard they were right. But not one of them spoke out directly against Ryzhkov's government or demanded his resignation.

Yeltsin, referring to a five-hour conversation we had had, said that 'we are moving together, we are implementing a common policy firmly and definitely; confrontation is unacceptable.' In his opinion, chaos was building up in the country not because of the declarations of sovereignty by the republics, but as a reflection of the crisis of the former system of government. He admitted that the leadership of the Russian republic, after the attempt to create its own Russian programme for a transition to a market economy, had realized that it was impossible to implement this programme within the framework of a single republic.

'To do this it is necessary to destroy the Union,' he added. 'We have rejected this notion and proposed that the President of the country use our ideas for an all-Union programme, which in fact is the object of the Shatalin-Yavlinsky co-ordinating commission.' Yeltsin expressed his confidence that the Russian Supreme Soviet would approve this programme, which called for an economic union among the republics, and would also define its attitude to the Union government. But the Russian leader thought the joint programme should be implemented by a special committee under the President, not by the Union government.

In spite of the fact that the majority was in favour of the Shatalin-Yavlinsky programme, a number of speakers pointed to flaws in it. Academician Yu. A. Osipyan, a member of the Presidential Council, noted that the programme lacked what any state, be it unitary or federal, must have – a federal tax.

Medvedev, in spite of his generally favourable evaluation, objected to the fact that the programme, while mentioning an economic union, circumvented the question of a political union of republics. 'Who must in practical terms carry out the programme of economic recovery and conversion to a market economy at the Union level?' he asked. 'The answer is clear: of course – the government. If it is denied this function, it cannot do anything at all. Such a government is simply unnecessary. And no committee can replace it.'

The debate over the Union government flared up anew. Khasbulatov, in his rough, outspoken manner, called for the government to resign. Representatives from other republics opposed him. An angry Ryzhkov declared that in the final account the problem was not the government, but the struggle of certain republican leaders against the centre. He turned to me and declared: 'You yourself undertake the functions of government, but the next blow will be directed against you.'

In deciding not to replace the government, I took into consideration that Ryzhkov and especially Maslyukov had shifted their position dramatically in favour of a market economy, and therefore hoped that the government would be capable of carrying out the reforms. My main objection to the resignation of the government was that it would have dragged us into a new and difficult round of political struggle. Some highly respected people from my own inner circle thought differently.

The joint session of the Presidential Council and the Council of the Federation did not adopt any formal decisions, since it did not even have the full text of both programmes. This was simply an exchange of views, which ended with the statement that it was necessary to continue work on the programmes and to try to find a way of bringing them closer together before their official submission to the USSR and Russian Supreme Soviets.

Unfortunately this agreement about postponing the submission of the programmes to the USSR and Russian Supreme Soviets was not kept. On 3 September the 500-day programme was distributed and the Russian Parliament's deputies began discussing it. This was an obvious attempt to put pressure on the centre, to thwart the development of a common programme, and to present us with a *fait accompli.*

The very next day, in spite of being very busy (this was also the opening day of the Russian Communist Party Congress, which was a significant event in the political life of the country), I conducted a detailed discussion and comparison of the two programmes, inviting their authors, the leaders of republican governments and academics to join me. However, this was not a broad political forum but a relatively narrow business meeting. Yavlinsky rather aptly represented the 500-day programme, and was opposed by Abalkin.

Again the authors of the programmes did everything they could to stress what they felt to be the fundamental differences and the 'incompatibility' between the two documents. On the other hand, the republican representatives, being more inclined to support the 500-day programme, found it necessary and possible to bring the two programmes closer together.

By this time a detailed analysis of the two programmes had been carried out, both in academic institutes and by my own staff, and I had a more complete idea of what they were. I still felt that the 500-day programme was preferable, but the main subject of disagreement and discord was not economic – it was really about the future model of our society. The government's programme was based not only on an economic union among the republics, but also on the retention of the single Union state with regulatory functions and what could be called the fundamentals of a socialist system.

On the other hand, the Shatalin-Yavlinsky programme, while recognizing the need for an economic union of republics, left aside the problem of their political union and lacked precise social content. It did not even mention a new Union Treaty.

The authors argued that the programme was not supposed to deal with political issues; but this was disingenuous – an unprejudiced analysis showed that the programme was in fact based on the prospect of ending the existence of the Union as a single state. Here is just one example: the programme called for the introduction of a one-way tax system, in which all taxes would go to the republics, and then, according to a rate that they would establish, they would make allocations to the Union budget. The existence of a federal state is of course unthinkable without federal taxes.

In fact, the 500-day programme prejudged the fundamental decisions that were the subject of the talks on a new Union Treaty. Its adoption would give a strong push to the forces of disintegration, first of all in the political sphere. And this in turn would unavoidably affect the economy.

Indeed the political problems turned out to be the stumbling-block to combining the two programmes. As far as the socio-economic content was concerned, there were no insurmountable barriers. The problems connected with the transition to a market economy were basically the same. It was just that the approaches were different: aggressive and decisive in the 500-day programme, and balanced and smooth in the programme submitted by the government.

On prices, Ryzhkov and Abalkin proposed that we should carry out a gradual liberalization of prices after an initial price reform, i.e. after less distorted wholesale, procurement and retail prices and tariffs had been established. Shatalin and Yavlinsky, on the other hand, suggested freeing prices from 1991 onwards, after some stabilization measures.

In short, in spite of Yeltsin's caustic comment that 'Gorbachev wants to cross a hedgehog with a grass snake', there was enough room for agreement. Moreover, it was soon discovered that the Russian leadership, which ostensibly was zealously defending the principles of the 500-day programme, was in practice not at all inclined to follow those principles at that moment. For example, the Russian government had sharply raised procurement prices for meat from 1 October (higher than was specified in the price reform that was due to go into effect on 1 January 1991). I do not want to imply that this was an incorrect or unfounded act – in the situation that existed then it was necessary. The fact is that this measure was preceded by a sharp increase in procurement prices for meat by the governments of the Baltic republics, which was claimed to result from price increases for grain and mixed feed. As a result, livestock from Russia and Belorussia streamed into the Baltic countries to be sold there, so that corrective measures had to be taken. The sad thing is that they acted separately, giving rise to a kind of trade war, instead of resolving issues on a co-ordinated basis at the Union level.

Without question, the 500-day programme was attractive because of its freshness, the unusual way it posed the problems of the transition to a market economy, and its more concrete and thorough development of these problems. However, these merits somehow turned into shortcomings. As some critics said, it had the stamp of economic romanticism or, more plainly, it was not realistic enough. There seemed to be a desire to represent the programme as a kind of railway timetable, with instructions that such-and-such must be accomplished by a certain date. Even then it was doubtful whether achieving financial and monetary stabilization of the economy in 100 days – as was proposed in the programme of Shatalin and Yavlinsky – was feasible, and today it is completely clear that it was not.

On the other hand, the government programme, despite being in some ways traditional and imprecise, had certain strong aspects. In particular, the measures to ensure the social security of the people in the transition to a market economy had been worked out more thoroughly.

Eventually I became convinced that neither of the proposed programmes could be adopted in the form in which it had been submitted. This was a considered and firm decision. I realized that it would not be popular. The supporters of the government, as well as Nikolai Ivanovich himself, did little to disguise their resentment. They dropped hints or even said directly that I should have backed my government against the newly declared democrats. To this I can give only one answer: 'Plato is my friend, but truth is more important.'

AN ATTEMPT AT SYNTHESIS

At the session on 4 September, I announced my decision: the two groups should come together for a conference, with Aganbegyan acting as arbitrator, so as to create an integrated document. As work progressed on merging the two programmes I knew that it was not going well, mainly because of Abalkin's unwillingness to participate. Nevertheless, it was completed and then sent to the USSR Supreme Soviet and the Russian leadership. It must be said that the basis of the new document was the Shatalin-Yavlinsky programme but without those points that anticipated the future solution of problems in the Union Treaty: in particular, the principle of the supremacy of republican legislation had been removed, and it provided a financial base for the Union in the form of federal tax and so forth.

On 27 September and 1 October I held two lengthy and frank talks in the Walnut Room on the subject of further development of the plan and 'bridge building' in the prevailing political situation. Participants in the discussion included Ryzhkov, Abalkin, Maslyukov, Medvedev, Primakov, Petrakov, Pavlov, Boldin, Sitaryan and Shcherbakov. Shatalin appeared briefly on 27 September, but he was not present on 1 October; I was told that he had gone to the United States for medical treatment.

In response to my invitation, some of the participants spoke out on a broader range of general political problems. The main theme was strengthening central power in the presidential type of government. For example, Abalkin spoke in favour of reorganizing the government and the Presidential Council on a broader socio-political basis. Medvedev and Pavlov were in favour of concentrating all executive power directly in the hands of the President, although they admitted that at that particular moment it was not possible to do without a government. These remarks were important for me, since I myself was also thinking more and more about the structure of presidential power.

Initially we proposed that the work on the new version of the President's market transition programme should be entrusted to the same people: Shatalin, Abalkin, Petrakov and Aganbegyan. However, as I have already said, Shatalin was absent, and, moreover, joint work between these academicians was really impossible because of their disagreements. The preliminary work would therefore have to be done by one person operating on his own. Abalkin offered his services and I agreed. However, the draft programme that he submitted turned out to be too closely tied to the government's version. Then Aganbegyan and Petrakov joined in the work. I also joined in, refusing literally all other business for several days. As a result, a sixty-page document was drafted and submitted to the USSR Supreme Soviet precisely on the day specified (15 October). The republics were to be given the right to decide which specific measures should be implemented and when. The centre, on the other hand, was to ensure overall co-ordination of the reforms. Hence the name of the document: 'Basic directives for the stabilization of the national economy and transition to a market economy'. Intensive work on this draft continued for three weeks. It may have seemed that passions over the market programme had died down, but this impression was deceptive. In fact, positions were becoming even more polarized.

On 8 and 9 October the Central Committee plenum discussed the situation in the country and the tasks the Party faced during the transition to a market economy. This time I limited myself to a brief introductory speech so that no-one could say that I was dictating my own programme. Ivashko's speech provided detailed calculations. At first the speeches at the plenum were not as strident as at the pre-Congress plenums. Evidently the new Central Committee members were taking the measure of one another. However, the overall atmosphere was still conservative. Gidaspov objected to transition to a market economy before a Union Treaty had been concluded, calling it a political mistake. Polozkov said that we must defend the chairman of the Council of Ministers. Passions flared up over the draft resolution. The prepared draft was discarded, and eventually we adopted a more or less satisfactory draft.

The debate moved on to a different plane – how to move to a market economy. The speakers were unsparing in their criticism of the 500-day programme. Followers of the old ways simply could not reconcile themselves to the changing role of the Party and the loss of its right to determine every step in political and economic life. This was the source of their unwillingness to recognize that the Central Committee and the Politburo could no longer play the roles they had played before. It is not by chance that a number of speeches asked the same question: why is the CC debating the market reform programme after it has been discussed in the USSR Supreme Soviet, and not before? Speakers insistently accused the President of being slow to raise the fundamental problems of reform in Party bodies, or claimed that the Party was isolated from the discussion of fundamental issues and being presented with decisions that had already been made. I replied that the accusations against me were completely unfounded, since the policy of transition to a market economy had been laid down by the XXVIIIth CPSU Congress. Regarding specific steps and decisions within the competency of the President and government, they were not supposed to be determined in Party organizations. Incidentally, there were already Party decisions on this matter.

These were the attitudes I had to face at the Central Committee plenum, attitudes shared by a significant proportion of those deputies who were closely connected to the Party apparatus and who gravitated towards the 'Soyuz group'. This group influenced the development of events in the USSR Supreme Soviet in subsequent months. Little by little, Lukyanov became their spokesman (while remaining extremely cautious!). First among themselves and then out in the open, some people complained that the President had stopped consulting with the supreme representative body and preferred to rely on his own apparatus, the Presidential Council and the Council of the Federation, and on direct contact with Yeltsin.

I sensed that Ryzhkov was increasingly uncertain which side he should take. On the one hand, he was pleased that a stop had been put to the petty interference in government activity by the Central Committee, about which he had complained when he became Chairman of the USSR Council of Ministers. On the other hand, it seemed that he did not object to criticism of the President for 'not taking the opinion of the Politburo into consideration' – especially since the onslaught on the President and his 'team' by Party leaders had been combined with a defence of the government against attack from the market advocates and radical democrats. Neither Ryzhkov nor Lukyanov spoke at the plenum. Nevertheless, I sensed intuitively that even if they were not wholly in tune with the Party conservatives, they were at least sympathetic to them in some ways. At that time, I took these to be no more than acceptable nuances in the positions of my colleagues. The further course of events confirmed my impression that Ryzhkov and Lukyanov were becoming closer.

There was much to think over in the autumn of 1990. Only the first step had been taken in the establishment of presidential power; its ability to exercise supreme executive-managerial functions was largely illusory. The problem could have been resolved by creating a powerful executive apparatus – comparable to that of government – but this would have given rise to an even greater muddle at the higher levels of state power. The Presidential Council could not be an effective tool of management and, moreover, had come under fire in the mass media as a 'new Politburo'.

One must take into consideration that the problem of constructing a 'vertical' presidential power structure was immeasurably complicated by the claims of sovereignty by the republics, which were jealously guarding the autonomy they had gained and had resisted sharing their prerogatives with the centre. Lengthy talks were inevitable, but time was pressing. Leaving the authorities toothless bordered on irresponsibility. The only way out was to ask for temporary additional powers.

Meanwhile the situation continued to heat up in the Russian Supreme Soviet. Speeches in favour of the 500-day programme took on a tone of ultimatum, even to the point of calling for strikes if it were not approved by the Union. Towards the evening of 16 October Yeltsin took the floor. His confrontational speech was full of unfounded accusations: that the centre took a hard line towards the republics, that it desired to limit the sovereignty of the Russian Federation and to undermine the transition to a market economy, and to preserve the supremacy of the command-administrative system. Not content with absurd accusations of sabotage (although it was not quite clear whom he was accusing), he presented what could only be described as an ultimatum: either accept his demands or divide power, property and armed forces. His speech was full of thinly veiled calls for street demonstrations.

That very day, *Moskovskiye Novosti* printed an interview with Gavriil Popov, which shed some light on the nuts and bolts of decision-making by DemRossiya. The interview spoke of the tough steps that would be taken by the President of the Russian Federation if the 500-day programme were not adopted. As Chairman of the Moscow city council, Popov also threatened to resign. This was indeed a co-ordinated attack on the Kremlin, using every 'weapon'.

The next day I convened the Presidential Council. Yakovlev was absent – he was said to be in hospital. Bakatin interrupted a meeting of the board of the USSR Ministry of Internal Affairs to attend. Shatalin arrived at the end of the meeting, but did not participate in the discussion. Kryuchkov, Lukyanov and Revenko were in favour of a 'proper rebuke'. Shevardnadze and Medvedev, who also agreed that Yeltsin's speech was intended to provoke, took a more flexible position: we should answer the attack, but not get into a head-to-head battle. Eventually we decided to show restraint.

I should mention that Yeltsin's speech had a quite unexpected effect, directly opposite to what he had counted on. No street demonstrations or strikes followed. His decisive tone and threatening appearance produced bewilderment: why were passions being inflamed over this issue? Apparently this escapade did not even garner unanimous support in the Inter-Regional Group. The Russian Supreme Soviet, which met the next morning, continued its discussion of current issues as if nothing had happened.

The discussion of the 'Basic directives for the transition to a market economy' in the Union Parliament likewise went off calmly. The speeches by radical democrats were restrained and delivered in a conciliatory, even (it seemed to me) apologetic, tone. The draft of the programme was adopted immediately after my speech and, out of approximately 400 members of the USSR Supreme Soviet, only 12 deputies voted against the programme, with 26 abstentions.

ECONOMICS – HOSTAGE OF POLITICS?

The voting on the 'Basic directives' seemed to reflect better understanding between deputies who held different positions. But neither side was very satisfied with the results. The prestige of the government was undermined. The radical press portrayed it as a reactionary obstacle to the salvation promised by the market. The government itself assumed the pose of the injured party, declaring the prime cause of the economic mess in the country to be political anarchy, the fault of the opposition and the political leadership: in other words, the President.

A further deterioration of relations between the Union and the Russian leadership was one of the costs of the battle over the market programme. The Russian leadership used the fact that the 500-day programme had not been adopted as one more argument in favour of forcing the pace of Russia's movement towards sovereignty. The leaders of some of the other republics increasingly followed Russia's example.

Implementation of the programme we had adopted required constructive relations with the republics, the reorganization and strengthening of presidential authority, and the promotion of new people. At a gloomy session of the Presidential Council on 31 October, I called for a dialogue with the opposition and for an understanding with the Russian leadership and the republics.

On 2 November the Council of the Federation examined closely the draft Union Treaty and ordered that its drafting should be speeded up. At a session of the Presidential Council three days later, we discussed draft measures for the transition to a market economy. Again debate on the general political situation flared up.

In answer to Ryzhkov's assertion that the economic problems were engendered by the weakening of power due to the actions of the opposition and the republics, and his hints at the indecisiveness of the higher political leadership, Yakovlev declared that the main source of the problems lay not in policies, but rather in the poor state of the economy and its management and the delay of economic reforms. Medvedev also criticized the government. 'This is plain folly,' he declared, 'speeding up expensive social programmes while closing our eyes to the unbridled growth of monetary incomes when an absolute decrease of production has begun.' Ryzhkov and Maslyukov both reacted heatedly.

Strain among the leadership was tremendous, and vacillation and hesitation began even in my inner circle. Yakovlev, who was unhappy that I had refused to give unqualified support to the 500-day programme, adopted a pose full of meaning, expressing his disagreement with my actions towards the opposition, towards the Party and its leadership structures, and with my policy of preserving a renewed Union of republics. Shevardnadze was upset by increasingly frequent attacks on our foreign policy from fundamentalists and 'the colonels' – people's deputies from the armed forces.

I decided to try a frank discussion with Yeltsin. It was a difficult meeting; Yeltsin complained of 'neglect of the interests of Russia', 'infringement of the rights of the Russian authorities' and so forth. In turn, I said that as a result of his attempts to weaken and undermine the Union, to 'pull all the covers over himself', we had reached a stage beyond which collapse of the country would begin.

I proposed that Yeltsin should declare clearly and unequivocally that he was in favour of preserving the Union of republics as a single state, and that he should switch the emphasis from a one-sided stress on the sovereignty of the republics to the need to preserve and renew the Union. After all, the disintegration of the state would be difficult to stop at the borders of the Russian Federation. 'The sovereignty fever is beginning to affect the autonomous republics as well,' I said. 'The suspicion that we want to urge them into a fight with the Union republics is ridiculous. We occupy a position of principle both with regard to the Union and the unity of the Russian Federation. They are inseparably linked.'

We also discussed other subjects, including matters related to the market. Generally speaking, in spite of the sharpness of the discussion, it eased tension somewhat in the relations between the Union centre and Russia. However, at this point I was attacked by the Soyuz group of people's deputies. Essentially,

503

this group served as a legal parliamentary cover for the intra-Party conservative opposition. On 14 November, at the opening of the session of the USSR Supreme Soviet, the deputies refused to discuss the agenda and instead debated current affairs. In harsh, nearly hysterical speeches they criticized the situation in the country and the actions of the government and President. A continuing theme of the speeches was resentment that the USSR Supreme Soviet was not being taken seriously and that the President was allegedly circumventing it and solving problems in the Presidential Council, the Council of the Federation, and back-room meetings with Yeltsin. Eventually, the delegates decided to invite the President for a general political discussion.

On 16 November I spoke to the deputies, giving my analyses and proposals. However, this did not calm things down. The discussion went haywire. The deputies savaged not only the government but also the President. In the fierce criticism one could perceive a merging of extremes – the fundamentalists and the radicals.

Immediately afterwards Nazarbayev, Karimov, and all the other republican leaders except Yeltsin came to see me in a room next to the auditorium in which the sessions were held. They considered it necessary to take immediate and decisive steps, otherwise the situation threatened to get out of control. First of all, they felt that it was important to strengthen presidential authority and the mechanism for more effective interaction with the republics. In this regard our thoughts coincided. Nazarbayev and the others proceeded to formulate their own proposals. I went back to my office to prepare for the morning speech.

I had to use drafts on the reorganization of the supreme authority of the country, which were already on paper and, moreover, had been tested in working conferences, sessions of the Presidential Council and the Council of the Federation and, in particular, in the discussion of the draft Union Treaty. This included reorganization of the government, its conversion to a Cabinet of Ministers operating under the direct guidance of the President, strengthening the role of the Council of the Federation, giving it a more precise official status, creation of a Security Council, and the dissolution of the Presidential Council.

I finished the speech at four a.m. I phoned Ryzhkov in the morning and briefly told him what changes I would propose affecting the status of the government. In principle, these were not new to him. Nikolai Ivanovich himself had raised the issue of the reorganization of executive power.

The USSR Supreme Soviet meeting opened in the morning with my speech. It lasted only twenty minutes, but the reaction was completely different from the one only two days earlier. Indeed the response to the proposals I advanced came in the form of general and, I am convinced, sincere applause. It was an interesting phenomenon – such a sharp change from total rejection to warm support. I believe that the deputies were starting to recognize the impending danger of chaos in the country, with its unforeseen and unpredictable results. The conservative deputies saw that the Union was being preserved and unified presidential power even strengthened. They had achieved something, while enjoying the opportunity to criticize the President. At the same time, they saw that things might go too far if the radical democrats succeeded in bringing down the government and undermining the centre. Of course, they would like to have achieved more, to have changed our policy, and to have forced me to abandon the economic and political reforms. But they seemed to understand that this was beyond their reach.

The radical democrats – at least those who were capable of interpreting the developments without prejudice – had to realize that I had resolved to move the reforms forward. They too sensed that they had achieved something, though their main goal – bringing down the government – had not been attained. Still, this would be a different government now and they could fight to have a say in government policies.

The representatives of the republics likewise seemed to recognize that criticism of the centre was just at the point beyond which a backlash would occur, with unpredictable results. Moreover, in my proposals the role of the republics in the Union system was increased.

To sum up, the proposals that I introduced and that were warmly approved by the USSR Supreme Soviet eased the tension in the nation and in the political leadership. However, this did not eliminate the deep contradictions in the positions of the main socio-political forces, which were quick to show up in the IVth Congress of People's Deputies. One need only recall the surprise sprung by the Soyuz group of deputies when the Congress opened on 17 December. I have in mind the 'absolutely spontaneous' speech by Umalatova proposing that the first item on the agenda should be a vote of confidence in the President. The vote was rather curious – among the 400 deputies who voted to place the item on the agenda were the extreme wings of both the Inter-Regional Group and the Soyuz faction. Yeltsin, Popov, Stankevich and many of their supporters voted against.

There was heated discussion both of my speech about the current state of affairs and of the amendments to the Constitution connected with changes in the structure of state institutions. Shevardnadze stunned everyone by dramatically announcing his resignation, supposedly because of the threat of an approaching dictatorship. He had not consulted me beforehand. Then there was a harsh battle over the adoption of the resolution on the general concept of a new Union Treaty, which ended in a roll-call vote on the preservation of the USSR as a renewed federation of equal sovereign republics. I proposed that the Congress should pass a resolution to hold a referendum, which, as the reader may know, took place on 17 March 1991.

To some degree the political events of November and December held back the implementation of 'Basic directives'. The government was not able to give its full attention to these questions, since everyone realized that the composition of government would be altered. The impending formation of a Cabinet of Ministers led me to discuss its functions, structure and even composition with my colleagues.

It goes without saying that the most difficult question was who would be the next Prime Minister. I did not discuss this issue with Ryzhkov at the Congress, although his behaviour and his remarks suggested that he did not intend to claim this position. It would have been impossible to get the Council of the Federation to concur in his reappointment, as was required by the amended constitution. However, the matter was dropped when Ryzhkov suffered a massive heart attack, which put him out of commission for a long time.

Both preliminary soundings and discussion in the Council of the Federation revealed that V. S. Pavlov was the preferred candidate to succeed Ryzhkov. The fact that he was a professional in financial affairs played an important role. The Cabinet needed exactly this kind of leader when the President was vested with executive power. People were familiar with Pavlov, and the leaders of the republics knew him, which was also appealing: after all, the Premier would have to work primarily with these leaders. Ryzhkov, whom I visited in hospital, and Maslyukov both supported this choice. Yeltsin was not enthusiastic about Pavlov, but said he would not object.

There were also certain doubts, especially among my close colleagues. Pavlov's political views were unclear. He was not independent enough and was easily influenced. Someone mentioned that at times he was impulsive and failed to think through his actions and statements. Ryzhkov said he had heard rumours that the Minister of Finance had a certain weakness for alcohol. I believe I overestimated Pavlov's positive qualities, and failed to pay enough attention to indications that he possessed negative qualities as well.

On 11 January I signed the decree on the Prime Minister and the First Deputy Ministers, and on 14 January they were approved by the USSR Supreme Soviet. In the next few days the Supreme Soviet approved new heads of the 'power' ministries,[1] the Ministry of Foreign Affairs, and other ministries. The Cabinet was put together. This was the first government formed on the basis of proposals by the President co-ordinated with the Council of the Federation.

WHAT BECAME OF PAVLOV'S CABINET

Formation of the Cabinet took up a few more weeks. Some time was needed to form the USSR Security Council, and for a reshuffle in the presidential administration. I took every step I

---

[1] Ministry of Internal Affairs, KGB, Ministry of Defence.

could to prevent problems in government. However, the discord and lack of co-ordination caused by the republics' claims to sovereignty and the disruption of economic ties were already having their inevitable effect – in January–February 1991 produced national income fell 10 per cent compared with the same period in 1990, industrial production fell by 4.5 per cent and procurement of meat products fell by 13 per cent. The slump embraced not only the means of production but also the production of consumer goods, which in recent years had been steadily growing. The economy was rapidly sinking into crisis.

This crisis was probably unavoidable. However, the fact that it became so severe resulted not just from objective factors, but also from the inadequacy of our actions and our mistakes in economic policy and management.

The rapid expansion of monetary incomes was not curtailed (in January–February 1991 personal incomes increased 19 per cent compared with the same period of 1990) – while production was declining, even in the consumer sector. A state of market imbalance prevailed. Hidden inflation grew. The country's budget was falling to pieces. Russia, and following Russia the other republics, began to operate a one-channel system of taxation for the Union budget.

At the end of 1990 I signed several decrees proposed by the government on financial matters, which, it turned out, contained serious flaws. For example, one of the decrees set up non-budget funds for the stabilization of the economy. Essentially, they were 'generating' money from nothing. The money did not represent real value and for this reason intensified inflation.

On 20 January, only a few days after he had been approved as Prime Minister, Pavlov implemented yet another half-baked idea that caused a stormy public response – the exchange of 50- and 100-ruble notes for new ones.[1] The argument behind this measure was that a large quantity of such notes were in the hands of speculators, criminals in the black economy, or abroad. However, such calculations proved illusory. Trying to find some justifica-

[1] Only a limited number of old notes could be exchanged for new ones within a certain period.

tion for this generally fruitless though dramatic operation, the Prime Minister, in a mid-February interview for *Trud*, made the sensational announcement that there was a conspiracy among foreign banks intended to upset monetary circulation in the USSR.

Initially, I had done everything I could to support Pavlov. However, I started to have some doubts about his professional expertise, and I became more and more convinced that we had made a mistake.

One of the most urgent tasks was retail price reform, which could no longer be delayed. We had allowed the most favourable period for this (1988–90) to slip through our hands, and now the reform had to be carried out under increasingly difficult conditions. Strictly speaking, the transition to the new price system had already begun – new procurement prices had been introduced for grain and meat and new wholesale price lists operated in industry. The new retail prices had to be put into effect urgently, in order to take the pressure off enterprises producing finished goods. The entire chain of economic circulation slowed. Alarming signals reached me, warning of calamity.

At the same time, the Cabinet of Ministers needed at least a few weeks to prepare considered decisions. A mistake here would have been highly dangerous. Current events also had an effect. The events in Lithuania in January,[1] Yeltsin's demands for my resignation, the referendum of 17 March – all these forced us to put off the price reform.

One more stumbling-block had to be removed before we could carry out price reform – the consent of the republics. This problem was discussed on 12 February in the Council of the Federation, where the members reached a unanimous opinion – we had to act immediately, rapidly and in concert. Talks began with the republics on basic principles and parameters for raising retail prices, issues of social security, and the formation of a common Union-republic people's support fund. The problem was that there was a discrepancy between income from higher

---

[1] On 11–12 January 1991 troops had attacked the TV tower in Vilnius, leaving fifteen dead.

prices and expenditure on social security in the republics because of differences in their economic structure. Nine republics had to contribute about 80 billion rubles to this fund, including 56 billion from Russia, while six republics were to be given 16 billion in compensation. In addition, 66 billion rubles were to be allotted to pay workers employed in the general state systems. The negotiations were difficult. The Baltic republics refused altogether to sign an accord and began to act on their own.

Some problems also came up with Russia. Specific formulae had been agreed and the agreement was signed by Khasbulatov and Silayev – undoubtedly, both with the concurrence of Yeltsin. Suddenly, however, Yeltsin began to disavow the agreement, on the grounds that the reform did not meet Russia's interests. Probably one of his advisers had suggested this action. The agreement was signed by all the supreme officials in the republics, except for Yeltsin – it was eventually signed by Yeltsin's deputy. The Cabinet of Ministers adopted the decision on 19 March, and in the next few days published extensive materials on this issue.

Just what were the results of the price reform that had taken so long to implement? The market normalized somewhat. Meat, milk, pastries and many other consumer goods returned to the shop shelves, which had emptied in the preceding period. It is true that this stabilization was shaky and unstable. One must keep in mind that the central government no longer had sufficient control over the economic situation or the necessary financial levers, which to a large degree had passed into the hands of the republics. It was unable to establish any real control over the unrestrained increase of monetary income or the expenditure of the income obtained from increased prices.

The republics failed to transfer money to the people's social support fund or to the non-budget economic stabilization fund. It was not just a matter of unwillingness on the part of the republican authorities. Their enterprises and organizations had spent a significant portion of this money on unforeseen wage increases. Everyone was beginning to act on his own, which threatened to jeopardize any attempts at centralized regulation.

It must be noted that the reform did not have anything in common with the 'shock therapy'. The existing prices for medicines, certain kinds of fabric, shoes, knitwear, toys, petrol, paraffin, electricity, gas, coal and vodka were unchanged. Ceilings for price increases were established for a large group of basic consumer goods. The numbers of goods that were sold to the public at regulated retail and (free) contracted prices[1] expanded significantly (by mid-1991 up to 40 per cent of goods were sold at free market prices). This promoted the future transition to free prices. The country could have avoided freeing prices all at once if these measures to improve the financial and monetary situation had been carried out consistently.

Perhaps the chief shortcoming of the price reform of 1991 was that it had been developed and implemented outside the overall context of economic transformation. Pavlov's attitude did not help. There were no grounds to complain about his lack of activity. He started many things, but he acted impulsively, haphazardly, unsystematically. This was why, back in February, I had raised the question of the need for the government to work out a 'minimum programme' – in fact, an anti-crisis programme.

The reader should take into account that at this time every step in the improvement of the economy was achieved only by enormous political effort. Behind it all was the struggle for power.

The experience of the last few months and weeks had shown that problems could not be solved by methods of confrontation, pressure and ultimatums. Such actions only aggravated the situation, increasing the danger of the disintegration of the country, of plunging it into the abyss of internecine strife. I emphasized in a session of the Council of the Federation that nothing was more important than stopping the process of disintegration. Work on the anti-crisis programme accelerated, particularly with the launching of the Novo-Ogarevo process.[2] The republics, too, participated actively and, in spite of serious difficulties, the task was successfully completed. On 5 July I approved the anti-crisis programme.

[1] Prices agreed and confirmed by contract.

[2] On 23 April 1991 a meeting of the President of the USSR and the leaders of nine republics was held at Novo-Ogarevo, near Moscow, to discuss the situation in the country. The participants issued a statement favouring the immediate preparation of a new Union Treaty. The meeting marked the start of the Novo-Ogarevo process, leading to a new Union of Sovereign States (*see Part IV*).

THE JUNE 'DÉMARCHE'

A great scandal erupted in the USSR Supreme Soviet during the final stage of the work on the anti-crisis programme provoked by the irresponsible behaviour of Pavlov and the 'power ministers'. Pavlov declared that the Cabinet did not have the right to resolve pressing problems on an urgent or immediate basis. He requested therefore that the government be granted the right, for 1991, of legislative initiative and a wide-ranging authority to make decisions. He added that granting such powers would not mean that the Cabinet of Ministers was no longer under the control of the organs of legislative and presidential power. The Cabinet would immediately inform the USSR Supreme Soviet or the President of its decisions.

The delegates showered him with questions, asking: 'Why do you need such powers when the President, under whose guidance you work, already has them?' 'Does this proposal come from the Cabinet of Ministers or have you co-ordinated this with the President?' 'What does the President think about your demanding this authority – does this reflect your disagreements with the President?'

Passions heated up even more after a speech by Kucherenko, the chairman of the planning and budget commission, which was delivered in dramatic tones, bordering on panic. It seemed that this was what the hawks from the Soyuz group were waiting for. One after the other they stepped up to the podium. They sensed that it was now possible to resume 'playing the old record', one that they had not been able to play for some time, now that the Prime Minister and the President were at loggerheads. Lukyanov poured oil on the fire with his dubious comment that 'we must separate the administrative activity of the Cabinet of Ministers from the activity of the President himself and his decrees.'

The discussion was not limited to economic problems and quickly spilled over into politics. Blokhin demanded to hear an account from the heads of the power ministries, saying there had been a preliminary agreement about this. Lukyanov hastened to say that no such proposals had been submitted, but if there were questions, the ministers were present and could answer. The delegates agreed that this should happen in the afternoon in a closed session of the Supreme Soviet.

However, at four p.m., when the session began, these ministers delivered lengthy and thoroughly prepared speeches, especially Kryuchkov. It was then that he launched the phrase 'agents of influence', trying to frighten the deputies with the spectre of massive pressure from Western intelligence services. No speech by the KGB chairman ever omitted this theme.

How did the democratic wing feel and act? The radicals felt a certain degree of sweet satisfaction that the President was again being pushed and knocked about. Most of them preferred to stay silent. However, some, although timidly, spoke out against granting additional powers to the Prime Minister. Ryabchenko, Lubenchenko and Yudin took a clearer stand against granting emergency powers to the government.

The democrats did not wake up to what was happening until the power ministers had spoken. However, the reaction of their leaders was quite unique; instead of declaring themselves openly in the Parliament, they preferred to contact the American leadership through closed channels. Not until two years after these events did we learn, from an article published by Gavriil Popov, about his hurried meeting with the US Ambassador Jack Matlock, and the transmission through him of a warning (apparently intended for Yeltsin, who at the time was in the USA) that reactionary forces were conspiring in Moscow. Moreover, the information contained the clear hint that these events were taking place with the knowledge, and, moreover, practically according to the scenario and under the guidance, of Gorbachev himself. It goes without saying that this information was intended mainly for Bush, who according to Popov then forestalled this conspiracy.

I was not present at that ill-fated Supreme Soviet session of 17 June. I had not attached much importance to the Prime Minister's speech and had not been informed of his intention to raise the issue of additional powers for the Cabinet. In the morning I was participating in the work of the founding Congress of the Peasants' Union and in the afternoon I chaired the session of the preparatory committee, at which the draft Union Treaty was to be signed in order to send it to the USSR Supreme Soviet and the Supreme Soviets of the republics. I had discussed this the day before with Lukyanov and he conveyed the substance of our talk to the deputies, noting that in the next few days Gorbachev would find the time to attend the Supreme Soviet session.

In the evening I had a stern talk with Yanayev, Pavlov and Lukyanov on the mess that they had created. Pavlov admitted his mistakes, with the excuse that he had raised these questions a number of times in conversation with me. He also attributed his behaviour to the fact that he was upset by the collapse of the economy, the budget and the tax system, and that everything was slipping out of his hands, although he himself in his speech had assured the deputies that the government was in control of the situation.

I drew Yanayev's attention to his passiveness in the Supreme Soviet. Unfortunately, at that time I could not say anything definite to Lukyanov, since I was not yet aware of the nuances in his comments and remarks. Only a subsequent close reading of the verbatim record made it clear to me that he was playing a double game.

Somehow I had to put an end to this scandal. On 21 June, when the Supreme Soviet met at its next session, I spoke and explained what had happened. The Prime Minister did not look his best, but I did not want to aggravate the situation. I did not try to justify his démarche, but neither did I raise the question of any censure.

Just how should we analyse what happened in the USSR Supreme Soviet between 11 and 21 June? Of course this was a renewed attack on the President and his policy from revanchist forces. It is also clear that Lukyanov sympathized with the Soyuz group, in reality encouraging their attacks on presidential policy. From everything that happened I sensed that the Soyuz group's speeches and its tactics were co-ordinated and well thought out.

The attack by the revanchists was beaten back. However, this incident aggravated the situation in the country. We were already up to our knees in fuel. All that was needed was a spark for everything to explode.

PART III

THE CHANGING SOVIET UNION
AND THE WORLD

18

NEW THINKING IN FOREIGN POLICY

THERE IS PROBABLY NO NEED TO PROVE THAT PERESTROIKA AND the fundamental reform of both our economic and political systems would have been impossible without the corresponding changes in Soviet foreign policy and the creation of propitious international conditions. As a first step, we had at least to clear up the 'snow-drifts' left over from Cold War times and to alleviate the pressure that had borne down on us due to our involvement in conflicts all over the world and in the debilitating arms race. We had to understand that 'we couldn't go on living like this', both inside our country and in world politics. This understanding was the starting-point for everything. And one should not imagine it as a 'sudden revelation': a number of factors had convinced me of the need for a serious re-examination of our foreign policy even before my election as General Secretary. I won't claim that I entered my new office with a detailed action plan in my briefcase, but I had a pretty clear idea of the first steps to be taken. Thus perestroika began simultaneously in domestic and foreign policies, success in one area encouraging progress in the other, set-backs slowing down progress in both.

But the General Secretary, however decisive his views and intentions, could not make the foreign policy alone, especially as what I had in mind was not simply cosmetic changes, but practically a U-turn. I had to convince the country's collective leadership of the need for change. And the problem did not end there. The international agencies of the Central Committee, the Ministry of Foreign Affairs, the KGB and the foreign trade

517

organizations were, as a rule, at least as conservative and ideo-
logically 'drilled' as most of the bureaucrats in our domestic
administration. However, one must say that quite a few of our
international analysts and experts supported the idea of change in
foreign policy. One of my main tasks therefore became the
promotion of these people to leading positions in foreign affairs.

Still, changes were far too slow. The XXVIIth Party Congress
had adopted a number of decisions, we had worked out a plan of
progress towards a nuclear-free world and replaced a number
of the cadres, but the diplomatic wagon train was moving slowly
along the same old beaten track. Our diplomatic style was toughness for toughness' sake. The main thing was to demonstrate an
unyielding spirit and an attitude of arrogant pride which was justified neither by political nor practical considerations.

In late May 1986, we discussed the new role of Soviet diplomacy at a conference held at the Ministry of Foreign Affairs. We
had invited all the ambassadors and Moscow's 'diplomatic elite'
to attend this meeting. The Minister of Foreign Affairs made a
speech which was then discussed by the participants, and I later
addressed the conference. The gist of my speech was the lagging
behind of our international agencies, which did not keep up with
the policies and practical steps undertaken by the country's political leadership. Today I consider this meeting the starting-point
for the full-scale implementation of our 'new thinking'.

It is hard to say how the international situation might have
evolved after this initiative, since the steps we took to carry out
our new policy were met by a wall of prejudice and refusal in the
political centres of the West. But in the end Western politicians
yielded to pressure from the general public, who understood that
the world was on the brink of a catastrophe, and that we could not
allow this to continue.

Some philosopher has said that the most important virtue is not
sympathy or compassion, but understanding. I wanted to be
understood, and expressed my views on the necessary changes in
the book *Perestroika: New Thinking for Our Country and the
World*. There I defined the theoretical principles on which, in my
eyes, the new world order – which was to supersede the post-war
order – had to be based: interdependence of countries and nations,

the balance of interests, freedom of choice, common responsibility and the finding of universally accepted solutions for today's global problems.

We realized that it was vitally important to correct the distorted ideas we had about other nations. These misconceptions had made us oppose the rest of the world for many decades, which had negative effects on our economy as well as on the public consciousness, science, culture and the intellectual potential of our country.

We understood that in today's world of mutual interdependence, progress is unthinkable for any society which is fenced off from the world by impenetrable state frontiers and ideological barriers. A country can develop its full potential only by interacting with other societies, yet without giving up its own identity.

We realized that we could not ensure our country's security without reckoning with the interests of other countries, and that, in our nuclear age, you could not build a safe security system based solely on military means. This prompted us to propose an entirely new concept of global security, which included all aspects of international relations, including the human dimension.

All these ideas are widely known today. They have been repeated millions of times in speeches, articles and scientific monographs. But at that time, they did not gain easy acceptance – neither in our country nor abroad – and each attempt to put them into practice was an arduous undertaking, indeed. Take for example the proposal I made on 15 January 1986 to abolish nuclear weapons. It was met with mistrust and jeering, as just another propaganda trick from the traditional Soviet 'struggle for peace' act. Only a few believed at the time that in a period of but a few years we would be able to make real progress on the road towards nuclear disarmament, put an end to the Cold War, cross the moat separating East from West and untie – rather than cut – other international 'Gordian knots'.

The most difficult one to untie was undoubtedly the military rivalry between the superpowers. I and my associates in foreign affairs all shared the view that we must first deal with the United States. America is the acknowledged leader of the Western world; without its consent, any attempt to change East-West relations was bound to fail, and might even be regarded as 'intrigue', 'trying to drive a wedge into the Western alliance' etc. Our task was by no means easy: we had to find common ground not with a social democrat like Olof Palme or a socialist like François Mitterrand, but with Ronald Reagan, who had called the Soviet Union 'the evil empire' and was under propaganda fire from us for his 'Reaganomics', the invasion of Grenada and similar unseemly acts.

After extended negotiations Reagan and I eventually agreed to meet in Geneva in the autumn of 1985. The last summit meeting between American and Soviet heads of state had taken place six and a half years before, in the summer of 1979. The international situation was heated to the limit, the powerful NATO and Warsaw Pact groupings had fenced themselves behind palisades of nuclear missiles, and people all over the world were full of anxiety. Small wonder that the whole world focused on the Geneva summit meeting, which was covered by 3,500 journalists.

We viewed the Geneva meeting realistically, without grand expectations, yet we hoped to lay the foundations for a serious dialogue in the future. It was important that the leaders of the superpowers should have a chance to get a close look at each other, to share their views on the world and the role their countries played in it, and discuss options to ease tension and normalize co-operation. I learned later that the Americans wanted to see for themselves whether Mrs Thatcher was right in praising me as a man 'you can do business with'. I think this was the main thing that interested them – a perfectly understandable objective for a first meeting.

According to long-time practice, the Politburo drew up, discussed and adopted in advance instructions for the General Secretary. I participated in these preparations, together with Foreign Ministry officials, the Central Committee international department, and the KGB. Obviously, there could be different types of instructions. For a simple exchange of views, they would be limited to a list of viewpoints to be made clear to the other side at the meeting, and several instructions were designed to probe his thinking on the issues under discussion. For concrete negoti-ations, the directives would precisely delineate our proposals and how far we could go. I mention this because of the number of superficial and incompetent judgements, some of them completely false, that the General Secretary allegedly decided everything for himself and made unjustified concessions etc.

Besides the main guidelines, some fallback positions were drawn up to be kept in reserve and used only if all else failed to achieve a reasonable compromise. If no agreement could be reached and the issue had to be postponed for further discussion later, it was generally agreed that each side should do a supplementary analysis of the question. Let me illustrate this by a particularly controversial example, which raised most speculation – the reduction of nuclear and conventional weapons.

The agencies set out by drawing up draft proposals. In the first years the Foreign Ministry played the co-ordinating role at this initial stage. Later a special Politburo commission was created with the task of co-ordinating the decision-making process once the agencies had presented their draft instructions or final documents. The commission heard the Foreign Ministry, the Ministry of Defence, scientific institutes, Gosplan, the Council of Ministers' military-industrial committee, and major specialists and experts (including academicians), trying to find a reasonable compromise between their inevitable disagreements. The General Secretary, and later the President of the USSR, was kept informed on the most important conclusions and questions that remained open. It was usually Zaikov and Shevardnadze who would brief me, sometimes joined by Yazov or Akhromeyev, Chebrikov or Kryuchkov. We would have regular discussions of this kind even before the scheduled Politburo meeting.

After a series of consultations, a version was finally agreed that took into account my directives. This version was submitted to the Politburo together with the other opinions. Politburo members were thus informed about the discussion and had the opportunity to study alternative viewpoints.

Zaikov chaired the Politburo commission over many years. There are two aspects to arms issues – the military purpose of a certain weapon and its production. Lev Nikolaevich was familiar

with both. He had vast experience in the field of military production and extensive technical knowledge, and he was nobody's
fool. In addition to being a qualified expert, he was a deal-maker
who would always try to harmonize the diverging suggestions.
He could cool down any heated argument, mediate in conflicts
between agencies and prevent the Ministry of Foreign Affairs
from taking rash decisions on highly specialized issues. At the
same time, he could also pressure the Defence Ministry by
exposing the conservatism and parochialism of the military-
industrial complex. Incidentally, although the Defence Ministry
was well aware of the price the arms race exacted from the
country, in all the years of my work in Moscow they never made
any suggestions for cuts in defence spending.

The passionate Caucasian Shevardnadze often lost his temper
with the Defence Ministry officials during work on major arms-
control initiatives. He would come to my office and declare: 'I
can't work with these people any more!' I would try to calm him
down and ask Zaikov to mediate. Whenever I realized that things
had gone too far in their dispute, I played mediator myself. On
such occasions, I invited Shevardnadze together with Defence
Minister Sokolov, later Yazov and Akhromeyev or Moiseyev,[1] to
my office. We would discuss and sort out everything together.

Obviously, it was the Politburo's and the General Secretary's
prerogative to set the basic course on questions of principle and
decide the positions which would correspond both to Soviet interests and to the realities of world politics. Hence decision-making
was a thorough and collective job. We had prepared a significant
number of ideas and specific suggestions for the summit with the
American President, and the meeting could therefore raise
the curtain on the process of resolving the most acute problem
of the day – nuclear disarmament. In Geneva, we spent a total of
some fifteen hours in negotiations and other meetings. I met
President Reagan in private on five or six occasions, each time
exceeding the time-limit set by our schedule. This fact alone
shows that our conversations were not simply guided by protocol,
when the partners look at their watches more than they do at each

---

[1] Chief of the General Staff.

other. On the contrary, our dialogue was very constructive and intensive, sometimes even emotional. But what is more important, it was frank, and increasingly friendly the better we got to know each other. Tempers became heated whenever we touched upon topics such as human rights, regional conflicts and the notorious Strategic Defense Initiative (SDI). Nonetheless, I realized by the end of our two-day meeting that Ronald Reagan too was a man 'you could do business with'.

But let us start at the beginning. On the morning of the first day, we had a private meeting which lasted over an hour instead of the scheduled fifteen minutes. As I reread the minutes, I am amazed at the extremely ideological stands taken by both partners. In retrospect, they read more like the 'No. 1 Communist' and the 'No. 1 Imperialist' trying to out-argue each other, rather than a business-like talk between the leaders of the two superpowers. I myself spent time trying to fend off accusations of human rights abuses, even though I was not always convinced that these were not justified. For his part Ronald Reagan was busy warding off my judgements on the role of the military-industrial complex in American politics and the existence of a powerful propaganda machine directed against the USSR. To top it all, we traded accusations of responsibility for the mad arms race which had led the world to the brink of a catastrophe.

We were both right and wrong at the same time. Both countries shared responsibility for splitting up the world into two blocs and fomenting the threat of war, as well as for the extreme tension that prevailed in Soviet-American relations. Yet neither of us was ready to admit this then at the Geneva summit. Nonetheless, we had a frank, meaningful conversation from the start. Incidentally, I also mentioned – as a general remark – that we did not intend to remain in Afghanistan and supported a political solution to the Afghan conflict.

The first round of talks showed the extent and sharpness of the existing antagonism, mutual mistrust and 'political deafness'. This impression was reinforced when we set out to discuss regional conflicts. President Reagan dwelt at length on our alleged interference in Third World affairs, deploring the negative effect this had on the already strained relations between

Washington and Moscow. The gist of my reply, which I gave at a broader meeting with our delegations, was that we only helped other nations to attain their freedom, without planning to establish any military bases or to 'export revolution' – and that our actions were in many ways similar to those undertaken by the United States in what they considered their areas of vital interest, which covered practically the entire world.

We had lunch at our residence, and I shared my impressions of my tête-à-tête with Reagan with my colleagues. Reagan appeared to me not simply a conservative, but a political 'dinosaur'. We agreed that we must take a firm stand in the talks but at the same time stick to our principal objective, without missing the slightest opportunity to achieve a breakthrough towards reasonable solutions.

I returned after lunch to the villa on the lake which the Americans had rented for the negotiations. The topic was arms control. My partner was eager for action – I later learned that the American strategy consisted of being the first to set forth their prepared positions in order to make us play their game. He proposed significant cuts in offensive weapons and a simultaneous transition to defensive weapon systems. With righteous indignation, President Reagan tore apart the American policy of deterrence, which had triggered the arms race and led mankind to the brink of destruction. He concluded his proposals by claiming that the Soviet Union had no reason to fear SDI. He tried very hard to get his point across, suggesting 'open labs' and promising to share the technology with us once it was ready for use.

Ronald Reagan's advocacy of the Strategic Defense Initiative struck me as bizarre. Was it science fiction, a trick to make the Soviet Union more forthcoming, or merely a crude attempt to lull us in order to carry out the mad enterprise – the creation of a shield which would allow a first strike without fear of retaliation? Yet I had consulted scientists on the issue beforehand, and the volley of arguments President Reagan launched at me did not catch me unprepared. My answer was sharp and strong. I said that Mr Reagan's words simply proved that the Americans mistrusted us. Why should we trust them any more than they did us?

524

'SDI is the continuation of the arms race into a different, more dangerous sphere,' I continued. 'It will only foment mistrust and suspicion, with each side fearing the other is overtaking it. The Soviet Union strongly opposes an arms race in space. But if the Americans remain deaf to common-sense arguments and to our appeal to seek a way out of the arms race and reduce the existing nuclear stockpiles, we will have no choice but to accept the challenge.

'I think you should know that we have already developed a response. It will be effective and far less expensive than your project, and be ready for use in less time.'

Statesmen are not entitled to disclose everything they learned in office. Even today I cannot reveal certain facts to the reader. Still, I can assure you that we were not bluffing. Our studies had proved that the potential answer to SDI could meet the requirements I had mentioned.

'It looks like a dead end . . .' I concluded. An uneasy silence fell upon the room. The pause was becoming oppressive.

'How about taking a walk?' the American President suddenly asked.

'That seems like a good idea to me,' I replied.

We left the table and went out into the courtyard, accompanied by the interpreters. We strolled towards an outbuilding which housed the swimming pool. A fire was burning in the hearth of the adjoining 'living room', the small room we had entered. The walk, the change of scene, the crackling of burning wood – all these helped to alleviate the tension. But as soon as we sat down, Reagan rushed back to his old tactics. Seemingly anxious that I might take up SDI again – this time 'one on one' – he decided to anticipate my move by taking out a list of arms control proposals and handing them to me. As I understood it, the paper was not intended for discussion but, rather, for acceptance on a 'take it or leave it' basis. It was then to be sent to our negotiators as instructions.

It was a nine-point package, written in English and in Russian. The list included many issues we had already discussed without reaching any agreement. President Reagan stressed that the American side saw these suggestions as a package deal.

I read the list unhurriedly and replied that even on a first reading I noted points that were unacceptable to us. In the first place, the package deal would have allowed the United States to proceed with the SDI programme. We were going round in circles. The fire was burning and the room was warm and cosy, but the conversation had not improved the general mood. We went outside again and I suddenly felt very cold – maybe in contrast to the warmth by the fireside or to our heated discussion. At that point, the President unexpectedly invited me to visit the United States, and I reciprocated by inviting him to Moscow.

As it seems to me now, something important happened to each of us on that day, in spite of everything. I think there had been two factors at work – responsibility and intuition. I did not have this impression after lunch, and in the evening we were still clinging to our antagonistic positions. But the 'human factor' had quietly come into action. We both sensed that we must maintain contact and try to avoid a break. Somewhere in the back of our minds a glimmer of hope emerged that we could still come to an agreement.

The following day it was the Soviet delegation which acted as host for the talks. I greeted President Reagan at the entrance to the Soviet residence. We went upstairs, stopping occasionally for the photographers, and the negotiating teams were again left face to face. Everybody was in a somewhat better mood; we had become 'used' to each other, and the exchange of invitations on the day before had aroused expectations.

I had another private talk with the American President, this time about human rights. Ronald Reagan apparently hoped that discussing this controversial issue in private would ease the tension. I think he anticipated my reaction and wanted to avoid a possible confrontation in the presence of our teams.

However, his arguments were nothing new to me. The Americans had focused on the human rights issue even before our actual meeting, and they did not confine their actions to diplomatic channels alone but also worked through the media. Reagan began by saying that if the Soviet Union intended to improve its relations with the United States, it would do well to change its reputation with respect to individual freedom. He argued that the American public was very sensitive about this issue and that therefore no American politician could ignore it. I said that I did not think the United States had a right to impose their standards and way of life upon other countries.

We continued our conversation in the presence of the delegations. I told the American President and his colleagues that SDI stood in the way of a 50-per-cent cut in strategic arms, and that the American administration must do something about this if it wanted to reduce our nuclear stockpiles. Reagan stood his ground, but we did not yield either. The occasionally heated discussion dragged on, showing our irreconcilable differences. I suppose the American negotiating team asked itself the same question we did – how should we conclude the summit?

There was just one encouraging factor – neither side wanted the Geneva meeting to end without any tangible results. Such an outcome would have been seen as a personal failure by the leaders of the superpowers and disappointed the hopes that millions of ordinary people had set on our meeting. And the tried and tested stratagem of blaming any failure on the other side would have been of little or no avail this time. People expected as a minimum a joint communiqué that the talks would be resumed.

During our afternoon meeting we agreed to entrust Foreign Affairs Minister Shevardnadze and Secretary of State George Shultz with the task of finding a way to some kind of agreement. I spent the afternoon with the American President at the Soviet mission, waiting for results. By five p.m. it was clear that the remaining disagreements left little hope of a breakthrough. They parted to explore possible solutions within the delegations. Reagan and I instructed our colleagues to resume negotiations and to brief us in the evening on the progress achieved. I added, half-jokingly: 'I hope they won't ruin the evening.'

Parallel to the talks, there were also social events; we took turns acting as hosts for the other side. We had dinners together with our wives and the officials participating in the talks. In addition, it was agreed that the first ladies should meet for tea on two occasions. Raisa Maksimovna had brought drawings made by Soviet children – the winners of an international children's drawing contest in 1984. Many people went to see them at the Soviet mission; they were so full of spontaneous warmth and friend-liness. Raisa Maksimovna invited Nancy Reagan on a short excursion, from which both returned very pleased. Then both of them participated in the ceremony of laying the foundation stone for the Museum of the International Red Cross and Red Crescent. Raisa Maksimovna's programme also included visits to a farming family, to the World Health Organization, to the university and to a library.

After dinner at the house where they were staying in Geneva, Ronald and Nancy Reagan again invited us to sit by the hearth, and we had a friendly conversation. The fireside had indeed a beneficial effect, warming the general atmosphere and tempering the harshness of some of our remarks. Heated exchanges were gradually giving way to a desire to understand each other.

From our first meeting, I had noticed President Reagan's dislike for detail. I was told that briefings put on Reagan's desk never exceeded two or three typewritten pages. Anything more extensive was rejected. In contrast, my desk was always piled high with briefings, files and drafts. I never used to read 'pre-digested' information, but I am not sure whether this was an advantage or a drawback. In our country, information for top officials was handled with an appalling lack of professionalism, which made you lose a lot of valuable time. There should be – just as in everything else – some 'golden mean' in these things.

President Reagan preferred discussing general politics; it helped us get to know each other better. Specific issues were relegated to the talks with the delegations in the presence of Shultz, Shevardnadze and others.

Meanwhile the experts were working at full speed. The whole world expected some sort of joint communiqué from us. The Americans spoke of two possible solutions: a joint document or separate declarations made by each side. We strongly advocated a joint document, considering anything else as a failure. People would not understand if the leaders of the two superpowers limited themselves to an exchange of views and separate declarations, having met for the first time after such a long interval.

The dinner given by the Reagans was nearing its end and still there was no document in sight. We left the table and went to a small adjacent living-room. Reagan and I sat down. When the negotiators finally arrived, Deputy Minister Kornienko started briefing us. George Shultz reacted heatedly and that sparked off an argument. Kornienko was virtually leaning over me and speaking in a harsh and extremely nervous tone. Shultz, usually calm and even-tempered, suddenly burst out: 'Mr General Secretary, you can now see for yourself how we work. How are we supposed to achieve anything in this way?'

President Reagan and I were quietly watching the scene. 'Let's put our foot down,' he suggested.

'Agreed,' I replied.

We separated and I went to discuss the problem with my colleagues. From Kornienko's tone and behaviour, I assumed that there must be some fundamental disagreement or serious threat to our interests. But from what Bessmertnykh was saying it became clear that they simply could not agree on the wording, and the problem was quickly taken care of.

What else? There were disagreements about resuming Aeroflot flights to the United States: our Ministry of Air Transport had raised some objection and this 'made a joint communiqué impossible'. I picked up the receiver and telephoned Minister Bugaev. He said that everything was going fine and that there were some minor problems which they were about to solve.

'Then go ahead and solve them,' I replied.

Was there anything else? Nothing. We had settled all the 'problems' in fifteen minutes.

The joint communiqué was thus ready by morning, in time for the closing ceremony of the summit meeting. The conference hall, adorned with the Soviet and American banners, was filled with journalists. Arriving from different directions, the American President and I walked towards each other and shook hands. Needless to say, this was a sight the whole world had hoped for after so many years of relentless ideological war.

We signed the joint communiqué. In this truly historic document the leaders of the two superpowers declared that 'nuclear war cannot be won and must never be fought'. Admitting this and implementing it in practice made meaningless the arms race and the stockpiling and modernizing of nuclear weapons.

'The parties will not seek military superiority.' This fundamental statement was not just a general phrase to soothe the public. The American President and I had already committed ourselves to giving the necessary instructions to the negotiating teams at the nuclear arms talks in Geneva.

Both parties declared their intention to improve bilateral relations – in particular, humanitarian exchanges and contact between our young people – and to resume air traffic between the two countries.

The President and I each gave a short address. I stressed that the summit meeting was too important an event to be judged by simplistic standards. It had shed light on our differences and allowed the overcoming – 'at least I hope so' – of some biased judgements about the Soviet Union and its policies.

'You cannot establish trust in one day; it is not an easy task. We highly value the assurances given by the American President that the United States does not strive for military superiority, and we expect these assurances to be followed by deeds.'

Reagan spoke about extending the political dialogue. He mentioned that we had each accepted invitations to visit the other country. Both countries would develop bilateral co-operation and sustain and extend consultation on regional problems. It had been a long time since any Soviet or American leader had expressed such proposals in such a cordial tone. Experienced observers were reluctant to take the risk of invoking a new era in Soviet-American relations and world politics in general – they had burned their fingers too often in the past. But everybody sensed that a breakthrough had been achieved.

What was the importance of the Geneva meeting for our own policy? I think one can say that we set to the tasks of defining our new priorities with increased energy. We prepared a policy statement containing a step-by-step programme for moving towards a nuclear-free world. This time we did not use the issue as a means of propaganda as had been done in the past. I did not meet any opposition within the Soviet leadership. Maybe some people concealed their doubts, and some cynics probably saw this as just another 'strong propagandist move' in the Cold War.

Eduard Shevardnadze devoted a lot of time and energy to the

preparation of this statement, which was published on 15 January 1986. We agreed on the necessity for such a step during a conversation we had soon after his appointment as Foreign Minister. By the autumn we had made a start – a scientific analysis of the international situation, contacts and meetings we had had in the past months. It was then that we decided to formulate our ideas and intentions in a long-term agenda which would serve as a basis for our 'peace offensive'.

During one of the preparatory meetings, the question arose of when we should come out with the statement. Initially I had intended to include it in my opening speech for the XXVIIth Party Congress; experience, or rather past stereotypes, told me not to waste significant ideas and to save them for the Congress, or at least for a plenary meeting or another such important event. But when we discussed the question we decided that to include the statement in the opening speech would reduce its importance as an independent move, while publishing it beforehand would still allow discussion of these major initiatives. What we had expected happened: the Party Congress supported both the theoretical basis of our new policy and the specific plan, which thus became a governmental action programme. Support for the plan shown by the Congress was not just another display of Party loyalty, a reminder of Stalinist times when any suggestion from the Central Committee was greeted with storms of applause and unanimously approved. It was a manifestation of the changing general mood – a first timid result of glasnost and democratization. Party politics basically remained the same, a lot was still governed by inertia, the old, rusty mechanisms serving the powers that be. But the people already felt the first signs of freedom.

THE SETBACK AFTER GENEVA

The general public throughout the world showed genuine interest in the 'new thinking' presented at the XXVIIth Party Congress. And our Statement of 15 January received an enthusiastic welcome. Foreign politicians reacted differently. A few cautious ones did not dismiss our initiative from the start and declared that it 'needed careful study'. But the majority viewed it with scepticism, and many branded it as just another Soviet propaganda trick. Top officials in Washington, who set the tone for the West, openly denounced our declaration. In addition to allegedly 'lacking seriousness', this move of ours was seen as a dangerous attempt to improve Moscow's prestige at the expense of Washington.

The Western governments resorted to their usual strategy of simply ignoring our initiative. To undermine the Soviet Union's peaceful policy, which was becoming increasingly popular, they provided new fuel for the ideological war. Again, it was Reagan who led anti-Communist hysteria, reiterating his attack on the 'evil empire'. No effort was spared to discredit our initiatives and to dismiss our genuine invitation to disarm as a utopian scheme. The tragedy of Chernobyl was exploited as an alleged proof that we had no intention of really 'opening up', that we remained treacherous and not to be trusted.

The Americans continued to proclaim in public their readiness for serious arms control negotiations, but in reality they were again undermining the talks and adopting new weapons programmes which sent the arms race spiralling ever upward.

Try as I would, I simply could not understand this behaviour. We had just come home from Geneva, where we had signed a highly promising joint communiqué – and now such a blunt repudiation of the commitments made there. Was President Reagan perhaps overruled by the powerful American military-industrial complex? Maybe his aides had got at him, hinting that he had yielded to Gorbachev's 'magnetism' in Geneva? Maybe he himself was suddenly seized by fear lest he had made too many 'concessions to the Soviets'? I finally arrived at the conviction that it was yet another attempt to provoke us and to make us deviate from the new course we had been pursuing since April 1985, returning to a policy of open confrontation. Right-wing circles in the West feared a renewed, dynamic and more democratic Soviet Union, offering peace and co-operation to other nations. Such an outcome did not conform with their strategies of the time.

I shared these views with my colleagues in the Soviet leadership, suggesting that we should not obstinately try to counter these provocations, which would only serve the purpose of the 'hawks', but must steadfastly continue our dialogue, pressing the West to reciprocate our moves. Everyone agreed that this was the right course to take. I had a meeting with an American congressional delegation led by Congress Speaker 'Tip' O'Neill. He avoided discussing the substance of the issues, saying that he did not have the authority to interfere in the policies of the American administration, but that he was prepared to listen to my arguments and convey them to President Reagan. I candidly told the American congressmen everything I felt, adding that I intended to inform our people how things stood.

I carried out my promise during a trip to Kuibyshev and Togliatti. In my speech in Togliatti, I mentioned that shortly after the Geneva summit there was a flare-up of anti-Sovietism in the United States, a campaign that did not shun insinuations and insults of all kinds. The Americans demanded that the Soviet Union reduce its diplomatic staff in New York by forty per cent. American warships approached the Crimean shores – a move openly sanctioned by the American leadership. The United States attacked Libya, in a demonstration of its might and impunity. On the last day of the unilateral moratorium on underground nuclear testing which the Soviet Union had declared, the Americans carried out a nuclear test in the Nevada Desert; the powerful explosion was obviously meant as a provocation. When I suggested an early meeting with President Reagan to discuss the issue of nuclear testing, Washington declined the offer.

The United States, I said, apparently believed that they were dealing with weak-kneed opponents. Did the Americans think we would not notice how they used the fledgling Soviet-American dialogue as a cover for new weapon programmes? Despite public pressure, Western European governments were meekly following suit, with European politicians suddenly arguing that it would be unwise to remove the American missiles because of the Soviet Union's superiority in conventional weapons – despite our January statement offering reductions in conventional weapons and troops. West European governments and financial circles were becoming involved in a dangerous project and were becoming accomplices in a new, even more deadly spiral of the arms race, I said in my speech. Détente or even a simple warming in Soviet-American relations did not conform with the interests of certain people in the West, who would use any pretext to undermine the improvement in international relations initiated in Geneva. Nevertheless, I emphasized that we intended to stick to the course set at the XXVIIth CPSU Congress.

REYKJAVIK: THE CONCEPT

I received a letter from Reagan during my holiday in the Crimea in the summer of 1986. It looked to me like an attempt to uphold the pretence of a continuing dialogue, another tactical move in the 'double game' played by the Americans. Eduard Shevardnadze telephoned me to say that he had already sent a draft reply for approval, adding that we did not need to give a detailed reply since there were no significant proposals in Reagan's message. Still, we could not leave it unanswered.

On the next day, Anatoly Chernyaev (who had accompanied me to the Crimea) made his daily report and showed me Shevardnadze's draft reply to President Reagan's message. It was a short, routine statement, and as I was reading it, I suddenly realized that I was gradually being forced into accepting a logic that was alien to me – a logic that was in open contradiction to our new attitude, to the process we had started in Geneva and – most important – to the hopes of ordinary people. I said that I could not sign such a letter, and told Anatoly about the thoughts that had been haunting me for days. In the end, I decided to take a strong stand, suggesting an immediate summit meeting with President Reagan to unblock the strategic talks in Geneva, which were in danger of becoming an empty rite. A meeting was needed to discuss the situation and to give new impetus to the peace process. It could take place in England or Iceland.

I immediately telephoned Shevardnadze, Gromyko, Ryzhkov and Ligachev. They all agreed to my idea. We sent an urgent message to the American President. Reagan replied agreeing to the meeting, and suggested Reykjavik as equidistant from both our countries. We contacted the Icelandic government and received a positive reply. It was time to announce another Soviet-American summit meeting.

I had to ask myself why Reagan had been so quick to accept my proposal. In all likelihood, the Americans had reckoned with the possibility that we might have leaked the news had Reagan turned down our invitation. The Reagan administration would have been hard put to explain the refusal, and American presidents were known to be quite sensitive about these questions.

There seemed to be yet another important factor. Reagan might have been induced to believe that he could force me into making major concessions by sustaining his tough policy towards the Soviet Union. American political analysts maintained that the Soviet economy was exhausted and the Soviets desperate for a break in the arms race. According to them, the Soviet Union yearned for a respite to free the resources needed to attain the goals set by the new Soviet administration – and Gorbachev could, therefore, make important proposals in Reykjavik which would meet the interests of the United States.

I tried to put myself in Reagan's place. The more I reflected on the question, the more I was convinced that the American President had decided to carry a big enough basket to Reykjavik to 'gather the fruit Gorbachev would yield, squeezed out by US policy.' The Reykjavik meeting showed that I had been right. My partner was not quite prepared for detailed talks, although our task had been clearly defined – we had to give new impetus to the strategic arms negotiations.

There must have been an additional element in Reagan's logic. He did not like to see Gorbachev setting in motion the international peace process all by himself, without American participation.

The world was increasingly responding to our agenda, and Washington may have decided that it was better to join in this process.

At the Politburo meeting on 8 October, I said that we had to prepare bold but realistic proposals for Reykjavik. If the Americans accepted our initiatives, it would indeed mean a fresh start in disarmament and normalization in world politics. If they rejected them, it would show the true intentions of the Reagan administration. In either case, the stakes were high. The world was meanwhile buzzing with excitement at the forthcoming event. Political circles in the United States joined in the discussion, with the 'hawks' trying all known means to exert maximum pressure on the American President. But, in my view, President Reagan could hardly ignore worldwide hopes for a positive outcome. It was widely accepted that the first four years of 'Reaganomics' had stabilized the US economy and that the Reagan administration had contributed to the strengthening of the 'American spirit'. However, there was a tempting opportunity to go down in history as the 'President of peace' – and the elections were drawing nearer.

Everyone agreed at the Politburo meeting that Reykjavik would improve our image in the world, demonstrating our determination to prevent a new arms race. But our generals and even some people in the Foreign Ministry and in our negotiating team in Geneva were doubtful. They were firmly stuck in a logic of antagonism, and the military sought to protect their corporate interests. The existing state of affairs seemed to suit some of our negotiators in Geneva, who enjoyed having their wages paid in hard currency, thinking 'the longer the negotiations, the better for us'.

Shevardnadze, Akhromeyev, Yakovlev, Dobrynin and Chernyaev accompanied me to Reykjavik. We also decided to fly in a group of journalists, public figures, scientists and experts. It was the first time that Pavel Ruslanovich Palazhchenko accompanied me as interpreter. He has since translated for me on various major occasions. In addition to his command of English, he is a professional diplomat and devoted to his work. I highly value the moral stand he took. He remained with me even after I had stepped down as President of the Soviet Union, working as tirelessly as ever.

THE DRAMA OF REYKJAVIK

We arrived in Iceland on the afternoon of 10 October 1986. An unknown world opened before us – no trace of vegetation, nothing but rocks and boulders. And every half an hour it would rain.

Reykjavik means something like 'smoking place'. It appeared indeed as in a fog, which turned out to be steam produced by geysers. Reykjavik is a major seaport and our entire delegation stayed on the *George Otts*, an ocean liner which had sailed from Tallinn for this occasion.

The meeting opened with a private conversation between the two leaders. Our initial exchange of views proved disappointing. The American President had little to say in answer to the arguments I advanced, in spite of the importance of the issues at stake – the growing tensions throughout the world, the setback after Geneva, the dangers we had to overcome. I outlined the proposals we had prepared in Moscow, through which we hoped to bring about a fundamental change in international politics.

Reagan reacted by consulting or reading his notes written on cards. I tried to discuss with him the points I had just outlined, but all my attempts failed. I decided to try specific questions, but still did not get any response. President Reagan was looking through his notes. The cards got mixed up and some of them fell to the floor. He started shuffling them, looking for the right answer to my arguments, but could not find it. There could be no right answer available – the American President and his aides had been preparing for a completely different conversation.

I sensed his nervousness and said: 'Well, we are talking about specific problems, so let us invite our Foreign Ministers to join the talks.' George Shultz and Eduard Shevardnadze came in, and I repeated in detail our proposals to cut strategic nuclear arsenals, which boiled down to the following: negotiations were stuck in endless discussions, the argument was going round in circles and getting nowhere. What was needed was a new approach. Our strategic nuclear stockpiles consisted of three main groups: ground-based intercontinental ballistic missiles, submarine-launched ballistic missiles and strategic bombers. Each country had its own armament structure to meet its specific requirements, but our overall strategic nuclear arsenals were approximately equal. We therefore suggested cutting each of these three groups by 50 per cent.

It was the first time that the Soviet Union had agreed to such a big reduction in its ground-based ICBM force. This was our most powerful strategic weapon and was considered a major threat by our 'potential enemy', as we used to call the Americans. But we would have agreed to this step to unlock the stalemate in the disarmament process, by now completely blocked by decades of fruitless talks. It was not meant as a one-sided offer, since the United States were supposed to cut by 50 per cent their major striking force – their nuclear submarines and their strategic bombers, in which they were superior to us.

The logic was simple: to reduce the arsenals which guaranteed nuclear deterrence to a much lower level. Our far-reaching proposals seemed to have caught President Reagan off guard; he appeared confused, although we had suggested something the United States had always wanted us to do, i.e. a radical cut in our intercontinental ballistic missiles. But since this proposal was part of a package, the American President apparently feared some sort of trick. His Secretary of State saved the day by saying that our approach was fundamentally acceptable. During the exchange of views that followed we managed to reach an agreement in principle on a 50-per-cent cut in strategic arms.

The American delegation was clearly not prepared for such a turn of events, and we often had to interrupt the talks for consultations within the teams. The breaks would occasionally last for quite a while, the White House experts obviously needing additional consultations. The American team kept a 'hot line' open to Washington for inquiries and consultations.

Since we had put forward the proposal, both our delegation and our experts' group under Marshal Akhromeyev had done their homework. Obviously a lot of additional questions arose in the process of working out the details of the agreement. Most of these questions were to be looked into at the talks in Geneva, but some aspects required immediate clarification. In order to remove some of these obstacles, we came out with a fallback proposal we had kept in reserve, removing the question of forward-based systems from the agenda, i.e. our demand that Western intermediate-range nuclear missiles be counted as strategic weapons.

Our second proposal aimed to find a solution to the problem of intermediate-range nuclear missiles. We decided to drop the link with the French and British nuclear arsenals and suggested returning to the American zero option, dismantling all intermediate-range missiles based in Europe. At the same time, we offered to start talks on the missiles based in Asia and to freeze the number of missiles with a range of less than one thousand kilometres.

But, paradoxical as it might seem, the Americans would not accept their own zero option in Reykjavik. I think it was probably less for fear of a negative reaction from their European allies than because they were reluctant to harm the American arms industry. A compromise was finally found, not without difficulty. Alas, as it turned out, our greatest trials lay still ahead.

Both the negotiating teams and the media realized that this was a unique opportunity to break out of the vicious circle of the nuclear arms race. But the moment we had seemingly reached an agreement, some invisible force suddenly stayed the hand of the President of the United States.

In all the previous negotiations, the Americans had always viewed verification procedures as the most important factor. And suddenly they started manoeuvring on this issue. Our position was clear: if we were to begin dismantling nuclear weapons, we necessarily had to intensify inspection and verification to prevent either side from attaining military superiority. Hence, slackening existing arms control and verification mechanisms – and the ABM treaty in the first place – was out of the question. On the contrary, it would have been logical to reinforce the treaty, both sides committing themselves not to withdraw from the agreement over a period of ten years – the time needed to dismantle the nuclear arsenals.

We were aware of President Reagan's commitment to SDI and suggested allowing continued laboratory research and testing in this area. But the American President insisted that the United States had the right to conduct virtually any kind of tests within the framework of SDI, refusing to set any restrictions. Reykjavik became the site of a truly Shakespearean drama. We would interrupt the talks, get back together and break up again. Success was a mere step away, but SDI proved an insurmountable stumbling-block.[1]

The Reykjavik meeting was drawing to its end. We had not been able to overcome our differences. The talks had reached a stalemate and were becoming bizarre, with President Reagan starting to haggle – 'Meet me halfway and you'll feel the beneficial effects of American co-operation' – while I was desperately trying to get across to him that he was just one step away from going down in history as the 'peacemaker President'.

We left the house as it was getting dark. We stood by the car. Everyone was in a bad mood.

Reagan reproached me: 'You planned from the start to come here and put me in this situation!'

'No, Mr President,' I replied. 'I'm ready to go right back into the house and sign a comprehensive document on all the issues agreed if you drop your plans to militarize space.'

'I am really sorry' was Reagan's reply. We made our farewells and he left in his car.

THAT FAMOUS PRESS CONFERENCE

Only forty minutes remained before the press conference. Reagan had left for the American military base to take the aeroplane home. My first, overwhelming, intention had been to blow the unyielding American position to smithereens, carrying out the plan we had decided in Moscow: if the Americans rejected the agreement, a compromise in the name of peace, we would denounce the US administration and its dangerous policies as a threat to everyone throughout the world.

I walked from the building where the talks had been held. It

[1] At a February 1993 conference in Princeton, former ambassador Jack Matlock recounted a remark made by Robert McFarlane immediately after Reykjavik. The American President's former National Security Adviser had been taken aback by Ronald Reagan's refusal to accept our proposal, commenting that 'Gorbachev's offer in Reykjavik was quite consistent with our goals. Once we had reached an agreement to cut intercontinental ballistic missiles, we could have well accepted a ten-year delay [for SDI testing].'

was a distance of some 400 metres and I was feverishly collecting my thoughts. One thing preyed on my mind – had we not reached an agreement both on strategic and intermediate-range missiles, was it not an entirely new situation, and should it be sacrificed for the sake of a momentary propaganda advantage? My intuition was telling me that I should cool off and think it all over thoroughly. I had not yet made up my mind when I suddenly found myself in the enormous press-conference room. About a thousand journalists were waiting for us. When I came into the room, the merciless, often cynical and cheeky journalists stood up in silence. I sensed the anxiety in the air. I suddenly felt emotional, even shaken. These people standing in front of me seemed to represent mankind waiting for its fate to be decided.

At this moment I realized the true meaning of Reykjavik and knew what further course we had to follow.

My speech has been published in newspapers and commented on by scores of journalists, political scientists and politicians. I therefore do not quote it *in extenso*. The key phrase of the speech was: 'In spite of all its drama, Reykjavik is not a failure – it is a breakthrough, which allowed us for the first time to look over the horizon.' The audience came out of its state of shock, greeting the sentence with thunderous applause. One journalist wrote later in an article characterizing the mood of the press conference: 'When the General Secretary presented the failure of the Reykjavik meeting as a victory, Raisa Gorbachev was sitting in the conference-hall, looking with awe at her husband, with tears rolling down her face.'

On that day, we had sensed the public's prevailing mood, thus saving the process of worldwide change and restoring the hope that Reykjavik would be followed by further progress.

I soon received the information that George Shultz had characterized Reykjavik as a failure during a briefing he had given to journalists at the military base. Upon his return to the United States – and having read about my speech and the worldwide reaction to it – he was, however, quick to 're-adjust', speaking of a 'breakthrough', and of the work that lay ahead. One must give him his due – he was a man you could do business with.

Reykjavik showed that an agreement was possible and that the new Soviet Union was not into propaganda but wanted genuine disarmament. Political leaders were given the opportunity to see for themselves who Gorbachev was. It inspired hopes in some of them, while others appeared to be worried. Margaret Thatcher – more about her later – rushed her fences: 'We must not allow a second Reykjavik to happen.'

Reykjavik strengthened our conviction that we had chosen the right course.

THE DELHI DECLARATION

History has its own peculiar way of setting landmarks, and it often requires the distance of hindsight to perceive the logical pattern of events. When, after the summit meeting with President Reagan in Reykjavik, I flew to India to sign – together with Rajiv Gandhi – the Delhi declaration on the principles of a nuclear-weapon-free and non-violent world, many people could not see any connection between these two events.

The Soviet Union had established good relations with India in the late 1950s. Our nations have been traditionally friendly, and India welcomed Soviet support in consolidating its independence and maintaining peace in the region. Perestroika created new opportunities to strengthen ties between our nations. The Indian leadership welcomed the new thinking. I established a warm personal rapport with Rajiv Gandhi. We met on many occasions and regularly exchanged letters. Our thoughts went along the same lines, and our conversations ranged far beyond the agenda. I was deeply impressed by the way he organically combined the profound philosophic tradition of India and the East with a perfect knowledge and comprehension of European culture. He had great personal charm and was endowed with many human virtues. Rajiv was devoted to the cause of his grandfather, Jawaharlal Nehru, and his mother, Indira Gandhi – his life's aim was the renaissance of India.

Over the years, the similarity in our views grew into mutual confidence. We did what we could to help India to defend its national interests and we could count on India's unfailing support for our international initiatives. But our relations were no mere exchange of mutual aid. Far from it, they significantly contributed to the ideas which eventually formed the theoretical basis for the new world order, as reflected in the Delhi declaration Rajiv Gandhi and I signed on 27 November 1986, during my visit to India.

> In the nuclear age [the declaration reads] mankind must develop a new political thinking and a new concept of the world which provides sound guarantees for the survival of mankind.
> The world we have inherited belongs to present and future generations alike – hence we must give priority to universal human values.

We suggested a number of principles for the new world order:

> human life must be acknowledged as the supreme value...
> non-violence must become the basis of human co-existence...
> the right of every state to political and economic independence must be acknowledged and respected...
> the 'balance of fear' must be replaced by a global system of international security.

We declared that progress towards a world free of nuclear arms and violence demanded urgent disarmament measures: the total elimination of nuclear arsenals by the end of the century, the prevention of an arms race in space, a ban on nuclear weapon tests and the destruction of all existing chemical weapons, the reduction of conventional forces etc.

For the transitional period preceding the total elimination of nuclear weapons, the Soviet Union and India proposed an international convention which would ban the use or the threat of use of nuclear weapons and which would take effect immediately.

It all began in May 1985, when Rajiv Gandhi came to Moscow on his first official trip abroad. It was some six months after he became Prime Minister and a little over two months after my election as General Secretary. The meeting marked the change of generations, this alone making it a major political event. We had to re-appraise the progress our countries had made in political, economic, cultural and military co-operation, smooth out problems that occurred from time to time, and discuss opportunities for a new level of co-operation. In spite of all the differences, our countries had much in common. Both the Soviet Union and India faced problems of modernization, renewal and radical reform.

Rajiv and I signed a number of agreements on the development of trade and economic, scientific and technological co-operation by 1990, and on joint ventures for the building of various industrial plants in India.

The international situation at the time was very difficult, worldwide tensions having reached threatening dimensions. Unorthodox, courageous decisions were called for to reverse the fatal course of events. Aside from global issues, we needed to discuss the situation in the Asia-Pacific region, which was of vital interest for the Soviet Union and India.

I expressed my support for the initiative launched by Argentina, India, Greece, Mexico, Tanzania and Sweden, calling for a worldwide moratorium on the testing, production and development of nuclear weapons and delivery systems, the prevention of an arms race in space, and the conclusion of a treaty which would ban nuclear weapons worldwide. But this significant step, made by six countries on behalf of the non-aligned movement, was unfortunately ignored by the United States.

In the final communiqué, the Soviet Union and India declared that they opposed any infringement of the right of every state and nation to its own independent and peaceful development and any form of imperialism, colonialism, neo-colonialism, domination and hegemony.

We proposed that all disputes and conflicts among states should be settled by negotiation, without the threat or use of force. We stated our common views on the Middle East conflict, the situation in South-East Asia, the Pacific region, southern Africa, the role of the non-aligned countries and other issues.

Rajiv Gandhi was presented with the Lenin Peace Prize awarded posthumously to Indira Gandhi, and participated in a ceremony to name a Moscow square after his mother. Our Indian guest went on trips to Belorussia and Kirgizia, where he was cordially received. Raisa Maksimovna and Sonia Gandhi spent many hours together and established a cordial personal rapport they have maintained ever since.

One day we had some free minutes left and, trying to play the role of a tour guide, I invited Rajiv Gandhi on a guided tour of the Kremlin. In the park, we came across some beautiful blooming lilac. I broke off a few branches from a bush and presented them to my Indian partner and friend. He thanked me for the gift, while tactfully expressing his concern about the lilac. I allayed his fears – lilac bushes and bird cherries grow better if you break off their branches.

I paid a return visit to India in November 1986. It is a wonderful season – the blazing summer heat is gone and you find yourself, as it were, in a Central Russian summer. Never before or since have we been greeted by such masses of people: there must have been hundreds of thousands. The crowds lined the road from the airport to the presidential palace, thousands of banners floating in a sea of flowers. In some places, skilful gardeners and artists had arranged flowers to form our portraits, Raisa Maksimovna's and mine. We plunged into a country of sunshine, passionate hearts and flowers.

We had maintained regular contact since Rajiv Gandhi's visit to Moscow, exchanging letters and messages through our ambassadors. But events had been developing with growing speed since our last meeting. In the meantime, I had met Ronald Reagan in Reykjavik, a number of public figures and politicians from East and West had visited Moscow, and I had made a visit to France. The Soviet Union had proposed a fifteen-year programme to free the world of nuclear weapons and significantly reduce other types of armaments, and we had redefined our foreign policy at the XXVIIth Party Congress in 1986. The situation in South-East Asia remained uncertain and tense, particularly along the Indian borders with Pakistan and China.

A few months before my visit to India, I had made a speech in Vladivostok on the development prospects of the Asia-Pacific region. The Indian Prime Minister welcomed the ideas I had expressed on general security, adding, however, that one should take into consideration Asian traditions, the spirit of the non-aligned movement and the principles of Bandung,[1] which were proclaimed in this very region. He also drew my attention to the fact that progress towards the solution of security problems could only be gradual. At a certain point, I had the impression that Rajiv was not too happy with my Vladivostok speech. And I realized how much tact and caution one needed to show in launching global initiatives. There may have been some jealousy on the part of my young friend, who was the leader of a great country in the region I had spoken of and maybe thought it would have been more appropriate to make a joint declaration, possibly with the participation of other countries. But this was precisely what I had in mind when I stressed that we did not intend to impose our views on anybody and that we were open to co-operation with everyone – be it China, the United States, Japan or all the other countries of the region, and obviously with our friends in India.

Be that as it may, this episode cast no shadow on our relations.

Rajiv Gandhi welcomed the changes in the Soviet Union and perceived them as an opportunity to reach a new, superior level of co-operation between our countries. I remember his words: 'We must reach new horizons: we need creativity and innovation.'

The Indian Prime Minister expressed his support for the position we took in Reykjavik and for the initiative on the elimination of nuclear weapons we had launched on 15 January 1986.

From the Indian capital, I appealed to the international community to adopt the new political thinking and new philosophy of international relations. In these times of turmoil, I declared that the survival of mankind must be set above all other interests, and that the security of each nation is coupled with the security of all members of the world community.

I was given the opportunity to address the Indian parliament. Since I wanted to avoid abusing their hospitality, I asked in advance how much time had been planned for the address. In

[1] A conference of Asian and African states held in Indonesia in 1955, which adopted a ten-point declaration on the promotion of world peace and co-operation, incorporating the principles of the United Nations Charter and the five principles of Indian Prime Minister Nehru.

reply, my cordial hosts said: 'Feel free to speak for as long as you wish.' In the end, my speech and the ensuing answers to the questions from the deputies lasted more than two hours. Incidentally, it was the first time that the speech of a foreign leader had been transmitted on national television and radio.

I laid a wreath and planted a tree at Mahatma Gandhi's tomb, and visited the Jawaharlal Nehru museum and the Indira Gandhi memorial. We learned many interesting things about this outstanding family and were deeply touched to be shown the spot where Indira Gandhi had been murdered. On the evening of 26 November, Rajiv and Sonia Gandhi invited us to a private dinner at the Prime Minister's residence.

At a meeting with a group of Indian women, Raisa Maksimovna suggested launching a joint Indo-Soviet journal for women. The first issue of *Dialogue* was published in 1988, in both Russian and Hindi. The journal appears in India to this day, but ceased publication in our country after the disintegration of the Soviet Union.

Rajiv and I agreed to organize an Indo-Soviet festival which would take place in India and the Soviet Union to commemorate the seventieth anniversary of the October revolution and the fortieth anniversary of India's independence. The festival was officially opened in the summer of 1987 in the Kremlin, marked by a concert in the Moscow Luzhniki sports stadium. This colourful manifestation of Indo-Soviet friendship toured the entire Soviet Union.

I visited India for a second time in late November 1988, to participate in the closing ceremony of our festival. Many outstanding Soviet artists and sportsmen, as well as a number of amateur drama groups and ensembles, took part in the final events, and our fellow citizens received a cordial welcome everywhere they went. The festival drew the Indian and Soviet people even closer together, which is in my view at least as important an achievement as concluding inter-governmental agreements. I am convinced that 'people's diplomacy' will play an ever-increasing role in the future.

In my talks with Indian leaders, I focused on the establishment of a new world order. Rajiv Gandhi was concerned about the appearance of 'power blocs' which claimed a special standing in world affairs. We fully agreed that the Soviet Union and India should resist the temptation to act along such lines – we had no intention of creating closed groups or alliances directed against other nations. The best way to counteract such tendencies was to deal with global issues at the United Nations and other continental or regional international organizations. We also reaffirmed our commitment to the universal principles proclaimed in the Delhi declaration.

Rajiv was keen to receive first-hand information about the changes in the Soviet Union, and asked many questions. We were about to launch a number of political reforms and I told him in detail about these. I did not hide from him that we were worried about separatist movements and ethnic conflicts, and the Indian Prime Minister mentioned his own concern about the increasing aggressiveness of some Sikh leaders. To this day, I remember our discussion about the appropriate means to settle ethnic and religious strife. We agreed that one could not always avoid the use of force, but that one should be aware of the fact that this would only delay the outbreak of violence, often making it thus even more destructive.

Another important subject discussed during my visit in November was China. We felt that the time had come to strive for an improvement of relations with the People's Republic and that it was essential to avoid creating the impression that the Indo-Soviet rapprochement could be directed against the Chinese. The understanding we reached on this issue was to bear fruit in the future.

When you reach a certain level of trust with a political partner – as I had with Rajiv Gandhi – you can progress from discussing day-to-day politics and co-operation to envisage broader horizons for the future. We started looking for new, dynamic and integrated forms of co-operation, better adapted to the challenges of the day. India had tried to modernize its economy with the help of the Western industrialized countries, but Western technologies and investments had not yielded the expected results. Rajiv Gandhi realized – learning by doing – that the road his grandfather Nehru and his mother Indira Gandhi had chosen for India had been the right one and had served India's national interests best.

During this second visit to Delhi, I was awarded the Indira Gandhi Prize – a moving ceremony and an award I cherish and value to this day. I decided to donate the money to the Soviet cultural centre in Delhi.

We met Rajiv and Sonia on another two occasions. In mid-July 1989, the Indian Prime Minister made a stop-over in Moscow on his way home from a meeting of the leaders of the British Commonwealth of Nations. In the evening, we gave a dinner in honour of our Indian guests at our official country residence. I remember this evening for its particularly warm and frank atmosphere. Rajiv told us about the unrest in neighbouring Sri Lanka – you could see that the situation caused him much concern. He shared his impressions of the Commonwealth meeting and drew a parallel between India and the Soviet Union, which had taken the road of radical reform. He commented that many people in the West entertained an over-simplified view of the changes, analysing them exclusively from the point of view of whether these changes corresponded with their own ideas and expectations. Rajiv was taken aback by the cynicism displayed by some Western leaders, who would apparently have preferred a weakening of the Soviet Union's role in international affairs. I had observed the same worrying trend. It seemed that the Soviet Union's growing prestige did not suit some of my Western partners.

On that occasion, Rajiv Gandhi imparted to me some confidential information he believed was absolutely reliable: reviewing its foreign policy, the Bush administration had reached the conclusion that the growing popularity of perestroika and of the Soviet General Secretary went against American interests. A special group was to be set up in the President's administration to counteract this 'threat'. This was unexpected corroboration of earlier information I had received from various sources. I often mentioned this issue in my talks with American officials, including the President, usually adding that I was informed about their assessment of the situation in the Soviet Union and the policy of the Soviet leadership. Ignoring the visible embarrassment caused by my remarks, I tried to convince my partners that our reforms were designed not only to meet the vital interests of the Soviet people but were also in the best interests of our partners abroad – and that it was about time they freed themselves and their policies from the ideological remnants of the Cold War.

The last time we met, Rajiv Gandhi had already resigned as Prime Minister to become leader of the Indian opposition. I could understand the way he must have felt, and Raisa Maksimovna and I did everything we could to show our sympathy and support. However, the moment we met our Indian friends we realized that they had already swallowed the bitter pill: Rajiv made a sound analysis of the reasons for his party's defeat and criticized both the policy of the Congress Party and his own political errors, particularly concerning the pace of reforms. Like a mature statesman, he weighed up the pros and cons of his new situation– he had become an experienced, tough politician. When later I learned of his successful election campaign, I felt sincerely glad for my Indian friend, and I was deeply shocked on hearing of the untimely, tragic death of this outstanding man.

19

EUROPE – OUR COMMON HOME

I HAVE ALREADY MENTIONED MY VISIT TO GREAT BRITAIN IN December 1984, when I headed a delegation of the USSR Supreme Soviet. That trip led me to reflect on the role and place of Europe in the world. In an address to Members of the British Parliament, I recalled that in the 1970s Europe had become the cradle of détente and of the Helsinki process – continued at the conferences in Belgrade (1977–8) and Madrid (1980–3). However, the work of these forums had been hampered by another sharp deterioration in the international situation, and the two conferences resulted only in a number of ideas and documents – which proved to be of use for the future. The Stockholm Conference on Confidence and Security-Building Measures, which opened in early 1984, was not making any progress. At the time, we in the Soviet Union used to blame the West for any setback. But in my address to the British Members of Parliament, I deemed it necessary to say that 'the nuclear age inevitably dictates a new political thinking'.

In short, we did not start from zero with the new foreign policy we initiated in spring 1985 – including its European direction. The fortieth anniversary of the end of the Second World War served as another sharp reminder of the urgent need to find a solution to European security problems. I discussed this question with Willy Brandt during a meeting in late May. I could see that the best solution would be to free the European continent completely of nuclear and chemical weapons. But I realized the difficulty of agreeing on full-scale measures at once and suggested making gradual progress towards this goal.

It was my firm intention to reactivate and to give a strong impulse to the 'European process', i.e. pan-European integration, and for this very reason I chose France as the destination for my first official visit as General Secretary of the CPSU. We in the Soviet Union remembered that détente in the 1970s was to a large extent made possible by our co-operation with the French. On the eve of my departure, I gave an interview to French television. It was the first time a Soviet leader had talked directly to a group of Western journalists in front of live cameras. To be frank, I could not have imagined beforehand the psychological and intellectual stress one is exposed to during such an interview, what with the blinding spotlights and the journalists' crossfire interrogation. At the time, both I and my compatriots could not understand why the French journalists were so aggressive and tactless, not to say rude. Today I realize that this was due largely to the novelty of the situation and to the fact that the times in which we lived, and Soviet-French relations, were marked by mistrust and suspicion – in short, it was a time of confrontation.

In 1981 the French had in fact drastically reduced political contacts. Afghanistan and the events in Poland had led to grave discord between our nations. In addition, the French leadership seemed allergic to any mention of the role France's nuclear forces played in Europe's nuclear balance. And the unprecedented, undoubtedly 'political' expulsion of a large number of Soviet officials and diplomats did not contribute to an improvement in the climate. In spite of continuing commercial ties, there was an obvious cooling in the atmosphere.

At the press conference I was trying to drive home to the French – and to others as well – that compliance with the Final Act[1] would improve the climate in Europe and dispel the clouds. In reply to a question, I confirmed our special interest in Europe and used a metaphor which had just come to my mind – 'Europe is our common home'.

The idea of Europe as our common home had been a spontaneous thought, but the symbolic image eventually acquired an

[1] The Helsinki Final Act, signed in 1975.

552

existence of its own. People in Europe tended to be particularly aware of the instability of the international situation and of the threat of war. It was here that the two antagonistic military blocs stood face to face, accumulating mountains of weapons and deploying sophisticated nuclear missiles. On the other hand, Europe possessed the most valuable experience of co-existence between countries belonging to different political systems – both members of military alliances and neutral states.

Reflecting on the goals to set for our new foreign policy, I found it increasingly difficult to see the multicoloured patchwork of Europe's political map as I used to see it before. I was thinking about the common roots of this multiform and yet fundamentally indivisible European civilization, and perceived with growing awareness the artificiality of the political blocs and the archaic nature of the 'iron curtain'.

It was important that both the general public and, as far as possible, the politicians should rid themselves of the notion of Europe as a potential 'theatre of war' – this was incidentally the name used for Europe in various military headquarters. I was convinced that Europe's mission was to serve as an example for the co-existence of sovereign and peaceful, albeit different, states, which fully realized their interdependency and founded their mutual relations on trust. I realized that we were still a long way from such an ideal. But this was one more reason not to waste time and to make the first steps.

My proposal to eliminate nuclear weapons by the year 2000 was considered another Soviet propaganda trick by many politicians in Western Europe, who pointed to our superiority in conventional forces. However, this cold reception did not discourage me and I suggested to my West European partners that they should take another look at the situation. The West could reduce the types of armament of which it had more than the Eastern countries, and we would reciprocate by eliminating our 'excess' weapons – we could strike a new military balance at a lower level. It was a realistic, urgent task, and I felt that we had the right to expect a positive Western response.

There was yet another theme I constantly reiterated – the potential opportunities for a pan-European policy which lay in 'the spirit of Helsinki', a unique achievement in itself. The Stockholm conference, which was nearing its end in the summer of 1986, was in danger of failing. The only way to make it a success was to accept the idea of significant reciprocal concessions, based on equality and mutual security. I suggested to François Mitterrand during our meeting in Moscow that the Soviet Union and France – the countries which were in a way responsible for the Stockholm forum – should agree on ways to promote the process.

Mitterrand came to Moscow in July 1986 to reciprocate my visit to France. East-West relations remained rather difficult. Hopes for major changes in world politics – kindled by our summit meeting with President Reagan in Geneva – were waning. Hence I attached particular importance to the continuation of a fruitful dialogue with France. Just as in our previous meeting, I discussed with President Mitterrand questions of bilateral co-operation and disarmament problems.

We had a certain convergence of views on the Strategic Defense Initiative, the ABM treaty and SALT II. François Mitterrand said in particular: 'I am opposed to the idea of SDI – I perceive it as a potential opportunity for a first strike. I am profoundly convinced that it would be far better to search for possible ways to disarm, instead of constantly carrying the arms race to extremes. It is obvious that SDI will not replace nuclear weapons, but will become a substantial addition to the existing arsenals.'

He added that France would not participate in the implementation of any kind of military-industrial strategy that excluded France from the decision-making process – which was precisely the case with SDI.

Some days before his visit to Moscow, Mitterrand had a meeting with President Reagan. He told me that he considered the arguments the American President had advanced as unconvincing, commenting ironically that Reagan's belief in the effectiveness of the Strategic Defense Initiative as a panacea for all ills was, in his view, more mystic than rational.

'In my talks with the Americans,' Mitterrand said, 'I asked quite frankly what specific results they sought. Do they want the

Soviet Union to be able to invest additional resources in its economic development – resources obtained by cuts in its defence budget? Or does the United States intend to wear out the Soviets in the arms race, uprooting the Soviet people and pressuring their leadership into allotting more and more funds for unproductive purposes, i.e. military build-up? I told Reagan frankly: the former means peace, the latter – war.' It turned out that we had converging views on many of the main problems in international relations, while differing on certain specific problems, for example, our commercial ties. The French trade balance with the Soviet Union had been unfavourable for a number of years, and the French suggested at virtually every meeting that we should increase our imports. In practice, it turned out that almost all the goods we were interested in buying could be found in the strategic lists of Cocom[1] (the Co-ordinating Committee on East-West Trade Policy), which were controlled by the Americans.

I mentioned this problem during a meeting with the French President, but alas even François Mitterrand could not overcome the notorious Cocom. We would continue to come across this difficulty in our trade with France – thus, we had to wait for over three years to get the go-ahead to purchase equipment for our telephone exchanges.

Soviet-French relations suffered a setback shortly after the Reykjavik summit meeting, due to the fact that the French leadership – in spite of publicly proclaiming its support for the new political thinking – was in practice still devoted to the concept of nuclear deterrence. This conflict of views on the very principles of security led to contradictions and inconsistencies in practical questions.

As prospects for an agreement on the elimination of Soviet and American intermediate-range nuclear forces in Europe and negotiations on a 50-per-cent cut in strategic weapons were becoming more and more tangible, sceptical voices in Paris grew

---

[1] An organization, comprising NATO countries and Japan, which drew up a strategic list of goods – especially advanced technology, which might be useful to the military – which were not to be sold to a communist country.

louder. The French, who had only recently called for the elimination of the Pershing and SS-20 missiles, were now saying that disarmament in Europe had 'started at the wrong end'. France had taken up the toughest position among the Western countries against the reduction and eventual elimination of tactical nuclear weapons and dual-purpose conventional weapons. The French parliament passed a bill providing for a significant upgrading of the French nuclear forces. The French leadership was hostile to any suggestion that it should eventually join in the process of nuclear disarmament or in any talks that might involve a reduction of the French nuclear forces.

The French government was also playing a waiting game when it came to discussing talks on cuts in conventional forces in Europe at the Vienna meeting. Publicly supporting the idea of an international convention that would ban chemical weapons, France insisted at the same time on its right to produce binary chemical weapons. There was a growing gap between the words and deeds of the French leadership.

I mentioned all these concerns to Prime Minister Jacques Chirac during his visit to Moscow in May 1987. 'I should like to put a direct question to you,' I said. 'What do Western Europe and France, which is one of its pillars, really want? . . . Today, we have a historic opportunity to make a first step towards disarmament. But the political leaders can't get themselves to move in that direction.'

The Vienna CSCE meeting was scheduled shortly after the protracted Stockholm conference, in November 1986. We intended to promote the pan-European process in every field – political, economic, humanitarian and cultural. It was our aim to fill all three Helsinki 'baskets' with fresh and useful fruits.

The situation called for a development of the 'common European home' idea, the more so because some people had already criticized the formula as being too abstract. I decided to state my views on the question in full and was offered a suitable occasion in April 1987 during my visit to Czechoslovakia, the geographical centre of Europe. This inspired me to dwell on the 'European theme' in the public speech I made in Prague.

The 'pan-European idea' met with a favourable reception from politicians and public figures both in Eastern and Western Europe – including people whose political views significantly differed from ours. Yet, mutual distrust, nourished by the huge arsenals piled up in Europe, was still too strong. After the Reykjavik summit meeting, I met leading politicians from a number of West European NATO states: Great Britain, Denmark, the Netherlands, Norway, Iceland and Italy. The main topic of discussion at all the meetings was 'Europe and disarmament'. By agreeing not to include the French and British nuclear arsenals in a first stage of nuclear disarmament, the Soviet Union had shown its goodwill and made a great step towards establishing trust.

For a long time, the question of asymmetries and imbalances in conventional forces remained a major stumbling block. We discussed the problem with the leaders of the Warsaw Pact states. In order to speed up negotiations on conventional forces, we agreed to propose a three-stage programme which would as the very first step eliminate existing imbalances – primarily in tanks and attack aircraft, i.e. offensive weapons. At the same time, we suggested reducing the military forces and weapons stationed along the dividing line between the two alliances and thus creating a 'low-level weapons zone' in order to further reduce the risk of a surprise attack.

We had to break out of the vicious circle of mistrust and finally begin the process of conventional disarmament. In a speech to the Polish parliament, I suggested a kind of 'European Reykjavik' – a summit meeting of all European leaders, in the hope that we could achieve a similar breakthrough in European affairs as we had in Soviet-American relations during our meeting with Ronald Reagan in Iceland.

The question arose of whether the concept of a 'common European home' was compatible with the maintenance of the two military-political alliances, NATO and the Warsaw Pact. The way I saw it, we had to face the realities and accept the existing structures, pushing them at the same time towards co-operation – and hence towards a gradual transformation of both NATO and the Warsaw Pact, their relations shifting away from tension towards eventual stability. In this context, we suggested creating a permanent centre to reduce the risk of war in Europe, which would establish regular contacts between representatives of both alliances.

The concept of a 'common European home' touched also the triangle Soviet Union–Europe–United States. Growing tension between the two superpowers worried both the public and politicians in Europe, who exerted themselves to reduce it, sometimes even acting as mediators. At the same time, the European NATO states frowned on any signs of mutual understanding between Moscow and Washington, fearing a Soviet-American deal that would leave them out in the cold.

We made great efforts to try to dispel their doubts and convince the Europeans that we had no intention of establishing a 'superpower condominium', i.e. an agreement between the superpowers to rule the world – just as we did not intend to leave either the United States or Canada outside the 'common European home'. We realized that such a policy would have been simply unrealistic. And what is more, we believed that Europe could benefit from improved Soviet-American relations. In fact, it would have been difficult to persuade the Europeans to co-operate without the Americans. And the Europeans could for their part significantly help in achieving further progress between the Soviet Union and the United States.

Obviously, we could not accept geo-political doctrines aimed at isolating the Soviet Union. One could perceive such a tendency in some of Henry Kissinger's speeches at the time. His 'recipe' was to see Europe as a whole, reaching from the Atlantic to the Ural mountains, when it came to acknowledging strategic realities. But so far as economic, scientific, technological and cultural ties were concerned, the East European countries could be brought in, but not the Soviet Union. We simply could not agree with such a view and I openly protested against it in my speeches and talks with foreign leaders, including Henry Kissinger himself.

GREAT BRITAIN: LAUNCHING A DIFFICULT DIALOGUE

Margaret Thatcher, leader of the Conservative Party, had headed the British government since 1979. Her election platform had consisted mainly of cuts in social security, reduced state intervention in the economy and the promotion of private enterprise. 'Thatcherism' became a symbol of a rising tide of neo-conservatism in the world.

The new British Prime Minister managed to improve the situation in British industry and stop its fall in competitiveness on the world markets. The jubilant Conservatives won a second term in 1983. But changes in international relations were in the air.

At my first meeting with Mrs Thatcher in late 1984, we had established what proved to be a good and lasting relationship. We both appreciated the contact and got on very well. This first meeting might be the reason why the Soviet-British dialogue made such a good start on my taking the helm of the Soviet Union in 1985 – although British policy towards us during the first years of perestroika was not exactly what you would call friendly. Great Britain was the first Western country to support the American Strategic Defense Initiative and to participate officially in its development. Margaret Thatcher viewed the Reykjavik meeting as a failure and fully supported Ronald Reagan's position, blaming the Soviet Union for the lack of an agreement. The British government made a big show of expelling a group of Soviet embassy officials, accusing them all of being agents of the KGB.

But at the same time the British spoke out in favour of a 'constructive long-term dialogue' with the Soviet Union. It is revealing that Margaret Thatcher took the initiative in visiting the Soviet Union after my election as General Secretary. She was a frequent guest in Washington, and it seemed as if she intended to represent Western European interests in the dialogue between the superpowers.

Mrs Thatcher came to Moscow in late March 1987. Our talks took place in the Kremlin, in the presence only of our personal assistants and interpreters. Stressing the significance of her visit,

I remarked that the last high-level visit to the Soviet Union by a British Prime Minister had taken place more than twelve years earlier. She corrected me immediately, saying that the last time a British *Conservative* Prime Minister had visited the Soviet Union had been more than twenty years before.

Before getting down to business, I expressed my astonishment at a speech she had made in Torquay only a week before leaving for Moscow, delivered in the spirit of Reagan's anti-Communist crusade. I said that we even had the impression that she might cancel her visit.

Mrs Thatcher had maintained that the Soviet Union aspired to 'establish Communism and domination worldwide' and that 'Moscow's hand' could be seen in virtually every conflict in the world. Obviously, I could not leave it at that and replied that much of her speech in Torquay as well as most of the accusations she had made were conservative stereotypes going back to the 1940s and 1950s. But Mrs Thatcher stood her ground: 'You are supplying weapons to the Third World countries,' she rejoined, 'while the West supplies them with food and aid in addition to helping establish democratic institutions.' The discussion became very heated.

Looking back I must admit (and it seems to me that I have already done so) that our policy towards developing countries had been highly ideological and that, to a certain extent, Mrs Thatcher had been right in her criticisms. However, it was well-known that the West had always been the prime supplier of weapons to the Third World and thus supported authoritarian and even totalitarian regimes, working on the principle that 'that dictator is a son of a bitch, but he is our son of a bitch'.

Our discussion had reached a point where I considered it necessary to say: 'We have frankly expressed our respective views on the world in which we live. But we have not succeeded in bringing our standpoints any closer. It seems to me that our disagreements have not become less after this conversation.'

My partner struck a more conciliatory note. Suddenly changing the course of our conversation, she said: 'We follow your activity with great interest and we fully appreciate your attempts to improve the life of your people. I acknowledge your right to have your own system and security, just as we have the right to ours, and we suggest taking this as a basis for our debate.

'In spite of all the differences between our systems,' she added, 'we can still exchange some useful experiences. We are deeply impressed by the vigorous policy of reform you are trying to implement. We have a common problem here – how to manage change.'

We went on to discuss our main topic, arms control. At the time, Soviet-American talks on strategic arms were being held in Geneva. I went on the offensive, asking Mrs Thatcher directly: 'Is the West ready for real disarmament or have you been forced into negotiations under pressure from public opinion in your countries? I would appreciate it if you could clarify your position.'

Mrs Thatcher advanced the familiar argument that nuclear weapons represented the best guarantee for peace and that there could be no other guarantee in present conditions. 'We believe in nuclear deterrence,' she continued, 'and we do not consider the elimination of nuclear weapons practicable.'

In reply, I delivered quite a long harangue, the gist of which was that the West did not want a solution, but was only interested in complicating the issue. I concluded: 'Today, we are closer than ever before to making a first step towards genuine disarmament. But the moment we were given this opportunity, you hit the panic button. Is the Tory policy exclusively aimed at hindering disarmament and the reduction of the level of confrontation in the world? It is amazing that Great Britain should feel comfortable in such a position.'

Mrs Thatcher seemed somewhat taken aback by my tirade. 'That's what I call a speech!' she exclaimed. 'I don't even know where to start.' And she assured me that the West did not in any way intend to make life difficult for us or to complicate reform in the Soviet Union by rejecting disarmament.

Again and again, Margaret Thatcher reiterated her main argument: nuclear weapons are the only means to ensure the security of Great Britain in the event of a conventional war in Europe. For this reason, Britain did not intend to commit itself to limiting in any way its nuclear arsenal. In short, our conversation was going round in circles. In an attempt to ease the tension, Margaret

Thatcher told me about a 'funny occurrence', as she put it, which happened during a meeting with Hua Guofen. The meeting was scheduled to last one hour. The Chinese leader spoke for forty-five minutes and when Mrs Thatcher asked one single question, he continued his monologue for another twenty minutes. Seeing this, Lord Carrington (the British Foreign Secretary) handed the Prime Minister a written note: 'Madam, you tend to speak too much . . .'

Incidentally, this did not keep her from repeating her main arguments. But in spite of the rather heated exchange, Margaret Thatcher assured me at the end of our conversation that she intended to hold her press conference in a constructive tone.

A TALK AT THE BRIZE NORTON AIR BASE

I should say that the 'constructive polemics' we engaged in with the British Prime Minister did no harm to our relations – on the contrary, they even seemed to strengthen our mutual sympathy. In December 1987, Mrs Thatcher suggested that I should stop over in Britain on my way to Washington for the signing of the INF[1] treaty. She came to meet me at the Brize Norton air base, where we had a brief and interesting talk – in a sense, a continuation of the conversation we had in Moscow. It was apparent that the British Prime Minister was genuinely interested in developments in the Soviet Union. Incidentally, she mentioned that she had already read my book *Perestroika*, which had just been published in the United Kingdom.

We touched upon strategic arms, an issue I intended to discuss in detail with the American President. Mrs Thatcher showed that she was quite well-informed on these questions too. Discussing first-strike and second-strike weaponry, she suddenly stopped to remark: 'However, it seems that I am using an outdated language. At this stage, it appears somehow inappropriate to speak of first strike or retaliation – we should better speak of arms reduction and co-operation.'

[1] Intermediate-range nuclear forces.

'I won't argue with that,' I replied.

But Mrs Thatcher immediately rejoined: 'In any case, it is necessary to keep a small number of nuclear weapons for deterrence.'

'It seems to me that we continue the old argument about nuclear deterrence.'

'But it proved its effectiveness – it has preserved peace in Europe for over forty years.'

'You will probably agree that one feels more at ease sitting in a comfortable armchair than perched on a powder keg. On the latter, one tends to think less about dialogue and more about how to avoid being blown up.'

Mrs Thatcher was seemingly eager to continue the discussion, but time was running short.

'One has the impression that we had just started our conversation,' she commented, 'and it's already time to part.'

It will be obvious from this that, in spite of our good rapport, we had serious difficulties in starting a dialogue between our countries. I discussed the problem with the British Foreign Secretary, Geoffrey Howe, during his visit to Moscow in February 1988, in connection with an interview Mrs Thatcher had given to *The Sunday Times* on the eve of Howe's arrival. According to the British Prime Minister, the Soviet Union's policy had not changed, with the Soviets pursuing the same goals as before, i.e. 'spreading communist influence world-wide'.

'Could you draw the line between "Mrs Thatcher – the politician" and "Mrs Thatcher – the ideologist"? How much of this is politics and how much mere propaganda?' I asked Howe.

Mr Howe did not question my interpretation of the interview. On bidding farewell, he added: 'We are looking forward to your visit to Great Britain. Your talks with Mrs Thatcher are simply breath-taking. You work like two "Stakhanovites"[1] to fulfil your plans at an unprecedented pace and thoroughly discuss every topic.'

---

[1] Exceptionally hard workers, a term originating in the 1930s after A. G. Stakhanov, a Russian coal-miner.

'I like the comparison you've just made,' I replied. 'Let us all work like "Stakhanovites" to improve our relations.'

THE VIENNA CONFERENCE OPENS NEW PERSPECTIVES

Step by step and brick by brick, I was developing my idea of a 'common European home'. The Vienna CSCE meeting was a significant step forward in this direction. It opened in November 1986, and reached a successful conclusion in early 1989. A noteworthy coincidence – the final document was agreed upon in Vienna three years to the day after I had launched the initiative to rid the world of nuclear weapons, which proved that my proposal had been neither a Utopian dream nor mere propaganda.

The 'Vienna mandate' gave the go-ahead to negotiations about conventional forces in Europe and further developments on co-operation and security. We had proved that we were serious about disarmament by taking a number of unilateral measures and – no less important – we had acknowledged the human rights issue as an integral part of the European process.

The principle of reasonable sufficiency in defence we in the Soviet Union had adopted was in full accord with our concept of a common European home. Developing this new doctrine had been far from easy, however. Indeed, two factors formed one psychological knot: on the one hand, the constant worry about a secure peace (the Soviet people remembered Hitler's attack in 1941) and, on the other, the need drastically to reduce our defence budget – an indispensable condition for improving our economy.

Negotiations on conventional forces in Europe began in March 1989, in the Hofburg Palace in Vienna. For us, it was essential to prevent upgrading of any types of weapons; this would have dealt a fatal blow to everything we had achieved by then and to the trust we had taken such pains to establish.

The Vienna mandate also helped to consolidate our dialogue with Western European leaders.

'You advanced the idea of a "common European home",' François Mitterrand said during his visit to Moscow in the autumn of 1988. 'What a wonderful formula! But what can we do to make it a reality – how can we avoid fostering isolationism on a regional level and, on the contrary, promote integration both in Eastern and Western Europe?'

I supported President Mitterrand's suggestion for a pan-European action programme on environmental issues, and for our participation in scientific and technological co-operation between European states and the European *Eureka* satellite communication project.

The French President thought it possible to start talks on reducing short-range nuclear weapons once the problem of more powerful nuclear missiles had been settled. Concerning negotiations about conventional forces – he seemed to be particularly interested in this issue – Mitterrand agreed to the idea of a conference at ministerial level to be called after the Vienna CSCE meeting. A summit meeting that we were proposing could take place once negotiations had made some headway. This approach was not incompatible with our proposal – we were not in a hurry to fix the day for such a meeting.

I had another encouraging conversation about European integration with the Italian Prime Minister, Ciriaco De Mita, in October 1988. I asked him how we were supposed to build our 'common European home' if the then fashionable plans for the military integration of Western Europe were to be carried out. Must we really draw another dividing line which we would again have to erase in the future?

I should mention here my first meeting with the German Chancellor, Helmut Kohl, in the autumn of 1988. I will talk about it in detail later, but I would just like to make some comments at this point. Our spontaneous mutual trust was probably due to the fact that both he and I saw our 'political mandate' not only in establishing neighbourly relations between the Soviet and German people, but in achieving peace in all of Europe. He took this problem to heart, considering it a personal duty to ensure a safe future for his own family and children. At the time, it crossed my mind that such a rapport between leaders in East and West (not only with Helmut Kohl but also with other leading politicians) proved that the Cold War was about to become a thing of the past.

20

TOWARDS A NEW WORLD ORDER

1987 WAS FRAUGHT WITH PROBLEMS AND COMPLICATIONS IN foreign affairs. The previous year we had reached an agreement in principle between the leaders of the superpowers on the inadmissibility of nuclear war. We had established a productive dialogue with the French leadership, and signed the Delhi declaration during my visit to India. I issued a statement on step-by-step progress towards a nuclear-weapon-free world and the reduction of all types of armament. Finally, the Reykjavik summit had opened up new horizons.

On the other hand, a succession of crises and provocations now threatened to cancel all we had achieved in 1986. I am still convinced that various forces – mostly connected with the military-industrial complex – attempted then to undermine improvements in Soviet-American relations. Reykjavik had frightened many people. A press campaign was launched to convince Americans that the success of the Soviet 'perestroika' and 'new thinking' ran contrary to American interests and Western interests in general.

In the best tradition of its Wild West, America was again flexing its muscles and accusing the Soviet Union of all the deadly sins.

The Americans (and not only they) employed their mass media to manipulate public opinion, to recapture the initiative in international affairs and to force us to accept their rules. I often discussed the issue with my colleagues. All of us felt that we must not surrender the initiative.

After reviewing the options, we arrived at the conclusion that we had to 'untie' the package deal we had proposed in Reykjavik.

We had discussed the package deal even before the summit meeting. At the time, the Politburo had agreed to let me decide in Reykjavik whether or not to accept separate agreements – depending on the turn the talks might take. We had to take a firm stand at the summit, accepting only an overall agreement on our package deal. Now we had to cover the last trump cards that the enemies of disarmament had kept in their hands. The Politburo supported my plans. In a television address I gave on 1 March 1987, I spoke of the Soviet Union's continued commitment to the cause of disarmament, and said that we had agreed to treat the issue of intermediate-range nuclear forces in Europe separately, apart from other problems of nuclear arsenals. The Americans were thus forced to make a move.

On 14 April 1987, I welcomed George Shultz in Moscow. Today I view this meeting as a milestone. The American Secretary of State focused the conversation on intermediate-range nuclear forces and the continuation of strategic arms negotiations. But the issues we discussed went far beyond our prepared briefs. It was the first time that we touched on the philosophical aspects of the new policy, on the roles and responsibilities of our countries.

It seemed that the Americans' main objective had been to learn more about our views and intentions – an entirely justified purpose. But what was to follow? Another round of propaganda campaigns and battling for public support? Or were these soundings a prelude to real politics?

Incidentally, my own aim had been to find out what lay behind the Reagan administration's rhetoric. I wanted to see whether there was any chance of improving relations with Washington. During the talks, I therefore applied a strategy which encouraged our American partner to be frank, to show us his 'fallback positions' and the extent of Mr Shultz's powers.

I think that both sides basically pursued the same object. Rhetorical exchanges of 'compliments' – including the traditional accusations of excessive spying – were one thing. But the talks had shown that underlying considerations and intentions were far more important. As we could see from his subsequent actions, the Secretary of State genuinely wanted to sustain the dialogue. His position seemed to influence the American administration in general, President Reagan in particular.

I realized, maybe for the first time, that I was dealing with a serious man of sound political judgement. Subsequently, he developed his potential even more – as a statesman, an intellectual, a creative and at the same time a far-seeing person.

Mr Shultz invested a lot of effort in transforming our agreement in principle into productive co-operation. He managed to rally the President and his aides as well as his allies. Contacts were intensified and co-operation increased between ministries and general staffs, and the pace of the Geneva talks picked up. I do not know whether it was maybe due to a decrease in whisky consumption, but we were getting more results.

We discussed the progress made in the Geneva and Stockholm talks at a special Politburo meeting called in spring of 1987. The procedural routine at the negotiations and the inclination shown by some of our diplomats for hair-splitting arguments – remnants of past traditions – were strongly criticized. We drew practical conclusions and decided to continue negotiations at a higher level, with Eduard Shevardnadze and Marshal Akhromeyev taking an active part. The top leadership of both countries had thus assumed direct control over negotiations, which could now advance at a quicker pace, and we were finally able to make progress.

In the early autumn of 1987, Shevardnadze went on a visit to Washington, and in October the American Secretary of State was back in Moscow with his team. This meeting proved that we were close to an agreement on intermediate-range nuclear weapons in Europe. The understanding we had reached in April was starting to show results.

At the meeting in the Kremlin on 23 October, we concentrated our attention on the problem of a radical reduction in strategic arms. We had made significant progress on this issue in the last months. But our heavy missiles remained a worry to the Americans, while we were still uneasy about SDI and their strategic bombers. We also kept an eye on their mobile intercontinental ballistic missiles. We discussed in detail the ABM treaty and a ten-year commitment not to withdraw from it following the signing of the strategic arms treaty.

Our conversation was not confined to arms control. We also discussed other aspects of Soviet-American relations – this time not only on a philosophic, conceptual level, but with reference to specific issues. Our exchange of views on the Iran-Iraq war and the American reaction to it is a telling example of how the talks went.

'You are seemingly offended,' I told Shultz, 'by the fact that we did not support your demands for further sanctions in the second resolution of the Security Council, and therefore you have decided to go ahead on your own, just like in the "good old days". I do not want to dwell on the reasons why this happened. I would simply like to repeat that we are disappointed by your unwillingness to co-operate.'

Shultz assured me that the United States had not intended to act alone and preferred to co-operate within the framework of the United Nations. But he pointed out that the conflict represented a serious threat to America's 'friends' in the Gulf – friends who supplied Western countries with oil, their prime energy source.

This example proved that, in spite of a certain progress in our relations with the United States, influential political circles in Washington had not yet decided how to respond to the Soviet Union's perestroika and new thinking. There was obviously also some jealousy about the influence our new foreign policy was having on public opinion in European countries and throughout the world, including the United States.

SOVIET–AMERICAN RELATIONS AND WORLD POLITICS

We were gradually freeing ourselves of stereotyped thinking and the habit of blaming everything on the 'imperialist Western states', while praising our own domestic and foreign policies and actions. This change did not pass unnoticed.

The broadening and intensification of our contacts with the

so-called Third World countries – including influential states like India, Argentina, Indonesia and Mexico – played a major role. Neither did we forget the neutral countries, such as Sweden, Austria or Finland. We did not conceal – neither from 'left-wing' nor 'right-wing' politicians we met – that we considered effective co-operation and understanding with the United States our top priority. But our policy was not exclusively oriented towards this goal. Seeing our intense activity and understanding its potential effects, the Americans were gradually realizing that a negative response to our invitation to co-operate could in the end undermine the authority they had as the leader of the West. Everything was indeed inter-related.

The process of perestroika in the Soviet Union was being discussed throughout the world, as we were intensifying contacts with politicians and influential public organizations in other countries. At the same time, we felt the need for new ideas and new approaches to problems and decision-making. It was becoming increasingly apparent that we had to put an end once and for all to the antagonism of military-political blocs and revive the role of international organizations – first and foremost the United Nations. The divided world of the Cold War had impeded the UN from carrying out the tasks defined in its Charter. It was high time to make good use of the opportunities provided by this universal organization. I discussed this issue in an article published by *Pravda* in September 1987.

MY VISIT TO WASHINGTON, AND THE FIRST NUCLEAR ARMS REDUCTION TREATY

Our Ilyushin-62 landed at the Andrews Air Force Base on 7 December 1987. Mr and Mrs Shultz met us – myself, Raisa Maksimovna and our delegation – at the airport. We exchanged greetings, and then our motorcade sped towards Washington. The Secretary of State shared my car: he was in high spirits as we discussed the summit programme. The highlight was to be the first nuclear arms reduction treaty. START 1 and START 2 were to come later, but the INF treaty set the whole process in motion.

It is doubtful whether we would ever have been able to sign the subsequent agreements without it – the INF treaty represented the first well-prepared step on our way out of the Cold War, the first harbinger of the new times.

The signing ceremony was indeed a solemn occasion, and all the participants were moved by the event. President Reagan and I entered the East Room of the White House, the television networks went on air, and the guests rose to their feet to greet us. The signing procedure took a few minutes. We exchanged the Russian and English copies and pens which had been manufactured for the occasion. President Reagan and I shared a firm handshake and proceeded to deliver addresses to the American and Soviet peoples and to the entire world.

In my address, I mentioned the long and winding road that had eventually brought us to this point – a long, difficult quest to overcome accumulated negative feelings and ingrained stereotypes. What we had achieved was a mere beginning, a starting-point for nuclear disarmament – although, as we all know, the greatest journey starts with a first step: 'We can be proud of planting this sapling, which may one day grow into a mighty tree of peace. But it is probably still too early to bestow laurels upon each other. As the great American poet and philosopher Ralph Waldo Emerson said: "The reward of a thing well done is to have done it". So let us reward ourselves by getting down to business.'

Back at home the INF treaty eventually came under fire, a number of hotheads and amateur politicians claiming that the agreement had undermined the Soviet Union's security and upset the balance of weaponry between the superpowers. The only reason Gorbachev accepted the treaty, according to this theory, was to score a success for his 'new thinking'.

The decision to deploy SS-20 missiles in Eastern Europe had reflected the style of the Soviet leadership at the time, decision-making fraught with grave consequences for the country. I had arrived at the sad conclusion that this step, fateful both for our country and Europe and for the rest of the world, had been taken without the necessary political and strategic analysis of its possible consequences.

It was Soviet Defence Minister Ustinov who had suggested to

571

Brezhnev replacing the missiles based in the European part of the Soviet Union. But it was not merely a question of replacing 'obsolete' equipment. Technological progress allowed the creation of SS-20 missiles far superior to their predecessors in terms of range, precision, guidance and all other properties. Essentially they had the characteristics of strategic weapons. Whatever the arguments advanced at the time to justify the deployment of such missiles, the Soviet leadership failed to take into account the probable reaction of the Western countries. I would even go so far as to characterize it as an unforgivable adventure, embarked on by the previous Soviet leadership under pressure from the military-industrial complex. They might have assumed that, while we deployed our missiles, Western counter-measures would be impeded by the peace movement. If so, such a calculation was more than naive.

Former German Chancellor Helmut Schmidt often returned to this question in our later meetings, openly expressing his amazement at our decision. He remembered that in his time as West German Chancellor, he had a talk with one of Kosygin's deputies during a brief stop-over at Moscow airport (on his flight to Japan or another Far Eastern country). Schmidt had warned that the deployment of SS-20 missiles by the Soviets would force the West to take serious counter-measures, such a move altering the entire military and political situation.

In fact, our decision to deploy the SS-20s suited America's interest in the Cold War. Even more important is the fact that the counter-measures adopted by NATO resulted in a serious threat to Soviet security – the most densely populated part of the USSR suddenly finding itself within reach of the Pershing II. Since the American missiles would take a maximum of five minutes to reach their targets, we were practically unprotected against a possible strike.

By signing the INF treaty we had literally removed a pistol held to our head. Not to mention the exorbitant and unjustifiable costs of developing, producing and servicing the SS-20 – funds swallowed up by the insatiable Moloch of the military-industrial complex.

Incidentally, our military experts were fully aware that to

deploy the SS-20 was a dangerous venture, since we would be unable to protect ourselves against the Pershing II. Marshal Akhromeyev also shared this view. An expert in the field and a straightforward person, he did not conceal his negative view of this fatal adventure – and he later contributed greatly to the removal of the hazard we had brought upon ourselves. I had the opportunity to form an impression of the potential dangers during a briefing with top experts at a defence installation near Moscow. I was accompanied by representatives of the political leadership, the military-industrial complex, and the USSR Council of Ministers. We spent the whole day listening to their reports. I inquired about possible defence systems that could ward off a Pershing attack – and was told that we did not have any.

In short, we had to make haste to prevent full implementation of the American Euromissile programme. It is doubtful whether NATO would have given up their newly acquired advantage once all the missiles had been deployed. I would venture to say that it certainly would have been far more difficult to reach an INF agreement under such conditions.

Hence I deemed it my duty to avert the deadly danger to our country and to correct the fatal error made by the Soviet leadership in the mid-1970s. In a sense, I believe this to be as important an achievement as the withdrawal of Soviet troops from Afghanistan.

Besides its direct application, the INF treaty contained a number of points which, it was hoped, would pave the way for an eventual agreement on strategic long-range weapons. This applied in particular to the verification procedures spelled out in the treaty. We had reached a new level of trust in our relations with the United States and initiated a genuine disarmament process, creating a security system that would be based on comprehensive co-operation instead of the threat of mutual destruction.

Once again, the most important topic during my visit to Washington was strategic arms control. We were progressing step by step on problems of sub-ceilings,[1] sea-launched cruise

---

[1] A numerical limit on a sub-category of weapons within a broader category.

missiles, telemetry and scores of similar essential details. But one stumbling-block remained – President Reagan's Strategic Defense Initiative.

What were the limits imposed by the ABM treaty on testing for the 'Star Wars' programme? What would happen after the period of non-withdrawal from this agreement ended? These were the crucial questions discussed heatedly up to the last moment. The Americans wanted a joint communiqué that would specifically mention the right to deploy defence systems after a period of ten years. (Just imagine – had we accepted these conditions, there could have been nuclear and laser weapons in space by 1997!) We insisted on an indefinite commitment to the ABM treaty, with the treaty remaining in effect and each side required to give prior notice of its intention to withdraw at least six months in advance.

I reiterated what I had repeatedly said both to the American President and to the world – extending the arms race into outer space would rob the strategic arms reduction talks of their sense.

We discussed strategic arms control virtually throughout the visit. President Reagan and I were about to go to the White House South Lawn for the farewell ceremony, but our teams were still working on the final communiqué. A fine drizzle was falling. It was time for us to leave, but there was still no document. All the guests had assembled, as well as the orchestra and the military guards of honour. Reagan and I waited in the White House lobby. Marshal Akhromeyev came to brief me on the compromise reached by the arms-control group: our teams had finally agreed that both sides would commit themselves to observe the ABM treaty, as signed in 1972; research, development and testing must not be contrary to the ABM treaty; the Soviet Union and the United States would not withdraw from the ABM treaty for a specified period of time.

As the reader can see, the joint communiqué did not remove our differences – which made a strong comeback the moment each side began interpreting the results of the summit meeting.

Former Defense Secretary Frank Carlucci has said since that the Soviet leadership overestimated the significance of the Strategic Defense Initiative. I see it differently. For us it was a matter of principle. We were thinking in strategic terms, aware of our responsibility to prevent an arms race in outer space – and I believed then, as I still do, that this would have been the end of the fledgling disarmament process.

DIALOGUE WITH AMERICA

The programme for my visit to the United States was limited to Washington. It was not merely a question of time. Both we and the Americans viewed this first visit – the first since 1974 – as a test run of sorts. Both sides were concerned about the format of the summit meeting. President Reagan had repeatedly said that he wanted me to see different parts of the United States – but apparently his wish was somehow forgotten when it came down to mapping out the programme. Security services (especially on our side) wanted to avoid complications and strongly recommended confining ourselves to Washington on this first trip. I started thinking how I could meet American people outside the official events. We eventually managed to organize meetings with influential American citizens – leading publishers, editors and businessmen.

Raisa Maksimovna's programme included a sight-seeing tour of Washington, a visit to the National Gallery and an invitation from Pamela Harriman for tea with prominent American women.

All in all, we were quite satisfied with our first trip to the United States and returned home with many impressions. Later Raisa Maksimovna and I visited America on numerous occasions; we went both to the east and west coasts of the United States and to the American heartland.

What I like about the Americans is their natural, uninhibited and very down-to-earth manner, their spirit of democracy and obviously their commitment to freedom. But for non-Americans, it is quite difficult to adapt to the American way of life – it is just too different from ours. Maybe it is also a question of different traditions and standards, with the United States being a nation of immigrants.

My first visit to the United States left me with contradictory impressions. Both the American President and his aides had been anxious not to let their guest 'score too many points' – and had tried to draw up a summit programme accordingly. I cannot find any other explanation for the fact that, although we had discussed the possibility of a speech to Congress, nothing came of it. In addition, President Reagan had to manoeuvre. As I see it, the Democrats did not want a Republican President to get all the credit for US foreign policy achievements. The issue was also discussed by the American press, and in the end the programme included only a meeting with congressional leaders.

Something similar had happened in France, where I was not given the opportunity to address the National Assembly, but could speak only to the French deputies – although the main 'players' were present at the meeting. The same had happened in Great Britain, and the Americans had apparently decided to follow this example.

Strange things were happening with Raisa Maksimovna's programme too. It had been planned that on the Washington sight-seeing tour she would be given the opportunity to get out of the car to visit a number of locations. But the motorcade sped past the scheduled sites, where people had gathered in the hope of meeting the General Secretary's wife, without halting; the crowds had to content themselves with the sight of a passing limousine. Everyone was taken aback, Raisa Maksimovna most of all. When she inquired why they did not stop, she was told that this was for security reasons. The press voiced its discontent with the behaviour of the Soviet 'First Lady', since the organizers were openly maintaining that this had been her own wish. And this was far from all. Throughout the visit, American newspapers gossiped about an alleged 'cold war' between the First Ladies, Raisa Maksimovna and Nancy Reagan.

Raisa Maksimovna and Nancy Reagan are very different persons, both from their life experiences and in their professional interests. Nancy is an actress, Raisa an academic. And our countries have their own different traditions, especially concerning the leader's wife's position. Our society did not have a tradition of according the First Lady a special status, and Raisa Maksimovna did not regard this as a problem. But after my election as General Secretary she tried to help me in any way she could – particularly in establishing human contacts during our visits abroad and when we received foreign guests in Moscow. She did not 'wage war' with anyone – in fact she did a lot for mutual understanding and goodwill.

Besides the problems we had on the issues of disarmament, Ronald Reagan and I had occasional skirmishes that echoed in a way the old ideological antagonisms. During one of our meetings, the American President started lecturing me. I was obliged to interrupt him and calmly replied: 'Mr President, you are not a prosecutor and I am not on trial here. Like you, I represent a great country and therefore expect our dialogue to be conducted on a basis of reciprocity and equality. Otherwise there simply will be no dialogue.'

Now and then, there appeared a feeling of mistrust and we would exchange biting remarks – but these moments gradually grew fewer. Both partners were becoming used to each other and stopped getting worked up at every word and snubbing every remark they disliked. Obviously, there were still critical situations – you cannot avoid them completely during such talks – but we tried to play them down with a joke. The Americans have a marked sense of humour. And it seemed to me that during my visit Reagan re-appraised many things and succeeded in overcoming some of his own stereotypes and misconceptions – although I must say that George Shultz went furthest in this sense.

The American public literally bombarded the Soviet embassy – my residence during the summit meeting – with letters, greetings and appeals. I invited many distinguished American citizens to a meeting in the Soviet Embassy's Oval Room. There were also outstanding Soviet scientists and artists present. The meeting stimulated great interest both in the United States and in our country.

It was – and still is – my conviction that there can be no fruitful co-operation between two nations without economic ties. Apart from our grain imports, there were practically no such ties between the United States and the Soviet Union. We were isolated from each other by political decisions and restrictions aimed at preventing the transfer of new technologies.

The notorious Cocom lists impeded not only the United States but also many other countries from co-operating with us on a modern technological and economic level. Linking trade to human rights caused many difficulties for those who genuinely wanted to do business with us. Few American businessmen managed to break into our market.

In my meeting with leading American media executives I focused on one theme – we all have to learn to live in a new world. The American press depicted the meeting as quarrelsome. Maybe I was a little emotional, and I regret it. But I was bombarded with prickly questions right from the start – questions I had incidentally answered dozens of times. I was troubled by the fact that our meeting was about to turn into a run-of-the-mill press conference. But we finally succeeded in calming down and getting to the point.

One of the reasons for the success of our 'invasion' of Washington was that we did not harbour any 'subversive' plans. The 'invading force' included not only myself, Raisa Maksimovna and our closest aides, but all my compatriots who accompanied me to the United States – distinguished scientists, intellectuals and artists and an army of journalists. They had arrived earlier and established contact with their American colleagues, participating in a number of discussions and giving numerous interviews. The Soviets spoke openly, without resorting to the old clichés and dogmas. They had attained freedom of thought, showing that they knew how to use it responsibly, without indulging in demagoguery. This was the first fruit of glasnost.

The participants in the numerous discussions did not insist on stubborn defence of ideological principles, but concentrated instead on trying to hear and understand each other. And this was as important an achievement as the signing of the INF treaty.

During those days so full of interesting meetings there were some truly emotional moments. One was the dinner at the White House. Van Cliburn gave a recital after dinner. We remembered him as the young pianist who had won the 1958 Tchaikovsky Prize in Moscow for his rendering of the great Russian composer's first piano concerto. After exchanging an affectionate hug with us, Van Cliburn sat down at the grand piano and started softly playing and singing *Moscow Nights*. This was a genuine gift for the Soviet guests. The song, which had been written by Soloviev-Sedoi for the 1957 Moscow Youth Festival, had become virtually an informal popular anthem. We could not resist the temptation and joined in, Russian and English lyrics blending into one emotion.

George Shultz played the part of the perfect host at the reception at the State Department, creating a warm and friendly atmosphere. There were guests from all over the United States, the 'crème de la crème', and Shultz had also invited all his surviving predecessors in office.

I think that my speech at this meeting was the best I gave during this visit. Obviously I spoke about the INF treaty and its significance, but I built the speech around a different central theme:

'Today, hundreds of millions of people are gradually realizing that the end of the twentieth century represents a watershed for mankind – a watershed which separates not so much political systems and ideologies, but common sense and the will to survive on the one hand, and irresponsibility, national egoism, prejudices – in short, the old thinking – on the other hand. Mankind has come to realize that it has had enough wars and that it is time to put an end to them for good. Two World Wars, the exhausting Cold War and the minor wars which have cost and are still costing millions of lives – this is a more than sufficient price to pay for adventurism, ambition and the neglect of the other's rights and interests, for the unwillingness and inability to cope with realities and for failure to respect the legitimate right of every nation to decide its own future and to have its place in the sun.

'The world of today is not a monopoly of one nation or group of nations, whatever their power. The world is a common home and a common cause for a plurality of individuals. And where you have a number of actors, you cannot do without reciprocity and compromise. Peace from a position of force is inherently weak, whatever people say about it. It is in the nature of such peace to be founded on confrontation – hidden or open – on the permanent danger of flare-ups and the temptation to use force.

'For centuries, mankind has been obliged to accept this truly bad peace. We cannot allow ourselves to continue like this any more. Some people believe that the Soviet side has conceded too much for the INF treaty, others think that the Americans have made many concessions. It seems to me that both views are wrong. Each side conceded just as much as was needed to start the process of disarmament, to establish a minimum of mutual trust without endangering anyone's security. To put it in simple, human language, what we have achieved is – both in Russian and in English – the revival of hope.'

There was another event I would like to mention. In accordance with protocol, George Bush was to accompany me to the airport – and we had a substantial conversation in the car on the way there. As a matter of fact, our conversation laid a foundation stone of mutual understanding and trust. We often referred to this conversation in our subsequent meetings, when George Bush had become President of the United States. I greatly appreciated the attitude he had shown then, at that turning-point in Soviet-American relations. And I was always frank with him, leading to a responsible and open dialogue – which in my view has been of enormous significance both for our countries and for world politics in general.

MAINTAINING THE MOMENTUM

In spite of being completely taken up with domestic affairs, I kept an eye on developments in Soviet-American relations after the visit to Washington in 1987. The Americans were getting ready for their election campaign, with the usual effect on American foreign policy. Yet it was essential not to lose momentum; at this stage of Soviet-American relations, a pause could have resulted in a setback.

The American public welcomed the improvement in Soviet-American relations, and the INF treaty stood a good chance of being ratified by the American Congress. Yet we could not rest on our laurels. Washington's reaction to our proposal to search jointly for a solution to the Afghan problem had been disappointing and the disarmament talks in Geneva were dragging along, 'smelling of mothballs again', as I commented to my colleagues.

Ronald Reagan's official visit to Moscow was scheduled for summer 1988. We wanted this visit to become another milestone marking the end of the Cold War, instead of a mere symbolic act of friendship. It was therefore essential to achieve a breakthrough on disarmament. Ideally we would work out an agreement on strategic arms cuts in time for President Reagan's visit – which seemed feasible, considering how much progress we had already made in the negotiations.

Hence the significance I attached to the meeting with George Shultz in Moscow on 28 February 1988. We had established quite a good rapport during our previous meetings and negotiations and could hope for success. Mr Shultz and I began with a brief exchange of views on the domestic situation in the Soviet Union and the United States and went on to discuss ratification of the INF agreement. He agreed that ratification procedures should be completed in time for President Reagan's visit to Moscow, adding that he was convinced the American Senate would ratify the treaty in time.

Our talks moved to strategic arms. We focused our attention on a number of questions that remained to be settled, such as the verification procedures. I said that the Soviet Union would agree to comprehensive verification of production and deployment of strategic arms – i.e. land-based, ship-based, submarine-launched and air-launched missiles. We were also ready to exchange more information and proposed the setting up of a special working group of scientists and military experts to deal with all aspects of verification. Shultz supported the idea, suggesting that we should establish a strict timetable: since the Soviet Foreign Minister was to visit the United States in March, the working group should provide us with the results by then.

Again we discussed the link between strategic arms agreements and the ABM treaty. I insisted that we should take the joint statement we had agreed upon in Washington as a basis for further negotiations. Mr Shultz initially seemed to agree, but then began expressing reservations and trying to back out of the commitment. Despite having accepted the formula we agreed upon in Washington, the American administration was still trying to play hide-and-seek with us on the ABM treaty.

I also brought up the question of a ban on chemical weapons. The Americans seemed to have lost some of their initial enthusiasm and I wanted to clarify the situation. Hence I suggested preparing a joint statement on this issue for the Moscow meeting; our countries could express their firm intention to promote a worldwide ban of these weapons and do everything in their power to conclude an appropriate international convention. The American Secretary of State agreed, and I proposed taking an additional step in this direction: verification being the issue of the day, the United States and the Soviet Union could each designate one chemical plant where verification procedures could be tested, before being included in a future international convention banning the use and production of chemical weapons. Mr Shultz approved the proposal, adding, however, that he 'risked a dressing down back home'.

We briefly touched on the question of conventional forces, agreeing that we 'should push on', and concentrated on regional conflicts. Incidentally, Mr Shultz and Eduard Shevardnadze had spent nearly the whole night discussing this issue.

I reiterated my declaration, made six months earlier, that we would withdraw our troops from Afghanistan. We had no intention of creating a bridgehead in Afghanistan or of pushing towards the southern seas, I told Mr Shultz. I asked for American co-operation in helping Afghanistan to become an independent, non-aligned, neutral state and allowing the Afghans themselves to decide what kind of government they wanted.

On the eve of Mr Shultz's arrival, the American Ambassador in Moscow, Jack Matlock, had transmitted to us the written proposals for a Middle East settlement which George Shultz intended to make public during his forthcoming trip to a number of Middle Eastern states. The proposals became known later as the 'Shultz Plan'. I welcomed the fact that we were given the proposals in advance – for me, it was a sign of fledgling Soviet-American co-operation in trying to find a solution to this chronic international problem.

This exchange of views led to a discussion about the

'philosophical' aspects of the global challenges of today. George Shultz was greatly interested in my ideas and said that he had been 'moving in the same direction'. 'I don't have a crystal ball to see the future,' he said. 'But I can see worldwide trends which require, I would say, a new thinking. And if we follow the spirit of the new thinking, we might perceive our interests differently – many things will appear in a different light.'

'There is a real chance to harmonize national interests,' I told him. 'Developed countries judge this unacceptable at first glance, fearing another raid on their wallets. But this is only at first glance. If you take a second look, worldwide progress is in the interest of developed countries. Lack of progress means the accumulation of economic, social and other problems which will eventually backlash and hit everyone – including the developed nations – disrupting established ties.'

After this meeting with the American Secretary of State, I tried to see what new elements it had added to our relations with the American administration. I asked myself whether we had been right to pursue co-operation with the present and future American administrations. It was obvious that Mr Shultz personally favoured this approach and that we could count on him to use his influence to further improve Soviet-American relations, while naturally defending the interests of the United States. At the same time, you could see that he enjoyed only limited freedom of action and that many people from the presidential team, the Congress and influential political circles and government agencies were not about to accept such a policy. The American Defense Secretary, Caspar Weinberger, a known foe of Shultz's ideas, could count on the support of a powerful lobby.

Subsequent developments showed that there was a fierce battle raging in the American administration about future policy towards the Soviet Union. On the one hand, Eduard Shevardnadze had achieved significant progress on a number of prickly disarmament questions during his meetings with leading figures in the Reagan administration. In Geneva we had finally succeeded in reaching an agreement on Afghanistan. On the other hand, remarks made by a number of American government officials, including President Reagan himself, were not helpful to the new relations we hoped to establish.

When I met George Shultz again on 22 April, after the usual exchange of greetings and jokes, I asked him directly about the President's real intentions. 'Could it be that President Reagan's recent remarks represent the groundwork for his visit to the Soviet Union? Does he really intend to bring this ideological luggage to Moscow? He must realize that we will answer back. And with what result? We'll have an argument, and we might as well forget everything we have achieved with so much effort! Who needs that?'

Shultz made an attempt to dispel my doubts, saying that the American President viewed our relations as 'a new page in history', and making a detailed inventory of what had been achieved in the past few years.

We were still making little progress on disarmament. By May it was clear that we could not expect to sign a strategic arms reduction treaty at the summit meeting. In 'compensation', we agreed to push for a ratification of the INF treaty in time for the President's visit. The American Senate ratified the agreement on 27 May and the USSR Supreme Soviet on 28 May, the eve of Mr Reagan's arrival in Moscow.

RONALD REAGAN IN MOSCOW

On 29 May the President stepped onto Soviet soil, closing a fourteen-year break in official visits by American heads of state to the Soviet Union. We had our first private meeting in the Catherine Hall at the Kremlin that day.

Looking back to that period and re-reading the notes I made then, it appears to me that the significance of those first Moscow talks lay not so much in the subjects we discussed as in the friendly atmosphere and the mutual desire to strike a well-meaning, trustful tone from the start. We spoke of the need to develop our dialogue on major aspects of Soviet-American relations and expressed our satisfaction with the progress hitherto achieved. I proposed to make a joint statement at the end of the visit, declaring that in the world of today, with its ideological and other differences, controversies could not and should not be resolved by military means. The nations of the world should live in peace, peaceful co-existence being a universal principle of international relations.

President Reagan agreed in principle with the idea, saying that we should defer this question to the experts, and immediately raised an issue which always seemed to concern him greatly: he asked me to decide a number of specific cases linked to the re-unification of families and permission to emigrate. I promised to look into all the cases he had mentioned.

Mr Reagan then turned to the question of religion and freedom of worship in the Soviet Union, stressing that I should regard his comments as 'nothing more than personal, well-meant advice'. He was sincere and I respected it. Since the American President planned to meet the Russian Orthodox Patriarch Pimen and visit a monastery, I expressed the hope that he would receive more comprehensive information on the problems of religion in our country.

During that first meeting with the President, Raisa Maksimovna took Nancy Reagan on a sight-seeing tour of the Kremlin. There were the usual crowds of tourists from all over the Soviet Union – the holiday season had just begun. The Soviet citizens warmly greeted our American guests and wished us all good luck with the negotiations. Mr and Mrs Reagan and the other members of the American delegation found themselves surrounded by an atmosphere of goodwill from the start.

Disarmament was the topic of the day. I started by briefly recalling our position on the issue. I remarked that we were as worried about the American submarine-launched ballistic missiles as they were about our intercontinental ballistic missiles. 'We realize that sea-launched cruise missiles cannot be included in the subceilings for strategic nuclear arms and have to be treated separately,' I said. 'But they have to be linked to the fifty-per-cent reduction of strategic arms. Otherwise we would leave the door open for a continuation of the arms race in another area. We must agree on a ceiling for these missiles and it would be marvellous if we could agree on such a ceiling here in Moscow.' I added that we would very much like to sign a strategic arms reduction agreement while our guest was still in office.

As expected, Ronald Reagan brought up the Strategic Defense Initiative. He confirmed the American position that a reduction of strategic nuclear arms could be accompanied by an agreement not to withdraw from the ABM treaty for a specified period of time. If we did not reach another agreement during this period, each side would have the right to decide what future course to take. At the same time, Mr Reagan stressed that the United States would not give its consent for a period of non-withdrawal from the ABM treaty as long as the Soviet Union continued violating the treaty; his remark was aimed at our radar station in Krasnoyarsk.[1]

He added that another essential question was how much research, development and testing was to be permitted during the period of non-withdrawal from the ABM treaty. The United States were against imposing stricter limitations than the ones provided by the treaty.

The ensuing discussion focused on the logic of SDI. Since we were talking about Ronald Reagan's 'pet project', the exchange quickly became rather heated. 'What is SDI for?' I asked. 'What missiles is it supposed to bring down if we eliminate all nuclear weapons?'

'It will be there just in case,' Reagan replied. 'The know-how for developing nuclear weapons won't evaporate from people's minds. No-one will be able to take it away from them. And there will be the technology for building missiles. A madman might appear who will appropriate these secrets. There have been examples before, like Hitler – they occasionally appear in history . . .'

The American President made an unfortunate gesture, knocking over a glass of water, and apologized.

'Never mind, Mr President,' I commented jokingly. 'A careless move with a glass of water is no big deal. If it had happened with missiles . . .'

We all laughed at the joke and the tension eased.

---

[1] The US regarded the Krasnoyarsk facility as a violation of the ABM treaty.

Returning to the subject, I argued that the Strategic Defense Initiative was not a purely defensive programme: it opened the way to the development of space-based weapons that could hit targets on the earth. Reagan repeated his suggestion made in Geneva that we could observe the Americans' SDI research and be present during testing.

'I am afraid I have some doubts about this,' I replied. 'Before making such a proposal, you should maybe first try to convince Mr Carlucci,[1] Mr Shultz and the US Navy to open just two types of your warships for inspection of sea-launched cruise missiles. But as far as we know, your Navy people balk at consenting to the inspection of their warships, and Mr Carlucci supports them. How do you intend to open sensitive SDI research for inspection if you cannot even grant our inspectors access to two types of warships? It seems to me unrealistic.'

Frank Carlucci intervened, assuring us that SDI could not function as an offensive weapon.

'The arguments you advance do not convince us, Mr Carlucci,' I told him.

We went on to examine verification procedures, and discussed the American proposal to sign a separate agreement providing for prior notification of ICBM and SLBM flight tests conducted both within and outside each nation's territory. We agreed to prepare and sign this agreement during President Reagan's stay in Moscow.

Discussion of conventional forces was facilitated by the fact that only two weeks before, George Shultz and Eduard Shevardnadze had finally agreed on the agenda for negotiations: armed forces, conventional weapons and equipment – all types would be included in the negotiations. There was a chance to agree on a mandate for the negotiating teams. However, Mr Reagan again raised the question of Soviet superiority in conventional forces. I reminded him that we had discussed the issue back in Washington and suggested exchanging and publishing data about the size and structure of our respective conventional forces, to put an end to the argument once and for all. My

---

[1] Frank Carlucci, the American Secretary for Defense.

partners responded rather coolly to this proposal.

I wanted to get things moving and suggested starting the talks proper: 'We suggest three stages for these talks,' I said. 'As a first stage, we would define and eliminate existing imbalances and asymmetries. In order to do this, we make the following new proposal: let us verify the data which will serve as a basis for negotiations by way of on-site inspection right at the start of conventional forces reduction talks in order to eliminate differences in our respective estimates. At this stage, we would also agree on how to eliminate imbalances and asymmetries and reduce armed forces and weapons under strict surveillance.

'In a second stage, having eliminated the imbalances and asymmetries, both sides would reduce their conventional forces by approximately half a million men each.

'In the third stage, conventional forces on both sides would be restructured to become purely defensive and unsuited for offensive warfare. At all stages of the negotiations, we are prepared to reduce offensive weapons on both sides – tactical nuclear weapons, strike aircraft and tanks. We could also discuss such measures as the creation of nuclear-free disengagement zones between our respective forces.

'This is our logic. I can't understand why it doesn't suit you. What is it that stops you from seriously discussing these questions?'

The American Secretary of State's reply spoke for itself: 'We can see that you want to achieve progress on the question of conventional forces. We and our allies also want to make headway. The question is how to do it. We should start in Vienna and conclude work on the mandate. The formula you have just read has indeed been discussed by us in Geneva. It's a good formula. We must now "sell" this formula to our allies, yours and ours. The deal will be made easier if it looks like a proposal considered by all parties, and not just like a formula we worked out by ourselves. They fear that we will make a deal behind their backs. Hence this process must start in Vienna. As to the essence of the deal, the formula suits us. The main thing is a careful presentation in Vienna.'

At the end of the meeting, President Reagan brought up the

problem of the proliferation of ballistic missiles. 'This is becoming a critical issue in the Middle East and Southern Asia,' he said. 'And if we don't stop this proliferation, it might become a serious threat. Countries like Iran and Libya could combine missile technology and the technology used for chemical weapons, with the most dire consequences. We should therefore consider what pressure we could exert on the countries in question and how to influence our friends in order to stop this trend or get it under control.'

I agreed that this was indeed a serious problem, adding that I was prepared to examine its specific implications.

Next morning we met for another private talk. Ronald Reagan asked me to give him a detailed account of the progress of perestroika, the difficulties we had encountered and our future plans. I directed his attention to the fact that the United States persisted in maintaining a discriminatory trade policy towards the Soviet Union. I expressed the fear that American policy might still be to ask: 'Why on earth should we help the Soviet Union to become stronger, if it is easier to deal with a weak nation?' or something along that line. President Reagan naturally protested, at the same time trying to justify the discriminatory trade policy by pointing out a number of unresolved problems with Soviet emigration policy.

The general sense of my reply was that now that we had agreed in principle on the need to promote bilateral co-operation, we should join efforts to clear away the ideological debris of the past.

'I am convinced it's God's will that we should co-operate,' I added. 'Incidentally, a greater interdependence ensures greater predictability in our respective policies.'

The American President promised to do everything in his power to preserve the constructive spirit in the Soviet-American dialogue, adding that he sometimes prayed to God for George Bush to become his successor, since he shared his views on fundamental issues and they were both seeking to improve relations with the Soviet Union.

FAREWELL TO THE 'EVIL EMPIRE'

After the morning talks, Mr Reagan and I went on a walk around the Kremlin. The American President was greeted by groups of tourists. He answered their greetings good-humouredly, occasionally stopping for a chat. During one of these spontaneous 'press conferences', which incidentally happened next to the famous *Tsar-Pushka*[1] ('The Tsar of Cannons'), someone from the crowd asked 'Mr President, do you still see the Soviet Union as the evil empire?' Ronald Reagan's reply was short: 'No.' I was standing next to him and thought to myself: 'Right.' I recounted this incident the next day at my press conference, and the journalists reminded President Reagan of it during the press conference he gave a few hours later. A reporter insisted on learning the reasons which had prompted the American President to change his view: 'Mr President, did you discover something that made you change your mind?' he asked. 'Did you have the opportunity to get a better look at this country? And who deserves credit for it – you or Gorbachev?'

'Mr Gorbachev deserves most of the credit as the leader of this country,' President Reagan replied. 'And it seems to me that with perestroika things have changed in the Soviet Union. Judging from what I read about perestroika, I could agree with a lot of it.'

For me, Ronald Reagan's acknowledgement was one of the genuine achievements of his Moscow visit. It meant that he had finally convinced himself that he had been right to believe, back in Reykjavik, that you could 'do business' with the changing Soviet Union – the hopeful business of preventing a nuclear war. He could congratulate himself on having made the right choice – and I now realized why he had told me the other day he prayed to God that the next President would be a man who would support this choice. In my view, the 40th President of the United States will go down in history for his rare perception.

We strolled through the Kremlin and emerged from the Spassky Gate on Red Square, close to the Lenin Mausoleum. President Reagan was greatly interested by the architectural sites

[1] The huge cannon which can be seen in the grounds of the Kremlin.

of Russia's historic centre. He was excited and seemingly pleased with the visit.

We returned to the Kremlin and went to the Great Kremlin Palace to attend the official signing ceremony. The guests had already assembled. Eduard Shevardnadze and George Shultz signed the agreement on a joint verification experiment and an agreement on prior notification of ICBM and SLBM flight tests. We also signed a co-operation and exchange programme for 1989 and 1990, including an annual school exchange of 1,000 pupils from 100 Soviet and American schools – an idea President Reagan had suggested (incidentally, I do not know whether this project is still in effect).

The final meeting took place in the morning of 1 June, in the presence of our delegations. Shevardnadze and Shultz briefed us on the results of their talks.

On this occasion, we discussed in detail the problem of regional conflicts. I explained to President Reagan our approach to resolving these conflicts, stressing that we proceeded on the premise that both the interests of our allies and political friends and the legitimate interest of the United States must be taken into account. Afghanistan was a good example for this approach. The significance of this unprecedented settlement went far beyond its regional implications. It was the first time that the Soviet Union and the United States, together with the conflicting parties, had signed an agreement which paved the way for a political solution of the conflict. We also made progress on the question of an international Middle East conference. In the course of the discussion, we perceived a possibility of finding settlements for the conflicts in southern Africa, Central America and Cambodia.

We turned to the text of the joint statement, and I repeated the proposal I had made during our first official talk: a joint statement on the unacceptability of resolving conflicts by the use of military force, the acknowledgement of peaceful co-existence as an internationally accepted principle, the equality of all nations, non-interference in domestic affairs and the freedom of social and political choice as inalienable and binding international standards. The American President then agreed to study my proposals with his colleagues.

591

The 'colleagues' opposed the idea. The 'softened' version we suggested was not accepted either. The reader can turn to the published text of the statement to learn what remained in the end.

The last official round of talks came to an end and we proceeded to the Vladimir Hall of the Great Kremlin Palace for the official exchange of ratification documents for the INF treaty.

The first step had been made. But there was still a long way to go. The world was crammed with deadly weapons and the great powers still confronted each other. We had to continue our work.

THE WATERSHED: MY SPEECH TO THE UNITED NATIONS

By 1988 we had fully developed both the conceptual basis and the policies of our new political thinking. I outlined these in a speech to the United Nations.

We started preparations for this trip to New York in good time; I had been thinking about it even during my summer holiday and convened my closest associates on international affairs – Shevardnadze, Yakovlev, Chernyaev, Dobrynin and Falin – on 31 October to discuss the general direction and content of the forthcoming speech. Everyone agreed that the time had come to make significant cuts in our armed forces and that the next five-year period should be dedicated to disarmament. My speech to the United Nations was to be the exact opposite of Winston Churchill's famous Fulton speech. And we could substantiate our ideas through facts, showing the real progress achieved in the past few years. It was clear that people would believe us only if we translated our intentions into deeds.

I intended to include a section about the role of the United Nations as an instrument of peace, and to stress that the time had come for the organization to develop fully its potential and to make use of the powers with which it had been endowed at its founding. It seemed to me feasible to propose a realistic 'action plan' for the United Nations which would be adapted to the new realities in the world. Again it was necessary to stress the need for 'demilitarizing' thinking in our community of nations and for building international relations on a more democratic and human basis. And, last but not least, to present our ideas about the role of the United Nations in establishing a new economic world order and creating equitable economic ties between developed nations and the Third World.

The Politburo agreed to the initial concepts and suggestions that were to be included in the final draft of the speech. Incidentally, there were no objections of principle.

We spent a long time working out the suggested figures for planned unilateral armed forces reductions. Marshal Akhromeyev spared no effort to get the work done – the rumours about his alleged opposition to that disarmament proposal are sheer nonsense. On the contrary, he supervised all the preparatory work for this initiative.

We then set to work on the text of the speech. I used to rewrite, or rather 're-dictate', my speeches several times – three times in this case. But even so, my colleagues and I continued working on it (another custom I had introduced) on board the aeroplane that took us to New York, exchanging views, discussing last-minute information and refining different aspects.

I had only a few hours left before landing to marshal my thoughts and 'switch off'. The next days were bound to be stressful and I had to muster all my energy and concentration. Everything seemed thoroughly thought out, planned and replanned, but all the same I tried to review the priorities we had set for this visit.

The highlight was obviously the address to the United Nations General Assembly. In the forty years of its existence, it had heard a great many speeches, including some delivered by master orators. But this aspect was of the least concern to me. By the end of 1988, I had formed a comprehensive concept of a proper world order and a view of how to achieve it, as well as the contribution our great country could make to progress in this direction. The United Nations General Assembly seemed to me the appropriate forum for presenting these views. Since they reflected not only my personal assessment of the international situation but also the interests of a great nation, they could become an important factor in the process of shaping a new international consciousness. I will not deny that I also hoped that a positive international response to my programme would strengthen my position and help overcome the growing resistance to change in the Soviet Union.

What did I consider to be the most important part of the speech? It included a number of concrete proposals aimed at further improving the international climate. I informed the United Nations of our decision to reduce the Soviet armed forces by half a million men and the corresponding number of weapons and equipment in the coming two years, of the agreement we had reached with our Warsaw Pact allies to withdraw and disband six Soviet armoured divisions from the GDR, Czechoslovakia and Hungary by 1991, and of a number of additional measures aimed at reducing our offensive military potential. However, my main intent was to show the international community that mankind was on the threshold of a fundamentally new era, the traditional principles governing international relations, which were based on the balance of power and rivalry, to be superseded by relations founded on creative co-operation and joint development.

If I were asked today to summarize the main ideas of the speech, I would confine myself to the few universal axioms and principles:

- Every nation, and in particular the major powers, must exercise self-restraint and refrain from the use of force in international relations;
- Freedom of choice is a *sine qua non* for preserving diversity in the social development of nations;
- Relations among states must be freed from ideology;
- We must join forces to ensure the primacy of universal human values over the numerous centrifugal forces nourished by possibly legitimate but egoistic motives.

The practical steps I proposed in my speech were centred around the new role of the United Nations, with new opportunities for the organization opening up in virtually every sphere, be it military-political or economic, scientific, ecological and humanitarian.

This concerned, first and foremost, the problem of development. The conditions of life for hundreds of millions in the Third World were such that they posed a real danger to the world. 'Exclusive clubs' or even regional organizations, despite their significance, could not undo the Gordian knots tied along the main economic axes: North–South, East–West, South–South, South–East, East–East. It was imperative to act jointly respecting the interests of all groups of nations, and the United Nations was the sole organization up to the task. In particular, it could help to find a way out of the international debt crisis. With a number of regions facing ecological problems, I suggested as a first step the creation of a United Nations centre for urgent ecological relief, which would co-ordinate and send international expert teams to regions struck by acute environmental pollution.

I dwelt on the question of international law, which was to play a significant role in the new world order. Ideally the international community would be composed of states founded on the rule of law which would subordinate their foreign policy to law and nothing but law. A significant step in this direction could be achieved by agreeing on a uniform interpretation of the principles and standards of international law, their codification and the development of legal standards adapted to the new fields of co-operation. In our age, the effectiveness of international law should be ensured not by coercion, but by developing standards which would reflect the international balance of interests. This would help every nation to realize that it acted in its own interest by matching the standards of international law.

The legal aspect of international affairs was closely linked to the need to humanize them. International relations could serve the genuine interests of nations and global security only if man – his concerns, rights and freedoms – was placed at the centre of the international system.

I have re-read the text of my speech as I worked on my memoirs. We have learned much in the past few years and if I were to write it now, I would probably correct or add some points and express a number of them differently. Yet even today I would not retract any of the fundamental ideas I wrote down at the time, and I would say that the message of the speech is as relevant as ever.

I started speaking somewhat hesitantly, with occasional pauses. But gradually I felt the growing interest of the audience, sensing that my words and ideas were coming across and gaining self-confidence and perhaps eloquence. I ended my speech to a storm of applause, which was apparently more than a mere sign of courtesy.

I was curious about the reception my speech would be given by the American press. The press service later prepared a report. Naturally many newspapers centred on the specific disarmament proposals. But the more respectable publications had grasped the profound meaning of my United Nations speech.

The *New York Times* wrote in its editorial:

> Perhaps not since Woodrow Wilson presented his Fourteen Points in 1918 or since Franklin Roosevelt and Winston Churchill promulgated the Atlantic Charter in 1941 has a world figure demonstrated the vision of Mikhail Gorbachev, displayed yesterday at the United Nations. Like the others, the Soviet leader called for the basic restructuring of international politics – for the rule of law, not force; for multilateralism, not unilateralism; and for economic as well as political freedoms. Like them, he used occasion and oratory to command global stage. Unlike them, he promised to lead the way unilaterally, by reducing Soviet military forces and converting defense industries to peaceful uses.
>
> Breathtaking. Risky. Bold. Naive. Diversionary. Heroic. All fit. So sweeping is his agenda that it will require weeks to sort out. But whatever Mr Gorbachev's motives, his ideas merit – indeed compel – the most serious response from President-elect Bush and other leaders.

Robert Kaiser commented in *The Washington Post*:

> In a speech as remarkable as any ever delivered at the United Nations, Mikhail Gorbachev today proposed to change the rules the world has lived by for four decades

... Gorbachev invited the world literally to beat its swords into ploughshares, declaring that 'the use or threat of force no longer can or must be an instrument of foreign policy' ... Gorbachev's invitation to move beyond the Cold War to a new era of international co-operation is one that no elected Western leader will easily be able to reject or resist. And, by surrounding this offer with stunning acknowledgements of Soviet shortcomings and errors in the past, the Soviet leader has conveyed a sense of candor and sincerity that is likely to increase the appeal of his propositions. The boldness of today's speech was remarkable ...

Governor's Island lies at the south end of East River, some fifteen minutes by car from the city centre. There I was to meet President Reagan and Vice-President Bush. Initially, I had planned to relax somewhat and collect my thoughts during this brief trip, but things never turn out the way you think they will.

A MEETING AT GOVERNOR'S ISLAND

I learned of the earthquake in Armenia from a telegram Mrs Thatcher sent me the same night. I had a telephone conversation with Ryzhkov from the car on the ferry to Governor's Island. He briefed me on the extent of the disaster, the devastation and the enormous losses in human lives. It was an unprecedented tragedy, at least in recent years.

We arrived on the island and I went directly to the Admiral's House to dictate a message of sympathy and solidarity to the Armenian people.

The reader can easily imagine the state I was in. I had already decided to cut short my visit to the United States. I had planned to go on to Cuba, but I would apologize to Fidel Castro and fly back home immediately.

But for the moment I had to think of the agenda. A ceremonial welcome had been prepared and hundreds of reporters were already waiting. I tried to keep my countenance, exchanging polite remarks with President Reagan and Vice-President Bush and pressing them to retire to the 'fireside lounge' of the small cottage set apart for our meeting. We spent the first minutes discussing the tragedy in Armenia and were later joined by Shevardnadze, Yakovlev, Chernyaev, Dobrynin, Bessmertnykh, Dubinin, Shultz, Powell, Duberstein, Ridgway and Matlock. It was important for me to gauge the prospects for our American policy in view of the impending change in the American leadership. The informal discussion meandered from one topic to another. Ronald Reagan was speaking for the Americans, in spite of the fact that he was merely completing his term in office, a 'lame duck', as the American newspapers called him. George Bush, though President-elect, was keeping a low profile, tactfully playing his part as a loyal Vice-President.

All in all, I had a good impression of this meeting on Governor's Island. The conversation had been frank and friendly, and we could hope to make further headway with the next President of the United States.

Ronald Reagan accompanied me to the car-ferry. A few minutes later, our motorcade was speeding down Broadway, which was lined with crowds. We drove for an hour along the city streets, and I got out of the car on two occasions to shake hands and exchange greetings. But time was pressing, and I still had a number of meetings to attend.

A grand reception was given in the evening by the United Nations Secretary-General. But I had only one thing on my mind – the tragedy in Armenia. I left the reception and returned to the Soviet Embassy to give instructions to prepare for our departure and to inform the press of my decision. We left New York for Moscow on the morning of the following day.

21

PERESTROIKA AND THE SOCIALIST COUNTRIES

THE END OF THE 'BREZHNEV DOCTRINE'

AFTER THE CENTRAL COMMITTEE PLENUM HAD ELECTED ME General Secretary in 1985, I decided to meet the leaders of the Warsaw Pact[1] countries without delay. I spoke on the telephone to each of them, introduced myself in my new capacity, and offered to meet them when they arrived in Moscow. The meeting was held in the Kremlin after Chernenko's funeral. Those present were Todor Zhivkov of Bulgaria, Nicolae Ceausescu of Romania, Erich Honecker of the German Democratic Republic, János Kádár of Hungary, Gustav Husák of Czechoslovakia, and Wojciech Jaruzelski of Poland. Participating on our side were Tikhonov, Gromyko and Rusakov.

I will not say that this was an easy meeting for me. By that time I was already personally acquainted with all the leaders of the Socialist countries, and I had met a few of them – Zhivkov, Kádár, and Ceausescu – several times. That was one situation, though, and this was quite another. I had to build bridges with men who for the most part had already been leaders of their countries for dozens of years and were used to following established stereotypes in their relations with the Soviet leadership.

[1] In the Soviet Union, the official name – the Warsaw Treaty Organization – was used. The more familiar term 'Warsaw Pact' is used in this translation.

Moreover, this is only one aspect of the matter, and perhaps not even the most important one. By that time it was clear that relations with these countries were badly in need of revitalizing. The 'formula' I took to the meeting thus included two chief elements – continuity and the need for change.

For understandable reasons, the meeting was not lengthy, but it did have far-reaching consequences. In opening it, I said that we were in favour of relations on an equal footing, respect for the sovereignty and independence of each country, and mutually beneficial co-operation in all spheres. Recognition of these principles also meant all parties taking full responsibility for the situation in their own countries.

The partners expressed their support for what I said, but I had the feeling that they were not taking it altogether seriously. In fact, something similar had been declared several times before, and nothing had changed. This time, too, they probably thought they would just wait and see. In essence, however, our statement at this meeting signified a shift to new relations, a rejection of the Brezhnev doctrine, which had never been officially proclaimed but which had in fact defined the USSR's approach towards its allies.

On 14 March 1985 a meeting was held with the head of China's delegation, Li Peng, Vice-Chairman of the People's Republic of China's State Council. Li Peng had graduated from the Moscow Energy Institute and spoke Russian. The very fact that it was he who was sent at the head of this delegation to Moscow by the Chinese leadership was a good sign. I began my conversation with him in a spirit of good-will and expressed my conviction as to the necessity of and the potential mutual benefit to be derived from full normalization of our relations.

Li Peng said that China was prepared to normalize those relations gradually to put them on a genuinely equal footing, but it did not want to find itself in the role of a younger brother and subordinate to the Soviet Union. I not only agreed but developed this concept at length, emphasizing that our relationship simply could not be normalized or make progress otherwise than on a basis of equal rights, mutual respect, and consideration for national interests. In short, the leadership of both states at this meeting gave and received important signals.

My reader would doubtless say that similar intentions had been proclaimed several times in the past – during the Khrushchev era, the Brezhnev era, and even subsequently. This is true, of course. But starting in March 1985 we strove to put these principles into practice, although this was not easily done. We had to overcome persistent opposition to any change from the existing system of leadership in the Socialist community, which had scarcely known any changes since Stalin's day. The forms and protocols might have become more polite, but the essence and methods had stayed the same, with rare exceptions. The Party-state institutions that had run this aspect of international relations agreed to perestroika only with great difficulty and much reluctance. The cadres, of course, who were used to a specific style, were in no rush to dispense with arrogance and conceit in their official and even their human everyday contacts with our allies.

The inertia of paternalism made itself felt for a long time. In the Socialist countries themselves, the traditions of dependency and obedience to the leader, the desire to agree with the 'big brother' on nearly every relatively important step, so as not to call down the wrath of the Kremlin, had put out deep roots. Naturally, the degree of this 'obedience' differed substantially from country to country, determined by its dependence on economic ties with the Soviet Union, the stability of its regime, its international status, historical factors, and, last but not least, the personality of its leader. By the time I took up the reins of power, figuratively speaking, the Socialist community was already far from being as homogeneous as it had been in the immediate post-war period; it had its heretics and troublemakers, like Ceausescu. On strategic issues, however, discipline was observed, and the first word always remained with the recognized vanguard, the Socialist superpower.

The new policy towards the Socialist countries was not formulated immediately. It took shape gradually, as a component part of the new political thinking and in that general context.

A month later I had the opportunity to meet the leaders of the

Warsaw Pact countries once again in Poland, in connection with the renewal of the Warsaw Pact for another twenty years. There had been some discussion on the subject, but an agreement was eventually reached. A remark I made in private had an effect. 'Let's not force anyone,' I said. 'Let each country decide what it should do.'

For me this meeting was no less important for another reason as well. On 25 April we had just held our Central Committee plenum. Naturally, I wanted to clarify my colleagues' attitude towards its results, and I found a very positive reaction to the ideas that had been voiced in Moscow. In any event, my colleagues raised no perplexed questions or concerns.

As for foreign policy issues, we let our allies know that Soviet diplomacy was steering a course towards a broad peace offensive, in all seriousness, moreover: on a practical rather than a propaganda level. We needed to work together in order to break down the confrontational tendencies, and at the next meeting of the Warsaw Pact's Political Consultative Committee in Sofia (October 1985), we compared notes on the eve of the Soviet-American summit in Geneva. Actually, this was the first time in many years that the Soviet leadership had not simply presented its allies with a *fait accompli* and demanded formal approval for its initiatives, but instead considered it necessary to discuss its decisions jointly before putting them into action. Our allies appreciated this consultation. As to the substance of the matter, our attempt to come to an agreement with the United States on halting the exhausting arms race and on effective measures for disarmament was supported enthusiastically by all the participants at the Sofia conference.

In an effort to establish a relationship of trust with my partners, I offered to hold an informal working session outside the conference. Seven of us gathered round a table, with one aide apiece at separate tables. An exception was made for the Soviet delegation. In addition to my aide Sharapov, also present was Medvedev, whom I had nominated to be a department head of the Central Committee.

According to the general wish, the meeting began with my speech. I candidly related our problems to my colleagues and explained why we in the Soviet Union so badly needed renewal, and what we intended to do to accelerate socio-economic development.

I recall Jaruzelski's substantive and emotional speech, the entire tone of which attested to his commitment to change. He complained of excessive ideology, which was slowing reforms and hindering any solution to Poland's 'besieged fortress' situation. The others, too, commented favourably on our innovations. We talked freely about who hurt where. Everyone agreed in their criticism of the Council for Mutual Economic Assistance (Comecon or CMEA).[1] They railed against its bureaucracy and inefficiency and stressed the need for a fundamental overhaul of the co-operation mechanism. Everyone complained about the fact that in the economic sphere – especially in matters of technological progress, advanced technologies, and integration – the Socialist countries were obviously losing ground to the West. In summary, we agreed to devote a special high-level meeting to the problems of restructuring economic relations and co-operation among the Comecon nations.

Several of the Socialist countries had attempted to find their own solutions to these problems. The Bulgarians, for example, like our other Comecon partners, saw that the Soviet Union lagged behind the West in many areas of science and technology. Therefore a one-sided orientation towards us condemned our partners as well, at least in part, to inferiority. They were attempting to compensate for this by developing scientific-technical links with the West, which in and of itself was quite natural. The problem was that this was being kept secret from us – but when complications arose, they turned to us for help.

Bulgaria had been living beyond its means for years. By the early 1990s, its foreign debt had grown to US $10 billion, for a population of only about 9 million. Zhivkov had managed to develop relations with Brezhnev in such a way as to obtain major

---

[1] The socialist trading community, established in 1949, but always dominated by the Soviet Union. Eventually it became a liability for the Soviet Union as its allies became dependent on Soviet inputs of raw materials and energy, at below world market prices, and Moscow received in return sub-quality goods.

hard currency support. In exchange for widely publicized plans for 'fraternal co-operation', significant supplies of energy and raw materials as well as financial subsidies were forthcoming from the Soviet Union.

A serious attempt to rectify these distortions was made in July 1985, when during Zhivkov's visit to Moscow a 'Long-Term Programme for the Development of Economic and Scientific-Technical Co-operation between the USSR and the People's Republic of Bulgaria Until the Year 2000' was signed. Its implementation was hampered, however, by changes in the world market that were extremely unfavourable to us: a sharp drop in oil prices cost the Soviet Union nearly half of its hard currency earnings. We were forced to cut our supplies of oil to our Comecon partners, including Bulgaria. There, as in East Germany, this was a very painful experience. The fact of the matter was that the Bulgarian side, like East Germany, was involved in re-exporting to the West some of the oil it got from us.

At that point it became quite clear that the economic model that had been accepted in Bulgaria, as well as in several other Comecon countries, could work only thanks to 'artificial respiration' – which is to say, injections of foreign capital. The Soviet side could no longer continue economic relations along those lines. We raised the question of transferring economic ties to a basis of equivalent exchange, which would mean the cessation of annual subsidies to Bulgaria for agricultural production amounting to 400 million rubles.

Here the gap between Zhivkov's assurances about the continuation of close co-operation with the Soviet Union and some of his practical steps in domestic and foreign policy became more noticeable. He surrounded himself with men who supplied him with new projects, now oriented more towards the West than the East. Soviet citizens holidaying in Bulgaria, on the famous Golden Sands, sensed an abrupt change in attitudes towards them. The attention of the local administration and service personnel had switched to the holders of dollars and marks.

The Hungarian experiment was in some ways similar, but in other ways different. János Kádár's democratic inclinations and his respect for people's freedom to choose their own way of life allowed him to resolve the peasant question with brilliant simplicity, you might say. In essence, he recognized the peasants' right to leave the collective farms freely, after which most of them voluntarily organized into co-operatives. City dwellers, too, were given the opportunity to acquire plots of land for gardens and holiday cottages.

The co-operatives introduced new technologies for cultivating maize and managed to obtain high yields. They developed great quantities of their own fodder mixes, which they began selling freely all over the country. The peasants and the workers in the villages, even in the small towns, took up animal husbandry. Eventually, as much as 80–90 per cent of the fruit produced in Hungary came from the private sector. This was a well thought-out strategy. After all, the country is not rich in raw materials for heavy industry, but the natural conditions for agriculture are propitious. At the time, it was quite appropriate to emphasize the development of agriculture and the export of its produce.

In the development of industry, the Hungarians, in a way copying us, allowed themselves to get carried away with a kind of 'gigantomania' – if that term can be applied at all to little Hungary. I have in mind large enterprises like the plant that produced the Icarus buses and the metallurgical combine at Sztálinváros (as it was called at one time). Hungarian heavy industry and machine-building prospered for no more than fifteen years. Apart from the conscientious work of Hungarian engineers and workers, they were aided by the raw materials and fuel made available by the Soviet Union. Since they were paying for their energy in rubles and earning hard currency for their agricultural exports, the Hungarians were able to manoeuvre quite success-fully and make a decent living.

Not everything went well in Hungary's economy, of course. Even in the best times Kádár had to go to the Soviet leadership about once every ten years for substantial financial assistance, and hundreds of millions of dollars were apportioned to Hungary. In time, though, this option disappeared, and the Hungarians began turning more and more to West Germany and the West. Having re-oriented much of their production in that

605

direction, Hungary became dependent on deliveries of components, a few types of raw materials, and semi-finished products. Payment for these virtually consumed their export earnings, and their hard currency foreign debt mounted. Eventually matters reached a point where the interest alone on their debts swallowed 40–60 per cent of all their hard currency earnings. This led to bottlenecks and disruptions in production involving Western suppliers. It also led to a drop in production.

Hungary too was living beyond its means. This became the country's main problem and drama. There was a strategic miscalculation here, and not just by the Hungarians. Nearly all the Eastern European countries had based their plans for the future on the assumption that the favourable terms of trade with Europe and the world would continue. The oil crisis upset these calculations, and our allies found themselves up to their ears in debt.

The Hungarian debt to the West reached US $12 billion – or $14 billion, according to some statistics – in fact, no-one really knew precisely how much. The Hungarians looked for a way out by accelerating economic reform. On Kádár's instructions, this work was supervised by the prominent economist Rezsö Nyers. But the development of reform was difficult and inconsistent, partly due to its novelty, and partly due to resistance from conservative forces. Kádár himself had his doubts and acted more by trial and error. He would weigh all the factors and consider the various political currents, the ebbs and flows of society's moods. The reforms touched the lives of millions of people. Kádár would draw Nyers closer and then pull away.

On the whole, though, Kádár understood the need for changes and sought new approaches to the efficient administration of the economy. The Hungarians were among the first to abandon strict directives from the centre and to place the emphasis on enterprises formulating and implementing plans themselves. This is also how they approached price formation: they placed only some prices under control, especially food prices, and gradually introduced contract prices.

All these steps towards liberalizing the economy provoked numerous questions from the Soviet leadership. Our orthodox Communists literally booed when they saw 'those "troublemaker

Hungarians" intentionally violating the "objective economic laws of socialism" formulated by "the classics themselves"'. 'Reprimands' were issued to the Hungarian leaders several times, and those particularly jealous of Marxism-Leninism's purity even began to talk about how we needed to apply pressure on Hungary economically.

The Sofia conference helped me penetrate deeper into the affairs of the Socialist community, which was one of the General Secretary's most important prerogatives and, simultaneously, most important concerns, and to get a better look at my partners. However, I still did not have a complete picture. In my speech to the XXVIIth CPSU Congress, our approach to relations with our allies was set forth fairly traditionally, except for a few 'novelties'. Immediately after the Congress, however, work began on a detailed analysis of the situation of the Socialist community and the preparation of specific proposals for the future. At that time, Rusakov retired as head of the Central Committee's Department for Liaison with Communist and Workers' Parties in Socialist Countries and was replaced by Medvedev; Shakhnazarov became his First Deputy, replacing O. B. Rakhmanin, who had been well-known for his conservative views.

We were knee-deep in primary material, including statistical data and all kinds of memoranda submitted to us by the USSR Council of Ministers, our representatives in Comecon, our embassies, the USSR Ministry of Internal Affairs, research institutes, and so forth. It was no easy task to sort through this stack and reduce it to a set of fairly pragmatic proposals. After solid work, my memorandum to the Politburo 'On Issues Concerning Co-operation with the Socialist Countries' emerged. I purposely chose this form because it allowed me from the very outset to lend our new assessments and initiatives the status of an official political direction reinforced by decisions of the collective leadership.

The memorandum concluded that there was a need for real change in the whole system of co-operation with our allies.

Re-reading this memorandum now, I can clearly see the influence of traditional views and stereotypes. Not that it could have been otherwise, inasmuch as we had barely started reviewing all the things that had been knocked into our heads for decades and had taken on the status of a creed. There was an exchange of opinions on the subject of my memorandum at a May 1986 session of the Politburo. The members' support was not merely formal: they were not just yielding to the General Secretary's authority, they supported it enthusiastically. With rare exceptions, everyone in the leadership saw the gaping holes in the system of co-operation with the Socialist countries, especially in economic matters. The first practical step became reform of foreign trade relations, initiated in August 1986.

In November of the same year, the 'Socialist summit' on the problems of economic co-operation we had agreed upon in Sofia was held in Moscow. The discussion was thorough. We sought out the root causes for our general economic backwardness. We did not reduce the matter to superficial details, but dug deep. Singled out above all were the deficiencies of the economic model in operation in the countries of the community. There was talk too about our flawed economic policy, which failed to ensure an optimal balance between efficiency and social justice, between social programmes and work incentives. It goes without saying that the very atmosphere of this 'free' discussion was possible only because the ideological taboo had been lifted from all these issues.

The futility of abstract arguments about the advantages of a planned economy, and about how socialism *a priori* ensures the harmonious development of productive forces and guarantees a co-ordination of interests, was becoming more and more obvious. Scholars and specialists who had dared in the past to raise doubts about these postulates had been declared anti-Soviet. In other Socialist countries they had been tagged with other labels, driven out of academic life, and excluded from the Party. Some had been forced to emigrate. Now the dam had burst and a serious conversation had begun, moreover not in the auditorium of the Institute of the Socialist Countries' Economy, not even at a session of Comecon, but at a meeting of the supreme guardians of orthodoxy.

The main thesis of my speech was that the old forms of co-operation had become obsolete. The usual model for economic relations, which had Soviet raw materials flowing primarily to our allies and their finished products to us, was not going to work any more. It was becoming more and more unprofitable for both sides. In addition, trade between Comecon countries had been growing more slowly than gross domestic product in recent years, whereas in Western Europe it was the other way around. Most important, within the framework of the community, domestic producer co-operation was not moving forward, and the 'Comprehensive Programme for the Integration of Comecon Countries' passed by the governments was running into all kinds of obstacles, including the frankly pro-Western orientation of some of the administrative institutions.

On the whole, the participants in the meeting welcomed our proposal for a 'trilevel' mechanism for regulating economic relations. We proposed leaving the principal problems of the strategic orientation of economic relations, particularly in the spheres of finance and scientific and technical co-operation, at the top level, that is, at the level of relations between the states. Specific tasks for interaction were supposed to be concentrated at the sectoral level. Direct ties between enterprises and associations would become the lowest, basic level. The main idea of the proposed 'trilevel model' lay in giving producers maximum freedom to select their partners and forms of co-operation. To reduce it to its bare structure, laws would be written on the 'top floor', programmes composed and 'framework decisions' passed on the 'first floor', and agreements reached and business conducted on the ground floor.

In August 1986 we in the Soviet Union adopted decisions for a fundamental restructuring of our foreign trade activities. The state monopoly over foreign trade was significantly restricted, and a few dozen of the largest enterprises were given the right to enter the world market independently. All without exception were given the right to establish contacts with partners in Socialist countries. We proposed leaving the hardest issues – prices for mutual trade – to the co-operating enterprises for them to resolve, within certain general parameters.

Aware that Mongolia, Vietnam, and Cuba would not be able to

join in the new forms of co-operation in the near future, we suggested working out a separate programme for improving economic relations with these countries.

With certain qualifications, you can say that the measures we proposed implied an invitation to base economic relations within the Socialist community on market principles. Here we did not find the familiar unanimity. Advisers and Council of Ministers chairmen feverishly calculated what the end-result of this might be – increased earnings or, as they feared, losses. Critical as well as approving notes were heard in the leaders' speeches. While Kádár and Jaruzelski wholly supported the proposals I had advanced, Husák and Zhivkov did so only with qualifications. Honecker and Ceausescu, having come out in favour of improving co-operation on an inter-state level, reacted with great reserve – negatively, in point of fact – to the idea of expanding the enterprises' rights.

During those November days we exchanged candid opinions on social issues as well. The discussion focused on the eternal theme of the correlation between social justice and economic efficiency, a theme Kádár and Jaruzelski raised quite pointedly. Their main idea was that we were all in favour of equality, but we had taken it too far, to the point of mindless levelling, which inevitably entailed the suppression of individual interests. This had left its mark on the economy and on all social processes. Husák was laconic, but as always he revealed an understanding of long-term prospects. Zhivkov theorized in his usual manner, not without pretence. Ceausescu and Honecker recognized the importance of the issues under discussion, although they claimed that these had already been successfully resolved in their own countries. To support this assertion they cited a long list of accomplishments – some of them real but some, as became clear later, illusory.

The working session in Moscow was a serious attempt to find ways of jointly overcoming the economic and social difficulties that had mounted in all the Comecon countries, which threatened to turn into a crisis unpredictable in its force and consequences. At the time, though, no-one realized its true depth. We thought we were discussing matters thoroughly. We were not shying away from painful, 'unpleasant' problems. Nonetheless, I still felt as if we were maintaining a certain theoretical distance from reality. It was hard to believe that our debates would provide an impetus for immediate action. The advanced age of my partners may have been to blame for this. It was not yet senility, but the weariness of leaders who were over seventy or nearly so, and who in addition had been at the helm for two or three decades, was quite obvious.

A SPECIAL POSITION

Nicolae Ceausescu's special position had become particularly pronounced when in August 1968 the troops of five Warsaw Pact countries crossed the border of Czechoslovakia. He began to distance himself from the Soviet Union and to emphatically demand respect for the independence and sovereignty of Romania. In and of itself an elementary demand, repeated on every occasion and even for no reason at all, it became an incantation that yielded a double dividend. Romania's 'special status' was encouraged by the West with loans, a little investment, most-favoured-nation trade status, and so forth. Second, and I think more important, Ceausescu deftly took advantage of this to strengthen his already firm control over the Romanian people. In essence, he established absolute personal rule. The bulk of the population was cut off from both the West and the Soviet Union by an impenetrable administrative curtain.

I had known Ceausescu even before I became General Secretary. As a Secretary of the CPSU Central Committee, I had met him when he came to the Soviet Union from time to time. He was not particularly welcome in Moscow. He was not forgiven for his ambitions and his demonstrative flirtations with the West. In reply to such accusations, he declared more and more loudly his 'special' views and put forward ambitious foreign policy initiatives – initiatives which would never be implemented but which were calculated to emphasize the originality of Romania's position. It gave me a strange feeling to watch Ceausescu going out of his way to demonstrate the independence of his opinions.

All this was unnatural, and anyone with the slightest political experience could see his delusions of grandeur as well as his psychological instability.

I thought that it was worth attempting to remove the confrontational overtones in Soviet-Romanian relations. Hence my approach to Ceausescu, with whom I strove to speak respectfully and to penetrate to the essence of his statements. I admitted, for example, that there was a great deal of truth in his opinion that the tension between Moscow and Beijing could be explained at least in part by blunders and miscalculations on the Soviet side. Ceausescu, it must be said, was very proud of the fact that he maintained good relations with the Chinese leadership, and he sought to act as mediator between Beijing and Moscow.

Generally speaking, the role of intermediary was attractive to the Bucharest leader. Thus he strove to maintain broad contacts with Middle Eastern politicians, including both Arafat and the Israeli leadership. It is probably easier to list the countries of Africa and South-East Asia where Ceausescu did not go than those which received his widely publicized visits. The Romanian President was not indifferent to the non-aligned movement either, obviously envying Yugoslavia's popularity. He attempted to fortify these global ambitions by establishing economic ties everywhere, offering a broad assortment of Romanian output, from petro-chemical products, agricultural machinery, compressors, and diesel assemblies to aviation technology, automobiles and locomotives. All this was produced by Romanian industrial enterprises, although they were overburdened and suffered shortages of energy, supplies, and raw materials. The Romanian economy was wholly subordinate to its ruler's great-power ambitions and was coming to look more and more like a horse being mercilessly whipped and driven by a cruel rider.

From 1986 on we began to receive signals that despite the strict censorship of information about the Soviet Union in Romania, interest in the perestroika process had begun to emerge there. Everyone understood, of course, that the matter rested above all on Ceausescu's position. So much depended on this 'living god', his word alone. People knew that the leader's relatives as well as his wife had been placed in key positions in the country (there were as many as seventy of them on the Central Committee), and that anyone he didn't like faced disfavour. As soon as the talk turned to Ceausescu, people shrugged their shoulders.

I knew, however, that Ceausescu was interested in meeting me, aware of the necessity for him and for Romania (and he was unquestionably inclined to identify himself with Romania) to collaborate with the Soviet Union as a powerful neighbour, failure to reckon with which was not only not sensible, but plain dangerous. Behind this there were also economic needs, especially for Soviet oil, since Romanian oil production did not satisfy the demand of even half the oil refineries rashly built on the leader's orders.

He had another intention that was no secret to me either. By establishing good relations with the new and relatively young General Secretary of the CPSU Central Committee, and by obtaining recognition from his side, Ceausescu hoped to have a chance to implement his own ambitious pretensions, his own understanding of global politics. Elena Ceausescu once said, more in earnest than as a joke, that Romania was too small for a leader like Nicolae Ceausescu.

I have encountered many ambitious people in my life. Indeed it is hard to imagine a major politician without his share of vanity and self-confidence. In this sense, though, Ceausescu was in a class of his own. An absolute ruler for decades, he always wore an arrogant smirk, treating others with apparent contempt, everyone from retainers to equal partners.

The Romanian President loved to demonstrate his special importance at international forums. No single state or Party figure in Romania, not even the most highly placed, except Ceausescu himself, had the authority to approve the documents passed on such occasions. This was true at meetings of the Warsaw Pact, whose documents were passed by consensus. The Romanian representatives always left a few suggestions or comments that could be removed only by 'himself', and Ceausescu agreed to concessions – sometimes – only at the expressed request of the General Secretary of the CPSU Central Committee, usually demanding a couple of million tonnes of oil in return. This arrangement had been worked out back in Brezhnev's time, but I did not make a drama of it. Usually, I simply approached him in the course of the session or during a break, took him by the arm or shoulder, and in full view of everyone we left for discussion in private or with a few members of our delegations. This public demonstration suited him. It suited me too, although for a different reason. I managed not only to find solutions to disputed points but also to a certain extent to restrain Ceausescu's excessive pretensions by not giving in to obvious attempts at blackmail.

To be fair, some of his statements calculated for effect (for example, on issues of disarmament and relations between North and South, between developed and developing countries), for all their propaganda aura, were sensible. You have to bear in mind that everyone was so sick and tired of the Romanians' endless demands and whims that sometimes no-one wanted to listen to them, declaring their amendments, some of which contained a grain of sense, unacceptable.

There was one other notable circumstance. In meeting Ceausescu I noted that through the solid curtain of his usual 'mentor' role, a certain desire emerged for intimate dialogue, for an informal exchange of opinions, in short, as it seemed to me then, for normal human communication. At times, however, this took on a comic tinge. At Political Consultative Committee meetings, his people watched to see when the Soviet delegation was leaving for the session. A signal was immediately given to Ceausescu, who, as if by accident, would show up at the same time as me. I remember a session in Hungary when I was walking to the meeting through a park. The Romanian delegation was walking ahead of us. Suddenly, Ceausescu fell over on level ground, as if he had twisted his foot. They helped him get up. We drew level, and I walked over to inquire how he was feeling. Then, as if by magic, TV cameras appeared, out of nowhere, and later the press and television reported Ceausescu's meeting with Gorbachev. I understood his game. He wanted to show everyone that Gorbachev was meeting, chatting, discussing with him.

There were no personal prejudices or old scores undermining

my relations with Ceausescu. I wanted to choose my moment for a frank conversation with him, and I felt that I had patience and arguments enough to encourage him to make changes in line with the spirit of the time – most important, to get Romanian society to open up to contacts and co-operation. Then the process would acquire a momentum of its own. This, actually, was my intent when I agreed to accept Ceausescu's persistent invitation to make an official friendly visit to Romania. The last time a CPSU General Secretary had visited Bucharest had been in 1976.

We arrived in Bucharest on 25 May 1987. I was greeted by tens of thousands, if not hundreds of thousands, of people. It was, of course, an organized show. When I tried to engage individuals in conversation during a tour of the Romanian capital I was shocked to discover how frightened they seemed. It was clear to me that what their leader tried to pass off as a society of prosperity and democracy was nothing of the kind – in fact the whole country was ruled by terror, isolated from the rest of the world. One evening, when we were dining alone with our wives, Ceausescu provoked me into saying frankly what I thought, without mincing words. The discussion became so loud that one of his aides or attendants gave an order to close the windows, flung open on the warm night, and to move the guard further back into the park – no point in witnesses. Nicolae tried to object. He was nervous, but he could not say anything convincing in reply, of course. The evening was completely ruined. Nevertheless, we agreed that the next day the Ceausescus would show us Bucharest.

In the centre of the Romanian capital a complex of high-rise buildings intended for political administration institutions was being built, and housing was under construction. Huge funds had been poured into this and builders taken off other sites. The President was determined to immortalize himself by transforming Bucharest into a sea-port, a kind of Romanian Manhattan. For this the construction of a colossal canal had been started, the Bucharest-Danube Canal.

He took us to the dam and showed us what would be razed where and what would be rebuilt. He talked about the creation of agro-cities which, he said, would solve all the problems of agriculture and give the peasants a new way of life. I asked him

615

whether it made sense to tear peasants away from the land, to drive them away from the places where they had been born and where their ancestors were buried. I told him about our sad experience of eliminating 'futureless villages' in the non-black earth lands.

But Ceausescu didn't want to listen. His eyes burned: 'No, we are ready for a new agrarian revolution. Agro-cities are the only progressive way.' His other motive was that he hoped in this way to solve the problem of the Hungarian ethnic minority, since villagers of Hungarian nationality were being resettled from their native villages and would be mixed in artificially with Romanian peasants. I think, though, that this only exacerbated national feelings, rather than the opposite. After all, we know that ethnic minorities suffer forceable removal from their native places especially acutely.

Mistakes in investment policy had led to enormous volumes of incomplete construction and increasing numbers of half-idle industrial enterprises. There was an acute energy shortage, and as a result more and more new restrictions were being introduced on the consumption of electrical energy, to the point where the television operated only for a few hours a day. The accelerated payment of debts to the West had caused much hardship to the population.

All the best industrial goods and food were being exported, and domestic consumption was rationed. They decided to show us the abundance of food, not at the market, which we were not allowed to visit because, they said, the security service was unprepared for that, but in a store. We arrived there accompanied by 'himself'. It was a big store with tall windows like glass walls. There were no customers inside, but outside stood enormous crowds of people. There was an excellent assortment of different foodstuffs, at least forty kinds of sausage and meats alone, as well as various cheeses and so forth. No sooner had we left, however, than most of the goods were removed from the shelves and taken away. The people who flooded into the store instantly cleaned it out of everything that was left. People from our embassy observed this scene and told me about it later. It turned out that this was a movable 'Potemkin village', as we call it.

We were taken to the Bucharest Polytechnic Institute, which was located in a new district. Everything had been laid out and built quite well – classroom buildings, dormitories, teachers' housing. But it was sad to see the young people chanting without let-up: 'Ceausescu-Gorbachev! Ceausescu-Gorbachev!' I walked up to them and tried to start a conversation, but they kept on shouting. I took them by the hand and addressed them several times: 'Wait, wait! Why don't you stop!' I started a conversation, but in reply all I got was a couple of sentences and again the shouts: 'Ceausescu-Gorbachev!' I never did manage to get into conversation with anyone.

It was both tragic and comic to see Ceausescu proposing the Romanian economy as a model for emulation. After all, I had spent years trying to involve the public more actively in the administration of the state and in economic management at all levels. But, so long as the authoritarian-bureaucratic system was preserved, all these attempts would in the final analysis prove fruitless.

I cannot deny the useful work of the trade unions, the Komsomol organizations, or, say, the 'Knowledge' society,[1] the associations of the artistic intelligentsia, or the production conferences at many enterprises. On the whole, though, these and other public organizations were filling the roles predetermined for them. These groups provided the requisite support for the monopoly position of the ruling party, or, to put it more precisely, they formed a narrow group covering up for one another. Wherever there is a monopoly, tyranny, stagnation, and degradation are inevitable, and no pseudo-democratic decorations can hide that.

FACING UP TO HISTORY

In the late 1970s, Poland had found itself in a grave crisis, one that Moscow considered the result of weakness and indecision on the part of the Polish leadership. In fact, the situation was much

---

[1] Society for the propagation of scientific knowledge.

more serious than that. The imposition of a socio-political model alien to Poland – albeit greatly altered and partially adapted to national conditions – had run into opposition from the populace, including a significant portion of the working class. At first the discontent was of a passive nature and found an outlet in jokes about the authorities. As the years passed, however, it mounted, and there were explosions of social and political unrest, each more powerful than the last (1953, 1970, 1979). To top it all, the country recklessly amassed a colossal hard currency debt to the West. Poland was essentially the first to enter the stage that could be called the general crisis of socialism. State institutions found themselves on the brink of paralysis, and the country was literally one step away from total chaos and national disaster.

Under these conditions, the opposition, Solidarity, which had gathered momentum, advanced a programme for a self-governing Rzeczpospolita, which the orthodox leadership of the Polish United Workers' Party,[1] to say nothing of the CPSU and the other ruling parties of the Socialist community, saw, with some reason, as an agenda for dispensing with the existing system and deserting the Warsaw Pact for NATO. The Soviet leadership feverishly sought a solution between what were to them two equally unacceptable positions: the acceptance of chaos in Poland and the ensuing break-up of the entire Socialist camp; or armed intervention. The opinion that both positions were unacceptable predominated. Nonetheless, our troops, our tank columns along the border with Poland, and even a rather powerful northern group of Soviet troops stationed in Poland – all these could be put in motion, given extreme circumstances.

In this situation, Wojciech Jaruzelski, who had replaced S. Kania as First Secretary of the PUWP Central Committee in October 1981, weighed the various possible courses of events, all of which were obviously negative, and decided on what he considered the lesser evil: martial law was declared on the night of 12 December 1981. This was more an administrative-political measure than a military one, although it was prepared for and implemented by the army and the police.

[1] PUWP, the official name of Poland's Communist Party.

In early 1990 I travelled for three days through Lithuania and there were long discussions with citizens there. The conclusions were not very promising.

Below: I was in Kyrgyzstan in the autumn of 1991. Kyrgyz and Russians expressed their concern about the future of the Soviet Union.

Above: *During 1989 I visited China, where I met Deng Xiaoping for the first time. The result of our meeting could be summed up by the Chinese expression: 'Close the past, open the future'.*

Below: *During the visit to China in 1989, I spent many hours with the Chinese leader Zhao Ziyang. It appeared to me that the events in Tiananmen Square were a heavy burden for the General Secretary of the Central Committee of the Communist Party of China. Shortly afterwards Zhao was demoted.*

Wojciech Jaruzelski and I became friends after our first meeting. He was a true patriot, a friend of the Soviet Union, a moral person, a leading politician, a man with many human virtues.

As soon as I met Rajiv Gandhi there was considerable mutual understanding between us, and we worked together on promoting new co-operation between India and the Soviet Union.

Above: *My discussions with Margaret Thatcher were not always very easy. Nevertheless, I greatly valued the co-operation with the British Prime Minister.*

Below: *One of the greatest achievements of perestroika was the withdrawal of Soviet troops from Afghanistan. This was discussed during my talks with Najibullah, the Afghan leader, in Tashkent.*

Left: *The visits of the heads of state of the USSR and the USA to each other's country in 1987 and 1988 had a great impact on relations between our two countries. Here I am showing President Reagan Red Square.*

Right: *After Hans-Dietrich Genscher and I had got to know one another, each one found something in the other which made it possible to discuss the most difficult questions of European and world politics and to search for solutions.*

My meetings with President Bush at Camp David in June 1990 and in Novo-Ogarevo in July 1991 reflected the new nature of the relationship between the Soviet and American governments and demonstrated in many ways remarkable progress in Soviet-US relations.

New friends and partners (above): *Willy Brandt and Johannes Rau, here in June 1989;* (below): *my meeting with Chancellor Helmut Kohl in the Caucasus was of decisive importance during the final stages of drafting the documents on German unification. This photograph was taken in Arkhyz in July 1990.*

Left: *Speaking about our reforms during an address to the United Nations. The most important part of my speech was the message of peace to all people throughout the world.*

Right: *With Pope John Paul II in the Vatican, 1989.*

The hush before the beginning of the ceremony conferring on me the Nobel Peace Prize, June 1991.

Above: *President Bush and I opened the Madrid Middle East Conference on the morning of 30 October 1991. In the evening we were, together with the Spanish Prime Minister, Felipe González, the guests of King Juan Carlos. The main topic of our conversation was the situation in the Soviet Union.*

Below: *The '7 + 1' meeting with leaders of the G7 countries in London in July 1991: reality had to be recognized here.*

In the face of the West's blockade of the Jaruzelski regime, the substantial material and financial assistance to Poland from the USSR, East Germany, Czechoslovakia, and several other countries had a stabilizing effect. The Soviet Union allocated about US $2 billion and several billion rubles to the Poles, and supported them in later years as well. Our troops were categorically prohibited from interfering in events, and they behaved themselves irreproachably.

In addition to help, however, Jaruzelski was pestered with advice and suggestions as to whom to avoid and whom to rely on. The quality of this advice can be judged from the fact that the most unflattering characterizations concerned, for instance, such a distinguished figure as Mieczyslaw Rakowski. After martial law was imposed, Moscow and East Berlin transparently hinted that it was time to act more decisively and not to permit any spinelessness or liberalism. Politely but firmly, Jaruzelski deflected attempts to foist a line of conduct on him, and he followed his own course, calculated to calm the situation, placate the nation, and gradually transform the political system. But, as he later told me, he was naturally forced to reckon with the country's real dependence on Moscow.

Martial law under Jaruzelski did not put an end to the reforms; in its own way, it facilitated them. Polish reformers took advantage of the newly instituted law and order in the country not to turn back but, on the contrary, to rally all the healthy forces of society that supported political pluralism and a market economy.

In the first half of the 1980s the situation in Poland substantially mirrored ours, but when it came to economic reforms the Poles were clearly ahead of us. We were just beginning to understand the essence of what was going on in Poland and Hungary. Real understanding did not come until 1985–6.

The alienation between the two countries and the two peoples that had grown up in the late 1970s and early 1980s had to be overcome. To no small degree this feeling was the result of the activities of the Politburo's Special Commission on Poland, which Suslov headed for a long time. The Commission and its apparatus kept constant tabs on the course of Polish events, issuing assessments and recommendations to the Politburo, ministries, departments, and public organizations. A *cordon sanitaire* was erected around striking, rebellious, stormy Poland: all contacts were frozen or sharply curtailed.

Right up to the mid-1980s, reports reaching Moscow from Warsaw would frequently have even a phrase like 'Socialist renewal' – which was the official policy of the PUWP – crossed out! The fear of the 'Polish contagion' overshadowed even the obvious fact that a Polish society isolated from contacts with its neighbour to the East was left prey to those circles in the West that were taking advantage of the situation to promote anti-Soviet and anti-Russian moods.

On Jaruzelski's initiative, and supported by reformers in the PUWP and CPSU leadership, preparations began on a document whose goal was to promote rapprochement and co-operation between the two countries. The result was the 'Declaration on Soviet-Polish Co-operation in Ideology, Science, and Culture'.

Naturally, the document is not free of the ideological overtones of the period, but many of its ideas are still relevant. It was then that the go-ahead was given for revitalizing and significantly expanding contacts among sociologists, writers, journalists, scholars, cultural figures, and the creative intelligentsia and the youth of both countries. This effort on the part of the democratic circles in Polish and Soviet society to meet each other halfway helped to dispel the feelings of mutual suspicion, dislike, and fear that reactionary elements in our country and in Poland were stoking.

'History', this document said, 'should not be an object of ideological speculation or grounds for igniting nationalistic passions.' But we could put history behind us only if we were prepared to face the most painful episodes of the past.

After Jaruzelski's visit to Moscow in 1987, the work of the joint commission of Soviet and Polish historians, abandoned in 1974, was revived. We needed the whole truth about the Soviet-Polish war of 1920, Stalin's punishment of the Polish Communist Party, and especially the Katyn massacre, the most painful point of all for the Poles.

The creation of a commission of Polish and Soviet historians had significantly stimulated the activities of our researchers, who included N. S. Lebedeva, V. S . Parsadanova, and Ye. N. Zorya. They did not abandon their search even when the situation seemed absolutely hopeless. Now we know why those searches had reached an impasse: the documents had been destroyed on the orders of the former leadership of the KGB, when it had been run by A. Shelepin. The archive documents found by the group testified circumstantially but convincingly to the direct culpability of Beria, Merkulov, and their assistants for the crime in the Katyn forest. I stated this publicly, handing over the documents to Jaruzelski on 13 April 1990.

A TASS statement on 13 April 1990 expressed the Soviet Union's profound regret in connection with the Katyn tragedy, stating that it represented one of the most heinous crimes of Stalinism. As for the other documents referring to the Katyn massacre, I remember two files that were shown to me by Boldin on the eve of my visit to Poland. It was, however, a random set of documents meant to confirm the conclusions of Academician Burdenko's commission under Stalin.[1] We found the document that directly implicated those truly to blame for the massacre only in December 1991, a few days before I stepped down as President of the Soviet Union. It was then that the archive staff were able to convince Revenko, the director of the President's staff, to make sure I looked at one file kept in a special archive. The draft of my final speech as President was then being typed. I was totally preoccupied by this and other matters.

Nonetheless, Revenko continued to insist and handed me the file on the eve of my meeting with Yeltsin, in the course of which it had been agreed that I would hand over affairs to him. I opened the file. In it there was a memorandum from Beria concerning the fate of the Polish servicemen and representatives of other groups in Polish society who were being detained in several camps. The memorandum ended with a recommendation that all the interned Poles should be executed. This last part was marked off and above it was written in Stalin's blue pencil: 'Resolution of the Politburo.' And the signatures: 'In favour – Stalin, Molotov, Voroshilov.' It took my breath away to read this hellish paper,

---

[1] Putting the blame for the massacre on the Nazis.

which condemned to death thousands of people at a single stroke. I put the file in my safe and then took it out again in the course of my conversation with Yeltsin, when we had reached the point of signing the document about the transfer of the special Central Committee archive (which held one or two thousand so-called special files containing documents of special importance). I showed Yeltsin the document and read it to him in Yakovlev's presence, and we agreed on its transfer to the Poles.

'But now,' I said, 'this is your mission, Boris Nikolaevich.'

There was another paper in the file as well, written and signed in Shelepin's hand when he was Chairman of the KGB. Addressed to Khrushchev, it proposed the destruction of all documents connected with the NKVD's actions to eliminate the Polish servicemen.

It seemed to me that, just as it was essential for us to understand our own history, so, in establishing new relationships with our allies, it was important to clear away the débris of the past by admitting our often grievous mistakes. On a visit to Yugoslavia, for example, I felt it necessary to admit that the interruption in the good relations between our countries had been the Soviet leadership's fault, and that the resulting conflict had inflicted great damage on Yugoslavia, the Soviet Union, and the cause of socialism. Then came the words that appeared throughout the press and were met with applause in the Skupstina[1]: 'I felt it was essential to talk today about this so that no wariness, suspicion, mistrust or resentment remained. As history shows, these can easily arise in relations between peoples and are very hard to overcome afterwards. This is essential also in order to emphasize the significance of the conclusions that we have drawn from the lessons of the past, and in order to build our relations firmly and rigorously on a basis of full equal rights, independence, and mutual respect.'

At the time of my official visit to Czechoslovakia in April 1987 I was often asked how I assessed the events of 1968. This was the hardest question for me. I found it extremely awkward to repeat the positions agreed upon in the Politburo before my visit to

[1] The Yugoslav Federal parliament.

people who – I felt this – were drawn to me in all sincerity. Never had I experienced the kind of internal division I did at that moment.

The question of re-assessing the events of 1968 was being raised there with increasing frequency and intensity. Half a million people who had been excluded from the Czechoslovak Communist Party could not forget the fact that they and their loved ones were cut off from political and social life, that they had been humiliated, ostracized, and some even forced to leave their homeland. The reformers of the Prague Spring greeted our perestroika with enthusiasm and demanded changes in their own land as well.

In an interview, Zdenek Mlynar, my friend and fellow student at Moscow University, said: 'In the Soviet Union they are doing what we did in Prague in the spring of 1968, perhaps acting more radically. But Gorbachev is General Secretary and I am still in exile.'

The Czechoslovak leadership was well aware that the principal players in the Prague Spring were attempting to make overtures to us. If the Soviet Union repudiated the events of 1968, this would deal a tremendous blow to the Czechoslovak Communist Party. Therefore they did all they could to bolster our 'fighting spirit', sending us various statements to prove the historical correctness of the August action, which, they said, saved socialism, drove back imperialism, and thereby averted a world war.

The paradox consisted in the fact that both sides proceeded from a common point of departure. They assumed that the fate of Czechoslovakia had to be decided in Moscow. They simply could not believe that we truly had no intention of interfering in the affairs of other countries, that we intended to put into practice the principle proclaimed in the documents of the Socialist community and the Communist movement, according to which each Party was independent and responsible to its own people.

I cannot come to a full stop in my discussion of relations between Moscow and Prague without relating one more meeting.

On 21 May 1990 Alexander Dubcek, Chairman of the Federal Assembly of the Czech and Slovak Federal Republic (as it was called at the time), walked into the presidential office in the Kremlin, next to the hall where the all-powerful Politburo once convened. The last time he had come (or, rather, had been brought) to Moscow had been nearly twenty-two years before, in August 1968. Then he was forty-six years old and was First Secretary of the Czechoslovak Communist Party Central Committee, and it seemed as if his career was over for good. Relatively soon thereafter, following a brief sojourn as Ambassador to Turkey, he was excluded from the Party and sent into political oblivion under the surveillance of the secret police.

And here was Dubcek walking towards me with his invariable, somewhat shy smile, older but still quite slim. He walked with his arms opened slightly in friendly greeting. We met warmly, and Dubcek's eyes were wet.

TIME FOR NEW WALLPAPER?

Once we began the process of reform, this increasingly determined our relations with the leaders of the Socialist countries. According to information that reached me, and on the basis of numerous meetings and conversations, I can say that our very first steps towards reform evoked enormous interest in our allies, especially among students and the intelligentsia. Many aspirations and hopes found expression here – for revitalization of outdated forms of life; for democracy and freedom; and, probably most of all, for the long-awaited possibility of deciding the fate of their own countries independently.

The reaction of most of the leaders was quite different. For decades they had been part of authoritarian regimes that relied on outside support, and they had developed a taste for unlimited rule, so at first they did not take our intentions seriously but treated them with polite curiosity and even condescending irony: 'This isn't the first time a new Soviet leader has started out by criticizing his predecessors, but later everything falls into place.'

When they were convinced that we were in earnest and prepared for the long haul, however, they began to make clear their refusal to accept perestroika, especially when it came to democratization and glasnost. This put them in a somewhat awkward situation. After all, up until that time both the political course and the official propaganda of the 'fraternal parties' had been built on the thesis of the leading role of the CPSU and the USSR in building Communism. But following the path of reforms begun in the Soviet Union meant the end of the system they embodied. No longer could they count on Soviet tanks to prop them up. They were left face to face with their own people, and they had to prove their right to remain at the helm or else leave. This was an agonizing choice, and not everyone realized immediately that the end of the post-war era was approaching. Some were able to meet the challenge of the time with dignity; others would not accept it, failed, and left the political stage.

I believe I can pinpoint the moment when the reaction of rejecting Soviet perestroika manifested itself in some leaders. It was January 1987, when the plenum of the CPSU Central Committee considered issues of democratization and the Party's cadre policy. It was then that Honecker said that the path of perestroika did not suit East Germany. At his instruction – an unprecedented instance! – publication of the proceedings of the plenum in the East German press was prohibited. (Those proceedings became dissident literature and were sold at fantastic prices on the black market.)

Kurt Hager, the SED's chief ideologist, added to what his leader said: 'If my neighbour decides to change his wallpaper, that doesn't mean that I have to do the same.'

There was a total rejection of the plenum's decisions in Romania. The public was given no information about it whatsoever. Ceausescu declared openly to the Soviet Ambassador that he could not agree with what had been said at the plenum and that the CPSU was starting down a dangerous path.

The XVIth Romanian Communist Party Congress was held in late November 1989. It was called 'the congress of great victories, the triumph of socialism, the full manifestation of Romania's independence and sovereignty'. The CPSU delegation was led by Vitaly Ivanovich Vorotnikov. Talking afterwards in the Politburo about his impressions, he could not contain his amazement at what he had seen and heard in Bucharest: 'It was as if I had landed in the distant past, in some kind of different, strange world. Everything revolves around one man. There isn't any thought, there were just chants and eulogizing. The audience got to its feet forty-three times during Ceausescu's speech shouting praise and thundering applause.'

I have frequently been asked why the USSR did not intervene in the Romanian drama to assist the dictator's departure. I repeat once more that we did not intervene because to do so would have contradicted the principles of our new policy. The interventions undertaken previously had eventually turned into liabilities, Pyrrhic victories, for us. That was the lesson of Hungary in 1956, Czechoslovakia in 1968, and Afghanistan in 1979.

The Politburo of the Bulgarian Communist Party discussed the results of the January plenum three times. Under pressure from several Politburo members, the assessments proposed by Zhivkov were toned down, but even so, a statement was made about the unacceptability of the basic principles of perestroika for Bulgaria, which 'has its own April plenum' (an allusion to April 1956, when Zhivkov came to power). True, a few months later the Bulgarian leader would make a dramatic turnabout and initiate a shake-up of the political system and the economy in an attempt to be one step ahead of the Soviet Union. As for real democratization and glasnost, though, there was not a whiff of that.

Husák's common sense and caution were felt in the assessments of the January plenum by the Czechoslovak leadership, which in principle were positive. Practical policy in the Czechoslovak Communist Party, however, was determined ultimately by more conservative forces. The leadership, which was still haunted by the memory of 1968, would not permit any loosening of its grip on power. The result is well known.

From the very beginning, the greatest mutual understanding on the problems of perestroika was reached with Kádár and especially Jaruzelski. Soon after 1956 the Hungarian leader had come to the conclusion that fundamental reforms were necessary and had begun bringing them about, conducting a clever policy and acting cautiously, concerned about the reaction from Moscow. Serious steps in the direction of economic and political liberalization alternated with periods of regression; first the reformers' positions would be strengthened, then they would retreat into the shadows, giving way to hard-liners. I saw and felt that Kádár welcomed the changes in the Soviet Union with all his heart. They opened up the possibility for acting more consistently in Hungary. His physical powers, however, were on the wane.

Jaruzelski fervently supported the changes in the Soviet Union. He and I had formed a very close and, I would say, amicable relationship. I explain the General's devotion to reform by the fact that he had been convinced by his own experience that you cannot resolve a country's complex problems by force. Profound changes in the social system and government were required. The Poles and Hungarians had started their reforms before we did. Hence their sincere interest in perestroika's success.

In the latter half of the 1980s, it was the leaders' attitudes towards perestroika that determined how the social and political situation developed in the various Eastern European countries. Those countries like Poland or Hungary which had begun to implement reforms in response to public opinion were able to avoid major upheavals. On the other hand, those countries whose leadership bitterly opposed the changes saw the most acute social and political crises, and mass popular demonstrations swept away the old regimes.

Frequently I have heard criticism and even accusations directed against me for my policy towards the countries of Eastern Europe. Some say that Gorbachev did not defend socialism in those countries, that he more or less 'betrayed his friends'. Others, on the contrary, accuse me for having been too patient with Ceausescu, Honecker, Zhivkov, and Husák, who had brought their states to the brink of catastrophe.

I firmly reject these accusations. They derive from outdated notions about the nature of relations between our countries. We had no right to interfere in the affairs of our 'satellites', to defend and preserve some and punish and 'excommunicate' others without reckoning with the people's will. Such procedures were against the principles of equality, independence, non-interference in each other's internal affairs, and full responsibility of the leadership of each country before its own people, all of which had been formally proclaimed even in Communist Party documents. If I could not act immediately and fully in the new spirit, then it was because no individual could move the hands of the political clock forward at will. Many changes had to mature first, both in people's minds and in the real social situation.

Once I began perestroika, from the very outset I predicated my actions on the inalienable right of every nation to determine its own future independently. Naturally we kept patiently explaining the meaning and significance of the contemplated transformations, held discussions with our allies on the problems of socialism, and, if you like, influenced them by our own example, but we never imposed our choice on anyone else. Those who still blame Gorbachev are, in effect, lacking in respect for their own people, who have gained freedom and made use of it as best they could.

22

MOSCOW AND BEIJING: 'CLOSE THE PAST, OPEN THE FUTURE'

PEOPLE OF MY GENERATION REMEMBER WELL THE JOY IN THE Soviet Union at the development of relations with China after the Second World War. So it was with great alarm and worry, with disbelief even – I'm talking about myself, too – that we reacted to the many years of cooling, mutual insults, open conflicts, and eventually rift. Our people generally did not accept or approve of the way our political leaders were handling relations with China.

Today, the reasons for the break are known and understandable. The Chinese leadership, above all Mao Zedong, did not accept the manner or even the essence of Khrushchev's revelations at the XXth CPSU Congress in 1956. These disclosures were perceived by the Chinese as a blow to their own political and ideological system. The polemics began. Communist and workers' parties found themselves drawn into the political battle, which affected all left-wing organizations and movements.

There was another reason for the Sino-Soviet rift. The Chinese side was injured and indignant at the Soviet Union's refusal to provide the technology for producing the atomic bomb. I believe that this refusal was objectively justified, since by this time the idea of nuclear non-proliferation was becoming generally recognized. True, Khrushchev was probably guided not so much by this consideration as by a desire to maintain the Soviet Union's influence over China. Khrushchev's real mistake was his massive

629

withdrawal of Soviet specialists from China. The Chinese, with some reason, saw this move as high-handed.

It cannot be said that nothing was later done on our side to ease the confrontation, but it was done unsystematically and inadequately considering the importance of the problem.

The inertia of confrontation that had accumulated over the decades blocked the possibility of change, which in any case was resisted by most of the ruling cadres, who had grown up in an atmosphere of profound mutual hostility. Feeble attempts by sober-thinking politicians, diplomats, and specialists on both sides to ease the tension at least a little were perceived as virtually a betrayal of national interests. It would take a powerful impulse, a display of political will from the very top, a major initiative reinforced by systematic and painstaking work to build new bridges of trust to replace those burned so recklessly a quarter of a century before.

FROM HOSTILITY TO RAPPROCHEMENT

In early December 1988 I received China's Minister of Foreign Affairs, Qian Qichen, and asked him to tell the Chinese leadership that we were in favour of normalizing relations and that the conditions for doing so were now at hand. The minister was informed candidly about our domestic affairs and our new approaches to foreign policy.

The minister then conveyed to me greetings and good wishes from Deng Xiaoping and other members of the Chinese leadership, and invited me to Beijing.

On 14 May 1989 we flew into the Chinese capital. There was a mood of excitement and concentration all at once. On the approach we were informed by radio telephone that the official welcoming ceremony would take place immediately at the airport. Ten days earlier, Tiananmen Square had been occupied by students. This demonstration, or rather series of demonstrations, was unusual for China and had become an expression of protest by a significant portion of the young people and intelligentsia against corruption in government, infringements of civil rights and a lack of social protection for most of the urban population in the process of market reforms, which hit many working people very hard. Our hosts were extremely concerned about the situation.

On the morning of 16 May, in the building of the National People's Congress, I had a meeting with Deng Xiaoping. He was eighty-four, but he spoke in a free and lively manner, without referring to any notes. Deng asked me whether I remembered his message, transmitted through Romanian President Ceausescu three years before. He had proposed meeting me then once the 'three obstacles' to normalizing Sino-Soviet relations were removed. I said that I had appreciated this step and the message had stimulated our thinking, which was moving along the same lines.

'Today,' Deng Xiaoping said, 'we can officially declare that Sino-Soviet relations have been normalized.'

We shook hands, and Deng Xiaoping added that my talks with the General Secretary of the Chinese Communist Party's Central Committee, Zhao Ziyang, scheduled for later that same day, meant that relations between our Parties were being normalized as well.

Deng suggested that the result of our meeting should be expressed by a formula composed of eight Chinese characters that in Russian translation meant 'Close the past, open the future'. We accepted this formula. However, Deng Xiaoping was unable to refrain from commenting on the history of our relations. I responded by saying that we could not rewrite or recreate history. 'If we started restoring boundaries on the basis of how things were in the past, which people resided on what territory, then essentially we would have to recarve the whole world. That would lead to worldwide strife! The principle of the inviolability of borders makes the world more stable and helps to keep the peace.'

Above all, I was interested in Deng's thoughts on how to expand our bilateral relations and how soon this could be achieved. I had in mind political dialogue and economic ties, scientific and cultural exchanges, education and training – with the understanding, naturally, that each country would decide what was beneficial and acceptable for itself.

I don't think Deng was prepared for a discussion of these issues on the level of specifics. Nonetheless, he said that, now that relations between our two countries had been normalized, contacts and ties between us would increase, and the pace of their improvement would be fast.

I also wanted to use my meeting with Deng to promote normalization in relations between China and Vietnam. But, as soon as I suggested that dialogue between them should be resumed and expanded, Deng Xiaoping retorted that 'only the Soviet Union can influence Vietnam.' He did not believe that Sino-Vietnamese talks could be productive without that.

My conversation with Deng Xiaoping lasted in all at least two hours. He often used terms and phrases typical of times past. However, far from being a slave to those terms and phrases, he tried to subordinate them to the logic of real life, as it was evolving then. He is a man who perceives historical events and current developments with much insight. I think the key to his great influence over the course of events in China lies in his enormous experience and healthy pragmatism.

When I met Zhao Ziyang later that day, the whole conversation proceeded in a spirit of goodwill and mutual understanding. The theme of reforms arose in and of itself. The common and most important problem for our parties was how to work in an environment where both the state and society were becoming more democratic.

The General Secretary himself brought up the subject of Tiananmen Square. 'Naturally, the students have a naive and simplistic view of many things,' he said. 'They think all they have to do is put out a slogan, and the Party and government will solve all their problems in a single day. Right now there is the sense of a lack of mutual understanding between Party and state institutions on one side and young people and students on the other. We don't understand their moods well, and they don't really understand us. We have four generations living together in our country, and mutual understanding among them is very important. I belong to the second generation, the students to the fourth, and Deng Xiaoping to the first.'

I agreed with the logic of his arguments. 'We are running into the same general problems. We have our hotheads too.'

Then Zhao Ziyang posed a seemingly rhetorical question, stressing that we all had to answer it together:

'Can a one-party system ensure the development of democracy? Can it implement effective control over negative phenomena and fight the corruption in Party and government institutions?'

In this question I read all my own doubts – not mine alone, actually. After all, in the discussion of the content and framework of our political reform, we had talked about pluralism of opinions, about the fact that democracy can be developed under a one-party system. Pluralism in our country, however, had gone beyond the sphere of ideas but had begun to take on a political aspect as well. This was followed by reproaches from the orthodox, accusations that we had subjected the April plenum, the XXVIIth Congress, and the XIXth Party Conference to revision.

From Zhao's arguments it followed that the Chinese leadership was prepared to follow the path of political reform by giving the masses a chance to enjoy broad democratic rights under one-party rule. He concluded that if this did not work out, the issue of a multi-party system would inevitably arise. In addition, he emphasized the need to strengthen citizens' constitutional rights and create an optimal correlation between democracy and law. Law must be based on democracy, and democracy must rely on law.

Zhao Ziyang said that in China people were following political reform in the Soviet Union with great interest and attention. 'It has evoked special interest among the intelligentsia, which has demanded that China learn from you and emulate your experience.'

To be frank, the openness demonstrated at my meeting with the General Secretary of the Central Committee of the Chinese Communist Party amazed me. Even during the conversation I began thinking about what all this might mean. Only later did it become clear to me what this man was going through, what an internal struggle between assumptions and values. Here was a reformer close to Deng Xiaoping, his follower, a new-style politician, so to speak. Naturally, quite a few thinking people were following him, especially from the younger intelligentsia. Now here he was, faced with a democratic challenge from the student masses. Zhao Ziyang had to know that many were demanding the imposition of order, since the student demonstrations had taken on the character of civil disobedience. But most of these demonstrators were people who had followed him, after all, or at least who had been inspired by ideas he himself shared. Herein lay his drama.

On 18 May, after a farewell ceremony at the government residence, we set out for the airport, where we would fly on to Shanghai. We did not drive through the centre of the capital, but tens if not hundreds of thousands of Beijing's residents came out to see us off. These were by no means stooges brought out in an officially organized show.

In Shanghai we were met at the airport by Jiang Zemin, a member of the Politburo and secretary of the City Committee of the Chinese Communist Party, and Mayor Zhu Rongji. As in Beijing, there were many people on the streets that day. They had come out to meet us, some simply curious, but most of them ready to show us goodwill.

In Moscow when we were discussing possible itineraries for our stay in China, I had preferred, besides Beijing, to spend time specifically in Shanghai, although some advised me against it, stating that it would be impossible to provide the necessary security in this densely populated city with its narrow streets. In selecting Shanghai, I was guided by the fact that this was the country's largest industrial and cultural centre. I had probably heard and read about it more than any other city in China. I won't hide the fact that in choosing Shanghai I also had in mind the possibility of meeting Jiang Zemin.

Information had reached Moscow about his being one of the most notable and interesting leaders of the 'new wave'. He was a graduate of the Shanghai Polytechnic Institute; in the 1950s he had trained at a car factory in Moscow, and he had never forgotten the Russian language, as I found out when I spoke with him.

Jiang Zemin's good knowledge of the moods of the people of Shanghai, as well as perhaps his personal qualities as a calm, balanced, and gracious man – that is how he impressed me then – were important factors that help to explain why the mass student demonstrations in this city played themselves out, so far as I was told, without any tragic incidents. Therefore the news of his election in June 1989 to the post of General Secretary of the CCP Central Committee after the resignation of Zhao Ziyang, who was blamed for the student demonstrations and in general for the 'trend of bourgeois liberalization', came as no surprise to me.

The elevation of Jiang Zemin was not a victory for the hard-liners. Evidently Deng Xiaoping, the architect of Chinese reforms, had managed to find a political compromise and to balance the leadership of the Party and the state. The promotion of Zhu Rongji, who was actively promoting market reforms, to prominent posts in the Chinese government, also seemed logical to me.

In addition to my meetings with China's leaders, which were pivotal in the history of relations between the peoples of our two countries, my meetings with young people made an enormous, even somewhat unexpected, impression on me. Many of our China specialists had said that the desire for good relations with the Soviet Union was part of the nostalgia felt mostly by the older generations of Chinese. As for the younger people, during the years of Sino-Soviet alienation, it was assumed, if they hadn't become anti-Soviet, then at least they were indifferent towards the Soviet Union or had even oriented themselves in a pro-Western, pro-American spirit.

Mingling directly with young Chinese in Beijing and Shanghai, we were convinced otherwise. The young people – university and high school students, labourers, and office workers – entered eagerly into a conversation and spoke of their desire to spend time in the Soviet Union. I was deeply struck by their lively, unfeigned interest in what was going on in our country and their enthusiasm for the restoration of normal relations between our countries.

I recall, in particular, an encounter with demonstrators on our way back from the Great Wall of China. The security service, having spotted many columns of young people ahead, would have liked to direct the motorcade down a side street, but I asked them to drive straight on. Seeing my car, the students greeted us enthusiastically. We stopped, got out of our cars, and shook hands. The demonstrators maintained perfect order and themselves organized a living corridor, through which we calmly drove with our guard behind us.

In short, our diverse contacts with Chinese youth confirmed for me that I had acted correctly in deciding not to postpone my visit to China, even though some of our comrades had wondered whether the student demonstrations in Beijing might not interfere with its successful conduct. To be frank, in Moscow we had not imagined the scale of these demonstrations. The peak of the student protest coincided with my arrival in Beijing, but it would have been a great oversimplification and simply untrue, of course, to see any connection in this, as many of the twelve hundred foreign journalists who came to cover my visit tried to do.

On 20 May martial law was imposed in several districts of Beijing, and troops were brought in. On the night of 3–4 June, army and police forces cleared Tiananmen Square, and the adjacent streets, of demonstrators. As they did so, according to official statistics, there were casualties among the civilian population – more than 200 killed and 3,000 injured. Dozens of servicemen died and over 6,000 of them were injured.

My speech and the statement of the USSR Congress of People's Deputies adopted on 6 June expressed regret about what had happened in Beijing, sympathy for those who had suffered, and the hope that wisdom, common sense, and a balanced approach would prevail and that a solution worthy of the great Chinese people would be found for the present situation. In this way, our response to the tragic events in Tiananmen Square combined non-interference in the internal affairs of China with a sincere interest in the stable development of a friendly country along the path of reform and openness with civil peace and non-violence.

A year after my visit, Prime Minister Li Peng came to the Soviet Union. I received him in the Kremlin on 24 April 1990. Ties between our two countries, especially in the Far East, were expanding, and the Chinese premier and I expressed our satisfaction on that score. Our conversation also touched on 'big politics'. Li Peng described my visit to China as historic and called for a new level of political and economic relations between us. He also expressed interest in developing co-operation in aircraft construction, the acquisition of up-to-date military equipment from the Soviet Union, and contacts between the militaries of the two countries. He also shared his ideas on the international situation, which he saw as combining elements of détente and tension.

In closing our conversation, I had reason to say that more and more points in common were appearing in Sino-Soviet relations, and this was a good basis for their further development. I fully supported the talks between Li Peng and Ryzhkov on economic co-operation.

Sino-Soviet relations were improving steadily in all directions. An important moment in this was the visit of Jiang Zemin to the Soviet Union in mid-May 1991, exactly two years after my visit to Beijing.

Jiang and I met like good friends. One could see how pleasant it was for him to be in Moscow once again. He paid a visit to the Likhachev plant, where he had worked thirty-five years before. The engineers and workers greeted their high-ranking Chinese guest warmly.

We knew that considerable concern was being manifested in Beijing over the increasing domestic political tension in the Soviet Union. We also knew that 'Gorbachev's perestroika' was being subjected to fairly heavy criticism at closed meetings inside the Chinese Communist Party. But the Chinese leaders would not engage in open polemics. By all accounts, Beijing had drawn its own conclusions from the events that China had lived through in the spring of 1989. While reacting sharply to accusations of violating human rights, China's leaders nonetheless made corrections in their conduct of economic reforms and tried to improve relations with students and the intelligentsia. The change of approach had undoubtedly been an object of struggle in the upper echelons, and supporters of an evolutionary path had evidently proved stronger than the fundamentalists in the Maoist mould.

ABOUT CHINESE REFORMS

I am not convinced by the opinions of some of our politicians that we should have followed the Chinese path – that is, to implement economic reforms first and only later take up political reforms – and that we could thus have avoided upheavals and ensured stability. It is hard to say what there is more of in these judgements: naiveté and superficiality or political speculation.

I am too familiar with the sluggishness of our political structures to cherish any illusions concerning their tolerance for economic reforms. All attempts at any kind of serious economic transformation in our country were stifled and choked by political retrogradism. That is how it was under Khrushchev and Brezhnev, and that is what is happening even today.

What can I say? The economic reforms in China are a great success for the new leadership of the country and the Chinese people as a whole. Their experience, the strong and weak aspects, the pluses and minuses, merit the most attentive study. After all, in ten years or so an enormous country of more than a billion people was freed from the most ruinous effects of left-wing experiments. Hundreds of millions of people were given the opportunity to feed themselves, and tens of millions attained relative prosperity. The achievements are significant and obvious.

But an ecstatic assessment of the benefits of economic reform in China is not enough for an objective evaluation of the highly contradictory and far from unambiguous socio-economic and socio-political processes going on in that immense country.

Take the economic zones, which are located primarily in coastal regions. Thanks to foreign investors – for the most part, ethnic Chinese residing abroad – and to cheap labour and advanced technology, competitive modern goods earmarked for export are being produced in these zones. To this day, however, few people in our country know that these zones are essentially closed to most Chinese citizens.

It is also obvious that the issue of political reforms is still there. It has simply been put on hold. This was confirmed in its own way by the XIVth CCP Congress in the autumn of 1992 and the session of the National People's Congress that followed, which recognized the necessity of conducting a 'political restructuring' in parallel with economic reform. Characteristically, the Chinese politicians have not rejected this concept.

Naturally, it is for the people of China and the Chinese leadership to define their own political, economic, and social priorities and the strategies and methods for the implementation of reforms. But those who recommend that we reproduce the Chinese model, even the newest one, would do well to know a great deal more about it. As I see it, the methods of maintaining political stability that are considered possible and essential in China are in many respects not applicable to our conditions. In stating this I am not saying I am in favour of a so-called double standard with respect to China and the rest of the world. But to ignore the uniqueness of a country with such a huge population and an ancient civilization, to attempt to drive everyone into some new mandatory, uniform model of development, would be the height of dogmatism.

The historical significance of the normalization of relations between our countries is that the peoples of China and Russia and the other states of the CIS now have an opportunity to deal with each other openly and broadly, to their immense mutual benefit, and to the benefit of Asia and the world.

23

OVERCOMING DIVISIONS IN EUROPE

AN INTERMISSION

ON 23 JANUARY 1989 I RECEIVED A TELEPHONE CALL FROM
President George Bush. Since his election, the mass media had
been of the opinion that the new American administration was in
no hurry to further develop relations with the Soviet Union.
Informed observers with contacts in the presidential entourage
wrote about a 'pause for reflection', a 'strategic review' and a
'general reassessment' of American foreign policy.

At the meeting on Governor's Island, I had told the President-
elect that I would understand if the new administration needed
some time to get its bearings. So long as we had a basic understanding that it was essential to preserve continuity, we would
have no reason for concern.

Shortly before taking office, George Bush sent me a letter by
the hand of Henry Kissinger, who had come on a visit to Moscow.
Mr Bush wrote to confirm that he needed time to review all the
issues – particularly in the field of arms control – which were
central to our bilateral relations, and to formulate a course with a
view to further developing these relations. 'Our aim is to develop
a solid, consistent American approach,' he wrote. 'We are in no
way attempting to slow down or reverse the progress that marked
the past couple of years . . .'

When the anticipated telephone call from President Bush came,
the tone of our conversation was quite optimistic, and it seemed
that we could expect a constructive dialogue and quick progress.

But weeks and months passed. The American administration was apparently in no hurry to develop Soviet-American relations. The first meeting between Eduard Shevardnadze and Secretary of State James Baker, which took place in Vienna in mid-March – nearly two months after George Bush assumed office – left us with the impression that the new administration was biding its time, waiting for . . . what were they waiting for? Some of the signals we were receiving were quite alarming. There were people in our country and in the Soviet leadership who were ready to interpret the drawn-out interval as evidence that Washington was plotting against the Soviet Union, or at least had no intention of improving relations.

As a matter of fact, various sources in the United States provided us with rather contradictory information. Yevgeny Primakov, who headed a Soviet delegation there, reported a noticeable swing in American public opinion in favour of the Soviet Union, particularly at the grass-roots level. Ingrained mistrust was gradually giving way to sympathy and interest. There were reasons to believe that sooner or later the Bush administration would have to follow suit and adapt to the changing mood of the American public, whereas only recently the American government had been forced to dance to a conservative tune.

However, the confidential information we received about deliberations at the White House cast a somewhat different light on the general picture. The hawks were again on the move, interpreting developments in our country and Eastern Europe as the long-awaited harbingers of the coveted 'victory in the Cold War'; they therefore suggested increasing pressure on the Soviet Union to force further concessions.

Had this attitude fully prevailed in the Bush administration, much of what we had achieved in Soviet-American relations with President Reagan would have been lost, providing new fuel for those in our country who had argued from the start that normalizing relations with the United States and other Western countries was a dangerous and unacceptable policy. In my meetings with West European leaders – I saw quite a few of them in those months – I openly expressed my concern about the current state of Soviet-American relations. I was convinced that my partners would inform their principal NATO ally about it.

It seems to me that discussing the situation and the prospects for Soviet-American relations with Mrs Thatcher during my visit to Britain in April 1989 must also have been useful, considering the 'special relationship' between Great Britain and the United States.

ON AN OFFICIAL VISIT TO LONDON

My official visit to London had been planned for late 1988. I was due to stop in England on my way back from New York after addressing the United Nations General Assembly. But the earthquake in Armenia made me change my plans, and I had to return home immediately. I apologized to Mrs Thatcher and we postponed the visit to a later date. She had been the first to send me a telegram of condolence on the terrible tragedy that had befallen the Armenian people, which she took very much to heart. The United Kingdom was among the first countries to send humanitarian aid to Armenia.

My visit to Britain finally took place in April 1989, on my way home from Cuba. At midnight on 5 April our plane landed at Heathrow Airport. We were greeted by the Queen's representative, Lord Strathclyde, and by Mr and Mrs Thatcher. I started a conversation with the British Prime Minister immediately at the airport and continued it in the car on the way to the Soviet Embassy. Margaret Thatcher remarked that she had been very impressed by the recent Soviet parliamentary elections, especially by the turnout of the voters, and she told me about her recent trip to a number of countries in Southern Africa. Official talks were scheduled to begin the next day.

I arrived at the London residence of the British Prime Minister early the next morning. Some three hundred reporters from major television companies, news agencies and newspapers from all over the world were already waiting for us. It was my first visit to the famous No. 10 Downing Street. Margaret Thatcher led me up a narrow staircase, under the intent gaze of the portraits of British prime ministers since 1732.

Many changes had occurred in the world in the two years since our last meeting in Moscow. The West was gradually re-assessing its views on perestroika in the Soviet Union. This new approach was also reflected in our talks. Mrs Thatcher suggested the following agenda: East-West relations, arms control, regional problems and bilateral Soviet-British relations. However, she wanted to know first how things were going back in the Soviet Union and what progress had been achieved with perestroika, adding that she was intensely interested in the developments there.

I briefed the British Prime Minister in detail about the situation in my country, expressing concern about attempts in the West to counter the favourable impression that reforms in the Soviet Union were making on the general public. Knowing Mrs Thatcher's intimacy with Washington, I stressed the point. I wanted to hear her own opinion. She disagreed with my view, asserting that the West welcomed perestroika and wished us every success.

'It is a common position all of us have taken in the West,' Mrs Thatcher said. 'How could it be otherwise? Your policy leads to an improvement in human rights and civil liberties, an improvement in people's living conditions, the affirmation of such values as freedom of speech and freedom of assembly, free movement of ideas and other forms of co-operation across state borders. We are therefore very much in favour of the changes you are making and are ready to help you in practical ways – while of course maintaining our own Western values and our alliances and while remaining vigilant about our security.'

Margaret Thatcher was sincere. I believe that when she informed Washington about our conversation, she also conveyed her own views, which were apparently taken into account by the American administration. In any case, the American Secretary of State, James Baker, came to Moscow some six weeks later in a constructive spirit.

'As to the essence of your domestic developments,' Mrs Thatcher continued, 'I foresaw from the start that you are now reaching the most difficult stage. I have always believed that the most difficult task is to change people's attitudes towards their

643

work and towards themselves and to induce them to participate in economic changes. In a politically free society, such attempts are usually met with criticism, not with the desire to participate . . . It is one thing to tell people what to do and where to work, and another to make them work by themselves, as required by large-scale production and complex technologies. People start feeling uncertain of themselves and their future . . . The old order is being demolished and people do not know what will take its place – and what it means to rely on one's own work and the spirit of enterprise, and whether this will improve their lives.'

The British Prime Minister seemed concerned that growing difficulties and resistance by the Soviet nomenklatura could prove insurmountable obstacles on the road to reform. She also perceived another danger – hurried implementation of the reforms – and for this reason she stressed how much time had been needed to consolidate the existing system in England. Margaret Thatcher's own experience in introducing changes showed the importance of being both decisive and prudent at the same time.

We were able to record a number of positive results which had been achieved thanks to our joint efforts and the new spirit reigning in international affairs: the recent agreement on Namibia's independence, the spirit of co-operation at the United Nations General Assembly and in the Security Council which had produced a ceasefire agreement in the Iran-Iraq war, as well as some progress in the Middle East. However, I expressed concern that the Bush administration was taking so long to review Soviet-American relations. But the British Prime Minister replied that my doubts were unfounded.

We attended the signing ceremony on three protocols and agreements by our foreign ministers: an agreement on investment promotion and protection, a protocol aimed at clarifying and simplifying visa arrangements between our countries, and a protocol arranging for Great Britain to finance the building and equipment of a school in Armenia. Mrs Thatcher and I made a short statement for the waiting press outside 10 Downing Street. Margaret Thatcher characterized the talks as substantial, warm and friendly. I took the opportunity to thank the British government and people for reaching out to the Armenian people to help overcome the dire consequences of the recent earthquake. I added that our dialogue with Great Britain was both substantial and marked by growing mutual understanding.

Margaret and Denis Thatcher accompanied Raisa Maksimovna and me to Westminster Abbey, where we laid a wreath at the Tomb of the Unknown Soldier in memory of those who fell in the Second World War and those who, together with the Soviet soldiers, had liberated Europe from Nazism.

Our delegation was welcomed by cheering crowds lining the streets outside Westminster Abbey. I asked our driver to stop the car and went over to shake hands with Londoners. The enthusiastic acclamation made any conversation impossible, but the atmosphere of this short exchange spoke for itself.

On the second day of my visit, I was to make a speech at London's Guildhall. This famous hall had witnessed many major events in five centuries of English history, and foreign leaders were invited to speak from this most prestigious platform only on very special occasions. Outstanding political and public figures and city representatives had been invited to attend the meeting. At the entrance, we were greeted by the Lord Mayor and his wife.

I had prepared my speech thoroughly, concentrating on the significance of the period in which we lived. The international community found itself at a crossroads – having to decide whether to follow the past policy, based on power and force, or a newly emerging policy based on universal human interests and values. Today's political leaders bore the burden of crucial choices and of fateful decisions. We in the Soviet Union tried to answer frankly and candidly the most difficult questions with which we were faced. We were trying to re-assess our own experience and history, the surrounding world and our place in it, and we invited everyone to participate in the dialogue and to co-operate in the name of survival and progress.

'There is a genuine opportunity to turn the last page of post-war history and to make a first step into a new, peaceful world,' I continued. 'As to so-called "deterrence", we should not speak of deterrence by nuclear weapons but of deterring of the use of nuclear weapons.' I expressed the hope that Anglo-Soviet relations could make a significant contribution to establishing and strengthening trust, which was essential to resolve burning international problems.

From the Guildhall, we drove directly to Windsor Castle. The road led through a picturesque English landscape. We were greeted by Queen Elizabeth II and the Duke of Edinburgh. We had a warm exchange during the lunch held in our honour and afterwards the Queen personally showed us the sights of Windsor Castle and her wonderful collection of paintings. I expressed the hope that she would one day visit the Soviet Union, something no British monarch had ever done.

FIRST TALKS WITH THE NEW AMERICAN ADMINISTRATION

Secretary of State James Baker came to Moscow in mid-May. Shortly before this visit, President Bush had informed us that the Americans' 'strategic review' was completed and they were ready for serious discussion of all the items on the Soviet-American agenda, including disarmament, regional issues and global co-operation.

Mr Baker brought me a message from President Bush. By and large, it was positive, but I was somewhat surprised by the statement that a stronger Soviet Union could become more assertive in projecting its military might, 'which would cause concern to the United States.' The Americans were apparently still influenced by obsolete stereotypes. We obviously had no intentions of that sort. On the contrary, we had significantly reduced surplus weapons and arms exports (on the eve of Mr Baker's visit, I had informed President Bush of our decision to stop shipments of weapons to Nicaragua). However, there was another, far more important factor which I immediately mentioned to the American Secretary of State: 'I want to assure you that everything we do in the process of perestroika to revive our society and to strengthen our state and bring it nearer to the people will benefit not only the Soviet Union but also the United States.

'Obviously, I have closely followed the analysis of the

domestic and foreign policy of the United States you have been undertaking in the past months. And I know that in the course of your analysis you thoroughly examined in detail the issue I have just mentioned. You heard many different views, recommendations and advice on this question, including the following: "Why should we hurry if the Soviet Union is anyway heading for destabilization and break-up? Let the fruit ripen and fall into our lap." You should reject such an approach.'

I talked with Mr Baker in private for an hour after this introduction, and we were later joined by the members of our respective delegations. All in all, it seemed to me that we had established quite a good rapport. James Baker impressed me as a serious person who would firmly defend his stand but be prepared to listen to reasonable arguments. In addition, it seemed to me that his general attitude was constructive. Yet we still had no clear answer to the question whether the American administration was prepared to make fast progress.

TALKS WITH CHANCELLOR KOHL

My visit to the Federal Republic of Germany began on 12 June 1989. The West German Chancellor and I met in private on three occasions during this visit, twice at the Chancellor's office and once at his home.

Some two weeks before my visit to West Germany, at the summit meeting in Brussels, the leaders of the NATO states had agreed on a 'joint agenda for the future' which included President Bush's proposals for armed forces reductions in Europe. This was the American answer to the arms control initiative launched by the Soviet Union and its then Warsaw Pact allies. We aimed to correct asymmetries between NATO and the Warsaw Pact in Europe, in terms both of men and weapons, and to reduce radically the armed forces to a level that would make a surprise attack impossible.

I viewed the Brussels document with mixed feelings. It was the first time one of our disarmament initiatives had been met not with suspicion or criticism but with a serious and substantial response. I told Mr Kohl that West Germany's constructive approach had contributed significantly to this decision. He seemed pleased to hear this and repeated several times that he believed an agreement in Vienna was feasible within the coming twelve months. He told me that he was prepared to intervene personally to help find mutually acceptable solutions. Kohl suggested that he did not regard President Bush's proposals as NATO's final offer and that he would not be averse to further, more radical cuts in the armed forces on both sides.

On two or three occasions, the West German Chancellor insisted that a successful conclusion of the Vienna talks could pave the way for a settlement of all outstanding disarmament issues. Whether this was true was debatable, but I could understand the motives behind this approach. Having been for decades at the epicentre of the military confrontation between East and West, the Federal Republic of Germany was sensitive about the Vienna talks. Indeed, this time it was directly participating in the negotiations affecting its security.

There was no point in starting an argument about whether the Vienna talks were simply 'important', 'very important' or 'most important'. For us, it was essential to break the stalemate in the talks on armed forces reduction in Europe, which had been dragging on since the early 1970s. The time had come for us to acknowledge that, even by Cold War logic, Soviet superiority in conventional weaponry in Europe stopped making political sense the moment we had reached nuclear parity with the United States. On the contrary, this situation helped to maintain the image of the Soviet Union as the enemy, thus creating ever new threats to our own security. Soviet conventional superiority served as a pretext for the United States and NATO to push through all sorts of military programmes, including the upgrading of nuclear weapons – in a sense, we were even giving them a hand with it!

In a nutshell, Chancellor Kohl and I agreed that it was time to abandon petty military accounting and adopt a broader political approach.

Incidentally, Mr Kohl did not challenge my criticisms of the principle of nuclear deterrence, which apparently remained the basis of NATO strategy. Unlike Mrs Thatcher, who never missed an opportunity to try to convince me of the virtues of nuclear deterrence, he simply remarked that 'Everyone has a creed', and the matter was closed.

We quickly reached understanding on another important issue. I was very worried about NATO's decision to modernize its tactical nuclear weapons in Europe. We had agreed to include the Soviet SS-23 missiles in the INF treaty despite the fact that their range of less than 500 kilometres put them formally in another class. We therefore obviously strongly disapproved of NATO's intentions, as I bluntly told Mr Kohl.

We were aware that there had not been full agreement among the NATO allies on the planned modernization. Great Britain alone was an unconditional supporter of the American plan, the others having reservations and the Germans defending the view that tactical nuclear weapons should be negotiated simultaneously with the Vienna talks. As a compromise, the phrase about the upgrading of tactical nuclear weapons was included in the declaration but its implementation was postponed.

From Helmut Kohl's statements, I understood that the European NATO allies had not been very enthusiastic about this compromise formula. But – and this was the essential point – he seemed convinced that the planned modernization of tactical nuclear weapons in Europe would be cancelled at the first signs of a breakthrough in the Vienna talks. This was an important signal, all the more so that it was coming from the Germans, since the American Lance missiles, due to be upgraded as part of the modernization plans, were deployed on West German soil.

We obviously also discussed bilateral questions. While our joint working groups examined specific co-operation projects, the Chancellor and I concentrated on issues that were, as he put it, of 'particular psychological importance' for the Germans – namely German POWs declared missing in the Soviet Union, access to German soldiers' cemeteries in the USSR, the possibility of German citizens visiting Kaliningrad (formerly Königsberg) and the re-creation of an autonomous region for Soviet citizens of German descent in the Soviet Union. I assured Chancellor Kohl that we would show understanding in all of these issues.

All in all, I had the impression that we had achieved as much as we could have expected during the visit, with Soviet-West German relations reaching a new high. We signed eleven agreements, including a far-ranging joint political declaration – the centrepiece of the visit – reflecting our common vision of the pan-European process and relations between our countries.

Chancellor Kohl and I agreed to work together to overcome the division of Europe. The Soviet Union and the Federal Republic of Germany appealed to the member states of the Conference on Security and Co-operation in Europe (CSCE) to join their efforts to develop the future construction of Europe.

Indeed, progress was made in a number of areas. The first round of the CSCE conference on human rights was closed in Paris on 23 June. Contacts were established between NATO and the Warsaw Pact, between the European Community and Comecon, and between the European Parliament and the USSR Supreme Soviet. The Council of Europe parliamentary assembly granted the Soviet Union special guest status, and I was invited to address the assembly in Strasbourg.

A MESSAGE FROM EUROPE

I arrived in France in early July. François Mitterrand gave a welcoming address at the Elysée Palace.

'Your visit happens at a moment which is generally perceived as decisive for our continent,' the French President said. 'For the first time in fifty years, we are offered an opportunity to steer Europe away from the era of division and confrontation and take the course of conciliation and concord – and it depends on us not to miss this opportunity.'

In my reply, I supported the idea he had expressed, stressing that we had good grounds for believing that 'the post-war period has come to its close.'

A record number of agreements had been prepared for the Soviet-French summit meeting. Co-operation was to be developed in some twenty areas: culture, a youth exchange programme, the prevention of incidents on the high seas, mutual investment guarantees etc. The French approach to disarmament had also somewhat changed. We appreciated François Mitterrand's decision to reduce the defence budget by 85 billion francs over five years. Even during the preparations for the visit, the French President and I had had occasion to exchange views on the situation in various conflict zones, particularly Lebanon and the Middle East.

There was every reason to believe that our summit meeting could become a milestone in the history of Soviet-French relations – and our hopes were fulfilled. Our conversations were extremely frank and penetrating. Among other things, I shared with François Mitterrand my thoughts about President Bush's request for time to review Soviet-American relations. We had accepted this, but such reflections, when they take too much time, are inconsistent with dynamic changes in international relations. It was essential for me to get a clear idea of the new American administration's attitude towards the agreement we had reached to withdraw our troops from Afghanistan, and towards the strategic arms reduction talks in Geneva, where things were going badly. In this context, I wanted to know the French President's opinion.

François Mitterrand told me that the French had discussed the issues I had mentioned with the Americans and that both sides viewed things positively. But it seemed to me that he had got my message.

As to the sensitive issue of nuclear arms, I expressed the hope that the French position would not hinder the progress of talks in Vienna and Geneva (the negotiations on the 50-per-cent cut in strategic arms). President Mitterrand's reply was generally reassuring.

We had a symbolic meeting at the Sorbonne with French intellectuals and artists. The Rector accompanied me to the auditorium of this famous institution. In his welcoming speech, he spoke about the role that intellectuals play in a society and their relations with the powers that be – an issue I also treated in my speech. It was the eve of the 200th anniversary of the French Revolution: history, as well as my own experience, made me emphasize that great socio-political upheavals were always preceded by philosophical revolutions. Thus many of the ideals of the French Revolution reflected the beliefs of the Enlightenment – equality and natural rights, the supremacy of the law, the separation of powers, the sovereignty of the people and the social contract – ideas that Voltaire and Montesquieu, Diderot and Holbach, Mably and Rousseau had formulated in their works. The intellectual and political heritage of the French Revolution gave impetus to the development of democratic thought in the nineteenth century, which prepared the ground for the social revolutions of the twentieth century.

Mankind was facing fundamentally new, global problems at the end of the twentieth century. They called for renewed intellectual efforts, a re-assessment of many established ideas, the rejection of the stereotypes we had grown accustomed to – in short, it needed new thinking. Speaking of this, I stressed three points I considered of particular importance: 'First, we have no right to continue setting our hopes on "spontaneous development" – we have to learn to manage it. Secondly, we must revise traditional criteria of progress, harmonizing our needs with the available energy and other natural resources, environmental and demographic realities and the need to overcome the gap between rich and poor countries. Thirdly, we must finally admit that the human race can survive and renew itself only if it learns tolerance and respect for freedom of choice and seeks peaceful, political ways to resolve contradictions and conflicts.

'One of the most significant features of our times is the high qualitative demands that are made on politics in general. This depends to a large extent on the participation of intellectuals. They must show greater responsibility in social and international affairs.

'Lack of spirituality and anti-intellectualism are terrible dangers. But pure intellect that is deprived of a moral basis is just as dangerous a threat in today's world. Without this organic bond, contemporary science loses its humanitarian sense.

'It is even more important that the reinforcement of science's moral basis be reflected in its interaction with politics. A weakening, or worse, a breaking of any link in the triad "politics –

science – ethics" may have unpredictable consequences for mankind.'

I spoke these words in July 1989. In those areas where the new thinking was linked with politics, this synthesis yielded positive results and paved the way for progress. However, much of the new thinking has not been taken up by politicians – and we had to pay and are still paying a high price for this failure, particularly in Europe. One reason for this is that most politicians are completely absorbed by domestic affairs, another is the weakness or absence of the channels for regional and international co-operation.

In my speech at the Sorbonne, I considered it my duty to warn against over-reacting to the events in China. At the time, there was a powerful move to condemn the actions of the Chinese leadership in suppressing the student demonstrations. The freedom-loving French, who still remembered the student unrest in 1968, reacted very emotionally. And yet it seems to me that the audience acknowledged my main arguments: you cannot corner a great nation; isolation cannot be the answer to actions that are contrary to democracy and human rights; the international community has enough means to influence events positively without interfering in the domestic affairs of a country.

Some people claimed that I had tried to justify the Tiananmen tragedy because I did not exclude such a turn of events in my own country. All I can say is that by now it must be clear that I have never consented and will never consent to the use of force to crush similar unrest. Violence does not resolve any problems, it simply drives them deeper.

A VISIT TO ITALY

My first official visit to Italy at the invitation of the Italian government did not take place until late November 1989. Apart from its own significance, this visit to Rome served as a prologue of sorts to my subsequent meeting with George Bush in Malta.

Our Ilyushin-62 landed at Fiumicino Airport. It was a wonderful November day, clear and sunny. From the airport we drove directly to the Quirinale Palace to attend the official welcoming ceremony. Crowds of Romans greeted us enthusiastically as we sped by. After the welcoming ceremony, I had a short talk with President Cossiga and then drove to the Piazza Venezia to lay a wreath at the Altar of the Fatherland. Again, we were warmly greeted by crowds of Italians. The programme included a sight-seeing tour of the Eternal City. But it ran into difficulties, our progress towards the Colosseum being hindered by thousands of cheering people. Slowly making our way through the crowd, we exchanged greetings and handshakes. 'Enthusiastic Rome welcomes Gorbachev' wrote the newspaper *La Stampa* on the next day.

Another memorable event was the visit to the Roman municipality on the Capitol, where I was given the opportunity to deliver a speech. I shared my thoughts on the events and lessons of 1989. This is not the place to quote the speech, but its significance lay in the perception of the turning-point my country and the world had reached.

My programme included a visit to Milan. Meeting the Milanese turned out to be one of the most emotional moments I experienced during my trips abroad. It seemed as if all the inhabitants of this ancient Italian city had come out onto the streets to greet us. We decided to walk from La Scala to the city hall, but progress was made nearly impossible by the cheering crowds. The noise was so loud that you could not hear yourself speak. Tens of thousands of Milanese passionately displayed their genuine feelings, their heartfelt solidarity and sympathy. I was absolutely astounded by their behaviour. We were swallowed up by this human stream and could only escape from it some forty minutes later, with the active help of policemen.

To complete the picture, I should add that both before and during my visit to Italy, I received dozens of personal letters and telegrams from Italian citizens, public and academic organizations, and firms who invited me to 'drop in' if the programme allowed it. Obviously it was physically impossible for me to answer all of these letters and invitations.

Raisa Maksimovna travelled with some members of our delegation to Messina in Sicily. The city was devastated by an earthquake on 28 December 1908, when over 80,000 people had lost their lives. The first to reach out to the Messinese were Russian sailors. For two weeks, they participated in rescue operations and fed the survivors. A commemorative plaque was erected in their honour. And the Messinese were among the first to reach out to Armenia – they collected over 1,800 million Italian lire to build a hospital in Kirovakan and sent a CAT scanner. The Messinese welcomed our delegation with open arms, and Raisa Maksimovna expressed her gratitude and solidarity on behalf of the Soviet people.

During the three days of my stay in Italy, I met the head of the Italian government, Giulio Andreotti, the President of the Italian Senate, Giovanni Spadolini, and the leaders of the five governing parties. I also had a meeting with the General Secretary of the Italian Communist Party, Achille Occhetto.

Another event I would like to mention: in Rome, the pacifist Italian Centre of Documentation and the National League of Co-operation awarded me the 'Golden Dove of Peace'. Luigi Anderlini, the president of the centre, presented me with the award, and the novelist Alberto Moravia read the welcoming address. I was deeply touched by his words.

On 1 December an extraordinary event took place, the first visit by a Soviet head of state to the Vatican, at the personal invitation of Pope John Paul II. Soviet relations with the centre of Catholicism had always been extremely hostile. The Vatican was invariably described as 'the source of reaction and obscurantism'. During détente in the 1970s, the situation had improved somewhat and the Soviet embassy in Rome had established contacts with representatives of the Holy See. Nevertheless, official relations were not established, and problems accumulated. The time had come to search for new approaches. In summer 1988, I had met Cardinal Casaroli, State Secretary of the Vatican, who had come to Moscow to attend the celebrations of the 1000th anniversary of Russia's conversion to Christianity. He brought me a friendly message from the Pope and a memorandum which touched on questions concerning the Catholic Church in the Soviet Union. Casaroli had declared that the Vatican followed developments in the Soviet Union with great interest and hope, and expected the reforms to continue in spite of the inevitable difficulties. He did not hide the fact that the Vatican viewed 'socialism' with suspicion. However, I gathered from his explanations that he made a distinction between human, democratic socialism and the totalitarian practice known as 'real socialism'. Nevertheless, there was still a 'certain fear and reserve', as he had put it.

I had informed the Cardinal that we were preparing a law on freedom of conscience that would regulate the situation of the Catholic Church in the Soviet Union. I promised to examine John Paul II's message and to reflect on his ideas. Bidding farewell to Casaroli, I had said that I looked forward to meeting him in Italy.

AN AUDIENCE WITH JOHN PAUL II

We drove through the Arco delle Campane and entered the San Damaso courtyard, where an array of Swiss Guards in picturesque uniforms (which are said to have been designed by Michelangelo) had assembled in our honour. I went directly to meet John Paul II for a private audience.

Welcoming the mission of His Holiness in the modern world, I noted that there were many identical terms in my statements and his. 'This means that we must also have something in common "at the source" – in our ideas,' I said. As if in reply to my thoughts, John Paul II referred to perestroika as a process that 'allows us to search jointly for a new dimension of co-existence between people that will be better adapted to the needs of the individual, of different peoples, to the rights of individuals and nations.

'The efforts you undertake,' he continued, 'are not merely of great interest for us. We share them.'

He pointed out another important idea: 'No-one should claim that the changes in Europe and the world happen according to the Western model. This is contrary to my profound convictions. Europe must breathe with both its lungs.'

'This is a very precise image,' I replied.

The Pope said that this was precisely what he had in mind when, in 1980, he proclaimed Cyril and Methodius – two representatives of the Eastern, Byzantine, Greek, Slav and Russian traditions – patron saints of Europe, together with St Benedict, who represented the Latin tradition.

'This is my European creed,' John Paul II concluded.

Naturally we focused on freedom of conscience, as one of the fundamental human rights, and on freedom of worship. John Paul II spoke of 'our Orthodox brothers' and of the intensification of the ecumenical dialogue with the Orthodox Churches and the Russian Orthodox Church in particular. At the same time he dwelt on a number of questions connected with the situation of Catholics in our country.

I explained my approach to these issues. 'We intend to realize our plans by democratic means,' I said. 'However, I have been thinking about the developments of the past years and have come to the conclusion that democracy alone is not enough. We also need morality. Democracy can bring both good and evil – there is no denying it. You have what you have. For us, it is essential that morality should become firmly established in society – such universal, eternal values as goodness, mercy, mutual aid. We start from the principle that the faith of believers must be respected. This applies both to Orthodox believers and to representatives of other religions, including Catholics.'

We agreed in principle to establish official ties, and to exchange permanent representatives between the Vatican and Moscow.

After the meeting, we joined Casaroli, Raisa Maksimovna and the officials from my delegation, who were waiting for us in the ceremonial library of the Apostolic Palace. John Paul II spoke a few words with everyone.

This was the end of my visit to the Vatican, but afterwards our contacts intensified and we repeatedly exchanged views with the Holy See. His Holiness sent me messages of support and understanding in my most difficult hours.

The next day, we left Italy to meet President Bush in Malta.

THE MALTA SUMMIT

In July 1989 Marshal Akhromeyev returned from a visit to the United States with a message from President Bush, suggesting an informal preliminary meeting for December of the same year. The message was highly confidential; I learned later that only Mr Bush's closest aides were informed of the proposal.

I agreed to Mr Bush's proposal, and we immediately started intensive preparations. The Americans were also 'doing their homework' for the summit.

The day drew near. We had settled on the agenda for the meeting. Malta was to be the venue, and the talks were scheduled to take place by turns on the Soviet warship *Slava* and the *USS Belknap* in the lanes of the Valletta sea-port. We also sent the Soviet tourist liner *Maksim Gorky* to Valletta to serve as a hotel for us.

The Malta summit – the first since the new American President and his administration had taken office – could be regarded as symbolic in many respects. We met at the juncture of three continents, the crossroads of the world and the meeting-point of manifold interests. The talks were to take place on warships – symbols of the military might behind the Soviet and American leaders. The world was on the threshold of a new era.

I and my colleagues were looking forward to serious work, although we still hoped to find time to get acquainted with this exotic island. Malta is a country rich in architectural monuments, paintings and sculptures that are the surviving witnesses of a civilization that has its roots in the fourth millennium B.C. But I never had an opportunity to see any of this, the few days of my stay being fully taken up by work. Raisa Maksimovna made a sight-seeing tour of the capital – San Giovanni, the principal church of the Knights of Malta, and the sloping, narrow Market Street – and visited a newly-wed couple. She strongly advised me to find at least one or two hours to see the wonderful sights, and the summit programme had initially allowed for an excursion to Valletta. However, I hardly ever set foot ashore. All my impressions on land were reduced to the road from and to the airport – no bushes, no trees, nothing but cactus thickets and the interminable peculiar stone walls which girdled the island.

Well, another missed occasion to engage in some 'tourism' – I missed quite a few of them during my term at the helm of the Soviet Union. I had other priorities.

We arrived in Valletta on the evening of 2 December, direct from our visit to Italy. At the beginning, everything went according to the programme. We met the Maltese President, the Prime Minister, and other members of the government, and had very friendly encounters with the crowds who greeted us on the streets and at the presidential palace.

However, natural elements introduced some radical corrections into our programme for the next day. The sea was stormy and the transfer by boat to the Soviet cruiser *Slava*, where we had initially planned to hold the first round of talks, proved difficult. Both our sailors and the Americans were against such an operation, and it was suggested that we should organize the first meeting on board *Maksim Gorky*, moored in the port. The change in the programme fortunately caused only a slight delay.

The agenda provided for a number of meeting 'rounds': I had a private conversation with Mr Bush while James Baker and Eduard Shevardnadze exchanged views on foreign affairs, then a working lunch and expanded talks in the presence of both delegations. We decided not to sail in the teeth of the storm, which had grown stronger during the day, and cancelled our evening meeting.

'I fully agree with what you said in New York,' Mr Bush declared. 'It will be a better world if perestroika succeeds. Just a short time ago, many people in the United States had doubts about that. I won't claim that such attitudes are a thing of the past. But I can say with certainty that serious, thinking people do not support such views. This fully applies to those you are dealing with – the US administration and Congress, who want your reforms to succeed.'

Mr Bush went on to explain a number of positive steps which could, in his view, pave the way for an official summit meeting in the United States. Since it was necessary to set a date, the Americans proposed late June 1990.

According to Mr Bush, the American administration planned

to take the necessary steps to suspend the Jackson-Vanik amendment barring most-favoured-nation trade status for the Soviet Union. Considering the forthcoming reforms in the Soviet Union, the Americans suggested starting consultations on a new trade agreement, to be completed for the next summit meeting. The Bush administration had also decided to push for the abrogation of the Stevenson and Bird amendments which restricted credits to the Soviet Union.

The President stressed that the measures suggested by the United States for developing Soviet-American relations were in no way meant to be a show of American superiority.

'Naturally, we in the United States firmly believe in the advantages of our economic system,' he said. 'But that is not the point. We are trying to present our proposals in such a way as to avoid creating the impression that America is "rescuing" the Soviet Union. We are speaking not of an aid programme, but of co-operation.'

In this context, the American President mentioned the General Agreement on Tariffs and Trade. 'We used to oppose Soviet membership of this international organization,' he said. 'We have now reviewed our position: we suggest granting the Soviet Union observer status in GATT. However, the member states need some time.

'We already have a functioning Soviet-American working group for investment problems. This is a good thing. Maybe it is time to examine possibilities for drawing up an investment protection agreement.'

The American President spoke at length about disarmament issues. In particular, Mr Bush announced a somewhat modified position on the question of chemical weapons, saying that if the Soviet side agreed in principle with the American proposal he had put forward in his speech to the UN General Assembly in September 1989, the United States could abandon their modernization programme, i.e. the continued production of binary weapons, after a general ban on chemical weapons had come into force. In practice, this meant that we could settle on a significant reduction of our chemical arsenals in the near future, limiting each side's chemical weapons stockpiles to twenty per cent of the current American level and eventually to two per cent, eight years after the convention had come into force. With some effort, we could prepare a draft agreement by mid-1990.

For conventional weapons, Mr Bush formulated the following objective: to sign a treaty on significant conventional force reductions in Europe at the 1990 summit meeting of the participants in the Vienna talks. Concerning the strategic arms reduction treaty, he expressed the hope that our foreign ministers would try to resolve the outstanding issues quickly.

'The United States would welcome the Soviet Union's adherence to the non-proliferation regime for missiles and missile technology, which has already been adopted by seven Western states,' the American President said. He also suggested that the Soviet Union should publish data about its defence budget.

I welcomed Mr Bush's suggestions for bilateral economic co-operation and expressed the hope that the American President would show his political will. What was needed was a signal from the President; American businessmen were disciplined people and would react positively to the new thinking in economics.

Disarmament was obviously one of the issues of the day. I supported President Bush's proposal to sign an agreement on conventional forces in Europe in 1990. I thought we could realistically hope to draw up a strategic arms reduction treaty in time for the summit meeting in Washington in summer 1990. However, I drew Mr Bush's attention to the fact that he had left out the problem of sea-launched cruise missiles, where the United States had a significant advantage over the Soviet Union.

'Our Supreme Soviet,' I declared, 'will not ratify the treaty if we do not find an acceptable solution for the problem of sea-launched cruise missiles.'

The Americans were particularly interested in Soviet policy towards Central America, and Mr Bush brought up the subject during the first of our private meetings. He asked me to persuade Fidel Castro to stop supplying arms to 'states where the democratic government system is itself rather fragile'. He characterized the situation in Nicaragua and El Salvador as a 'giant thorn' in Soviet-American relations, reducing the problem again to arms supplies.

In my reply, I stressed that we did not pursue any special goals in Central America. We did not want to create bridgeheads or bases there. The American reaction to developments in the region gave me the impression that they were being supplied with one-sided information. We had agreed not to supply weapons to Nicaragua and we did not supply them. We also noted that the American Congress had stopped aid to the 'Contras'.

Concerning Cuba, I suggested that the simplest and most effective way to clear up misunderstandings would be to talk directly to Fidel Castro. Nobody could give him orders. In a private meeting, Fidel had asked me to help him normalize relations with the United States. The chief of staff of the Cuban armed forces had visited the Soviet Union shortly before our meeting and repeated this confidential request in a conversation with the Soviet Defence Minister and during a meeting with Marshal Akhromeyev. Should the Americans express such a wish, I said that we would be glad to help in establishing a dialogue.

I must say Mr Bush reacted very coldly to my proposal. He indicated that the United States were not ready for any compromise in the matter and went so far as to suggest that we should reduce our economic ties with Cuba, adding that he could not understand why we had not done so already, since the Cubans had openly condemned our perestroika.

I had to remind the American President that Cuba was an independent country with its own government, its own understanding of things and its own ambitions. We were in the process of reviewing our economic ties in order gradually to make them mutually beneficial, but we had no intention of telling the Cubans what to do.

In this connection, I asked the President about American relations with such countries as Panama, Colombia and, lately, the Philippines. People in the Soviet Union wondered why the independence of these nations did not seem to stop the United States from interfering in their affairs. What right had Washington to lay down the law, bring in the verdict and execute the sentence? Was the 'Brezhnev doctrine' about to be replaced by the 'Bush doctrine'?

Mr Bush strongly objected. I tried to clarify my position by citing the following example: 'Look at what is happening in Europe,' I said. 'It is changing, and lawfully elected governments are being replaced. What if somebody asked the Soviet Union to intervene? How are we supposed to react to such a request? The same way as President Bush?'

My American colleague naturally disagreed, admitting nevertheless that some people in the Soviet Union might feel like reacting in this way.

Another issue we discussed in private was the situation in Eastern Europe. I expressed my concern about the way developments in Germany were being handled. Unification was a serious business and required a cautious approach. There was no need to push events.

George Bush replied that he had personally no intention of storming the German border or 'jumping on the wall', as he jokingly put it. I rejoined that climbing walls did not seem to be a proper occupation for a President.

Defying the weather forecasts, the storm raged through the night, and in the morning it turned out that it was still too dangerous to transfer the delegations from one warship to another. Hence, we decided to meet again on board the Soviet passenger liner and the final round of talks took place in the ship's library – first a meeting in the presence of our delegations, and then another private conversation with Mr Bush.

I decided to outline some aspects I deemed fundamental. 'First,' I said, 'the United States should take as a starting-point that the Soviet Union will never, under any circumstances, start a war with the United States and, what is more, is prepared not to regard it as an enemy. Second, we propose to join efforts to ensure mutual security – we are committed to continuing disarmament in all areas and will do everything in our power to prevent the development of new, exotic weapons. Third, we have adopted a defensive doctrine and our armed forces are undergoing profound changes: the structure of our forces in Central Europe is changing – we have reduced the number of tanks per division, we are withdrawing airborne and amphibious equipment, repositioning our strike aircraft to the second echelon and so on.'

'However, there are some points that need clarification,' I

added. 'Why does the United States still adhere to the "flexible response" strategy? Why has the third pillar of their military might, the US Navy, not yet been included in negotiations?'

In this connection, I made the following additional proposal: 'The Soviet and US Navy have both strategic – i.e. submarine-launched ballistic missiles and sea-launched cruise missiles – and tactical nuclear weapons – short-range cruise missiles, nuclear torpedoes and mines,' I said. 'The strategic component is part of the Geneva talks; the tactical nuclear weapons remain. We propose that they be eliminated completely. Such a radical solution would also simplify verification procedures.

'Three major issues remain to be settled at the Vienna talks,' I continued. 'The first is the reduction of military personnel. I suggest reducing them by one million, to 1,300,000 men on each side. The second problem is the reduction of armed forces stationed on foreign territory; we propose setting a ceiling of 300,000 men. However, NATO is prepared to reduce only the Soviet and American forces; what about the British, French, Belgian, Dutch and Canadian troops? The third question is the size of the respective air forces, and we suggested a ceiling of 4,700 tactical combat aircraft for each alliance, with a sub-ceiling for interceptor aircraft. However, progress is still very slow.

'Incidentally,' I added, 'we endorse President Bush's proposal for "open skies",[1] which makes sense.'

We returned to European issues. I laid special emphasis on a number of fundamental points: Europe was undergoing profound changes and the dynamic developments called for careful and responsible action and consensus – a view supported by practically all the European leaders.

What were the practical implications of such an approach? First of all, we had to continue and develop the Helsinki process. We needed a Helsinki Two to agree on common criteria and objectives.

Another important question in the new situation was how to deal with international structures created under very different

---

[1] The superpowers were negotiating about the right of their reconnaissance aircraft to fly over each other's territory.

circumstances. Again, balanced and responsible action was called for. Instead of destroying the existing international instruments which contributed to maintaining stability, they had to be adapted to the challenges of our times. The political, economic and military alliances created in East and West should not compete but co-operate.

At this point Mr Bush and I had a brief argument about different interpretations of 'Western' and universal democratic values. I repeated that the new political thinking we adhered to provided for the right of each nation to choose its own course without foreign interference. We had to learn from the experience of others, selecting those aspects that were organically suitable for us.

The President agreed with me in principle. We continued by discussing the situation in Afghanistan and the Middle East.

During the final, one-to-one session that followed, the President and I discussed the situation in the Baltic region. Repeating the well-known American position, he added that American public opinion was sensitive to the developments in the Baltic republics. I explained the special nature of the situation which had emerged in the Soviet Union to the American President.

Finally, another precedent was set in Malta, the first joint press conference by the Soviet and American leaders. It was held on board the *Maksim Gorky*. We both concurred in the view that the summit meeting had brought our relations onto a new plane.

24

GERMAN UNIFICATION

THE MALTA SUMMIT CONVINCED ME THAT WE HAD FINALLY crossed the Rubicon. For the first time since the Second World War, the political barometer of East-West relations stopped skipping back and forth to steady on 'fair'. I firmly believed that we had succeeded in breaking out of the vicious circle, in which short springs of détente had been inevitably followed by long winters of confrontation. It took us some time to comprehend fully the significance of what had happened, and to realize that we were on the threshold of a new phase in the post-war history of international relations. The Malta summit had drawn the curtain on the Cold War, although we would still have to live with its difficult legacy.

Germany – the focus of many a European and international problem – was to become a crucial test of the progress we had achieved in our relations with the United States, and with the nations of Western Europe, including Germany herself. The process of German reunification was a difficult and painful period for everyone involved, particularly the Soviet Union, and it seems to me that, all in all, the main protagonists passed the test.

I should be less than sincere if I said that I had foreseen the course of events and the problems the German question would eventually create for Soviet foreign policy. As a matter of fact, I doubt whether any of today's politicians (in either East or West) could have predicted the outcome only a year or two beforehand. After the radical changes that had taken place in the German

Democratic Republic, the situation developed at such breathtaking speed that there was a real danger that it would get out of control. However, looking back I can say in all conscience that, in the circumstances, we did everything humanly possible to uphold the interests of our country, and to preserve peace in Europe and the process of European integration.

It goes without saying that back in 1985 the German question – as seen from Moscow – looked quite different from the way it does today. The German Democratic Republic was our ally, while the Federal Republic of Germany, albeit the Soviet Union's prime trading partner in the West, was, militarily, among our 'potential enemies'. The short 'thaw' in our relations with West Germany inaugurated by Willy Brandt's Ostpolitik in the early 1970s was over by the early 1980s. Given the general increase in international tension, Moscow viewed Bonn's political course primarily in the context of Soviet-American confrontation. Seen from that angle, the ensuing pattern of thought appeared quite logical: 'West Germany is America's closest ally and the champion of US policy in Europe; the Bundeswehr is NATO's "first army"; American Pershing missiles which can reach the Soviet Union in only a few minutes are stationed on West German soil.' I write this without irony – in the general context of global confrontation, the above-mentioned arguments could not be taken lightly, particularly if one bears in mind the psychological trauma of the Second World War.

The Soviet position on 'German reunification' stemmed from the same logic. It is not my intent to revive the old argument about who was more to blame for the division of Germany, although I believe that Stalin was prepared to pay a price for a neutral Germany up to the last moment. However, after the creation of the North Atlantic Treaty Organization (1949) and West Germany's joining the alliance (1955), speculations about German unification became a mere propaganda ritual of sorts, both in the West and the Soviet Union.

Brezhnev and Gromyko had obviously miscalculated when, in the early 1970s, they officially accepted the GDR leaders' attractively 'simple' idea of two fully-fledged German nations, which seemingly closed the debate on the German question for good.

Nevertheless, Ulbricht's and Honecker's theoretical concepts about the existence of two German nations were not the decisive motive behind the Soviet policy. Soviet leaders were genuinely convinced that our security could be guaranteed only by perpetuating the division of Germany at all costs. I must admit that my views on the question were rather similar, although I doubted whether you could preserve anything forever. The world is constantly changing, and you are bound to lose if you ignore this objective fact. Be that as it may, when I made my entrance on the stage of international politics, the existence of two German states was a fact, and German unification was simply not an issue.

West German President Richard von Weizsäcker brought up the question of German unity – very tactfully and cautiously – during a meeting in June 1987. In my reply I did not exclude the possibility of German reunification in the future, but I believed that, given the political situation at the time, it was premature and even harmful to raise the issue.

As the reader knows, the question was soon 'resolved' in connection with the profound changes which took place in Western Europe, induced to a significant extent by our own policy. It goes without saying that the improved relations between West Germany and the Soviet Union contributed significantly to its solution.

However, our relations remained strained throughout the first two years of perestroika. The government in Bonn followed President Reagan's course with German precision. Back in Moscow we had the impression that we were hearing a meticulous German translation of well-known American themes. The West German government seemed to lack either the necessary imagination or the political courage to react imaginatively to the changes in our country; and Chancellor Helmut Kohl's comparison of all the talk about reforms and new political thinking in the Soviet Union with Goebbels' propaganda made me doubt the West German leadership's ability to assess the new political situation.

I had already met President Reagan in Geneva and Reykjavik and established an active political dialogue with France, Italy and Great Britain, but there was still no sign of change in our relations with Bonn. At some point, both sides seemed to sense the abnormality of the situation. I realized that for us, there could be no serious European policy without German participation, and I brought up the issue at various Politburo meetings and discussions with my closest colleagues. Europe had a place of its own in Soviet foreign policy, and was in addition an important factor in our dialogue with the United States.

Some time in the second half of 1987, when the storm aroused by the Reykjavik summit had calmed down, Bonn started moving. I received several letters from Chancellor Kohl. In one of these, he formally apologized for his improper statements, putting most of the blame on the press for the misunderstanding. As I have already mentioned, I had met President von Weizsäcker in June, and we had a constructive and substantial exchange of views. I met Foreign Minister Hans-Dietrich Genscher for the second time, and I also met Franz Josef Strauss, who visited Moscow in December 1987. We established a good rapport, and I must say that – despite the derogatory clichés applied to this politician by our press – Mr Strauss impressed me as a man of character, with realistic, broad-minded views on world politics.

In early February 1988, I met the Deputy Chairman of the German Christian Democratic Union, Baden-Württemberg Prime Minister Lothar Späth. He came to Moscow to discuss the possibility of a summit meeting. By then, we were prepared for such a meeting and I had already asked Eduard Shevardnadze to transmit my invitation for the German Chancellor to visit Moscow in May. It was apparent that Bonn feared that the Germans might be left out of the new developments in Europe. 'Chancellor Kohl believes it is essential that you should meet,' Späth told me. 'Who should travel first to Moscow or Bonn poses no problem to him. His problem is that, if you plan trips to Western Europe, it would be desirable that the Federal Republic of Germany should be included in your plans. It is a very sensitive aspect. To be frank, the Chancellor would resent it – now that you have already visited France and Great Britain – if you visited other West European countries and left the Federal Republic aside.'

In the end the visit was postponed, and my first meeting with

West German Chancellor Helmut Kohl did not take place until he came to Moscow on 24 October 1988. The main point I made in our discussion then was that the present state of relations between the Soviet Union and West Germany was unsatisfactory both for us and for the Germans, as well as for the rest of the world. 'We want to build our relations on trust and realism,' I said. 'I am convinced that we need to start a new chapter in Soviet-West German relations.'

Kohl's reply was unequivocal: 'I fully agree with you,' he said. 'I have thought it over and this is the reason for my coming to Moscow.' He stressed his government's readiness to develop relations energetically with the Soviet Union in every area.

'I attach particular importance to a personal rapport with you,' he added. 'I have come to Moscow both in my function as Chancellor of the Federal Republic of Germany and as citizen Kohl. We are about the same age and we both lived through the war. It is true that I served for some time as an anti-aircraft auxiliary, but this cannot be regarded as participation in the war. However, our families lived through the war and all its horrors. Your father was a soldier and was severely wounded. My brother died at the age of eighteen. My wife was a refugee. We are a typical German family. You have a daughter, I have two sons, twenty-three and twenty-five. They are both reserve officers.

'We have a great task to perform. The twentieth century and the second millennium end twelve years from now. War and violence have ceased to be a means of politics, and to think otherwise is to head for the destruction of mankind. In the context of glasnost, we must also establish a completely new kind of personal contact. I would welcome an active personal dialogue with you – we could exchange letters, telephone each other and send personal envoys.'

I must admit that I was impressed by Mr Kohl's approach, both from the personal and business points of view. I believed that, in the new emerging international climate, personal 'compatibility' and understanding of your partner's motives would become increasingly important in world politics. We could achieve such understanding only if we worked together, maintaining regular contacts and mutually comparing each other's words and deeds.

Many difficult issues are far more easily and quickly resolved if there is trust between political leaders, without unnecessary diplomatic moves and formalities. Without the good political and personal rapport that Helmut Kohl and I gradually established, it would have been far more difficult to cope with the complex of problems which unexpectedly confronted us as a result of the grass-roots landslide towards unification of Germany.

In October 1988 we succeeded in establishing constructive long-term relations between our countries. We signed a number of agreements on economic, scientific, cultural and environmental co-operation. For the first time in the post-war history of Soviet-West German relations, our defence ministers sat at one negotiating table and could see for themselves what the 'potential enemy' of a little while ago looked like in reality. The Germans agreed in principle to promote the establishment of ties between NATO and the Warsaw Pact – a breakthrough we could not even have imagined only three or four years before.

My return visit to the Federal Republic of Germany took place in June 1989. Shortly before, I had been elected Chairman of the USSR Supreme Soviet, and visiting Germany first in my new capacity acquired a symbolic dimension. We were thus endorsing the importance we assigned to co-operation with the Federal Republic.

The programme for my visit was full and varied, providing the opportunity to see a number of West German states and cities and meet politicians, businessmen, artists, workers and representatives of political parties and organizations. During the welcoming ceremony outside the residence of the West German President, I had my first opportunity to meet ordinary German citizens. A group of young people expressed their enthusiastic support for the reforms in the Soviet Union. And I will never forget our encounter with the citizens of Bonn in the Town Hall Square. We were literally overwhelmed by manifestations of goodwill and friendship, the cheering crowds expressing their support and solidarity. I remember some of the slogans people were shouting: 'Gorbi! Make love, not walls!' 'Please, Gorbachev, stay the course!'

Raisa Maksimovna visited the Soviet POW cemetery in

Stukenbrock. During the war this had been a camp for prisoners-of-war and civilians from different countries to be used in mines and armament factories and on farms. All they received for their back-breaking labour was a daily ration of 200 grams of ersatz bread. Hundreds of thousands of Soviet citizens, as well as people from Poland, Britain and France, passed through this camp, and some 65,000 of our compatriots perished – shot or killed by hunger or disease – and were buried next to the camp. The prisoners were freed by American troops on 2 April 1945. A group of Soviet POWs insisted that the graves of their comrades should be properly maintained, and a memorial obelisk was erected in May 1945 to commemorate the victims of Stukenbrock. The obelisk was designed by a former inmate of the camp, the artist and architect Aleksandr Antonovich Mordan.

During the Cold War, a small group of people, who took the name 'Flowers for Stukenbrock' in 1963, took care of the cemetery and the memorial. They adopted this slogan: 'On the graves of the fallen, let us reach out to the Russian people'. The local authorities initially viewed the activities of this group with suspicion. With their connivance, some right-wing radicals damaged the graves and attempted to destroy the memorial. Fortunately, some young people had decided to keep watch over the cemetery. In the 1970s, 'Flowers for Stukenbrock' had grown into an active anti-war organization with thousands of members all over West Germany. Sensing the wind of change, the authorities changed their attitude.

Once a year, in late August or early September, thousands of people from all over Germany gather at the cemetery, with delegations coming from various European countries. But we were told by the organizers that no official delegation – either West German or Soviet – had ever visited the cemetery.

Raisa Maksimovna was accompanied on her visit by members of our delegation and Soviet artists and writers who had come with me on my visit to Germany, as well as a representative of the Russian Orthodox Church, Metropolitan Pitirim. Their group was joined by Hannelore Kohl and Mrs Rau, the wife of the Prime Minister of North Rhine-Westphalia.

People from neighbouring villages had gathered at the

cemetery. The Soviet delegation laid a wreath adorned by a red ribbon, and Mrs Kohl and Mrs Rau each laid a bouquet of flowers. Metropolitan Pitirim gave a short address. It was what should have been done long ago; the last honours were paid to our compatriots who perished in the war forced upon us by the Nazis, and goodwill was expressed towards the citizens of the new Germany. The German press gave the event plenty of coverage, describing it as an important 'gesture of reconciliation'.

Raisa Maksimovna was asked by journalists for her impressions of the visit. 'Decades have passed,' she replied, 'but even today, there is no Soviet family that does not mourn relatives who met a tragic untimely death in those terrible years. We know that those years were also tragic for the German people. I would like to thank all those who tend the graves of our compatriots.'

Memories of tragic events and lasting, piercing grief – such moments make you realize how arduous has been the path that led towards Soviet-German reconciliation and rapprochement.

I also recall with emotion the meeting with workers at the Hoesch steelworks in Dortmund. We got out of the car and found ourselves walking down a human corridor of thousands of cheering people. The gargantuan workshop – it was several dozen feet high and you could barely distinguish the back walls – was filled with people. People were perched on the machines, balancing on cranes and sitting on each other's shoulders. Our delegation went up to the rostrum with the factory managers and the workers' representatives. The moment I heard the first welcoming address, I realized that there was no point in reading a pre-written speech. I started speaking freely, directly and without flourishes, as is the custom among workers. I spoke of the important place working people have in any society, of the German people and its merits and of our difficult relations in the past, the audience interrupting me with approving shouts and applause almost after every sentence. I stressed that the future relations of our great nations depended to a large extent on the working class, on practical and candid people.

The interpreter seemed to have a hard time keeping up with me – but I was gripped by a feeling of sympathy towards this huge audience, these warm and sincere people who had taken us in their arms, and I had the impression that they understood my words even without translation. People everywhere showed a keen interest in the developments in our country and expressed their heartfelt sympathy and support for our nation, speaking with enthusiasm about perestroika. I was deeply touched and quite excited. Fifteen years had passed since my last trip to West Germany in 1974, and the change in people's attitudes towards the Soviet Union was striking. I remembered one of Ludwig Erhard's favourite sayings: 'Foreign policy starts at home.'

THE COLLAPSE OF THE BERLIN WALL

In the autumn of 1989, precipitate developments in the 'socialist part' of Europe radically changed the situation – the Communists lost power in the first free elections in Poland and Hungary, Erich Honecker was forced to step down, and the Berlin Wall collapsed virtually overnight.

It goes without saying that the events in Hungary and Czechoslovakia and later in Romania and Bulgaria caused us great concern. However, not once did we contemplate the possibility of going back on the fundamental principles of the new political thinking – freedom of choice and non-interference in other countries' domestic affairs.

In our conversations, Kohl had repeatedly said that Honecker did not understand or accept Soviet perestroika and was set on implementing his own dogmatic, hard line. I had the impression that Kohl was trying to win me as an ally in case he decided himself to influence developments in East Germany. Be that as it may, I made it quite clear that we would not dictate to the East German leaders how they should run their affairs at home.

Obviously, we were not blind; we had our own views on Honecker's policies and were worried about the developments in the German Democratic Republic. We did not sit idly by – but I reject any insinuation that our contact with the East German leadership at this critical moment amounted to pressure or blackmail.

I had met Honecker on some seven or eight occasions since

1985 and had formed quite a consistent view of him as a person and as a politician. My cautious attempts to convince him not to delay the necessary reforms to the country and the Party had led to no practical results whatever. It was as if I had been speaking to a brick wall. We last met in October 1989. I had gone to participate in the ceremonies planned for the fortieth anniversary of the German Democratic Republic. Honecker had pressed me to come. Despite some hesitation on my part, I agreed to attend.

Some worrying information reached me a few days before my visit. A group of officials from the Soviet Culture Fund, just back from East Germany, passed on via Raisa Maksimovna a message about a conversation in the Kulturbund[1] that had greatly disturbed them. Their East German counterparts had characterized the political situation taking shape in the country as 'Five minutes to twelve'. A political crisis was coming to a head in society, and the population was expressing its dissatisfaction. Representatives of the intelligentsia were leaving the Party (SED). The Kulturbund's appeals to the leadership and its expression of concern went unheeded. People expected that acute problems in society and the necessity for public discussion would be openly declared during the fortieth-anniversary celebrations. If that did not happen, the Kulturbund planned to discuss the situation in the country immediately after the holidays and approve a critical public appeal to the East German authorities. Knowing the credibility the Kulturbund enjoyed, I took this information seriously.

So here we were in Berlin at the commemorative session. The impression it gave was not good, to put it mildly. Honecker's report spoke of the many accomplishments and achievements of the last forty years, but as for the present-day situation and prospects for the future – no analysis or conclusions.

I was given the floor to speak on behalf of the guests. I will say candidly that this turned out to be a difficult moment for me. My hosts were in a celebratory mood, but I did not have the heart to follow their lead. I found a solution in giving the citizens of East Germany their due for their labour and for having overcome so many difficulties and having done so much in this part of

[1] Official East German cultural organization.

Germany since the war. All these years, Soviet people had lent them their support, so today's anniversary was near to their hearts.

Most of my speech was devoted to our understanding of the new principles on which relations among the Socialist countries would now be built. 'Equality, independence, and solidarity. This is what will determine the content of those relations today.' In the most general way I said that there were problems in the republic connected with its internal development, and with the processes of modernization and renewal in all the Socialist countries.

It is hard to say how events might have developed in East Germany if Honecker, having given the past its due, had proposed cardinal reforms in his speech. It may already have been too late to change anything, but society was waiting, and it might have supported an initiative by the country's leadership if it had met their expectations. Instead, Honecker once more let the moment slip for a major initiative directed at the future. Dissatisfaction with the regime was already spreading into open mass demonstrations.

This was fully manifested that evening, during the torchlight procession down Unter den Linden. Columns of representatives from all the regions of the republic filed past the dais where the East German leader and their foreign guests were standing. The spectacle was impressive, I must say. Orchestras playing, drums banging, searchlights, torches gleaming, and most of all – tens of thousands of young faces. Participants in the march, I was told, had been hand-picked in advance. They were primarily activists in the Free German Youth Movement, young members of the SED and parties and public organizations close to it. So much the more indicative, then, the slogans and chanting in their ranks: 'Perestroika! Gorbachev! Help us!' Mieczyslaw Rakowski, who with Wojciech Jaruzelski was also on the platform, came over to me, visibly agitated: 'Mikhail Sergeyevich, do you understand these slogans they are shouting?' And he translated: 'They're demanding: "Gorbachev, save us once more!" These are Party activists! This is the end!'

I had sensed that something was wrong when we were driving into Berlin from Schönefeld airport. Along almost the entire route to the residence there were solid rows of young people chanting 'Gorbachev! Gorbachev!' – even though Honecker was sitting right next to me. No-one paid any attention to him when he and I were walking down a narrow bustling corridor from the Palace of the Republic. But I simply could never have anticipated what happened during the torchlight procession. Anyone who saw all that would have instantly dismissed Honecker's later statements about his removal from the leadership of East Germany being the result of an intrigue sanctioned by Gorbachev among the apparatus of the SED Central Committee. By the way, I also heard the words 'Gorbachev, save us again' in the Treptower Park from schoolchildren giving me flowers and an address. Thousands of boys and girls were there.

All this time, Honecker could not hide his inner agitation. In the evening, waving to the young people passing by the dais, he danced a few steps, hummed, and tried to put the best face on things in general, but it was obvious that he was not feeling right, and he behaved as if he were in a trance. The following day we met one-to-one. The conversation lasted about three hours. Despite all my efforts, I did not succeed in drawing him into a candid conversation. I had to listen yet again to a detailed account of the German Democratic Republic's accomplishments. Honecker did not accept the protests coming from society. But the situation in East Germany, after direct observation, was indeed just as it had been characterized by the Kulturbund representatives: 'Five minutes to twelve'. Somewhat timidly, members of the SED leadership were talking about this as well. After my meeting with their leader, some of them asked me whether or not he understood that the time had come for changes in East Germany. It was odd, of course, that they should put this question to me. I drew the conclusion that the situation in the SED Politburo did not allow them to put the question to the General Secretary.

The programme for my visit included a meeting with GDR leaders, which was held just before I left East Berlin. Sharing our experiences of perestroika, I told our German friends: 'Life punishes harshly anyone who is left behind in politics.' To make my point, I cited our decision to move forward the date for the

XXVIIIth CPSU Congress, where we intended to analyse the last few years of perestroika and lay down guidelines for the future. Simultaneously the USSR Supreme Soviet and Congress of People's Deputies would take up the issues of property, leasing, and entrepreneurship, among others, which in the near future would allow us to create a legal basis for extending reforms.

Turning to my interlocutors, I said: 'As I understand it, life demands that you too make courageous decisions.'

The meeting participants listened to me with extreme attention. Honecker took the floor first. Agreeing with me formally, he reduced the discussion to minor, ancillary subjects. The remarks or brief comments made by others did not go beyond the framework of routine questions, generally speaking.

I left Berlin with mixed feelings. The image of that enormous stream of humanity, the thousands of German boys and girls – healthy, strong, welcoming, thirsting for changes – had made an impression on me that instilled hope and optimism. But there was something else, too. In my memory there remained the cautious, concentrated faces of the SED leadership, each of whom, it seemed, was preparing to make his decision. Honecker was obviously offended by my attitude, and to emphasize this he did not come to see us off from Schönefeld airport. I returned to Moscow in a state of alarm. The country reminded me of an over-heated boiler with the lid tightly closed. The danger was there for everyone to see, and subsequent events vindicated my premonitions. The crisis reached its breaking point only two weeks later.

I learned later that a few days after the anniversary celebrations, the SED Politburo met to discuss the results of the celebrations and the general situation in the republic. Many came out in favour of active efforts to appease the mounting unrest. Honecker called on them 'not to overdramatize the situation' or to 'enter into dialogue with the class enemy'. This evidently provoked the Politburo, despite the General Secretary's position, to convene a plenum of the Central Committee. The Politburo passed a declaration stating its readiness to discuss and resolve the problems that had arisen through dialogue and glasnost, and to settle issues of foreign travel. The SED Central Committee plenum that convened on 18 October relieved Honecker of his duties as General Secretary of the SED Central Committee and Chairman of the East German Council of State. Egon Krenz was elected to both these posts, having previously been responsible in the Politburo for state security and the law-enforcing agencies, as well as young people and sport. This was a pre-programmed switch, so to speak. Even before he had been jokingly referred to as 'Crown Prince Krenz'.

Meanwhile spontaneous demonstrations in the city streets continued. Demands were made to democratize the regime, investigate abuses, and eliminate excessive privileges for officials. The authorities were losing control over events, and their perplexity and inability to recapture the initiative were taking their toll. On 8–11 November a Central Committee plenum replaced many members of the Politburo. The 'rebel' Hans Modrow, who soon after would lead the coalition government, was brought in. On the night of 9–10 November, huge crowds gathered by the wall that separated East and West Berlin. To avoid dangerous excesses, the checkpoints to the West were opened. The wall fell, or, rather, it was transformed into a monument to the Cold War, which had become a thing of the past.

Thank God, the new East German leadership had the courage and enough common sense to refrain from trying to quench the popular unrest in blood. I believe that the Soviet position had also contributed to this; the East German leaders realized that Soviet troops would not leave their barracks under any circumstances.

I find it difficult to say whether the leadership's 'second echelon' could have preserved the German Democratic Republic. Helmut Kohl later told me he had never believed that Egon Krenz was capable of getting the situation under control. I do not know – we are all wiser after the event, as the saying goes. For my part, I must admit I briefly had a faint hope that the new leaders would be able to change the course of events by establishing a new type of relations between the *two* German states – based on radical domestic reforms in East Germany.

On 1 November 1989 I met Krenz in Moscow at his own wish. We agreed that it would be naive to reduce the political crisis in his country to the developments of the past few months: in reality, the problems had been accumulating for years. Accordingly, there was a pressing need for radical reforms – cosmetic surgery would not do. A lot of time had already been lost and immediate action was called for. We parted on this note.

However, it soon proved that the majority of the population would not accept any government or party that tried to preserve the GDR, most East Germans seeing their salvation in unification with the Federal Republic. Mass exodus to 'the West', a growing tide of demonstrations, civil disobedience, and open threats against the authorities threatened a peaceful settlement of the crisis. In essence we were witnessing the disintegration of state power – in the first place at the local level, where the elections on 7 May 1989 had been marked by the most blatant cases of election fraud by the former East German leadership.

The German Democratic Republic was on the verge of social chaos and complete political and economic collapse.

HELMUT KOHL FORMULATES HIS 'TEN POINTS'

This critical moment called for a cool head and responsible political action by all the main protagonists. Indeed, the developments in East Germany had caused intense concern throughout Europe and obviously in the Soviet Union as well. The fate of the Helsinki process was at stake.

It seemed to me that the ten-point plan Chancellor Kohl announced in late November was not an appropriate answer to the challenges of the moment. The document came as a surprise to us, to the French and the British and even to the West German Foreign Minister, Hans-Dietrich Genscher. It looked as if the historical issues at stake – which concerned not merely the German people – were being used as a welcome boost to the Christian Democrats' election campaign.

In my view, any one-sided attempt to rush the unification process could only have a destabilizing effect on the situation in Europe, making feelings run even higher. Incidentally, in a telephone conversation only a few days earlier, Chancellor Kohl had assured me that the federal government was aware of its responsibility in connection with the developments in the German

Democratic Republic, and that it would take cautious and considered action in close consultation with the Soviet Union.

Barely two weeks after this conversation, Kohl announced his ten-point plan for unification of Germany on a federal basis – listing a number of categorical demands for domestic reforms in the German Democratic Republic as a precondition for the implementation of his plan!

I had a frank and rather sharp exchange of views on this subject with Mr Genscher, who came to Moscow in early December 1989. It was a piquant situation. The German Foreign Minister was forced to defend a political stand he had not been informed about beforehand and about which he was probably not very happy.

The tone was tense and the discussion unpleasant for both of us. I greatly esteemed Genscher as a politician who had personally contributed to the difficult rapprochement between our nations, but I felt compelled to give him my view – for the sake of future co-operation. We decided against publicizing the details of our conversation and came out with what we called a 'rounded' press statement. I expected, however, that Bonn would pay due attention to the signal from Moscow.

Hans Modrow's coalition government found it difficult to prevent the complete disintegration of the East German republic. I met him on several occasions and received first-hand information about the problems his cabinet had to face. Modrow performed a great task under extremely unfavourable conditions, clearing the way for free parliamentary elections in East Germany. By now the situation was changing daily. We met once again on 30 January 1990. 'The majority of the people in the German Democratic Republic no longer support the idea of two German states,' Modrow told me frankly on that occasion, 'and it seems that it has become impossible to preserve the republic. The trend in favour of unification is particularly strong in the border regions, Thuringia, for example. No party can control these tendencies, neither the old ones nor the new ones.

'The formulae we have employed until now,' Modrow concluded, 'do not function any more. The majority of public organizations, with the exception of a few insignificant Leftist

sects, are all in favour of unification. If we do not take the initiative now, the process will become uncontrollable and we won't
be able to influence developments in any way.'

This news was not entirely unexpected. We had arrived at the
same conclusion during a meeting I had called a few days before
to exchange views on the German question. I had invited
Ryzhkov, Shevardnadze, Yakovlev, Falin, Kryuchkov,
Akhromeyev and my aides Chernyaev and Shakhnazarov, and we
spent four hours discussing the issue. We agreed in the end that
German reunification should be regarded as inevitable; hence we
should launch an initiative to create a group of six, the four
victorious powers and the two Germanies; we should not cut off
contact with the East German leadership; we should more closely
co-ordinate our policy on the 'German question' with Paris and
London; and, finally, Marshal Akhromeyev should prepare for
the withdrawal of Soviet troops from East Germany.

Germany was the central issue in our talks with the American
Secretary of State, James Baker, who came to Moscow on 9
February. Baker summarized the American position, saying that
the outcome of the forthcoming elections was clear, with the
majority of East Germans expressing themselves in favour of
unification. Unification was therefore inevitable and the United
States and the Soviet Union should base their policy on this fact.

'I want you to know,' Baker reassured me, 'that neither
the President nor I intend to derive any advantage from the
developments.'

I took note of this statement and we went on to discuss ways
for co-operation. We soon realized that our views were quite
close on a number of key issues and we could therefore agree on
the general outlines for the policy to follow: the 'internal' aspects
of unification were the business of the Germans, and they should
discuss all these questions among themselves. However, the four
victorious powers should be involved in the negotiating process,
being responsible for the preservation of peace and stability in
Europe and focusing on the international aspects of unification.

We disagreed on one key issue – the military-political status of
a united Germany. James Baker tried to convince me of the
advantages of keeping Germany within NATO – as compared to

its 'neutralization'. He argued basically that maintaining the American military presence in Germany and Germany's membership of NATO provided the United States and the West with leverage over Germany's domestic and foreign policy, whereas a neutral Germany which would slip out of the network of NATO could again become a generator of instability in Europe.

'A neutral Germany,' Baker insisted, 'does not necessarily mean a demilitarized Germany. On the contrary, it could very well decide to create its own nuclear potential instead of relying on the American deterrent. I should like to ask you a question that you do not have to answer right away. Assuming unification takes place, what would you prefer: a united Germany outside NATO and completely autonomous, without American forces stationed on its territory, or a united Germany that maintains its ties with NATO, but with the guarantee that NATO jurisdiction or troops would not extend east of the current line?'

The second half of Mr Baker's last sentence eventually formed the nucleus of the formula that cleared the way for a compromise on Germany's military-political status. However, at the time I was not yet prepared to accept this. I too believed that we needed a 'safety net' which would protect us and the rest of Europe from any 'surprises' from the Germans. However, unlike the Americans, I thought that these security mechanisms should be provided not by NATO but by new structures created within a pan-European framework. James Baker, however, did not believe that the CSCE would ever be able to replace NATO.

I had another meeting with Helmut Kohl scheduled for the next day. His main purpose, as I understood it, was to convince me that the German Democratic Republic was heading for complete collapse. The West German Chancellor believed that the coming parliamentary elections would lead to the formation of a government that would favour unification, and that the people and the parliament would fully support such a decision. In his view, the main task was therefore to stabilize the situation in East Germany as far as possible, to prevent economic collapse and political chaos, and to reduce the flow of East Germans to the West. Kohl tried to convince me that the only way to achieve this was by implementing an active policy, by creating an economic and monetary union immediately after the elections. He was thus (with only a slight, intentional delay) presenting his arguments in favour of a decision he had already taken.

I could see that Helmut Kohl was set on pushing through the process of unification and I had good reason to believe that he had the support of the United States. However, the West German Chancellor never tired of repeating that circumstances compelled him to this course of action and that he still intended to co-ordinate his policy with Moscow.

I was prepared to answer the central question he put to me – about the Soviet Union's basic attitude towards the unification of Germany.

'One could probably say that there is no disagreement between the Soviet Union, the Federal Republic of Germany and the German Democratic Republic on the question of German unity,' I said. 'We have reached an understanding on the main starting-point – the Germans must make their own choice. And they must know our position on this issue.'

'The Germans know it,' Kohl replied. 'Do you want to say that the question of German unity is a choice for the Germans themselves to make?'

'Taking into account the realities,' I added.

'I agree with that,' said Kohl.

The 'German question' was not only one of unification and the satisfaction of German national aspirations, since it also affected the interests of neighbouring nations. Quite a few questions arose in this context: the guaranteed inviolability of borders and the recognition of post-war territorial and political realities, the future military-political status of a united Germany, the link between pan-European policy and German unification . . .

By and large, Kohl accepted the arguments I advanced, rejecting out of hand, however, any solution that provided for the 'neutralization' of Germany. We agreed that all questions concerning unification should be discussed by the 'group of six', i.e. the Soviet Union, the United States, Great Britain, France and the two Germanies.

The West German Chancellor said that he liked the idea of a '4

+ 2' conference (later the Germans – with the active support of the United States – insisted on calling it '2 + 4') but that he would strongly object to a separate conference of the four powers. I assured him that nothing would be decided without the Germans, and we parted.

We had managed to clear up the misunderstandings, which was most important at that particular stage. However, there was still a long and dangerous road before us.

THE FATE OF THE 'MODROW PLAN'

The political and social destabilization of East Germany offered unique opportunities for the competing political forces in West Germany. All the major parties – the Christian Democrats, the Free Democrats and the Social Democrats – started a feverish campaign for unification, their tactics differing only on the pace and procedures of the unification process. Initially, though, most of them favoured gradual rapprochement based on co-operation between equal partners. Hans Modrow's 'three-stage plan' corresponded with these goals: the East German Prime Minister suggested the creation of a 'treaty community' between East and West Germany, with close co-operation in economic and other areas, the confederacy of two sovereign states gradually acquiring neutral status and eventually transforming itself into a German federation or German union that would actively participate in pan-European policy.

Modrow presented his plan in public. On the eve of his trip to Bonn, scheduled for 13 February, I briefed him in a telephone conversation on my talks with Chancellor Kohl.

Modrow told me that he had learned about the West German Government's proposal for monetary union from the press. Shortly before, during a meeting in Davos (Switzerland) he had agreed with Chancellor Kohl on the creation of a joint team of experts (with four East and four West German members) to study economic and monetary co-operation. The East Germans had appointed their representatives, but they were never invited to West Germany and the planned talks on the monetary union never opened. This was the context in which the West German government made its unexpected proposal.

Meanwhile Bonn had apparently decided that there was no point in signing an agreement with the East German Modrow government and set out actively to support the opposition – including the anti-Communist organizations and parties that presented themselves for the parliamentary elections in March. The circumstances were favourable to them; the country was in dire straits, with shortages of heating, fuel and food and public disturbances. Waves of mass protest against the former regime shook the GDR, fuelled by sensational disclosures of corruption and delusions about the miraculous effects of a rapid union with West Germany.

The East German Communists were defeated at the polls, obtaining less than 17 per cent of the votes, with the other left-wing parties getting some 8 per cent. The Alliance for Germany, which was backed by the West German Christian Democrats, finished ahead. Together with its coalition partners, the Alliance controlled over two thirds of the seats in the East German parliament.

In April 1990 the newly formed coalition government under Lothar de Maizière called for German unification in accordance with Article 23 of the West German constitution, which provided for the direct incorporation of East Germany or parts of it into the Federal Republic of Germany without any transitional stage. It was the opposite to the solution Modrow had proposed.

As could have been expected, Lothar de Maizière proved to be a transitional figure. This lawyer, musician, churchman and politician had close ties with the Christian Democrats in both East and West Germany and reflected their desire for an absorption of the German Democratic Republic into West Germany as soon as possible. At the same time, he acknowledged the importance of maintaining good relations and economic ties with the Soviet Union, realizing that the well-being of most of the East German population depended on trade with the USSR.

At a Politburo meeting on 3 May, we discussed the forthcoming '2 + 4' conference to be held in Paris. There was general agreement as to the Soviet position – Shevardnadze was to insist on a 'neutral status' for the united Germany, or, if it came to it, on its membership of both alliances, NATO and the Warsaw Pact. However, at the conference it proved that we were the lone advocates of such a view.

We returned to the German question during President Mitterrand's visit to Moscow in May 1990. Perceptions of this issue in our society as well as my own views on the subject were changing fast. Only a couple of years before, I had considered it a problem to be decided some time in the future. Now the Germans' aspirations for the unification of their country were so strong that to disregard them could have jeopardized the entire European process.

The question was not how to prevent the unification, but what the pace and conditions of this process should be, how it would affect the situation in Europe and what consequences it would have for our security and European security in general. These were questions asked not only in Moscow, but also in Warsaw, Prague, Brussels, the Hague, London and other European capitals . . . and obviously, last but not least, in Paris.

Despite official declarations of support for a unified Germany made both by NATO and the European Community, the views on the developments in Germany were far from uniform, as I could see during my meetings with many West European politicians.

To sum up my impressions from these meetings, I would say that each country had its own ideas about the ways and means to react to the developments in Germany. Nobody was very enthusiastic about what was happening there.

At a certain point, I had the feeling that Bonn was trying to force the pace of the unification with the support of the United States, in order to present the other nations with a *fait accompli*.

I visited the United States in late May 1990. Discussing the agenda at our first meeting on 31 May, President Bush declared: 'We both agree that Germany must not represent a potential threat to anyone. It must be committed to democratic principles and provide guarantees that the past will not repeat itself . . . We have divergent views on the future military-political status of Germany – but both you and we feel concern about the future.

687

'Germany,' Bush added, 'can be trusted. It has paid its dues.'

We discussed the German issue at length during our second meeting the same evening. I insisted on a gradual, step-by-step solution for German unification which would be organically linked to the transformation of the Warsaw Pact and NATO and reduced confrontation between the military-political alliances. It seemed that President Bush had already reached an agreement with Chancellor Kohl, however. Referring to the results of the '2 + 4' conference in early May, he categorically disagreed with me.

'I can understand your fears,' Bush said. 'We also fought against Hitler, although we cannot compare the American losses with the 27 million Russian lives sacrificed in the war against Hitler. And yet for fifty years there has been democracy in Germany. This should not be ignored. It seems to me that our approach to Germany has a better sense of perspectives and timing. The unification processes have developed far more rapidly than any of us could have imagined, and nothing can slow them down. Mistrust that is based on the past is therefore particularly bad advice in this case.

'It appears to me that our approach to Germany, i.e. seeing it as a close friend, is more pragmatic and constructive, although I will say frankly that many people in the West do not share this view. Like you, there are some West Europeans who neither trust the Federal Republic of Germany nor Germans in general. However, all of us in the West agree that the main danger lies in excluding Germany from the community of democratic nations and forcing some special status and humiliating conditions upon the Germans. Such a development could lead precisely to a revival of the German militarism and revanchism you fear.'

Needless to say, I realized why the Americans were so keen on including a united Germany in NATO. George Bush and his colleagues feared – and to a certain extent with good reason – that with such a powerful nation outside NATO, the alliance's fate would be sealed, and the American military presence in Europe with it. Advancing different arguments and citing various statements I had previously made, I made several attempts to convince the American President that an American 'withdrawal' from Europe was not in the interest of the Soviet Union.

The discussion became rather heated, with both sides accusing the other of fearing the Germans and a renewed German threat to peace in Europe and the world. In the end, however, we managed to find a formula on which we could both agree: a united Germany, once a final settlement had been reached that took into account the realities of the Second World War, would decide for itself which alliance to join.

Mr Bush said that the United States declared itself clearly in favour of NATO membership for a united Germany, but would not contest its choice should Germany decide otherwise.

Helmut Kohl came to Moscow in mid-July 1990 to settle the complex of questions related to German unification. We had several one-to-one meetings, as well as talks in the presence of our Foreign Ministers, Shevardnadze and Genscher. Kohl was focused and determined, and we had an extremely frank exchange of views. We had reached agreement on the main points, but there remained a number of questions to discuss in greater detail, such as the non-extension of the NATO military structures onto East German territory and the continued presence of Soviet troops there for a specified transitional period. We had to define precisely the legal and financial basis for the presence of our troops on the territory of a united Germany. In addition, we needed guarantees that East German territory would not become a threat to Soviet security after the withdrawal of our troops. We finally reached an agreement on all these issues. I was able to insist on a significant reduction in the German armed forces, with a ceiling of 370,000 men for the united Germany, and we agreed that Germany would forever renounce the possession of nuclear, chemical and bacteriological weapons.

We shared the view that better synchronization between the pan-European process and German unification was called for, which could be achieved in particular by creating new security structures within the framework of the CSCE.

We discussed at length the fundamental principles that were to form the basis of a future treaty between Germany and the Soviet Union (it was later called the treaty on 'good neighbourliness, partnership and co-operation'). This was to set the course for the long-term development of Soviet-German relations.

In a nutshell, these were comprehensive talks that reflected our common understanding that German unification was not an isolated issue, but should be viewed as an integral part of our common progress towards a new Europe. At the risk of repeating myself, I told Kohl: 'Our public opinion is changing step by step, gradually accepting the choice made by the German people when it took the road towards unification. We cannot forget the past. Every family in our country suffered in those years. But we have to look towards Europe and take the road of co-operation with the great German nation. This is our contribution to strengthening stability in Europe and the world.'

ON A VISIT TO THE NEW GERMANY

On 9 November 1990 I went on a visit to the newly united Germany to attend the official signing ceremonies of the agreements which laid the legal, political and moral foundations for the establishment of normal, up-to-date relations and genuine friendship between Germany and the Soviet Union.

Thus we drew a final line under the past and recent history of our nations, opening, as I hope, a new, lasting period in relations between Germany and Russia, when all the positive common heritage built up over the centuries in German-Russian relations will finally bear fruit. Indeed, we let the past, which had brought so many sufferings to both our nations, be past.

In giving the green light to German unification, the Soviet Union and its former allies in the struggle against Hitler were guided, among other things, by the following consideration: a democratic, politically stable and economically healthy Germany, 'settled' in its borders, stable in its political system, and content with its role in Europe and the world, will eventually become a major factor for progress in European and world affairs.

Nevertheless, it would have been naive to believe that the unification of Germany would by itself be sufficient to achieve this goal. Today, probably everyone recognizes that Germany will be kept busy raising living standards in its Eastern parts to equal those in West Germany for quite a while, and that this will

690

require – in addition to huge efforts and immense financial investments – a well-planned, balanced social policy that will take account of the specific situation in the 'new' German Länder. And obviously the major, long-term task of changing attitudes, the development of a new mentality for the united nation and the overcoming of the psychological heritage of German division – all these are essential preconditions for the achievement of genuine political stability for the German state. This is important for the whole of Europe – any destabilization in its geographical centre being fraught, as history teaches us, with dire consequences.

However, this is but one aspect of the problem. It is also essential to overcome the gap between living standards in Eastern and Western Europe – and Germany and all the other Western nations will have to face up to this issue. All political, economic, social and environmental issues in both parts of Europe are tied together in one single knot, and to ignore this is to jeopardize one's own interests.

A German-Russian partnership is a key element in any serious pan-European integration process. It is my ardent wish that Russia and Germany may manage to preserve all the positive achievements of the late 1980s and early 1990s in today's difficult times.

25

UNDERSTANDING LEADS TO
PARTNERSHIP

AS I MENTIONED IN THE PREVIOUS CHAPTER, I MET PRESIDENT
Bush again some six months after the Malta summit, this time in
Washington. My last visit to the American capital had taken place
in December 1987, while Ronald Reagan was still at the White
House. Now, having reached a qualitatively new level in Soviet-
American relations, we had to make further headway along the
chosen road, taking a more stable and predictable course and
leaving behind the ups-and-downs in the relations between our
nations, when every warming was followed by a freeze.

This was far from being an easy task. Soviet-American
relations still lacked the necessary stability and, although we had
left the path of confrontation, the logic of military-political
competition was still present in our thinking and approaches. Co-
operation between our countries was improving steadily, but we
were a long way from genuine partnership. Last but not least, the
'confrontational infrastructure' was still in place.

Nevertheless, I was firmly convinced that there was no turning
back. The realization that we live in a single interdependent world
had made its way into common political thinking, and the 'enemy
image', used to fuel the Cold War confrontation for decades, had
lost much of its appeal. I believed that further progress was the
best way to prevent regression, this rule applying to every area of
co-operation – disarmament, which was still lagging behind the
political changes, co-operation on transnational issues, trade,

692

scientific and cultural exchanges, and simple human relations between people from different generations and backgrounds.

In Malta President Bush and I had outlined a long-term agenda for the development of Soviet-American relations. The time had come to implement our plans. Against the background of the stormy developments of the past six months, Malta appeared to me even more significant than immediately after the meeting, although I viewed it as a clear success even then. It was obvious that the Malta summit represented far more than a mere stopover on the road of Soviet-American rapprochement. Indeed, it had allowed us to establish a personal rapport, both between Mr Bush and me and between our foreign ministers – just in time to avoid being caught unprepared by the developments in Eastern Europe and in Germany in particular. It is quite probable that the 'international context' of the Baltic problem would have looked rather different had we not met.

However, we fortunately managed to avoid all these dangers. Arriving in Washington on 30 May 1990, I could reasonably expect that – despite possible disagreements on a number of specific questions – we would preserve the constructive spirit established in the Soviet-American dialogue and reach a number of important agreements.

'To bring about co-operation,' I told the President, 'we should first define how we would like to see each other – the Soviet Union, the United States and the United States, the Soviet Union. I will be frank: we do not believe that a weakened United States playing a less important role in world affairs would be in our interest. There can be no advantage for us in it, inasmuch as a weakened United States, or a United States which sees its interests infringed upon, means instability throughout the world.'

This was the central theme during the Washington summit. From my meetings with senators and congressmen and representatives from business and academic circles, I was left with the impression of a growing understanding among Americans that the new Soviet Union – which had taken the road of democracy and freedom and was open to co-operation with the outside world – was consistent with the interests of the United States.

For me, this outweighed the information that reached us about vacillation in the Bush administration's policy. However, in politics words must be followed by action. I realized that things were not that simple, given the fact that on the American political scene anti-Soviet circles were still quite influential. The situation called for promoting and stimulating our nascent understanding by every means, with a view to establishing a genuine partnership between our countries.

The summit agenda was extremely crowded. We planned to discuss disarmament, including basic provisions for the future strategic arms reduction treaty; the European process, primarily the international implications of German unification; prospects for the conclusion of a trade agreement; and regional conflicts. In addition, we were to sign a number of documents on economic, scientific and cultural co-operation – all in all some twenty-four agreements and protocols, although it is obviously not the number that counts, but their contribution to establishing a stable infrastructure for co-operation.

After discussing the German question (I have described our exchanges on this subject in the previous chapter), we turned to disarmament. The conventional and nuclear arms agreements reached in Washington were the end-product of four years of painstaking negotiations. This time we finally managed to settle the basic provisions for the strategic arms reduction treaty, which was designed to cut our strategic arsenals by fifty per cent – an idea launched four years ago in Reykjavik. The remaining disagreements were finally resolved.

For us, it was essential to exclude any scenario in which the United States would be able to take a sudden lead in these types of weapons and tilt the balance established at a lower level after the fifty-per-cent cut. The American agreement to settle the problem of sea-launched cruise missiles in a separate document annexed to the treaty and to reduce the range of air-launched cruise missiles to 600 kilometres significantly eased our fears.

There were obviously also a number of disagreements, even on issues we had previously viewed as non-contentious. Invoking their 'special relationship' with Great Britain in the area of strategic weapons, the Americans unexpectedly insisted on an unrestricted right to transfer know-how and any types of weapons to their European ally. We believed that this co-operation should be limited to their replacement of the submarine-launched missiles Trident I by Trident II, lest a channel be created which would allow the continuing development and build-up of strategic nuclear arsenals, by-passing the Soviet-American strategic arms treaty we were to conclude.

Hence we were obviously against such a broad interpretation of the limits to be set to British-American co-operation. The American and Soviet preparedness to slash their strategic arsenals in half increased the relative importance of the English, French and Chinese nuclear potentials in the overall nuclear equation, and applying a double standard to the future treaty was simply unacceptable to us. We failed to overcome the disagreement at the time, but at least I had stated our firm position on this issue.

We reached broad agreements on almost all the other principal provisions of the strategic arms reduction treaty.

We also signed an agreement on an eighty-per-cent cut in chemical weapons and their eventual complete elimination, finally opening the way for the multilateral convention on chemical weapons – talks on which had been stalled for years.

In Washington we adopted the addenda to the treaties limiting nuclear tests and governing underground nuclear testing for peaceful purposes, thus paving the way for ratification of the treaties signed in the mid-1970s.

I would like to stress the significance of the agreement on non-proliferation of nuclear and chemical weapons, delivery missiles and technology. Even then, some fifteen or more countries had the means available to develop and produce nuclear weapons in the near future, and preventing this proliferation was a *sine qua non*, without which the Soviet-American disarmament efforts would become meaningless.

We also discussed arms reductions in Europe. Noting the significant progress made in this field, Mr Bush and I agreed that it would be realistic to call a European summit conference to sign the conventional forces agreement by the end of the year.

To sum up the main achievement of this Washington-Camp David summit meeting, I would say that we significantly increased the pace of the clean-up of the gigantic powder magazine left over from the Cold War. In a report I gave to the Supreme Soviet on 12 June 1990, after my return from the USA, I emphasized the significance of the summit meeting in promoting disarmament: 'Both the Soviet Union and the United States bear their share of the responsibility for the fact that the post-war period was marked by a wasteful and dangerous confrontation, which exhausted resources and distorted not only the economy but society as a whole. In an unprecedented, far-reaching move, these same two countries took upon themselves the responsibility for dismantling, as soon as possible, the existing mechanisms of military confrontation between East and West, in order to employ the resources freed by disarmament to improve the well-being of the people. If it is true that the world has changed in the past few years, moving towards a period of genuine peace, the decisive contribution was made by the Soviet Union and the United States of America.'

George Bush and I had gone on to discuss bilateral issues. The trade agreement turned out to be the most difficult subject: up to the last moment we were not sure whether the Americans would agree to sign it. On the eve of my visit to Washington, opponents of the trade agreement spoke out in the American press and in Congress, arguing that there was no point in making economic presents to the Soviet Union unless Moscow adopted a law on freedom of emigration and allowed Lithuania and the other Baltic republics to leave the Soviet Union.

There were no major problems concerning the first item, freedom to emigrate. Mr Bush and the American administration were well aware of the fact that the immigration and emigration laws had been passed in a first reading by the USSR Supreme Soviet and were to be adopted soon. We did not view this step as a concession – it was a natural consequence of our policy of perestroika – obviously taking into account the interests both of Soviet citizens and of state security.

Lithuania proved to be the main stumbling-block. I knew that President Bush was under pressure on this issue – as a matter of fact, he did not hide it from me himself. About a month before my visit, I had received a confidential letter in which he attempted to explain the difficulty of his position, being hard-pressed by Congress, the American media and various lobbies to take a tough line on Lithuania. He brought up the subject again in Washington, acknowledging that the Lithuanian leader, Vytautis Landsbergis, was defying and provoking us.

I realized perfectly well that, in taking a decision, the American President had to reckon with the political balance in his own country. However, I had my own problems with the situation in Lithuania, which were no less difficult to resolve. We acknowledged Lithuania's right to self-determination, including the possibility of leaving the Soviet Union. We simply insisted on respecting legal procedures and a proper timetable for the 'divorce', if such were the express wish of the Lithuanian people.

George Bush showed understanding of the arguments I advanced, agreeing that such problems should be resolved in accordance with Soviet law and that it was not for him to tell me what to do and how to do it. Nevertheless, he stuck to his line, courteously explaining that unless we agreed to make certain concessions, he would not be able to put his signature to the trade agreement, however much he wished to do so.

On the second day of our one-to-one talks, there was a moment when I had the impression that we had reached deadlock on this issue. I got up, giving him to understand that this was my last word, and said: 'Well, I gave you my view on the subject and you gave me yours. We must make a choice. You seem to have chosen to support the Baltic republics and to ignore my arguments. Nor can I force the President of the United States to take some course of action. If, today, supporting the Baltic republics is more important to the American President than everything else, I will take note of it and we will have to live with it. This is all I can say. Let us join the delegations.'

Mr Bush tried to ease the tension by suggesting that we make another attempt to find an acceptable solution the next day – in the quieter atmosphere of Camp David.

CAMP DAVID

In the morning, we left by helicopter from the White House South Lawn for Camp David, the presidential retreat in the Catoctin Mountains of Maryland some 55 miles north-west of Washington. It was interesting to see the Washington suburbs from above – hundreds of comfortable-looking, compact towns to which the commuters returned by car from their work in the city. There are quite a few sites of local and national importance in the region and the President and his aides pointed those out to us. They did not fail to show us the Pentagon.

Camp David is a beautiful spot in the woods, designed for recreation, with many a shady nook and sports lawns and buildings. I was introduced to a new game there, horseshoes, and it seems to me that I picked it up rather fast. George Bush, who was very proud of his own skills at the game, was greatly surprised at my ability to 'hit the ringer' after only a few tries.

I was presented with a horseshoe, having distinguished myself in the impromptu contest. George invited me afterwards to his study to see a 'souvenir' I had given him in Malta – a map of the US military bases made by our intelligence services for this special occasion. 'Everything is correct,' he commented, tongue-in-cheek. 'There are only minor inaccuracies.' We laughed and I replied: 'You know as much about us as we do about you.'

We spent most of the day discussing regional issues. This was the first time that we had discussed the Afghan problem in a non-confrontational, 'constructive' tone. George Bush declared that the United States did not intend to 'play the Afghan card' and was 'not interested in the establishment of a radical regime in Afghanistan which would be hostile to the Soviet Union.' He outlined his views about a possible long-term settlement, which incidentally coincided with our own ideas on a number of points. It boiled down to the following: the organization of free elections under the control of the United Nations and the constitution of a broad-based coalition government which would run affairs until the elections. Bush assured me that following the start of such a transitional period, the United States would be prepared to stop supplying weapons to the Mujaheddin and to start withdrawing military equipment and arms on condition that the Soviet Union and the other countries involved would do the same.

'Our foreign ministers have already done some work on these issues together with our experts,' I replied. 'There seems to be an understanding about the need for a transitional period and the organization of free elections which would lead to the constitution of a broad-based government. We accept the role the United Nations should play in Afghanistan during the interim period and in the organization of the elections.'

The status of the Afghan President, Najibullah, was one of the difficult points that caused much speculation. Far from being a 'puppet in our hands', as some people believed, he represented a political force to be reckoned with, with support and influence in a number of provinces. We knew from our contacts that he was prepared to accept the outcome of the elections, but that he wanted to 'save face' and would therefore reject any ultimatum demanding his immediate resignation. I tried to get this message across to my American partners. Bush agreed with my arguments.

There was a clear shift in the American position on Afghanistan, the Bush administration showing its willingness to co-operate in settling the conflict. The Soviet Union and the United States were now more like partners rather than enemies on the Afghan issue.

We had rather a sharp – but never hostile – exchange of views on the situation in Latin America, Cuba in particular. Like his predecessors, George Bush harboured a strong dislike of the Castro regime. Obviously, this wasn't news to us and there was little I could do about it.

'We have no right to dictate to Fidel Castro how he should manage the affairs of his country. I never did so in relations with leaders of East European countries – or with anyone for that matter,' I said to Bush. He had to take note of this position.

But, on the other hand, I could not ignore the continuing support Cuba provided to the rebels in El Salvador, creating serious obstacles to a peaceful settlement there. Bush and Baker asked me to inform Castro that a normalization of relations could be discussed only after Cuba had stopped supporting the guerrillas fighting the government in El Salvador. I promised to do so, nevertheless advising Bush to launch a direct dialogue with the Cubans as soon as possible. The moment you treated the Cubans as equal partners, they adopted a balanced and reasonable attitude.

I should mention the joint Soviet-American declaration on Ethiopia. It was a demonstration of our common political approach; both countries favoured a political settlement in this war-torn, starving country. What is more, this was the first time that the Soviet Union and the United States had organized a joint operation to bring humanitarian aid: it was decided to deliver American food supplies in Soviet transport planes to alleviate the sufferings of the starving Ethiopians.

In the evening, Bush mentioned with a smile, as if in passing, that he had decided to sign the trade agreement. One must give the American President his full measure of credit: he had given priority to what really matters in world politics, instead of surrendering to short-lived considerations and in spite of the mounting pressure – a courageous choice.

I greatly appreciated his decision. The economic aspect was not even that important. Considering the level of Soviet-American trade, we could not quickly make full use of the advantages offered by the agreement. Far more important was the political impact of this symbolic gesture, which came at a decisive moment for the Soviet Union. Indeed, it was a turning-point, from verbal support for our perestroika to real action.

MEETINGS IN MINNEAPOLIS AND SAN FRANCISCO

The official part of the visit ended on 3 June. Our delegation boarded the helicopters for the Andrews Air Force Base taking the plane from there to Minneapolis, Minnesota.

The Mid-West represents, as we say, the granary of the United States, the traditional centre of agricultural production. The new Soviet-American grain agreement and the pressing need for a radical modernization of our food industries made it imperative to get a close look at the most interesting American experience in this field.

It was a rainy day in Minneapolis. The Minnesota landscape reminded me of Central Russia: you had the impression of being somewhere in the Orel region. As we were driving from the airport, we were really touched by the crowds lining the road for miles and miles, the people shielding themselves from the rain with umbrellas or newspapers and enthusiastically greeting us. When we entered the city, our motorcade literally drove through a human corridor.

We had lunch with our hosts, Governor Rudy Perpich and his wife. The atmosphere was pleasant, the conversation lively and we felt very much at home. We then attended the opening ceremony of the Soviet-American Institute of Global Technologies, which was to provide research facilities for American, Soviet and European scientists working on issues of global importance – environmental protection, global warming, health etc.

In the afternoon, there was a meeting with Mid-Western business and agricultural leaders.

It is occasionally quite useful to take a look at oneself from the other side and to verify one's own ideas and arguments in debate. The meeting in Minneapolis was a very enriching experience in this regard. The question-and-answer session after the speech was far from an exchange of niceties – I realized that, much as American businessmen were interested in co-operating with us, there was a lot of unhappiness among those who had already worked with the Soviet Union and strongly resented our disorganization, unreliability, and the confusion and red tape reigning in the decision-making processes and in the economic mechanisms in general. Of course, questions were put to me concerning investment protection, regulations for the repatriation and reinvestment of profits, and the convertibility of the ruble.

We were expected in San Francisco. You simply cannot remain indifferent to the charm and beauty of this wonderful city, as it gently rolls down from the hills to the ocean, surrounded by a picturesque landscape. Its cultural richness is reflected in the striking variety of architectural styles. This incomparable major West Coast sea-port is bound to cast a spell on any visitor.

The visit to Stanford University became the highlight of our trip to the West Coast. Our motorcade had to make its way through a crowd of thousands of cheering students even as we drove up to the campus. We finally got out of the car and continued on foot, stopping now and then to chat to the young people. At the entrance to the inner yard, we were welcomed by the Stanford University President, Donald Kennedy, and our old friend and colleague George Shultz. After the meeting with the faculty members and representatives of the student body, I addressed an audience of thousands of people, both professors and students, who had gathered in the auditorium and outside the building.

'Your task is not only to create a new world order, but to live in it,' I said. 'It will undoubtedly be different in many respects from anything we can imagine today and different from what I am telling you now. But the main thing is that all people should live better and enjoy more freedom in this new world. And this depends to a large extent on the scholars and scientists. I wish you every success in this great, unprecedented endeavour.' George Shultz responded with an eloquent and very substantial speech.

At the end of my stay in the United States, I had a meeting with South Korean President Roh Tae Woo at my hotel. We had agreed in advance that he would come from Seoul to meet me. It was clear that we could not, for obsolete ideological reasons (i.e. because of our ties with North Korea), continue opposing the establishment of normal relations with his country, which showed an exceptional dynamism and had become a force to be reckoned with, both in the Asia-Pacific region and in the wider world. I confirmed that we were in favour of a peaceful re-unification of Korea, adding that the general improvement of the situation in the region opened up the prospect of establishing diplomatic relations. Our relations with South Korea improved quickly after this meeting.

CONTINUING THE DIALOGUE

Mrs Thatcher came to Moscow in June 1990. I had returned from my trip to the United States and Canada on 5 June, a few days before her arrival. She seemed greatly impressed by the results of the visit and complimented me on the 'extraordinarily successful meeting' with George Bush. Indeed the talks with the American President had dispelled a number of mutual concerns, including issues we had often discussed with Margaret Thatcher.

During our first conversation, she remarked that she believed it was essential to emphasize the positive aspects in our relations and to point out our convergent views on a number of issues at our joint press conference. 'Journalists tend to highlight negative aspects,' she said, 'and we must therefore concentrate on the positive achievements.

'It seems to me that many people, including many of the press, have not yet fully grasped how far we have come and how much the summit meetings contributed to this.'

'In 1986 my idea of a nuclear-free world was perceived as wishful thinking,' I reminded Mrs Thatcher. 'Today we are about to conclude an agreement with the Americans on a fifty-per-cent cut in strategic nuclear arms, and we have agreed on the elimination of our chemical weapons stockpiles. We have made much headway in only three years! Or, to take another example, the idea of a political settlement of regional conflicts was seen as another utopia. Today, the process has begun. And I must say that you personally have greatly contributed to this.'

My last meeting with Margaret Thatcher in her capacity as Prime Minister took place in Paris on 20 November, on the occasion of the European conference. We concentrated on the situation in the Gulf, which I shall describe in detail in the following chapter. I had discussed the issue with Mr Bush on the eve of our meeting, and Margaret Thatcher 'OK'd' our exchange of ideas. However, she admitted that she did not believe that a political settlement was possible and thought the use of force was inevitable. Hence she proposed that the next UN Security Council resolution (we had discussed it with George Bush) should be formulated in more severe terms, complaining that the Americans seemed to be 'somewhat over-cautious'. Needless to say, we also talked about the situation in the Soviet Union. The British Prime Minister did not hide her concern – she was an experienced politician and she perceived the dangers. We bid farewell at the entrance to my residence. 'God bless you!' she said in a soft voice.

The elections to the leadership of the British Conservative Party took place in Mrs Thatcher's absence. She failed to obtain the necessary majority on the first ballot. She had told me that she had enemies – in eleven and a half years at the helm, this is virtually unavoidable. Yet she seemed to have no intention of capitulating. In Paris, when she was informed of the result of the election, she declared to the waiting press that she was 'going to show them' back home. Upon her return to London, however, she announced that she would resign. It was a noble act. Nonetheless, I regretted it.

I received her warm letter of farewell in late November and sent her a friendly message of support. I would like to reproduce here two of her letters to me, written at the time of her departure.

Dear Mr President,

By the time you receive this message, you will probably already have heard this morning's announcement from 10 Downing Street of my decision to make way for a successor, and to resign as Prime Minister as soon as the Parliamentary Party has completed the necessary procedures for electing a new leader. I shall of course remain in charge of the Government until my successor has been appointed.

I should like to thank you for the great co-operation and friendship which you have shown me during our time together in office, during which so much has been achieved, and I send you my warmest wishes for the future. I know that my successor will continue to attach the highest importance to the relations between our countries.

I was glad we were able to have a final meeting in Paris, and send you my very best wishes for the success of the great reforms which you are carrying through. We shall continue to watch your success with the greatest possible interest.

Denis joins me in sending you and Raisa Maksimovna our warm regards and good wishes.
Yours sincerely,

Margaret Thatcher

Dear Mikhail Sergeyevich,

I was most grateful to receive your warm and generous message. I remember every one of our meetings, from your visit to Chequers in December 1984 through to our most recent encounter in Paris, for their intense interest and their practical results. I believe that together we really did contribute to changing our world, and your own contribution to that has been outstanding. I share your hope that we can continue to meet on future occasions.

Meanwhile, Denis joins me in sending you and Raisa Maksimovna our warmest regards.
Yours sincerely,

Margaret Thatcher

We met six months later in May 1991, on the occasion of her private visit to Moscow. She gave a lecture at the Institute of International Relations, and had a number of meetings with students and young people. She was keenly interested in the situation in our country and asked many questions. We discussed the position of the West, the Group of Seven and the possibility of my participation in the forthcoming London meeting, and Mrs Thatcher promised to use her political influence and ties to help matters.

Margaret Thatcher did much to support our perestroika. Needless to say she had her own views on the reforms, perceiving them as winning the Soviet Union over to Western positions, as a Soviet version of 'Thatcherism'. Nonetheless, she genuinely

705

wanted to help us and to mobilize the efforts of the Western countries in support of our policies. During the August 1991 coup, she spoke out in defence of democracy and of the Soviet President and his family.

One must also give her credit for her services to her country. Mrs Thatcher took over at a time when the United Kingdom was lagging behind the other major Western nations, and she succeeded in radically changing both the domestic and the international situation of Great Britain. However, Mrs Thatcher's tough methods and her inherent authoritarianism soured even her closest supporters, not to speak of the opposition, and eventually led to conflict situations. I had the impression that, in order to work with her, you had to accept her style and character unconditionally. Her authoritarianism and her penchant for forceful methods were manifest in British foreign policy. In crisis situations, she spoke out in favour of military sanctions. Even after her resignation as Prime Minister, we would occasionally receive information that 'Mrs Thatcher is suggesting air raids'. She was particularly tough in her approach to the Gulf crisis.

Margaret Thatcher was not an easy partner for us, and her fierce anti-Communism would often hinder her from taking a more realistic view on various issues. Still, one must admit that in a number of cases, she was able to substantiate her charges with facts, which eventually led us to review and criticize some of our own approaches. All in all, she was a strong advocate of Western interests and values, indeed.

Margaret Thatcher had much of what I would call the 'Old English Spirit', at least as we Russians usually imagine it, which shows in her commitment to traditions and 'tried and tested' values. During our official meetings, she was always very considerate and courteous. We eventually came to know each other better and she showed genuine warmth towards both me and Raisa Maksimovna – despite the differences in our views and our political arguments.

THE PARIS SUMMIT

The developments in Eastern Europe in the autumn of 1989 made it necessary to review security issues. Indeed the creation of new security arrangements for all of Europe became a priority in the European process. We focused our diplomatic efforts on the '2 + 4' negotiations on the German question, the Vienna talks and the preparations for the forthcoming CSCE summit meeting. Linking these three priorities would allow us to synchronize the process of German unification with the creation of a new structure of European security. This was a recurrent theme in my talks with Bush, Thatcher, Mitterrand, Andreotti and obviously Chancellor Kohl in summer 1990, which opened the way for the Paris summit meeting.

In Strasbourg I had proposed calling a pan-European conference, the second since the Helsinki summit in 1975, before its scheduled date in 1992. The idea was initially viewed with suspicion, but eventually everyone took it up and joined in the preparations. Though the date for Helsinki Two remained unchanged, it was decided to organize a special conference in Paris on the occasion of the signing of the treaty on conventional armed forces in Europe. The Paris conference took place on 19–21 November 1990, with the participation of the leaders of the thirty-four CSCE member states.

The heads of delegation and foreign ministers convened at the Elysée Palace on the eve of the opening of the European summit for the signing ceremony of the conventional force reduction in Europe treaty (which had been negotiated in Vienna) and of the twenty-two-nation joint declaration. The signatory powers pledged that henceforth they were no longer enemies and would build new relations based on partnership and friendship.

This was indeed a historic event. An era marked by two world wars and nearly fifty years of 'nuclear antagonism' between the two military-political blocs and political systems was about to become a thing of the past. The conference adopted a final document, 'The Charter of Paris for a New Europe', which was signed by the leaders of the thirty-four CSCE member states and the President of the European Commission, Jacques Delors.

In addition to spelling out the principles generally acknowledged by the CSCE member states, the charter provided for the new structures and institutions that were to form the core of the European process. It was decided to create a council of foreign ministers, which was to become the main forum for regular political consultation, a committee of senior officials, a CSCE secretariat, a conflict prevention centre and a consultative committee.

The Paris conference heralded a new, post-confrontational era in European history. The next steps would be the ratification and coming into force of the conventional arms treaty, the organization of the third round of the CSCE Conference on Human Rights and preparations for Helsinki Two.

But, caught in the process of change, the new Europe proved unprepared for the dramatic events of 1991. The August coup in Moscow and the subsequent disintegration and break-up of the Soviet Union – which had become one of the mainstays of a new, peaceful balance in Europe and the world – and the civil war and disintegration of Yugoslavia radically changed the situation. The pan-European process was put to trial even before the newly created mechanisms became fully operational, and thus failed to contain the armed conflicts that flared up on the European continent.

THE NOBEL PEACE PRIZE

In October the Nobel Committee had awarded me the 1990 Peace Prize. To be frank, I learned of the decision with mixed feelings. Of course it was flattering to receive one of the most prestigious international awards, which had been bestowed upon such outstanding men as Albert Schweitzer, Willy Brandt and Andrei Sakharov. I received many congratulations from my colleagues and compatriots and from abroad.

However, Soviet society had, to put it mildly, a somewhat ambiguous view of Nobel Prizes in general, particularly if they were awarded for public or political activities. Pasternak and Solzhenitsyn had received the Nobel Prize for Literature in circumstances that emphasized their dissidence, and the awards were perceived in our country as anti-Soviet provocations. True, there was also an exception, the Nobel Prize for Literature awarded to Sholokhov. All in all, however, only awards for scientific achievements were taken seriously – and only in academic circles.

This mind-set also cast a pall on the Nobel Prize bestowed on me, and much of the reaction within the Soviet Union was far from civil or dignified. The situation in our country had come to a head, with all-out attacks launched at me from all sides. In this context, the Nobel Prize was viewed as a token of approval of my policies by people who, in the eyes of a significant part of the Soviet public, were acting as the mouthpiece of Western 'imperialist' interests. What amazed me was the particularly hostile reaction of the leadership of the Russian Federation.

I decided against attending the award ceremony in Oslo on 10 December. I asked Anatoly Kovalev, First Deputy Minister of Foreign Affairs, to go in my stead. He read my letter of thanks and received the award on my behalf.

It was the custom for the Nobel laureate to deliver the traditional lecture either at the award ceremony or within six months of the presentation. I was invited to give a lecture in early May 1991. However, the political situation in our country had meanwhile become even more critical, particularly after the January events[1] in Vilnius and Riga. I was under fire both at home and abroad, with some people going so far as to declare that to award me the Nobel Prize had been a mistake and that the committee should reconsider its decision. In this situation, I repeatedly postponed the decision to go to Oslo. I thought of going there in early May, but had to cancel the trip. I must admit that to this day I feel somewhat embarrassed, since my hesitation could have been perceived as a lack of respect towards the Nobel committee. However, in the end I decided to use this international forum to restate my creed about the role of perestroika and the new thinking for us and for mankind.

---

[1] In January 1991 armed troops stormed the TV tower in Vilnius, leaving fifteen dead. There was also violence in Riga.

I delivered my Nobel lecture in Oslo on 5 June 1991. I naturally apologized for the delay. I emphasized that I perceived the committee's decision as an acknowledgement of the global significance of the changes in the Soviet Union, as an acknowledgement of the new thinking, and as an act of solidarity with the great endeavour which had already required enormous efforts, sacrifices, privations, will-power and endurance from our people. The leitmotif of my speech was that a modern state deserves solidarity if it attempts, both in domestic and in foreign affairs, to harmonize the interests of its people with those of the international community.

26

THE MIDDLE EAST KNOT: TRIAL BY AGGRESSION

THE INTERNATIONAL CRISIS PROVOKED BY THE IRAQI aggression against Kuwait was a milestone in the development of post-Cold War relations between East and West. It was a major test for the new political thinking. During the Cold War, this conflict could have led the opposing blocs to a military, even a nuclear, confrontation. In any event, curbing the aggression would have been more than problematic. Now it was possible to unite the entire world community to oppose aggression, and this determined its defeat, closing the era when aggressors could go unpunished.

Events in the Gulf posed especially difficult problems for Soviet policy. The Soviet Union and Iraq had a friendship and co-operation treaty, and much of the Soviet public resented the prospect of 'betraying' an ally. Ingrained mistrust of American foreign policy motives also played its part. Thousands of our people were in Iraq in various capacities – as military advisers, technical specialists, and so on. Finally, billion-dollar economic interests linked us to Iraq, an especially sensitive point considering our difficult economic situation.

Nonetheless, without delay or hesitation, I immediately condemned the aggression and spoke out in favour of forming an international coalition to oppose Iraq within the framework of the United Nations. We followed this principle consistently, despite all the complications and unforeseen hazards.

711

At the same time, I also called for political rather than military means for resolving the crisis – not only because they were the more appropriate means of settling international disputes after the end of the Cold War. I was thinking above all of the devastation and human suffering that military action would inflict. I was also thinking about how Saddam Hussein might try, as was later confirmed, to exploit the situation to feed anti-Western moods in the Arab and Muslim world, which could prove a serious blow to the entire healing process in international relations.

Unfortunately our efforts were not successful. We ran into Hussein's blind stubbornness and irrational conduct. But these efforts did not always meet with sympathy from the United States either, where American politicians who wanted the United States to lower the military boom, so to speak, demonstrating its might, had a noticeable influence.

On 2 August 1990 Iraqi tanks invaded Kuwait. Annexed by Iraq, this small state was declared its nineteenth province. Why did Iraq undertake such a risky adventure? The Iraqi leadership was behind the times internationally. They clung to the idea, which had taken root in the confrontational era, that in the event of a crisis in this part of the world the United States and the Soviet Union would inevitably wind up on opposite sides of the barricades.

This is where Baghdad made its biggest mistake. Events in the Persian Gulf marked a watershed for the superpowers: for the first time they acted in concert to solve a regional crisis. We immediately and decisively condemned the act of aggression and demanded the unconditional withdrawal of the invaders' troops from Kuwait and the restoration of its sovereignty. Resolutions to this effect, including harsh economic sanctions, were passed by the UN Security Council, with our active participation. At the same time, we started working towards a peaceful solution, using our contacts with the United States and other countries to this end, and encouraging the Arabs to exercise their influence over Hussein.

I felt it was important to maintain contact with Iraq. We tried to rid the Iraqi leadership of any delusions of invulnerability and to convince them that they had to implement the Security Council's resolutions.

On 5 September 1990 I had a long conversation with Iraq's Minister of Foreign Affairs, Tariq Aziz. To give an idea of the tone of the conversation, I will quote a rather extensive excerpt:

'For us, the purpose of this conversation,' I said, 'is to see whether the Iraqi leadership has any new ideas that might facilitate a political settlement. This is why we wanted you to come here on the eve of my meeting with Bush . . . We have collaborated with you in the past, and we would like to continue this collaboration. It is quite clear to us that if Iraq is going to participate constructively in the political efforts to solve these problems, a solution is possible. However, if there is no such participation, then it could all end badly. I would like to say quite candidly that the conflict that has flared up is fraught with great danger.

'I advise you to move as quickly as possible to a search for political ways out of the crisis. More and more, voices are being heard on the international scene calling for "tough measures" against Iraq. It is clear what they mean by this. Is that all right with you? I can't believe that the Iraqi leadership would want such a harsh fate for its people. Speaking candidly, constructive and realistic steps are needed from your side. These are what we were expecting to hear about when we asked Iraq's President whether new elements had appeared in the Iraqi position.'

I asked Aziz bluntly: 'Do you have any new proposals?'

Aziz assured me that the Iraqi leadership was playing a constructive role in the region. He complained of a plot against Iraq. But Iraq 'is completely confident of its powers and is not afraid of a confrontation with the Americans . . . we know that confrontation could lead to a wide-scale conflict, the consequences of which would affect not only the Arab region but the entire world. That prospect does not frighten us, though.'

The Iraqi leaders were 'not frightened' by the possibility of global catastrophe! Such were the kind of people with whom the world community had to deal.

Aziz linked the Kuwait problem to all the other problems of the

713

Middle East. In so doing, the Iraqis were attempting to obscure the issue of their aggression against Kuwait in a cloud of other, albeit undoubtedly real, problems.

I rejected these arguments: 'We have been searching for years for the key to the most important problems of the Middle East, especially the Palestinian problem, the Arab-Israeli conflict as a whole, and the Lebanese crisis. A solution has yet to be found, though. Now, after what Iraq has done, the task has been complicated many times over. It is unrealistic,' I emphasized, 'after all that has happened, after the Security Council has passed five resolutions and a large US military contingent has been sent into the Persian Gulf zone, to talk about negotiations without displaying a readiness to withdraw Iraqi troops from Kuwait.'

In reply, Aziz once again unleashed a tirade about the Iraqi leadership's 'confidence' that 'the present confrontation between Iraq and the United States will eventually bring Iraq success.' He reproached us for talking 'the same language as the Americans.'

Concluding our conversation, I said: 'You may be receiving instructions direct from the Almighty, but I would still like to give you some advice. You should not reject the search for a political solution on a realistic and constructive basis. We get the feeling that you still don't see it that way. You should bear in mind, though, that in the future the situation is only going to deteriorate.'

Four days later I met President Bush in Helsinki. This meeting, undertaken at his initiative, was of fundamental importance. Its crux was the issue of maintaining and consolidating the American-Soviet partnership in the face of the crisis that had broken out.

'I'm glad that the Soviet Union and the United States have demonstrated to the whole world that now, during this crisis in the Persian Gulf, they are together, side by side,' the American President said.

I stressed that as a result of our joint efforts a great deal had already been achieved. Moving troops into the Persian Gulf region and active policy in the UN Security Council had accomplished several strategic tasks: the Iraqi armed action had not spread to other countries on the Arabian peninsula; the oil crisis that had threatened the world economy ever since Kuwait and Iraq had stopped exporting oil had been averted; and the idea of firm resistance to aggression had received wide international support. All this had created the necessary prerequisites for continuing political efforts that could prove effective in resolving the problem. At the same time we were counting on economic sanctions against Iraq to yield speedy results and force Saddam Hussein to quit Kuwait.

I must say that our orientation towards non-military solutions to the problem met with understanding from Bush at that point. He said several times that he 'did not want the conflict to escalate' and favoured a peaceful solution. These statements by the American President were especially valuable for, as I understood – and said in Helsinki – he was under pressure from certain quarters to use force immediately. Coming out in favour of a political settlement as the preferable, one might even say the only appropriate, path, at the same time I was in complete agreement with Bush's point that 'Saddam Hussein cannot be permitted to profit from his aggression.'

Our conversation covered another topic too. I put the question like this: while naturally rejecting Saddam Hussein's attempts to lump together all the serious problems that had accumulated in the Middle East, we should use a political settlement of the crisis to help advance the resolution of the Arab-Israeli conflict. I envisaged the possibility of convening an international conference of the members of the Security Council and the Arab states, to discuss not only the problem of restoring Kuwait's independence but also other problems in the region, including the Palestinian-Lebanese question, beginning, obviously, with Kuwait.

In the end, this topic was reflected in a joint Soviet-American statement which said that it was essential to work actively for a settlement of the conflict in the region. The United States would not go beyond this vague language, but it did open up opportunites for political moves.

From my point of view, the Helsinki meeting yielded two fundamental results that did not, however, lead to equal practical consequences. On the one hand, we had demonstrated our readiness and ability to take our new relationship, our partnership, through a difficult crisis, thus strengthening that relationship. On the other, we had come to an agreement, at least in principle, to work towards a peaceful, political resolution of the problem, although the influence of those thirsting for blood could be felt as well.

After Helsinki, we energetically pursued our policy of persuading Iraq to implement UN Security Council Resolution 660 – which demanded the unconditional withdrawal of Iraqi troops from Kuwait – rejecting any scenarios that could be looked on as a reward for the aggressor. In the process we made use of dialogue with Iraq, inasmuch as that channel was available chiefly to us. If I were to characterize our approach on the broad, strategic level, so to speak, its essence consisted above all in reversing the aggression, but without the use of military methods, which would entail heavy political, human, and environmental costs. This approach assumed that after Iraq withdrew its forces from Kuwait – after, not in conjunction with – specific actions must follow designed to help stabilize the situation throughout the Middle East. In this spirit I sent several strongly worded letters to Saddam Hussein, in particular with Primakov, who went to Iraq in early October.

The Soviet Union's line, which was aimed at seeking opportunities for a peaceful solution of the crisis, met with approval from virtually everyone who had any interest in finding an alternative to war. The leaders of many countries with whom I or our representatives had contact – Mitterrand, Andreotti, and the Arab leaders, for example – expressed their support for our efforts. The only exception was Margaret Thatcher, who preferred military methods. In time the policy directed at not just achieving the withdrawal of Iraqi troops from Kuwait but also inflicting a crushing blow on Iraq, 'breaking' Hussein's back, wiping out the country's entire military and possibly even industrial potential, began to gather momentum in the United States. As for Bush, he seemed to be hesitating, still not completely sure that military action was the correct option.

Under these circumstances, I decided to send my personal representative to Iraq again, in yet another attempt to bring

Hussein to his senses. He seemed to have no real idea of how the situation was developing. He remained captive to the illusion that the world community would never take extreme measures. Primakov also had to raise the issue once again, and pointedly, of the evacuation of Soviet specialists and foreign hostages still being held at military and other strategic sites in Iraq. Finally, he was instructed to make the rounds of several Arab states to discuss the possibilities of working together more actively to settle the crisis. It is worth noting that in all the Arab capitals Primakov visited, support was expressed for a political solution to the situation. This was the case in Cairo, Damascus, and Riyadh. However, contacts with Hussein did not yield the desired result, although a change of tone could be observed.

Time was running out, and the supporters of a military solution were becoming more and more insistent; Iraqi stubbornness gave them additional arguments. In the middle of November, with our full support, the UN Security Council approved a resolution setting a deadline for Iraq to withdraw. While for some this resolution opened the way for the decision to apply military force, for us its significance consisted above all in providing the last chance to avert war. I sent I. S. Belousov, Deputy Chairman of the USSR Council of Ministers, to Baghdad to attempt to convince Hussein to agree to a meeting with American representatives in Geneva. The meeting was arranged and took place in Geneva, but the seven-hour conversation led nowhere. Tariq Aziz had not packed anything new in his diplomatic baggage, and Baker demanded the unconditional withdrawal of Iraqi troops.

Nevertheless, I did not stop trying to avert war, especially since encouraging notes had begun to appear in Hussein's statements. A few days before the Security Council's ultimatum elapsed, I telephoned Bush and informed him of my readiness to send a representative to Baghdad again, in a final effort to avert war. He generally welcomed this proposal, but asked that the deadline set by the Security Council should not be changed. Simultaneously, a concrete version of the so-called invisible package[1] proposed

---

[1] The implication that efforts to promote the peace process between the Arabs and Israel would be reactivated immediately after the withdrawal of Iraqi troops from Kuwait.

earlier, which was to facilitate a political solution, was conveyed to Washington.

A positive reaction to the Soviet Union's proposal came in Bush's speech over the radio. However, a few hours later our ambassador in Washington was told that the United States did not object to the Soviet representative travelling to Baghdad if his sole purpose was to tell Saddam Hussein to get out of Kuwait. There had been a very important shift in the US administration's position. Now that mutual understanding had broken down, the trip made no sense.

Saddam Hussein's irrational stubbornness, his barbaric behaviour, especially the pillaging and wrecking of Kuwait and taking the specialists working in Iraq hostage, strengthened the war party in Washington and other Western capitals.

THE GULF WAR

On the night of 16–17 January, the United States began air strikes against Iraq. Baker had telephoned the Soviet Minister of Foreign Affairs at home and informed him.

I asked the Americans to postpone their attack at least for a while so that I could try to convince Iraq to withdraw its troops from Kuwait. Baker replied that military actions had already begun, however.

I then made the following statement: 'This tragic turn of events was provoked by the Iraqi leadership's refusal to meet the demands of the world community and withdraw its troops from Kuwait. From the very beginning of the Iraqi aggression, the Soviet Union has done everything in its power to resolve this serious international conflict by peaceful means. Up until the very last moments we were involved in energetic efforts to avert war and return Kuwait its independence by political means.'

Simultaneously, I instructed our ambassador in Baghdad to get in touch with Hussein and inform him of my appeal to Bush. I emphasized the need, in the interests of the entire Iraqi people, in the interests of peace in the region, for Iraq to declare its readiness to leave Kuwait. I expressed the hope that, guided by the higher interests of its people and the world community, Iraq would take this only remaining possible step.

That night we appealed to the leaders of France, China, Great Britain, Germany, Italy, India, Iran, and the heads of most of the Arab states to undertake joint parallel steps to localize the conflict and to prevent its dangerous spread. In response to powerful air strikes, the Iraqis attempted to expand the theatre of military action by subjecting Israel and Saudi Arabia to missile attack. They were clearly hoping that this would provoke a counter-strike from Israel, which would in turn trigger an all-out Arab-Israeli struggle, with the attendant political consequences. The Soviet Union unambiguously condemned the strikes against Israel and Saudi Arabia, and praised the restraint and responsible approach of the two countries at this extremely dangerous moment.

Meanwhile there was a clear military escalation. Whereas at first the targets had included mostly Iraqi military sites, later industrial enterprises were subjected to attack, and not just those working for the army. The United States emphasized strikes against nuclear reactors, chemical factories, and centres that might be developing biological weapons.

On the third day of military action, 19 January, I took a new political initiative. I instructed our ambassador in Baghdad to contact Hussein and convey to him the following: if we received confidential assurances from Iraq of its readiness to carry out unconditional and unqualified withdrawal of its troops from Kuwait, then we would propose a cease-fire to the United States.

By the way, this initiative of mine was interpreted in very bad faith by certain Western politicians and members of the Western press. Not knowing the true circumstances, or else consciously distorting the truth, they declared that we had gone behind Washington's back. In fact, in my telephone conversation with Bush on 18 January at 5.15 p.m. Moscow time, I had informed him about the efforts I was undertaking. I emphasized: 'Hostilities have begun, and right now we have to think above all about how to shorten them, how to prevent them from spreading.' To this Bush replied: 'I am very worried about that too. I think when Hussein intentionally fired missiles at Israel, he wanted the fighting to spread.'

I also stated: 'We want to be entirely with you in a common rejection of the aggression and a common position towards the actions of Hussein's regime. We have no hesitations or doubts that the blame and the responsibility for what is going on lie with him.'

That same day I had a telephone conversation with Kohl, whom I also informed of our initiative.

Baghdad maintained silence for two days. Then we were told that proposals of this type must be addressed to the American President.

Even this discouraging reaction from Hussein did not induce me to back off. The stakes were too high, especially since we were now witnessing increasingly alarming military action. Bombings and missile attacks were hitting residential sections of Baghdad and other cities more and more, and the country's infrastructure had incurred tremendous losses. All electric power stations had been destroyed, water treatment plants and sewerage pumps had been knocked out. There was now a real danger of mass epidemics. Iraq released a huge quantity of oil into the Persian Gulf, creating a terrible threat to the environment. Nor were we inclined to ignore Iraqi threats to use weapons of mass destruction – you never know what to expect from a dictator who has been driven into a corner. Especially since we were talking about territories lying close to the Soviet Union.

We were alarmed by references in the American press and American political circles to the possibility and appropriateness of using tactical nuclear weapons against the Iraqi army.

I repeat, I saw all this as confirming the correctness of the policy we chose, emphasizing the preference for political methods of ending the crisis.

On 29 January Aleksandr Bessmertnykh, our Minister of Foreign Affairs, visited Washington. The resulting joint Soviet-American statement underscored that a cessation of military actions was possible 'if Iraq gives an unambiguous commitment to leave Kuwait'. The ministers also assumed, it said further, that this pledge would have to be reinforced immediately by specific measures leading to full implementation of the UN Security

Council resolutions. Elimination of the sources of conflict and instability in the region was impossible without a fully fledged peace process that included reconciliation between Israel, the Arab states, and the Palestinians.

In the United States the two latter parts of the statement met with rather sharp criticism. However, I thought it very important. First of all, while clearly stating the main task – to restore Kuwait's sovereignty and independence – it opened up a kind of political window for a peaceful solution. At the same time, it reaffirmed and delineated the scope of the Security Council resolution, confining the task unambiguously to making Iraq leave Kuwait unconditionally, thus rejecting any broader interpretation of the resolution.

The hostilities were becoming increasingly fierce, sowing destruction over virtually the entire territory of Iraq, and military action had already gone well beyond the limits of the Security Council resolution. This, and the increasingly likely prospect of the ground forces being brought in, moved me to make one more step. On 9 February I issued a new statement and simultaneously decided once again to send my own personal representative to Baghdad.

The statement read: 'Events in the Persian Gulf region are taking an increasingly alarming and dramatic turn. The flywheel of the largest war in recent decades is gathering momentum. The number of victims is multiplying, including innocent civilians. Military action has already inflicted enormous material damage. Entire countries – first Kuwait, now Iraq, and later possibly others – are threatened by catastrophic devastation.' The statement reaffirmed the Soviet leadership's strong support for the UN resolution; at the same time, however, it noted that the 'logic of military operations and the nature of military actions create a threat that the mandate contained in these resolutions could be exceeded.' Even earlier, when I received US Ambassador Matlock on 24 January 1991, I had made similar points.

NEW TALKS WITH IRAQ

At long last, evidently under the influence of their defeats, there was a shift in the Iraqi position. Hussein did not limit himself to statements about how Iraq would not capitulate and would offer effective resistance, and so on. We were given a written statement which said that the Iraqi leadership was seriously studying the ideas advanced by the Soviet side and would respond to them through Tariq Aziz, who would fly to Moscow on Sunday. On 15 February, two days before his arrival, Baghdad radio ceased regular broadcasts and issued a statement from the Revolutionary Command Council stating that Iraq was ready to act in accordance with Security Council Resolution 660.

On the evening of 17 February Tariq Aziz arrived in Moscow on a Soviet plane. We met the next morning. In talking with him, I emphasized that Iraq's position looked contradictory. On the one hand, this was an important step towards a political settlement, since the Iraqi side was recognizing Resolution 660. At the same time, this recognition came equipped with qualifications, whereas the resolution demanded Iraq's unconditional withdrawal from Kuwait. I acknowledged the existence of what the Iraqis in their statement called 'important Middle East problems'. But those could not and should not be linked directly to the withdrawal of troops. That was unacceptable and unrealistic. It was especially important to know whether these questions were brought up as a precondition for settling the Kuwait crisis or whether they were merely a reference to the existence of profound problems in this region.

Aziz was forced to agree that the list of problems in the statement was not a 'condition for withdrawal' but a kind of programme that should be implemented in the future.

I proposed the following plan:

'Iraq must declare its readiness to withdraw its troops from Kuwait;

'The withdrawal of troops must start the day after the cessation of hostilities, which is necessary for its practical implementation;

'The deadline for the withdrawal of troops must be clearly defined;

'There must be a full UN Security Council guarantee for the safe withdrawal of troops from Kuwait.'

If the Iraqi leadership had issued this kind of plan to back up its statement, this would have been grounds for us and other countries immediately to call a session of the Security Council to analyse the situation in a comprehensive manner and undertake an examination of the whole complex of problems involved in a Middle East settlement.

To Aziz's question about tough economic sanctions against Iraq, I replied that they would be reconsidered by the Security Council, after the withdrawal of Iraqi troops.

At the close of the conversation, I appealed to Aziz: 'If you value the lives of your fellow countrymen and the fate of Iraq, then you must act immediately.'

All in all, we had a difficult discussion lasting approximately three hours. I got the impression that the Iraqi representatives, presumably reflecting the position of Hussein himself, were inclined to be more realistic. They did not reject our proposals outright, but naturally they said they could respond only after Aziz reported the 'Gorbachev plan', as he put it, to President Hussein and the entire Iraqi leadership. The Iraqis left for home immediately after this conversation.

I telephoned the American President and the leaders of several Western European countries immediately afterwards and told them about the nature of the conversation and my impressions, pointing out the possibility of changes in Hussein's position. I felt that the new points that had appeared had to be taken into consideration in planning military action over the next few days, and it seemed to me at the time that my information met with understanding.

Aziz returned to Moscow on the night of 21 February. A few hours before that, however, Hussein spoke over the radio. His speech was rambling, unconstructive, and contained a full panoply of propaganda clichés and even threats. I understood that all this was addressed primarily to the Iraqis and designed to mask the Iraqi leadership's acceptance of the UN ultimatum, which it had previously rejected in strong and provocative terms. However that may have been, this speech by Hussein was later cited by Bush during my telephone conversation with him on 22 February as testimony to Hussein's insincerity and the impossibility of trusting him, even when the Iraqi side was talking about accepting Resolution 660.

At midnight Aziz was taken directly from the airport to the Kremlin. I basically never left there during that entire period. Our discussion lasted until nearly three in the morning.

This time our conversation was simpler, although the Iraqi leadership continued to hold unrealistic positions on several points. In the final analysis, we were able to reach a more or less acceptable – from our point of view – line. Most important, the point about Iraq accepting Security Council Resolution 660 and being ready to withdraw all its troops from Kuwait was formulated precisely and unambiguously. The Iraqis asserted, however, that they could not do this within extremely tight deadlines. To my argument (also made by the American side, by the way), that their invasion had taken a matter of hours, but the Iraqis were now asking (at first) for several months to withdraw, four weeks as a minimum, Aziz replied that they had invaded with only a couple of divisions, but in seven months an army of half a million men had been concentrated in Kuwait. I declared firmly that the proposed time-frame could and must be cut to the minimum.

As before, Aziz also raised the issue of repealing all Security Council Resolutions on sanctions simultaneously upon Iraq's announcement of its withdrawal of troops from Kuwait. I remarked that those issues could be examined, but there could be no conditions attached to Iraq's acceptance of Resolution 660.

We decided that a final text with these fundamental points would be formulated by Soviet and Iraqi representatives, who would start work immediately.

At the same time – and it was already four in the morning – I got in touch with Bush and talked with him for an hour and a half. I said that my conversation with Aziz had proceeded on the basis of serious shifts on the Iraqi side and that the Iraqis had 'reached a position that was quite realistic, which meant that the chances for finding a solution to the conflict were good'. Bush expressed his appreciation for the efforts being made by the Soviet Union and its President and asked to be told immediately about any information coming from Baghdad. He added significantly: 'Time is running out, and running out very quickly.'

Meanwhile, the talks between the Soviet and Iraqi representatives led to the formulation of six points, chief of which was the following: 'Iraq agrees to implement Resolution 660, that is to withdraw all of its troops immediately and unconditionally from Kuwait to the positions they occupied on 1 August 1990.' At the same time, despite all objections from Soviet representatives, Aziz clung to the point that stated: 'Immediately upon completion of troop withdrawal from Kuwait, the reasons for the passage of the other Security Council resolutions will no longer exist, so said resolutions shall cease to be effective.'

Of course, it would be hard to call this document ideal, and the point just cited was unacceptable. But it could undoubtedly – and I am convinced of this still – have been a point of departure for the cessation of hostilities. Having made the qualification that the agreed document had to be approved by the entire leadership, above all Hussein, Aziz added that he was confident of a positive response. In order to speed up the matter, we suggested that he should send a telegram through the Soviet embassy in Baghdad, even in Iraqi code. In this way the six points were transmitted to the Iraqi leadership on 23 February, and at two in the morning, Moscow time (in Washington it was still 22 February), we received a positive reply.

Even before this, however, at 19.00, Moscow time, President Bush had presented Iraq with an ultimatum demanding withdrawal of troops from Kuwait within a week, including withdrawal from the city of El Kuwait in 48 hours, and insisting that this withdrawal begin the next day, at 20.00, Moscow time.

In our opinion, the Iraqi leadership's statement had led to a new situation, and there was now a real chance to shift from a military to a political means of resolving the dispute. The problem now was that the coalition, above all the United States, did not accept this statement as a reply to its demands. On 23 February, at 12.05, Aziz informed journalists of the Iraqi leadership's decision to withdraw its troops from Kuwait immediately and unconditionally, but in so doing he alluded to the whole complex of issues worked out in Moscow. He ended his remarks by saying that the decision to withdraw unconditionally from Kuwait was a response to President Bush's demands.

In another telephone conversation with Bush, on the evening of 22 February, I suggested that a Security Council session should be called in the next twenty-four hours to examine the entire situation. In reply, Bush once again emphasized the 'highly constructive' role that the Soviet Union had played and was continuing to play during the Persian Gulf crisis. At the same time the American President expressed doubts about the opportunity presented by the changes in Iraq's position, changes that, as I have already mentioned, he had recognized. Bush said that Hussein could not be trusted; that he, Bush, was particularly alarmed by the Iraqis' destruction of Kuwait and by the fate of the prisoners, who were being held in the worst possible conditions. He felt it was also impossible 'to ignore the enormous material damage inflicted by Iraq's aggression on Kuwait.' Agreeing that I had managed to persuade the Iraqi leadership not to tie the withdrawal of their troops to other problems and to agree to the 'concept of troop withdrawal', Bush emphasized that 'this is far from an unconditional withdrawal of troops.' The President also considered the Iraqi time-frame for the troop withdrawal unacceptably long.

I referred to Aziz's assurances that the Iraqi leadership had decided to withdraw its troops and would do so. Moreover, holding to my convictions and my chosen political line, I insisted: 'It seems to me that we must ask ourselves where our priorities lie in working out a final solution to the Persian Gulf problem. Do we favour a political approach or search for a military solution?

'We do not disagree with you as to the assessment of Saddam Hussein. But we must take advantage of what we have already achieved and take the next major step towards achieving our objectives through political means and thus avoid a dramatic or even tragic ending.'

The curtain went up on the final act. The situation had become extremely complex. On the one hand, the Iraqi leadership, after prolonged blindness or perhaps swaggering (or, more likely, both), had shown signs of realism and was now inclined to accept the demands of the world community. Aziz's statement in Moscow had been confirmed by an official statement in Baghdad about Iraq's willingness to make a total and unconditional withdrawal of its troops from Kuwait within four days, in accordance with Resolution 660 of the Security Council.

On the other hand, the anti-Iraq coalition, mainly the United States, was determined to call the aggressor to account, irritated by Saddam Hussein's provocative conduct and by his insulting personal attacks on the American President. Fired by the success of its military action, during which sophisticated weapons had been tested, the coalition was showing its definite and growing preference for the military option.

A FINAL ATTEMPT

I made one last attempt to halt the escalation of the war. On 23 February I never left the telephone, as I tried to convince my principal partners around the world that there was still a possibility of shifting to a non-military track. First I sent telegrams to all the members of the Security Council. Between 12.45 and 9.10 p.m. I talked with Major, Andreotti, Mitterrand, Mubarak, Assad, Kohl, Kaifu (the Japanese Prime Minister), Iran's President Hashemi Rafsanjani, and again with Bush (in that order).

The conversations differed, of course. They were influenced by the nature of the relationship involved. But the political content was the same. I emphasized the following points: first, since the Iraqi leadership had agreed to an unconditional withdrawal of troops from Kuwait, the situation had changed; second, this turnaround had been achieved thanks to joint action by the entire world community; and third, Iraq's unconditional agreement created a real possibility of a political settlement.

I proposed convening the UN Security Council to reconcile the plan already accepted by Iraq with the demands of the United States and other governments. I felt that the differences could be resolved in the Security Council within a day or two.

Reaction to my proposals varied, but most of the leaders I spoke to supported my efforts. At dawn on 24 February, however,

727

the American President told the world that he had given the order to start the land invasion. We all know what happened after that. The coalition participants, mainly the Americans, unleashed a powerful offensive that brought them complete success in a short space of time but entailed tremendous loss of life on Iraq's side.

On the night of 26–7 February, the Soviet Ambassador in Baghdad was invited to Iraq's Ministry of Foreign Affairs, where he met Aziz and Deputy Prime Minister Hammadi. They asked him to transmit to the UN Secretary-General and the President of the Security Council immediately through Soviet channels the Iraqi government's acceptance of Resolution 660. The full withdrawal of Iraqi forces from Kuwait would be completed within a few hours, they told him. Aziz also declared their agreement to implement Resolutions 662 and 674, which provided for the restoration of legal rule in Kuwait and the payment of reparations and compensation for the damage inflicted on that country by Iraq. On 28 February Baker informed Bessmertnykh that, in response to Iraq's agreement to implement all of the UN Security Council's resolutions on the Kuwait crisis, the United States had decided to halt military action.

Thus the curtain was lowered on events in the Persian Gulf. What did we have as a result?

One unquestionably positive result was the restoration of Kuwait's sovereignty and independence, the reversal of aggression, and the punishment of the aggressor, which in a way signified a victory for morality in international affairs. Another important achievement was the fact that, for all his efforts, Hussein had been unable to split the world community, which opposed the aggressor to the end.

But the other results of the events were the devastation of Kuwait and Iraq, tens of thousands dead and wounded, ecological disaster, and many other regrettable consequences, not to mention the fact that we had entered the new era, announced as the era of the new world order, to the thunder of cannon – not the best accompaniment.

Looking back, I want to say the following. We played a fundamental role in shaping the world community's common reaction to the aggression and its reversal, and we helped consolidate the

United Nations' role. We were able, of course, in conjunction with the leadership of the United States, not just to preserve but also to reinforce Soviet-American mutual understanding, trust, and partnership, sustaining them throughout this acute conflict – the first such test since the Cold War's end.

Finally, we persisted in seeking a political solution to the situation, one that would rule out war, casualties, and suffering, and although we did not achieve full success, that was not our fault.

Let me be completely frank. I cannot help thinking that the implementation of the plan for a political settlement of the Persian Gulf crisis was possible and that this did not happen because of the position of the United States, which at the last moment chose the military option. I believe that Washington preferred the arguments that a political settlement would be a mistake for the United States, since this would have raised the Soviet Union's prestige, something that many of the President's advisers always perceived as not in American interests.

From my point of view, it was these kinds of approach that prevailed in that dramatic moment. The United States needed another victory to demonstrate to the whole world what it could do and to put an end to any doubts at home about the President's resolve. There was evidently another serious motive, the desire to destroy Iraq's military potential, to deal a crushing defeat to Hussein's regime and to remove him from power.

TOWARDS A MIDDLE EAST SETTLEMENT

In the end, events in the Gulf were a stimulus for settlement between Israel and the Arabs. The Soviet-American relationship, tested in the flame of war in the Gulf, was now quite solid, and virtually for the first time, as Bush told me in Helsinki, the Americans began to co-operate with us in the Middle East. Having encountered aggression from within, the Arabs were more receptive to the idea of a peaceful settlement. Israel moved in this direction as well: its position was strengthened after Iraq's military defeat, but at the same time it felt even more acutely that the lack of peace was dangerous. Finally, the erroneous line adopted by the Palestinians in the crisis caused them much damage, which made them sit up and re-examine their position.

Assuming a similar assessment of the situation, we and the Americans, interacting closely, undertook active efforts to seize the opportunity to come closer to what was now our common goal, an international conference. When, on 11 September 1991, I received Baker, it was a sign of the times that now not only I but also the American Secretary of State were speaking out actively in favour of our co-operation in the Middle East.

Although the Americans were seen more often in public, and Baker really did do an enormous amount of work in the course of shuttling back and forth to the Middle East, in fact there existed something like a division of labour. The United States were talking mainly with Israel and its other friends; we were talking with Syria and the Palestinians.

Our efforts were rewarded. The International Conference on the Middle East opened in Madrid on 30 October 1991. This was a genuine breakthrough for the Middle East problem. Of course, ahead lay – and still lies – the long and difficult process of negotiations and the search for mutually acceptable solutions.

In the autumn of 1993, a ceremony was held in Washington for the signing of the accord between Israel and the PLO. A historic event. I say with great satisfaction that it would have been impossible without the tremendous efforts partially recounted above, in which ministers Shevardnadze, Bessmertnykh, and Pankin, and other Soviet diplomats participated together with their American colleagues, among whom I would like to name in particular Jim Baker. I am mentioning them because in 1993 their efforts were 'inadvertently' forgotten.

PART IV

1991, THE STORMY YEAR

27

THREATS AND HOPES

IT IS IMPOSSIBLE TO UNDERSTAND AND ASSESS THE EVENTS OF 1991 without an excursion into the past, however brief. What stages did we go through and what had happened to us and the country in the perestroika years?

The initial period, from 1985 to 1988, was a time of quests, trials and errors, as we hoped to remedy the glaring flaws of the system. And although we considerably exceeded all earlier attempts at renovating the system, we had, nonetheless remained within the traditional framework, without venturing to encroach upon the fundamentals of the Communist faith.

The second period, starting in the spring of 1988 and lasting until the beginning of 1990, was that of democratization. Having realized that a cosmetic job alone or even a major repair would not do, and that no innovative economic measures would work without a radical reconstruction of the political system, we introduced free elections, a parliament, and a multi-party system, and paved the way for the formation of an opposition. Briefly, we restored political freedom to society.

Finally, the third period, from 1990 to 1991, saw a struggle between the newly unleashed social, national and political forces. By the end of 1990 the very future of our society was being questioned: should the Soviet Union continue?

That was the message I tried to express in the New Year's greeting of the President of the USSR to the Soviet people. It contained an evaluation of the outgoing year and a brief account of our hopes and plans for the new year. Here is an excerpt:

733

'Next year will be special. In the coming year decisions will have to be made concerning the fate of our multinational State. For all of us, Soviet people, there is no more sacred task than preserving and renewing the Union where all peoples can live freely and prosperously. The peoples of our country have cohabited for centuries. They also share common values acquired during the Soviet years as well as the memory of the victory in the most destructive of wars. Perhaps at the present time there is a particularly keen awareness that we must not shut ourselves off from each other. And it is only by joint effort that we shall be able to emerge from the crisis, rise to our feet and firmly embark upon the path of renewal. It is in the Union and its preservation and renewal that the key to the solution of the enormous, momentous tasks that confront us in 1991 is to be found.'

With these hopes we entered the year 1991. But a storm broke out in the first half of January.

THE LITHUANIAN SYNDROME

Many a dramatic page in Russian history has been linked to Lithuania. Recent history has been no exception. On Lithuanian territory, many of the issues affecting the future of the whole country were first put to the test. It was a battle for people's hearts and minds. Despite the fact that the population of the republic was 80 per cent Lithuanian, and only 20 per cent Russian and other nationalities, Sajudis – the Popular Front – fomented the fear that if Lithuania were to remain part of the USSR, Lithuanians might become a minority on their ancestors' soil – as had already almost happened in Estonia and Latvia. Needless to say, such fears touched a chord not only among the intelligentsia or people close to the émigrés, who had always been hostile towards the Soviet Union, but also among many ordinary Lithuanians.

Besides the political arguments there were possibly weightier practical ones, on these lines: 'Even though we in Lithuania have the most developed agriculture in the USSR and deliver a great deal of livestock to Leningrad, Moscow and various Russian

oblasts, we sometimes have shortages of meat.' But such arguments conveniently ignored or underestimated the vast extent of
supplies flowing in the other direction, from Russia – grain, oil
and metals, as well as industrial and consumer goods. Not a word
was said about the considerable privileges granted for political
reasons to the Baltic states by the Soviet government since the
initial post-war years. Thanks to these privileges and, of course,
to greater productivity, their standard of living had always been
higher than in other regions of the Union. Few people have given
serious thought to that balance. Listening to the speeches of the
Sajudis propagandists, not only Lithuanians but people of other
nationalities living in Lithuania were fired by the idea that they
would live much better once they had shaken off the obligation
to 'pay tribute' to Moscow.

The fact that it needed no great effort for Sajudis to sway the
consciousness of an overwhelming majority of society may be
attributed, to a certain extent, to the weakness of the incumbent
Party leadership. After Griskevicius' death, Songaila was elected
first secretary of the Central Committee of the Communist Party
of Lithuania. A man of even temper and integrity, who had spent
a lifetime in agrarian work, he was not equipped to cope with such
a complex political situation. I talked to Songaila several times
and realized that he was totally at a loss. Brazauskas replaced him
as first secretary, and in fairness it should be pointed out that he
assumed the leadership at a time when the initiative was already
in the hands of Sajudis. Many Sajudis members were also
members of the Communist Party, and they reacted sharply to the
accusation that they owed their allegiance to Moscow, not to
Lithuania.

This was the situation that Brazauskas had to cope with. And
after some hesitation he embarked upon the path of proclaiming
the independence of the Communist Party of Lithuania and its
withdrawal (possibly via certain transitional stages) from the
CPSU. That was obviously a blow to the unity of the CPSU. The
result was that the 'Lithuanian syndrome' acquired a dual
character and developed concurrently along Party and state lines.

I think that Brazauskas was fully aware of the problems that
would arise if the Lithuanian Communists withdrew from the

CPSU. But he realized that the Party was doomed if it did not affirm its national character.

At the time I deemed it possible to preserve the unity of the CPSU while ensuring the independence of the republican Communist Parties or, at worst, creating a kind of federal union between them.

I suspect that the decision to leave the CPSU was made only after the will of the people to achieve full independence had fully crystallized. Until this point, both sides had been searching for an acceptable way to co-exist within the framework of a single political structure – the Party and the state. I still believe that it would have been possible, but for the stand taken by Russia.

I considered it of the utmost importance to understand what was going on in Lithuania and to see whether those who favoured complete secession could be persuaded to change their minds. In January 1990 I undertook a fact-finding trip there, on which I was accompanied by the chief editor of *Pravda*, Frolov, who had by then been elected a Central Committee secretary. At Vilnius Airport we were met by Brazauskas and Burokiavicius, Central Committee secretary of the Communist Party of Lithuania 'based on the CPSU platform',[1] as well as other officials. The details of that journey are engraved in my memory. We were met everywhere with friendliness and goodwill, but virtually from my initial talks with the population of the Lithuanian capital on Lenin Square up to the moment of my departure, the sole topic of discussion was the secession of Lithuania from the USSR. I urged the Lithuanians to reconsider the situation, and to realize that the change being foisted upon them by the separatist movement was fraught with danger. 'We must have a renewed Party, a renewed federation, a renewed democratic structure, a renewed society. We must build it up by interacting and co-operating and not by destroying, not by excluding, not by denouncing and not by sowing distrust and hostility among each other.'

At a factory where the work-force consisted of 30 per cent Lithuanians, about the same percentage of Poles, 20 per cent

[1] A minority in the Lithuanian Communist Party that was opposed to severing ties with the centre.

Russians, Belorussians, etc., all these arguments were, I believe, correctly understood. It was also comparatively easy to arrive at a mutual understanding in talks with the peasants, whose down-to-earth common sense enabled them to visualize the adverse consequences of a break with Russia.

It was a different matter altogether with the artistic and academic intelligentsia I met at the Vilnius Press House. There, I am afraid, I was unable to make any contact with my listeners, since most of them were adamant supporters of secession. Before and after that meeting I had repeated encounters with educated, well-disposed people, tolerant by nature, who nonetheless failed to respond to the most weighty and irrefutable arguments because they were obsessed by a fanatical determination to act in accordance with what had become their creed.

'The path towards political sovereignty,' I stated, 'to economic independence, cultural development and the preservation of all traditions is a single one – through a union of sovereign states united in a federation. And do you know what a federation means?'

From the meeting came shouts: 'We do, we do!'

'How do you know? We have not lived in one. The Lithuanians are a rather reserved people. But what happens to this reserve, what happens to your open-mindedness, when I ask you to listen to my arguments?'

I am afraid it was a rhetorical question. The answer was to be found in the fact that by this time Sajudis had taken over all the mass media. With television drumming propaganda into them every day, the entire population soon came to believe that separately they would live much better.

The participants in the Press House meeting stood firmly on their position. Here, for example, is what an assistant professor of Vilnius University, Jurgis Karosas, said to me:

'During a meeting with artists, you, esteemed Mikhail Sergeyevich, attempted repeatedly to encourage our speakers to come up with a clearer analysis of the decision for independence made at the XXth Lithuanian Party Congress. Obviously it is based on the national revival of Lithuania engendered by perestroika. Both are intertwined and that is exactly how we see it. After the CPSU resolved to base our political life on democracy, we in the Republic have considered it, first and foremost, as a proclamation of the right to self-determination. To us, democracy is identical with this right. You, Mikhail Sergeyevich, have taken democracy seriously and we, in turn, also took our right to freedom seriously. Hence our being rebuked for the separatist tendency in Lithuania and the Communist Party of Lithuania sounds very bad. We contend that freedom is the inalienable right of the nations and not a luxury that one can do without.

'Dear Mikhail Sergeyevich,' continued the academic, 'we are convinced that you are sincere in wishing all people well and understand that you cannot make a people happy against its will.'

It was an indisputable argument. In our talks another argument was brought up: that Lenin had recognized Lithuanian independence in 1918; the present leadership – if it were sincere – must do likewise. I did not dodge the subject. But invariably I stressed: *'We need a constitutional mechanism for the implementation of that right*. A relevant draft law exists already and will be presented for all-Union discussion. If anyone imagines in a simplistic manner that on the very first day after elections you could immediately withdraw from the Soviet Union – well, political decisions are not taken that way!'

In short, I must confess that, while admitting the possibility of secession in principle, I had hoped that the development of economic and political reform would outpace the secession process. Having experienced the real benefits of a federation, people would no longer be obsessed by the idea of full independence, and the problem would be resolved to everybody's advantage.

The beginning had already been made: the Supreme Soviet was about to make decisions on land and property problems. Next on the agenda was the law on the division of competence between union and republic organs.

'The Lithuanian situation,' I said on one of my last days in Vilnius, 'does not only have a republican but also a nationwide significance. It is a matter relevant to the fate of the country, its role, its impact and the implementation of our plan that we consider in a broad historical context a transition from an authoritative and centralistic model of society to a humane, democratic socialism that works for the individual. How can it possibly divide us?'

I left Lithuania with mixed feelings of concern and hope. But very soon it turned out that we had failed to stem the course of events. Less than two months later Sajudis scored a landslide victory in the elections to the Lithuanian Supreme Soviet. Without waiting for the second round of voting its leaders convened the deputies on the night of 11 March, opened the session and adopted a decree on the independence of Lithuania, proclaiming the abrogation of the Soviet constitution and declaring null and void our state laws on the territory of the republic. The reasons for such haste were easily understood. On 12 March the special third session of the Congress of People's Deputies (CPD) was to open and at that session the first Soviet President was to be elected. Landsbergis and his 'team' obviously intended to use the session to proclaim the secession of Lithuania from the USSR, thereby lending an ostensible legitimacy to their patently anti-constitutional actions.

Transparent hints were dropped to my aides to the effect that if I were to adopt 'a sensible position' on the independence of Lithuania, the deputies from the Baltic republics would vote in favour of my election to the presidency. It goes without saying that such proposals were spurned.

By the time the debate on the Lithuanian problem started at the Congress I was already President of the USSR. Many speakers were outraged at the ultimatum presented by the Lithuanian parliament. Its newly elected President, V. Landsbergis, showed disdain for the CPD by refusing to come to Moscow to explain the intentions of the new legislative body. It was pointed out that the deputies of the Lithuanian Supreme Soviet represented just over 40 per cent of the population and were therefore not qualified to take a decision on such a fateful question as secession from the Soviet Union. Some deputies who represented the Russian-speaking population of the Baltic states expressed concern lest an emotional over-reaction of the Congress to the illegal action of the new Lithuanian leadership provoked ethnic tensions. Others, however, reproached me for not taking firmer action.

I endorsed, with some amendments, the draft resolution of the Congress, prepared on my instruction by V. M. Falin. It may be summarized as follows: re-affirming the right of each republic to withdraw freely from the USSR, the Congress pronounced the decisions adopted by the Lithuanian Supreme Soviet invalid until the adoption of a law defining the procedures and effects of secession from the Soviet Union. The President of the USSR was entrusted with safeguarding the legal rights of all peoples living on the territory of the Republic of Lithuania.

The Lithuanian Supreme Soviet officially refused to recognize the Congress decisions or to abrogate its Declaration of Independence. Nonetheless, in Vilnius they were wary of acting under the provisions of that declaration and in its spirit and letter. In fact, things remained as they had been before: Soviet laws continued to be enforced in Lithuania and the entire structure of relations between the republic and Union bodies of government remained intact. Except for individual acts of provocation, no serious attempts were made to obstruct the functions of Soviet Army units stationed in the republic and so on. It was a war of nerves. Landsbergis was biding his time until the Union centre – overwhelmed by problems and increasingly drawn into the tough, exhausting struggle with the Russian leadership – would give up Lithuania as a lost cause.

Obviously we saw through these manoeuvrings and tried to counter them. We decided to create a commission, headed by Ryzhkov, to conduct negotiations with the Lithuanian leadership. But Landsbergis was obstinate from the start. He declared that negotiations might be initiated only in accordance with the protocol to be adopted in relations between sovereign states. We could not accept this, so the matter was deadlocked for months. Meanwhile the USSR Supreme Soviet had already adopted a law governing the withdrawal of a Union republic from the USSR, thus enabling the Lithuanian leadership to avail themselves of a legitimate course of action. But the point was that Vilnius did not want to act under the provisions of the law, fearing that the outcome of the referendum stipulated by that law would be negative for them. They feared that they might fail to obtain the required majority for secession. There were reasons for these fears, very serious reasons indeed, because the economic situation in the republic began to deteriorate rapidly.

The chairman of USSR Gosplan, Maslyukov, had warned at the Congress that cutting economic ties would inevitably entail losses of about 14 billion rubles for the economy of Lithuania and the other Union republics. In switching its trade with other republics to a freely convertible currency Lithuania would end up with an annual balance of payments deficit of 3.7 billion rubles. Perhaps these warnings were laid on somewhat thick, but the statistics were objective. The Lithuanian leadership took no notice of such warnings, relying on the benevolent attitude of the West.

In his speech Maslyukov quoted an excerpt from an interesting article published by the commission for the independence of Lithuania. It stated that the strategy for the republic's foreign economic ties should concentrate on the increased import of basic raw materials and fuel from the USSR, the acquisition of advanced equipment and technology through joint ventures with Western countries, and the export of production initially to the East and then, as standards rose, to the West. In other words, the intention to use Russia as a source of cheap raw materials to build a 'high-tech' Lithuania was bluntly and brazenly stated. One of the Moscow papers published a cartoon depicting a long-necked cow being fed fodder in Russia while being milked in Lithuania.

Landsbergis's policies had led the republic into a profound crisis, which he blamed on the Prime Minister, Prunskiene. The situation was aggravated by ill-considered economic experiments aimed at racing ahead of the Union, the so-called 'big leap'. Presumably great hopes were pinned on generous help from Scandinavian countries; they were long on promises, but slow to loosen their purse-strings.

The self-confidence of the Lithuanian leadership was undoubtedly buttressed by events in Russia. Landsbergis had seemed to be wavering, as he put out feelers to us. But as soon as the radical democrats secured Yeltsin's election as Chairman of the Russian

Federation's Supreme Soviet, the Lithuanians dropped their 'peace-making' initiatives. Moreover, as if regretting wasted time, the Lithuanian Supreme Soviet adopted one discriminatory decree after another against the Union and all-Union interests, infringing the rights of non-Lithuanian citizens. I have no doubt that Vilnius had ventured all this because an assurance of support and perhaps even a recommendation to take a harder line had been received from the Russian leadership.

Against this background, the Kremlin was bombarded with telegrams demanding the introduction of presidential rule. The Communist Party of Lithuania 'based on the CPSU platform' – that part of the Communist Party led by Burokiavicius, which opposed severence from the CPSU – was also getting bolder. The atmosphere had reached boiling-point, heated by the increase of retail prices. This stirred up discontent among workers of all nationalities.

First economic and then political demands were made: 'Down with the government, down with Landsbergis!' His poll rating dwindled. It became known that the deputies had discussed replacing him. How ironic that he should have been saved by his opponents! Had there not been a 'Lithuanian putsch', history might well have then taken another turn.

'DIVORCE' OUTSIDE THE LAW

The fate of Lithuania was being decided according to which of three tendencies would gain the upper hand. Landsbergis and his followers were firmly resolved to attain independence at any cost. It did not matter to them in the least that a considerable part of the population, including some ethnic Lithuanians, opposed a break with the Soviet Union.

Burokiavicius and his followers were ready to fight secession at any cost; their determination was nurtured to a large extent by the belief that the Union would not allow Lithuania to secede and would give them every kind of support.

The President of the USSR occupied the only position possible for him in full compliance with the Soviet Constitution and the resolutions of the Congress of People's Deputies, namely to use all available political means to avert the secession of the republic from the Soviet Union. And should this fail and the people of Lithuania express their will to separate in a referendum – to negotiate a legal 'divorce', to ensure normal relations based on future co-operation and partnership.

Today, when attempts are made to evaluate the events of 13 January in Vilnius, both politicians and analysts often ignore the context of the Vilnius tragedy. What did the facts look like at that time? On 8 January a large-scale demonstration against the price increases which had been announced the previous day took place in front of the government building in Vilnius. Prime Minister Prunskiene had to resign. Another mass demonstration in the Lithuanian capital followed the next day, its participants demanding the immediate establishment of presidential rule.

In a memorandum dated 7 January the Central Committee of the Communist Party of Lithuania based on the CPSU platform had proposed that I should introduce presidential rule. One after another, alarming telegrams were sent from the republic requesting measures to restore order there. But even in that situation I still believed that I had no right to resort to that extreme measure. On 10 January I addressed the Lithuanian Supreme Soviet appealing for the restoration of the USSR Constitution immediately and in its entirety, since the situation was becoming explosive.

The message was meant to avert further escalation of the situation – and to do so not by making them renounce their demand for independence but by a commitment to attain this goal within the framework of constitutional legality. Landsbergis failed to seize this opportunity. Why? I believe there is only one explanation. He realized that the clear fiasco of the political strategy implemented so far by the uncompromising faction of Sajudis would once and for all discredit them in the eyes of the population and compel them to yield power to a more moderate and sensible trend within the national liberation movement. Any compromise would have been fatal for Landsbergis's future as a political leader. He acted according to the principle 'the worse, the better'; he provoked the creation of the Committee of

National Salvation on 11 January. The anti-constitutional action of the Lithuanian Supreme Soviet in discarding the Union Constitution was followed by the creation of that unconstitutional body. The struggle now shifted from the constitutional track to overt confrontation.

In the two following days Vilnius was in the grip of a classic situation of dual power, when neither of the two sides succeeded in overcoming the resistance of the other. Yazov, Kryuchkov and Pugo reported to me that they had taken measures to prevent the situation in Vilnius from getting out of control, which would render the introduction of presidential rule inevitable. Only this matter was discussed and nothing else, that is, how to act in case of bloodshed.

A telegram from General Varennikov, who had arrived in Vilnius on 10 January, described the situation as dangerous and once again raised the issue of presidential rule. On the very eve of the tragic events in the Lithuanian capital, another attempt was made to assist the feuding groups to find a reasonable solution. On 12 January the situation in Lithuania was debated in the session of the Council of the Federation. Pugo presented a report. I stated that bloodshed was only one step away and proposed to send representatives of the Council of the Federation to Lithuania on a fact-finding mission.

Yeltsin said that the information available to us was of a one-sided character and that Union authorities were flexing their muscles. He argued, in particular, that the message of the President of the USSR to the Supreme Soviet of Lithuania 'was not worded in the proper way. It was not an ultimatum but neither was it an appeal to come to an agreement.'

The Chairman of the Supreme Soviet of Latvia, Gorbunovs, referred to Pugo's report as simplistic. And here is what Savisaar, the Estonian Prime Minister, said: 'We had arrived at a compromise with Yazov on the problem of the military draft. I asked: do we also have to expect a landing force? He flatly denied it. But an hour ago I learned that these units had already landed.' Yazov, however, asserted that no such troops had been sent to Estonia.

I reminded the participants that the hasty decisions made by the

Supreme Soviet of Lithuania on 11 March 1990 were the source of the current events.

'If we fail to observe the Constitution and the laws, we will plunge the country into an abyss . . . We must ease the confrontation and move towards an economic agreement between republics and a Union Treaty.'

I suggested to Yeltsin that deputies in the Supreme Soviet of Russia should refrain from statements that would only encourage the Lithuanian leadership to adopt a more aggressive position. In conclusion, I stressed that the reasons for the growing discontent in Lithuania were not to be attributed to the price issue alone. It was a matter that concerned the feelings of many hundreds of thousands of people – both the indigenous population and the Russians as well as the Poles, who now found themselves in the situation of pariahs.

After discussion, it was agreed that the fact-finding delegation would go to Vilnius immediately. On the same day, I announced that the crisis would be resolved by political means. But even before the delegation had arrived, the TV tower and the radio station in Vilnius were seized with the help of Soviet troops, resulting in loss of life.

The mechanism that was triggered off during the night of 12–13 January has to this day not been clarified; neither have the people who gave the command been identified. But as the saying goes, all secrets will out. Gradually many important details of the past are coming to light. I was recently given a book by the veterans of the 'Alpha' unit,[1] entitled *Alpha – the Top Secret KGB Detachment*. An excerpt from the book reveals that a KGB operation co-ordinated with the military was being planned. Some people may argue that this was undertaken in case an escalation of events resulted in a state of emergency which would require the intervention of the Union authorities. Maybe so. But on 12 January the Council of the Federation had discussed the situation and had approved political measures to ease it. We may therefore assume that the leaders of the power ministries did not agree with these decisions, though no objections had been voiced.

---

[1] Elite unit of the KGB, used only in emergencies.

Together they decided to launch this reckless operation, assuming that it would easily succeed. The main consideration was to complete it before the arrival of the Council of the Federation delegation. Thus they might confront the President with a *fait accompli*, thereby making him a party to this adventure.

I contacted Kryuchkov immediately after receiving news about the events in Vilnius, and demanded an explanation. The KGB Chairman replied that neither he nor Pugo had ordered the use of force. The decision was made locally, and he was not sure who was behind it. He tried to understate the extent of the clash, depicting it as the outcome of the obstructionist actions of local authorities and an aggressive nationalistic crowd. I interrupted him, reminding him that people had been killed and that the authorities would have to account for this. I was increasingly sceptical about the extent of popular support for Burokiavicius and his followers. Even if they had been supported before, Landsbergis would now look like a hero in the eyes of the Lithuanians. I demanded that Kryuchkov should support the efforts of the Council of the Federation delegation, headed by Dementei.

I also rang Yazov. 'Who sanctioned the use of force?' I asked. He replied that he thought it was the chief of the garrison. It was hard to believe that such a junior officer could have done so without the approval of the Minister. But at the time I trusted Yazov.

Many months were to elapse before documents relevant to the Vilnius events were discovered by the RSFSR Prokuratura, in the course of the investigation of the August 1991 putsch. A paragraph in the so-called 'Information on the results of the mission to Vilnius' revealed that some 'authorities' had sanctioned the operation. But since the President and the Council of the Federation had opted for a political solution and sent their envoys to Vilnius, what kind of 'authorities' were implied?

My worst apprehensions about the outcome of the violence in Lithuania were very soon confirmed. It was not only that the effort to avert the secession of Lithuania as well as that of the other Baltic republics from the Union failed after the bloodshed of 13 January. With the exception of some Russian-speaking people in the Baltics, public opinion began to change throughout the Union. People asked themselves: 'Is it really worthwhile to keep the Balts by force and shed blood? If they really are so anxious to become independent, for God's sake, let them go.'

The situation in the Baltic states worsened again a week after the bloodshed in Vilnius, when bloody clashes broke out in Riga. And events there developed according to a similar scenario. On 13 January a plenum of the Central Committee of the Communist Party of Latvia declared that it backed the demands of workers' collectives to dissolve the Supreme Soviet and all local Soviets in the Republic, to remove the government and hold new elections. Otherwise, the 'All-Latvian Committee of Public Salvation' was willing to assume full powers.

Underlying this statement was the hope that a return of Communist power in the Baltic states would trigger a 'chain reaction' in the rest of the Soviet Union. But the opposite was to happen. The weakness of their position led to defeat.

A few days later, a skirmish in the Latvian capital, between OMON (the special task-force MVD Units) and republican forces formed after the proclamation of the independence of Latvia, escalated into a real conflict. As in Lithuania, loss of lives served only to buttress the intentions of the Latvians to achieve total independence.

In the early morning hours, Yazov reported to me that during the night he had received three telephone calls from Gorbunovs' office. The chairman of the Latvian Supreme Soviet, 'who was out dining somewhere with a foreign delegation and could hear the shooting', had told his office to ask the USSR Ministry of Defence to send in troops to stop the bloodshed. Yazov told me that he had answered three times with a flat 'no', and had given an order not to react to similar requests whoever they might come from.

There was something strange about the whole business, I thought at the time. How was it that on such a matter Gorbunovs would not himself have picked up the phone and called the Minister?

There were reasons to assume that the armed clash in Riga had been deliberately instigated. The clues seemed to point to radically minded local separatists. After the Vilnius tragedy strict orders had been issued to refrain from the use of force. Moreover, a broad campaign launched in the national and international press must have influenced the leaders of our 'power ministries'. I doubt if at that time they were anxious to be accused of committing acts of violence.

Having embarked upon the path of attaining independence at any cost, the separatist parties who had seized power acted wilfully and, one might say, with neo-Bolshevik methods. And they were able to act in that manner only because they enjoyed the backing of the Russian leadership. As we all know, immediately after the Vilnius clash Yeltsin flew to Tallinn, where he met the leaders of the three republics and signed a document on the recognition of their sovereignty by Russia. Meanwhile – and this was without precedent in international practice – the leaders of Russia and the three Baltic republics addressed the Secretary-General of the United Nations proposing an international conference on the settlement of the problem of the Baltic states. In other words, it was a direct invitation to interfere in the internal affairs of the USSR.

The Russian separatists (the phrase sounds strange, indeed, but such was the political reality) exerted every effort to incite the Balts to secede. They used the Vilnius and Riga incidents to launch an all-out attack on the Union and the Union centre. On 20 January, a demonstration was staged in Moscow to protest against the events in Vilnius. Demands were voiced then and there for the resignation of Gorbachev, Yazov and Pugo. The press, inspired mainly by radical democrats, railed against the President. Aflame with 'righteous indignation' and not bothering to examine properly the secret springs that had triggered the bloodshed, they hastily declared the incumbent Union regime to be criminal, castigating the President of the USSR. I am referring, in particular, to the statement by Abuladze, Ambartsumov, Bovin, Golembiovsky, Petrakov, Popov, Ryzhov, Shatalin, Stankevich, Starovoitova and Zaslavskaya on the events in Lithuania, published in *Moskovskiye Novosti* (*Moscow News*). By the way, none of them mentioned the unconstitutional actions of the Lithuanian authorities.

Meanwhile, on 22 January, I made a statement on television about the events in Lithuania. I emphasized that what had happened was contrary to my policy. I said that the use of armed forces for the solution of political problems was inadmissible. At the same time I emphasized the need to remove the sources of conflict and to restore constitutional order. A statement of the USSR Prokuratura was issued on the same day, calling for the provisions of the law to be observed and denouncing the use of force. It was announced that the incidents where military force had been used would be investigated and the perpetrators punished under the law, regardless of their position.

Without further delay it was decided to appoint delegations to discuss the entire spectrum of political, social and economic problems with representatives of the Baltic states. Meanwhile an opinion poll on the issue of independence was conducted in Lithuania. The initiative reflected a certain shift in Landsbergis's policies. Sajudis leaders now realized that they would have to win the consent of the population before seceding from the USSR. Moreover, after the dramatic events of 12–13 January they had a unique chance to expect a positive outcome in the opinion poll. Upon the advice of my associates I adopted a decree, stating *a priori* that the results of the opinion poll could not substitute for the referendum prescribed by the law on withdrawal from the USSR. To be frank, I now feel that the decree was too hasty. The poll results showed an impressive majority in favour of independence.

Turning it over in my mind time and again, I still believe that events might have developed differently had it not been for the August coup and the conspiracy at Belovezh Forest in December.

THE BARRAGE – AND THE DECLARATION OF WAR

In August 1993, threatening to dissolve Parliament against its will, Yeltsin declared September to be the time of 'propaganda barrage'. Precisely that kind of barrage, using every available weapon, was launched by DemRossiya at the beginning of 1991, blazing away in an organized political frontal assault to weaken and eventually destroy the Union, the centre and the President. Not only the events in the Baltics but almost anything that was happening in the country was presented as the insidious plotting of reactionaries ensconced in the Kremlin. According to the press I had allied myself with the rightists, backed down, become a different man etc. Any government action was grossly misinterpreted. The most odious publications contained a direct appeal to disobedience and resistance. There can be no doubt that DemRossiya was ready to break up the Union even then. Clear evidence is provided by the press conference Yeltsin gave on 14 January, after his trip to Tallinn. He declared that the leaders of four republics – Russia, Ukraine, Belorussia and Kazakhstan – had decided to sign an agreement, without waiting for a new Union Treaty. He argued that attempts were being made to pressure them into accepting a draft that had been 'approved by the Party Central Committee and the USSR Supreme Soviet'. To dispel any illusions about the stance of the Russian leadership, Yeltsin added that 'we shall probably be unable to defend our sovereignty without a Russian army'.

Hence a Russian army was supposed to defend the independence of Russia against . . . the Union army, 80 per cent of which was made up of Russian soldiers. It is difficult to imagine a more irresponsible, not to say mad, idea. I was therefore forced to condemn categorically this declaration at a meeting of the USSR Supreme Soviet on the following day. At the time Yeltsin decided against carrying out his threat to create 'his own' armed forces, but the radical democrats continued their attacks on the Union centre.

Thus, instead of dealing with the country's critical economic problems, settling inter-ethnic disputes and the resulting conflicts, we were drawn deeper and deeper into the frustrating struggle with the 'democratic' opposition. We were exhausted, open to assault by conservative forces and, subsequently, also by radical democrats, who dealt the final blow.

Need I say, the ideologues of DemRossiya depicted it altogether differently. According to them, the President had withdrawn from the 'left centre', drawn close to the nomenklatura, and was now dancing to their tune. Any action by Union authorities and all presidential decrees were interpreted from that point of view. Measures designed to maintain public order came under particular fire, first and foremost my decree of 26 January, 'On measures to support the struggle against economic sabotage and other economic crimes', which granted the internal affairs and state security agencies rights of access and inspection at industrial and other official premises, the right to obtain documents and other information from the heads of enterprises and establishments, to seek banking information etc. Then there was another decree dated 29 January: 'On the interaction of the militia and units of the armed forces in law enforcement and the struggle against crime.' This requires special comment. Our long-suffering people were weary of the arbitrary repression practised in the past and the defenceless position of citizens exposed to the wilful actions of the authorities. Consequently even the slightest strengthening of the law enforcement agencies gave rise to apprehension. I believe such an attitude to be justified. Society should be vigilant and possess reliable mechanisms of defence against a nascent police state. On the other hand, it should be considered that the deepening economic crisis, the intensification of political struggle and the weakening of the central power had led to a steep up-surge in crime. Corruption had begun spreading in state organs. Moreover, abuses concealed previously from the eyes of the public during the stagnation period[1] had come into the open, thanks to glasnost. The press published articles on corruption involving a number of high-ranking officials, including the leaders of some republics, Union ministries and Party officials. All of this called forth justified alarm and outrage, and people demanded the adoption of firm measures.

Being guided by this, I signed decrees drafted by the relevant agencies. I saw nothing reprehensible in allowing assistance to be given to the militia by garrison servicemen to maintain order in the city. The enlisting of help from the army when police units are unable to cope with criminals is nothing unusual, not only in

[1] i.e. the Brezhnev era.

our country but in many others. Obviously, I could not have anticipated that the decree would be discredited from its inception because of stupid orders issued by local commanders. Ordering armoured carriers into the streets of Leningrad the day after its promulgation justly outraged the population and provided grounds for asserting that this entire action was not really targeted at criminals, who are, of course, never caught that way, but rather at demonstrations and rallies of opposition forces.

Regarding the intensification of the struggle against economic crime I believe the furore raised against that decree was inspired by the emerging mafia-like structures and shady elements. They were not anxious to see conscientious investigators endowed with the right to demand exhaustive documentation, study the content of safes whenever necessary etc. Therefore a counter-propaganda campaign was launched, with an earth-shaking protest about the repression of allegedly honest businessmen, violation of business secrets, and infringement of the rights of citizens. I am afraid that this din must have been nerve-racking for law and order officers, compelling them to display excessive caution so as not to gain notoriety – heaven forbid – as the oppressors of free initiatives. Let us reflect upon this. The situation then was not comparable with the rampant crime and corruption that we are facing today. At that time, the press was still debating whether the mafia had appeared in the Soviet Union. Now it is no longer debated; the bloody mafia shoot-outs in Moscow outdo those in Chicago during the prohibition era. Billions of dollars are flowing abroad, deposited in foreign banks to await the arrival of their gangster owners from Russia. All this goes on with the connivance of, and due to the inertia of, the authorities. I myself assume some of the blame for having failed to launch an anti-corruption struggle early enough and on a proper scale. However, it is a fact that all attempts undertaken to that end were blocked by the opposition, which was already becoming enmeshed in the corrupt structures of our nascent business world, and which once in power provided a reliable cover for them.

I should like to remind all those who still suspect me of devious intentions that on 13 February I addressed the staff of the USSR and republican Prokuratura and the republics with clear-cut guidelines on legal enforcement without any political bias. I stated that we were renouncing an administrative-bureaucratic system, but a new one – a democratic and law-based system – had not yet been created. In this interim state, our ship was being tossed about, and not everybody could take it. But we could neither back down nor support those who advocated ultra-radical solutions. Attempts to destroy the country and create parallel power centres could not be tolerated. The Prokuratura must prepare for work under the new conditions, based on creating an all-pervasive dictatorship – the dictatorship of the law.

I thus took a centrist position, trying to keep the state organs committed to the maintenance of order in the country, away from the sway of rightist or leftist extremes. Both these wings had initiated their long-term strategy: one, to break up the Soviet Union, and the other, to reinstall an over-centralized unitary state. We now know from a later admission by S. Shushkevich[1] that a secret 'preparatory' agreement had been drafted in February as a basis for the document adopted at Belovezh Forest some months later. Meanwhile, also in February, A. I. Tizyakov set about drafting documents on the introduction of a state of emergency. Two groups of conspirators were trying to undermine the Kremlin, each hurrying to get ahead of the other.

At the time I had no precise knowledge of all that intrigue. Although some information was available to me from various sources, it was mere conjecture. I was becoming increasingly aware that the political struggle in the forthcoming period would evolve primarily around the issue of the fate of the Union: to be or not to be – and if it were 'to be', what shape would it take? In the final analysis, the success or failure of economic, political and legal reforms also hinged on answers to these questions. I believed that none of these problems could be resolved without the participation of our people. I was honestly convinced that, on the whole, they would favour the preservation of the Union and its transformation into a full-fledged federation. The Supreme

[1] Chairman of the Belarus Supreme Soviet, one of the 'Belovezh three'.

753

Soviet endorsed my proposal for a referendum, and as early as 16 January a presidential decree was promulgated, setting the date for the referendum as 17 March.

There were many arguments about the wording of the question to be put to the referendum. My aides and I discussed this at length, and the subject was examined in the Council of the Federation and, of course, at the meetings of the USSR Supreme Soviet. We finally decided to ask the people: 'Are you in favour of preserving the USSR and forming it into a federation of sovereign states?' When we announced this to the public, the democratic press met it with hostility. Two arguments were adduced. Some were unhappy that the question linked the problem of preserving the Union of Soviet Socialist Republics with that of its renewal and transformation into a federation – the wording was, allegedly, too vague, providing a basis for alternative interpretations of the referendum results in future. The other argument alleged that there would be a distortion of the will of the people in small republics, since numerically their population was not comparable to that of Russia. Russian people would probably opt for the preservation of the Union and that would be decisive for the outcome.

Neither of the arguments stood up to criticism. Responding to them, I had to assert repeatedly that the mention of preserving the USSR was not a trick and that there was no hidden agenda behind it. By that time, the draft agreement on the Union of Sovereign States had already been completed. In answering the question about the preservation of the Union, citizens were therefore well aware that it was not the old Union that was implied but a new transformed and genuinely federal Union.

As to the republics, the arguments of the opponents of the referendum were simply ridiculous. The results of the referendum were to be published not only for the whole Union but for each republic individually. We had not the slightest intention of ignoring the will of the peoples of the smaller republics.

Perhaps the wording of the referendum could have been improved. But in such cases it is always difficult to come up with ideal solutions that satisfy everybody. I believe that the opponents of the referendum were decrying the wording only because they could not admit openly that they were actually opposed to the will of the people.

From the moment it became clear that the referendum could not be prevented, the separatists in all the republics unleashed a fierce campaign to convince the voters to choose a flat 'no'. Back in late January the founding assembly of the Democratic Congress bloc, with the participation of DemRossiya and a number of associated parties from the republics, convened in Kharkov, Ukraine. It opposed the retention of the USSR as a federal socialist Soviet state. And the so-called consultative council of that Congress, working in Moscow, appealed to all citizens to say 'no' to the renewed federation 'imposed upon them by the Kremlin leadership'. On 10 March the council launched a campaign under the slogans 'No – to the question of the union referendum' and 'Support the Chairman of the RSFSR Supreme Soviet, Boris Yeltsin'.

Yeltsin and his followers understood that a positive outcome of the referendum would strengthen the Union centre and would provide the USSR President with legal and moral grounds to sustain his policy of preserving and transforming the Union. Obviously it was at variance with their plans, postponing the possibility of seizing power in the country for quite a while, possibly even permanently. Hence the fierceness of the radicals in attacking the referendum.

On 19 February Yeltsin made a sensational statement on television, calling for the immediate resignation of the President of the USSR and the transfer of all power to the Council of the Federation. His speech teemed with rude and offensive remarks about me. His hands were trembling. He was visibly not in control of himself and laboriously read out a prepared text. Twenty days later, on 9 March, at a regular appearance in the Dom Kino,[1] Yeltsin urged his followers 'to declare war on the leadership of the country that is dragging us down into the mire.' He stated that I was 'deceiving our people and our democracy'. On 10 March a rally in Moscow was held 'in support of Yeltsin, the coal-miners and the sovereignty of Russia.'

---

[1] Headquarters of the cinematographical union.

755

The purpose of these confrontational actions was obvious. They were generated by a desire to undermine the results of the referendum in advance. Radical democrats realized that the answers to the referendum were likely to be positive. They regarded it as a likely success for Gorbachev, and that was at variance with their plans.

I had already anticipated Yeltsin's reaction to the referendum. He was sitting on my right in the Presidium of the Congress of People's Deputies and in a fit of fury threw down his earphones when the Congress voted in favour of a nationwide referendum. He felt he had been 'outwitted' and that his ambitious plans might be thwarted.

But by the kind of paradox which occurs occasionally in politics, Yeltsin then succeeded in improving his position somewhat, owing to the very opposition to him which had formed in the Russian Supreme Soviet. I am referring to the statement by six members of the Presidium of the Russian Supreme Soviet who denounced the actions of their leader in strong terms and called for his resignation. It was a bold step, motivated by a growing perception of a confrontation fanned by Yeltsin's followers. I have to dispel any suspicion that this action had been planned in the Party Central Committee. Nonsense! The Presidium members acted quite independently – besides, they were not the kind of people who would do as they were told. To begin with, they had been willing to work loyally with Yeltsin as his deputies. However, it had not taken them long to realize that he was more interested in power than in solving the practical problems that beset Russia at the time. But 'the six' committed a psychological error and in fact came to Yeltsin's rescue. The radical democrats reacted to their statement by contending that a Kremlin-inspired plot was in the making. They mobilized all their forces and organized several demonstrations in Moscow in defence of their leader. This tried-and-tested method, playing on the compassionate nature of our people towards those who are insulted and persecuted, worked once again. The initially unfavourable impression created by Yeltsin's address was defused. In the eyes of onlookers the contest he had launched ended in a kind of draw.

Yeltsin had demanded my resignation and Yeltsin's associates, in turn, wanted to 'dismiss' him. People didn't like such infighting and failure to co-operate at the top. And it was an expression of the popular mood that thousands of letters were sent to the President's office with urgent requests for me to reach out to Yeltsin. Apparently a similar flood of mail was directed to the Russian White House.

The IIIrd RSFSR Congress of People's Deputies opened in an extremely tense atmosphere. On the eve of the Congress, participants in a rally had threatened to 'storm the Kremlin'. In order to avert unrest, militia units and Interior Ministry forces were deployed in the capital on the opening day. The confrontation had reached a dangerous point. Both sides realized this and acted accordingly.

When the Congress continued its work on 29 March, Yeltsin refrained from antagonistic statements, and even spoke in favour of dialogue and co-operation with the centre. Nevertheless, throughout his entire report he insisted that two political courses – the policy of DemRossiya, aimed at radical transformations, and that of the Union leadership, allegedly retrograde in spirit – were incompatible.

The debates at the Congress were heated, since by then Yeltsin's conciliatory gestures lacked credibility. In the end his supporters had to exert great efforts to prevent their boss from being ousted. For obvious reasons I agreed with those who criticized Yeltsin at the Congress. Yeltsin was helped out of trouble by Aleksandr Rutskoi, who announced the creation of a new group of deputies, Communists for Democracy, in support of Yeltsin. This changed the balance of forces at the Congress. And, finally, Yeltsin received backing in the least expected quarter: the leader of the RCP, Polozkov, denied that the Communists had demanded the resignation of the Chairman. I was told that Polozkov believed that we wanted to use him in the struggle against Yeltsin; hence his decision to take such a step. It helped Yeltsin not only to retain his speaker's chair but to be granted even broader powers by the Congress and to push through the decision to hold elections for the post of president of Russia.

A CALL FOR CENTRISM

A week after Yeltsin's provocative statements I went to Belorussia. It was a fact-finding mission, its main purpose being to investigate the situation in the regions most affected by the Chernobyl accident. At the same time I decided to use the opportunity to explain why Yeltsin's assault on the political course of the Union leadership was specious and meaningless, and to warn that political extremists were threatening to drive the country into an abyss.

Preparing for my visit to Belorussia, I was well aware of the mood that prevailed in the population of the republic. Economically it was better off than many others and seemed more stable in the face of the crisis that affected the country. But the consequences of Chernobyl caused great heartache to the Belorussians. Notwithstanding the substantial funds allocated to cope with that disaster, many problems remained unresolved such as pensions, the treatment of the victims and the relocation of the population from the areas affected by radiation. I was showered with letters requesting help. It was imperative to do everything in our power and to use all available resources to respond to this vital need. The problem was debated in the Union government, and it was decided to allocate additional funds to overcome the consequences of the Chernobyl tragedy.

Thus I did not come to Belorussia empty-handed. I also visited the disaster areas in the Gomel and Mogilev oblasts. The Belorussian trip was particularly memorable because it also provided an opportunity to set forth some important conclusions from the experience of perestroika, consolidating observations and evaluations made on various previous occasions. I believe my speeches during the meetings with the Belorussian representatives of the scientific and artistic intelligentsia (on 26 February) as well as with municipal and regional leaders, directors of enterprises, heads of farms and institutions, and war and labour veterans of Mogilev oblast are relevant to this day.

To begin with, I drew the attention of the audience to the danger of separatist tendencies. All that was positive and inherent in the process of democratization and decentralization and in the process of upgrading the level of independence of enterprises, republics, and regions – all this would inevitably backlash to its opposite extreme whenever it exceeded the framework of a balanced system. We had to remember that we needed each other, that we shared a common destiny, that we faced common problems. And it was only jointly that we would be able to solve them.

'Disintegration is fraught with danger,' I told my listeners. 'It opens up the path towards civic conflicts and I do not know how we shall determine where one or the other would live and where the boundaries would pass. And what are we going to do about the seventy-five million who live beyond the borders of "their" republics?

'We have renounced the monopoly of power held by the CPSU and welcome the political pluralism that allows diverse social strata and groups to express and defend their interests through parties, trade unions and other organizations within the incumbent legal procedures and under the provisions of the constitution. This is the ABC of democracy. Meanwhile, some of the nascent political movements are striving to implement their objectives not in accordance with existing laws but at variance with them. Impatience and radicalism are turning into intolerance and aggressiveness. Attempts are made to substitute reckless demands of total privatization for a course of action aimed at the creation of a mixed economy. The legitimate desire of the peoples to gain autonomy and bring about a national revival is being distorted, resulting in nationalist self-imposed isolation and autarchy. The "war of laws" that is being waged in accordance with that ideology has paralysed power in many respects, disrupted the market and is disorganizing the vital ties that took decades to establish.

'The groups that work under the banner of democracy are a motley crowd but the programme aims of their leaders are already clearly visible. Where do these "latter-day friends of the people" want to lead us? The first item on their programme concerns defederalization that involves splitting our great multi-national state into forty to fifty states, a migration of entire populations and a recarving of the boundaries between republics. Political

759

action under the programme's provisions consists of vitriolic attacks at the centre and the referendum on the future of our multi-national state. It is not surprising that the "democrats" formed a political alliance with separatists and nationalist groups. They have a common goal: to weaken and, if possible, destroy the Union.'

Noting the danger threatening from the right and the left, I quoted Aleksandr Solzhenitsyn: 'The most difficult task in social development consists in tracing a centre line. It does not help to invoke the throat, the fist, the bomb and iron bars. A centre line requires utmost self-control, the most steadfast courage, the highest degree of deliberate patience and the most precise knowledge.'

To me the centre does not represent a geometrical middle between two points. 'It is not a matter of occupying an interim position – this would be dead and deprived of a momentum. To me a centre is a direction that strives to reform society in a new way – although not by setting one against another, and not by means of confrontation, especially by declaring the opposite side an enemy, but on the basis of the consolidation of an over-whelming majority of society.

'In any society common sense prevails – that is the realistic basis of a political centre. It is not as vociferous and boisterous as the extreme wings but it encompasses the basic mass of people who are concerned over the fate of their country and at the right moment will say the decisive word. We must not disregard their opinion. This is what perestroika is all about, to make headway through far-reaching revolutionary reforms but not via confronta-tion and not by way of a new version of civil war. We had enough of the fight between the white and the red, the black and the blue. We are one country and one society and we must find answers by comparing the programmes before the eyes of the people and within the framework of political pluralism, answers that would satisfy the essential interests of the country and get it moving.

'A genuine centrist position would not tolerate either a return to Stalinism and stagnation or the recklessness of the radicals who are trying to drive the country into the market at one stroke. A centrist policy is a course of action aimed at consent and the consideration of objective interests inherent in society.' Speaking of its content, I defined it then as a *socialist orientation*. And even today I would not change that characteristic.

'We do not believe,' I said in Belorussia, 'that only adventurers are busy on the right and the left. True, there are leaders who sway back and forth without any sense of direction – some call for a reversal while others gallop forwards without considering reality, the state of mind and, in general, the situation in society. Yet even there, many sound forces exist. The main idea of centrism today and in perspective is, undoubtedly, the idea of civil and national accord. Not an accord void of principles and attained at any cost but one that is relevant to the goals acceptable to the majority of the people.'

That was the gist of my statements in Belorussia. I felt that these words were properly understood there. Yet the central press disregarded them. It seems that they chose such tactics because it would have been difficult to say anything sensible in response. They refused to propagate these ideas even by way of criticism.

Meanwhile the radicals, having completed their preparations, threw their reserves into the battle. I refer to the second widespread miners' strike, launched on 1 March, which called for the resignation of the President of the USSR. The demonstrations of the miners' collectives played a fatal role in the destiny of the Union. Nothing so undermined the position of the centre, as well as my own position as President. It was not solely and not so much a matter of the economic damage inflicted by many months of idleness in the mines of the Kuznetsk basin, Pechora etc. The situation in the country was affected still more painfully by the psychological consequences of the miners' actions. Essentially they were aimed at defending the interests of the workers in one of the toughest industries – but at the time they served to discredit perestroika. The situation was skilfully exploited by radical democrat ideologues who used it as a ram to destroy the walls of the besieged fortress. We had underestimated the danger.

The initiators of the miners' strike had prepared their plans in detail, including the outbreak of the strike on 1 March – the eve of my sixtieth birthday. The members of the Politburo, ministers, and many deputies, writers and journalists with whom I

761

maintained good relationships congratulated me on that occasion. My aides expressed their best wishes warmly. On that day we gathered at home in our family circle, there were many flowers, messages, congratulatory telegrams, from my foreign colleagues too.

Well, as to the press . . . I was congratulated by *Rabochaya Tribuna*, and *Komsomolskaya Pravda* published greetings by the Komsomol Central Committee, as well as a few of its own ambiguous remarks. The *Vecherka* (*Vechernaya Moskva*, the Moscow evening newspaper) carried an unflattering selection of statements.

The most joyous event associated with my sixtieth birthday happened on the following day, 3 March, when it was announced that the draft Union Treaty had been initialled by nine republics. The laborious efforts of the preparatory committee and, subsequently, the Council of the Federation had borne fruit. At the time I believed that we would succeed in overcoming the centrifugal forces, and that the life of the country would soon return to normal.

THE REFERENDUM OF 17 MARCH

With the approaching referendum, political activity increased dramatically. New organizations sprang up. At the end of February the creation of the Movement for a Great and United Russia was announced, its main protagonists being Prokhanov, Starodubstev and Polozkov. At the same time, the Scientific and Industrial Union[1] was formed, led by Arkady Volksky. I have already mentioned the Democratic Congress, which united several parties into an electoral bloc.

As to the March 1991 referendum, the deployment of forces was extremely simple. On one side was the DemRossiya movement, whose ideologues brazenly and overtly urged the voters to answer 'no' to the question on the preservation of the Union. On the other was the CPSU, and practically all the other parties and

[1] An association of leaders of science and industry.

groups existing at the time, which championed the preservation of our Union.

Public polls held a week before the voting suggested an unpromising outcome for the radicals. Anticipating the inevitability of defeat on the fundamental question of the referendum, they decided to save face by including on the Russian ballot-paper a question asking whether the post of President of the RSFSR should be created. It was easy to guess that the answer would be positive, inasmuch as by that time many republics had already acquired their own President or were preparing to do so.

The Ukrainian Supreme Soviet tacked its own question onto the referendum. The motive of the separatists who had insisted on it was manifest: to keep a loophole that would allow them to interpret the results of the referendum in their favour or, at least, as neutral. By using this 'peg' they succeeded eventually in conducting another referendum, and, following the Russian leadership, inflicted the second blow to the Union.

On 15 March I addressed the citizens of the country on television. The speech was short but its preparation had involved great effort. It was a matter of using the right words to reach the minds and hearts of the people. It was important to remember that the same idea would be perceived differently in Russia, Central Asia and the Caucasus. One single address was obviously not decisive, but I believe it played a positive role. Here is an excerpt from my statement on that occasion:

'In participating in the referendum, each of us should be fully aware of the fact that in our multinational state it will decide the crucial question relevant to today and tomorrow. The issue before us concerns the fate of our homeland, our common home. It concerns the future of all of us, of our grandchildren.

'The magnitude and significance of this question overrides the interests of individual parties, social groups and political and public movements. It is solely up to the people to decide upon it. I appeal to all of you, dear fellow citizens, to take part in the all-Union referendum and answer the question at stake with a "yes". Our "yes" will preserve the integrity of a thousand-year-old state, created by the toil, intellect and innumerable sacrifices of many generations – a state in which the destinies of the peoples and millions of human fates are insolubly intertwined – yours and ours.

'Our "yes" signifies our respect for the state that has repeatedly demonstrated its ability to stand up for the independence and security of the people united in it.

'Our "yes" signifies a guarantee that the flame of war will never again scorch our country, which has already suffered so much.

'Our "yes" does not signify the preservation of the old order, involving the dominance of the Centre and the lack of rights of the republics. A positive outcome of the referendum would pave the road for a renewal of the Union State and its transformation into a federation of sovereign republics where the rights and freedoms of citizens of all nationalities would be safeguarded.

'Our "yes" at the referendum and the conclusion of a Union Treaty will make it possible to put an end to the destructive processes in our society and to work more decisively to restore normal conditions for life and work.

'As I understand it, that is what the people need, it is that which they want most of all. They are sick and tired of the interminable arguments and the fanning of passions. They demand the solution of practical issues concerning production and the consumer market, legality, law and order and efficiency of State bodies. Briefly, people want life to return to normal.

'The success of the referendum – and this I want to emphasize – would open up new opportunities for the continuation of all reforms begun in the country to which we link all our plans.

'Let me add the following. It is difficult, if not impossible, to cope with the tasks that confront us without the consent and co-operation in our society. Therefore, before it is too late, we must halt the build-up of intolerance, bitterness and even animosity in some quarters. That too would have to be a joint effort by all. A positive outcome of the referendum would lay the ground for the consolidation of society.

'I am absolutely convinced that should society be split down the middle, there would be no winning side. We would all be losers . . .'

And thus the referendum took place. The victory of the forces for unity over the forces of schism and the break-up of the country was undeniable and convincing. Notwithstanding the all-out efforts of the radical democrats and the doubts voiced by the sceptics, the people voted decisively for the preservation and renewal of the Union – not only on an all-Union scale, but in each republic where the referendum was conducted.

Russia answered positively also to the question of whether it should have a president. I shall not weary readers by giving precise figures. The results of the referendum were published and repeatedly discussed in the press. But here is what I want to say. Two years later Russia would conduct another referendum – this time a vote of confidence in the President and the Supreme Soviet. Well, the somewhat dubious victory of the democrats would be used, as we say, 'up to the hilt', so as to implement strategic aims that had been planned long before. Competent lawyers, some of whom I had known personally and whose integrity I did not question, maintained against all the evidence that the voting results 'legitimized' the plans of the President to dissolve the Supreme Soviet. And so forth. None of these people bothered to look back, to remember how the sovereign will of the Soviet people expressed in the 17 March vote was later blatantly disregarded. But 76 per cent of the population of the whole country and 71.43 per cent of the population of Russia had at the time voted in favour of the Union. The referendum results in Ukraine and Belorussia had been just as impressive. However, this did not stop Yeltsin, Kravchuk and Shushkevich at their meeting in the Belovezh Forest. Their hands did not falter when they signed a document at variance with the explicit will of the Russians, Ukrainians and Belorussians and, I venture to point out, all the other peoples that inhabit our country.

Notwithstanding the efforts of radical propaganda to belittle the significance of the referendum, Yeltsin and his entourage had to consider its outcome. The meetings in Novo-Ogarevo, which served to defuse the atmosphere in the country for a time and laid the ground for overcoming the crisis, would not have taken place without that vote.

It was also reflected in our relationship. Yeltsin was preparing for the presidential elections in Russia and I felt obliged to maintain a strictly neutral position, although, to be quite frank, my sympathies were not on his side. The citizens of Russia had the right to decide freely which of the candidates they preferred. Yeltsin was the favourite. His choice of vice-presidential candidate was important; Rutskoi was undoubtedly a great help to Yeltsin, since he attracted the votes of the section of the electorate that continued to favour socialism.

But all this would occur later. At the time, the presidential campaign was in its infancy and the future candidates were anxious to be on good terms with anyone who could in any way influence the results of the elections.

In the spring months Yeltsin and I met and talked on several occasions. We discussed the whole range of current problems, usually in a good atmosphere. During these consultations we exchanged views in a serious and business-like manner, and no ultimatums were either given or accepted. However, when he was on television or speaking to the press, before the deputies of the Russian Supreme Soviet or at meetings in the Dom Kino, Yeltsin interpreted our talks rather strangely. It may well be that he was consumed by the desire to project a public image as a victor whose ultimatums were humbly accepted by the President of the USSR. Once or twice I responded to this by noting that the public should know how our meetings were conducted. He tried to justify himself, arguing that I had not been briefed correctly about his remarks.

In the following months, clashes between the Union and Russian leaderships did occur for a number of reasons. Not all the members of Yeltsin's entourage displayed a peace-loving mood. Some were simply unable to cool down after the 'anti-centrist' excitement. They had worked themselves up to fever pitch, and continued to condemn and castigate the President whenever the opportunity arose. Nonetheless, I had the impression that at that time a truce prevailed. Their attitude was: let us first have the boss elected to the Russian presidency, and then we shall see what happens.

Realizing the precariousness of this lull, and almost certain that the extremists in the 'democratic' camp would continue to invite Yeltsin to revive the attack on the centre and the Union President, I nevertheless deemed it necessary to make use of this respite in order to achieve practical results in the long-drawn-out work on the draft Union Treaty. I believed it important to bind the Russian leadership by a commitment that would be difficult to break. That was the origin of what became eventually known as the Novo-Ogarevo process.

THE NOVO-OGAREVO PROCESS

In order to explain the complexities and contradictions of this co-operation I should like to recall that at the IIIrd Extraordinary Russian Congress of People's Deputies on 30 March, Yeltsin expounded his programme while describing the actions of the centre as a return to the policies of the past. Two weeks later, in an interview with *Izvestiya*, Yeltsin said that those who claimed that he had made an 'irreconcilable break' with Gorbachev were mistaken; should the issue of defending the country from the rightists arise, 'we shall unite'.

Needless to say, the fears of a fundamentalist threat were not unfounded. The results of the referendum had strengthened my opinion (shared by my supporters) that the incipient trans-formation of the state structure of the country – that is, turning the unitary state into a federation – must be completed; but the conservative elements in the Party had decided that the refer-endum provided a mandate to preserve the Union in its original form, without any substantial changes. They simply ignored the patent fact that the electorate had voted for the preservation of the Union undergoing transformation. Moreover, inasmuch as the new Treaty on the Union of Sovereign States had already been published, the vote should have been understood as explicitly approving that new treaty.

Party leaders at the centre and locally were concerned that they were no longer all-powerful – in fact power was slipping away from them daily. After the amendment of article 6 of the Constitution, the Party remained for a long time the *de facto* leading force in society and ruled, so to speak, under its own momentum. But this could not last forever. An opposition with a hard-line programme came into being and dozens of other parties and organizations sprang up, encroaching upon the territory of the Communists and gaining control over certain groups and strata of the population. Instead of drawing the right conclusions and learning how to wage a struggle for the support of the masses, those Party officials who were accustomed to consider their power almost as a gift of God blamed the Central Committee, the Politburo and, first and foremost, of course, the General Secretary for their diminishing political power.

The Party was shifting, with natural feelings of bitterness, from the position of a ruling party to that of an opposition. This situation generated frustration among the rank-and-file members and animosity at the top. At a meeting of first secretaries on 30 December 1990, an undertone of resentment and lack of understanding of the course taken by the leadership crept into the speeches. And on the following day at the Central Committee plenum, where Ivashko presented a report 'On the current position and the tasks of the Party', my reformist aides took the full volley. Only respect for the post of the General Secretary curbed the rudeness towards me. But at the next plenum in April even that barrier crumbled, and a change of leadership was demanded.

The top Party group tried to bolster its revolt from the bottom. Groups were formed proclaiming as their goal a struggle against revisionism and a drive to restore the dictatorship of the proletariat. On 2 April the conference of the All-Union Unity for Leninism and Communist Ideals Society in Leningrad completed its work by calling for my resignation as General Secretary. This was the brain-child of the not unknown Nina Andreyeva. At the beginning of April, the Kiev gorkom, the Leningrad obkom and, finally, the Central Committee of the Communist Party of Belorussia made the same demand, and requested that an extraordinary plenum of the CPSU Central Committee should be convened to call the leadership to account.

Hundreds of messages from Party committees were piling up on my desk, stressing the need for extreme measures to save the socialist system, including the declaration of a state of emergency. On 22 April, while discussing the report of the Cabinet of Ministers on measures to cope with the economic crisis in the Union, the deputies, upon Pavlov's initiative and with

Lukyanov's tacit approval, began discussing the possibility of introducing a state of emergency in the country as a whole or in crucial sectors of the economy. Once more I had to intervene and return Parliament to its regular business.

I and my associates repeatedly discussed the situation, and after thinking it over for a long time, I decided to accelerate the preparation and signing of the Union agreement and to convene a meeting of the leaders of the Union republics. Eventually it became known in popular parlance as '1 + 9' or 'The Ten'. I should like to point out that there was no intention of turning these meetings into a body authorized to make official decisions. It was simply a more efficient way of completing the work on the Union Treaty. Nothing was done behind the backs or without the knowledge of the legislators, that is, the Union and republican Supreme Soviets.

I mention this because some have asserted that Yeltsin merely 'followed in Gorbachev's footsteps' in 1993.[1] A very superficial analogy, that one. I have never taken the liberty of encroaching upon the rights of the Parliament, still less have I created unconstitutional bodies by virtue of my personal decree. On 13 March I sought the approval of the USSR Supreme Soviet to create the USSR Security Council, a small cabinet composed of the Vice-President, the Prime Minister, the Ministers of the Interior, Foreign Affairs and Defence, the Chairman of the KGB, plus Primakov, whom I was going to appoint to supervise foreign economic relations, and Bakatin. Moreover, the Parliament gave the President an object lesson when it rejected Boldin, whom I had proposed as another member of the Security Council.

At that time we decided that the only rational response to the growing threat represented by the conservative revanchist forces was an agreement between the centrists and the democrats. That is simplifying the issue and speaking in general terms. As a matter of fact, the Novo-Ogarevo process was a considerably more complex, multifaceted phenomenon. To begin with, there was a meeting with Yeltsin in the country retreat of the government, where Brezhnev had negotiated with Nixon and where I

---

[1] When Yeltsin dismissed the Supreme Soviet, thus violating the Constitution.

met Reagan, Bush and other foreign heads of state.

We inched our way to that meeting, as if probing each other's mutual willingness to agree to a compromise renouncing the endless attacks and, particularly, the 'war of laws'. My staff prepared the text of a press release about the meeting, while Yeltsin kept his draft in his briefcase. However, eventually, both versions had to be thrown out. After a talk that lasted most of the day we issued a joint press release.

But only the following day Yeltsin convened a press conference in which he openly upset the balance we had achieved and tried to present the agreement as primarily a personal victory. As we say – you cannot do anything about it, such is his nature.

In those days I frequently consulted those around me and was strengthened in my conviction that only a mechanism that reflected the true alignment of political forces could sustain the reform effort. This type of political mechanism was needed both for the anti-crisis programme and for the Union Treaty. My meeting with the leaders of nine republics was scheduled for 23 April, on the eve of a Central Committee plenum, which was to convene on 24 April. It was important to have a clear plan of action to solve the economic and political crisis, co-ordinating it with the leaders of the republics and, subsequently, presenting it at the CC plenum, thereby forcing critics on the left and right to take a public position on what was in effect a national salvation programme.

From 16 to 19 April I made a planned visit to Japan. After my return, on the 23rd I held a meeting with the leaders of the supreme state organs of Russia, Ukraine, Belorussia, Azerbaijan, Kazakhstan, and the four Central Asian republics at the same Novo-Ogarevo country retreat. I addressed my colleagues, looking them straight in the eye. The circumstances were of extreme gravity, calling for unusual, co-ordinated and effective action. We had to put aside all our differences, which concerned relatively minor issues, even more so our personal likes and dislikes. It was our duty to place the interests of our country above all else. We should, I stated, draft a document, short and comprehensible to the people, which should make it clear to them that their leaders intended to act decisively and together. This would immediately defuse the stormy atmosphere. My message was picked up by the participants in the discussion. One after another, and each in his own way, they spoke in favour of issuing an agreed statement. There was a brief exchange of views about its content. Then I announced a break and went to my office, where Revenko and Shakhnazarov were waiting for me. I called a secretary and dictated the text. It was edited, typed and submitted to 'The Nine'.

Under the impact of the referendum we were able to formulate a clear statement on the Union. The states, united in the Union, would grant each other the most-favoured-nation status, while developing their relations with the other republics according to the generally accepted international rules. The President of the USSR and the heads of the republics called upon the workers to end their strikes and urged all political forces to act within the framework of the Constitution.

The document confirmed our intention to carry on with the reforms. There were minor amendments to the text. After final editing it was promptly passed on to TASS and *Pravda* for publication.

Having completed our business we had dinner. Toasts were proposed. A load was taken off our minds, mine and those of my colleagues, and a glimmer of hope emerged. And though afterwards some people tried to misinterpret the statement, the participants staunchly defended it. This was of major importance, since it lent weight to the joint document.

A characteristic fact: at the time, the Independent Trades Unions of Russia were planning a general warning strike in protest against price increases for food and industrial goods. The workers had been incited by the radicals, as part of their 'war with the centre'. After the April statement of the '1 + 9', however, that tension too was eased. With the exception of some workers' collectives who suspended work for only a few hours, no-one joined the strike.

PEALS OF THUNDER

The Party nomenklatura had no intention of surrendering without a fight. In the spring of 1991 the leaders of the opposition within the Party decided to launch an offensive. They clearly intended to make use of the increasing social discontent provoked by the price increases for food and industrial goods introduced on 2 April.

On 16 April Party officials from the hero-cities of the RSFSR, Ukraine and Belorussia gathered in Smolensk. Most of the participants were first and second secretaries of Party organizations. The official occasion was the preparation for the fiftieth anniversary of the outbreak of the Great Patriotic War. The organizers of these encounters and, in particular, Prokofiev, a Politburo member and first secretary of the Moscow gorkom, and Melnikov, a Central Committee secretary of the RCP, clearly had not come there to pay tribute to the veterans. In their speeches they sharply attacked the Politburo, the General Secretary most of all, and called for emergency measures to 'save the country'.

Smaller groups which met within the framework of the conference discussed how to present tough demands to Gorbachev and insist on an extraordinary CPSU Congress and a change of the leadership. Those members of the Politburo who tried to influence the General Secretary to use presidential power for the introduction of a state of emergency and the restoration of the diktat of the CPSU leadership had been informed of these conversations and perhaps even initiated them.

On the eve of the April Central Committee plenum, motions calling for the resignation of the General Secretary surfaced at the plenums of the Moscow gorkom and the Leningrad obkom. They had been approved by Prokofiev and Gidaspov, though they did not raise the issue themselves. They explained that they came 'from below', and reflected the sentiments of rank-and-file Communists. It is noteworthy that the calls for the General Secretary to resign dovetailed with the appeals from the leaders of DemRossiya to oust the President.

In brief, the conservative forces within the CPSU decided to confront me at the April CC plenum. Aware of this, I decided to take the bull by the horns, letting my opponents know that I would never capitulate. I was prepared for the worst, and resigned myself mentally to a possible split within the Party. But I was determined to fight it out with the 'retrogrades' who were driving the CPSU into the abyss.

Here are my introductory remarks: 'We have gathered at an exceptionally difficult time. The atmosphere in the country is heating up to boiling point. The atmosphere within the Party is also becoming charged. What is most important now is not to yield to the temptation of emotional decision-making. Obviously the current time is not one for quiet academic analysis. Attempts are being made to deflect the country from the course of reforms, either by driving it into another ultra-revolutionary venture which would jeopardize our statehood or by reverting to a thinly disguised totalitarian regime. I am referring to the plans of the rightist and leftist radicals.

'Both these trends are pernicious. And the greatest danger at the moment lies in their convergence notwithstanding their ostensibly irreconcilable animosity. Just look at the unanimity they display in their slogans! For several months now the extremist leaders of DemRossiya have been exploiting the – mostly justified – discontent among the workers, bred by the economic hardships, hoping to incite them to support their political demands, such as the dissolution of the Congress of People's Deputies, the Supreme Soviet of the USSR and the dismissal of the President and the Cabinet of Ministers. Now the Party committees in the RSFSR, some other republics and also a number of the Soyuz group of deputies echo these demands.

'Well, then, let us imagine what would happen if these claims were implemented. The breakdown of legitimate state structures would create an explosive power vacuum. The diverse political forces which coincide today in their extremist claims would find themselves confronting each other. A fierce struggle, possibly a free-for-all strife, would inevitably erupt. And whoever got the upper hand, arbitrary rule would take the place of democratic institutions. Let me put it bluntly – it would be a true dictatorship, not the fictitious one that according to some people exists in our present constitutional order. The historical chance to modernize the country through reforms, that is, by peaceful means, would be missed.'

The first day of the plenum passed relatively calmly. The publication of the Novo-Ogarevo statement had come as a tremendous surprise, and the firebrands were probably restrained by my opening speech. However, the peace was not to last. It seems that they consulted each other overnight, and the next day an array of speakers pounded the General Secretary. Gurenko spoke aggressively, not to say rudely: 'Even our enemies were unable to do to the country what has been done now.' He demanded 'that the status of a ruling party be safeguarded for the CPSU by law, and that the former system of appointing leading cadres be restored, as well as the supervision of the mass media by the Party.' It seemed incredible that anyone could be so divorced from reality. Prokofiev, Gidaspov and Malofeyev were not far behind: the first secretary of the Communist Party of Belorussia explicitly demanded that the President should declare a state of emergency. Others implied the same: let him either introduce a state of emergency or quit. After the most strident speech – I believe it was by Zaitsev from the Kuznetsk Basin – I took the floor. I said: 'I've had enough of demagoguery. I am resigning.'

I have been asked whether my decision was made on the spur of the moment, provoked by irritation and frustration, or whether it was a tactic, coolly planned in advance. Strange as it may sound, both assumptions are to some extent correct. Tempers were clearly running high. On the other hand, I was prepared for such an outcome. When the moment of truth came, I said to myself that there was no longer any room for wavering, and that a decision had to be made.

Many of my associates and well-wishers had tried to persuade me to step down as General Secretary. Although personally I could do without it (a horrific burden!), yet I felt that this was still not the time to divide the posts. After all, the Party was already being pulled asunder into national segments, and the Union state was exposed to the same danger. As far as I was concerned, I was committed to playing a unifying role.

The meeting was suspended and the Politburo met during the

break. I dropped in briefly to say, in no uncertain terms, that the Politburo members, especially Gurenko, were responsible for what had happened. Let them now unravel the predicament and make up their minds what to do next! Gurenko fiercely denied everything, jumping up and down.

People tried to persuade me to withdraw my resignation. I refused and withdrew to my office. The debates in the Politburo continued. By that time many of the Central Committee members who had objected to the attacks on me and strongly opposed my resignation began gathering in the meeting hall around Volksky, Latsis, Bakatin, Grachev and other comrades – I believe there were about seventy-two in all. They drafted a statement condemning the present composition of the Central Committee and demanding that a new CPSU Congress be convened.

Upon a proposal tabled by the Politburo an hour and a half later, an overwhelming majority (with only thirteen against and fourteen abstentions) voted not even to consider the question of my resignation.

After the vote the climate was somewhat cooler. I believe it was Nazarbayev who made the most strongly worded but equitable evaluation of the developments. 'We are dealing with an attempt,' he said, 'to bury the idea of a renewal of society and state, returning to a command system, to a totalitarian regime.'

The plenum adopted a well-balanced resolution. In my closing statement I noted that the necessary dialogue on the problems of future Party theory and policy still lay ahead, and this would be part of the discussion of the draft Party programme. The Party must change with society. Many Party officials were nostalgic for the CPSU's former monopoly of power. The difficulties experienced by Party organizations were comprehensible. However, that was no reason to spoil for a big and unnecessary fight. Instead, the right course to take was a centrist one, emphasizing the interests of the majority. The Party should focus on the implementation of the anti-crisis programme, thereby gaining authority in the eyes of the people. In conclusion, I called for responsible analysis of the joint declaration of the leaders of the Union and nine republics.

The attempt to force me to embark upon a revanchist path had failed. I had no illusions. The Central Committee majority had not voted against my resignation because they approved of perestroika or liked me personally. Being pragmatists, they realized that without me the Party would have no political influence at all and its leaders would have to console themselves with memories of past grandeur.

Today, turning over these developments in my mind, I often wonder whether I should have insisted on resigning the post of General Secretary. Such a decision might well have been preferable for me personally. But I felt that I had no right to 'abandon the Party', for this might well have jeopardized the reforms.

THE LAST PLENUM

I have attended many congresses and plenums in my time. Most of them are no longer remembered, though at the time there was the usual ballyhoo in the press. Some Central Committee plenums had a direct personal significance for me or remained engraved in my memory because of major problems that were decided there or clashes over policy. Some of them I have described already in this book. But without exaggeration I would say that the July 1991 Central Committee plenum had the greatest impact on the Party and on the development of our conception of the future. That plenum was the final round between the exponents of new thinking and the orthodox group. The draft of a new CPSU programme was adopted, signifying a final break with the past.

Quite a few hurdles had to be surmounted along the way. Attempts to water down the positive outcome of the XXVIIIth CPSU Congress were already being made at the RCP Congress, which convened in early September 1990.

Reform-minded delegates had no intention of surrendering. They instantly demanded that the discussion and the adoption of the programme be removed from the agenda, inasmuch as it was incompatible with the decisions of the XXVIIIth CPSU Congress. Furthermore, a proposal was tabled to consider whether the first secretary should be replaced. Heated debates flared up and were suspended personally by Polozkov, who informed the meeting that he was going to make a special statement at the next day's meeting.

I remember having tea in the Presidium room and asking Ivan Kuzmich what kind of statement he intended to make.

'I have thought the matter over once more,' answered Polozkov, 'and for the sake of normalizing the situation I shall not ask for a vote of confidence, as suggested by some people, but rather offer my resignation from the post of first secretary of the Central Committee.'

I arrived at the Congress to see for myself how Polozkov's statement would be received – but there was no statement. I learned that the first secretaries of the Party obkoms had met and unanimously rejected his resignation. Polozkov had had to bow, so to speak, to the common will. It was a cleverly orchestrated show.

This episode clearly revealed that the nomenklatura, having failed to get its way at the XXVIIIth Congress, had decided to recoup its losses at the Russian Party Congress. Opposition to the reforms, and to the General Secretary as their embodiment, was shifting to the obkoms and the emerging central structures of the RCP. It was directed from behind the scenes, at first covertly but eventually more openly, by the new Politburo.

I am not here referring to the leaders of the Communist Parties of the republics, who, absorbed by their own problems, paid little attention to the activity of the central bodies. I do not wish to suggest that amid the new members of the leadership there were not open-minded people. However, they were not the ones who set the tone.

From the previous pages the reader knows about the dramatic events in the early months of 1991. Confrontation in Lithuania and the other Baltic states, the 'declaration of war' by the radicals against the centre, the quest for an acceptable compromise initiating the Novo-Ogarevo process – all these testified to the need for the Party to adopt a new direction. The decisions of the XXVIIIth Congress laid a fairly good basis for such a process. Alas, the Party leaders were unable and unwilling to take the necessary action. They gave only half-hearted approval to every measure proposed by the President and the government.

I had warned that, unless the Party changed, it would lose all credibility. But all those warnings were in vain. My Party colleagues had other thoughts on their mind. They wanted an enforced restoration of the Stalinist model, or at least the Brezhnev variety. Their resentment towards me was constantly growing, as they blamed me for their own inability to march in step with the times.

The role of the instigator was increasingly assumed by the Moscow gorkom. At its regular plenum, attended by secretaries of CPSU hero-city gorkoms, Prokofiev blamed me for all the trials the country was enduring. The speeches of Gidaspov, Gurenko and Shenin said much the same. The fundamentalists clamoured furiously for the 'revisionists' to be punished and for groups such as Rutskoi's and Lipitsky's Communists for Democracy to be expelled from the Party.

The inability of the Party structures to adapt to reality and to grasp the new status of the CPSU, as well as their attempts to thwart and even wreck the democratic transformation, gave rise to disillusionment among the majority of Communists. In 1990 about 2.5 million people left the ranks of the Party. This process gained momentum after the publication of the debates of the April plenum. By 1 July 1991, only 15 million Party members remained. Thus, within eighteen months, over 4 million or 22 per cent had either left the Party or been expelled from it.

I repeatedly discussed the developments in the CPSU with my associates and Party members whom I trusted. There was but one conclusion: we must accelerate the transformation of the CPSU into a modern political party based on democratic socialism. To that end a new programme had to be rapidly drafted and adopted. The Congress commission preparing the draft in Volynskoe had already submitted five versions – but none of them satisfied me, as they all remained within the traditional framework. Under these circumstances my aides and I joined the drafting process. As a result a document was produced, approved by the commission and presented to the July plenum for consideration.

I raised the following question in the introductory part of my report to the plenum: 'Why does the Party need such a document now?' I began by giving a short answer:

'The former theoretical and practical model of socialism has turned out to be a failure. Hence a deep-rooted perestroika is needed, i.e. a democratic refashioning of all aspects of public life. It involves the renewal of the Party itself.

'Within the CPSU there are forces that openly challenge the course of action of the XXVIIIth Congress and question the current policy in its entirety. But those who are flaying perestroika and its architects are at variance with facts. Back in the early 1980s the country approached a state of depression: the old and new diseases of society were not laid bare and certainly not treated but driven underground. This practice brought on a severe crisis. It was not a crisis of some individual parts of the public organism; it affected the very model of "barracks communism".

'The totalitarian and bureaucratic system created by Stalin was able to achieve major results by concentrating the forces and resources of this enormous country,' I continued.

'Yet these extraordinary efforts gradually sapped the health of society, led to the waste of resources and removed the incentive to work productively and creatively. Lenin's idea that socialism could not be built on bare enthusiasm was corroborated in practice. It had been understood a long time ago that the potential of the system was nearly exhausted. It was for that reason that after Stalin's death an attempt was made to change the situation. Times were changing, mass repressions had ended and many aspects of a totalitarian heritage were denounced. Yet, at the root of power and government, the same bureaucratic system was at work, buttressed by an absolute dominance of state property. In substance, this was *post-Stalinism*.

'Perestroika was also vitally important because the country lagged behind the developed countries of the world in virtually all spheres of scientific, technical, economic and social progress.'

From a multitude of significant questions raised by the programme I singled out one which had been the stumbling-block for many generations of socialist advocates, the correlation of socialism and the market.

779

'In the past we thought these ideas incompatible, on the premise that market relations were contrary to the principle of 'distribution according to labour' (i.e. according to the work done by the individual), and allegedly served as a basis for the exploitation of man by man. In fact, the market *per se* does not determine the character of the relations of production. Since ancient times it has always been and still is the sole mechanism that allows an impartial assessment of each producer's labour contribution, excluding, to some extent, the interference of bureaucracy. The entire worldwide experience of the last decades leads to the conclusion that the principle of distribution according to labour cannot be implemented other than in a market economy. Not only are socialism and the market compatible, but they are indivisible in substance.

'Taking into account the characteristics and traditions of our society we do not want the total dominance of state property to be replaced by a similar dominance of private property. We need a mixed, multi-layer economy; the free development of all types of property, with an emphasis on share-holding and leasing, thus making it possible for more and more working people to become owners, proprietors and holders.

'Last but not least, a market economy would allow the country to become integrated in the world economy. For that purpose we need to have common rules applicable to entrepreneurial activity, a free exchange of goods, a stable currency and, first and foremost, a law-based state and civic society. Only by satisfying all these conditions shall we be able to occupy a worthy place in the worldwide division of labour. This may all sound like truisms, but we have arrived at such truths belatedly and by a tortuous path!'

Remembering the nature of my audience I chose examples that would strike a chord with those who had been brought up in the ways of unconditional acceptance of Lenin's legacy, and I spoke about his insistence on NEP – the New Economic Policy with free enterprise and foreign concessions – immediately after the civil war.

Referring to the Party, I said:

'Different trends have already formed within the CPSU, each

trying to shape it according to their own orientation, while the very fact of their activity provides a testing ground for a potential split. I am not at all inclined to make a sweeping accusation of those Communists who for various reasons adhere to one or another of these trends. In many cases they are motivated by an understandable dissatisfaction with the situation in the country and in the Party.

'The past pattern prevails over public consciousness, hampering an understanding of the meaning of ongoing changes. The representatives of what I would call Communist fundamentalism accuse us of a 'social-democratization of the CPSU.' They are harking back to the ideological divergences in the days of the revolution and the civil war, when Communists and social democrats found themselves on opposite sides of the barricades. Let historians unravel the vicissitudes of the past; but it is quite obvious that the criteria underlying such divisions then have lost their original significance. We have changed and so has social democracy. The course of history has swept away many demarcation lines in the workers' democratic movements among exponents of socialism.'

In my report I called upon all movements and groups to critically evaluate their behaviour, control their emotions and give priority to sound political planning. 'But, of course, nobody needs the "let's all live in friendship" kind of peace-making. The departure from the CPSU of some movements that oppose its strategic course of action and venture directly to violate the provisions of its rules would not damage the Party. On the contrary it would strengthen it.'

I concluded with a proposal to convene the next Congress in November–December, when the Party programme would be adopted.

Next came the speeches. Notwithstanding the advice of well-wishers who recommended me to be on the safe side and follow the example of former leaders in 'organizing' the debate (i.e. giving the floor to the greatest number of my followers and restraining my critics after a preliminary talk with some of them etc.), I refrained from such manoeuvring. I decided that it was high time to let those who opposed me come out into the open.

Should the majority reject the draft, lines would be drawn. Should we succeed in getting the draft approved at the plenum – the test of strength between the fundamentalists and reformers and the parting of their ways would be deferred until the XXIXth Party Congress. To be honest, I preferred the second alternative, since it would be more seemly and more appropriate for the Congress and not a plenum to decide upon the fate of the Party.

As might have been expected, the first speakers started with a flurry of critical comments and castigation of the draft programme: the adherence to Marxist-Leninist ideas was not affirmed with sufficient clarity, the transition to a market economy was considered in over-simplified terms, the services rendered to the people by the CPSU deserved greater emphasis etc. However, the greater the clamour and the more glum the faces of my aides, who feared that the editorial commission of the plenum would mutilate the draft, the calmer I felt at heart.

I was struck by the contrast between the content of the remarks and the tone in which they were made. There were no more than two or three hysterical outbursts cursing renegades and professing an ineradicable faith in our everlasting ideological dogmas. The overwhelming majority of the speakers assessed the draft programme from a position of greatly enhanced social consciousness.

Even those conservatives who longed nostalgically for the old order, or at least for some of the features of the cherished past, realized that, after heated discussion at the Congrees of People's Deputies and the sessions of the USSR Supreme Soviet, as well as in the press and on television, such concepts as the market, a civic society, a law-based state, free elections, political pluralism, a multi-party system, human values, integration in the world community and many other ideas of that kind were here to stay.

And what about the fanatics: were they out in the audience? Why did they keep mum instead of denouncing such heresy? I believe there were several reasons. First, the April plenum, when the hard-liners had to retreat from their attempt to oust the General Secretary, was still fresh in their memory. The alignment of forces had not changed since and another mutiny was bound to fail. Moreover, they must have realized that in early July the

Novo-Ogarevo process had begun to bear fruit and the public was in the mood for conciliation. Under the circumstances a split in the CPSU would boomerang, affecting primarily the Party bosses. Last but not least, many of them no longer believed in the possibility of achieving their goals through discussion; they began aiming at 'decisive' and coercive measures instead.

At any rate, the plenum entrusted the editorial commission with the final version of the draft and the commission approved it without major amendments.

Concluding the work of the plenum, I underlined the need for broad-mindedness and tolerance towards dissent. Society, weary and unwilling to suffer new upheavals, confrontation and excessive social tension, welcomed with relief the appeal to place the interests of the people, the country and the state over and above all Party and political disputes. Grasping this general principle, it was of major importance to stay the course of reform and to learn to engage in democratic politics in a civilized manner.

For those who were put off by the notion of 'reformism' I quoted Lenin: the revolutionary approach, 'in the sense of a direct and complete break with the old', must be replaced by 'an entirely different approach of a reformist type.

'We are facing the need for another radical change in our concept of socialism. We shall not find any answers within the framework of the old model, just like our foreign friends whom we helped to "experiment" with this model in their respective countries. It is indeed a crisis of socialism and the socialist idea, but it can be resolved.'

My impression of the July plenum may be summed up as follows: a realistic prospect of reforming the CPSU had opened up. Yet whether this possibility would be realized still hung in the balance.

28

ECONOMIC RECOGNITION FOR A CHANGING SOVIET UNION: THE GROUP OF SEVEN IN 1991

PERESTROIKA WITHIN THE SOVIET UNION REQUIRED A CHANGE IN the way we conducted our foreign trade, an organic integration with the world economy. This had been one of the main themes in my speech to the United Nations General Assembly in December 1988 and in my subsequent conversations with representatives of the influential non-governmental Trilateral Commission, which was preparing a report on the state of and prospects for relations between East and West at the time. A large group of its members, including Henry Kissinger, former French President Valéry Giscard d'Estaing, former Japanese Prime Minister Yasuhiro Nakasone, and the American banker David Rockefeller, had come to Moscow looking for first-hand information to help them write the report. For several hours I discussed with them the prospects for our entry into the world market, forms of participation in world economic ties, the rules of multilateral co-operation, conditions for the Soviet Union's inclusion in the activities of the international economic organizations, and so on.

Later, when I learned that there was to be a Group of Seven meeting in Paris, I decided to address a special letter to President Mitterrand in order to put these questions directly before the leaders of the most important Western nations. This letter was essentially the beginning of our rapprochement with the Group of Seven which led two years later to my meeting with that Group in London in the summer of 1991.

There were many obstacles to be overcome first, however. At the next annual meeting of the Seven, in Houston, the situation in the Soviet Union and Eastern Europe was the main topic of discussion. I sent the participants a new message. I was increasingly convinced that we needed direct dialogue with the Seven.

In my meetings with representatives of the West in the autumn of 1990, I kept stressing that it was our job to solve our economic crisis and reform our economy, and no-one could do that for us. We understood this. But I told them that the West ought to have an interest in our success as well. After all, the creation of a healthy economy in our immense country was in the Western interest. Therefore, at the most acute, critical stage in the reforms, we had the right to expect that our partners would take steps in our direction.

I must say that the initial reaction was cautious – sceptical, actually. Directly or indirectly, I heard the same theme in the statements of our Western partners: reform in the Soviet Union was not moving quickly enough, the Soviet economy was still not sufficiently 'market-oriented', and this limited the opportunities for action by the West.

This theme also came through in the remarks of James Baker, whom I received on 15 March 1991. The background was very complex: a critical domestic political situation on the eve of the referendum on the fate of the Union; a beleaguered consumer market; and a troubled international scene. Baker did not try to conceal the Americans' concern. 'Today, we often hear that President Gorbachev's policy has taken a turn to the right,' he told me. 'It is said that you've changed your course. I have to be frank, sometimes we do get concerned when we see certain indications of this, especially on arms control. However, we have no doubt that the adjustments you have made in your policies are meant only to ensure success for the reforms and democratization and that there has been no fundamental change. We want to believe this and we do.'

'Still,' I had to ask, 'do you just want to or do you really believe it?'

'Both,' Baker replied. 'Recently I was talking with President Bush, and we both came to the conclusion that your place in history is assured if you don't change course. All your enormous achievements will go down in history if you do not turn back. This is one of the main reasons why we don't believe that there will be that kind of turnabout.'

That day I was frank with Baker. He deserved as much, this thoroughly unsentimental and thoughtful man who had already understood much about our affairs. But I did have to remind him of something. In an increasingly strained situation, I told the Secretary of State, 'it takes huge reserves of strength, faith, and conviction to keep matters under control. It also takes a certain amount of tactical manoeuvring.' The goal was the same, though: 'to neutralize both radical wings, left as well as right, and avoid civil strife. I am determined to act exclusively by constitutional, democratic methods.'

The Secretary of State's ideas on the economy were rather straightforward. 'As we see it,' he stated, 'things are not moving in the right direction.'

I objected: 'That assessment of our economic course is mistaken.'

'I hope I am wrong,' he reacted immediately.

'We are not changing our course,' I continued. 'We want to go all the way to a mixed market economy. But not the way we did with collectivization. In time we shall be able to move forward more rapidly, but first we have several matters to take care of. We are open to developing co-operation with Western countries more rapidly.'

'Of course,' said Baker, 'only the Soviet President himself can decide what he is prepared to agree to. America cannot decide for you. However, we do know what you should not do if you want to open the country up to business and capital from the West: your Prime Minister should not go talking about some plot by Western bankers to undermine the Soviet economy . . . That scares Western investors off. You have to act very cautiously if you don't want to trample the first seeds of a market in the Soviet Union.'

'There's a problem here,' I told Baker. 'What you consider

legal business people here consider criminal speculation. When I meet our workers, they always ask me, why have we let all this get started here? Why aren't dealers like that in prison?'

As this conversation shows, the words I had used in my talks with foreign leaders several years before were once again relevant: *we want to be understood*. A correct understanding of our economic situation and policy was especially important because the West's industrialized countries now had an opportunity to help our country along towards a market economy and its integration into the world economy.

By the spring of 1991, the chances of inviting the Soviet President to the Group of Seven meeting in London had increased significantly, the idea having received support from Kohl, Mitterrand, and Andreotti. John Major, who was to take over as G7 chairman on 1 July, was also favourably inclined. Mrs Thatcher actively supported the idea when we met in Moscow in late May. 'It would be truly a tragedy,' she said, 'if your efforts should end in failure merely because the West proved incapable of coming to your assistance in a timely fashion. Future generations will never forgive us for that.'

The situation was complicated, however, especially because of the American and Japanese positions. Bush was obviously in no hurry. We had some problems about the interpretation and implementation of the Paris treaty on conventional armed forces, and outstanding issues remained in the talks on cutting strategic arms. Quite possibly, Washington would link these snags in the disarmament process to our joining the Seven.

Meanwhile the idea of our participation in the Seven had already taken on a life of its own. In the first ten days of May, the British newspapers had reported that Major wished to invite me to London. My Nobel lecture in Oslo on 5 June was widely discussed and helped the European powers to insist that I should be invited to London.

I received my formal invitation in mid-June, but we had begun our preparations well before. The moment demanded urgent action. The Novo-Ogarevo process was pointing to a way out of the country's acute social and political crisis. The issue of the international community's support for our reforms had taken on great urgency. Our ties with the Seven now had more than merely general strategic significance: they had acquired a purely practical importance, ensuring substantial economic support for the country in its most critical hour.

In mid-May the USSR Security Council discussed the USSR Council of Ministers' memorandum on our joining the International Monetary Fund. At this session I raised the question of our possible participation in the London meeting of the Seven. The Council agreed with my policy. In late May I signed an order on the drafting of texts and proposals for the London meeting. Medvedev was instructed to co-ordinate the work, and leading specialists, academics, and heads of economic agencies were recruited for the task.

By 6 July all the documentation was in hand. Our only remaining problems were with the reports on finance and monetary policy. Finance Minister Orlov once again attempted to reduce everything to general talk, with Pavlov's support. The old habit of drawing the blinds over mistakes in the country's financial management, such as the unsatisfactory results of the recent price reform, a habit that had become part of our flesh and blood, took its toll here. Only after I insisted did we get a true picture of the budget, its deficit, and the amount of money in circulation. The London preparations helped us probe other problems of the economy as well – balance of payments, hard currency debt, and defence conversion.

On 8 July the results of our work were presented to the leaders of the republics at a meeting in Novo-Ogarevo, which was conducted in an atmosphere of mutual understanding that in itself was a surprise to many. Prior worries about tough demands being presented to Gorbachev before his London meeting proved groundless. All the republican leaders, starting with Yeltsin, supported my ideas and positions. The President of the USSR had a mandate for the meeting from the republics as well. I emphasize this because there was quite a lot of speculation and not a little nonsense put out about it, both then and afterwards, in particular by the coup-plotters, and especially by Kryuchkov's aides, those masters of dirty tricks.

On 11 July I sent a personal letter summarizing the conclusions of the working group to our Western partners by diplomatic courier. Bessmertnykh travelled to Washington to hand it to Bush. The reaction followed just two or three days later. 'This is a fantastic letter,' Bush declared at a press conference, 'although the United States does have certain disagreements with some of its points.'

I will reproduce here only the basic points of the message:

> We feel that the time has come to take resolute steps to undertake co-ordinated efforts for a new type of economic interaction that would integrate the Soviet economy – with its vast productive, scientific-technical, and human potential, its rich natural resources, and its colossal domestic market – into the world economy. This would reinforce the positive political process in international relations as well.

The letter said that our strategy for the organic inclusion of the Soviet economy in the world economy was based on the following considerations:

> We are counting, above all, on the mobilization of our own forces and resources in order to stabilize our economy and bring it into the world economy;
>
> We feel there must be reciprocal movement on the part of the Soviet Union and the Group of Seven, in which major measures in economic reforms and the opening up of the Soviet economy to the outside world would be reinforced by reciprocal steps facilitating the implementation of these measures;
>
> We are in favour of shifting the centre of gravity in economic co-operation to direct market relations between companies and banks, with governments providing the necessary guarantees and a most-favoured-nation treatment;
>
> We feel that bilateral economic relations must be supplemented by the Soviet Union's active participation in the system of multilateral relations and the activities of international financial and other institutions.

This was followed by 'Ten Points' containing an appraisal of the developments under way in the Soviet Union and the prospects for political and economic reforms.

Preparations for the London meeting also included intensive contacts with Western leaders: telephone conversations and an exchange of letters with Bush; meetings and conversations with Mitterrand, Andreotti, and the Spanish Prime Minister, Felipe González. My discussion with Kohl in Kiev was especially productive. On 15 June I received Jacques Attali, the President of the European Bank for Reconstruction and Development (EBRD), and on 20 June Jacques Delors, President of the Commission of the European Communities.

On the eve of our meeting, Bush sent me a letter that, while reflecting the new level of relations between our country and the West, was also remarkable for its subtext and even contained an element of pressure. Judging by the letter, the US administration had taken a special position, and this later became apparent at the London summit.

Because of the doubts and reservations of some leaders of the Seven, my participation was arranged as a special meeting held outside the framework of the Seven's annual session. I was not about to make much of this detail, aware that the '7 + 1' formula, even without its transformation into the 'Eight', was an immense step forward and the high point of the London meeting.

On 16 July we arrived in London, gathered at the embassy, and exchanged opinions on the situation once again. There had been a change of tone in the media – from optimism and even euphoria to restraint and even scepticism. Someone may very well have leaned on the journalists. A similar tone appeared in the statements of some of the leaders. They probably wanted to warn me not to expect too much.

On the morning of 17 July, before our meeting began, I held talks with Bush, Mitterrand, and Attali. The American President and I came to a final agreement on the strategic arms reduction treaty. Then came my meeting with the Seven at Lancaster House, which was staged with quite a bit of ceremony.

Opening the meeting, Major welcomed me. He congratulated Bush and me on our final accord on the strategic arms reduction treaty. This announcement was greeted with applause – a rare thing at this type of gathering. Major called the meeting historic because it was the first of its kind and especially important for all its participants. He said that my letter had been studied, and the participants in the meeting agreed with much in it. There were several questions, however, on which they were awaiting clarification from me, concerning our plans for privatization and liberalization of the Soviet economy, ways to resolve problems of monetary emission, prices and the budget deficit, problems of financing and debt in relations between the centre and the republics, and how our future market would operate. The West, Major said, was in a position to help us at the macroeconomic level, primarily in the form of consultative assistance, and on the microeconomic level along several specific lines, especially in the area of energy. In all this, he noted, the investment climate was key.

I began my speech by saying that I saw the London meeting as a symbol of the profound changes taking place in international relations. What had been unthinkable only two or three years before, to say nothing of five or ten, had now become perfectly natural and logical.

The Soviet leadership felt that positive processes in the world could be sustained if the political dialogue we had established were to become rooted in the new economic co-operation.

Our concept of the country's inclusion in the world economy stemmed from the need for radical changes in the Soviet Union, but also for reciprocal measures on the part of the West (the lifting of legislative and other restrictions on economic and technical ties with the Soviet Union, the Soviet Union's participation in international economic organizations, and so forth).

I had made an irrevocable choice in favour of the further continuation and deepening of democratic changes in society and of accelerating movement towards the market. But the logic of events had convinced us that it was impossible to conduct radical economic reforms outside the world market, just as democratization and the guarantee of human rights and freedoms were inconceivable outside the general process of mankind's development at the turn of the twenty-first century.

I directed the meeting's attention to our package of specific proposals for co-operation. Thus my speech answered virtually all the questions posed at the beginning of the session.

Then a discussion began in which all the leaders of the Seven took part. Bush expressed concern about the distribution of responsibility within the framework of a Union Treaty. 'This is important from the standpoint of investments,' he stressed. He singled out as key points the mechanism for follow-up action, mutual understanding among participants in the meeting, co-operation with international organizations, and the political impetus from the current chairman and the next year's, Chancellor Kohl. Bush explained that by 'political impetus' he meant Major's trip to Moscow for consultations and then his report to the Seven. This, he said, would leave individual countries sufficient flexibility for action on the bilateral level.

After Bush's rather dry and purely pragmatic considerations, Kohl's speech was more emotional and sympathetic. 'We are experiencing an exceptional, historic moment,' he said. 'If this process we are initiating in London goes successfully, it will have the utmost importance for Europe and the entire world.' As for practical conclusions, Kohl too was quite restrained. Citing the position already agreed upon, he spoke in favour of creating a mechanism for interaction around the chairman, who would work in co-ordination with existing structures.

Mitterrand's speech made a great impression on me. Taking the floor after Delors, he continued, as he said, the 'theme of disbelief' touched upon by the latter, that is, the West's lack of confidence in rendering us assistance. 'There is a classic dispute over which came first, the chicken or the egg,' said Mitterrand. 'There is also a desire to evaluate an experiment before it has been completed. But the very best argument against disbelief is what President Gorbachev is doing. In the final analysis,' Mitterrand added, turning to me, 'you could have behaved like your predecessors, and the result would be catastrophic. History will record this. It will note not only the fact that you are transforming a country that does not have democratic traditions, but also how its relations with other countries have changed. Nations have been freed from the presence of foreign troops. Germany has been unified. All this is a result of your policy. And all this is an argument for belief, not disbelief. What you are faced with are grounds for hope.'

Mitterrand was trying to present his colleagues with weighty arguments in favour of a more positive approach and more effective assistance in rebuilding the Soviet economy. He supported the entry of our country into world economic organizations and advocated concrete assistance in specific areas and projects. Of course, he also spoke about what concerned everyone: political instability and the preservation of the Union.

There was also a passage in his speech about privatization. 'I would not advise you to privatize everything. The essence lies in the synthesis of private entrepreneurship, democratic contest, competition, and, at the same time, the role of the state. The state acts in all our countries; the difference is a matter of degree. We cannot tell you to do it one way or another. The traditions of the Soviet Union must be respected. In your country you have traditions of collective property, so you must find a middle way. If you follow that way, you will be able to get help. We will have something in common, but not everything. What we do have in common will make you receptive to assistance. For the rest you bear responsibility yourself, responsibility to the present and the future.'

Andreotti's speech was also very positive. 'Much has been said here about the fact that the Soviet Union is beginning its transition to the market under difficult conditions,' he said. 'President Gorbachev faces colossal tasks, of course. But I must say that our economy was not strong either when we began its transformation. Therefore we understand, perhaps better than anyone else, why prudence is essential in restructuring the Soviet economy, why price controls, for example, cannot be lifted overnight. The direction of the movement must be clear, however.'

I thanked all the participants for the atmosphere in which the meeting had been held – very open and at the same time permeated with a sense of responsibility and interest.

Major agreed with me. 'This was a frank, informal discussion,' he said, 'not a collection of formal speeches. Hard questions were put to which answers were given. As a result of the discussion, all of us share the intention of working together to facilitate the Soviet Union's integration into the world economy.'

Major summed up the agreement reached in the following six points,[1] which he set out a few hours later at our joint press conference:

'The first relates to a special association with the International Monetary Fund and the World Bank. The Summit participants very much welcome a special association for the Soviet Union with the IMF and with the World Bank. We believe that will be an enormous step towards helping the Soviet Union become more closely integrated into the world economy.

'Secondly, we are asking all the international institutions – the OECD, the European Bank for Reconstruction and Development, as well as the IMF and the World Bank – to work closely together and intensify their efforts in their support of the Soviet Union. They can provide the Soviet Union with practical advice, with know-how, with expertise to help create a market economy.

'Thirdly, we talked of technical assistance, we agreed on the importance of intensifying our technical assistance for the Soviet Union. We believe there should be greater co-operation and in particular greater co-operation in the following sectors: energy; defence conversion; food distribution; nuclear safety; and transport.

'Fourthly, we discussed trade. As President Gorbachev said during his remarks this afternoon, he was very conscious that trade had collapsed between the Soviet Union and its immediate neighbours and it would be desirable to re-establish it. We also wish to see improved trade access to markets for Soviet goods and services and we believe that would help to attract more inward private investment and that will govern our policies.

'Fifthly, and vitally I think, we discussed the follow-up to the meeting we had this afternoon. We agreed that the Chairman of the G7 summit, on behalf of all summit colleagues, should keep in close touch with developments on behalf of the whole of the G7. There was a general wish following that, that as the current

---

[1] What follows is an edited version of Mr Major's statement.

chairman I should visit Moscow before the end of the year to meet President Gorbachev, discuss with him the matters of mutual concern to us all and to review progress. I am happy to do so and I look forward to that visit. Next year my successor as Chairman of the G7, Chancellor Kohl, will liaise and will undertake similar visits.

'Sixthly, we decided to take this contact a little further. We will encourage our Finance Ministers and Ministers for Small Business to accept invitations to go to the Soviet Union and to discuss a range of matters with their counterparts in the Soviet government. We see this as a part of widening and deepening the continuing dialogue between the Soviet Union and the G7 governments.'

The next day I had wide-ranging and detailed conversations with the British Prime Minister. We discussed the practical steps needed to implement the agreements reached. Major proposed sending his Chancellor of the Exchequer, Norman Lamont, to Moscow in the near future. He also confirmed that he himself intended to go to Moscow before the year was out, as co-ordinator within the framework of the '7 + 1' formula. For my part, I proposed that preparations should be made beforehand on other levels, both political and technical, with a view to drawing up proposals for later discussion with all the leaders of the Seven. I reminded Major of the list of specific projects I had submitted and asked Major to study ways to eliminate Cocom restrictions preventing their implementation. Major promised to look into the matter and discuss it with his foreign colleagues.

He told me about the 'know-how fund' created in Great Britain to help the countries of Eastern Europe and the Soviet Union in creating a market. With the Seven discussion as his point of departure, Major asked several specific questions about the political changes in our country, the balance of political forces, the prospects for a Union Treaty, the future system of taxation in the Union, and so on. His comments in the course of my answers showed his desire to grasp the essence of the developments in our country.

On 19 July I met Mrs Thatcher and had an opportunity to thank her personally for all she had done to make the meeting with the

Seven possible. 'It is very important that your meeting with the Seven took place,' she said. 'These days virtually everything has focused on your presence and on making the Soviet Union part of the world economy.' She told me that she was quite disappointed that the Seven had not worked out more specific and practical measures to support the Soviet Union in its reforms. She urged me to seize on the Seven pledge to provide support and cooperation. 'Don't let go of them,' she insisted. 'Demand specific, more practical manifestations of support!'

Mrs Thatcher was quite optimistic about the prospects for foreign investment in the Soviet Union. Her conversations with American businessmen had convinced her of this. It was important, she emphasized, that the ground rules with respect to joint enterprises, foreign investment, property and so forth, remained in force and did not change. As for private property, some American businessmen had told her outright that they would be quite happy with an arrangement for ninety-nine-year leasing of land.[1] Nor were they concerned about whether the problem of the ruble's convertibility was solved immediately. They felt they could use the rubles they earned in the Soviet Union to purchase equipment and raw materials. She added: 'Convertibility will not come until the economy can sustain it. Otherwise it will only lead to the further devaluation of the ruble.'

Some of my radical critics assert that the London meeting of 1991 was fruitless, that I returned empty-handed. On the other hand, their opponents from the camp of fundamentalists and 'patriots' sing their own song: Gorbachev 'mortgaged' the country and sold out to the West.

Both versions are ridiculous. I did not go to London to beg for credits; a meeting of top leaders is not the place where money is given out. I did not sell the Azerbaijan oilfields to the British or the Kuril Islands to the Japanese.

However, while I did not bring back any cheques from London, I did return with a significant gain. I achieved a fundamental political agreement about the integration of our country in the

---

[1] Foreign businessmen could not buy land, but could lease it for up to 99 years.

world economy, and we had defined ways of resolving specific problems, including that of foreign debt. In these talks the President of the Soviet Union took fundamental steps forward that entirely fulfilled the national and state interests of our country.

29

BUSH IN MOSCOW THREE WEEKS BEFORE THE COUP

LATE IN JULY 1991, THE PRESIDENT OF THE UNITED STATES CAME to the Soviet Union to sign the Strategic Arms Reduction Treaty.

Before writing these pages, I have carefully re-read the notes I made at the time, and have once again felt the full import of what occurred during those few days. There were several meetings: a private conversation on the morning of 30 July; talks with delegations present; an exchange of opinions during a working breakfast; and an especially significant discussion at Novo-Ogarevo on 31 July. Two qualities were characteristic of all of them: a high degree of mutual trust, despite divergent opinions on some issues; and a high degree of agreement not only on current but also on new, emerging problems. In any event, a great deal of what we discussed at the time is now being debated by both diplomats and the media.

ON THE PORCH AT NOVO-OGAREVO

Bush and I had agreed in advance that when he came to Moscow we would arrange something similar to what he had arranged for me at Camp David during my visit to the United States. Specifically this meant gathering in an informal situation, in a small group, preferably in the country, in our shirt sleeves, without any protocol or mandatory agenda, and talking freely and openly.

I arrived at Novo-Ogarevo before our guests. With me was Raisa Maksimovna. Soon after, we were joined by Baker and Brent Scowcroft.[1] A photographer ran up and captured us all together. We were waiting for the President, who, as we soon saw from the cars passing in the distance, had gone first to his quarters, the house set aside for him in the Novo-Ogarevo grounds. A few minutes later, George and Barbara Bush arrived. We engaged in small talk and joked. Then Raisa Maksimovna and Barbara left us and Bush and I began our session.

We chose as the spot for our talks the open porch that looked south towards the Moskva River. For the whole conversation, which lasted the entire first half of that day, only Bessmertnykh and Chernyaev, Baker and Scowcroft were present (and of course the interpreters).

My main theme was the prospect for creating a new common security system through a world policy conducted *jointly* (for the first time in history) and based on new criteria that had already undergone some testing in practice.

I noted the considerable gains as a result of efforts to improve the international situation. It was time to think about a new concept of strategic stability, which in the past had boiled down to military parity, equality, the military aspect of security. Now that we had rejected the emphasis on force and the arms race and were building a completely different relationship, it made sense to emphasize the components of political and economic stability, especially since inter-ethnic and also, in several instances, religious conflict increasingly threatened to destabilize the world.

It was extremely important to stimulate the democratic nature of the current changes, I continued. We had brought about these changes by our actions and wanted them to continue. The problem, however, was how to keep this process developing along peaceful, legal lines.

Another point was the emergence of other influential power centres besides the two nuclear superpowers – for example, the

[1] The President's National Security Adviser.

integrating European continent. The Nordic countries and the states of Central and Eastern Europe were drawing closer and closer towards the European Community. We could soon see here a locus of economic, political, and military might that could affect the entire geopolitical situation.

Complex processes were under way in Africa. Much was still uncertain, but the first stage of post-colonial development was over, with the results more on the minus than on the plus side. Africa's place in the world's balance was still far from clear.

The geopolitical importance of both China and India would continue to grow, in a unique way that was not traditional for twentieth-century world politics. Together, they accounted for two billion people. These were very ancient peoples, in which the will to set their own course had awakened. In this regard I was able to note that the US President was right not to attempt to play the China card against us. We too would not permit any actions that might upset the balance of world interests. Moreover, we would welcome the return of US-China relations to a positive track.

In the Asia-Pacific region, there could be great changes if Japan, in addition to its role as a great economic power, decided to become an influential political and military factor.

I also cited the problems of resources, the environment, and population growth. All these, albeit to varying degrees, were giving rise to the question of the role our two countries should play under the new circumstances and what our relationship should be in future.

Bush spoke along the same lines. He stated once more that the United States would like to see the Soviet Union strong and with a sound economy, capable of fundamental changes in a democratic spirit.

'I trust your intentions,' he said. 'And now more than before coming here I am sure that you know where you are going and how to move towards your goal.'

Turning to the problem of Europe, Bush confessed that the United States had certain difficulties with the Europeans. 'Our choice,' he said, 'is to maintain our involvement in Europe. We shall continue to support the CSCE process, with the Soviet

Union's participation, naturally. We will try to convince our Western European friends that we want to be in on the take-off as well as the landing. We do not want to be presented with facts, with economic initiatives – not only with respect to the Soviet Union – without having been consulted first.'

Moving on to the issue of Africa, Bush stressed that the United States would welcome any steps of ours in support of F. W. de Klerk. He spoke rather critically of the policy of the African National Congress, which, in his opinion, lagged behind on democratic changes and was too 'friendly' with Libya's Colonel Gadaffi. The President agreed to continue co-operation on the problems of Namibia, Angola, and other countries of Africa.

Bush's thoughts on China seemed balanced and well considered. 'We are still bitter about the events on Tiananmen Square. First of all, though, there can be no talk of "playing the China card", and secondly, we want to influence China positively, not to break off contact with it. This will not be easy to do. Congress is in a mood to punish China. I don't think we should, though – globally China is a very important country.'

He expressed the hope that the Soviet Union would be able to convey to India the United States' concern about the issue of nuclear weapons.

'We have also been hearing concerns from the Asia-Pacific region,' Bush said, 'about Japanese expansion. Anti-Japanese attitudes exist in the United States too, although for different reasons. Difficulties have arisen due to insufficient mutuality and a lack of openness in the Japanese market.

'If you, the Soviet Union, were to establish economic co-operation with the Japanese,' he said, 'that would promote stability.' In this connection, Bush mentioned we would do well to look for a way of resolving the Soviet-Japanese territorial dispute.[1]

Baker seemed to think that the President had not been sufficiently diplomatic. He therefore decided to elaborate: the Japanese, according to him, wanted to increase their political weight rather than their military might; US-Japanese security ties

[1] Over the ownership of the Southern Kuril Islands.

had significantly eased whatever worries the ASEAN countries might have had.

Talking about prospects for Soviet-American relations, Bush strongly confirmed that his administration had chosen to 'support Gorbachev's policy'. At the same time he spoke of the pressure he was under from various sides. 'In my own party,' he reported, 'there are extremists saying that it is in the interests of the United States to try to achieve the break-up of the Soviet Union or its economic collapse, and we are being attacked on the left by liberal Democrats who are constantly raising the issue of human rights and demanding that the administration should take advantage of your difficult situation and oblige you to accept various demands.

'The media have been attacking us. First Baker and I were criticized for being overly cautious in our relations with the Soviet Union and not seizing the newly available opportunities. Now the attacks are from the other side. Bush likes Gorbachev too much, they say, and is putting all his eggs in one basket.

'Several of our European friends and allies have been accusing us of dawdling and a failure to act. Actually, sometimes you get the impression that they're using this excuse to hide behind the United States' back. I want the reforms in the Soviet Union to be successful just as much as any European does,' Bush emphasized again. 'And we can do more to make that happen than any Western European country. We have a bigger economy, better technology, and more ingenuity.'

Bush assured me that neither he nor any of his people would allow his upcoming trip to Kiev to be interpreted as support for separatist tendencies. Landsbergis had pressed for Bush to stop over in Vilnius on the way home. Naturally, Bush assured me, they were not about to do that. At the same time, in his opinion, it would be best if we could find a way to sever our ties with those republics and let them go. This would make a very good impression internationally.

As during previous visits, economic problems occupied an important place. Actually, they had been discussed in more specific terms the previous day in Moscow, where Nursultan Nazarbayev had taken part in the discussions. Bush had mentioned the difficulties that had arisen in connection with Chevron's contract to develop oil fields in Kazakhstan.

Appealing to the trust that we had developed in our relationship, I reminded Bush of the serious obstacles that the discriminatory laws of the United States and the Cocom lists were creating for our economy. I drew his attention to the most striking examples.

Bush acknowledged that in some cases those bans were probably a legacy of the Cold War and promised to look into this problem. Despite this pledge, the problem of discriminatory American legislation and Cocom lists was not resolved either at that time or even two years later.

I asked Bush how we could get around the 'probation period' which had been set for the Soviet Union before joining the International Monetary Fund. For us it was important to take advantage of its services at once, not some time later. From his reply I realized that we could not count on serious support from the United States. Before large loans were possible, certain economic conditions had to be met, and those matters were not entirely up to the Americans. The necessary information had to be submitted and the rules of the World Bank, the IMF, and the Paris Club observed. We agreed to continue discussion of all these issues at the finance minister level.

One other set of problems involved further progress in the dismantling of arms. Here Baker and Bessmertnykh actively joined in the conversation on arms control. We agreed to resume the talks on anti-ballistic missiles and space in Geneva and to convene a meeting of biological weapons experts. We reaffirmed our shared commitment to completing a convention on the elimination of chemical weapons and removed several obstacles that had slowed this work.

The ministers reported on progress in negotiations on arms limitation: the renewal of multilateral 'open-skies' talks; the intensification of the Vienna-1A talks so that they could be concluded before March 1992, that is, before the start of Helsinki Two; and the provision of information to the American side on SS-23 missiles in Eastern Europe.

The situation in the Middle East was the subject of detailed discussion at Novo-Ogarevo. In recent months we as well as the Americans had been actively engaged diplomatically, pushing both sides to an agreement. The immediate goal of our efforts was a peace conference on the Middle East. I proposed sending out invitations to this conference in the names of the Presidents of the Soviet Union and the United States and that those two Presidents should open the conference. Bush supported the idea.

At the same time he pointed to obstacles that might hinder our efforts. Israeli settlements in the occupied territories were a very serious issue. The United States, Bush said, was trying to convince Israel to change its policy on this issue, but nothing had come of it so far. I, in turn, talked about the pressure to which we were being subjected by the Arabs.

'They are demanding an end to the emigration of Soviet Jews to Israel. When President Mubarak was here in Moscow, he frankly warned me that he would raise this question publicly, and did so at a press conference. Naturally, we have no intention of yielding to pressure, but this is something we have to reckon with eventually.'

I told Bush that we were prepared to establish diplomatic relations with Israel as soon as a date was set for the international peace conference. 'You can tell the Israelis that,' I said.

We talked at length about Yugoslavia, and I said something I want to repeat today:

'Even a partial break-up of Yugoslavia could set off a chain reaction. It's not just a matter of Yugoslavia. There are an enormous number of real and imaginary international and inter-ethnic problems. Carving up states along these lines means provoking utter chaos. If I were to start listing the potential territorial problems, I wouldn't have enough fingers – not just on my own hands but on everyone's here. For example, here in the Soviet Union, 70 per cent of inter-republic borders have not been definitely drawn. Before, no-one cared about that, and everything was decided pragmatically, virtually at the district Soviet level. The Bulgarians, with their Turkish minority, and the Romanians, with Transylvania, have inter-ethnic problems of their own. There is the problem of relations between the Czechs and the Slovaks in Czechoslovakia, and so on. Not long before London, I was discussing this issue with Helmut Kohl, and he asked me what we were supposed to do about the principle of self-determination of nations if we were to insist on territorial integrity and the inviolability of borders. I replied that I saw no insurmountable contradictions between these principles, but it had to be an internal process within a constitutional, legal framework.'

Since this problem, like several others, had to be reflected in the official document, I proposed finding a formula to make it clear that inter-ethnic problems could be resolved only by constitutional processes, with a reference to the principles proposed by the CSCE regarding the inviolability of international borders. Bush did not object in principle. Nonetheless, a few of his remarks seemed to imply that the forces working towards redrawing the map of Europe were gaining influence among Western Europeans and exerting pressure on the US President. To my deep regret, further events confirmed this feeling.

A MOMENT OF GLORY

The time had come to return to Moscow and the Kremlin, where an official ceremony for the signing of the Strategic Arms Reduction Treaty, which had been in preparation for more than nine years, awaited us in the St Vladimir Hall. Speaking at the ceremony, Bush said in particular: 'With this treaty we are solidifying the new opportunities being created between our countries, which promise further progress towards a stable peace.' These words were wholly consistent with my thoughts and assessments of this step.

I recall this visit of the US President – the last ever to the Soviet Union – with a certain sadness now. We did not know then what would happen just three weeks later. We were living for the future. Although we spoke about many current problems, in a way we were summing up the journey we had travelled over the last five or six years. These years had led world policy to a fundamentally new and historic watershed, where it was now being made as a *joint* policy of powers that had until only recently considered themselves mortal enemies and had in this enmity been prepared to push the entire world towards catastrophe. In this sense, the meeting between the Presidents of the United States and the Soviet Union at Novo-Ogarevo on 31 July 1991 could be considered a moment of glory for the new thinking and the foreign policy stemming from it.

TWO MOMENTS OF EMBARRASSMENT

Two stories connected with Bush's visit shed light on what was then going on inside the Soviet 'elite'.

Within the framework of the visit there were two official dinners: one that we hosted in the Chamber of Facets,[1] and another hosted by the Americans at their ambassador's residence.

The first was our dinner. According to protocol, Raisa Maksimovna and I introduced our guests to the American presidential couple. Among the first to approach turned out to be Yeltsin's wife, who for some reason had been escorted by Gavriil Popov. When the guests had all passed through the reception line, Yeltsin appeared in proud solitude. He walked up and invited Barbara Bush into the Chamber of Facets. Everyone was dumbfounded – except for me. I knew Boris too well. The night before, he had telephoned and asked me to let him go in to dinner with Bush and me. Naturally I refused. Why had he even asked?

Mrs Bush was confused; she was waiting for an invitation from the Soviet President, the reception's host. 'Is that really all right?' she exclaimed, astonished.

The Russian President was very anxious to draw attention to himself. Later, at the dinner in the American embassy, Nazarbayev and Yeltsin were annoyed that they had not been seated at the top tables. Right in the middle of the reception they got up and headed towards the American President. In and of itself this wouldn't have meant anything, had there not followed from Yeltsin and Nazarbayev fervent claims to the President that they 'would do everything for the success of democracy in this country.' Those seated at the tables observed all this not only with

---

[1] A famous room in the Kremlin.

curiosity but above all with amazement, and the natural question as to what it all might mean. Only our heroes experienced no embarrassment. Of course this behaviour went beyond all bounds of protocol. It was a signal to the Soviet Union's President of hard times still ahead.

30

THE COUP

IT IS COMMON KNOWLEDGE THAT, AT THE TURNING-POINTS OF history, time is condensed and infinitely compressed. Months, weeks and even days saturated with events may sometimes equal centuries. That was the case in the second half of 1991. A fierce struggle raged around three main questions.

First, the integrity of the country and the fate of our Union State: whether it would continue as a real federation in a renewed form or would disintegrate and crumble, with dire consequences for the people.

Second, the fate of perestroika and the economic and political reforms initiated in 1985 concurrently with democratization. Would these be sustained or curtailed? And if the reforms were to be sustained, what methods would apply, how quickly would this happen, and what was the price we would have to pay for a transition to a more effective economic and management system?

Third, the power struggle: what social forces, parties, movements and leaders would be at the helm in this new stage of our history?

These fundamental issues were, of course, inextricably entwined. Unfortunately the outcome was to be decided not only on the basis of so-called objective laws and pressing social needs, but also by the fierce rivalry of political groups, the aspirations of national elites, and simple human ambitions and passions.

Reaching final agreement on the new Union Treaty on 23 July was of decisive importance. I have already described the tremendous difficulties involved in this act. Following the example of

Russia, the republics had declared their sovereignty and exerted every effort to secure as many rights as possible for themselves. In all fairness it should be said that with rare exceptions the republics' leaders realized the need for a strong centre capable of resolving common problems. In short, a sound balance in the distribution of power had to be established.

Most importantly, we were able to solve the problem of the subjects[1] of the Union of Sovereign States. The new status of the autonomies[2] as co-founders of the Union safeguarded equal rights for all nations, making it possible for them to tackle their affairs on their own. At the same time the integrity of Union republics was not violated, and the historically established borders of states and national territorial entities were not questioned. I am far from contending that a final solution had been found. The problem is an extremely difficult one. Today it is more acute than ever. However, let me repeat: by sustaining and renewing the Union State in the draft Treaty it was resolved in the best possible way, avoiding conflicts and making urgent changes in relations between nationalities by legal means rather than by force of arms.

It is of equal importance that the new Union Treaty was accepted not only by the republics but also in the fundamental institutions of power, above all the USSR Supreme Soviet. Lukyanov[3] and Nishanov[4] participated in virtually all the Novo-Ogarevo meetings and often suggested compromises. After each session an updated version of the draft was sent to the Presidium of the USSR Supreme Soviet for the information of deputies. In the course of discussions a great number of comments were made in the committees and commissions. They were submitted to a working group, where they were considered together with the proposals tabled by the parliaments of the republics.

Lukyanov briefed the members of the Council of the Federation frequently on the attitudes of the deputies and the apprehensions some of them had that the Union Treaty would

[1] Constituent members of the Union.

[2] Autonomous republics, oblasts and districts that are part of Union republics.

[3] Chairman of the USSR Supreme Soviet.

[4] Chairman of the Council of the Nationalities, USSR Supreme Soviet.

weaken the central bodies, including the Union Parliament. But all of this was part of the discussions in Novo-Ogarevo. In the end, the Supreme Soviet approved the draft in principle and its chairman and the chairmen of its chambers were to sign it, together with the delegations of the republics.

While the work in Novo-Ogarevo was going on the different versions of the Union Treaty were also being discussed by the government. Prime Minister Pavlov and economic leaders submitted their observations. The State Bank and its chairman, Gerashchenko, actively advocated a single money and credit policy. Memoranda were presented by the Ministries of Foreign Affairs, Internal Affairs, Communications and Rail Transport, and most of the other ministries. Needless to say, their papers concentrated on the need to maintain a high level of power within the Union bodies. These arguments were painstakingly examined, and often their authors were invited to meetings of the Council of the Federation. It goes without saying that not every proposal of the government was approved, but all in all it expressed no objection to the Treaty. Nor did any of the political parties (at least, not overtly) denounce the draft. Many of them hoped that the new Union Treaty would serve to normalize the political situation in the country. As to the CPSU, the draft was repeatedly discussed in the Politburo and the plenums. The last version of the draft was considered at the 25–26 July plenum and was approved in substance.

Another event in July suggested that the power struggle, although not conclusively decided, would at least be deferred. Yeltsin's inauguration took place at a solemn meeting of the RSFSR Supreme Soviet. I made no secret about my misgivings. But I adopted an attitude of good faith, hoping that, having reached his goal, the President of Russia and his team (actually a party) would get down to the business of running the republic and put aside their ambitious plans, at least temporarily.

In that same month of July – and this is certainly not a coincidence – the implementation of the anti-crisis programme began after much arduous work and vacillation. It was a difficult decision, affecting the lives of millions of people. We were criticized both by those who clung to the old economic system and by those who were eager to destroy it overnight. However, we finally succeeded in drafting a text that was approved by the republics. Let me reiterate that this programme had become not only a Cabinet programme but also the programme of republican governments.

There was another concurrent event: the London G7 meeting where the problem of the interaction of the Soviet economy and the world economy at this crucial phase of our reforms was discussed.

On 29 July, almost at the last moment, we succeeded in removing the final obstacle to the signing of the Union Treaty. This was the long-standing objection of the Russian leadership to the introduction of a Union tax. Eventually a compromise was reached, and Yeltsin withdrew his last objection. The agreed text of article 9 (Union Taxes and Levies) read as follows:

'For the purpose of financing the expenditures of the Union budget necessary for exercising the powers entrusted to the Union, common Union taxes and levies will be imposed in accordance with fixed percentage rates to be determined in consultation with the republics on the basis of the items of expenditure presented by the Union. Control over the expenditure of the Union budget will be exercised by the parties to the Treaty.'

We had come a long way since April 1985. It seemed feasible that we could pull the country out of the crisis, and continue the programme of democratic changes. I left for a holiday on 4 August convinced that in sixteen days the Union Treaty would be signed in Moscow, opening a new stage of our reforms.

In a television address two days earlier I had tried to explain the significance for the country of the new Union Treaty. First of all, it was the implementation of the will of the people, expressed in the 17 March 1991 referendum. A unified state would be preserved, embodying the labour of many generations and of all the peoples in our country. Meanwhile a new, truly voluntary unity of sovereign states was being created, in which the peoples would independently administer their own affairs and freely develop their own cultures and traditions.

Preparatory work for the signing ceremony was under way.

During my holiday in the Crimea I followed this process closely. Considering the fact that the Ukrainian Supreme Soviet was to decide on that issue only in September,[1] I thought it appropriate to sign the treaty in three stages. However, the republics that were invited to sign the treaty 'at the second stage' objected to this arrangement. Following an exchange of opinions the second stage disappeared, while the third stage planned for the beginning of October became the second. Ukraine and Azerbaijan were to sign at that stage.

Despite the high level of agreement that had been reached, so that ostensibly nothing stood in the way of signing the treaty, the assaults from the left and the right gained momentum as the date drew nearer. In the press, whatever its orientation, fierce battles were raging. On 14 August I talked to Yeltsin on the telephone, and sensed an uncertainty and wavering on the part of the President of the Russian Federation. He asked me whether I appreciated the impact of the attacks targeted at him. I answered – and here I am relating the gist of our conversation – that I was being equally castigated. I was criticized for wanting to sign a treaty which would jeopardize the integrity of the State, while the President of Russia was attacked for doing the same and thus extending the life of the empire. However, considering that both the extreme right and the extreme left were dissatisfied, we must be on the right track. Concluding the conversation on this topic, I said: 'Boris Nikolaevich, we must not retreat a single step from our agreed positions, wherever the attacks come from. Let us keep a cool head and carry on with the preparations for the signing.'

As the President of Russia was interested in the way the ceremony would proceed, I briefed him on all the details. At first he questioned the proposal to seat the delegations of the republics in alphabetical order at the table where the signing would take place. But after I had told him that Russia would thus be at the centre, I seemed to have dispelled his doubts.

On the whole we parted on good terms. However, I could not

---

[1] The Ukrainian Supreme Soviet was to take a decision on the treaty in September, after it had been signed by some states in August.

get rid of the feeling that Yeltsin was holding something back. I did my utmost to warn him against wavering at this crucial and historic moment. As I was to learn later, Yeltsin was under pressure from his associates to attach some conditions to his signature of the treaty.

But this is hindsight. At that time I was convinced that the treaty would be signed. Any attempt to prevent it from happening, knowing the position of the people as it was expressed in the referendum and aware of the difficulties in advancing reforms without cohesion in the Union, would have involved too much risk.

Now we can only guess what Yeltsin would have done. I am inclined to think his political instincts would have warned him against wrecking the process of signing the treaty. As to reservations or attempts to thwart the coming into force of the treaty – these could not be ruled out.

It was the putschists, acting from another direction and for different motives, who unleashed an all-out attack in violation of the Constitution and perfidiously embarked upon the path of high treason.

It goes without saying that I did not rule out the possibility of a head-on clash between the forces of renewal and reaction. Moreover, since November–December 1990 the conservative forces had been making ample use of every opportunity to attack the President and the reformers at Supreme Soviet sessions, Congresses of People's Deputies of the USSR, Party plenums and all kinds of meetings and conferences, clamouring for the introduction of presidential rule or the declaration of a state of emergency.

I was not simply observing the situation – I acted to foil the designs of the reactionaries. From the very inception of the crises brought about by the radical transformation of society I tried to defuse conflict by resorting to tactical manoeuvres in order to gain time for the stabilization of the democratic process, phasing out the old system and strengthening the new values in people's minds.

In brief, my main goal was to bring the country to a stage at which any reckless attempt was doomed to failure, to sustain the course of transformation in spite of all difficulties and assure the development of society along constitutional lines.

I would not say that my holiday that year was a real rest. Events in the country were acquiring an increasingly alarming character. While staying at Foros[1] I had to cope with many problems. I had a strong feeling that I should quickly return to Moscow. Every day I urged all those involved in the preparation of the signing of the Union Treaty to expedite their work. The plane for my return was already scheduled. I discussed my speech at the signing ceremony with G. Shakhnazarov, who was holidaying in the neighbouring Yuzhny Sanatorium. On the 18th I told him of my final amendments, and that was, incidentally, our last conversation, after which my telephones were cut off. Now we know that officers stood behind the backs of the telephone operators, who were to interrupt communications at 4.30 p.m.

At about five p.m. on 18 August, I was informed that a group composed of Baklanov, Shenin, Boldin, Varennikov and Plekhanov had arrived at the dacha. I was surprised, because I had not invited anyone. The head of my security guard was patently at a loss. It turned out that the guards had let the visitors enter because they were in the company of Plekhanov and Boldin. Nothing like that could have happened otherwise. For security reasons no-one was allowed to enter the grounds of the dacha without my consent.

I decided to find out what was going on. I tried to contact Moscow and talk first of all to Kryuchkov, only to discover that all five telephone lines, including the strategic communications line, were dead. Even the city telephone did not work. I walked out to the verandah where Raisa Maksimovna was reading the newspapers, and told her that we had unexpected guests. Their intentions were unpredictable, but we could expect the worst. She was shaken by the news, but remained cool. We went to the nearby bedroom. My thoughts were racing: I shall not retreat, I shall not yield to any pressure, blackmail or threats. Raisa Maksimovna said: 'It's up to you to make a decision, but I am

[1] The official summer residence of the President of the USSR in the Crimea.

814

with you whatever may happen.' Then we summoned Irina and Anatoly. Having listened to me, they said that they were prepared for anything.

This took about thirty to forty minutes. The guards told me that the visitors were edgy, wondering why they had not been received. When I left the bedroom I discovered that they had come up to the second floor without being asked. Their general behaviour was uncivil, almost as if they were the hosts. I invited them into my study and asked them the purpose of their mission. Baklanov declared that an emergency committee had been created. The country was sliding into disaster, he declared – 'You must sign the decree on the declaration of a state of emergency.' In fact they had come with an ultimatum. Eventually I learned that they had brought with them different versions of documents prepared for my signature.

Baklanov named the members of the emergency committee, mentioning Lukyanov as one of them. He claimed that Yeltsin was under arrest, but immediately contradicted himself by saying that Yeltsin would be arrested on his return from Alma Ata. The conspirators wanted me to believe that they had already seized control of the situation.

I had promoted all these people – and now they were betraying me! I refused to sign any decree. If they were truly worried about the situation in the country, I told them, we should convene the USSR Supreme Soviet and the Congress of People's Deputies. 'Let us discuss and decide. But let us act only within the framework of the Constitution and under the law. Anything else is unacceptable to me.' Baklanov's response to all my arguments was to display profound 'concern' about my health, which, he said, must have suffered during the stressful perestroika period. If I didn't want to sign the decree on the state of emergency myself, Baklanov suggested, I could authorize Yanayev to do it for me. He told me that they would take care of all the 'dirty work', then I could return. Needless to say, I rejected this despicable proposal.

'Why then don't you resign?' said Varennikov.

I told them that they were criminals who would be held accountable for their folly. That put an end to the conversation.

As they were departing, I lost my cool and swore at them, Russian-style.

I should like to answer a question which is often addressed to me: why did I not detain them, since I had armed guards at my disposal?

First of all, I expected the instigators of the plot to come to their senses after my refusal to accept their ultimatum. It was not the first time that I had restrained them from rash action, and I hoped that this time too a firm stand on my part would have its effect. Moreover, an attempt to detain them at the dacha would not have served any purpose. After all, the masterminds were in Moscow, controlling the levers of power. I had no doubt that the plotters had taken precautions against any such reaction on my part here in Foros. My assumption was confirmed. Arrangements to isolate the President totally had been made in advance. Communications were cut. A double line of guards was deployed around the dacha and on the sea. No-one was allowed to leave or enter the dacha and its area.

To call a spade a spade, it was an act that involved the arrest of the President and the usurpation of power. The conspirators realized that they would be unable to win me over, but hoped to force me to sign decrees lending an appearance of legitimacy to their venture. My flat refusal to do so branded them immediately as criminals.

As we know now, that night was not easy for them. When the delegation returned from Foros, their report sowed discord in the midst of the conspirators. Yanayev wavered and reached out for the bottle. It seems that Pavlov also went on a drinking bout, feigning illness. Lukyanov wasted no time in preparing his fall-back positions. Marshal Yazov was pensive, and later said: 'What the hell possessed me, old fool, to get involved in this mess!' Voices were heard suggesting that it might be better to stop. But it was too late. They had gone too far to sound a retreat. Boldin told the others: 'I know the President; he will never forgive such treatment.' There was no other way for them but forward.

FROM THE DIARY OF RAISA MAKSIMOVNA

In order to convey to the reader how we felt during the days of confinement I shall quote some excerpts from Raisa Maksimovna's diary, which were published on 20 December 1991 in *Komsomolskaya Pravda*.

18 AUGUST, SUNDAY

We are straining to get some news over our small Sony pocket transistor radio. What a stroke of luck to have brought it along! While shaving in the morning Mikhail Sergeyevich uses it to listen to the 'Mayak' station. He brought it with him to the Crimea. The fixed receiver here in our residence is not working on any of the wavelengths. Only the tiny Sony is working. But there is no special news. Nothing unusual . . .

We agreed that Anatoly should hide the transistor radio. And nobody is to know that we have it. Nobody at all. I shall make more detailed entries.

I cannot sleep . . . I am tormented by bitterness at the betrayal of people who worked side by side with Mikhail Sergeyevich.

. . . What is happening in the country now and in Moscow? What is going on in the President's residence outside Moscow?

19 AUGUST, MONDAY

Around seven in the morning Anatoly and Irina managed to get the following information over the transistor (it was not Mayak, probably the World Service of the BBC): a State Committee for the State of Emergency has been created. The state of emergency has been declared in some regions of the country. An appeal from the committee to fellow citizens and an address to foreign countries, as well as a decree allotting 15 sotka[1] per person, have been transmitted . . . Further, 'in view of the illness of the President of the USSR and his inability to fulfil his functions, his powers will be assumed by Vice-President Yanayev.' All the documents must have been prepared in advance.

In the small hours of the morning – according to Anatoly, it must have been about five a.m., several large warships headed towards our bay. The patrol ships came unusually close to the shore, stayed for about fifty minutes and subsequently left. What was that? A threat? Isolation from the sea?

No mail. No newspapers. We were told: 'There won't be any.' The

---

[1] One sotka is equivalent to one hundredth of a hectare.

state communications service officer was detained yesterday right here, in the grounds. The radio fell silent, the television is disconnected. Anatoly and the security staff are trying to make an aerial for a stationary receiver. Boris Ivanovich[1] found a piece of wire. However, their attempts failed.

Through the senior security guard, Mikhail Sergeyevich transmitted to Generalov[2] the following demands to be forwarded to Moscow: restore telephone communications, deliver the mail and the newspapers, turn on the television sets, and send an aeroplane for his immediate return to work in Moscow.

'New faces' with machine-guns on the premises . . .

A. Chernyaev came. We talked on the balcony, fearing eavesdroppers. The security officers do not rule out such a possibility. Anatoly Sergeyevich complains: he has nothing here, not even razor blades. All his things were left behind at the Yuzhny Sanatorium, where he, the stenographer, Olga Vasilievna, and his secretary, Tamara Alekseyevna, were staying. Normally they come to work here every day. Chernyaev said that he had spoken to Generalov. He insisted on being released. 'I am, after all, a USSR People's Deputy. Moreover I am not interned. Why do you keep me here?'

We went for a walk in the grounds and to the sea. It was important that people – 'our' people and those who are watching us from the cliffs and from the sea – see Mikhail Sergeyevich fit and well and in normal health.

Boris Ivanovich and Igor Anatolievich[3] relate the news they have heard over an old radio set with a makeshift aerial attached to it. Reports from abroad affirm that Yeltsin has not been arrested. 'Whereas Generalov told me yesterday that he had been arrested at his dacha,' said Boris Ivanovich. 'All in all, the information on the latest developments varies greatly. It's difficult to make sense of it . . .'

There is also news at the residence here: a fire engine and a street-cleaning vehicle have been parked blocking the helicopter pad. In front of the entrance, the road is barred by trucks. Sub-machine-gunners are deployed at the garage, at the gates and at the helicopter pad. There are strangers all around.

Oleg Anatolievich[4] and Boris Ivanovich have stated once more: 'Mikhail Sergeyevich, we'll stick by you. Until the end.'

The sea is calm: there are no pleasure boats, no passenger liners, no trawlers, no barges . . . The usual patrol vessel is there. Normally there

[1] Boris Ivanovich Golentsov, a personal security guard.
[2] The Emergency Committee's head of security at Foros.
[3] Igor Anatolievich Borisov, Gorbachev's doctor.
[4] Oleg Anatolievich Klimov, Gorbachev's senior guard officer at Foros.

are people on deck, engaged in some kind of activity, sometimes swimming or fishing . . . Now, not a soul on the deck. Tatyana Georgievna, the nurse, is indignant: 'You wouldn't believe it, "friends" and "supporters" they were supposed to be – traitors, that's what they are! When she saw her boss, Boldin, Olga said: "There's trouble ahead! He is the worst of the lot in the apparatus."' She told me that Pugo had been taking a holiday in the Yuzhny Sanatorium. 'He left yesterday, he had to leave early. They say that he and his wife had food poisoning.' She told us that nobody, strictly nobody, had been allowed to leave the grounds, 'obviously, so that people wouldn't find out the truth – that Mikhail Sergeyevich is well.'

Mikhail Sergeyevich and I are sitting in his study. Anatoly and Irina rush in. News: the television is working, music is being broadcast right now. More patrol vessels appear on the sea, keeping a distance from the shore. BBC news on the transistor: Boris Yeltsin has publicly denounced the conspirators and called for resistance to them. Nazarbayev appealed to the population of his republic on Kazakh television to remain calm and cool and maintain public order. Not a word about the ousting of the President of the USSR.

At five p.m. the senior security guard reported that the signalling unit has been withdrawn.

At 5.30 p.m. Mikhail Sergeyevich asked A. Chernyaev to see him. He told me that he had instructed him to transmit his demands to Yanayev once more regarding the restoration of government communications and making an aircraft available for his departure to Moscow. In case of refusal or silence, he asked him to transmit his demand for a meeting with Soviet and foreign reporters.

After Anatoly Sergeyevich had left, he asked me to write down a political statement. He dictated it to me:

'1. The decision by the Vice-President to assume the duties of the President of the country under the pretext that the President of the USSR was ill and, consequently, unable to fulfil his functions is fraudulent inasmuch as I am in a normal state of health. Moreover, I have had a rest and was scheduled to leave today, 19 August, for the signing of the Union Treaty and a meeting of the Council of the Federation. Hence this decision can be considered only as a coup d'état.

'2. All decisions made on this basis by the Vice-President and the State Committee for the State of Emergency are illegal.

'3. The escalation of measures taken in connection with the illegal introduction of the state of emergency may lead to a drastic aggravation of the situation in the country, social confrontation and upheaval, and may be fraught with unpredictable consequences.

'4. I demand that the implementation of the aforementioned decisions be immediately suspended and that Comrade Lukyanov as

Chairman of the USSR Supreme Soviet urgently convene the Congress of People's Deputies or the USSR Supreme Soviet to consider the current situation within the leadership of the country.'

. . . A televised press-conference by the members of the Emergency Committee. What perfidiousness, lawlessness, infamy! Needless to say, they are ready for anything, even the worst. To lie to the whole world about the incapacity of the President . . .

The guards outside the house are reinforced at night. Now the President's personal security officers will have to work more or less around the clock.

We have agreed – Mikhail Sergeyevich, the children and I – to save the food, using up only old supplies purchased before 17 August. We made up a fruit package for the children. To be on the safe side, Irina hid it in the cupboard under the air-conditioner. We collected all our personal medical supplies, pills. We decided not to use anything else.

We spent a sleepless night . . .

We recorded Mikhail Sergeyevich's Address to the People on our video. We are planning to try to transmit it to the outside world, and if we fail, to hide and preserve the tape. Whatever happens to us, the people should know the truth about the fate of the President. We found a room that we considered safe, since it was invisible from the sea or the cliffs, and drew the curtains. At about four a.m. we were watching the film we had made, the sound turned down very low, when we suddenly heard a door slamming below, on the ground floor. Mikhail Sergeyevich and Irina went downstairs to check all the doors. Everything was closed. Mikhail Sergeyevich went outside. Two sentries guarded the door. Irina and Anatoly processed the film until six in the morning. They checked it through the vision slot of the camera, then took the cassette apart and cut the film, using manicure scissors, into four parts – we had made four recordings. Each piece of tape was wound around a thin paper reel, sealed with Scotch tape and wrapped in paper. They were hidden in various places around the house. The cassette was reassembled so as not to show that it had been taken apart.

20 AUGUST, TUESDAY
Still neither mail nor newspapers. Several patrol vessels are cruising at the entrance of our bay.

Once more Mikhail Sergeyevich transmitted his demands to Moscow, requesting that the telephone lines should be reconnected, newspapers delivered, and an aeroplane sent without delay to enable him to return to his work in Moscow. He added a new demand: to announce over the radio and on television that he was in good health.

There are no visible results, except for Generalov's assertion that all our demands are being transmitted to Moscow. Mikhail Sergeyevich warns: unless my demands are met I shall resort to extreme measures.

Outwardly we try to behave as usual: follow the doctor's orders, walk around outdoors and stroll to the seashore. We stick together: Mikhail Sergeyevich, Irina, Anatoly, I and the grandchildren: anything may happen.

We give each other moral support. It is not only us, the members of the family, but all those who happened to have been with us at the time are also interned. I am concerned about the women, to keep them calm and self-controlled. And, of course, to shield the grandchildren from any knowledge of what is happening.

The senior guard voices concern about the food: i.e. 'the food is supplied from elsewhere', brought in by an outside car – 'it may be dangerous.' They have the same suspicions as we do ourselves. We have now adopted a common decision: to draw on our own available supplies and those of the guards' mess. We discuss matters once more in detail with the cook, Galina Afrikanovna. We instructed her to use only boiled food.

I had a talk with the senior guard officer and asked him: 'Oleg Anatolievich, is there any chance of sending a message outside, by-passing Generalov?' (I did not explain what was at stake.) He answered: 'None. We are totally blocked from the sea. On land we are surrounded so closely that it isn't possible to get through.'

I have nothing but my notebook with me.

Next we attempted to make use of a real-life situation: Olga Vasilievna's young child, whom she left behind in Moscow, has fallen ill. Her father has a cardiac condition. Mikhail Sergeyevich instructed Chernyaev to demand that Generalov should allow Olga Vasilievna to return to Moscow.

. . . Mikhail Sergeyevich and I are discussing the situation. How is it that Lukyanov and the USSR Supreme Soviet are silent? Why is Ivashko silent? And what about the leaders of the republics? After all, today the Union Treaty is supposed to be signed.

Yesterday Kravchuk[1] spoke on Ukrainian television. He called for 'calm, common sense, compliance with the law and prevention of a confrontation.' Not a word about the President . . .

Are Mikhail Sergeyevich's demands really being transmitted? Is there any way of sending a message out?

Nobody is allowed to leave the dacha. Perhaps we should attempt a breakout? According to Oleg Anatolievich our combat unit is small but well-armed.

Western radio broadcasts the news that the state of emergency has

[1] Chairman of the Ukrainian Supreme Soviet.

821

been declared in Moscow; armed forces are deployed; Moscow and Leningrad do not support the conspirators. A clear explanation about Gorbachev's situation is requested – his whereabouts and his state of health. The news also refers to a possible suspension of economic aid to the USSR.

Our news: someone from outside was trying to gain access to the grounds of the dacha. They failed, the area is off limits . . . Generalov suddenly appeared in the service building where the security officers are staying. For two days he had not come to see them . . . But he had brought Yanayev's answer to Mikhail Sergeyevich's demands: supposedly, they will be met. Generalov commented that he had 'forwarded everything to Moscow through Plekhanov. The answer has also come through him.'

The senior guard officers are concerned about the growing activity on the sea. Oleg Anatolievich warns against taking the children for a swim in the evening, or even letting them go walking in the grounds. Kseniya and Anastasiya[1] were told: 'You mustn't go out, there'll be very strong wind, you must stay indoors.'

I have a feeling that something could happen at any moment. Part of the guard unit will be staying in the house. Igor Anatolievich and Nikolai Feodosievich – the doctors – will also stay in the house with us. Irina took Kseniya and Anastasiya into her bed. Anatoly slept on the floor next to them.

It is three o'clock in the morning.

21 AUGUST, WEDNESDAY
Morning news: clashes in Moscow. There are casualties – some wounded and killed. Has the most terrible started . . . ?

Mikhail Sergeyevich insists on transmitting immediately a message to Yanayev: stop using the army, return the troops to the barracks.

At about ten a.m. the outlines of two groups of ships appeared on the horizon. At the entrance of the bay three vessels are 'laid up'. There are five new ships. They are landing craft. They were heading straight towards the shore, towards us. They almost reached the patrol vessels but then sharply changed their course, turning in the direction of Sebastopol and disappearing behind Cape Sarych. What were they trying to demonstrate? A blockade? The possibility of arresting us? Rescue? I have no doubt – they know the President is alive and well.

Oleg Anatolievich and Boris Ivanovich recommend us to stay indoors. They fear a possible skirmish, jeopardizing the President's life.

Two-day-old newspapers are delivered to the house.

---

[1] The Gorbachevs' granddaughters.

No official announcements, neither on television nor over the radio, about Mikhail Sergeyevich's state of health. How preposterous: the President is 'ill and incapacitated' and not a word about it! Meanwhile, information is being broadcast about Prime Minister Pavlov's condition and state of health.

. . . At about three p.m. Irina and Anatoly heard on the BBC news on our Sony that Kryuchkov had permitted a group of people, a 'delegation', to fly to Foros to see for themselves that Gorbachev was indeed gravely ill and incapacitated. We consider this a sign that the worst is to come. Within the next few hours actions may be carried out to translate the infamous lie into reality.

Mikhail Sergeyevich has ordered the guards to block all drives leading up to the house as well as its entrance and not let anyone in without his permission; to be ready for action and to use force if necessary.

Guards with machine-guns have been deployed along the staircase of the house and at the entrance door.

The children, Kseniya and Anastasiya, have been locked in a room. We have asked Aleksandra Grigorievna, our housekeeper, to stay with them.

I am seized by an apprehension of impending danger. 'What are they going to do?' My head was throbbing, there was but one thought – we must hide Mikhail Sergeyevich. But where? The dacha spread before my eyes. And suddenly, within seconds, I felt a numbness and a limpness in my arm and the words would not come, impossible to say anything . . . A thought flashed across my mind: 'Stroke . . .'

Thank God, help was nearby: my family, the doctors. They were all in the house. I was put to bed and given medicine.

. . . A knock at the door at about five p.m. Oleg Anatolievich enters: 'Mikhail Sergeyevich, cars have arrived – two Zils and a Volga. Inside are Yazov, Kryuchkov, Baklanov, Ivashko, Lukyanov and Plekhanov. They are asking to see you.' He added: 'What are they planning? Why have they come?' Mikhail Sergeyevich ordered: 'Take them into custody. Transmit the demand – I refuse to see anyone unless government communications are restored.'

Within minutes Oleg returned with the answer: 'It would take too long, they say. It would take at least thirty minutes to connect the lines. They are asking to meet you now.' Mikhail Sergeyevich replied: 'Let them wait. There will be no negotiations until communications are fully restored.'

At 5.45 p.m. communications were switched on – after 73 hours. Isolation has ended! So has the arrest!

Irina came in. 'Plekhanov and Ivashko were trying to enter the dacha. Boris Ivanovich stopped them at the entrance: "Orders – no-one is to go in. We will shoot!" Plekhanov said: "I knew it . . . They would shoot." They turned around and went back. Father is still on the telephone.'

Mikhail Sergeyevich came in. Asked how I am feeling. Told me that he refused to talk to any of the plotters (despite repeated attempts on their part). He immediately got in touch with Boris Nikolaevich Yeltsin: 'Mikhail Sergeyevich, my dear man, are you alive? We have been holding firm here for forty-eight hours!' He talked to other leaders of the republics. George and Barbara Bush sent their greetings to me, said that they had been praying for us for the last three days. He showed me a note signed by Lukyanov and Ivashko: 'Dear Mikhail Sergeyevich, this is an urgent request for a meeting with you now if possible. We have something to report to you.' He said: 'I'll not see Kryuchkov, Baklanov or Yazov. I have nothing to say to them. As to Lukyanov and Ivashko . . . maybe, later. I am waiting for the Russian delegation to arrive.'

. . . The delegation arrives: Rutskoi, Silayev, Bakatin, Primakov, Stolyarov, Fedorov, some deputies and the press. All came into the house. Joyous, excited voices are heard on the ground floor, below . . .

I asked Irina to call the women who have been here with us all these days. We embraced and shed a tear or two. I thanked them for all they have done for us and shared with us.

Anatoly came in. 'Mikhail Sergeyevich has issued instructions to get ready. We are leaving. Never mind our belongings, leave them behind. They'll pack our things and put them on the next flight, which will carry all the other "Muscovites".'

FAILURE OF THE PLOT

As the reader can see from the entries in Raisa's diary, we lived through those three August days on the brink of human endurance. Yet I retained my presence of mind and was active. Having discovered from the televised press conference that the plot hinged on 'Gorbachev's illness and incapacity', I began taking strolls around the grounds to show to the crews of the patrol vessels, the guards officers and all those others who were watching the dacha that I was in good health.

I made a taped statement, as described in Raisa Maksimovna's diary. I was exposed to some ironic remarks on that score. However, I had to provide for the possibility that the worst might happen. If I had disappeared, this tape would have become an important political document.

It all ended quickly, but it could have been otherwise. Polls conducted subsequently showed that about 40 per cent sympathized with the coup. And the leaders of the republics – with the exception of Yeltsin and perhaps Akayev – took their time to think it over. Even some foreign leaders adopted a wait-and-see attitude. The coup was defeated, but had it happened a year earlier, another outcome could not have been ruled out. This may well be the most convincing argument in favour of my policy of evolutionary change, trying to bring the majority with us.

Listening carefully to the radio, I had sensed already by 20 August that the situation was not developing in favour of the conspirators. This impression was subsequently confirmed by the arrival of the plot leaders: Kryuchkov, Yazov and Lukyanov. Ivashko was on the flight with them.

I don't think they were coming to say they were sorry. This was another desperate attempt to sway me to their side. Otherwise the deployment of fresh marine reinforcements at Balbek airport and the order to fire on any aircraft that tried to land without permission made no sense. They were obviously concerned about the possible arrival of members of the Russian leadership.

I insisted that no discussions should take place until communications had been restored. I talked on the telephone with Yeltsin, Nazarbayev, Dementei and leaders of the other republics. I also got in touch with President Bush. I began issuing orders. Yazov was dismissed and his duties as Minister of Defence were entrusted to Moiseyev, who was to ensure that the flight carrying Rutskoi and his comrades could land at Balbek. The chief of government communications was instructed to disconnect the telephone lines of all the plotters. The Kremlin commandant was to secure the buildings and to isolate all the conspirators who had stayed behind there.

The Russian delegation arrived. It was then that I really felt that I was free.

I talked to Lukyanov and Ivashko in the presence of Bakatin and Primakov. I said that the two of them could have foiled the coup, or at least unmasked its criminal character. The Chairman of the Supreme Soviet knew my supposed illness to be a lie, yet he hoped that the fruit of the plot would drop into his 'basket', seeing himself already as President. Ivashko could have firmly dissociated himself from their actions, demanding an urgent meeting with me on behalf of the Party leadership. He had not done so. On the contrary, the Secretariat issued an order to the local Party organs to support the coup.

I decided against a meeting with Kryuchkov and Yazov. After my return from Foros they were arrested, along with the other conspirators, and an inquiry was initiated. I was shown their initial statements: they admitted having committed a crime, although each of them tried to underplay his own guilt. I received a handwritten letter from Kryuchkov, telling me that 'on the whole, I do feel very remorseful.'

THE FATE OF THE PARTY – WHO BETRAYED WHOM?

I returned to Moscow on 22 August, at two a.m. Our plane landed at Vnukovo, where we were warmly welcomed. Raisa Maksimovna, Kseniya and I got into the same car. Irina, Anatoly and Nastenka took another car. And that is when the tension that had been accumulating in the last days gave way. Irina had a nervous breakdown. Our eldest granddaughter, Kseniya, had understood much of what had happened. As a consequence of Foros and subsequent events in the country, Raisa Maksimovna was not well again for two years.

On 23 August I went to the Kremlin. On my way to the office I made a statement to reporters that was subsequently quoted and interpreted in different ways: 'I have come back from Foros to another country, and I myself am a different man now.' That was a spontaneous impression. At the time I was not yet fully aware of the extent of the tragedy.

As a matter of fact there was much that I did not know and it was simply impossible to digest all the information at once. My working days were spent in continuous consultations, studying documents, and urgent decision-making. Late at night I would take home several heavy briefcases and read memoranda, embassy dispatches and telegraph agency briefs until the small hours of the morning. Gradually a complete picture of the events took shape.

I found out later that some of those whose appointments I had confirmed upon my return to Moscow had been ready to run with the hares and hunt with the hounds. I had to revise these appointments. Allusions were made to Gorbachev's loss of willpower, his going round in circles and treading water. Not so. Such errors were due to lack of information. Much would be disclosed only months later and certain issues have not been fully clarified to this day. We can only hope that 'there is nothing hid that shall not be revealed.'

It was disgraceful that a majority in the Secretariat of the Central Committee and many regional Party bodies supported the Emergency Committee. I have to give credit to Central Committee secretaries Galina Semenova, Andrei Girenko and Yegor Stroyev: in that highly complex situation they proved to be mature politicians and honest people. But the Central Committee as a whole failed the test of collective leadership and in effect made common cause with the Emergency Committee, although many members spoke against the coup.

Nazarbayev and Karimov resigned their membership of the Politburo, while some of the leaders of the Communist Parties of the republics left the Central Committee.

In September articles began to appear which asserted implicitly or explicitly that I had been 'in collusion' with the conspirators. According to one version, I had been unwilling to sign their declaration overtly but had promised to join them if everything went smoothly. Needless to say, both versions were false. The Union Treaty, the transformation of the country into a viable democratic federation as well as the general plan of perestroika, the sweeping reforms and the new thinking in the sphere of international politics – these had become my life's work. Why then would I want to lift my hand against it?

Political blindness and a narrow-minded vision, fanned by mercenary self-interest, had provoked the actions of the conspirators. The separatists and extreme radicals now possessed the most devastating argument in favour of the break-up of the Union. The leaders of the coup had dislodged the stone that started a landslide.

I am not vindictive by nature and would not want to see these mostly elderly and sickly men exposed to physical deprivation. The deliberately postponed trial, suspended under the terms of an amnesty, was discontinued in February 1994 by the military board of the Russian Supreme Court. Nonetheless, history will pass a harsh judgement on them. Even assuming that the defendants were motivated solely by their patriotic concerns, not by self-interest, their reckless venture had disastrous consequences. In fact there is evidence that they acted from self-interest.

At the very end of July, just before I went on holiday, I met Yeltsin and Nazarbayev at Novo-Ogarevo. We discussed measures to be taken after the signing of the Union Treaty. Until then we had assumed that the treaty would be followed by six months' work drafting the new Constitution, and that its approval would entail the election of new organs of power. Now the question arose as to whether the elections should be so delayed. Yeltsin and Nazarbayev were in favour of bringing the structures of the Union bodies into line with the provisions of the treaty without delay, in view of the dangerous disintegration in all spheres of public life. We agreed to discuss this with the leaders of the other republics.

Then there was a discussion concerning the cadres. It began, of course, with the candidacy of the President of the Union of Sovereign States. Yeltsin proposed to nominate me to that post. In the course of our discussion a proposal was made to recommend Nazarbayev for the post of head of the Cabinet. He said that he would be prepared to assume that responsibility, provided that the Union Cabinet of Ministers would be able to work independently. Mention was made of the need for a substantial revamping of the upper echelons of executive power, replacing the Deputy Prime Ministers and, especially, the heads of key ministries. The replacement of Yazov and Kryuchkov was specifically mentioned. I remember that Yeltsin was ill at ease – he behaved as if someone were sitting next to him and eavesdropping. I realize now that Yeltsin's intuition had not deceived him. Plekhanov had prepared the room in advance. Our conversation was being taped. When they heard that we intended to replace them, Kryuchkov and the others lost their heads. The claim that the plotters were driven by patriotic feelings alone is sheer demagoguery.

The most important problem I had to face on my return to Moscow was the question of the Party. Throughout 24 and 25 August I held consultations about it with my advisers and aides – Yakovlev, Medvedev, Primakov, Chernyaev, Shakhnazarov, Revenko and Kudryavtsev, as well as some of the Party leaders. As a result of agonizing reflection, certain decisions were made: to relinquish my duties as General Secretary of the Party, and to recommend to the Central Committee that it should dissolve itself and let the Party organizations decide independently on their future.

I had to shoulder a great deal of criticism from my former Party comrades for that attitude. While denouncing the coup, some of them disagreed about the need for such measures as regards the Party. Turning it over again and again in my mind, I still believe that no mistake was made. First of all, the charges of betrayal, that I had 'abandoned the Party', have no basis in fact. Certainly it was not I who had been disloyal to the Party. I had remained as General Secretary of the Party even though in the end it became detrimental to my status as President of the country. On the contrary, it was the Party leadership and a large number of the Party nomenklatura that had let down their leader.

It is wrong to blame me for the dissolution of the Party. In the extreme circumstances after the coup I took the decision that the future should be left to the Party organizations to decide. And when, at a meeting of the Supreme Soviet of Russia, Yeltsin ostentatiously signed his decree banning the CPSU, I protested against this action, arguing that it might unleash a wave of anti-Communist hysteria which would be unfair and dangerous. For this, I was booed at the Supreme Soviet by intolerant radicals who were called, not without justification, the 'neo-Bolsheviks'. One of them took the microphone to declare in a hysterical voice that all Communists 'must be swept out of the country with a broom.'

I made then a statement that I will not retract to this day: 'Such ravings only prove that you need to have your head examined. Even Stalin's sick brain did not breed such ideas. Do you really intend to expel eighteen million Communists from the country – if you include their families, 50 to 70 million people? If you call yourselves democrats you have to act accordingly.'

The press ignored this statement.

The meeting at the Supreme Soviet of Russia was filmed. Those who saw it on television have understood a great deal. At that encounter Yeltsin was gloating with sadistic pleasure. Meanwhile it seemed to me that some of my associates in the meeting hall were also gloating. Aleksandr Yakovlev kept silent.

After that meeting Yeltsin and I went to his office. He tried to defuse the situation by saying that the deputies' behaviour was understandable after what they had gone through. And he added: 'I won't point the finger at anyone. You will soon find out how people behaved on 19 and 20 August – including those towards whom you harbour good feelings. We who opposed the conspirators were virtually alone; the rest preferred to wait and see.'

Still, the banning of the Party had a pernicious effect on millions of innocent members. The majority of Party members had favoured both perestroika and the reforms. I categorically disagree with attempts to malign the whole history of the Party, portraying its founder as a villain, denying credit to the Party for what it has done for the country, and accusing it of stashing away billions of dollars in foreign banks. Fortunately the Constitutional Court took a decision that prevented the launch of another witch hunt.

These developments have to be examined in a broader historic perspective. The break-up of the Party was inevitable at a certain stage, because of the different ideological and political trends in its membership. I advocated proceeding by democratic means: convening a congress in November and making an amicable divide. According to some opinion polls, the version of the programme adopted by me and my followers was favoured by nearly a third of the Party members.

The rest would have been scattered – some joining Nina Andreyeva and Anpilov and others adhering to Buzgalin and Kosolapov, Medvedev and Denisov, Lipitsky and Rutskoi. And a considerable group would probably have joined DemRossiya, Travkin's Democratic Party or the Christian Democrats. That is what eventually happened. Regrets about the collapse of the Party are therefore meaningless. Having played its historic role, it had to leave the scene. New left-wing parties have now been formed, including Communist-oriented parties.

It all happened in an extremely painful and even scandalous way. Responsibility for this and the tremendous moral damage inflicted on millions of Party members should weigh heavily upon the conscience of the conspirators and their supporters. Primarily, it is the fault of the conservative wing of the RCP. I do not wish to condemn anyone – let historians pass the final judgement. Yet I cannot remain silent concerning one person, a former university comrade whom I had promoted to the second-highest post in the state and who played a key role in the plot. I am referring to Lukyanov.

Assuming for a moment that Lukyanov was really unaware of the plot and was misled by the conspirators – at least that is how he justified himself to me in Foros – why then did he fail to convene the USSR Supreme Soviet, as was his duty under these circumstances? Had he done so, everything would have fallen into place. He failed to do this, because like an inveterate gambler he hedged his bets. He reckoned that in a week, a delay that was not against the regulations, the situation would have crystallized: either the plot would have succeeded, leaving him in a good position, or it would have failed, and he would escape the consequences. He played a double game, as the saying goes. But he miscalculated.

Had the USSR Supreme Soviet, the country's supreme legislative body, convened at the outset of the adventure, it would undeniably have defended constitutional order and resolutely condemned the conspiracy. Unfortunately there was no clearly established procedure for convening Parliament in emergency situations.

But the most important thing is to draw the lessons from what happened then. The events of August 1991 laid bare the Achilles heel of the democratic system that we had created – the weakness of our representative bodies.

31

THE LAST EFFORTS AND THE BELOVEZH CONSPIRACY

IN THE AFTERMATH OF THE COUP, I WAS ANXIOUS TO RELAUNCH the reform process. To be frank, I had some doubts about whether the task could be completed under the new circumstances. The coup had given a strong impulse to disintegration. All the republics declared their independence in September and October 1991. The separatists felt that their day had come. The Russian President was in a frenzy: even though the USSR President had resumed his duties, Yeltsin continued for a few days to issue decrees applying to the entire Union. This was even more reason for the republics to cut themselves off quickly from the Union centre.

Still we had no right to give up – and I could invoke the results of the 17 March referendum. The country's entire history spoke in favour of preserving its unity. Moreover, this choice was dictated both by vital economic needs and the necessity to ensure the security of the state and its citizens.

My optimism was bolstered by the results of opinion polls conducted in major cities (Moscow, Kiev, Alma Ata, and Krasnoyarsk) in early October. They showed that public opinion in favour of preserving the Union had not significantly changed over the last six months. In the 17 March referendum, 73 per cent of the voters in three republics (Russia, Ukraine and Kazakhstan) had expressed themselves in favour of the Union – and, according to the October polls, some 75 per cent of those questioned in major cities of the same three republics favoured its preservation. In Moscow, the number of Union supporters had actually risen from 50 to 81 per cent, evidence that in the 17 March referendum some Muscovites had been heavily influenced by the 'anti-centre' propaganda campaign waged by the democrats and were not voting against the idea of the Union in itself. It seemed that the very real threat of disintegration had led to a surge of pro-Union feeling in the capital, a shift which was also visible in most of the Russian provinces. The results of the survey were less impressive in Kiev; even so, more than 50 per cent continued to support the Union. In Alma Ata, 94 per cent had voted 'yes' in the referendum, compared with 86 per cent in the October poll.

In short, there could be no doubt that the people did not want the disintegration of the country. However, the key to this vital issue lay in the hands of national elites and political leaders, which made the situation far more difficult.

Nursultan Nazarbayev was the most consistent advocate of the Union. We had frequent and extended talks on this issue. His position was influenced by objective factors, such as the make-up of the population of Kazakhstan and its high, not to say unique, level of economic integration with Russia. However, one should not forget Nursultan Abishevich's personal qualities, both as a statesman and as an individual who embodied the indissoluble blending of the Russian and Kazakh national cultures. One could see that for him it was a question of principle rather than a political calculation. I had watched Nazarbayev for a long time and always valued his business-like approach – and I deeply regret that circumstances prevented me from proposing him as USSR Vice-President or USSR Prime Minister.

The leaders of the Central Asian republics – Karimov, Akayev, Niyazov and Iskanderov, who at the time represented Tajikistan – held similar views. What fate awaits them in our turbulent times I cannot say, but I must state that in this watershed period, while the fate of the Union was being decided, these national leaders showed a genuine understanding of the colossal losses the break-up of the Union would inflict on their peoples. This is not to say that they unconditionally supported every proposal tabled by the

Union agencies. Each aspired to free his republic from the heavy burden of excessive centralism. Nevertheless it ought to be said that they never lost their common sense and refrained from transforming independence into a fetish, an end in itself, to be pursued regardless of the consequences.

I started meeting leaders of the republics immediately after the coup. On 23 August I had a talk with Yeltsin, Nazarbayev, Akayev and Mutalibov. Not all of the leaders were able to come to Moscow yet, but we soon organized another meeting at Novo-Ogarevo, which was attended by more of the republican leaders.

The coup had left the machinery of power and administration in a state of disorder. Republican authorities more often than not implemented only those decisions of the Union ministries they considered advantageous for themselves. Meanwhile, the centre was in a state of growing confusion, owing to the fact that the power – if not *de jure*, then *de facto* – was being divided between the Kremlin and the Russian White House. The capital was so taken up by this infighting that it was gradually losing all control over the national economy, which fuelled the desire of local authorities to act on their own.

All of us realized that the only chance of restoring order was to create an efficient organ that guaranteed co-ordination of the republics' and the Union's interests. The initial idea of making republican leaders members of the USSR Security Council was eventually abandoned and it was decided to create the USSR State Council instead.

We saw the concentration of power in the hands of the State Council as a transitional measure, which was to remain in force until the signing of a new Union Treaty defining the structure of new Union agencies, their relations with the republics etc. The question of recommencing work on the Union Treaty was raised at the very first Novo-Ogarevo meeting after the coup. In September it still seemed feasible to resurrect and conclude the Union Treaty, this time making sure it was signed without interference.

At the same time we understood that, given the situation, we could hardly expect all the republics to join the renewed Union. It was therefore decided to implement a proposal that had been actively discussed since mid-1990: an economic agreement to be signed along with the Union Treaty.

This could be seen as the second level of association, making it possible not to lose those republics which were, like all the others, in great need of economic co-operation but which for some reason were not prepared to join the Union. I do not make a secret of the fact that we hoped the economic ties would eventually help overcome mistrust towards the Union structures.

The August coup had shattered the process of establishing new Union ties between sovereign states. Aware how dangerous the new situation was for democratic transformations, I considered work on the Union Treaty as the top priority. This belief guided all of my actions during the extraordinary session of the USSR Supreme Soviet, convened immediately after the attempted coup, which decided to call an extraordinary Congress of People's Deputies without further delay.

In analysing the atmosphere on the eve of the Congress and discussing its agenda, both I and the republican leaders wanted to avoid becoming absorbed in fruitless debates from the very beginning. It was essential for the President and the republican leaders to come to the Congress united – this was far more important than my report, however brilliant that might be. In discussions that went on far into the night the idea was born of a joint declaration, signed by the leaders of ten Union states (another, Georgia, also participated in the drafting – hence the formula '10(11) + 1'). Some people even went as far as to suggest that Gorbachev and the republican leaders had effectively organized their own *coup d'état* after the failed August putsch. This was sheer nonsense, of course – for a start, in September all the decisions were taken by the Congress, in other words, in accordance with the Constitution. Furthermore, the supreme legislative authority, the USSR Supreme Soviet, had been preserved. Finally, the fundamental reorganization of the power structures was not a whim of the country's leaders but a necessary temporary measure dictated by the aftermath of the coup and the new realities.

In other words, there had been no violation, however slight, of the Constitution. Whether these decisions could work is a different question altogether. Alas, the following months showed that the newly created system was not viable: not because of inherent flaws – the main reason was that it did not correspond to the ideas of the Russian President's circle.

Be that as it may, at that time Yeltsin spoke out, both in public and in private, for the preservation of a reformed Union, which made it possible for us to agree on the organization of power structures in a transitional period relatively quickly. In the declaration of the USSR President and the leaders of the ten republics, it was proposed to prepare and sign the Treaty on the Union of Sovereign States, in which every republic could independently define the form of its participation; to call on all republics, regardless of the status they proclaimed, to conclude an Economic Union without further delay; to create a council of representatives of people's deputies which would 'decide general questions of principle', a State Council 'to co-ordinate decisions on domestic and foreign policy issues that affected the common interests of the republics', and an 'Inter-republican economic committee for the co-ordination of economic management and joint implementation of economic reforms'; to prepare and submit to the parliaments of the Union republics a draft constitution; to conclude an agreement on principles of collective security in the field of defence, with the aim of preserving common armed forces and a common strategic military area and radically reforming the armed forces, the KGB, the Ministry of Internal Affairs and the USSR Prokuratura, to take into account the sovereign status of the republics; to confirm strict observance of all international agreements and obligations assumed by the Soviet Union; to adopt a declaration that guaranteed the rights and freedoms of citizens; and to ask the Congress of People's Deputies to support the Union republics' request to the United Nations for recognition as subjects of international law and consideration of their application for membership in the United Nations.

The Vth Extraordinary Congress of People's Deputies began on 2 September. The debates centred on the document we had submitted to the Congress. The discussion was heated and sometimes highly emotional, but the proposals were eventually passed without major amendments, with the exception of the point suggesting that legislative functions be vested in the council of representatives of people's deputies during the transitional period. After debating the issue the Congress decided – rightly, it seems to me – that the USSR Supreme Soviet should continue its work until the signing of the Union Treaty and the creation of new authorities. This decision guaranteed supervision of the decrees of the State Council and a more reliable constitutional succession.

Speaking at the Congress, Kravchuk said that Ukraine was ready to 'participate actively in the creation of inter-state structures in the fields of economic ties, co-ordination and economic management, joint decisions on domestic and foreign policy, the development of a concept of collective security and the reorganization of the armed forces.' Less than six weeks later, the same Kravchuk would back out of practically all of these commitments.

Passions flared up at the session on 4 September, when a number of deputies accused the Presidium of undemocratic behaviour. I must admit that there were grounds for such accusations. The Presidium was indeed compelled to chair the sessions in a strict manner, lest we be faced with a Soviet version of the 'Long Parliament',[1] a situation which had to be prevented at all costs, given the tense atmosphere after the coup. Needless to say, the question lay not so much in the procedures, in spite of all their importance. Some of the deputies simply refused to take a realistic view of the situation and accept that the preservation of the USSR in its former shape had become impossible after the August events. The only way to preserve the country's unity was to conclude the Treaty on the Union of Sovereign States, and the majority of the deputies – one could even say, the overwhelming majority – were aware of this. The Congress resolution, the law on state power and management agencies in the transitional period and other decisions were passed by a majority of between three and four fifths of the deputies.

[1] Session of the English Parliament summoned by King Charles I in November 1640. It lasted until either April 1658 or March 1660 (depending on the source).

The Congress progressed in never-ending meetings, negotiations and consultations. Commissions and committees worked feverishly during the breaks. We had to answer the inquiries of the deputies and jointly find a formula for the participation of autonomous republics in the Union, without which their leaders refused to support the decisions of the Congress. Obviously I could not refuse the many deputies who simply wanted to express their support for the President and their sympathy for what we had been through during the coup, or those who wanted to ask for some explanation, to complain or to raise some issue vital for their constituency. Needless to say, I was also beleaguered by reporters.

I must admit that I was utterly exhausted. Yet my spirits were boosted by the realization that we had prevented the break-up of the Union. It seemed to me that, having enjoyed the delights of independence, we would eventually reunite to form a single state built on a new foundation. My hopes were bolstered by the results of opinion polls. Forty-six per cent of the Congress preferred the USSR to become a federation and 27 per cent wanted a confederation; only 15 per cent wished the Union to break up into separate, independent states. I have no doubt that if the same question were put to the citizens of Russia and the other republics today, the result would be quite similar.

However, the Russian leadership, albeit not openly, held a different view. Indeed, soon after the Congress, it began the methodical, step-by-step subversion and destruction of the agreement for the transitional period approved and passed by the Vth Extraordinary Congress of People's Deputies.

The first act of the State Council was to recognize the independence of the Baltic republics. I had tried to prevent these republics from leaving the Union. At the same time, I refute all allegations that, to achieve this, the Union leadership resorted to the use of force. The tragic incidents in Vilnius and Riga[1] were in no way directed from the presidential office. Subsequent events have proved that we were right to insist on a civilized and democratic solution to the question of independence for Latvia,

---

[1] In January 1991.

Lithuania and Estonia. Had it not been for the pressure – fuelled by separatists – and short-sightedness of the Russian leadership, it might well have been that today we would not be faced with the dramatic problems caused by the violations of the rights of the Russian and Russian-speaking population of the Baltic states.

Having decided to recognize the independence of the Baltic states, we were not able to start proper negotiations on the procedures because of the Belovezh conspiracy.

THE REBIRTH OF THE UNION TREATY

On 5 September the Congress of People's Deputies, on the proposal of the President and the republics' leaders, decided to establish a Union of Sovereign States and speed up the preparation of the draft treaty.

The members of the State Council entrusted me and the President of Russia with the drafting of a new treaty. We set to work immediately after the Congress.

On 10 September I had a meeting with Yeltsin at which we discussed the relevant issues. On 16 September the question of the future of the Union was examined by the State Council, with eight republics (Russia, Belarus, Uzbekistan, Kazakhstan, Turkmenistan, Azerbaijan, Tajikistan, Kyrgyzstan) adopting a positive approach.

At the same session, the State Council examined the draft treaty on the proposed economic community. After its signing on 18 October by eight sovereign states, including Ukraine, it was submitted for ratification to the parliaments of the republics. Meanwhile work on the package of concomitant agreements was in full swing.

At the same time, the Union power structures were being formed in accordance with the new conditions; new leaders were named and we set to work reorganizing the Ministries of Foreign Affairs, Internal Affairs, and Defence, and the KGB, and creating the inter-republic economic committee.

Thus, having recovered from the shock of the August coup, the leaders of the Union and the republics resumed their work on political and economic reform of the Union. There were grounds to believe that we had succeeded in reviving the Novo-Ogarevo process. However, progress during the autumn months was slow and interrupted by periodic setbacks.

The pace of the preparations depended to a large extent on whether we could use the text agreed on and ready for signing in August as a basis for the draft (obviously taking into account the new conditions), or whether we would have to begin again on an altogether different basis. When Yeltsin and I set to work on an updated draft, his team made an attempt to push through their own text. It was clear from the first reading that he was proposing neither a federation nor even a confederation. The document seemed to aim at creating a community like the European Union but with even weaker functions for the central organs.

I told Yeltsin bluntly that nothing would come of our work if we used that text as a basis. The republics' leaders, to whom the Russians had sent an unofficial version of the text in the hope of raising additional support, adopted a similar position. After some wavering (apparently, he was under great pressure from his circle), the Russian President agreed to resume work on the basis of the pre-August draft – obviously taking into account the 'Russian' version.

Argument in the working group resumed immediately on the distribution of power between Union and republican power agencies and authorities. In the end, it was agreed to leave out the details; the Union Treaty would provide for 'spheres of joint competence', whereas subsequently multilateral agreements would be concluded on the economic union, joint defence, state security, foreign policy, scientific and technological co-operation, co-operation in the fields of education and culture, protection of human rights and national minorities, the environment, energy, transport, communications, space and crime prevention.

This decision had an obvious disadvantage: the creation of a clearly defined power structure, which was vital to get the country out of the crisis, was delayed for an indefinite period. On the other hand, it also had some positive aspects: the transfer of these issues to the level of multilateral agreements would make it possible to set forth in greater detail the questions to be resolved jointly and the procedures to be adopted.

The revised draft Union Treaty was dated 1 October. While we were working on the draft in Moscow, Yeltsin, who was in Sochi, received a memorandum labelled 'top secret' – 'The strategy of Russia in the transitional period'.

Much of what is happening today in Russia and in the states of the Commonwealth can be traced back to such 'research papers' produced by the 'brains trust' of DemRossiya. The following are a few quotations from this document, which reminds me of a sort of 'mine-laying' scheme, with the difference that its application was political rather than military.

Until the August events, the Russian leadership, in its opposition to the old totalitarian centre, could rely on the support of the leaders of the overwhelming majority of the Union republics, who strove to strengthen their own political positions. The liquidation of the old centre inevitably brings to the fore the objective conflict of interests between Russia and the other republics. For the latter, the preservation of existing channels of resource transfers and financial and economic ties represents a unique opportunity to rebuild their economy at the expense of Russia. For the Russian Federation, which is faced with a serious crisis, it means a severe additional burden on its economic structures, undermining the prospects of its economic revival.

Objectively speaking, Russia has no need for a higher-level economic centre redistributing its resources. However, a number of other republics are interested in the existence of such a centre. Having established control over property on their own territory, they strive for a redistribution of Russian property and resources to their own advantage by way of Union organs. Such a centre being viable only with the support of the republics, it will – regardless of the make-up of its staff – conduct a policy that is contrary to the interests of Russia.

It was therefore suggested that Russia 'should refrain from participating in long-term, strictly regulated and comprehensive economic unions', 'is not interested in creating permanent supra-republican organs of overall economic management', 'categorically refuses the transfer of tax payments to the federal budget', 'must have its own customs agency', etc.

At the same time, in an attempt to pay off their former fellow countrymen, the authors suggested recognizing the existing borders between the republics (in particular, it was asserted that the 'rights of the Russian-speaking population do not require any real protection') and assisting them in obtaining full international recognition as independent states.

Essentially, according to this concept, Russia was to renounce its role as the 'nucleus' of a world power. The underlying idea was that retaining Russia's resources for its own use would allow it to get rich quickly. I do not know who wrote this memorandum, but reading it you could clearly perceive the influence of DemRossiya's leading ideologists, who advocated precisely these views and had apparently succeeded in foisting them on their leader. To me, they appear fundamentally wrong.

Does Russia bear no responsibility for the fate of the peoples with whom it has lived side by side for centuries, for the future of the vast territories it developed? Of course, it seems pointless to expect a moral approach from people who put their selfish interests above everything else. But it is not only Russia's moral duty to avoid a break with the republics; it is its paramount economic interest. A unified economic structure is no empty phrase or fib of communist propaganda. It is a reality. Now that it has been practically destroyed, against all common sense, it is clear for all to see who was proved right in this historic dispute. And what about territorial questions, demographic problems, human rights, culture and science and, last but not least, the environment and security?

As I understand it, back in September 1991 the Russian President was not yet prepared to unconditionally adopt this erroneous philosophy and act in accordance with it. It seems that the memorandum was written to persuade him. But, by criticizing their leader for allegedly 'losing the fruits of the August victory', the authors unintentionally disclosed their own hidden agenda. They perceived the prospect of a break-up of the Union, which had emerged as a result of the coup, as a 'victory' rather than a tragedy. One could say that the leaders of the coup, supposedly their sworn enemies, had given it to them on a silver platter. Could this be the reason why the democrats, normally fierce and merciless towards all whom they perceive as 'from the other camp', treated the prisoners of Matrosskaya Tishina (the jail in Moscow where the leaders of the coup were held) so leniently?

On 28 to 30 October I was in Madrid, where, in my capacity as co-chairman, I was to open the Middle East conference with George Bush. In the meantime, my misgivings concerning the Russian President's vacillation proved to be correct. On 28 October Yeltsin outlined his programme of reform to the RSFSR Congress of People's Deputies, requesting special powers for the transitional period. The measures he proposed either undermined the agreement on the economic union or directly contradicted it. Indeed it was another assault on the Union. In a shocking gesture, Yeltsin proclaimed his intention to put Gosbank under Russian jurisdiction, to cut the staff of the USSR foreign ministry by 90 per cent, to disband eighty ministries etc. True, after a talk with Silayev, the Russian President desisted from his 'take-over' of Gosbank, which had alarmed the republics and caused bewilderment in the West, in spite of all Western sympathies for our newly fledged reformer.

Yeltsin and I met on 2 November. It seemed to me that the time had come for a man-to-man talk. I spoke frankly, accusing him of backing out of agreements already reached. I insisted on the need for co-ordinated action. Yeltsin appeared to agree. He protested that he had no intention of changing the policy we had agreed. He readily admitted that he had been a bit 'over-zealous' concerning the staff of the foreign ministry. However, it often happened that you would talk with Boris Nikolaevich, convince him and reach an agreement, and the next day he would suddenly yield to some other influence and do exactly the opposite.

At the session of the State Council on 4 November, I decided to continue our talk on these same issues. Yeltsin was fifteen minutes late, deliberately demonstrating his independence and disrespect for his partners. I did not wait for his arrival, and made a strong statement in front of television reporters, warning that we were squandering the capital we had received after the coup by indulging in political games.

Yeltsin was present during most of my speech, and he seemed to strongly resent it. He either frowned or affected indifference. A heavy tension reigned throughout the session. No-one took up my suggestion to put forward alternative views. Nazarbayev was the only one to speak. 'The situation is clear to us,' he said. 'What is important is that you and Boris Nikolaevich have talked and have reached agreement.' Yeltsin nodded approval. 'Good,' I concluded, 'then let us act in this spirit.'

Putting the question in very strong terms at a meeting of the State Council had its effect. Yeltsin was forced to agree formally to complete the ongoing work on the Union Treaty and to initial it at the next session.

THE LAST SESSIONS OF THE STATE COUNCIL

In the 14 November session of the State Council, a heated argument broke out over whether the peoples living in this vast country needed a 'union state' or a 'union of states'? The reader may have the impression that this is merely a question of semantics. However, the issue at stake was whether we should preserve one country or divide into a number of states, with all the ensuing consequences for the country's citizens, its economy, science, the armed forces, foreign policy etc.

After a four-hour discussion, we eventually agreed on a 'confederative union state'. All the republics' leaders made televised statements at the press conference. I had the impression that some of my partners tended to over-simplify the arguments in favour of a union state. I was the last to speak. I stressed that the Treaty on the Union of Sovereign States was vital to the reform of our unitary multinational state and to the fulfilment of our most urgent tasks.

The State Council spent most of the time debating the status of the future Union. Three possible options were examined. The first proposal was a union of sovereign states without a supra-national state structure. The second was a union with centralized state power – either federative or confederative. The third was a union that carried out a number of state functions, albeit without the status of a state and without a specific name. A number of compromise proposals were also discussed. In the end, the participants agreed on a 'union of sovereign states', a confederative state which would carry out the functions delegated to it by the parties to the treaty.

The next day, the newspaper *Izvestiya* reported Yeltsin's remark at the press conference that followed the State Council session: 'It is difficult to say how many states will join the Union,' he said, 'but I am convinced that there will be a Union.' Nazarbayev and the leaders of Belarus, Kyrgyzstan, Turkmenistan and Tajikistan spoke in the same vein.

It seemed that everything humanly possible had been done to preserve the Union State and conclude work on the draft treaty, which had been criminally interrupted in August. However, there remained one more river to cross in this three-year marathon: the 25 November session of the State Council, in which Yeltsin reiterated his demand for the formula 'Union State' to be replaced by 'Union of States', refusing to initial the text before its consideration by the Russian Supreme Soviet.

Yeltsin's referring to the Supreme Soviet was but a subterfuge. I knew the prevailing mood in the Russian Parliament and was convinced that only a few delegates would support Yeltsin's formula.

I was exasperated by this perfidious move. Still I kept my temper and tried to reason with Yeltsin, insisting on compliance with the decisions we had made only ten days earlier. However, the new balance of forces was making itself felt. First Shushkevich and then a few other leaders wavered, apparently anxious to avoid a rift with the Russian leader. On seeing this, I declared that I'd had enough. 'I will not participate in the destruction of the Union. I will leave you alone; the decision is up to you. Bear in mind that the entire responsibility for the fate of the country will fall on you.'

My colleagues attempted to stop me, but I got up and left,

accompanied by all the 'unionists'. Half an hour later, Yeltsin and Shushkevich came down to my office. Hardly able to conceal their disappointment at having been forced to retreat, they handed me a press release which had been approved by the remaining members of the State Council. I read the text and found it satisfactory. I made a few minor corrections, which the 'peace negotiators' accepted.

A press conference took place immediately afterwards. I informed the journalists that all the fundamental provisions remained unchanged, in spite of a few amendments: thus it had been decided to abolish the post of chairman in the future bicameral Supreme Soviet of the Union of Sovereign States (USS). In addition, the republics' leaders insisted on 'reinstating' the State Council as a co-ordinating body for foreign and domestic policies, chaired by the President. The status of the Union Procurator's office was specified; it was to be attached to the USS Supreme Court and would supervise the compliance with laws. The formula defining the principles for the co-ordination of foreign policy was also somewhat 'fine-tuned'.

At the press conference, reporters asked me whether I believed it was still feasible to sign the Union Treaty in early December. That seemed unlikely, I replied, but there was a good chance of signing it in mid-December, perhaps before 20 December. There was still work for the committees and the Supreme Soviets, which would be followed by debates and approval procedures and finally the appointment of plenipotentiary delegations entrusted with the task of agreeing a final version and signing the Treaty.

I remember someone asking whether I still hoped that the other republics which had not participated in the final round of talks at Novo-Ogarevo would eventually sign the Treaty. I replied in the affirmative, and added that I thought that Ukraine would participate too. 'I cannot imagine a Union Treaty without Ukraine,' I said.

PERFIDY

At the time I sensed that the Russian President was prevaricating, playing a waiting game. This could only mean that he had a different plan in store. On the eve of the meeting in Minsk,[1] I asked him therefore what proposals he was taking there. My approach was that we already had a draft treaty to which Ukraine could adhere, at least partially. In explaining the delay in the examination of the Union Treaty, Yeltsin suddenly declared that the question of a different type of association might come up again. I replied that we should continue this discussion in Moscow, together with the leaders of Ukraine and Kazakhstan.

But when the three Presidents of Russia, Belarus and Ukraine met in Minsk and in Brest, they adopted decisions that openly contradicted what we had agreed on at the State Council sessions.

Only two weeks had passed since 25 November – but Yeltsin put his signature to a document which put an end to the Union, perfidiously going back on all of his earlier commitments.

Even assuming for a moment that at the time the participants of the Belovezh agreement felt that they had no other choice – as now they assert – and genuinely wished to save what could be saved by forming at least a commonwealth if it was impossible to create a confederation, developments since then have refuted all those assertions.

Indeed, what I was relentlessly and unsuccessfully trying to drive home to my partners has been confirmed: the losses incurred as a result of the break-up of the USSR proved to be a terrible shock, which could not in any way be compensated for by the gains attained from sovereignty. Nothing worthwhile has come of the Commonwealth. At the same time, the trend towards integration, towards saving what can still be saved by joint efforts, is becoming stronger. But this work will have to start from zero and can be achieved only by the leaders of the next generation, by people who will have learned from our bitter experience.

During our meetings I drew Yeltsin's attention to the fact that,

---

[1] The meeting in Belovezh Forest, near Minsk, between Yeltsin, Kravchuk and Shushkevich, which ended in the decision to dissolve the USSR and establish the CIS.

in spite of the worries he had expressed, it was unlikely that the Russian Supreme Soviet would oppose the Union Treaty. On the contrary, the evidence showed that most of the deputies believed that it was necessary.

Until recently I was not quite sure whether Yeltsin was playing a double game during all these months. I simply could not believe him to be capable of such perfidy. However, at a meeting in 1993 with members of the 'Smena' deputies' group in the former Russian Supreme Soviet, one of the deputies – who in the past had been among Yeltsin's most fervent supporters – told me the following inside story.

After his return from Minsk in December 1991, the Russian President called together a group of deputies close to him, in order to ensure support for the ratification of the agreements reached in Minsk. He was asked whether they were valid from a legal point of view. The President broke into a forty-minute tirade, telling excitedly how he had managed to 'dupe' Gorbachev just before leaving for Minsk, misleading him about the purpose of his trip, when in reality he intended to do the exact opposite of what he said. 'We had to get Gorbachev out of the way,' Yeltsin added.

The Russian President and his entourage thus sacrificed the Union for the sake of realizing their ardent desire to reign in the Kremlin.

BLACK DAYS FOR RUSSIA AND THE UNION

The first days of December were filled with worry. I was contacted by reporters as well as foreign political and public figures. They all wanted to know what was happening.

A day passed without news from Minsk. I thought they had decided to 'relax' (with maybe a drink or two), which proved to be true. However, I wanted to know what was going on. It turned out that they had gone over my head and were talking with ministers, including Defence Minister Shaposhnikov – who had not found it necessary to inform me. I telephoned Shaposhnikov and asked what it was all about. He wriggled and squirmed 'like a grass snake on a frying-pan' and finally said that they had telephoned him to ask how he envisaged the joint armed forces in a future state structure. It was, of course, a lie. Shaposhnikov is still trying to explain away his behaviour in those days.

In the evening I finally received a telephone call from Shushkevich, whom Yeltsin and Kravchuk had asked to inform me in their presence on the decisions they had reached. He said that they had already talked to Bush, who 'supported' them.

I asked Shushkevich to pass the receiver to Yeltsin. 'What you have done behind my back with the consent of the US President is a crying shame, a disgrace!' I said, demanding to be briefed in full. We agreed to meet the following day, which was a Monday.

I expressed my official view of the Minsk agreement in a statement that was published on 10 December. I emphasized in particular that:

' . . . The fate of our multinational state cannot be decided by the leaders of three republics. This issue can only be decided in accordance with the Constitution, with the participation of all sovereign states and taking into account the will of the people. The declaration concerning the abrogation of all-Union legal norms is also illegal and dangerous, as it can only increase chaos and anarchy in our society. The rash appearance of this document is bewildering. It was discussed neither by the people nor by the Supreme Soviets of the republics, on behalf of whom it has been signed. What is more, this happened at a time when republics' parliaments were examining the draft Treaty on the Union of Sovereign States drafted by the USSR State Council.'

I declared that it was necessary to call a Congress of People's Deputies, and I did not exclude the possibility of organizing a nationwide referendum on this issue.

Yeltsin came to see me upon his return from Minsk. He had telephoned beforehand to find out whether it was safe for him to come. Nazarbayev participated in the meeting, as agreed, although this was seemingly not to Yeltsin's liking. The conversation was painful. I said that I was standing by my position but would respect the choice that the republics, their parliaments, would make. 'If we want democracy and reforms we must act according to democratic rules.'

As I look back to the events of December 1991, each time I come to the conclusion that I had no right to act differently. To act counter to the decisions made by eleven republics, whose Supreme Soviets approved the Minsk agreement, would have meant to unleash a bloody slaughter, which might have developed into a global catastrophe.

The act staged in Minsk presented the Asian republics with a *fait accompli*. This 'rejection', a hint at the 'secondary role' of the Asian states, will cost us dear. A major, maybe historic error was committed. At the time, both the leaders and the parliaments of Kazakhstan and the Central Asian states showed realism, adopting, as it seems to me, a more civilized approach than their European colleagues. The meetings in Ashkhabad[1] and then in Alma Ata[2] counterbalanced some of the effects of the gross error committed in Minsk – the Commonwealth which replaced the Soviet Union gained a greater measure of legitimacy. Nevertheless, the documents adopted at these meetings failed to stop the logic of disintegration. Many issues that are vital for the Commonwealth were merely written down as declarations of intent, which are subject to differing interpretations. The subsequent behaviour of Ukraine, as well as other events, are clear evidence of this. Speaking in general, I find no other word than 'irrational' to characterize everything that happened after the Belovezh meeting. In the Russian Parliament, with the exception of thirteen deputies, everyone voted 'for'. But a year or two later, Khasbulatov deeply regretted his efforts to obtain ratification of the Belovezh agreement and his appeal to Zyuganov to try to convince the Communist deputies to vote 'yes'.

At a meeting with the press on 12 December, I was asked whether my view of the events in Minsk was affected by the bitter taste of defeat. 'No!' I replied. 'In the final account, everyone makes his own choice in politics. I initiated the referendum, the first in the history of our country, in which the people voted in

---

[1] In Turkmenistan, when the Central Asian states met to discuss the situation after the founding of the Commonwealth of Independent States (CIS).

[2] This meeting expanded the membership of the CIS to include Central Asian republics.

favour of a Union. By agreeing to reform the Union and create a Union of Sovereign States as a confederative state we were departing to some extent from what was understood by the renewed Union and what the voters had supported in the referendum. Still, we could speak of a united country, of a common home.

'In all fairness, the new formation, the Commonwealth of Independent States, should be submitted to a popular vote. The people should decide whether or not they agree to divide the country.'

On 18 December I sent a letter to the participants of the Alma Ata meeting on the creation of the Commonwealth of Independent States. The letter was published on 20 December and had no effect whatsoever.

I met Yeltsin on 23 December to discuss issues connected with the transition from the Union State to the Commonwealth. The talks lasted many hours, with a few short breaks. On 25 December I signed the decree relinquishing my duties as President of the USSR.

32

THE SOVIET UNION AND THE WORLD
AFTER THE COUP

THE AUGUST COUP LEADERS HAD FAILED TO TAKE INTO ACCOUNT the fundamental changes that had occurred in the international standing of our country, particularly in regard to its relations with the United States and the European nations. Initially there may have been some wavering, but soon most governments condemned the coup and rejected the Emergency Committee's claim to represent the Soviet Union. The only foreign leaders who expressed approval of the coup were Gadaffi and Saddam Hussein.

I spoke with a number of international leaders in the very first hours and days after my return to Moscow – Bush, Mitterrand, Kohl, Major, Andreotti, Mulroney, Hawke, Kaifu, Mubarak and other heads of state and government. The better relations we had succeeded in establishing with the outside world – along with the democratic achievements of perestroika – were one of the main factors that made the defeat of the coup inevitable.

The Moscow Human Rights Conference had been scheduled for early September, 1991, a few days after the failed coup attempt. Initially we had serious doubts whether we should hold it at all, or maybe postpone it or organize it in some other country. Much was still unclear. However, the European, American and Canadian governments were all in favour of holding the conference in Moscow as originally agreed; they indicated to us that they regarded it as a sign of solidarity with victorious democracy.

852

I focused my opening speech at the Moscow conference on those aspects of the protection of human rights that had been brought into full relief by the situation in our own country. One of these aspects was the rights of minorities. At that time, I was thinking first and foremost about the fate of the Russians in the Baltic states, which had just seceded from the Soviet Union and become members of the CSCE. Even then I was genuinely alarmed by the treatment of national minorities in these countries. I said that unless Europe wanted to be faced with a wave of refugees, armed conflicts, ethnic hatred, deaths and devastated cities and villages, it must strictly ensure that minority rights were protected in all European countries. Otherwise the entire European process would collapse, burying human rights too under its ruins.

I believed that after the conclusion of a new Union Treaty it was essential for all European countries to work together to avoid playing into the hands of separatist and extremist nationalist forces or jeopardizing the process of building a new Europe. I assumed that both the Europeans and the international community as a whole, having learned a lesson from the tragedy unfolding in Yugoslavia, would have a stake in preserving the integrity of a state which covered one sixth of the globe, as one of the mainstays of a new world order. At the time, some people, both in our country and abroad, advocated the preservation of the Soviet Union as a counterweight to the newly unified Germany. For my part, I believed that a renewed Soviet Union and the new, united Germany could jointly become powerful factors for international co-operation and peace in Europe and, through friendly interaction, could give a strong impetus to the pan-European process.

The high-level international forum held in Moscow provided me with an opportunity to meet many of my old friends and partners and to discuss issues that worried both us and them. In my talks with Baker and other Western foreign affairs officials, I emphasized my belief that the future Union of Sovereign States would inherit the positive legacy of the foreign policy the Soviet Union had conducted in the international arena for the past few years.

The Spanish government had reacted most sharply to the August coup. On 11 September I met the Foreign Minister, Fernandez Ordonez, who had come to Moscow to attend the conference. 'Felipe González has asked me to convey to you this message,' he said. 'First and foremost, he asked me to tell you that, during the days of the coup, all of us felt extreme tension and were deeply worried about your own fate and the fate of your cause. The tension was intensified by the extreme vagueness of the first information we received from the Soviet Union. We were also genuinely alarmed by the 'fuzzy' reaction of a number of our partners to the events in your country. We therefore set ourselves the task of achieving the necessary firm reaction of the international community to the developments in the USSR.'

Later, in late October, when I visited Madrid as co-chairman of the international Middle East conference, González told me what he had done upon receiving the news of the coup.

'On the morning of 19 August, when I was informed of the coup, I took the helicopter to Madrid and, during the two-hour flight, I drafted an official communiqué which unambiguously characterized what had happened. We discussed this draft with my deputy and the Minister of Foreign Affairs. I considered three main elements of vital importance: to characterize the events as a *coup d'état*, to demand the continuity of the entire perestroika policy, and to call upon the international community to take co-ordinated steps in order to inform the people in the Soviet Union that the world would not accept the situation.

'Our Minister of Foreign Affairs, who by then had already contacted all of his Western colleagues, said bluntly that we were the only ones to have adopted this position. I replied that this could in no way influence our position of principle, namely that the coup leaders were not to be permitted to consolidate their power. I added that it was necessary to try to co-ordinate our steps with our allies. I personally telephoned Bush, who was on his way from Maine to Washington, to inform him of our communiqué. Bush told me frankly that the main thing for him was not to have to tell the American public and the US press that the entire East-West security system was threatened by the events in Moscow. After the Gulf War, he could not afford once again to rally the

US public because of tensions in Europe. I could understand his position, but I replied nevertheless that I was not going to alter my communiqué.

'I also asked Bush,' González continued, 'to use the "hot line" to call the Kremlin directly – I have no access to such a direct line, and I could not get through to anyone in Moscow by regular telephone. Let the Kremlin tell the American President what was happening and where Gorbachev was. Bush agreed with me, but I added that this was not enough. It is necessary to use all official channels to exert pressure on the coup leaders. And there is one more thing – let us not, I told him, speak of Gorbachev and his cause in the past tense. He agreed to this too.

'Mikhail,' González told me bluntly, and one could see that he was quite upset by having to say this, 'during those days I had the impression that the West had accepted what had happened as a *fait accompli* and was ready to resign itself to it. I perceived such moods even among my closest colleagues. From this I conclude that today Western political leaders are in doubt about the ability of the Soviet Union to preserve itself and, therefore, proceed from two possible scenarios, including the disintegration of the USSR.

'It's quite depressing,' Felipe admitted. He could not hide his indignation at the schoolboyish, short-sighted position of some of his NATO colleagues: the foreign minister of one NATO country declared in his presence that he could not see anything wrong if there appeared one hundred states in Europe instead of the thirty-four countries who signed the Paris charter.

A UNIQUE MEETING

During my stay in Madrid, I had another meeting which was truly unique. Since both the American and the Soviet Presidents had come to Madrid, the King of Spain decided to seize the opportunity and invite both me and Bush to a 'friendly dinner', which was also attended by Felipe González.

The conversation at dinner started with an exchange of views on the Middle East conference, which was to open the following morning. However, my partners were most interested in the

situation in the Soviet Union. The ensuing four-hour conversation was amazingly candid, a real man-to-man talk.

'The actions of the coup leaders,' González declared, 'are an
example of people destroying something they are allegedly trying
to save. No-one has given a stronger impulse to centrifugal
tendencies in the USSR. Meanwhile Europe and the whole world
need the Soviet Union. In Europe, two circles are in the process
of being created – one in the West, which gravitates towards the
European Community; the other must be in the East. It is today's
Soviet Union, the Union of Sovereign States that you are
advocating. Without a second circle, Europe and the world will
lack an essential stabilizing pillar. This will create a dangerous
vacuum.'

'We are all worried,' George Bush said, 'about the future of the
Soviet Union. How should we interpret Yeltsin's latest speech?'
he asked me. Apparently the political part of the Russian
President's speech had made my partners doubt (and with good
reason) his commitment to the new, already agreed draft Union
Treaty.

Needless to say, I attempted to smooth away this impression,
pointing to Yeltsin's entourage and to the fact that he was rather
easily influenced. However, I had to admit that there were some
points in the speech that were contrary to the concept of a Union
State. (Incidentally, Yegor Yakovlev, who accompanied us on
this trip, said after reading the speech that Yeltsin clearly
intended to destroy the Union, but in a way that would put the
blame on the other republics.)

My partners were also interested in the position of the
Ukrainian leadership – particularly Kravchuk – and the leaders
of the other republics. For these rational people, it was difficult
to understand the actions of some of the republic leaders.
Everyone agreed that, in modern states, one could not take the
concept of self-determination to the point of absurdity. Secession
is absurd. How much can a country be divided? To the point of
self-determination for every village? This would be the logical
outcome once the process of division started. Indeed: the centre,
which embodied the totalitarian structures, was no more, but the
battle 'against the centre' continued.

At the time, I was convinced – and I said so to my partners at this unusual meeting – that there still was a chance of creating a full-fledged new Union in which the republics would be truly sovereign. My actions in October and November 1991 were based on this belief.

Bush complained that the coming year was going to be rather difficult for him, with the presidential elections forthcoming. 'Obviously, I do not intend to compare these worries with the colossal task you are facing today,' he told me. 'This is a staggering, breathtaking drama. We are following it with bated breath and we wish you every success.'

RENEWED EFFORTS TO PROMOTE REFORM

The August coup had created an entirely new situation. On the one hand, many stumbling-blocks on the road to radical change were removed and we were given a unique opportunity to accelerate the reform process and move more quickly towards the market. On the other hand, the coup had intensified the political struggle, giving a strong impulse to centrifugal trends in the Union and deepening the economic crisis.

We were faced with the threat of an imminent breakdown of life-support systems, primarily the food market and fuel and energy supplies. Convertible currency problems had come to a head. Loans already agreed upon were frozen during the coup attempt, and short-term credits on international financial markets were no longer available. All operations involving foreign currency had become far more difficult.

Hence the most urgent task at hand was to unblock the credits already granted and find an additional US $5-8 billion by the end of the year. Otherwise, the unavoidable decline in imports would lead to a sharp fall in production, particularly in the machine-building and consumer goods industries.

Given this situation, the question of Western economic support for the reform process took on great urgency. In general our Western partners understood this too. However, they were still undecided and 'shifting from one foot to the other'. In

September–November 1991 – in spite of being completely taken up by domestic affairs – I held meetings practically every day, usually in the evenings, with foreign leaders (sometimes two or three in a day), trying to prompt them into providing us with assistance. During this period, I had talks with Major, Kohl, Mitterrand, Bush, Andreotti and González, the foreign ministers and ministers of finance of all the G7 countries as well as a number of other European countries, parliamentarians and business leaders.

The talks with John Major, who at that time was G7 co-ordinator, opened the round of meetings. His position was of considerable importance in defining the course adopted by the other G7 countries. Obviously I bore in mind that before the London meeting he had not been among those who actively supported the idea of meeting us halfway in the process of integrating the Soviet Union into the world economy. Still one ought to give the British Prime Minister his due; he was the first Western leader to come to Moscow (on 1 September) in order to appraise the situation on the spot and to discuss ways for implementing the agreements reached in London.

Our talks took place on the eve of the opening of the Vth Extraordinary Congress of People's Deputies. Needless to say, I focused immediately on what I considered to be our priority: we needed more significant and open assistance from the Western countries. We discussed specific ways and means to support our imports, which we would have been forced virtually to stop without a rescheduling of current payments; the problem of foreign debt servicing; concerted action to achieve convertibility of the ruble as quickly as possible; and structural changes involving major international investment projects. Finally we discussed assistance in the development of the private sector and training for a market economy.

Major admitted that Western politicians were alarmed about the situation in the Soviet Union. His remarks confirmed my impression that the Europeans had a better understanding of the developments than, say, the Japanese or the Americans. He spoke of the 'great relief' he and his colleagues had felt on receiving the news that the coup had failed. However, he also mentioned that the West was quite concerned about several outstanding problems – such as the preparations for a new Union Treaty, the ties to be established between the republics and the centre, control over nuclear arms, and obviously the prospects of economic reforms and the 'manageability' of our economy.

Major assured me that the West genuinely wished the reforms to succeed. He enumerated the areas in which the United States and Great Britain were willing to provide immediate assistance (food products, medical supplies, expert advice etc.), and added that they would ask the other members of the G7 to do the same.

Later the same evening, we had a second meeting, since I had had to break off to finish work on a joint declaration with the leaders of the republics. As we talked in my Kremlin office, it was already dark outside. I explained the joint declaration to the British Prime Minister. He asked a number of questions, in particular about continuity in matters of international economic relations (on the following day, we included in the joint declaration a commitment to respect all USSR international economic obligations). My British partner was clearly impressed by the document we had produced.

At John Major's request, we continued our talk in private. We discussed control over nuclear weapons, and new information the West had received which fuelled its suspicions concerning work in the Soviet Union on biological weapons. I promised to hold an additional inquiry and to name a new team for this task.

The British Prime Minister asked me another question. I believe that I have no right to quote it here, but it seems to me that I can quote my answer: 'You can take as a starting-point that the co-operation between Gorbachev and Yeltsin is a reality – such a reality that, should it be undermined, it would have disastrous consequences. We have reached an understanding that our interaction has entered a new phase.'

'We would very much like you to establish proper business-like relations under the new conditions,' Major replied. 'And, as it seems to me, this is happening already.'

This optimistic note was typical of the many meetings with foreign leaders which followed. Needless to say, all of my partners wanted assurances that the assistance they provided would not drain away in the 'war' between the centre and the republics. I was asked time and again: 'Who are we to talk to? How are the powers distributed between the centre and the republics?'

I expected the republics to respect the agreements we had reached. It was up to them to show the necessary political will and common sense to act reasonably in their own self-interest.

It appears to me that in September 1991 the outlines of a realistic programme of partnership with the G7 were emerging, which could help us to solve the urgent problems of our country and to lay the basis for co-operation on a far broader scale. Working together, the teams of experts on both sides were able to convince themselves that the problems, albeit quite serious, could nevertheless be resolved, particularly if one took into account the enormous potential of our country. 'In the final account,' I used to say, 'what is a foreign debt of US $65 billion for a country like ours? The point is not just that other countries owe us a far greater sum – some US $85 billion dollars, but that one must consider the potential of our country.'

The experts – our group (from the centre and the republics) and a team of experts from the G7 and the European Community – worked intensively throughout the month of October. The time was right for decisions of principle. On 12 November John Major informed me that the G7 and the European Community had agreed on a US $10 billion programme for urgent relief. The G7 proposal for large-scale support was conditional on the readiness of the sovereign republics, including Russia, to assume the Soviet Union's foreign debt obligations and to show 'restraint' on whether to create their own armed forces.

By then we had reached an agreement on the Soviet Union gaining the status of associate member of the International Monetary Fund. The executive director of the IMF, Michel Camdessus, came to Moscow in late November. We discussed possible participation by the Fund in support of our economic reforms. It was understood that we would be admitted to full membership in the near future.

A few days later I received an important message from John Major, listing specific undertakings by the G7 to provide food and medical aid to our country and to integrate the Soviet Union into the world economic organization.

However, only a week later, Belovezh changed all that.

The British Prime Minister immediately sent a special envoy to Moscow. He explained to me that his mission was to receive first-hand information on the latest developments, and to clarify the question of the Soviet Union's international obligations. I explained my view of the new situation. I thought it necessary to add a few words: ' . . . Please convey to Mr Major that I am quite satisfied with our co-operation. After July he adopted a truly far-sighted position and I appreciated his genuine sympathy for us. I know he understands what is happening in our country and I ask you to convey to him that the assistance should not be cut off. It ought to be increased. Everything must be done to save democracy here. Hence we need food, consumer goods, medication – we must at all costs prevent people from taking to the streets.'

The envoy informed me that because of the Maastricht Conference Mr Major would not be able, as he had hoped, to come to Moscow before the end of the year. Needless to say, I realized that there was a different reason behind this decision. However, there was no reason to feel offended, and I replied: '. . . Life is overtaking us and history is again accelerating its pace.'

INTERNATIONAL REACTION TO THE BELOVEZH DECISIONS

The Belovezh agreement to break up the Soviet Union met with different reactions abroad. Among the 'lower echelons' of Western politicians, there were still quite a few who saw the break-up of the USSR as the main goal for which the Cold War had been fought. In these circles, the decisions made in Belovezh were received with satisfaction; some people even rejoiced on hearing the news. However, the major political figures in the international arena were alarmed by this action. As soon as the problem came up, they had made a political choice in favour of preserving the unity of our country, obviously guided by consid-erations of their own national interests. It was obvious to any serious statesman that the disintegration of the Soviet Union would leave a dangerous geo-political vacuum, with conse-quences that were difficult to foresee.

At the same time, some foreign politicians believed that the Commonwealth of Independent States proclaimed in Belovezh could realistically become the successor to the USSR. Hence the vagueness I noted in some positions in my telephone conversa-tions with Western leaders during those dramatic December days.

Helmut Kohl telephoned me even before the Belovezh meeting, sounding quite alarmed. I briefly outlined the situation and called upon the German Chancellor to help us prevent the developments from having dire consequences for the rest of the world. We agreed to return to the issue a week from then.

On 4 December, I had a telephone conversation with Polish President Lech Walesa. He showed solidarity with my concept of reforming the USSR and expressed his readiness, if need be, to call upon the peoples of our country to follow the evolutionary path of reforms.

On the next day I talked to Hungarian Prime Minister, Joszef Antall. He spoke of the need to keep the process leading to sovereignty for the Soviet republics within civilized bounds and prevent a 'Lebanonization' of our country, quoting the tragic example of Yugoslavia.

George Bush telephoned me on 13 December. In replying to his questions, I said that ' . . . The agreement between the three Presidents is but a draft, an impromptu. There are many open questions, the main problem being that there is no mechanism for interaction within the proclaimed CIS. My approach consists in providing a legal basis for the transformation of our state. I have appealed to the people's deputies. The will of the peoples and of the republics must be expressed. However, the republics' parliaments have been prevented from debating the draft Union Treaty. The agreements and decisions made after the coup have been violated. The arbitrary declaration made in Minsk by the heads of the three republics essentially means that, since the USSR no longer exists, there are no more laws to regulate public order, defence, the borders, or international ties.'

Mr Bush decided to send Baker to Moscow for first-hand information. We met on the eve of the meeting in Alma Ata. I emphasized that I saw my role as working to prevent further disintegration. We agreed that the agreement reached in Minsk was in many respects contradictory. Baker told me that the American administration was doing everything it could not to get involved in our domestic affairs. But it was in the interests of the United States that the process of transformation of our country should follow an orderly and constitutional course – a failed transformation would give a strong impulse to disintegration, with negative consequences for the Soviet people and the rest of the world.

James Baker doubted whether the CIS would be able to create a common defence system. 'From the talks I had here in Moscow,' he told me, 'I understood that there will be ten fully independent states. Each of them will have its own foreign policy. The question in this case is: what common defence can there be if there are ten independent foreign policies? And who is to give the instructions to the commander-in-chief of the joint armed forces, from whom is he supposed to receive directions?'

I agreed that the situation was very difficult. I said that today the most urgent need for the new Commonwealth was additional food aid.

Baker asked me what was meant by the 'transitional period' Yeltsin had mentioned in a conversation with him.

I replied that a comprehensive agreement on the creation of the Commonwealth was essential in order to channel the process in the right direction in all areas: it must be clear what the world can expect from this 'space'.

I repeated what I had been arguing before our citizens: we needed at least a final meeting of the USSR Supreme Soviet, as well as an agreement on foreign policy. The international community had a right to know who it would be dealing with – ten states and ten foreign policies or a political entity with a concerted foreign policy that would act as the successor to the Soviet Union? This was a particularly important question for the United Nations Security Council, as well as with regard to the major international agreements signed by the USSR.

Helmut Kohl telephoned me again in the evening of 19 December, to ask how I saw developments in our country. I could sense that he was rather upset, even alarmed, which was quite unusual for him.

François Mitterrand was the first foreign leader I spoke to after the meeting in Alma Ata. I sensed from his very first words, which were full of goodwill and sympathy, that he was mostly concerned about my emotional state and my projects for the future. I informed him that I would soon be relinquishing the office of President of the USSR.

On 23 December I had a talk with John Major. Though we had come to know each other only relatively recently, we had quickly established a good personal rapport. He too was alarmed by the latest developments. 'Looking to the future,' Major said, 'it appears to us that what has hitherto been achieved cannot be lost. Hence our desire to help your country, which rests on the understanding of what you have achieved in the past few years. Whatever happens following the decision you intend to announce in the coming two days, there can be no doubt that you have secured for yourself a special place in the history of your country and in world history. We are aware that the coming months are going to be very difficult.'

On 25 December I had another telephone conversation with George Bush. I told him I would announce my stepping down in about two hours, adding that I had just sent him a farewell letter. I used the opportunity to repeat that I genuinely appreciated what we had achieved together – both in his time as Vice-President and particularly after we both had become Presidents.

I said that there should be no doubt that he ought to recognize the states of the Commonwealth of Independent States. The second priority, I continued, was the support of Russia. I told Bush that I was transferring the right to use nuclear arms to the President of the Russian Federation. It was most important to ensure that nuclear weapons remained under reliable control. I said that he could celebrate Christmas without worry. We concluded by exchanging warm greetings and good wishes for the future.

Later on 25 December, I signed the farewell letters to the statesmen with whom I had co-operated to solve complex international problems for over six years. A new stage in my life was about to begin.

GOODBYE TO THE KREMLIN

In Alma Ata the council of leaders of the Commonwealth of Independent States made a decision concerning my status after I ceased to be President of the USSR.

At my request, the Russian President signed a decree providing premises for the political and socio-economic research fund I had decided to create and direct in order to continue my activities under the new conditions. (Yeltsin retracted this decision only a few months later.)

There were no farewells. None of the leaders of the states of the CIS telephoned me, neither on the day of my departure nor since – in over four years.

The transfer of Supreme Command to the Russian President was scheduled for the evening of 25 December. We had agreed that the ceremony should take place in my Kremlin office. Defence Minister Shaposhnikov, with a group of generals and the officers who were continually keeping guard over the famous presidential 'briefcases' with the control system for nuclear arms, was already waiting for us. A few minutes passed – the Russian President was apparently late. Then I was told that he had refused to come, in spite of our agreement. It turned out that Yeltsin, together with his entourage, had listened to my televised speech[1] and flown into a rage.

After a while, I was told that the Russian President proposed to meet on 'neutral territory' – in the Catherine Hall, i.e. the part of the Kremlin where talks with foreign leaders were usually held. Yeltsin and his team apparently saw this as a symbolic gesture. However, their action looked rather comical, not to say stupid. I therefore decided to send immediately a package to

---

[1] The text of this speech is given at the beginning of this book.

865

Yeltsin containing the decree of the USSR President on the transfer of Supreme Command over the armed forces to the President of Russia. I handed the briefcase to Shaposhnikov, asking him to take it to its new owner as quickly as possible and report back to me. The entire procedure took only a few minutes.

Thus even in the first minutes after stepping down I was faced with impudence and a lack of courtesy. Ensuing events proved that this action, rather than an isolated backlash of Yeltsin's feelings of revenge, was part of the policy he had adopted towards me.

Yeltsin put off his presidential duties to supervise personally my 'expulsion' from the Kremlin. He gave instructions for the lowering of the Soviet flag and the hoisting of the flag of the Russian Federation, and personally saw to it that the procedure should be completed according to schedule and filmed by television cameras. We had initially agreed that I should vacate my Kremlin office by 30 December. An interview with journalists from the Japanese newspaper *Yomiuri* was scheduled for 27 December. However, on the morning of the 27th, I received a telephone call from the Kremlin reception-room: I was informed that Yeltsin, Khasbulatov and Burbulis had occupied my office at 8.30 a.m. and held a party there, emptying a bottle of whisky... This was the triumph of plunderers – I can find no other word for it.

I was told to vacate both the country residence and the presidential apartment within three days. On 25 December, even before my television address, a group of people appeared at the house in Kosygin Street to seal the presidential apartment. Everything had to be done in a rush; we were forced to move to different lodgings within twenty-four hours. I saw the results in the morning – heaps of clothes, books, dishes, folders, newspapers, letters and God knows what lying strewn on the floor.

Following this 'exodus', we settled into our new apartment. I busied myself with my personal belongings (the library, all sorts of papers that had accumulated over the years – notes, letters, telegrams, photographs, documents . . .). Waves of recollection swept over me, pictures of both remote and recent events. These caused me to meditate on the past.

I was under the spell of painful reflections. Time and again I reached the same conclusion: we were still only at the beginning of the road we had chosen in March 1985. Let people talk about the end of the Gorbachev era as much as they want – the main act was only just about to begin. The lessons and conclusions to be drawn were needed now, not in some distant future. Thus in the first days of 1992 I was already absorbed in thoughts about the writing of my memoirs.

Meanwhile developments in the country took an alarming turn. The so-called 'shock therapy' – a 'cavalry attack' on our economy – brought enormous hardships for the people of Russia. Power was in the hands of irresponsible, incompetent people, who were both ambitious and ruthless. With every passing day, it becomes more and more obvious that what the country needs is a new balance of political forces and a new policy. Not only Russia, but all the other states of the CIS, the former republics of the USSR, are in this difficult situation.

All of this is to a great extent an aftermath of the December coup, a black page in the history of Russia and the Union. However, it is obviously not the last page. Life continues and the peoples of the republics, once they have 'mastered' the newly gained freedom, will find new paths towards reunification and the renewal of their lives. This is my hope and my belief.

EPILOGUE

AFTER LEAVING THE KREMLIN — AND THE CIRCUMSTANCES surrounding my departure were most uncivilized, in the worst inherited Soviet traditions – I faced the question: what to do next? Naturally, the first days were very emotional for me and my family. I had to get used to the new situation; I did not go anywhere, and hardly met anyone. Nevertheless desperation and hopelessness never overcame me. And my conscience was clear. The promise I had made to the people when I started the process of perestroika was kept: I gave them freedom. This was reflected in many quite specific things: glasnost, freedom of speech, the ending of ideological persecution, the right to live anywhere one wanted, the removal of the monopoly on property and power, the creation of the foundations of a genuine parliamentary system, the end of the nightmare threat of nuclear war, and openness to the world, which responded with understanding and support for our desire to become a normal democratic state.

Perestroika did not give the people prosperity, something they expected of me, as head of state, based on an ingrained, traditional feeling of dependence. But I did not promise that. I urged people to use this new-found freedom to create prosperity, personal and social prosperity, with their own hands and minds, according to the abilities of each.

When I was asked by a journalist on the first anniversary of the attempted coup how I felt, I answered: 'For me, there has never been a gulf between my conscience and my inner convictions. Otherwise I could not have endured what I am now experiencing.

I do not know anyone against whom so many slings and arrows have been launched as against Gorbachev at present. But I am at peace with my conscience. I, like everyone else, made mistakes, miscalculated. But my conscience is at ease. And my thoughts and ideas are exactly the same as they used to be.'

'You must be a happy man,' commented the journalist.

Nevertheless my heart ached for the future of my country. Though subject to slander and abuse, I decided to remain in politics, to participate in a new capacity, using other methods of public activity. In this I could count on those whose ideas were similar to mine and who remained close to me and faithful to the aims of perestroika. We had a basis for renewal of our activity in the new conditions: the Foundation for Socio-economic and Political Studies, which had been set up on the site of the former Lenin School.[1]

During my last, informal and seemingly friendly meeting with Yeltsin in the Kremlin on 23 December 1991 when the actual 'transfer of power' took place, it was decided that he, as President, would guarantee the transfer of the premises and all the property of the former Lenin School to the Foundation, which I intended to chair. I realized even then, though, that Yeltsin's word, like many of his promises, could not always be trusted.

In mid-January 1992, a small group of my former Kremlin colleagues, including Yakovlev, Chernyaev, Revenko, and Shakhnazarov, gathered to discuss the future of the Foundation and the choice of people who might become heads of its main departments. They were, as a rule, well-known members of the academic community, authors, highly knowledgeable people who had been pained by the dogmatic ideology to which they had had to adjust, and from which perestroika freed them. We also formulated the main tasks and the main ideas of the Foundation, which later became our motto: 'Towards a new civilization.'

Immediately after the Foundation was set up, one of the leading

[1] The Lenin School, or, as it was publicly known, the Institute of Social Sciences, was founded in 1958 to teach the basics of social science to students sent to the school in Moscow by the communist and revolutionary-democratic parties of foreign countries. It worked under the guidance of the Central Committee of the CPSU and was financed from the Party budget.

Italian newspapers, *La Stampa,* invited me to write a monthly column on current affairs. The contract appealed to me because my articles would be syndicated through the New York Times Corporation to more than a hundred papers around the world. The main topic of those articles was relations between Russia and the West. I wanted to help foreign readers to understand the incredibly complex nature of Russian political life and to share my view of our problems and to warn them against dangerous and false over-simplifications. I was more and more worried, I told my readers, by the readiness of Western leaders, under the pretext of desiring stability, to turn a blind eye to the deviations from democratic norms by our authorities, to the anti-constitutional activities and violations of human rights, to their slide towards authoritarianism.

It was important to draw the attention of foreign readers to the new problems of world politics which had arisen because of the disintegration of the socialist community and the dissolution of the Soviet Union, to the fact that the geopolitical structure of the world had changed, and the international situation had become more complicated. In this situation the main actors in world politics had to redefine their places in the world, their interests and their capabilities. Because the previous equilibrium had been disturbed, Western powers, first and foremost the United States, were tempted to take advantage of the situation. Drawing the attention of readers to the possible negative consequences, I wrote in one of the articles: 'There are two questions which we must constantly ask ourselves. Are we judging the changes in the world correctly? And how can we find a common denominator in our evaluations, so we can develop agreed, truly global policies? The world expects that American policies will reflect, above all, these qualities that made America great – its commitment to democracy, its love of freedom, its pioneering spirit.'

Naturally, when President Clinton was elected, I took the occasion to develop these ideas. I had high hopes for this young and vigorous politician. This was my advice to him: 'America, politically and economically, has an interest in sharing with other countries the responsibility for civilized development of events in the world. President Clinton would demonstrate his wisdom if he succeeded in using American influence to lead this process of redistribution of responsibility and to significantly enhance the role of the United Nations.'

Unfortunately a different approach prevailed in the policies pursued by the West – a rather selfish approach relying on force, clearly illustrated during the Yugoslav drama. 'In Yugoslavia, Europe did not pass the test' was the title of one of my articles, published at the beginning of May 1993. Instead of putting out the Yugoslav fire, more fuel was being poured on it. Russian public opinion reacted to the one-sided, biased position of the West on the Yugoslav tragedy with particular anguish, for understandable reasons.

The increasing tendency for confrontation between Russia and the West over NATO's planned expansion prompted me to remind Western politicians that during the negotiations on the unification of Germany they gave assurances that NATO would not extend its zone of operation to the east. We must tell our American friends, I wrote, that 'the policy of enlarging NATO will be considered in Russia as an attempt to isolate it. But it is impossible to isolate Russia. It would mean disregarding both history and reality.'

The pro-Western stance of the new Russian foreign policy caused additional tension in the country. In his address to the United Nations in September 1994, President Yeltsin therefore had to make a strong statement of Russia's national interests, of its intention to defend these interests and to participate in world affairs at a level appropriate to its status. I responded to that by commenting that if we wished Russia's interests and its global initiatives to be taken into account, we must first of all begin with the economic revival of the state. 'And for that we need a different policy.'

MY TRIPS ABROAD

One of the most vivid impressions of this period was my trip to the United States in May 1992. In two weeks I covered 14,000 kilometres and visited eleven American cities, including Los

Angeles, San Francisco, Chicago, Atlanta, New York and Boston. Everywhere I made speeches, had meetings, gave interviews, and participated in animated discussions.

At Fulton (Missouri) I made a speech in the very same Westminster College where forty-six years before Winston Churchill had announced the Cold War. The platform was in the open air, on a dais, near the impressive monument created by Churchill's granddaughter out of blocks from the Berlin Wall, symbolizing the drama of the Superpower confrontation. Thousands of people arrived to hear me speak. The main thesis of my Fulton speech was that, after the Second World War, the leaders of the USSR and USA had let slip the chance of peace.

My speech to the US Congress was wholly devoted to the problems of contemporary Russian-American relations. I expressed the opinion that the changed reality placed new demands on the foreign policies of every country, especially the United States. Movement towards new forms of co-operation required the breaking of old stereotypes.

Every trip abroad led to a wide dialogue on the problems of the world. The Russian authorities were rather nervous about my foreign trips, and whenever possible tried to create obstacles. Russian embassies were ordered to 'ignore Gorbachev'.

At the end of 1992 I visited four countries in Latin America (Argentina, Brazil, Chile, Mexico). It was one of the most unusual and interesting trips for me. I saw for myself the effects of the neo-liberal economic reforms of the International Monetary Fund, and realized that the mechanical application of the foreign experts' recommendations had resulted in huge social problems.

I tour Europe more often than any other part of the world. In December 1993, for example, I went to Edinburgh to lecture on problems of European policy.

A number of my foreign speeches are devoted to the role of leaders. In 1992 I went to the USA to receive the Albert Schweitzer Leadership Award, given by the Hugh O'Brien Youth Foundation. In the autumn of 1992 I made a speech at the funeral of Willy Brandt, who, in my opinion, was an example of wisdom, decisiveness, and responsibility in a political leader, courage, the ability to respond to the challenges of destiny, the highest example of morality in politics. These words would also describe Olof Palme. I mentioned this in Sweden, where I went in November 1995 to participate in the International Day of Leaders.

Many of my trips were connected with my activities as the President of the Green Cross, a non-governmental organization for the environment. I see the formation of a global ecological consciousness as the aim of this organization. I put forward the idea of an international ecological code. It will be ready by 2000, maybe 2005, and I hope it will be approved by the whole world.

CHARITY

I shall mention here one of my activities in this period: charitable help to child health care in one of its most difficult and neglected areas – oncology.

Children suffered more than anybody else from the turbulence in our society; the whole system of child health care practically collapsed. Especially tragic was the situation of children suffering from cancer and leukaemia.

While I was still President of the USSR, my family, and first and foremost Raisa Maksimovna, supported the appeal of a group of doctors, headed by Professor Rumyantsev, for help in combating these dreadful diseases in Russia. Raisa Maksimovna donated US $100,000 from the royalties of our books published in the West to the international association, Haematologists of the World for Children. With this and the generous help of our foreign friends, the first Russian Institute for Paediatric Haematology was founded in the autumn of 1991.

The Foundation continued this work. We decided to make humanitarian aid to children suffering from leukaemia and cancer a priority for the charitable activities of our organization. Between 1992 and 1995 the Foundation spent more than US $100,000 to finance international seminars on child oncology and haematology and the rehabilitation of children suffering from these terrible diseases. Thanks to our support, approximately two hundred young doctors and nurses went abroad for training. We helped the Institute for Paediatric Haematology to attract humanitarian aid, mainly from the USA and Germany, in the form of vital medical equipment. In June 1993 the building of the first bone marrow transplantation unit for children in our country was completed. Fifty per cent of the cost (US $2 million) was covered by the Foundation and its foreign partners.

It goes without saying that we would not have been able to accomplish anything without the help of our friends. In order to streamline this support and better organize it, we decided to form a special International Fund for Child Health Care in May 1995. In addition, the Fund gave targeted support to those needing medical and humanitarian aid – and there are a lot of those in our country now. The results are evident. Eighteen large regional child health centres are functioning in Russia at present, where 70 per cent of children suffering from leukaemia and cancer are receiving treatment. By October 1994 Russia reached international standards in the treatment of these childhood diseases by chemotherapy for the first time. The number of children who survived increased from 10 to 70 per cent, which is comparable to the results in the developed countries of the world.

We of course understand that all this is only a drop in the ocean of disasters which has befallen Russia. But, as the ancient Romans used to say, even one drop can wear away a stone.

WORK ON MY MEMOIRS

I considered writing my memoirs one of the first of my duties after stepping down as President. I have explained why in the foreword. Here I would like to describe very briefly how this work went.

The idea of writing my memoirs had occurred to me long before, while I was still General Secretary. The success of the book *Perestroika*, which sold in large numbers in different languages, reinforced Raisa Maksimovna and myself in our conviction that my memoirs were needed.

Vanity did not drive me. The historic significance of

perestroika was obvious to both its supporters and its adversaries. This was a period in the development of the country and the world whose objective importance earned it the right to be described in some detail. And of course the testimony of the main participants in the events of the time have special value – not only to historians but also to our contemporaries who continue to debate perestroika. But to make a proper assessment of perestroika, irrespective of one's point of view, one must know the person who became its 'author' and why he became what he did and how life prepared him for it.

I discussed the sequence of the work, the provisional list of contents, their chronology, and the chapters with a group of my closest colleagues. I gave myself a tight schedule, and the work started. Two, sometimes three times a week a group of my colleagues visited me. These people were close to me during the time of our work in the Central Committee and in the Kremlin. They brought with them their notes, documents, their memories of what we did together. I also went through my many notes, documents, and drafts. At our disposal we had volumes of documents, books and articles, which could be used for the exact recreation of the events with which my life was concerned.

The German publishers Bertelsmann, with whom I had been working for a long time on the publication of my previous books, undertook to publish my memoirs. They were published first in Russian, then in German and Japanese. Now they are becoming available in other languages, in English, French and Spanish.

I DID NOT LEAVE POLITICS

The main thing which was debated after the disintegration of the USSR, in serious discussions and sometimes in silly articles, was the question: how did it all happen, and why? So the first task to be accomplished in the Foundation was to compile the book *December 1991* – essentially, a collection of documents, compiled not as self-justification, but to put on record the actual events connected with the disintegration of the USSR, for posterity and for anyone who is capable of thinking and learning lessons for the future. This book was published abroad as well.

For the past few years I have had to struggle against those who tried to consign the name of Gorbachev to oblivion, to distort the truth about my perestroika activities. In Russia, on orders from the authorities, all sorts of clichés have been promoted, among them the assertion that Gorbachev was unpopular and rejected by his own countrymen. In fact this is untrue, even though many of my compatriots associate our current troubles with perestroika, which I started. But when one of my interviews was published in *Komsomolskaya Pravda* readers responded with over 14,000 letters, 60 per cent of them expressing ardent support.

In 1993 the magazine *Sobesednik* published the results of opinion polls held in seven republics of the former USSR. People were asked to name popular figures. The editors thought that those named would be mainly from the world of entertainment, but in fact there was only one of these – the singer Alla Pugacheva. The rest were all politicians. And in three of the republics I came top. In Russia Gorbachev received 21 per cent, while Yeltsin received 23 per cent, and in Ukraine was way ahead of Kravchuk.

Press and television poisoned the atmosphere around me. They were mainly encouraged from above. And during the CPSU 'trial' in the Constitutional Court there were attempts to make it primarily a trial of Gorbachev.

From the very beginning I declared that I was not going to participate in this bizarre trial. 'I am not being stubborn, or capricious,' I explained, 'nor am I showing disrespect towards the court and the law. I am a Russian citizen and I do not claim any special rights. As a witness I have given evidence in the investigations of those involved in the attempted coup of August 1991, of CPSU finances, of KGB officials exceeding their authority, and other cases. I have no problems abiding by the law. But I cannot participate in a trial which discredits the very notion of court proceedings, which undertakes to judge history and is, in essence, a place where political scores are settled.'

In connection with this case the Nuremberg trials of 1946 were invoked. The analogy was absurd from the beginning to the end. There specific people were judged for committing specific atrocities. But the CPSU leaders who were really guilty of crimes had passed away, and they can be judged only by history. To put Stalin on trial would be the same as putting on trial Napoleon or Nicholas II or Wilhelm II, each of whom was to blame for hundreds of thousands or even millions of deaths. As far as ideology is concerned, to equate communist and fascist ideology is stupid and absurd. Communist ideology in its pure form is akin to Christianity. Its main ideas are the brotherhood of all peoples irrespective of their nationality, justice and equality, peace, and an end to all hostility between peoples. It is true that communism was used to camouflage a totalitarian regime. But in its essence communism is a humanist ideology, and it never had anything in common with the misanthropic ideology of fascism.

For refusing to attend this absurd and unjust trial, the outcome of which – had the guilty verdict been pronounced – would have been the 'transformation' of millions of former communists into criminals, I was scandalously banned from going abroad for several weeks. Nevertheless, exactly as I predicted, the trial in the Constitutional Court ended in failure. It could not have been different.

At about the same time, in the autumn of 1992, the authorities launched a direct attack on the Foundation, hoping perhaps that this would put an end to my activity. On the morning of 8 October, when the employees of the Foundation reported to work, they discovered that the building had been sealed and surrounded by the militia. Nobody was allowed in. I immediately went to the Foundation and there, at the entrance, gave a press conference to the surprised journalists and the large crowd that had gathered. I vigorously denounced this act of arbitrary vandalism, incompatible with any legal norms, and demanded an explanation. Shortly afterwards senior government officials and officials of the Moscow administration arrived at the scene. It turned out that the building, which Yeltsin had guaranteed to the Foundation only a year before, was being transferred to the Academy of Finance of the Russian government. It was done in a typical Yeltsin fashion – noisily, rudely and unskilfully – in order to humiliate Gorbachev once more and 'clip his wings'.

As a result the Foundation was given several rooms on two

floors of the building, which of course made our work more difficult, not to mention the fact that the new landlord, the Academy of Finance, charged us rent not only for the rooms, but for even the slightest service. I must say that even though I had more than enough grounds to be angry with Yeltsin, I did not allow my emotions to get the better of me. Very serious considerations – the continuation of reform, the preservation and strengthening of democracy in Russia, the future of my country – mattered more to me than personal slights. I was, of course, critical of the 'shock therapy' policies which from the very beginning had been associated with sky-rocketing prices. But I sincerely wanted to help the reforms and did not conceal the fact that at that time Yeltsin and I had, in principle, the same goal – the democratic transformation of Russia and its integration in the global evolution of civilization. To prove my loyal attitude to the Russian leadership I can cite an interview for the Canadian Broadcasting Corporation on 25 November 1992, that is, after everything which had been done to me and to the Foundation with the knowledge and support of the authorities.

The correspondent asked me: 'You recently accused Yeltsin of playing political games. Do you trust him now?'

I answered, 'I do not accuse, but warn that it would be very bad for Russia if the President's only aim were to win another political round. I could give the very same warning to the Russian Supreme Soviet and the Congress of People's Deputies. If everything were reduced to scoring points it would not be worthy of the times, which demand much of Russian politicians. They must understand this. If they do not, everything will degenerate into a political free-for-all.'

Several months later, when the situation had become even more tense and there was talk of a referendum on the continuation of the reforms and support for the President, I declared: 'This noisy campaign is designed to hide the main question – what led to today's situation? I think that the policies pursued since 1992 could not solve the main problems, could not even find an approach to their solution. We did not get what we were promised. In fact, we found ourselves on the brink of a precipice, so that the democratic transformation is now in jeopardy.'

AMNESTY FOR THE COUP-PLOTTERS

The question of responsibility for the break-up of the USSR and its consequences was of more than academic importance in our country. A lot of speculation on this score was associated with the protracted investigation of the August 1991 coup-plotters, whose actions accelerated the disintegration of the USSR and undermined prospects for democracy. At first, they admitted everything and even expressed their regret. Later, however, seeing how disappointment with the worsening situation in the country was mounting, how the state was disintegrating, and how the authority of would-be democratic government was being undermined, they decided to deny what they had confessed to, and portray themselves as heroes who had suffered for their attempt to 'save the Union'. And with the help of the unscrupulous, unprincipled press they picked up the theme of Yeltsin and his team: 'Blame it all on Gorbachev'.

I insisted that the investigation into the activities of the Emergency Committee should be conducted in the most careful way and that an open, fair trial should take place, a trial which would be able to reveal and evaluate the truth. But many people – and not only those on the side of the accused – had no interest in this. Important 'details' of the coup remain a mystery, and this is being used by political profiteers from right and left. And it was not by chance that the trial never materialized. After the in-fighting among the upper echelons of power ended on 4 October 1993 with the shelling of Parliament by tanks, the new parliament, now named the State Duma rather than the Supreme Soviet, suddenly declared an amnesty both for the members of the August 1991 Emergency Committee and for those who had confronted President Yeltsin in October 1993 (Rutskoi, Khasbulatov and others).

But that was not the end. The majority of the members of the Emergency Committee, by accepting the amnesty, acknowledged – *de facto* and *de jure* – the fact that they had committed a crime against the state. Only one of them – General Varennikov (former Commander-in-Chief of Ground Forces and Deputy Defence Minister) – refused the amnesty and demanded in court an official juridical rehabilitation. The trial took place in June–July 1994, and, like the CPSU trial before the Constitutional Court two years earlier, it was prepared and conducted in such a way that the accused was not General Varennikov, but . . . Gorbachev.

I was invited as a witness. I had considerable doubts about whether I should go. I understood why the trial was being held. My suspicions were vindicated on the first day. It was especially strange that among the witnesses at this trial were the coup-plotters who had just been released – but the witnesses on the other side, the eye-witnesses and the victims, were not present.

With the help of the press the trial was from the very beginning turned into a political trial of the ex-President. I described the events very fully, with facts and documents in my hands, and exposed the perjury of the witnesses for the Emergency Committee, showed the groundlessness of their excuses and the personal responsibility of General Varennikov during the coup. But the outcome of the trial was predetermined long before its end. It did not surprise me when the military prosecutor withdrew the charges. This squandered another opportunity (since the trial of the other members of the Emergency Committee never took place) to expose all the secrets of the state coup in August 1991 and to demonstrate the real responsibility of its organizers for the disintegration of the USSR.

The farce of the Varennikov trial served to energize even more the reactionary, anti-reformist elements in the country. It demonstrated their growing confidence that the Yeltsin government was not only indulgent towards those who would seem to be its ideological and political opponents, but was quite willing to use them in its own interests. Given the regime existing in Russia today, it was therefore quite logical that General Varennikov became a State Duma deputy in the December 1995 elections.

I should like to quote a few lines from my speech in court:

'If we react to such crimes as nothing more than a farce, we would have one coup after another. We have already lived through the conspiracy of Belovezh Forest, which finished off the USSR, by exploiting the consequences of the August coup. Then we had to live through the bloody events of 3-4 October 1993, when before our own eyes Parliament was fired on, and, together with it, all of us, the whole country. If our future is to be determined by new coup-plotters, we will never become a country in which everyone can feel a citizen.'

THE CRISIS ESCALATES

By the end of 1992 the economic situation in the country began to cause serious concern. My worst fears were being confirmed. People suffered irreparable, grave losses as a result of the 'shock therapy' policy. All their savings, accumulated over years, were made worthless by inflation. Sixty per cent of the population found themselves below the poverty line. Enterprises, having lost all their working capital, were unable to pay for supplies of raw materials, semi-finished products, or energy. For several months, people were not paid their wages, and this soon became the norm.

People were more and more angered by the behaviour of the authorities, who were ignoring their needs, and by the arrogance and rudeness of the new 'democratic nomenklatura'. Nostalgia for the old days began to spread among the population.

The disenchantment of the population could not fail to influence the behaviour of the Russian Parliament – the Congress of People's Deputies and the Supreme Soviet of Russia. The Deputies, who were close to their constituencies and saw the real situation, criticized the President and the government as a whole increasingly sharply. Just recently they had allowed themselves to be manipulated, obediently voting for 'shock therapy', granting the President what in essence were extraordinary powers, but now they began to protest strongly against the policies which they had earlier been responsible for. Colleagues, recently close to Yeltsin, to whom he was in debt for his victory over the coup-plotters in August 1991, began to distance themselves from the ruling group. The most noticeable among them were Chairman of the Supreme Soviet, Khasbulatov, and Vice-President Rutskoi. The conflict between the executive and legislative branches rapidly acquired the form of open struggle.

President Yeltsin and his closest associates resorted to the usual Soviet methods of exerting pressure to crush the growing opposition, instead of reacting to the worsening situation by adjusting their policies. In March 1993 there was an attempt to introduce emergency powers, but this was strongly resisted. A compromise was reached to hold a referendum on support for reform and confidence in the President and the Supreme Soviet. The results of the April referendum proved what had been already clear. A majority (more than 50 per cent of those who voted) voted for the continuation of market reform, for democratic freedoms. But a considerable number of participants in the referendum rejected this course. Yeltsin's leadership did not get the message, however. The results of the referendum were viewed as a *carte blanche* to crush the opposition in the Supreme Soviet.

We in the Foundation were constantly analysing the situation. It was discussed at symposia and conferences which the Foundation convened, inviting outside experts. The general conclusion was the following: the political course pursued since January 1992 was not capable of solving the main problems of the country. The people not only did not receive what they had been promised, but, on the contrary, found themselves on the brink of bankruptcy. Democratic changes which had already taken place were called into question.

Despite the information blockade established by the authorities, I used every opportunity to express my views to the public – at a press conference in the International Press Centre in Moscow on 5 March 1993, and in numerous interviews with Russian and foreign newspapers. Meanwhile, the situation was developing into an acute political crisis.

ANOTHER COUP

On 21 September 1993 the President, exceeding his powers, issued a decree annulling the Constitution and dissolving the Supreme Soviet. The majority of the deputies refused to comply, regarding the decree as a *coup d'état*. Forces loyal to Yeltsin surrounded the parliament building. In its turn, the Supreme Soviet deprived Yeltsin of power and proclaimed Vice-President

Rutskoi as provisional President. At the time I was in Italy, where I was giving lectures in various cities. On learning what was happening in Moscow, I interrupted my trip and returned home immediately.

At a press conference on 25 September I warned about the approaching tragic outcome and made suggestions about the resolution of the conflict. I urged President Yeltsin to return to the situation which had existed before 21 September and to announce presidential and parliamentary elections, to be held simultaneously and without delay. This would have given the people a chance to express their will and to make their choice.

My position was shared by others. The Constitutional Court was inclined to resolve the conflict in the same way; and the heads of most of the regions and a number of public organizations were also of that view. Even those who supported the President's decree of 21 September insisted on negotiations. The Patriarch joined the negotiating process. There appeared a hope that bloodshed would be avoided.

Meanwhile the siege of the Parliament became more provocative. Electricity, water and sewerage were cut off. People in the building, technical staff included (women amongst them), were left to starve. Yeltsin's opponents rushed to the Supreme Soviet's rescue. Crowds gathered for rallies organized in Moscow's squares. A crowd of many thousands marched to the White House. Violent clashes with the militia broke out. The blockade of the Supreme Soviet building was broken. Rutskoi called for the storming of the Mayor's Office, not far away. A large group of people, some of them armed, headed towards the television centre in lorries and a real battle took place there.

Nevertheless, late on 3 October the government was in control of the situation and could have continued to seek a mutually acceptable solution to the impasse, but it was at this moment that the inclination of the President to 'act decisively', which he understood as using force irrespective of the consequences and the number of victims, manifested itself.

When I turned on the television on the morning of 4 October, I was shocked by what I saw. Not even in my most terrible nightmares could I imagine that in the centre of Moscow Russian tanks operating at the command of the minister of defence would, methodically and in cold blood, be firing at Parliament!

A day before, the authorities had publicly announced that Rutskoi and Khasbulatov had made hundreds of people in the Parliament virtual hostages: service and administrative personnel, journalists, and deputies who were in fact sincerely trying to defend constitutional principles. The troops now started to kill these people without mercy. The building was ablaze. And, despite that, the machine-guns and the artillery carried on firing.

This was madness. The army was ordered to shoot at the people! It was unforgivable! This was a tragedy, for which both the leaders of the Supreme Soviet and the President with his entourage were responsible. Their aim seemed to be to frighten the country.

What were the roots of this bloody tragedy? They originated from the very moment when an erroneous course of action was chosen, and when Yeltsin, Rutskoi, Khasbulatov and the other participants in this tragedy were together: they were in favour of forcing the pace of economic reform, and the very same Supreme Soviet granted Yeltsin the right to issue law-making decrees.

After what had happened, the government in any normal parliamentary system would have resigned. But Yeltsin and his team sought to legitimize the regime by calling a referendum on the new constitution to be held on 12 December 1993, together with elections to the new parliament – the State Duma.

They gambled that the opposition was frightened, paralysed, decapitated. They thought that in the atmosphere of fear and demoralization the advocates of the pro-presidential policy would score a crushing victory. It turned out that these calculations were based on ignoring, or refusing to recognize, the mood of the majority of the people. True, the new constitution, with a very strong authoritarian tendency, was pushed through, even though doubts remained whether the vote had been rigged. But 'Russia's Choice', the party which at the time enjoyed the favour of the President, was defeated in the Duma elections. The extreme nationalist Zhirinovsky and his Liberal Democratic Party won. Much of the electorate voted not for that party, but against Yeltsin and the government, against their policies, against their treatment of society, which culminated in the attack on the legislative branch.

The assault on Parliament was a turning-point in the evolution of the regime created in Russia after the disintegration of the USSR, starting a slide towards authoritarianism under cover of the Constitution, which practically granted Yeltsin licence to act without any controls, indeed arbitrarily. I was therefore amazed that Western governments justified and even approved of this barbaric action, contradicting all democratic and humanitarian values.

Summing up the year 1993 in my interview to the newspaper *Rabochaya Tribuna* I said: 'In order to regain people's trust, the government must change its policies. If anyone believes that order and stability can be achieved by denying democracy, then this is a major mistake.'

The events which followed proved me right.

THE CRISIS DEEPENS

President Yeltsin and those around him ignored yet another signal which the results of the State Duma elections had sent them. They knew that in the new constitution, tailor-made for Yeltsin, the Parliament was made virtually powerless in the important areas of domestic and foreign policy, unable to influence the state decision-making process or to oversee executive power. Even its legislative prerogatives were considerably reduced by the President's veto.

It is true that his intention to ignore the election results and the State Duma did not manifest itself immediately. In February 1994 the President announced a number of measures which could be interpreted as a willingness to modify his policies, to make them less harsh on the majority of the people – at least this is how they were understood by many in the country. I would not conceal that I had some illusions too. Speaking publicly at the time, with some reservations, I said that the implementation of these measures could change the situation for the better.

Nevertheless my illusions were quickly shattered. The

executive power, feeling that its hands were free, continued its policies more cynically and mercilessly, without regard for the society.

The core of these plans was the so-called financial stabilization. But this did not mean a regime of strict austerity in government, removing unnecessary expenditure, streamlining the activities of the financial institutions, putting an end to massive tax evasion, etc. The bureaucratic apparatus continued to grow, privileges for many officials were multiplying, hundreds of millions of dollars were spent on renovation and new equipment for administrative buildings, abuses of power were multiplying. The government was making cuts in capital investment in the infrastructure, which was on the brink of collapse, and in the leading technological branches of industry. Very soon this was followed by criminal cutbacks in the funding of education, health care, maintenance of the army and law enforcement agencies. Tens of millions of workers were not getting paid for months on end. The state even stopped paying for the industrial output which it had ordered. As a result, industrial and agricultural production fell by more than 50 per cent compared to 1990.

It is true that these measures helped curb inflation. It dropped below levels of, for example, 1992, when prices sky-rocketed. Nevertheless, the whole economic infrastructure was on the brink of collapse.

All this time I was in close contact with our leading economists. Almost all of them agreed with this very pessimistic conclusion: they were very critical of what was being done to our economy. They offered alternative programmes for economic recovery. The department of economics of the Russian Academy of Sciences issued one such programme.

I did my utmost to make the public aware of the real state of affairs. But it would be wrong to just state the facts. We at the Foundation concentrated on exposing the mechanisms which had brought about this situation, and by doing so defining possible ways out of the crisis. We maintained that the main 'bleeding wound' was inflicted on the Russian economy by the destruction of the USSR, for which those who were now at the helm of

Russian politics were largely responsible. The other bleeding wound was the catastrophic consequences of the erroneous reform model, and the unskilful, amateur methods of its implementation. A very important rule was ignored, that, first, reforms should not be forced on people, and second, while being energetic and consistent, they should not be like a 'cavalry charge', or an avalanche. The attempt to solve difficult social problems at one stroke was doomed to failure.

As the situation worsened I became more and more worried by two important circumstances. First, the growing dissatisfaction with the way the reforms were being implemented began to weaken the commitment of our people to reform in general. I therefore did my best to show the fundamental differences between the necessary changes, which were in the interest of society, and the methods to which incompetent rulers resort. Secondly, I was worried about the obvious inclination of the authorities, faced with such recurring failures, to turn to authoritarian methods of running the country, and their attempts to convince the Russian public that such policies were necessary. As a result, people were beginning to distrust democracy as a form of government.

The gravity of the situation drove me to address an open letter to the mass media on 26 October 1994, stating that the people's patience was near breaking-point. 'Unfortunately, many people think that democracy is to blame for all this. With increasing frequency, one can hear democracy derided, and calls for dictatorship.' Noting that an authoritarian regime, like a drug, can give temporary relief, but that the Russia of the twenty-first century would not be built in this way, I proposed a programme to overcome the crisis, based on democracy, strict adherence to the rule of law, unrestricted freedom of speech, and human rights. At the same time I stated that the present regime was incapable of implementing such a programme. A decisive step towards the establishment of democratic authority, I added, would be to hold without delay free democratic elections of the President, parliament and local authorities. 'Only then can power in Russia become really strong and authoritative.'

Meanwhile the government was becoming increasingly alienated from the people. In an opinion poll conducted by the Institute of Sociology of the Russian Academy of Sciences in November 1994, 70 per cent of those questioned said that the Russian leadership was not in control of the country, and 76 per cent had no confidence in the President. The popularity of Yegor Gaidar's party, regarded as the main pro-governmental political force, was continuing to fall. The authorities began to realize that dissatisfaction was growing in the country. They cast around for something that would on the one hand distract public attention and on the other hand increase the popularity of the President. This is how the idea of a 'victorious little war' in Chechnya arose.

CHECHNYA

The Chechen tragedy has its roots in the past, distant and not so distant. As for its recent deterioration, this was caused by the break-up of the USSR, and the consequent aggravation of the centrifugal tendencies, which now affected Russia itself. I recall a private conversation with Yeltsin when I told him: 'Remember, our state is held together by two rings. One is the USSR, the other is the Russian Federation. If the first is broken, problems for the other will follow.' This is just what happened. And the Russian authorities did much to fuel this process.

In the years after the Union state was destroyed many problems accumulated between Chechnya and the federal authorities. Tensions also mounted in Chechnya itself. All these problems required a solution. What kind of a solution? In discussions at the Foundation, I constantly warned that *force should under no circumstances be used*. This was not only because I am categorically opposed to the use of force to solve political problems. Coming from Stavropol, which is in the same area, I know very well how difficult and delicate relations between the nationalities are there. I know the mentality of the mountain people. You can negotiate with them, but you can't coerce them. If you don't understand that, you are bound to fail, to be defeated.

There were a few experts on the East and, more specifically, on the Caucasus among Yeltsin's associates. How strange that they were unable – or perhaps they did not dare – to explain this to him. It could be that, as is his wont, he just decided to barge in, regardless of common sense. Whatever the reason, in November 1994 the federal authorities decided to intervene in the internal quarrels in Chechnya, and to seek the laurels as victors, as keepers of Russian unity.

Yeltsin made a speech which, while not altogether wrong, contained a land-mine of great destructive power. It was an ultimatum, one which made a peaceful outcome practically impossible. Immediately after this, on 26 November, I publicly objected to the use of military force in the region and expressed my readiness to be a mediator in seeking a sensible and just solution to the problem. Dudayev, who held power in Chechnya, agreed. The federal authorities gave no reply.

When the federal armed forces entered Chechnya, with the sanction of the President, and began to engage in large-scale hostilities there, I sharply denounced this action. My position in a nutshell was reflected in an interview broadcast by Radio Liberty on 29 January 1995. I said that the developments affecting Chechnya were a tragedy for all Russians. 'Is there a Chechen problem? Yes, there is. Should we be worried about the future of the Russian Federation? Yes, we should. I am one of those who cannot even imagine agreeing to the collapse of the Russian state. But the actions of our authorities have only humili- ated the Russian army and thrown our society into a state of shock. The majority of our citizens are against the use of the federal armed forces there. But the executive power has opted for a military solution and is not reacting to public opinion. Can we consider the country as democratic, if the President and those around him can ignore the press, public opinion, representative bodies, and the international community?'

I also criticized the position adopted by Western countries. Since Chechnya had no formal sovereignty under international law and was recognized by no-one, they hastened to say that it was an internal matter for Russia, preferring to turn a blind eye to the way the problem was being handled. Only after the conflict turned into a bloodbath, did they yield to public pressure, and call for an end to military action. The events which followed demonstrated graphically that the calculations of the President and his entourage regarding Chechnya were wrong from the start. This was not 'a victorious little war'. The longer hostilities continued, the clearer it was that, as should have been obvious in the first place, there is no military solution to the Chechen problem.

Like many others, I constantly searched for a way out of this dead end into which Yeltsin and those around him had driven the Chechen problem. I offered a package of proposals for the settlement of the conflict when tragedy struck the town of Kizlyar and the village of Pervomaiskoye, as the federal authorities responded to an act of terrorism by Chechen fighters with massive force, leading to loss of life and enormous destruction.

My conclusions were outlined in a press statement I made on 12 February 1996. I reiterated some of the points I had made before and developed some new proposals. Its essence can be summarized as follows: to solve the problem, it is necessary to face the facts. And the facts are these: the efforts of the Russian leadership to solve the problem by force have failed; similarly Dudayev has failed to ignite a jihad and to separate Chechnya from Russia; nor can the conflict be resolved by electing a new leadership in the republic with Doku Zavgayev as leader. The problem can only be solved through direct dialogue with those who bear responsibility for the conflict and are in a position to find a settlement. President Yeltsin, Dzhokhar Dudayev, Doku Zavgayev, and possibly other Chechen leaders must meet immediately and work out a political formula to resolve the problem. In my opinion it should include an agreement on the immediate cessation of hostilities, the denunciation of terrorism and use of force, and an agreement on a common approach to the whole range of issues, including, above all, the status of Chechnya, which would take account of the interests of the people of the republic as well as the interests of Russia. Approaches should be developed to the solution of other problems, such as the withdrawal of troops, the holding of free elections in Chechnya, the development of a programme of national reconstruction, and humanitarian issues.

At the moment when these lines are being written, the situation is still deteriorating. Every day brings new losses, new destruction. Soldiers and officers serving in Chechnya declare publicly, in front of the cameras, that they do not know why they are risking their lives: 'Who needs this war?' And the army, which has had to fight for an unjust cause, has indeed become hostage to a shameful policy.

CONSEQUENCES OF DISINTEGRATION

The events in Chechnya have once again reminded us of the tragedy of the disintegration of the USSR. Everything I warned about, insisting until the end on the unity of the country, has been confirmed. Even Russia with her mighty economic potential and immense natural resources could not be saved from industrial collapse, unprecedented in peacetime, and decay in every sphere of life.

The break-up of the Soviet Union halted the momentum of democratization, launched in the years of perestroika. The democratic institutions have been eroded and in some of the republics even dismantled. Very soon Russia began to slide towards authoritarianism.

Those who opted for the collapse of the Union tried to cover up its dissolution by the creation of a new entity, the Commonwealth of Independent States (CIS). One of the reasons why the Belovezh conspiracy did not cause mass protests, and why the republics' Supreme Soviets rubber-stamped it almost without a murmur, is the fact that people believed that the unity of the country was going to be preserved in a new form, with only slight changes to its membership.

Soon it became obvious that the CIS proclaimed in Belovezh and approved in Alma Ata was not a viable entity. It was created to draw the wool over people's eyes or, as Kravchuk expressed it later, to guarantee a 'civilized divorce'.

The burial of the CIS began immediately. Despite declarations and agreements to the contrary, the common economic infrastructure was destroyed. Former Soviet republics isolated themselves behind borders and customs barriers. Heated disputes began between them on a large number of problems, including territorial questions. Former national disputes not only did not abate; in several cases they escalated. New conflicts appeared. In Transcaucasia, Moldova, Central Asia and then in Russia, in the North Caucasus, blood was shed. The number of victims has now reached tens of thousands and the number of refugees, millions.

I used every opportunity to warn the authorities and the public, to urge them to resist the mounting estrangement of the former Soviet republics. When I was unable to get through the information barriers within the country, I used my foreign trips for this purpose, hoping that what I said abroad would reach Russia, if only by an indirect route.

It was very important to let the West, particularly the Americans, know that what was happening in the 'post-Soviet area' was not in their interests either. Many in the USA regarded the disintegration of the Soviet Union as a coveted trophy of victory in the Cold War, or a gift of destiny which rid them of a dangerous rival. Significantly, the American media, unlike the Europeans, ignored the very existence of the Commonwealth of Independent States. This term was rarely, if ever used there.

In the Foundation we prepared a number of analytical papers and held scholarly symposia and seminars on the subject of the CIS. In December 1994, on the eve of the third anniversary of the Belovezh agreements, the Foundation issued a statement entitled 'We need a new Union'. In it, we assessed the consequences of the collapse of the unified state, pointed out the failure of the CIS structures, and put forward a programme of practical actions to breathe new life into them.

Today many people in most of the former Soviet republics would like to re-establish the links between them and call for reintegration – on new foundations, of course. More and more, they think how to 'gather the stones together'.

The policies of the Russian government since the Belovezh agreements have not been conducive to reintegration. They assumed that for Russia, rapprochement with the former Soviet republics would be a net loss, including lower living standards. Much time has thus been lost.

The centuries-old habit of the Russian leaders to dominate our neighbours has had its negative influence, too. It is not always overt, but it is always easy to recognize. It feeds the fears of once again becoming dependent on Moscow.

I completely rule out the possibility of the re-creation of the former USSR, as demanded by 'national patriots' like Zhirinovsky and the communists. I envisage a rapprochement into an inter-state association based on the principles of democracy, equality and a common market, similar in concept to the European Union, but taking special account of the large numbers of Russians and Russian-speaking populations in the newly independent states. A common market is required to stimulate the movement of capital and goods, entrepreneurial activity, diversification and industrial links. An agreed labour and social law is also required. We need common instruments to guarantee collective security, in areas ranging from the environment to defence.

Recently, some positive steps have been taken in this regard, which I welcomed, even though they were taken in the context of the presidential election campaign.

THE WORK OF THE GORBACHEV FOUNDATION

Some members of the Moscow intelligentsia gravitated towards the Foundation after it was set up. Specialists from institutions and numerous academic and social organizations which had emerged during glasnost participated in our conferences and discussions. Among them were some who were quite critical of Gorbachev. Gradually a more or less constant circle of people emerged, who were willing to work seriously with us on Russian and international problems in the spirit of the new thinking.

The meetings, conferences and seminars in connection with the tenth anniversary of perestroika were particularly lively. We planned them for the whole year, from May 1994 to May 1995. I shall list the most interesting of them: the conference on the lessons and the future of radical economic reform, the conference on the role of the intelligentsia in perestroika, the conferences 'Perestroika: the Idea, its Implementation and its Lessons', 'The

Rule of Law in Russia: the ideal and the reality', and the conference on 'The Foreign Policy of the USSR and Russia', held in
conjunction with the Foreign Policy Association, headed by
former Foreign Minister Bessmertnykh. Of great interest were
the discussions of Russia's national interests and objectives, and
the problems of civilization and global development in the
twenty-first century. A symposium on 'Russia and the countries
of Eastern Europe' brought together representatives from
Belarus, Bulgaria, Hungary, Germany, Moldova, Romania, the
Czech Republic, and Yugoslavia.

Different views and approaches to the issues were put forward
at our conferences, but one conclusion stood out: there is a
distinct dividing line between the periods of 1985–91 and
1992–95.

The conviction that our country and the world need new
thinking, a new global understanding, a new interpretation of the
ideas of progress, humanism and justice, has united outstanding
people who work with the Foundation. We are open to co-
operation with various research teams, we try to publish our
discussions and findings in newspapers, brochures and books.
We have begun publishing documents on the history of
perestroika.

Russia's history has not been very fortunate – not only by what
happened in the past, but also in the way these events have been
treated by academics and others. Our history is either over-
simplified, painted red or black, or used for political ends. But
unless we understand our history we shall never understand
ourselves. And what kind of future shall we have without that?

This explains the Foundation's interest in history, and not only
the history of perestroika. We marked the centenary of the birth
of Khrushchev and the fortieth anniversary of the XXth Party
Congress with academic conferences. Together with the
Gorbachev Foundation USA we organized The State of
the World Forum in San Francisco in October 1995, to commemorate the fiftieth anniversary of the United Nations and to help
develop a vision of the world's future. I chaired the forum and
participated in a televised debate with former President George
Bush and former Prime Minister Margaret Thatcher.

EPILOGUE

CHANGING ATTITUDES TOWARDS ME

I have spoken above of some of my foreign visits, which began soon after the Foundation was formed. At first I refrained from trips within Russia because of the hostile atmosphere towards me created by the authorities and much of the media.

But in March 1993 I decided to break this embargo. At the invitation of the Nizhny Novgorod Foundation 'Vybor' I went to this famous old city on the Volga. Meetings and talks with the governor, Boris Nemtsov, and the mayor Dmitry Bednyakov were both interesting and friendly.

It was a sign that attitudes towards me were changing. Quite unexpectedly in the autumn of 1993 I received a telephone call from Peredelkino, a village near Moscow, where many of our writers have dachas. One of them telephoned me on behalf of fifteen others. This is what he said: 'We would like to apologize for the terrible things we said about you. Now we understand what we have lost, and that we ourselves helped this situation to come about.'

I started to receive a lot of letters. Those who criticized me yet again and those who supported me agreed on one thing: 'You have started the process, why don't you finish it? Come back, do not hide in your Foundation.' I began to receive telephone calls, some from people who had turned away from me after 1991.

I felt that it was time to establish closer contact with the people, to talk openly about the past, the present, and what to do. And I started to travel across the country.

In 1994–5 I visited St Petersburg (three times), Krasnoyarsk, Vladimir, Novgorod (twice), Novosibirsk, Kursk, and Cheboksary. In Vladimir I took part in the seminar of the Suzdal Club, where discussions concerned problems of stability in Russia. At a conference in Kursk on 'Contemporary Ecological Problems of the Russian Provinces' I spoke as the President of the International Green Cross. I participated in discussions on the revival and development of entrepreneurial activity in Chuvashia. And in May 1995 I participated in a conference 'On the role of perestroika in Russia's destiny' in St Petersburg.

I went to St Petersburg with some emotion. It was there in 1985

895

that I had made my first public speech about perestroika, which was shown on television. And here I was again in this very city, in a totally different Russia. I felt that despite everything an understanding developed between myself and the people, and I was glad.

I would like to describe my two trips to Novgorod. When I visited it for the first time, I noted that the region differed from many in Russia by greater stability, and the business-like qualities of the authorities. That is why we chose Novgorod oblast as the site for the project 'Breakthrough into a Post-Industrial Society'. The project was developed by our Foundation in co-operation with some Western communications companies.

During my second visit to Novgorod, together with businessmen from Europe and America, we outlined the concept of the project to the local business community. Its realization will give the citizens of Novgorod access to modern information and communications technology, and thus to a new world, with all the resulting benefits for education, the mass media, and culture. In other words, we would like Novgorod to enter the information superhighway.

My trip to Novosibirsk was undertaken at the invitation of a member of the Council of the Federation, Aleksei Manannikov. The programme of the visit included a meeting in the Akademgorodok, a visit to the 'Stankosib' plant, and a live television interview. Near the public library, where a meeting with the local intelligentsia was planned, a 'group of comrades' met us with slogans like: 'No audience for the traitor' etc. But the hall was full to capacity. I answered questions for an hour and then went on to a seminar on 'Russia on the eve of the twenty-first century'. My live interview on Novosibirsk television was extended because of unprecedented public demand.

My trips around the country, my talks with my fellow-citizens and their reaction to my speeches, together with the many letters I received, convinced me that the country needed Gorbachev and that inspired me to participate in the 1996 presidential campaign.

On 1 March 1996 I addressed all democratic forces of the country. The roots of all our problems, I said, are to be found in the mechanism of power. Though elected, our authorities have nevertheless put themselves above the people, trying to perpetuate their rule. This government has to be changed.

Public opinion is being persuaded that it has only the option of a lesser evil, as if besides the 'party of power' that wants to see Yeltsin re-elected and the Communist Party, there are no other forces able to rule Russia today.

This is a false choice, the more so because with all their obvious differences and sharp rivalry, they both employ neo-Bolshevik tactics. They both spring from the same root – the nomenklatura of the times when the CPSU reigned supreme. While one group would like to continue the policies that most people reject, the other group, which has still not abandoned the totalitarian habits of the past, would like to use the people's discontent in order to return to power.

The presidential elections in Russia have duly taken place. Whatever else one may say, they were a watershed in the historic passage that my country is traversing. Sadly, the democratic forces failed to unite or, to be more precise, they were not allowed to unite. Thus, they failed to make a strong enough showing to be able to affect decisively the further course of events. Yet the elections gave rise to hopes – and at the same time disappointments. The promises of the winner are clearly 'hanging in the balance'. There seems to be no will, nor the means, nor a serious understanding of the responsibility to the people or of the limits of the people's patience.

The crisis in our country will continue for some time, possibly leading to even greater upheaval. But Russia has irrevocably chosen the path of freedom and no one can make it turn back to totalitarianism.

Democracy is the only way to Russia's revival, to a life of dignity for its great people and, eventually, to prosperity in the community of other civilized nations.

July 1996

CHRONOLOGY

1917

25 October (Julian calendar)/ 7 November (Gregorian calendar): The IInd Congress of Soviets of Workers' and Soldiers' Deputies opens and declares that power has passed from the Provisional Government to the Soviets.
26-27 October (Julian calendar)/ 8-9 November (Gregorian calendar): At an all-night sitting the Congress confirms a new government, the Sovnarkom or Council of People's Commissars, consisting entirely of Bolsheviks and chaired by Vladimir Lenin.

1918

1 February: Soviet Russia moves to the Gregorian calendar.
3 March: Treaty of Brest-Litovsk between Germany, Austria-Hungary, Bulgaria and Turkey and Russia is signed. Russia loses 26% of its population, 27% of its arable land, 73% of its steel industry and 75% of its coal industry.
June: Civil War between Reds (Bolsheviks) and Whites (anti-Bolsheviks) begins, continuing until late 1920.
13 November: The Soviet government annuls the Treaty of Brest-Litovsk and sends the Red Army into the German occupied areas.

1921

8-16 March: The Xth Congress of the Communist Party (Bolsheviks) bans factionalism in the Party and introduces the New Economic Policy (NEP).

1922

3 April: Stalin is elected General Secretary of the Party.
30 December: The Ist All-Union Congress of Soviets votes for the formation of the Union of Soviet Socialist Republics.

1924

21 January: Lenin dies at Gorky, near Moscow. The struggle for the succession begins; by 1928 Stalin has emerged as leader.

1928

1 October: The 1st Five Year Plan begins (ends on 31 December 1932).

1929

16 January: Stalin's proposal that Trotsky be deported from the Soviet Union is adopted by the Politburo.

1931

2 March: Mikhail Gorbachev is born at Privolnoye, Stavropol krai, North Caucasus.

1936

5 December: A new Soviet constitution is adopted which establishes the USSR Supreme Soviet, consisting of two houses, the Soviet of the Union and the Soviet of Nationalities.

1939

23 August: Molotov and Ribbentrop sign in Moscow the Soviet-German Non-Aggression Treaty, including a secret protocol on their spheres of influence in Europe (also called the Stalin-Hitler Pact, the Nazi-Soviet Pact, the Molotov-Ribbentrop pact, etc.).

1941

22 June: German forces invade the Soviet Union.

1942

August: The Wehrmacht overruns and occupies Stavropol krai. It withdraws in January-February 1943.

1943

31 January: Field Marshal Paulus surrenders at Stalingrad.

1945

30 April: Red Army soldiers hoist the Red Flag over the Reichstag in Berlin.
9 May: German commanders sign the unconditional surrender of German forces, thus ending the Second World War in Europe.

1950

Gorbachev becomes a candidate member of the Communist Party. He becomes a full member in 1952. In September, he enters the Law Faculty of Moscow State University.

1953

5 March: Stalin dies after suffering a stroke on 1 March.
6 March: Georgy Malenkov becomes prime minister and head of the Party.
14 March: Malenkov leaves the Party Secretariat and thus ceases to be head of the Party. The main beneficiary is Khrushchev.
26 June: Beria is arrested (and executed in December).
13 September: Khrushchev is elected First Secretary of the CPSU.
25 September: Gorbachev marries Raisa Maksimovna Titorenko.

1954

2 March: Khrushchev launches his 'Virgin and Idle Lands' programme which envisages the rapid expansion of the sown area of north Kazakhstan, west Siberia, the Urals, the Volga and the North Caucasus.

1955

8 February: Malenkov resigns as Prime Minister and is succeeded by Nikolai Bulganin, a Khrushchev nominee.
June: Gorbachev graduates from Moscow State University. After a short period in the Prokuratura, he transfers to Komsomol work.

1956

14-25 February: At the XXth Party Congress Khrushchev delivers a secret speech attacking Stalin's personality cult and demanding a return to Leninist principles.

September: Gorbachev is appointed first secretary of the Stavropol city Komsomol committee.

1957

6 January: Raisa Maksimovna gives birth to a daughter, Irina.

19 June: The Party Presidium votes to dismiss Khrushchev as Party leader but he argues successfully that only the Central Committee can do this. On 4 July, he eventually defeats his opponents (known as the Anti-Party Group) and thereby becomes undisputed leader of the Soviet Union.

1958

25 April: Gorbachev is elected second secretary of the Stavropol krai Komsomol committee.

1961

March: Gorbachev appointed first secretary of the Stavropol krai Komsomol committee.

12 April: Yury Gagarin becomes the first man in space, circling the earth in his spacecraft, Vostok-1.

14 October: A Central Committee plenum adopts a new Party programme and statute replacing those of 1919. The new programme defines the Party as a Party of the whole people, rather than as a dictatorship of the proletariat.

17-31 October: At the XXIInd Party Congress Khrushchev proposes a twenty-year plan to usher in a communist society. It envisages that, over the years 1961-70, the Soviet Union will surpass the US in per capita production, and that by 1980, the Soviet Union will be close to introducing 'distribution according to need'. Gorbachev attends as a delegate.

1962

March: Gorbachev is appointed Party organizer of a Territorial Production Association, Stavropol krai.
22 October: President John F. Kennedy announces to the American people that there are Soviet missiles in Cuba and imposes a naval blockade. Eventually Khrushchev backs down and removes the missiles, but gains the concession from Kennedy that the US will not attempt to invade Cuba.

1963

1 January: Gorbachev is appointed head of department of Party organs, Stavropol agricultural kraikom.

1964

14 October: Khrushchev is dismissed as First Party Secretary by a Central Committee plenum, which elects Leonid Brezhnev as his successor. Aleksei Kosygin becomes prime minister. It is also agreed that in future the same person cannot occupy simultaneously the posts of Party leader and prime minister.

1965

9 December: Anastas Mikoyan resigns as chairman of the Presidium of the USSR Supreme Soviet and is succeeded by Nikolai Podgorny.

1968

21 August: Soviet and other Warsaw Pact troops invade Czechoslovakia, bringing to an end the era of 'socialism with a human face'.

1970

Spring: Gorbachev is appointed first Party secretary, Stavropol kraikom.

1971

March: Gorbachev is elected a member of the Central Committee.

1975

1 August: The Helsinki Final Act is signed by Leonid Brezhnev, thus bringing the third session of the Conference on Security and Co-operation in Europe to a successful end.
9 October: The Nobel Peace Prize is awarded to Academician Andrei Sakharov.

1977

16 June: Nikolai Podgorny resigns as chairman of the Presidium of the USSR Supreme Soviet and is succeeded by Leonid Brezhnev.

1978

27 November: Gorbachev is appointed Central Committee Secretary for Agriculture, and the family moves to Moscow.

1979

November: Gorbachev is elected a candidate member of the Politburo.
26 December: Soviet troops move into Afghanistan.

1980

Gorbachev is elected a full member of the Politburo.

1982

10 November: Leonid Brezhnev dies and is succeeded as General Secretary of the Communist Party by Yury Andropov, who also becomes chairman of the Presidium of the USSR Supreme Soviet (President). When Andropov is ill, Gorbachev often chairs Politburo meetings.

1984

9 February: Yury Andropov dies and is succeeded by Konstantin Chernenko on 13 February. Chernenko later also becomes President.

1985

10 March: Chernenko dies.

11 March: Mikhail Gorbachev is elected General Secretary of the Communist Party.

8 April: Gorbachev announces suspension of the deployment of SS-20 missiles in Europe.

23 April: Gorbachev proposes a vague reform programme, which is adopted by a Central Committee plenum. Viktor Chebrikov, Yegor Ligachev and Nikolai Ryzhkov are elected full members of the Politburo.

15 May: Gorbachev visits Leningrad, where he makes a vigorous speech advocating change.

1 July: Boris Yeltsin is appointed a Central Committee secretary.

2 July: The USSR Supreme Soviet elects Andrei Gromyko chairman of its Presidium. Eduard Shevardnadze takes over from Gromyko as Minister of Foreign Affairs.

27 September: Ryzhkov takes over from Tikhonov as Chairman of the USSR Council of Ministers (prime minister).

30 September: The Soviet Union proposes cutting half of all Soviet and American nuclear weapons.

2-6 October: Gorbachev visits France, on his first official visit abroad as Soviet leader.

18-21 November: Presidents Gorbachev and Reagan meet in Geneva and agree to further meetings.

24 December: Yeltsin succeeds Viktor Grishin as first secretary of Moscow gorkom.

1986

25 February-6 March: XXVIIth Party Congress in Moscow. Gorbachev calls for radical economic reform.

26 April: Explosion at the Chernobyl nuclear reactor.

14 May: Gorbachev speaks for the first time to the nation on the Chernobyl disaster but gives few details.

28 July: Gorbachev announces troop withdrawals from Afghanistan and Mongolia.

30 September: A Central Committee resolution criticizes the slow pace of perestroika.

10 October: Gorbachev flies to Reykjavik for a two-day summit with Reagan. The two Presidents almost reach agreement on extensive cuts in offensive arms.

November: Gorbachev flies to India, where he and President Rajiv Gandhi sign the Delhi declaration on the principles of a nuclear-weapon-free and non-violent world (27 November).

16 December: Gorbachev telephones Sakharov in Gorky (now Nizhny Novgorod), inviting him and his wife, Yelena Bonner, to return to Moscow after six years of involuntary exile.

16 December: Riots in Alma Ata and many other Kazakh cities after Dinmukhamed Kunayev is replaced as first secretary of the Communist Party of Kazakhstan.

1987

26 January: A much postponed Central Committee plenum convenes and Gorbachev proposes political reforms, including multi-candidate elections and the appointment of non-Party persons to senior government posts. He also advocates the expansion of co-operatives.

10 April: Gorbachev proposes further arms cuts during a visit to Prague.

6 May: About six hundred members of Pamyat, a new Russian nationalist organization, demonstrate in Moscow and are then received by Yeltsin.

28 May: Mathias Rust, a young West German, lands his plane near Red Square. Wholesale military personnel changes are announced in the wake of Rust's penetration of Soviet airspace. Dmitry Yazov becomes Minister of Defence.

25 June: At a Central Committee plenum Gorbachev criticizes the head of Gosplan and other top economic officials.

28-30 June: At a USSR Supreme Soviet session a law giving enterprises more independence is adopted.

22 July: Gorbachev proposes the global elimination of all inter-mediate-range nuclear missiles, and on 24 November this is agreed in Geneva.

1 November: Gorbachev's book *Perestroika* is published in Moscow.

11 November: After criticizing both Gorbachev and Ligachev at a Central Committee plenum in October, Yeltsin is replaced as first secretary, Moscow gorkom, by Lev Zaikov.

December: Gorbachev visits Great Britain and the United States. In Washington he signs a treaty banning intermediate-range nuclear missiles.

1988

8 January: Gorbachev calls for glasnost in a meeting with representatives of the media.

8 February: Gorbachev proposes to withdraw all Soviet troops from Afghanistan by spring 1989.

February-April: Violence and disorder in Nagorno-Karabakh, where Armenians are demonstrating for the transfer of the region from Azerbaijan to Armenia. Armenians and others are murdered in Sumgait, Azerbaijan.

13 March: *Sovetskaya Rossiya* publishes Nina Andreyeva's letter attacking reformers.

14 April: Accords ending the Afghan war are signed. The United States and the Soviet Union agree to guarantee the accords and pledge themselves not to interfere in the internal affairs of Afghanistan and Pakistan.

29 May-2 June: President Reagan visits Moscow.

28 June: Opening in Moscow of the XIXth Party Conference, where Gorbachev proposes a presidential system for the Soviet Union, a new parliament, to be called the Congress of People's Deputies, an increase in the power of local Soviets at the expense of the Communist Party, and the removal of the Party from state economic management.

June-July: Further turmoil in Armenia and Azerbaijan over Nagorno-Karabakh.

30 September: At a Central Committee plenum many members retire and Gromyko leaves the Politburo. The following day

Gorbachev replaces Gromyko as chairman of the Presidium of the USSR Supreme Soviet.

7 December: At the United Nations in New York, Gorbachev announces a reduction of 500,000 in Soviet military personnel within two years, withdrawing six tank divisions from Eastern Europe. He calls for a new world order to be based on the United Nations, and renounces the use of force.

7 December: Gorbachev breaks off his visit to the United States and abandons plans to visit Cuba and Britain after hearing news of the earthquake in Armenia.

1989

January: The Baltic states, followed by other non-Russian republics, pass laws giving precedence to their own languages.

15 February: The last Soviet troops leave Afghanistan.

26 March: Elections are held to the USSR Congress of People's Deputies. Many Party candidates lose and the pro-independence parties win in the Baltic states. Yeltsin wins in Moscow.

9 April: Police and soldiers attack demonstrators in Tbilisi.

14 May: Gorbachev's visit to China stimulates the democracy movement and severely embarrasses his Chinese hosts.

18 May: Estonia and Lithuania declare their sovereignty. Latvia follows on 29 July.

25 May: The USSR Congress of People's Deputies opens in Moscow and is televised live. Gorbachev is elected chairman and on 26 May members of the USSR Supreme Soviet are elected from among the Congress's members.

June: Elections in Poland result in an overwhelming victory by Solidarity candidates over Communists.

3-4 June: Chinese troops attack pro-democracy demonstrators in and around Tiananmen Square, leaving many dead.

4 June: Soviet troops are despatched to Uzbekistan after clashes between Uzbeks and Meskhetian Turks in Fergana leave many dead.

July: Coal miners in the Kuzbass, Siberia, go on strike, followed by miners in the Donbass, Ukraine.

7 July: Gorbachev declares that Warsaw Pact nations are free to choose their own road to socialism.

23 July: On the eve of the 50th anniversary of the Soviet-German Pact, it is officially acknowledged for the first time that the Pact contained secret protocols for the partition of Poland and the annexation of the Baltic states by the Soviet Union.

29 July: The Inter-Regional Group is formed in the Congress of People's Deputies to promote reform. Among the leaders chosen by these 250-odd deputies are Yeltsin, Sakharov and Gavriil Popov.

24 August: A non-Communist government takes power in Poland.

10 September: Hungary opens its borders with the West. Thousands of East Germans emigrate to West Germany.

7 October: Gorbachev, in East Berlin, tells the crowds that 'life punishes those who fall behind' and this further undermines the authority of Erich Honecker, the GDR leader. He is replaced by Egon Krenz on 18 October.

9 November: The Berlin Wall comes down.

November-December: A 'velvet revolution' leads to the resignation of the Communist government in Prague. Václav Havel becomes President of Czechoslovakia.

29 November-1 December: Gorbachev travels to Italy and the Vatican, where he meets the Pope.

2-4 December: Gorbachev and Bush meet in Malta and discuss recent developments in eastern Europe and arms control.

14 December: Sakharov dies.

December: Rioting in Timosoara triggers off the Romanian revolution, leading to the execution of President Ceausescu and his wife by firing squad (25 December).

20 December: The Communist Party of Lithuania declares itself independent of the Communist Party of the Soviet Union.

1990

January: Azerbaijanis riot near the border with Iran. Soviet troops are sent to restore order. Armenia asserts its right to veto

Soviet laws. Armenia and Azerbaijan begin to mobilize. Moldavians demonstrate for unification with Romania.

10-13 January: Gorbachev travels to Lithuania to discuss the republic's desire to break away from the Soviet Union. Lithuanians demonstrate for independence.

19-20 January: Clashes in Baku between Soviet forces and the local population leave many dead.

5 February: At a Central Committee plenum Gorbachev proposes that the Party abandon its leading role, accept a multi-party system and adopt 'humane, democratic socialism'. These proposals are accepted on 7 February after a stormy debate.

February-March: Local elections are held throughout the Soviet Union. Pro-independence candidates win in the Baltic states. In Moscow and Leningrad official Party candidates are rejected. The USSR Supreme Soviet, followed by the Congress of People's Deputies, votes for increased presidential powers.

6 March: The Congress of People's Deputies amends Article 6 of the Soviet Constitution, thus ending the Party's monopoly of power.

11 March: Lithuania declares independence and elects Vytautas Landsbergis President. Continuing tension with central government eases on 29 June when the Lithuanian parliament votes to suspend declaration.

15 March: Gorbachev is elected Soviet President by the Congress of People's Deputies.

24-26 March: Gorbachev chooses his fifteen-person presidential council.

13 April: The Soviet government admits that the NKVD, rather than the Germans, were responsible for the Katyn massacre of Polish officers during the Second World War.

29 May: Boris Yeltsin is elected chairman (or President) of the Presidium of the Russian Supreme Soviet.

30 May-4 June: Gorbachev travels to the United States for his second summit with Bush.

8 June: The Russian parliament declares that its laws take precedence over Soviet laws.

19-22 June: The founding Congress of the Russian Communist

Party convenes in Moscow. Ivan Polozkov is elected leader.

2 July: The XXVIIIth Party Congress opens in Moscow. Gorbachev is re-elected leader. The new Politburo contains only Party officials and will have no role in governing the country.

15 July: Gorbachev issues a decree ending Party control of the media and broadcasting.

16 July: Ukraine declares its sovereignty.

20 July: The '500-day' programme of the Russian Republic to move to a market economy is published.

23-24 August: Armenia, Turkmenistan and Tajikistan declare their sovereignty.

9 September: Gorbachev and Bush meet for a one-day summit in Helsinki to discuss Iraq's invasion of Kuwait. They agree to put pressure on Saddam Hussein to withdraw his forces from Kuwait.

24 September: The USSR Supreme Soviet grants Gorbachev special powers to rule by decree during the transition to a market economy, but cannot agree on an economic programme.

3 October: Germany is reunited.

15 October: Gorbachev is awarded the 1990 Nobel Peace Prize.

20-21 October: Founding Congress of DemRossiya.

24 October: Russia and Ukraine declare their laws sovereign over all-union laws; the USSR Supreme Soviet declares such assertions invalid.

November: Negotiations on the conventional forces in Europe treaty are concluded.

17 November: The USSR Supreme Soviet accepts Gorbachev's proposal to set up a new Soviet government, consisting of representatives from all fifteen republics, to be called the Soviet (Council) of the Federation.

23 November: The draft treaty of a new union is published, to be called the Union of Sovereign Soviet Republics.

2 December: Vadim Bakatin is removed as USSR Minister of Internal Affairs and succeeded by Boris Pugo.

17 December: Gorbachev says that the country needs firm executive rule to overcome the threat posed by 'the dark forces of nationalism'.

20 December: Shevardnadze resigns and warns of the threat of dictatorship.

26 December: The Congress of People's Deputies approves new executive powers for the President.

26 December: Gorbachev chooses Gennady Yanayev as the new Vice-President of the Soviet Union. He is rejected on the first ballot by the Congress but accepted on the second.

1991

2 January: Soviet troops seize the main newspaper publishing plant in Riga, Latvia.

11-13 January: Soviet forces fire at the main printing press in Vilnius, Lithuania, and on 13 January attack and take the television station. A 'national committee of salvation' is announced by local Communists still loyal to Moscow.

14-15 January: Valentin Pavlov becomes prime minister in succession to Ryzhkov, who has suffered a heart attack. Aleksandr Bessmertnykh succeeds Shevardnadze as Minister of Foreign Affairs.

19-20 January: A 'committee of national salvation' is announced in Latvia. Soviet troops attack the Ministry of the Interior in Riga.

January-February: The crisis in the Baltic republics eases as many Soviet troops withdraw.

24-28 February: Gulf War breaks out. American and allied troops attack Iraqi forces and drive them out of Kuwait.

17 March: Referendum on the future of the USSR, with additional questions (in Russia) on the creation of a presidency and (in Moscow) a directly elected mayor. The results show a large majority in favour of retaining a reformed Soviet Union.

23 April: In Novo-Ogarevo President Gorbachev and the heads of state of nine republics sign a joint statement on speeding up a new union agreement.

12 June: Boris Yeltsin elected President of the Russian Federation in Russia's first democratic elections. He receives 57.3% of the vote in a turnout of 74%. Zhirinovsky polls 8%. Popov is elected mayor of Moscow with 65.3% of the vote.

17-21 June: The USSR Cabinet of Ministers attempts to restrict the power of President Gorbachev.

July: Gorbachev attends the G7 Summit meeting in London and appeals for funds but receives only promises. Later in the month, Gorbachev and Bush meet in Moscow to sign the Strategic Arms Reduction Treaty.

10 July: Yeltsin is sworn in as President of the Russian Federation and receives the blessing of the Russian Orthodox Church.

18-21 August: Attempted coup against President Gorbachev by the Extraordinary Committee. Afterwards, many of those implicated, including Kryuchkov, Yazov, and Yanayev, are dismissed. Pugo and Akhromeyev commit suicide.

20 August-22 September: Estonia, Latvia, Ukraine, Belorussia, Moldavia, Georgia, Azerbaijan, Kirgizia, Uzbekistan, Tajikistan and Armenia declare independence; only the Baltic states are recognized internationally (Lithuania had declared independence on 11 March 1990).

23 August-5 September: Yeltsin orders the Communist Party of the Soviet Union to suspend its activities on the territory of the Russian Federation. The Central Committee building at Staraya Ploshchad is sealed (22 August). The Russian national flag flies from the Kremlin, alongside the Soviet flag. Gorbachev resigns (24 August) as General Secretary of the CPSU and advises the Central Committee to dissolve.

5 September: USSR Congress of People's Deputies dissolves itself.

18 October: Treaty on an economic community is signed by President Gorbachev and representatives of eight republics: Azerbaijan, Georgia, Moldavia and Ukraine decline to sign.

28 October: Russian Congress of People's Deputies elects Ruslan Khasbulatov its chairman and speaker of the Russian Supreme Soviet.

6 November: Yeltsin bans the activities of the CPSU and the Russian Communist Party on the territory of the Russian Federation.

9-10 November: IInd Congress of Democratic Russia (DemRossiya).

1 December: In a referendum, the Ukrainian electorate votes for Ukrainian independence.

8 December: In Belovezh Forest, near Minsk, the Presidents and prime ministers of Russia, Ukraine and Belarus declare the USSR dissolved and found a Commonwealth of Independent States (CIS).

17 December: Yeltsin and Gorbachev agree that by 1 January 1992 the Soviet Union will no longer exist.

21 December: In Alma Ata, eleven Soviet republics agree on the formation of the CIS.

25 December: Gorbachev resigns.

27 December: Yeltsin takes over Gorbachev's office in the Kremlin.

31 December: The Soviet Union ceases to exist.

1992

2 January: Russian prime minister Yegor Gaidar launches his price liberalization policy, also known as 'shock therapy'.

13-31 March: Yeltsin and representatives of all territorial and national regions of the Russian Federation, except Tatarstan and the Chechen-Ingushetia, sign a Federal Treaty on the delimitation of power between the centre and the regions.

7 May: Yeltsin signs a decree establishing the armed forces of the Russian Federation with himself as commander in chief.

6 July: The Russian Constitutional Court begins the case against the CPSU. Gorbachev gives evidence in the case against the coup-plotters, which is eventually dismissed.

30 November: The Constitutional Court ends the proceedings against the CPSU without reaching any verdict.

14 December: Yeltsin is forced by the Congress of People's Deputies to drop Gaidar as prime minister. He chooses Viktor Chernomyrdin to replace him.

1993

20 March: On television, President Yeltsin announces the introduction of a 'special regime' (with dictatorial powers) and a referendum on 25 April.

24 March: Yeltsin's decree of 20 March is published, but the expression 'special regime' has been removed.

26-29 March: Motion to impeach Yeltsin at the IXth Congress of People's Deputies just fails.

25 April: In a nationwide referendum voters express their confidence in the President and his economic policy.

12 July: A Constitutional Assembly, called by Yeltsin, adopts the text of draft constitution.

21 September: Yeltsin signs a decree dissolving parliament and announces elections for a State Duma on 11-12 December. Parliament deposes the President and appoints Rutskoi to replace him, also new ministers of defence and security.

3-4 October: Conflict between forces supporting parliament and President Yeltsin results in bloodshed, with Yeltsin's forces bombarding the White House.

15 October: Georgian President Shevardnadze signs a decree on Georgian entry to the CIS, which now consists of all the ex-Soviet republics except Moldova and the Baltic states.

12 December: Elections to the State Duma and the draft constitution confirmed.

1994

23 February: The State Duma declares an amnesty for all those involved in the attempted coup of August 1991 and the events of October 1993.

27 May: Aleksandr Solzhenitsyn returns to Russia after twenty years in exile.

1995

17 December: Elections to the State Duma reveal the Communist Party of the Russian Federation to be the most popular party.

1996

March: Gorbachev declares that he will stand for election as President of Russia on 16 June.

GLOSSARY

ABC weapons Atomic, biological and chemical weapons.

ABM treaty Anti-ballistic missile treaty, signed by the United States and the Soviet Union in 1972; part of the Strategic Arms Limitation Treaty (SALT I).

Agitprop Department of Agitation and Propaganda, Central Committee Secretariat. The task of its officials was to mobilize the population to achieve the economic goals set by the state by raising Party awareness. It was believed that the more dedicated a communist was, the better he or she worked.

All-Union Ministries could be either All-Union, i.e. responsible for the whole of the country, or republican, responsible for their own republic but subordinate to Moscow. Hence there was a USSR Ministry of Agriculture and fifteen republican Ministries of Agriculture.

Alma Ata meeting See CIS.

Anti-Party Group Those in the Presidium (Politburo) in 1957, almost all representing government ministries, who opposed Khrushchev's policy of transferring responsibility for the implementation of economic plans from the government to the Party. He was almost defeated but after victory he removed all his opponents from the Presidium. None of his defeated opponents ever made a political comeback. The Party dominated economic decision-making until 1988, when Gorbachev, at the XIXth Party Conference, removed the Party from economic management.

Apparatchik Paid Party official.

ASSR Autonomous Soviet Socialist Republic. A territory within a Soviet republic inhabited by non-Russians, indeed non-Slavs (e.g. Komi ASSR), which had its own government. The Communist Party organization in an ASSR was equivalent to an obkom. In reality an ASSR was totally subordinate to the capital of the republic in which it was situated. Hence 'autonomous' did not mean independent. Most ASSRs were in the Russian Federation.

August coup The attempted coup of 18–21 August 1991. An eight-man Emergency Committee, led by Kryuchkov (KGB), Pugo (MVD), Lukyanov and Yanayev, declared Gorbachev deposed as Soviet President on 19 August (due to ill health), placed him under arrest at Foros, his dacha in the Crimea, declared a state of emergency and put troops on the streets. They demanded that all administrative organs throughout the country implement their instructions. The timing of the attempted coup was linked to the proposed signing of an agreement to establish a Union of Sovereign States, which would have devolved much of the centre's powers to the republics, thus establishing a genuine federal state. The putsch collapsed and achieved the opposite of what the plotters had intended. Reform was given a powerful boost, the Communist Party was fatally weakened and Russia dominated the political scene with an agenda which favoured an independent Russian state.

BAM Baikal Amur Magistral. Mainly built under Brezhnev (1974–84), this railway-line of over 3,000 kilometres was built as a back-up in case the Trans-Siberian Railway was interrupted. With hindsight, it was constructed too rapidly.

Bandung Conference A conference in Bandung, Indonesia, in April 1955, attended by twenty-nine independent African and Asian states which led to the non-aligned movement of states positioned outside the East–West conflict. The conference propagated the end of colonialism, the recognition of the equality of races and nations, nuclear disarmament and peaceful cooperation. It was the first time the Soviet Union had participated in such an event in non-communist Asia.

Belovezh agreement See Minsk agreement; CIS.

Black earth zone or Chernozem One of the most fertile regions in the world, forming a triangle with its tip in west Siberia and its base across southern Russia and northern Ukraine.

Bolsheviks When the Russian Social Democratic Labour Party (RSDRP) split in 1903, those in the majority were known as Bolsheviks. In October 1917 the Bolsheviks or Communist Party took power.

Brezhnev doctrine The right of the Soviet Union to intervene unilaterally if it considered socialism to be in danger.

Cadres Personnel, or Party officials. Stalin coined the expression: 'Cadres decide everything!'

Candidate member (a) Before a person could become a full member of the Communist Party he or she had to serve a probationary period during which he or she was referred to as a candidate member; (b) candidate members of the Party Central Committee and Politburo could attend, speak but not vote at meetings.

Central Committee (CC) The Central Committee of the Communist Party acted in the name of the Party Congress when the latter was not in session. It contained all the most important Party officials, government ministers, leading army and navy personnel, top ambassadors, academics etc., and was elected at each Party Congress. Meetings between Congresses were known as plenums. According to the Party statutes there were to be at least two plenums per year. The first meeting was the 1st plenum, the next the 2nd plenum, until the next Party Congress; then the first meeting after that became again the 1st plenum, and so on. The Central Committee had its own secretariat known as the CC Secretariat.

Cheka The All-Russian Extraordinary Commission for Combating Counter Revolution and Sabotage. Founded in 1917, it was the first Bolshevik secret police force, whose task was to ensure the Bolsheviks stayed in power. It changed its name several times and under Gorbachev was known as the KGB (q.v.).

CIS (Commonwealth of Independent States) Established on 8 December 1991 by Russia, Ukraine and Belorussia (now known as Belarus) in Belovezh Forest, near Minsk, Belorussia. Their leaders reasoned they had the right to dissolve the Soviet Union because these republics had been the original signatories setting up the USSR in 1922. At a meeting in Alma Ata (now known as

Almaty), Kazakhstan, on 21 December, other states were admitted: Armenia, Azerbaijan, Kazakhstan, Kyrgyzstan, Moldova, Tajikistan, Turkmenistan, and Uzbekistan. Eventually Georgia also joined, leaving Estonia, Latvia and Lithuania outside.

CMEA See Comecon.

Cocom Co-ordinating Committee on East-West Trade Policy of the NATO countries (except Iceland) and Japan to ensure that strategically important technology (technology which could be used militarily) was not sold to socialist states. There was a Cocom restriction list which was updated from time to time. The restrictions were removed on 31 March 1994.

Collectivization Common ownership of the land had begun in 1917 but had made little progress until 1929 when peasants (there were about 25 million peasant households) were forced to join a kolkhoz [collective farm]. On land not previously farmed, sovkhozes or state farms were set up. Collectivization was completed in 1937. In practice, several villages were lumped together and declared a kolkhoz. Peasant opposition was dealt with brutally, by using military force, deportation or expulsion. Initially almost everything was collectivized but from March 1930 peasants were allowed to own the private plots around their cottages. As of May 1932, peasants could legally sell any surplus (after paying taxes) in an urban kolkhoz market where demand and supply determined prices. The more efficient farmers, kulaks, were not permitted to join the kolkhozes, as they were viewed as class enemies. Hence Stalin deliberately eliminated the most successful farmers from agriculture. The Soviet state never developed socialist agriculture to the point where the demand of the population for food was met. By the 1980s about one third of marketed produce came from the private plots, though these occupied less than 5 per cent of arable land. Gorbachev devoted considerable attention to agricultural production in Stavropol krai, and then from 1978 he became responsible for Soviet agriculture.

Comecon Council for Mutual Economic Assistance. Set up in 1949 by Stalin, it came alive after his death to assume the function of a socialist Common Market. Yugoslavia became an associate member in 1964. Its membership eventually included Cuba, Mongolia and Vietnam, but by the mid-1980s it was becoming a liability for the Soviet Union. It was dissolved in June 1991.

Commonwealth of Independent States See CIS.

Communist A member of the Communist Party. By 1990 there were about 25 million members.

Communist Party of Russia, Russian Federation See RCP.

Communist Party of the Soviet Union (CPSU) Founded in 1898 as the Russian Social Democratic Labour Party (RSDRP) it split at its IInd Congress in 1903 into Bolshevik (majoritarian) and Menshevik (minoritarian) factions. It assumed the name of Russian Communist Party (Bolsheviks), in 1918, and adopted the name CPSU in 1952. Throughout the Gorbachev memoirs this party is referred to as the Communist Party, the CPSU.

Conference Differed from a Party Congress in that not all Party organizations were represented (an exception was the XIXth Party Conference, 1988). In the early years of the revolution logistics made it difficult to convene a Congress rapidly to deal with urgent business. A conference did not have the right to elect members to the Central Committee and the Politburo.

Congress Most important meeting of the Party, soviet, trade union or other organization. At a Congress, which had to meet once during a five-year period, the Communist Party reviewed its record over the period since the previous Congress and laid down goals for the future. A new Central Committee was elected and it, in turn, elected a new Politburo and Secretariat. The last Party Congress before these were banned by Yeltsin was the XXVIIIth in July 1990.

Congress of People's Deputies See USSR Congress of People's Deputies.

Conventional forces Non-nuclear forces.

Council of the Federation The upper house of the Federal Assembly, the Russian Parliament, established in the 1993 Russian Constitution. See also USSR Council of the Federation.

CPD See USSR Congress of People's Deputies.

CPSU Programme The agenda of the Communist Party. The 1961 Party Programme, which envisaged the beginning of 'communism' by 1980, was still current when Gorbachev became General Secretary. It was urgently in need of revision, but became a battleground between radicals and conservatives.

CSCE Conference on Security and Co-operation in Europe. The inaugural meeting was in Helsinki on 3 July 1973. The foreign ministers of thirty-three European states, as well as Canada and the USA, participated in the follow-up conferences. The CSCE developed into a forum for East–West debate on political, economic, cultural and security issues. On 1 January 1995 it became the Organization for Security and Co-operation in Europe (OSCE).

Decembrists Those who attempted, in December 1825, to assassinate Tsar Nicholas I. They were exiled to Siberia and the Caucasus and other remote regions.

Delhi declaration Mikhail Gorbachev and Rajiv Gandhi signed a declaration in New Delhi on 27 November 1986 on a nuclear-free and war-free world.

Democratic Platform A group of Party members formed in the Congress of People's Deputies in 1990 which worked closely with DemRossiya. Most members later left the Communist Party and founded other parties, such as the Republican Party of the Russian Federation.

DemRossiya (Democratic Russia) This movement came into being in 1990 in order to support democratically minded candidates during the elections to the RSFSR Congress of People's Deputies, especially those associated with Yeltsin. It was an umbrella organization, containing a wide range of parties and views, which failed to develop into a viable political party. One of the issues on which it could not agree in 1991 was whether Russia would be better off if the Soviet Union were destroyed. Their views were close to those of the Inter-Regional and Memorial groups. With over 4,000 members, they became the main opposition to the Communists. Leading members included Boris Yeltsin, Yury Afanasiev, Anatoly Sobchak, Gavriil Popov, Nikolai Travkin and Sergei Stankevich. Yeltsin's victory in the presidential election of June 1991 owed much to the support of this movement. By 1996 it had shrunk to a small group.

Duma or State Duma The lower house of the Federal Assembly, the Russian Parliament, established in the December 1993 Russian Constitution.

Eurocommunism A reformist movement which emerged in Western Europe in the 1970s as a response to the Soviet and Warsaw Pact invasion of Czechoslovakia in August 1968. Eurocommunists rejected the Brezhnev doctrine and favoured Communists joining coalition governments; this occurred in France, for instance. The movement caused the Soviet Union considerable embarrassment. It died out in the 1980s as Gorbachev's reforms got under way.

Events of 3 and 4 October 1993 The conflict between those who wanted a parliamentary republic led by the Congress of People's Deputies and those who favoured a presidential republic (Yeltsin and his supporters). The conflict came to a head in September 1993, when the President dissolved the CPD and called new elections and a referendum on a new Russian Constitution. The CPD leaders, led by Ruslan Khasbulatov, Speaker of the Parliament, defied his order to leave the building, declared the President deposed and swore in Vice President Aleksandr Rutskoi as President. The conflict ended after tanks stormed and took the White House. The new Constitution abolished the CPD and replaced it with a Federal Assembly (q.v.).

Federal Assembly The Russian Parliament established by the new 1993 Russian Constitution, consisting of two houses, the Duma (the lower house), and the Council of the Federation (the upper house).

First secretary Party leader in an oblast, krai, city or republic. The Party leader was referred to as First Secretary from 1953 to 1966.

Five Year Plan The first Five Year Plan spanned the period October 1928–December 1932, the second, 1933–7, and so on. Plans were drafted by Gosplan and had the force of law. Non-fulfilment of the plan was, therefore, a criminal offence.

Food subsidies Food prices were more or less stable after 1960 while the state regularly increased procurement prices. This led to a yawning gap between budget revenues from food sales and budget expenditure on food. Gorbachev grappled with the issue of increasing food prices but as increases in the past (e.g. 1962) had led to riots, the leadership proceeded very cautiously.

G7 Group of seven advanced industrial states, consisting of the United States, Japan, Great Britain, France, Italy, Germany and Canada. Gorbachev attended the G7 meeting in London during the summer of 1991.

General Secretary Leader of the Party 1966–1991.

German Democratic Republic (GDR), also known as East Germany. From 1945 the eastern part of Germany, occupied by the Red Army, was called the Soviet Occupied Zone of Germany. In 1949 this territory was renamed the German Democratic Republic in response to the establishment of the Federal Republic of Germany. The ruling Communist Party was called the Socialist Unity Party of Germany (SED, q.v.), and there were other parties, such as the Christian Democratic Union of Germany, which were subordinate to the SED.

Glasnost A key element of Gorbachev's reforms was openness in economic and political decision-making and the open discussion of all questions and freedom of information. This latter aspect led to vigorous debate about the Soviet past, including the crimes of the Stalin era. Glasnost was a key theme at the XIXth Party Conference and was confirmed in the conference resolutions.

Gorkom City Party committee, headed by a first secretary.

Gosagroprom State Agro-Industrial Committee (1985–9).

Gosplan State Planning Committee of the USSR Council of Ministers, responsible for drafting economic plans and checking on their implementation. Founded in 1921, it continued until 1991. It produced Five Year Plans, annual plans, quarterly plans etc. Each Soviet republic had its own Gosplan, whose task was to provide inputs for USSR Gosplan in order to draft the next plan and check on plan implementation. After 1985 Gosplan lost influence as the Soviet economy gradually fragmented. In 1990, when Gorbachev replaced the USSR Council of Ministers with a Cabinet of Ministers, Gosplan became the Ministry for Economics and Forecasting.

Gosstroi State Committee for Construction.

Gosteleradio State television and radio: the Soviet equivalent of the BBC before it lost its broadcasting monopoly.

Group of Seven See G7.

GRU Main intelligence administration or military intelligence. GRU officers were posted to Soviet embassies but politically were monitored by the KGB.

GUM The largest departmental store in the Soviet Union, on Red Square.

Helsinki Final Act See CSCE.

Hero-cities Cities which had distinguished themselves during the Great Patriotic War against Germany (1941–5).

Hitler–Stalin Pact See Soviet–German Non-Aggression Pact.

ICBM Intercontinental ballistic missile.

Ideologists Those Party officials and academics who were concerned with propagating and developing Marxism-Leninism. Every university student was required to pass an examination in Marxism-Leninism before graduating. Gorbachev complains that the great majority of professional ideologists merely confirmed existing views and did not attempt to develop Marxism-Leninism creatively. The negative Western term for these officials is ideologue.

International Monetary Fund (IMF) Based in Washington, and concerned with macroeconomic issues, the IMF was founded in 1945 as a result of the Bretton Woods agreement.

INF Agreement Signed on 8 December 1987 by the United States and the Soviet Union to eliminate a whole category of nuclear weapons: land-based nuclear weapons with a range between 500 and 5,500 kilometres.

Inter-Regional Group Deputies in the USSR Supreme Soviet who formed a group in the summer of 1989. Its policies included the defence of human rights, the introduction of private property, a multi-party system and a democratic rule of law. Members of the group included Boris Yeltsin, Andrei Sakharov, Yury Afanasiev and Gavriil Popov.

Katyn About 15,000 Polish officers were captured by the Red Army after its push into eastern Poland in September 1939 and most of them were murdered in 1940. Their mass graves were discovered by the German Wehrmacht near Smolensk in April 1943. The Soviet authorities always denied responsibility for these murders, but Gorbachev, to his credit, finally admitted that they had been carried out on the orders of Stalin.

KGB Committee of State Security. Established as the Cheka (q.v.) in 1917 by Lenin to ensure that the Bolsheviks stayed in power; under Stalin its task became to keep him in power. Each Soviet republic had its own KGB, subordinate to the USSR KGB, whose headquarters were in the Lubyanka, Moscow. The KGB was responsible for domestic and foreign intelligence. In the military, the GRU was responsible for intelligence gathering, but the KGB checked on the political loyalty of the armed forces.

Kolkhoz Literally, collective economy, i.e. farm; members farmed the land as a co-operative but in reality had little say in what was produced, as this was laid down in the annual state plan. Before 1966 there was no guaranteed wage; if the farm made a profit wages were paid; if not, no wages were paid. Most peasants preferred to concentrate on their private plots.

Kolkhoznik A member of a kolkhoz.

Komsomol Lenin Young Communist League. Most young people between the ages of 14 and 28 belonged to it, and almost everyone who joined the Communist Party had previously belonged to the Komsomol. In the early 1980s the Komsomol had over 40 million members. There was a USSR Komsomol and one in each Soviet republic. Its leaders were full-time officials, like those of the Communist Party.

Kosygin reforms Launched by Aleksei Kosygin, chairman of the USSR Council of Ministers, 1964–80, to give enterprises more control over what they produced and marketed. One problem which arose was what to do with surplus labour in an enterprise, as it was not possible just to sack workers. Kosygin was a technocrat and his reforms promised well but were interrupted by the invasion of Czechoslovakia in August 1968. Afterwards reform was a term which fell out of use as centralization was reimposed. Kosygin lacked the willpower to fight for power, and although he had been seen as the Soviet leader in the years 1964–8, he was gradually pushed aside by Brezhnev, who was clearly *primus inter pares* by the early 1970s. The reining in of Kosygin's reforms was one of the reasons for the terminal decline of the Soviet economy.

Krai Administrative sub-division of a Soviet republic containing within it a territory inhabited by another (non-Slav) nationality, called an autonomous oblast. Can also be translated 'territory'.

Kraikom Krai Party committee, headed by a first secretary.

Kulak Peasant who produced a surplus for the market. In West European terms the kulak would have been a moderately well-off farmer.

Lysenkoism Trofim Denisovich Lysenko was an agrobiologist who made a glittering career under Stalin by undermining the existing scientific thinking in agricultural science and genetics. He very skilfully propagated the 'theory' of the inheritance of acquired characteristics, which promised higher yields. He was a vigorous opponent of genetics, arguing that it was bourgeois pseudo-science. Lysenko reached the pinnacle of his influence in 1948. Khrushchev would not listen to those scientists who condemned him as a charlatan, and it was only in 1966, under Brezhnev, that genetics was rehabilitated. Lysenko's pseudo-science cost Soviet agriculture dearly.

Memorial Group formed to remember the victims of Stalin's oppression. Politically it became active in early 1989 and concentrated on making public the Russian and Soviet past and laying bare the crimes of the Stalin period. It later became part of DemRossiya.

Minsk agreement This agreement between the leaders of three republics, Russia (Boris Yeltsin), Belorussia (Stanislau Shushkevich) and Ukraine (Leonid Kravchuk) on 8 December 1991 was the death blow to the further existence of the Soviet Union under Gorbachev.

MGU Lomonosov Moscow State University.

MVD Ministry of Internal Affairs, responsible for law and order. There was a USSR MVD and each Soviet republic had its own MVD, subordinate to Moscow.

NATO North Atlantic Treaty Organization, founded in 1949.

Nazi–Soviet Non-Aggression Pact See Soviet–German Non-Aggression Pact.

New Economic Policy (NEP) Introduced in 1921 by Lenin as a compromise when the country was facing economic ruin after the Civil War, in response to the fear that the peasants would not deliver food to the cities. It was not well received by Communists, who saw it as a retreat from socialism. Under NEP the commanding heights of the economy (energy, communications, heavy industry etc.) stayed in state hands while light industry and agriculture reverted to private ownership. Trade was again legal. Soviet Russia recovered and by the mid-1920s the country was again achieving the Gross Domestic Product of 1913. For the peasant it was the golden era of Soviet rule. NEP was brought to an end by the victory of Stalin in the struggle to succeed Lenin when he launched the first Five Year Plan (October 1928–32). Also during NEP there developed a system of producers' and consumers' co-operatives and a vibrant tradition of cottage industries, but all this was destroyed deliberately by Stalin who forced peasants to join collective (kolkhoz) and state (sovkhoz) farms, mainly to ensure that the state could feed workers during the industrialization drive. Detailed plans for farms were laid down by Gosplan and it was the responsibility of the Party secretary to ensure their implementation. Stalin's Five Year Plan eliminated the market. There was great interest in NEP during the Gorbachev era. A renewed NEP was seen as an option for the Soviet Union, allowing the re-creation of a mixed market economy under socialism. In reality NEP was not an option for Gorbachev, as Stalin had destroyed private farming and few farm workers in the 1980s wanted to farm on their own.

XIXth Party Conference A rare event (the previous conference had taken place in 1941), convened by Gorbachev between Party Congresses, and more significant than a Central Committee plenum, to push through radical policies. The Party was withdrawn from economic management and it also lost its right to nominate candidates for state and soviet posts. Glasnost was also promoted through conference resolutions.

Nomenklatura Nomenclatura or nomenclature: consisted of (a) a list of positions which the Party regarded as important and required Party assent to be filled; (b) a list of persons capable of filling these positions. There was the Party nomenklatura and the state nomenklatura. Each Party body, from the obkom upwards, had a list of nomenklatura appointments it could fill. The longer a first Party secretary remained in an oblast, for example, the greater the number of posts he could influence. In this way nepotism and corruption crept into the Party apparatus. For example, important Soviet ambassadors – to Washington, Bonn, etc – were on the nomenklatura list of the Politburo. Nomenklatura officials were full-time. Gorbachev uses the term negatively throughout his memoirs, as he links the nomenklatura to his conservative opponents.

Non-black earth zone or non-chernozem zone Not very fertile, but the Russian heartland, it extends from Moscow to southern Russia, where the black earth zone (q.v.) begins, and eastwards to Siberia. Under Brezhnev considerable attention and investment were devoted to this region, since there was a risk that vast tracts of the Russian heartland would go back to wilderness as a result of depopulation.

Novo-Ogarevo Gorbachev's dacha near Moscow where republican leaders (including Yeltsin) debated the formation of a genuinely federal state to succeed the Soviet Union with President Gorbachev during the spring and summer of 1991. The outcome was the draft Union of Sovereign States. These talks were also referred to as the 9 + 1, nine republican leaders and Gorbachev. The Baltic republics never participated in these deliberations, having demanded their independence.

Obkom Oblast Party committee, headed by a first secretary.

Oblast Administrative sub-division of a Soviet republic; oblasts were sub-divided into raions, as were cities. Can also be translated 'territory', 'province'.

Organ Agency.

Orgotdel Organizational bureau, Central Committee Secretariat. Its tasks included Party organization, cadres etc.

Orgpartotdel Department of Party Organs, Central Committee Secretariat, responsible for cadres, among other things.

OSCE See CSCE.

Perestroika Restructuring, renaissance, reformation, the word goes back to the eighteenth century and was also used by Stalin, often in the sense of changing Party structures. Under Gorbachev the word came to mean an all-embracing modernization of the Party and state. It was to touch and transform all aspects of life, from the cradle to the grave. In 1985 the term *uskorenie* (acceleration) was used, but in mid-1986 perestroika became a universal term for Gorbachev's policy of reform.

Plenum Meeting of all members of the Party Central Committee.

Politburo Political Bureau of the Central Committee. It was the key decision-making body of the Communist Party, set up formally at the VIIIth Party Congress, 1919. It was called the Presidium between 1952 and 1966. In 1987 there were 14 full and 6 candidate members, with Russians predominating.

Pood or pud Russian measure of weight, equivalent to 16.38 kilograms.

Presidential Council See USSR Council of the President.

Presidium Inner council or cabinet, hence supreme body. The Politburo of the Communist Party was known as the Presidium, 1952–66. The USSR Supreme Soviet Presidium contained all the worthies in the state and Party. The chairman of the Presidium of the USSR Supreme Soviet was the head of state, hence he was sometimes referred to as President. The term President officially enters the Soviet Constitution in 1989, when Gorbachev was elected Soviet President. The USSR Council of Ministers (Soviet government) also had a Presidium, consisting of key ministers – hence it was similar to a cabinet. At Central Committee plenums and other meetings, important persons would sit on a podium facing the delegates; this was also known as a Presidium.

Procurator General The top law official in the Soviet Union, in charge of the USSR Prokuratura. Each Soviet republic had its own Prokuratura, as did each raion, oblast and krai.

Prokuratura The state agency responsible for the observance of the law and which prosecuted those who broke the law.

Prosecutor General See Procurator General.

Raikom Raion Party committee, headed by a first secretary.

Raion Administrative sub-division of an oblast, krai or city. Can be translated as 'district'.

RCP Russian Communist Party, founded 1990, dissolved 1991. Between 1918 and 1925 the Communist Party was known as the Russian Communist Party (Bolsheviks), becoming the CPSU in 1952. The Russian Federation was the only Soviet republic which did not have its own Communist Party: in Ukraine there was the Communist Party of Ukraine, in Estonia, the Communist Party of

Estonia, etc. All these parties were subordinate to the CPSU in Moscow. Despite the form of organization it was a strictly centralized party. One of Gorbachev's proposals, in the late 1980s, was that the republican Communist Parties should become autonomous parties, running their own affairs but still under the umbrella of the CPSU. Hence he was proposing a federal Communist Party. The RCP was a disappointment to Gorbachev since it was dominated by conservatives, reluctant to implement perestroika.

Referendum On 17 March 1991 Gorbachev launched a referendum in order to gauge support for a successor state to the Soviet Union, the Union of Sovereign States. There was a majority in favour of preserving the Union but other republics added questions to the Union referendum, e.g. Russian voters were asked if they were in favour of a directly elected Russian President, which they were. As a result Yeltsin was elected President of Russia in June 1991, one of the unforeseen consequences of the referendum.

Rootless cosmopolitanism A term which became synonymous with anti-Semitism in the late 1940s in connection with the turn towards Russian nationalism and xenophobia.

RSDRP The Russian Social Democratic Labour or Workers' Party, founded in Minsk in 1898. In 1903 it split into Bolsheviks and Mensheviks. The Bolsheviks eventually assumed the name Communist Party of the Soviet Union (CPSU).

RSFSR Russian Soviet Federated Socialist Republic or the Russian Federation or, simply, Russia. It was the largest of the fifteen Soviet republics and its capital was also Moscow.

RSFSR Congress of People's Deputies First convened in March 1990 with Yeltsin as Speaker. It was a super-parliament and it elected from among its members an RSFSR Supreme Soviet with a rotating membership which exchanged some members at each new Congress. Russia was the only Soviet republic with a Congress, as all the others declined to elect one and proceeded directly to the election of a Supreme Soviet, which then enjoyed popular legitimacy. It was dissolved by a presidential decree in September 1991.

Rukh The Ukrainian Popular Front.

Russian Communist Party See RCP.

SALT Strategic Arms Limitation Talks. Discussions between the USA and the USSR on the limitation of nuclear weapons began in 1969. In 1972 the SALT I treaty was signed and in 1979 the SALT II treaty was agreed. Owing to the Soviet invasion of Afghanistan the Americans did not ratify SALT II.

Science The Russian word *nauka* is the same as the German *Wissenschaft* and has a much wider meaning than the English term 'science', embracing all intellectual activity. The word 'scientist' is therefore used to mean any person engaged in such activity.

SDI Strategic Defense Initiative. Conceived in 1983 by President Reagan as a space system to prevent incoming nuclear missiles penetrating the United States. It was feared that SDI might form a defensive shield to launch an attack. The threat was more psychological than military but it was a useful bargaining chip for the Americans, since the Soviets could never write it off, even though their scientists did not give it much credence.

Secret police The Soviet secret police were originally known as the Cheka (q.v.) in 1917, then became OGPU in 1922, later GPU, then NKVD (People's Commissariat for Internal Affairs), then, in 1941, the NKGB (People's Commissariat for State Security), and finally, in 1954, they were renamed the KGB (Committee of State Security). The KGB was formally dissolved in 1991, but many of its officers moved into Russian security.

Secretariat The administrative centre of the Communist Party, set up by the VIIIth Party Congress in 1919. Stalin was elected the first General Secretary but at that time the post was not regarded as conferring much power on the incumbent. Its key officials were called Central Committee secretaries. Between 1953 and 1966 the top man was called the first secretary. The Secretariat had various departments, each headed by an official; Central Committee secretaries each supervised a group of departments. After 1957 the Secretariat assumed responsibility for the economy and a Central Committee secretary became senior to a USSR minister. It was responsible for ensuring that Central Committee decisions were implemented. In 1987 there were eleven secretaries, including Gorbachev. When Gorbachev became General Secretary in 1985, Ligachev was elected to chair the secretaries' meetings.

SED Socialist Unity Party of Germany. The ruling Communist Party in the GDR, it was founded in April 1946 and dissolved in 1990. In the Gorbachev period, its General Secretary was Erich Honecker, until 1989; then Egon Krenz.

Shestidesyatniki The 1960s generation, affected by the thaw in culture and politics in the Khrushchev era. Among the most prominent were singers, poets, and writers, including Solzhenitsyn, and a host of politicians who gained prominence under Gorbachev, including Georgy Shakhnazarov.

Shock worker Sometimes called a Stakhanovite. A worker who leads by example and sets the norms for his fellow workers.

Short Course The official Stalinist version of Bolshevik history, published in 1938 as *The History of the Communist Party (Bolsheviks) Short Course.* It continued to come out in new editions until 1983.

Smolny A palace in St Petersburg, seat of Sovnarkom (government), 1917–18, until Moscow became the capital; afterwards occupied by the Leningrad Party organization.

Soviet Council. Soviets first emerged during the 1905 revolution and then blossomed after the February 1917 revolution. There were soviets of workers' deputies, soviets of peasants' deputies, soviets of soldiers' deputies, soviets of long-distance train travellers etc. The most influential was the Petrograd Soviet of Workers' and Soldiers' Deputies which spawned the October Revolution. The October Revolution was called a Soviet revolution, the government was called the Soviet of People's Commissars, etc. The term became synonymous with worker power. Lenin changed his mind about the future role of the soviets in 1917, when he stated that Russia would be a republic of soviets. Lenin and the Bolsheviks handed power to the IInd Congress of Soviets, October 1917, but power soon slipped away from them as they opposed Lenin's prescriptions for revolution. They had ceded primacy to the government by mid-1918 and it in turn to the Politburo of the Party by 1921. Soviets ran the countryside and towns and performed the function of local government, but they never had the power to tax independently of the centre or keep local state taxation. Their finances were determined in Moscow. They had to implement Gosplan directives. Gorbachev attempted to reinvigorate them in 1988 but by then Party bosses ruled the localities. He hoped they would take over from the Party at local level and implement perestroika but they lacked the skill and personnel to do this.

Soviet–German Non-Aggression Pact or Stalin–Hitler Pact An agreement signed by foreign ministers Molotov and Ribbentrop on 23 August 1939 (Stalin and Hitler never met), that the Soviet Union and Germany would not attack each other and that if war did ensue elsewhere both states would remain neutral. The key part of the agreement was the secret protocol (the existence of which the Soviets denied until the late 1980s) dividing Europe up into zones of influence, with the Soviet Union taking eastern Poland, Latvia, Estonia, Finland, Lithuania (as the result of an amendment) and Bessarabia, and Germany taking the rest of Europe. The original agreement turned up in the private papers of von Schulenburg, the German Ambassador to Moscow at the time, after his death.

Soviet Republics There were fifteen in the Soviet Union, of which the Russian Federation was the largest. Each republic had its own government, many ministries and its own Communist Party, which was, of course, part of the CPSU. The local Communist Party had its own Central Committee and a Bureau (playing the same role as the central Politburo). Ukraine was the exception and had a Politburo. The Communist Parties split in many republics into pro-nationalist Communist Parties and pro-Moscow Communist Parties. This occurred in all three Baltic republics.

Sovkhoz State farm but, literally, state economy; set up on land not previously cultivated, run like factories with a guaranteed minimum wage, higher than those of the average kolkhoznik. Operatives were classified as workers and enjoyed their social benefits.

Sovnarkhoz Council of the National Economy, adopted by Khrushchev in 1957. Initially there were 105 which covered the whole country and were responsible for all economic activity on their territory (except military, security and other vital tasks, which remained centralized). Khrushchev thought that devolving decision-making to the local level would promote economic efficiency. In fact the sovnarkhozes attempted to become mini-states in their own right. They were abolished in 1965, after Khrushchev's removal as Soviet leader.

Sovnarkom The Council of People's Commissars, the government of the country, 1917–46, when it was renamed the USSR Council of Ministers. Commissars then became ministers. There was a Union Sovnarkom, and each Soviet republic and autonomous republic also had its Sovnarkom. The government in each republic resigned formally at the end of each legislature period. In reality the Union government ruled.

Soyuz A parliamentary group of which people's deputies at all levels were members, established in December 1990 to defend the integrity of the Soviet Union. It argued that a state of emergency was the only way to restore order and ensure the survival of the Soviet Union. Among the membership were representatives of the military-industrial complex, the KGB, the MVD and the Party apparatus. In the Congress of People's Deputies and the USSR Supreme Soviet, Soyuz was the largest anti-reform faction but did not command a majority.

Stakhanovite See Shock worker.

Staraya Ploshchad Old Square, Moscow, the headquarters of the Central Committee until August 1991. It is very near Red Square.

State procurements Output bought by the state and laid down by the plan in advance. In industry this applied to most of an enterprise's output but in agriculture it could vary. Kolkhozes and sovkhozes had to meet state procurement plans first, before they disposed of any of their produce. Naturally they attempted to keep back as much for themselves as possible, sometimes stating that they did not have enough to meet the plan. The first secretary was responsible for ensuring that farms met their state obligations.

Strategic Arms Reduction Talks (START) Negotiations on the reduction of strategic weapon systems, between the United States and the Soviet Union, then Russia, resulted in the START I agreement in 1991 and the START II agreement in 1993.

Strategic nuclear weapons Those nuclear weapons which can be fired from one continent to another; as opposed to tactical nuclear weapons, used on the 'battlefield'.

Supreme Soviet Set up by the 1936 Soviet Constitution, the USSR Supreme Soviet was bicameral: Soviet of the Union and Soviet of Nationalities. The number of deputies in the former was based on population, while the number of the latter was fixed; the houses were of equal status and often met in joint session. It was a parliament only in name (until 1989), key decisions being taken by the Communist Party and the government. The chairman of the Presidium of the USSR Supreme Soviet was Soviet head of state. Each Soviet republic and autonomous republic had its own Supreme Soviet, but they were unicameral. Each house had its own commissions, and committees were joint bodies. All important state legislation was passed by the USSR Supreme Soviet, which normally met only twice a year, for a few days at a time. In 1989 the USSR Congress of People's Deputies elected a USSR Supreme Soviet with a rotating membership, some members being dropped and others elected at each new Congress. The RSFSR Congress of People's Deputies, convened in 1990, also elected an inner RSFSR Supreme Soviet, again with a rotating membership.

Tactical nuclear weapons Short-range and battlefield nuclear weapons.

Territory See krai.

XXth Party Congress Convened in February 1956, it is famous for the 'secret speech' (it was held behind closed doors) in which Khrushchev laid bare Stalin's crimes since 1934. He did not use the expression Stalinism to describe what he was analysing but referred to it as the cult of the personality. The speech ended the claims to infallibility of the Communist Party. It became a focal point of interest under glasnost.

Union of Sovereign States Gorbachev intended this to be the successor state to the USSR, but the August coup of 1991 was timed to prevent its signature. Afterwards it proved impossible to reform the Union and it was replaced by the much looser Commonwealth of Independent States.

Universal human values These were likened to perestroika and emphasized that the Soviet leadership no longer thought in terms of class or national interest. This was now replaced by universal human values, whose tasks included preventing war and resolving the economic, social and political problems of the world. Elements of these common human values were freedom, social justice and solidarity, and respect for human and minority rights. The Soviet Constitution guaranteed many rights but they remained on paper until Gorbachev came to power; according to the Constitution the state granted these rights to the citizen but they could be withdrawn. When the USSR ratified the UN agreement on human rights in 1973 and signed the Helsinki Final Act, Moscow accepted the Western definition of human rights for the first time. In the Soviet Union, Helsinki Monitoring Committees were established during the 1970s, pressing for the implementation of the human rights agreed at Helsinki. The KGB moved against these groups and imprisoned many of their members. Academician Andrei Sakharov and his wife, Yelena Bonner, became leading campaigners. This led to Sakharov being exiled to Gorky (Nizhny Novgorod), which was a closed city because of its defence industries; only his wife was allowed to visit and contact him. Gorbachev released him and brought him back to Moscow.

USS See Union of Sovereign States.

USSR Union of Soviet Socialist Republics: also known as the Soviet Union.

USSR Congress of People's Deputies (CPD) This was convened in March 1989 as the supreme agency of state power. Its 2,250 deputies were elected for five years and there was to be a Congress every year. Of the 2,250 deputies, two thirds were directly elected; there were to be multi-candidate elections, with open campaigning beforehand. The other 750 deputies were elected indirectly, according to lists proposed by political and social organizations. For instance, the Communist Party received 100 seats. Gorbachev chaired the USSR CPD. It was a super-parliament and from its membership it elected a USSR Supreme Soviet, or standing parliament, with a rotating membership which exchanged some members at the next Congress. The Congress could amend the Constitution, if a two-thirds majority approved. The Congress elected Gorbachev President of the Soviet Union.

The proceedings were carried live on television and this led to many workers and staff turning up for work very tired because of the Soviet habit of debating until the early hours. On 5 September 1991 the Congress voluntarily dissolved itself.

USSR Council of the Federation Established under Gorbachev as a supra-government for the Soviet Union, consisting of the President, Vice-President, and senior representatives from each of the fifteen Soviet republics. It ceased to exist in August 1991 and should not be confused with the Council of the Federation, the upper house of the Russian Parliament, established in December 1993.

USSR Council of Ministers The Soviet government, headed by a chairman or prime minister. The USSR Council of Ministers was dissolved in 1990 and replaced by a Cabinet of Ministers, headed by a Prime Minister.

USSR Council of the President or Presidential Council Established in March 1990, it functioned until December 1990, with all members being nominated by Gorbachev. Its precise functions were unclear. It was replaced in early 1991 by the newly constituted USSR Security Council, which lasted until the coup in August 1991.

USSR State Council Introduced by Gorbachev as the successor to the USSR Council of the Federation, with many of the same representatives. It functioned until November 1991.

USSR Supreme Soviet Founded in 1936, it was the supreme agency of state power in the Soviet Union, according to the Constitution. It was bicameral – the Soviet of the Union and the Soviet of Nationalities – and in 1985 had 1,500 members. It was elected for four years and had to meet twice a year, amounting to about a week altogether. It elected a Presidium (39 members since 1977) from among its members and the chairman was the head of the Soviet state. Until Podgorny became chairman of the Presidium in 1964, the position had never been politically significant. Brezhnev made himself head of state in May 1977; Podgorny was sent packing. Andropov and Chernenko also made themselves head of state, but Gorbachev, in July 1985, suggested Gromyko for the post and he remained there until 1988, when Gorbachev himself took over. The USSR

Supreme Soviet was superseded by the Congress of People's Deputies in March 1989. Confusingly the Congress of People's Deputies then proceeded to elect its own USSR Supreme Soviet but the latter was subordinate to the former.

VAZ Volga Car Company.

Verst Russian unit of measurement, equivalent to 1.06 kilometres.

Vladivostok initiative Gorbachev delivered a speech in Vladivostok on 28 July 1986 on peace in Asia and the world, concentrating on improving the international climate in the Far East and East Asia.

VLKSM All-Union Leninist Communist League of Youth or Komsomol.

VTsIK All-Union Central Executive Committee of the soviets. It became the USSR Supreme Soviet in 1936.

VTsSPS All-Union Central Council of Trades Unions, the central trade union body.

Warsaw Pact organization The Pact was founded in 1955 as a response to the Paris Treaties of October 1954, which had admitted the Federal Republic of Germany to NATO. The original members were the Soviet Union, Poland, Czechoslovakia, Hungary, the GDR, Bulgaria, Romania and Albania. Albania left in 1961. The Pact had also a Political Consultative Committee, which was attended by foreign ministers. The forces of the Pact were subordinate to Moscow. The Pact never permitted the East German Volksarmee to set up its own General Staff, for instance. All advanced military technology was manufactured in the Soviet Union and the Soviet Army was the best equipped. The Pact was dissolved on 1 July 1991.

White House The seat of the Russian Parliament in Moscow.

ZIL Likhachev Car Company; its limousines were for Party and state use.

Martin McCauley

BIOGRAPHIES

Abalkin, Leonid Ivanovich (born 1930), Director of the Institute of Economics from 1986, Deputy Chairman of the USSR Council of Ministers 1989–91, adviser to Gorbachev, member of the USSR/Russian Academy of Sciences.

Abuladze, Tengiz Yevgenevich (born 1924), Georgian film director.

Adamovich, Ales (Aleksandr Mikhailovich) (1927–94), Russian writer, from 1987 Director of the Research Institute of Cinema Art and Co-President/Chairman of the Memorial group, USSR People's Deputy 1989–91.

Afanasiev, Viktor Grigorievich (1922–94), journalist, chief editor of *Pravda* 1976–89, Chairman of the USSR Union of Journalists 1976–90.

Afanasiev, Yury Nikolaevich (born 1934), Rector of the Moscow Institute of History and Archives from 1987, Rector of the Russian Social Sciences University from 1991, co-founder of the DemRossiya movement.

Aganbegyan, Abel Gezevich (born 1932), economist, Vice-Chancellor of the Academy of Economic Sciences from 1989, member of the USSR/Russian Academy of Sciences.

Aitmatov, Chengiz Torekulovich (born 1928), Kyrgyz writer and founder of the international Issikul Forum, USSR People's Deputy 1989–92, Ambassador of the USSR/Russia to Luxembourg 1990–4.

Akayev, Askar Akayevich (born 1944), Vice President 1987–9, President of the Kyrgyz Academy of Sciences 1989–90, President of Kyrgyzstan from 1990.

Akhromeyev, Marshal Sergei Fedorovich (1923–91), First Deputy Chief of the General Staff 1979–84, Chief of the General Staff of the USSR Armed Forces and First Deputy Defence Minister 1984–8, military adviser to Gorbachev 1989–91, committed suicide.

Aleksandrov, Anatoly Petrovich

(born 1903), Director of the Kurchatov Institute of Atomic Energy 1960–86, President of the USSR/Russian Academy of Sciences 1975–86.

Alekseyevsky, Yevgeny Yevgenevich (1906–79), USSR Minister of Land Reclamation and Water Management 1965–79.

Aliyev, Geidar Aliyevich (born 1923), first secretary of the Central Committee of the Communist Party of Azerbaijan 1969–82, First Deputy Chairman of the USSR Council of Ministers 1982–7, full member of the Politburo 1982–7, President of Azerbaijan from 1993.

Ambartsumov, Yevgeny Arshakovich (born 1929), Russian People's Deputy 1990–3.

Andreyeva, Nina Aleksandrovna (born 1938), General Secretary of the Communist Party of USSR Bolsheviks, founded in November 1991 in St Petersburg.

Andropov, Yury Vladimirovich (1914–84), Chairman of the KGB 1967–82, General Secretary of the CPSU 1982–4, Chairman of the Presidium of the USSR Supreme Soviet (Head of State) 1983–4, full member of the Politburo 1973–84.

Anpilov, Viktor Ivanovich (born 1946), Communist Party official, leading member of the Communist and nationalist movement from 1992.

Antall, Joszef (1932–93), Hungarian politician, Prime Minister 1990–3.

Arbatov, Georgy Arkadevich (born 1923), Director of the Institute of USA and Canada of the USSR Academy of Sciences from 1967, member of the USSR Academy of Sciences, adviser to the Soviet leadership on foreign policy.

Astafiev, Viktor Petrovich (born 1924), writer.

Avaliani, Teimuraz Georgevich (born 1932), Communist Party official and trade unionist, Kemerovo oblast.

Bagirov, Kiamran Mamedovich (born 1933), first secretary of the Central Committee of the Communist Party of Azerbaijan 1982–8.

Baibakov, Nikolai Konstantinovich (born 1911), Deputy Chairman of the USSR Council of Ministers, Chairman of the USSR State Planning Committee (Gosplan) 1965–85.

Bakatin, Vadim Viktorovich (born 1937), first secretary of the Kirov Party obkom 1985–7, first secretary of the Kemerovo Party obkom 1987–8, USSR Minister for Internal Affairs 1988–90, Chairman of the USSR KGB 1991, Chairman of the Inter-republican Security Service 1991–2.

Baklanov, Oleg Dmitrievich (born 1932), USSR Minister of General Machine Building 1983–8, Secretary of the Central Committee (military-industrial complex, chemical industry)

1988–91, one of the initiators of the August 1991 coup.

Belousov, Igor Sergeyevich (born 1928), USSR Minister of the Shipbuilding Industry 1984–8, Deputy Chairman of the USSR Council of Ministers 1988–91.

Belyaev, Nikolai Ilyich (1903–66), first secretary of the Central Committee of the Communist Party of Kazakhstan and full member of the Politburo of the CPSU 1957–60, first secretary of Stavropol Party kraikom 1960.

Bendera, Stepan Andreyevich (1909–59), Ukrainian nationalist, underground activist, later in political exile; murdered.

Beria, Lavrenty Pavlovich (1899–1953), People's Commissar of Internal Affairs (NKVD) 1938–46, USSR Minister of Internal Affairs 1953, full member of the Politburo 1946–53, executed.

Bessmertnykh, Aleksandr Aleksandrovich (born 1933), Head of the American Department of the USSR Ministry for Foreign Affairs 1983–6, USSR Deputy Foreign Minister 1986–8, First Deputy USSR Foreign Minister 1988–90, USSR Foreign Minister 1991.

Biryukova, Aleksandra Pavlovna (born 1929), Secretary of the Party Central Committee (light industry) 1986–8, Deputy Chairman of the USSR Council of Ministers 1988–90.

Boitsov, Ivan Pavlovich (1896–1988), first secretary of the

Stavropol Party kraikom.

Boldin, Valery (born 1935), Gorbachev's adviser on agriculture 1985–7, Head of the General Department of the Party Central Committee 1987–91, one of the initiators of the August 1991 coup.

Bondarenko, Ivan Afanasievich (born 1926), first secretary of the Rostov Party obkom 1966–84.

Bovin, Aleksandr Yevgenevich (born 1930), *Izvestiya* journalist 1972–91, Soviet/Russian Ambassador to Israel 1991.

Brazauskas, Algirdas Mikolas (born 1932), secretary 1977–88, first secretary of the Central Committee of the Communist Party of Lithuania 1988–90, Chairman of the Presidium of the Lithuanian Supreme Soviet, Chairman of the Lithuanian Democratic Party of Labour 1990, President of Lithuania 1992.

Brezhnev, Leonid Ilyich (1906–82), General Secretary of the Party Central Committee 1964–82, Chairman of the Presidium of the USSR Supreme Soviet 1960–4 and 1977–82, full member of the Politburo 1957–82.

Bugaev, Boris Pavlovich (born 1923), USSR Minister of Air Transport 1970–87.

Bukharin, Nikolai Ivanovich (1888–1938), Communist Party and Comintern official, party theoretician, executed.

Bulganin, Nikolai Aleksandrovich (1895–1975), Chairman of the USSR Council 1955–8, full

member of the Politburo 1948–58, Chairman of the Council of National Economy, 1958–60.
Bunin, Ivan Alekseyevich (1870–1953), writer, awarded Nobel Prize for Literature 1933.
Burbulis, Gennady Eduardovich (born 1945), USSR People's Deputy 1989–90, Yeltsin's adviser 1990–2, First Deputy Chairman of the Russian government 1991–2.
Burmistrov, F. P. (born 1917), first secretary of the Karachai-Cherkess Party obkom 1968–75.
Burokiavicius, Mikolas (born 1927), first secretary of the Central Committee of the Communist Party of Lithuania 1990–3.

Ceausescu, Nicolae (1918–89), General Secretary of the Communist Party of Romania 1965–89, President 1974–89, executed.
Chazov, Yevgeny Ivanovich (born 1929), personal doctor of General Secretaries 1967–87, USSR Minister of Health 1987–90, Director of the Cardiological Centre 1975, member of the USSR/Russian Academy of Sciences, Co-President of the Organization Doctors of the World for the Prevention of Nuclear War 1975, awarded Nobel Peace Prize 1985.
Chebrikov, Viktor Mikhailovich (born 1923), Chairman of the USSR KGB 1982–8, Secretary of the Party Central Committee 1988–9, full member of the Politburo 1985–9.

Chernenko, Konstantin Ustinovich (1911–85), General Secretary of the Party Central Committee, Chairman of the Presidium of the USSR Supreme Soviet (Head of State) 1984–5, full member of the Politburo 1978–85.
Chernichenko, Yury Dmitrievich (born 1929), journalist, USSR People's Deputy 1989–91.
Chernomyrdin, Viktor Stepanovich (born 1938), USSR Minister of Gas Industry 1985–9, Chairman of the Russia Council of Ministers 1992.
Chernyaev, Anatoly Sergeyevich (born 1921), adviser to Gorbachev on foreign policy, member of the Gorbachev Foundation.
Chicherin, Georgy Vasilievich (1872–1936), People's Commissar for Foreign Affairs 1918–30.

Dementei, Nikolai Ivanovich (born 1931), Secretary of the Central Committee, Communist Party of Belorussia 1979–89, Chairman of the Belorussian Supreme Soviet 1989–91.
Demichev, Petr Milovich (born 1918), USSR Minister for Culture 1974–86, First Deputy Chairman of the USSR Supreme Soviet 1985–8, candidate member of the Politburo 1964–88.
Deng Xiaoping (born 1904), Chinese politician, Deputy Prime Minister 1952–67, member of the permanent Council of the Politburo, during the Cultural Revolution lost all his posts, rehabilitated 1973, Deputy Prime

Minister 1975–6, removed again, regained all his posts 1977, resigned as Deputy Prime Minister 1980.

Denisenko, Bella Anatolievna (born 1941), doctor, First Deputy Russian Minister for Health 1991–2.

Denisov, Anatoly Alekseyevich (born 1934), Party official, Chairman of the Socialist Workers' Party 1991.

Denmirtchyan, Karen Seropovich (born 1932), first secretary of the Central Committee, Communist Party of Armenia 1974–88.

Dobrynin, Anatoly Fedorovich (born 1919), Soviet Ambassador to the USA 1962–88, Secretary of the Party Central Committee 1986–8.

Dolgikh, Vladimir Ivanovich (born 1924), Secretary of the Party Central Committee 1972–88.

Dubcek, Alexander (1921–92), first secretary of the Communist Party of Czechoslovakia 1968–9, Chairman of the Czechoslovak Federal Assembly 1989–92.

Dubinin, Yury Vladimirovich (born 1930), Soviet Ambassador to the USA 1986–90.

Dudayev, General Dzhokhar Mussaevich (born 1944), President of the Chechen Republic from 1991.

Dyakov, Ivan Nikolaevich (born 1937), first secretary of the Astrakhan Party obkom 1988–90.

Falin, Valentin Mikhailovich (born 1926), Soviet Ambassador

to the Federal Republic of Germany 1971–8, Chairman of the Soviet News Agency APN 1986–8, Head of the Party International Department, Secretary of the Party Central Committee 1988–91.

Fedorchuk, Vitaly Vasilievich (born 1918), Chairman of the Ukrainian KGB 1970–82, Chairman of the USSR KGB 1982, USSR Minister for Internal Affairs 1982–6.

Fedorov, Svyatoslav Nikolaevich (born 1927), Director of the Institute of Eye Microsurgery 1980–91, Co-Chairman of the Party of Economic Freedom 1992.

Feodorov, Nikolai Fedorovich (1828–1903), philosopher.

Florensky, Pavel Aleksandrovich (1882–1937), philosopher, executed.

Florentiev, Leonid Yakovlevich (born 1911), USSR Minister of Agriculture 1965–83.

Foteyev, Vladimir Konstantinovich (born 1935), first secretary of the Communist Party, Checheno-Inghush Party obkom 1984–9, member of the Presidium of the USSR Supreme Soviet 1989–91.

Frolov, Ivan Timofeyevich (born 1929), chief editor of *Voprosi filosofii* 1968–77, of *Kommunist* 1986–7, of *Pravda* 1989–91, full member of the Politburo, member of the USSR Academy of Sciences, adviser to Gorbachev.

Gaidar, Yegor Timurovich (born 1956), Director of the Institute of

Economic Policy 1990–1, Deputy Chairman of the Russian Council of Ministers and Russian Minister for Economics and Finance 1991–2, Russian Finance Minister and acting Prime Minister 1992.

Gamzatov, Rasul Gamzatovich (born 1923), Degestani writer.

Garbuzov, Vasily Feodorovich (1911–85), USSR Minister of Finance 1960–70.

Gdlyan, Telman Khorenovich (born 1940), lawyer, USSR People's Deputy from 1989, Co-Chairman of the People's Party of Russia and New Russia Party.

Generalov, Vyacheslav Vladimirovich (born 1946), Deputy Head of the Department of the USSR KGB for the protection of the President and leading politicians.

Gerashchenko, Viktor Vladimirovich (born 1937), Chairman of the USSR State Bank 1989–91, Chairman of the State Bank of Russia 1991–4.

Gidaspov, Boris Veniaminovich (born 1933), first secretary of the Leningrad Party obkom 1989–90, Secretary of the Party Central Committee 1990–1.

Girenko, Andrei Nikolaevich (born 1936), first secretary of the Crimea Party obkom (Ukraine) 1987–9, Secretary of the Party Central Committee 1989–91.

Goldansky, Vitaly Iosefovich (born 1923), Director of the Semenov Institute of Physical Chemistry 1988, USSR People's

Deputy 1989–91, member of the USSR/Russian Academy of Sciences 1989–91.

Golembiovsky, Igor Nestorovich (born 1935), journalist, chief editor of *Izvestiya* 1991.

Golikov, Viktor Andreyevich (born 1914), adviser to Brezhnev on agriculture.

Gopkalo, Pantelei Yefimovich (died 1953), Gorbachev's grandfather.

Gopkalo, Vasilisa Lukyanovna, née Litovchenko, Gorbachev's grandmother.

Gorbachev, Aleksandr Sergeyevich (Sashka) (born 1947), Gorbachev's brother.

Gorbachev, Aleksei Moiseyevich, Gorbachev's great-uncle.

Gorbachev, Andrei Moiseyevich, Gorbachev's grandfather.

Gorbachev, Grigory Moiseyevich, Gorbachev's great-uncle.

Gorbachev, Moisei, Gorbachev's great-grandfather.

Gorbachev, Sergei Andreyevich (1909–76), Gorbachev's father.

Gorbacheva, Anastasiya and Aleksandra, aunts of Gorbachev.

Gorbacheva, Maria Panteleyevna, née Gopkalo, Gorbachev's mother.

Gorbacheva, Raisa Maksimovna, née Titorenko (born 1932), Gorbachev's wife.

Gorbacheva, Stepanida, Gorbachev's grandmother.

Gorbunovs, Anatolis (born 1942), Secretary of the Central Committee, Communist Party of Latvia (Ideology) 1985–8,

Chairman of the Latvian Supreme Soviet 1988.

Gostev, Boris Ivanovich (born 1927), USSR Finance Minister 1985–9.

Grachev, Pavel Sergeyevich (born 1948), USSR People's Deputy 1989–91.

Gramov, Marat Vladimirovich (born 1927), journalist and Party official in Stavropol 1962–7, Deputy Head of the Party Central Committee Propaganda Department 1977–83, Chairman of the USSR Sports Committee 1983–9, friend of Gorbachev.

Granin, Daniil Aleksandrovich (born 1919), writer, USSR People's Deputy 1989–91.

Grechko, Marshal Andrei Antonovich (1903–76), USSR Defence Minister 1967–76, full member of the Politburo 1973–6.

Grishin, Viktor Vasilievich (born 1914), Chairman of the All-Union Council of Trades Unions 1956–67, first secretary of Moscow Party gorkom 1967–85, full member of the Politburo 1971–86.

Griskevicius, Petras (1924–87), first secretary of the Central Committee, Communist Party of Lithuania.

Gromyko, Andrei Andreievich (1909–89), USSR Foreign Minister 1957–85, Chairman of the Presidium of the USSR Supreme Soviet (Head of State) 1985–8, full member of the Politburo 1973–88.

Gurenko, Stanislav Ivanovich (born 1936), second secretary

1987–90, first secretary of the Central Committee, Communist Party of Ukraine, and full member of the Politburo 1990–1.

Gusev, Vladimir Kuzmich (born 1932), Deputy Chairman of the USSR Council of Ministers 1986–91.

Honecker, Erich (1912–94), German politician (GDR), Secretary of the SED Central Committee 1958–71, first secretary of SED and Chairman of the National Defence Council 1971–89, Chairman of the GDR Council of State 1976–89.

Hua Guofen (born 1921), Chinese politician, Chairman of the Communist Party Central Committee, Military Committee 1976–81.

Husák, Gustav (1913–91), first secretary of the Czechoslovak Communist Party 1969–87, President of Czechoslovakia 1975–89.

Ilyin, Ivan Aleksandrovich (1882–1954), philosopher.

Iskandarov, Akbarsho Iskandarovich (born 1951), Chairman of the Supreme Soviet of Gorno-Badakhash (Tajikistan), acting Chairman of the Supreme Soviet of Tajikistan 1992.

Ivanov, Nikolai Veniaminovich (born 1952), State lawyer, USSR People's Deputy 1989–91.

Ivashko, Vladimir Antonovich (1932–94), second secretary 1988–9, first secretary of the

Central Committee, Communist Party of Ukraine 1989–90, Chairman of the Ukrainian Supreme Soviet 1990, Deputy General Secretary of the Party Central Committee 1990–1.

Jaruzelski, Wojciech (1923), first secretary of the Polish United Workers' Party, 1981–9, Chairman of the Polish Council of Ministers 1981–5, Chairman of the State 1985–9, President of Poland 1989–90.

Jiang Zemin (born 1926), Chinese politician, member of the Central Committee of the Communist Party of China 1982, General Secretary 1989.

Kachura, Boris Vasilievich (born 1930), first secretary of Donetsk (Ukraine) Party obkom 1976–82.

Kádár, János (1912–89), First/General Secretary of the Hungarian Socialist Workers' Party 1956–88, Prime Minister of Hungary 1956–8 and 1961–8.

Kaganovich, Lazar Moiseyevich (1893–91), First Deputy Chairman of the USSR Council of Ministers 1953–7, full member of the Politburo 1930–57.

Kalinin, Yury Petrovich (1918–79), Deputy RSFSR Minister for Agriculture 1975–9.

Kamenev, Lev Borisovich (1833–1936), Party official, executed.

Kania, Stanislav (born 1927), first secretary of the Central

Committee of the Polish United Workers' Party 1980–1.

Kapitonov, Ivan Vasilievich (born 1915), secretary of the Party Central Committee (personnel matters, light industry) 1965–83, Chairman of the Party Central Revision Commission 1986–8.

Kapitsa, Petr Leonidovich (1894–1984), physicist, Director of the Institute for Physical Issues, member of the USSR Academy of Sciences, awarded Nobel Prize for Physics 1978.

Karamzin, Nikolai Mikhailovich (1766–1826), historian.

Karimov, Islam Abduganievich (born 1938), first secretary of the Central Committee, Communist Party of Uzbekistan 1989–91, full member of the Politburo 1990–1, President of Uzbekistan 1990.

Karlov, Vladimir Alekseyevich (1914–94), Head of Department of Agriculture and Food, Party Central Committee.

Kautsky, Karl Johann (1854–1938), German socialist, politician, journalist.

Kazannik, Aleksei Ivanovich (born 1941), lawyer, USSR People's Deputy 1989–91, Russian Procurator General 1993–4.

Khasbulatov, Ruslan Imranovich (born 1942), First Deputy Chairman of the Russian Supreme Soviet 1990–1, Chairman of the Russian Supreme Soviet 1991–3.

Khmel, Valentina Petrovna (born 1939), USSR People's Deputy 1989–91.

Khmelnitsky, Bogdan (1595–1657), Ukrainian Cossack leader.

Khrennikov, Tikhon Nikolaevich (born 1913), first secretary of the USSR Union of Composers 1948–91.

Khrushchev, Nikita Sergeyevich (1894–1971), first secretary of the Party Central Committee 1953–64, Chairman of the USSR Council of Ministers 1958–64, full member of the Politburo 1939–64.

Kirichenko, Nikolai Karpovich (1923–86), first secretary of the Crimean Party (Ukraine) obkom 1967–77, of the Odessa Party gorkom (Ukraine) 1977–83.

Kirilenko, Andrei Pavlovich (1906–90), secretary of the Party Central Committee 1966–82, full member of the Politburo 1962–82.

Klimov, Elem Germanovich (born 1933), film director, first secretary of the USSR Union of Cinematographic Workers 1986–91.

Klyamkin, Igor Moiseyevich (born 1941), sociologist.

Klyuchevsky, Vasily Osipovich (1849–1911), historian.

Kniga, General Vasily Ivanovich (1882–1961), military leader in the Red Army during the Civil War, later a General of the Soviet Army.

Kolbin, Gennady Vasilievich (born 1927), first secretary of the Central Committee, Communist Party of Kazakhstan, Chairman of the People's Control Committee 1986–9.

Koldunov, Marshal Aleksandr Ivanovich (born 1923), Air Force Chief Commander and Deputy USSR Defence Minister 1978–87, dismissed in connection with the Rust affair.

Kornienko, Georgy Markovich (born 1925), First Deputy Foreign Minister 1977–86.

Kosmodemyanskaya, Zoya Anatolyevna (1923–41), partisan in the Second World War, executed.

Kosolapov, Richard Ivanovich (born 1930), chief editor of *Kommunist* 1976–86, Dean of the Faculty of Philosophy, Moscow University 1986–8.

Kostomarov (Ukrainian Kostomariv), Nikolai Ivanovich (1817–85), Russo-Ukrainian historian, folklore writer.

Kosygin, Aleksei Nikolaevich (1904–80), Chairman of the USSR Council of Ministers 1948–52 and 1964–80, full member of the Politburo 1960–80.

Kovalev, Anatoly Gavriilovich (born 1923), diplomat, First Deputy USSR Foreign Minister 1986–91, received Nobel Peace Prize on behalf of Gorbachev 1990.

Kozlovsky, Ivan Semenovich (1900–93), tenor.

Kraiko, Aleksandr Nikolaevich, USSR People's Deputy 1989–91.

Krasnov, Petr Nikolaevich (1869–1947), White Cossack general, executed.

Kravchuk, Leonid Makarovich (born 1934), secretary, second secretary of the Central

Committee, Communist Party of Ukraine 1989–90, Chairman of the Ukrainian Supreme Soviet 1990–1, President 1991.

Krenz, Egon (born 1937), German politician (GDR), member of the SED Politburo 1983, SED General Secretary and President 1989.

Krestinsky, M. Nikolai (1883–1938), Bolshevik politician, Soviet Ambassador to Germany 1921–30, shot.

Kryuchkov, Vladimir Aleksandrovich (born 1924), Head of Foreign Intelligence, USSR KGB 1974–88, Deputy Chairman 1978–88, Chairman of the USSR KGB 1988–91, full member of the Politburo 1989–90, one of the initiators of the August 1991 coup.

Kudryatsev, Vladimir Nikolaevich (born 1923), Director of the Institute of State and Law 1973–89, Vice President of the USSR/Russian Academy of Sciences 1988.

Kulakov, Fedor Davydovich (1918–78), first secretary of Stavropol Party obkom 1960–4, Secretary of the Party Central Committee (Agriculture) 1965–78, full member of the Politburo 1971–8.

Kulidzhanov, Lev Aleksandrovich (born 1927), first secretary of the USSR Union of Cinematographic Workers 1965–86.

Kunayev, Dinmukhamed Akhmedovich (1912–93), first secretary of the Central Committee, Communist Party of Kazakhstan, 1960–2, 1964–86, full member of the Politburo.

Kuptsov, Valentin Aleksandrovich (born 1937), first secretary of Vologda Party obkom 1985–90, Head of Department and Secretary of the Party Central Committee 1990–1, first secretary of the RSFSR Party Central Committee 1991.

Kurchatov, Igor Vasilievich (1903–60), nuclear physicist, member of the USSR Academy of Sciences.

Kuznetsov, Aleksei Aleksandrovich (1905–49), secretary of the Party Central Committee 1946–9, victim of the Leningrad affair, died in prison.

Landsbergis, Vytautas (born 1932), Chairman of the Lithuanian independence movement Sajudis 1988–93, Chairman of the Lithuanian Parliament 1990–2.

Laptev, Pavel Pavlovich (born 1928), adviser to Andropov and Chernenko.

Larionov, Aleksei Nikolaevich (1907–60), first secretary of the Ryazan Party obkom 1948–60.

Latsis, Otto Rudolfovich (born 1934), journalist, first deputy editor of *Kommunist* 1987–91, and of *Izvestiya* 1993.

Lazurkina, Dora Abramovna (1884–1974), old Bolshevik.

Lebedev, Ivan Kononovich (1907–72), First Deputy Head of the RSFSR Council of Ministers

1955–6, first secretary of the Stavropol Party kraikom 1956–60.

Legasov, Valery Alekseyevich (1936–88), First Deputy Director of the Kurchatov Institute of Nuclear Energy, member of the USSR Academy of Sciences 1972–88, committed suicide.

Lenin, Vladimir Ilyich (1870–1924), founder and leader of the Russian Communist Party (Bolsheviks), Chairman of the Council of People's Commissars 1917–24.

Leonov, Leonid Maksimovich (1899–1994), writer.

Lermontov, Mikhail Yurevich (1814–41), Russian poet.

Ligachev, Yegor Kuzmich (born 1920), first secretary of Tomsk Party gorkom 1965–83, Secretary of the Party Central Committee (personnel, ideology, Party administration 1983, agriculture 1988), full member of the Politburo 1985–90.

Likhachev, Dmitry Sergeyevich (born 1906), specialist in Old Russian literature, Chairman of the Soviet Cultural Fund 1989–92, Chairman of the Russian International Cultural Fund 1991, member of the USSR/Russian Academy of Sciences.

Li Peng (born 1928), Chinese politician, Prime Minister 1987.

Lipitsky, Vasily Semenovich (born 1947), leading member of the Communist democratic movement 1990–1, Chairman of the People's Party of Free Russia 1991.

Lisichkin, Gennady Stepanovich (born 1929), economist.

Lobov, Oleg Ivanovich (born 1937), second secretary of the Central Committee, Communist Party of Armenia 1989–91, First Deputy Chairman of the RSFSR/Russian Council of Ministers 1991, 1993, Secretary of the Russian Security Council 1993.

Logunov, Anatoly Alekseyevich (born 1926), physicist, Rector of Moscow State University, Member of the USSR Academy of Sciences 1977–92.

Logunov, Valentin Andreyevich (born 1938), deputy editor of *Moskovskaya Pravda* 1987–90, USSR People's Deputy 1989–91, chief editor of *Rossiskaya Gazeta* 1990–3.

Lubenchenko, Konstantin Dmitrievich (born 1945), USSR People's Deputy 1989–92, Chairman of the Soviet of the Union, USSR Supreme Soviet.

Lukyanov, Anatoly Ivanovich (born 1930), Head of the Party Central Committee General Department 1985–7, Secretary of the Party Central Committee 1987–8, First Deputy Chairman of the Presidium, USSR Supreme Soviet 1988–90, Chairman of the USSR Supreme Soviet 1990–1, one of the initiators of the August 1991 coup.

Luxemburg, Rosa (1870–1919), socialist politician.

Lysenko, Trofim Denisovich (1898–1976), pseudo-scientist, agrobiology.

Malenkov, Georgy Maksimilianovich (1902–88), Chairman of the USSR Council of Ministers 1953–5, Secretary of the Party Central Committee 1939–53, full member of the Politburo 1946–57.

Malofeyev, Anatoly Aleksandrovich (born 1933), first secretary of the Minsk Party obkom, Belorussia 1985–90, first secretary of the Central Committee, Communist Party of Belorussia 1990–2, full member of the Party Politburo 1990–1.

Maltsev, Terenty Semenovich (born 1895), Soviet model agronomist, honorary member of the All-Union Agricultural Academy.

Manayenkov, Yury Alekseyevich (born 1936), first secretary of the Lipetsk Party obkom 1984–9, Head of Party Central Committee Department (Party work and personnel) 1989–91.

Manyakin, Sergei Iosifovich (born 1923), first secretary of the Omsk Party Committee 1961–87, Chairman of the People's Control Committee 1987–9.

Mao Zedong (1893–1976), Leader of the Communist Party of China and of the People's Republic of China.

Maretskaya, Vera Petrovna (1906–78), actress.

Masherov, Petr Mironovich (1918–80), first secretary of the Central Committee, Communist Party of Belorussia 1965–80.

Maslyukov, Yury Dmitrievich (born 1937), Deputy Chairman 1985–8, First Deputy Chairman of the USSR Council of Ministers and Chairman of the USSR State Planning Committee (Gosplan) 1988–91, full member of the Politburo 1989–91.

Mayakovsky, Vladimir Vladimirovich (1893–1930), Russian poet, committed suicide.

Mazurov, Kirill Trofimovich (1914–89), first secretary of the Central Committee, Communist Party of Belorussia 1956–65, First Deputy Chairman of the USSR Council of Ministers and full member of the Politburo 1965–78, Chairman of the All-Union War and Labour Veterans Council 1986–9.

Medunov, Sergei Fedorovich (born 1915), first secretary of the Krasnodar Party kraikom 1973–82.

Medvedev, Vadim Andreyevich (born 1929), Rector of the Academy of Social Sciences 1978–83, Head of Department of Science and Education 1983–6, Head of Department for Liaison with Communist and Workers' Parties of Socialist Countries, Party Central Committee 1986–8, Secretary of the Party Central Committee 1986–90, full member of the Politburo 1988–90, adviser to Gorbachev and member of the Gorbachev Foundation.

Melnikov, Aleksandr Grigorievich (born 1930), Head of the Construction Department, Party Central Committee 1986–8, first secretary of Kemerovo Party obkom 1988–90.

Melnikov, Vladimir Ivanovich (born 1935), first secretary of the Komi Party obkom 1987–9.

Mendybaev, Marat Samievich (born 1936), first secretary of the Alma Ata Party obkom, second secretary of the Central Committee, Communist Party of Kazakhstan 1988–9.

Merezhkovsky, Dmitri Sergeyevich (1865–1941), writer.

Merkulov, General Vsevolod Nikolaevich (1900–53), People's Commissar for State Security 1943–6, USSR Minister for State Control 1950–3, imprisoned, executed together with Beria.

Meshalkin, Yevgeny Nikolaevich (born 1916), USSR People's Deputy, Novosibirsk 1989–91, member of the USSR Academy of Medical Sciences.

Mesyats, Valentin Karpovich (born 1928), USSR Minister for Agriculture 1976–85.

Migranyan, Andranik Migranovich (born 1949), sociologist.

Mikhailov, Vasily Mikhailovich (1894–1937), Party official, died in prison.

Mikoyan, Anastas Ivanovich (1885–78), First Deputy Chairman of the USSR Council of Ministers 1955–64, Chairman of the USSR Supreme Soviet Presidium (Head of State) 1964–5, full member of the Politburo 1935–66.

Mironenko, Viktor Ivanovich (born 1953), first secretary of the

Komsomol Central Committee, Ukraine, 1983–6, first secretary of the Komsomol Central Committee, USSR from 1988.

Mlynar, Zdenek (born 1930), secretary and member of the Presidium of the Communist Party of Czechoslovakia 1968, signed Charter 77, emigrated to Italy 1977, friend from Gorbachev's student years.

Moiseyev, General Mikhail Alekseyevich (born 1939), Chief of Staff, USSR Armed Forces, First Deputy USSR Defence Minister 1988–91, acting USSR Defence Minister August 1991.

Molotov, Vyacheslav Mikhailovich (1890–1986), USSR Foreign Minister 1939–49, 1953–56, First Deputy Chairman of the USSR Council of Ministers 1953–7, full member of the Politburo 1926–57.

Mordvinov, Nikolai Dmitrievich (1901–66), actor.

Mozhaev, Boris Andreyevich (born 1923), writer.

Murakhovsky, Vsevolod Serafimovich (born 1926), first secretary of the Stavropol Party gorkom 1970–4, first secretary of the Karachai-Cherkess Party obkom 1975–8, of the Stavropol Party kraikom 1978–85, First Deputy Chairman of the USSR Council of Ministers and USSR State Agro-Industrial Committee (Gosagroprom) 1985–9.

Mutalibov, Ayas Niyazievich (born 1938), Chairman of the Council of Ministers, Azerbaijan 1989–90, first secretary of the

Central Committee, Communist Party of Azerbaijan, full member of the Politburo 1990–1, President of Azerbaijan 1991–2.

Nazarbayev, Nursultan Abishevich (born 1940), Chairman of the Council of Ministers, Kazakhstan 1984–9, first secretary of the Central Committee, Communist Party of Kazakhstan 1989–91, full member of the Politburo 1990–1, President of Kazakhstan 1990.

Nenashev, Mikhail Fedorovich (born 1929), chief editor of *Sovetskaya Rossiya* 1978–86, Chairman of the USSR State Committee for Publishing and Book Trade 1986–9, Chairman of the USSR State Committee for Television and Radio 1989–91, USSR Minister for Press and Information 1991.

Nikolsky, Boris Nikolaevich (born 1931), chief editor of *Neva*, Leningrad, USSR People's Deputy 1989–91.

Nikonov, Viktor Petrovich (born 1929), RSFSR Minister for Agriculture 1983–5, Secretary of the Party Central Committee (Agriculture) 1985–9, full member of the Politburo 1987–9.

Nishanov, Rafik Nishanovich (born 1926), Chairman of the Supreme Soviet, Uzbekistan 1986–88, first secretary of the Central Committee, Communist Party of Uzbekistan 1988–9, Chairman of the Council of the Nationalities, USSR Supreme Soviet 1989–91.

Niyazov, Saparmurad Atayevich (born 1940), first secretary of the Central Committee, Communist Party of Turkmenistan 1985–91, full member of the Politburo 1990–1, President of Turkmenistan from 1990.

Novikov, Ignaty Trofimovich (born 1906), Deputy Chairman of the USSR Council of Ministers and Chairman of the USSR State Committee for Construction (Gosstroi) 1962–83.

Novotny, Antonin (1904–75), first secretary of the Communist Party of Czechoslovakia 1953–67, President 1957–68.

Nuriev, Siya Nurievich (born 1915), Deputy Chairman of the USSR Council of Ministers 1973–85.

Nyers, Rezsö (born 1923), Hungarian economist and politician.

Obolensky, Aleksandr Mitrofanovich (born 1943), engineer, USSR People's Deputy 1989–91.

Obukhova, Nadezhda Andreyevna (1886–1961), singer.

Odoevsky, Aleksandr Ivanovich (1802–39), poet, participant in the Decembrist uprising, 1825.

Ordzhonikidze, Grigory (Sergo) Konstantinovich (1886–1937), People's Commissar for Heavy Industry 1932–7, full member of the Politburo 1930–7, committed suicide.

Orlov, Vladimir Pavlovich, Chairman of Central Electoral

Commission, USSR Supreme Soviet.

Orlov, Vladimir Yefimovich (born 1936), USSR Minister of Finance 1991.

Osipyan, Yury Andreyevich (born 1931), Director of the Institute of Solid Substances 1980, adviser to Gorbachev, member of the USSR/Russian Academy of Sciences 1990–1, President of the Russian-German Society 1992.

Palazhchenko, Pavel Ruslanovich, Gorbachev's interpreter.

Pankin, Boris Dmitrievich (born 1931), chief editor of *Komsomolskaya Pravda* 1965–73, Chairman of the All-Union Copyright Agency 1973–82, USSR Ambassador to Sweden 1982–90, to Czechoslovakia, 1990–1, USSR Foreign Minister 1991.

Parada, Petr Stepanovich (died 1937), grandfather of Raisa Gorbacheva, executed.

Pasternak, Boris (1890–1960), poet and writer, awarded Nobel Prize for Literature 1958.

Pastukhov, Boris Nikolaevich (born 1933), First Secretary of the USSR Komsomol 1977–82.

Paton, Boris Yevgenevich (born 1918), Director of the Paton Institute of Electrowelding, Kiev 1953, President of the Ukrainian Academy of Sciences, member of the USSR/Russian Academy of Sciences 1962.

Pavlov, Georgy Sergeyevich (1910–91), Head of Department,

Party Central Committee 1966–83, committed suicide.

Pavlov, Ivan Petrovich (1849–1936), physiologist, member of the Russian Academy of Sciences, awarded Nobel Prize for Medicine 1904.

Pavlov, Valentin Sergeyevich (born 1937), Chairman of the USSR State Committee for Prices 1986–9, USSR Finance Minister 1989–91, USSR Prime Minister 1991, one of the initiators of the August 1991 coup.

Pelshe, Arvid Yanovich (1899–1983), first secretary of the Central Committee, Communist Party of Latvia 1959–66, Chairman of the Party Control Commission, Party Central Committee, full member of the Politburo 1966–83.

Petrakov, Nikolai Yakovlevich (born 1937), Deputy Director of the Central Institute of Economics and Mathematics 1971–90, economic adviser to Gorbachev 1990–1, Director of the Institute on Market Issues, member of the USSR/Russian Academy of Sciences 1991.

Pimen (Sergei Mikhailovich Izvekov) (1910–90), Patriarch (Russian Orthodox Church) of Moscow and all Russia 1971–90.

Pitirim (Konstantin Vladimirovich Nechayev) (born 1926), Metropolitan (Russian Orthodox Church) of Volokolamsk and Yurevsk, Head of the Patriarch Publishing House, Moscow, 1986.

Plekhanov, Georgi Valentinovich

(1857–1918), philosopher, exponent of Marxism.

Plekhanov, Yury Sergeyevich (born 1930), KGB Head of Security for the President and leading politicians.

Podgorny, Nikolai Viktorovich (1903–83), Chairman of the USSR Presidium of the USSR Supreme Soviet 1965–77, first secretary of the Central Committee, Communist Party of Ukraine 1957–63, full member of the Politburo 1960–77.

Polozkov, Ivan Kuzmich (born 1935), first secretary of the Krasnodar Party obkom 1985–90, first secretary of the Central Committee, Communist Party of Russia, full member of the Politburo 1990–1.

Ponomarev, Boris Nikolaevich (born 1905), Secretary of the Party Central Committee (International Affairs) 1961–86, candidate member of Politburo 1972–86.

Popov, Gavriil Kharitonovich (born 1936), Professor of Economics, Moscow State University, 1977–88, chief editor of *Voprosy Ekonomiki* 1988–90, Mayor of Moscow 1990–2.

Preobrazhensky, Yevgeny A. (1866–1937), Bolshevik politician and economist.

Primakov, Yevgeny Maksimovich (born 1929), Director of the Oriental Institute 1977–85, Director of the Institute of World Economy and International Relations 1985–9, Chairman of the Soviet of the Union, USSR

Supreme Soviet, 1989–90, Director of Russian Foreign Intelligence Service 1991, member of the USSR/Russian Academy of Sciences, personal envoy of Gorbachev during the Gulf War 1991.

Prokhanov, Aleksandr Andreyevich (born 1938), writer, journalist, opponent of reforms.

Prokofiev, Yury Anatolyevich (born 1939), first secretary of the Moscow Party gorkom 1989–91, full member of the Politburo 1990–1.

Prunskiene, Kazimiera (born 1943), Chairman of the Lithuanian Council of Ministers 1990–1.

Pugo, Boris Karlovich (1937–91), Chairman of the Latvian KGB 1980–4, Chairman of the Control Commission, Party Central Committee, 1990–1, USSR Minister for Internal Affairs 1990–1, one of the initiators of the August 1991 coup, committed suicide.

Qian Qichen (born 1928), Chinese politician, Foreign Minister 1988.

Rakosi, Matyas (1892–71), General Secretary of the Hungarian Socialist Workers' Party 1945–56.

Rakovsky, Khristian Georgievich (1873–1941), State and Party official, Chairman of the Council of Ministers, Ukraine 1919–23, died in prison.

Rakowski, Mieczyslaw (born

1926), Chairman of the Council of Ministers, Poland 1988–9, first secretary of the Polish United Workers' Party 1989–90.

Rashidov, Sharaf Rashidovich (1917–83), first secretary of the Central Committee, Communist Party of Uzbekistan 1959–83.

Rasputin, Valentin Grigorievich (born 1937), writer, Secretary of the USSR/RSFSR Writers Union 1986–92, USSR People's Deputy 1989–92, member of the Presidential Council 1990–1.

Razumovsky, Georgy Petrovich (born 1936), first secretary of the Krasnodar Party kraikom 1983–5, Secretary of the Party Central Committee (Personnel) 1986–91.

Revenko, Grigory Ivanovich (born 1936), first secretary of the Kiev Party obkom, Ukraine 1985–90, Chief of Staff to Gorbachev 1991, Vice-President of the Gorbachev Foundation 1992.

Roerikh, Svyatoslav Nikolaevich (born 1904), Russian artist, living in India.

Romanov, Grigory Vasilievich (born 1923), first secretary of the Leningrad Party obkom 1970–83, Secretary of the Party Central Committee (Defence Industry) 1983–5, full member of the Politburo 1976–85.

Rubiks, Alfred (born 1935), first secretary of the Central Committee, Communist Party of Latvia, full member of the Politburo 1990–1.

Rudenko, Roman Andreyevich (1907–81), USSR Procurator General 1953–81, judge at the Nuremberg War Crimes Tribunal 1945–6.

Rusakov, Konstantin Viktorovich (born 1909), head of the Department for Liaison with Communist and Workers' Parties in Socialist Countries, Party Central Committee 1968–73 and 1977–86, Secretary of the Party Central Committee 1977–86.

Rutskoi, Aleksandr Vladimirovich (born 1947), Russian Vice President 1991–3.

Ryabov, Yakov Petrovich (born 1928), Secretary of the Party Central Committee 1976–9, First Deputy Chairman of the State Planning Committee (Gosplan) 1979–83.

Rybakov, Anatoly Naumovich (born 1911), writer.

Rykov, Aleksei Ivanovich (1881–1938), Chairman of the RSFSR/USSR Council of Ministers 1924–30, full member of the Politburo 1919–29, executed.

Ryzhkov, Nikolai Ivanovich (born 1929), Secretary and Head of the Industry Department, Party Central Committee, 1982–5, Chairman of the USSR Council of Ministers 1985–91, full member of the Politburo from 1985.

Ryzhov, Yury Alekseyevich (born 1930), Vice-chancellor of the Moscow Aviation Institute, USSR People's Deputy, Russian Ambassador to France 1991.

Sakharov, Andrei Dmitrievich (1921–89), physicist, USSR

People's Deputy 1989, member of
the USSR Academy of Sciences,
human rights activist, awarded
Nobel Peace Prize 1975.
Savinkin, Nikolai Ivanovich (born
1913), Head of Administration
Department, Party Central
Committee 1968–87.
Savisaar, Edgar (born 1950),
founder and Chairman of the
Estonian Popular Front and
Chairman of the State Planning
Committee, Estonian SSR
1989–90, Prime Minister 1990–2.
Sechenov, Ivan Mikhailovich
(1829–1905), Russian scientist.
Semenova, Galina Vladimirovna
(born 1937), chief editor of
Krestyanka 1981–90, Secretary of
the Party Central Committee and
full member of the Politburo
1990–1.
Serebryakov, Leonid P.
(1890–1937), Communist,
politician, leader of the opposition
1923–9, expelled from the Party
1927–30, executed.
Shakhnazarov, Georgy
Khozroevich (born 1924), member
of the Gorbachev Foundation,
adviser to Gorbachev from 1988,
USSR People's Deputy from 1989.
Shaposhnikov, Marshal Yevgeny
Ivanovich (born 1942),
Commander-in-Chief of the USSR
Air Force and Deputy Defence
Minister 1990–1, Defence Minister
1991, Commander-in-Chief of the
Strategic First Strike Forces
1991–3.
Sharapov, Viktor Vasilievich (born
1931), adviser to Andropov,

Chernenko and Gorbachev
1982–8, USSR Ambassador to
Bulgaria 1988–92.
Shatalin, Stanislav Sergeyevich
(born 1934), economist, member
of the USSR Presidential Council,
member of the USSR/Russian
Academy of Sciences 1990–1.
Shchelokov, Nikolai Anisimovich
(born 1910), USSR Minister for
Internal Affairs 1968–82.
Shcherbakov, Vladimir Ivanovich
(born 1949), Chairman of the
State Committee for Labour and
Social Questions 1989–91, Deputy
and First Deputy Chairman of the
USSR Council of Ministers and
Minister of Economics 1991.
Shcherbina, Boris Yevdokimovich
(born 1919), first secretary of the
Tyumen Party obkom 1961–73,
USSR Minister for the Oil and
Gas Construction Industry
1973–84, Deputy Chairman of the
USSR Council of Ministers
1984–9.
Shcherbitsky, Vladimir Vasilievich
(1918–90), Chairman of the
Ukrainian Council of Ministers
1961–63, 1965–72, first secretary
of the Central Committee,
Communist Party of Ukraine
1972–89, full member of the
Politburo 1971–89.
Shelepin, Aleksandr Nikolaevich
(1918–94), Chairman of the USSR
KGB 1958–61, Secretary of the
Party Central Committee 1961–7,
Chairman of the All-Union
Central Council of Trades Unions
1967–75, full member of the
Politburo 1964–75.

Shelest, Petr Yefimovich (born 1908), first secretary of the Central Committee, Communist Party of Ukraine 1963–72, full member of the Politburo 1964–73.

Shenin, Oleg (born 1937), first secretary of the Krasnoyarsk Party kraikom 1987–90, Secretary of the Party Central Committee, full member of the Politburo 1990–91, one of the initiators of the August 1991 coup.

Shevardnadze, Eduard Ambrosievich (born 1928), first secretary of the Central Committee, Communist Party of Georgia 1972–85, USSR Foreign Minister 1985–90, full member of the Politburo 1985–90, Head of State, Georgia from 1992.

Shibayev, Aleksei Ivanovich (born 1915), first secretary of the Saratov Party obkom 1959–76, Chairman of the USSR Central Council of Trades Unions 1976–82.

Shmelev, Nikolai Petrovich (born 1936), economist, Head of Department, USA and Canada Institute 1983–92.

Sholokhov, Mikhail Aleksandrovich (1905–84), writer, awarded Nobel Prize for Literature 1965.

Shumilin, Boris Tikhonovich, Deputy USSR Minister for Internal Affairs 1966–83.

Shushkevich, Stanislav Stanislavovich (born 1934), Chairman of the Belarus Supreme Soviet 1991–4.

Silayev, Ivan Stepanovich (born 1930), USSR Minister of Civil Aviation 1981–5, Deputy Chairman of the USSR Council of Ministers 1985–90, Chairman of the RSFSR Council of Ministers 1990–1.

Sitaryan, Stepan Aramaisovich (born 1930), Deputy 1983–6, First Deputy Chairman of the USSR Council of Ministers and permanent representative to Comecon 1989–91, Director of the Institute for Foreign Economic Relations, member of the USSR/Russian Academy of Sciences 1991.

Slavsky, Yefim Pavlovich (1898–1991), USSR Minister of Medium Machine Building 1957–86.

Slyunkov, Nikolai Nikitovich (born 1929), Deputy Chairman of the USSR State Planning Committee (Gosplan) 1974–83, First Secretary of the Central Committee, Communist Party of Belorussia, Secretary of the Party Central Committee, (Economic Administration, Comecon) 1983–7, full member of the Politburo 1987–91.

Smirnov, Leonid Vasilievich (born 1916), Deputy Chairman of the USSR Council of Ministers 1963–85.

Smolentsev, Yevgeny Alekseyevich (born 1923), Deputy Chairman 1977–87, Chairman of the USSR Supreme Court 1989–91.

Snieckus, Antanas (1903–74), first secretary of the Central

Committee, Communist Party of Lithuania 1940–74.

Sobchak, Anatoly Aleksandrovich (born 1937), USSR People's Deputy 1989–91, Mayor of Leningrad/St Petersburg 1990.

Sokolov, Yefrem Yevseyevich (born 1926), first secretary of the Central Committee, Communist Party of Belorussia 1987–90.

Solomentsev, Mikhail Sergeyevich (born 1913), Chairman of the RSFSR Council of Ministers 1971–83, Chairman of the Party Control Committee 1983–8, full member of the Politburo 1983–8.

Soloviev, Vladimir Sergeyevich (1853–1900), philosopher.

Soloviev, Yury Filipovich (born 1925), first secretary of the Leningrad Party obkom 1985–9.

Soloviev-Sedoi, Vasily Pavlovich (1907–79), composer.

Solzhenitsyn, Aleksandr Isaevich (born 1918), writer, awarded Nobel Prize for Literature 1970.

Songaila, Ringaudas-Bronislavas (born 1929), Chairman of the Council of Ministers 1981–5, of the Supreme Soviet of Lithuania 1985–7, first secretary of the Central Committee, Communist Party of Lithuania 1987–8.

Stalin, Iosef Vissarionovich (1879–1953), Party General Secretary 1922–53, Chairman of the USSR Council of Ministers 1941–53, full member of the Politburo 1919–53.

Stankevich, Sergei Borisovich (born 1954), USSR People's Deputy 1989–91, First Deputy Chairman of the Moscow City Council 1990–2.

Starodubtsev, Vasily Aleksandrovich (born 1931), Chairman of the All-Russia Kolkhoz-Council 1986–91, USSR Farmers' Union 1990–1, one of the initiators of the August 1991 coup.

Starovoitova, Galina Vasilievna (born 1946), USSR People's Deputy 1989–91, adviser to Yeltsin on inter-ethnic relations 1991–2.

Stolyarov, Nikolai Sergeyevich (born 1947), Chairman of the RCP Central Committee 1990–1, Deputy Chairman of the KGB, Russia 1991.

Stroyev, Yegor Semenovich (born 1937), first secretary of the Orlov Party obkom 1985–9, Secretary (Agriculture) of the Party Central Committee 1989–91, full member of the Politburo 1990–1.

Sukharev, Aleksandr Iakovlevich (born 1923), First Deputy 1988, USSR Procurator General 1989–90.

Sukhov, Leonid Ivanovich (born 1940), USSR People's Deputy 1989–91.

Suslov, Mikhail Andreyevich (1902–82), first secretary of the Stavropol Party kraikom 1939–44, secretary of the Party Central Committee 1947–82, full member of the Politburo 1952–3, 1955–82.

Sverdlov, Yakov Mikhailovich (1885–1919), Chairman of the All-Russia Central Executive Committee 1917–19.

Talyzin, Nikolai Vladimirovich (born 1929), Deputy Chairman of the USSR Council of Ministers and USSR representative to Comecon 1980–5, 1988–9 First Deputy Chairman of the USSR Council of Ministers and Chairman of the USSR State Planning Committee (Gosplan) 1985–8.

Tereshchenko, Nikolai Dmitrievich (1930–89), chairman of a collective farm, candidate member of the Party Central Committee.

Tikhonov, Nikolai Aleksandrovich (born 1905), Chairman of the USSR Council of Ministers 1980–5, full member of the Politburo 1979–85.

Tikhonov, Vladimir Aleksandrovich (born 1927), economist, USSR People's Deputy, Chairman of the Union of Cooperatives 1989–91, member of the Russian Agricultural Academy.

Timiryazev, Kliment Arkadievich (1843–1920), scientist, plant physiologist.

Titorenko, Aleksandra Petrovna (born 1913), mother of Raisa Gorbacheva.

Titorenko, Maksim Andreyevich (1907–86), father of Raisa Gorbacheva.

Tolpezhnikov, Vilen Fedorovich (born 1928), doctor, USSR People's Deputy, Riga 1989–91.

Tomsky (Yefremov), Mikhail Pavlovich (1880–1936), trade union official in the 1920s, full member of the Politburo 1922–9, committed suicide.

Trapeznikov, Sergei Pavlovich (1912–84), Head of the Department of Science and Education, Party Central Committee 1965–83.

Travkin, Nikolai Ilyich (born 1947), member of the CPSU, Deputy USSR Construction Minister 1988–9, USSR People's Deputy 1989–91, co-founder of the Democratic Party of Russia 1990, its Chairman 1992–3, Russian People's Deputy 1990–3.

Trotsky (Bronstein), Lev Davidovich (1879–1940), organizer of 1917 October Revolution, USSR People's Commissar for War 1918–25, lost all posts 1925, deported to Turkey, later emigrated to Mexico, murdered.

Ulbricht, Walter (1893–1973), German politician (GDR), member of the Politburo of the Communist Party of Germany 1929, co-founder of the GDR, First Secretary of the SED 1953–71, at the same time Chairman of the Council of State 1960–73, Chairman, National Security Council 1963–72.

Ulyanov, Mikhail Aleksandrovich (born 1927), actor, Chairman of the Russian Union of Theatre Workers 1986, Artistic Director of the Vakhtangov Theatre 1987.

Umalatova, Sazhi Saindinovna (born 1953), member of the USSR Supreme Soviet 1989–91.

Uoka, Kazemiras (born 1951), Chairman of the Lithuanian Union of Workers, and deputy of the USSR Supreme Soviet.

Ustinov, Marshal Dmitry Fedorovich (1908–84), USSR Defence Minister 1976–84, full member of the Politburo 1976–84.

Varennikov, General Valentin Ivanovich (born 1923), Commander-in-chief of the USSR Border Troops, Deputy USSR Defence Minister 1989–91, one of the initiators of the August 1991 coup.

Vedernikov, Gennady Georgievich (born 1937), first secretary of the Chelyabinsk Party obkom 1984–6, Deputy Chairman of the USSR Council of Ministers 1986–91.

Velikhov, Yevgeny Pavlovich (born 1935), nuclear scientist, Vice President, USSR/Russia Academy of Sciences, Director of the Kurchatov Institute of Nuclear Energy 1988–92, adviser to Gorbachev.

Vezirov, Abdul Rahman (born 1930), Komsomol and Party official, Diplomatic Service 1976–88, first secretary of the Central Committee, Communist Party of Azerbaijan 1988–90.

Virgansky, Anatoly (born 1957), Gorbachev's son-in-law.

Virganskaya, Anastasiya (born 1987), Gorbachev's granddaughter.

Virganskaya, Irina (born 1957), Gorbachev's daughter.

Virganskaya, Kseniya (born 1980), Gorbachev's granddaughter.

Visbor, Yury Iosifovich (1934–84), singer.

Vlasov, Aleksandr Vladimirovich (born 1932), first secretary of the Rostov Party obkom 1984–6, USSR Minister for Internal Affairs 1986–8.

Volksky, Arkady Ivanovich (born 1932), adviser to Andropov, Chernenko and Gorbachev 1983–5, Head of the Department of Machine Building, Party Central Committee 1985–8, Presidential representative, Nagorno-Karabakh 1988–90, Chairman of the USSR Science and Industry Union 1988–90, President of the Union of Industrialists and Entrepreneurs of Russia 1992, Chairman of the Civic Union Party 1993.

Voronin, Lev Alekseyevich (born 1928), First Deputy Chairman of the USSR State Planning Committee (Gosplan) 1980–5, Deputy Chairman of the USSR Council of Ministers, Chairman of the USSR State Committee for Supply (Gosnab) 1985–91.

Vorontsov, Yuly Mikhailovich (born 1929), USSR Ambassador to France 1983–6, First Deputy USSR Foreign Minister 1986–90, Permanent Representative of the USSR at UN 1990–1, Russian Ambassador to the USA from 1994.

Voroshilov, Marshal Kliment Yefremovich (1881–1969),

964

Chairman of the Presidium of the USSR Supreme Soviet (Head of State) 1953–60, full member of the Politburo 1926–60.

Vorotnikov, Vitaly Ivanovich (born 1926), Chairman of the RSFSR Council of Ministers 1983–8, Chairman of the Presidium of the RSFSR Supreme Soviet, full member of the Politburo 1983–90.

Voznesensky, Nikolai Alekseyevich (1903–50), Chairman of the USSR State Planning Committee (Gosplan) 1937–49, full member of the Politburo 1947–9, executed.

Vysotsky, Vladimir Semenovich (1938–80), singer and actor.

Walesa, Lech (born 1943), Polish politician, leader of Solidarity 1980–90, awarded Nobel Peace Prize 1983, President 1990–5.

Yakovlev, Aleksandr Nikolaevich (born 1923), USSR Ambassador to Canada 1973–83, Director of the Institute for World Economy and International Relations of the USSR Academy of Sciences 1983–5, secretary of the Party Central Committee (Propaganda, culture, foreign policy) 1986–90, full member of the Politburo 1987–90, adviser to Gorbachev 1990–91.

Yakovlev, Yegor Vladimirovich (born 1930), chief editor of *Moskovskiye Novosti* 1986–91, USSR People's Deputy 1989–91, Chairman of the USSR/Russian

Television and Radio Committee 1991–2.

Yanayev, Gennady Ivanovich (born 1937), Chairman of the USSR Committee for Youth Organizations 1968–80, Secretary 1986–9, Deputy Chairman 1989–90, Chairman of the All-Union Central Council of Trades Unions 1989–90, Secretary of the Party Central Committee, full member of the Politburo 1990–1, USSR Vice President 1990–1, one of the initiators of the August 1991 coup.

Yanshin, Mikhail Mikhailovich (1902–76), actor and director.

Yaroslavsky, Yemelyan Mikhailovich (1878–1943), Party official.

Yavlinsky, Grigory Aleksandrovich (born 1952), economist, Deputy Chairman of the RSFSR Council of Ministers 1990, Chairman of the Centre for Economic and Political Research (Epitsentr) 1991, co-leader of the YABLOKO party.

Yazov, Marshal Dmitry Timofeyevich (born 1923), Commander of the Central Asian Military District 1980–4, Far East Military District 1984–6, USSR Defence Minister 1987–91, one of the initiators of the August 1991 coup.

Yefremov, Leonid Nikolaevich (born 1912), first secretary of the Stavropol Party kraikom 1964–70, First Deputy Chairman of the USSR State Committee on Science and Technology 1970–88.

Yeltsin, Boris Nikolaevich (born 1931), first secretary of the Sverdlovsk (now Ekaterinburg) Party obkom 1976–85, Head of the Construction Department of the Party Central Committee, Secretary of the Party Central Committee 1985, first secretary of the Moscow Party gorkom 1985–7, First Deputy Chairman of the USSR State Committee for Construction (Gosstroi) 1987–9, Chairman of the RSFSR Supreme Soviet 1990, RSFSR/Russian President from 1991.

Yezhevsky, Aleksandr Aleksandrovich (born 1915), USSR Minister for Agricultural Machinery 1980–8.

Yuzhkov, Serafim Vladimirovich (1888–1952), Professor at Moscow State University, lawyer, specialist in state law.

Zaikov, Lev Nikolaevich (born 1923), first secretary of the Leningrad Party obkom 1983–5, Secretary of the Party Central Committee (Military-industrial complex) 1985–91, first secretary of the Moscow Party gorkom 1987–9, full member of the Politburo 1986–91.

Zamyatin, Yevgeny Ivanovich (1884–1937), Russian writer.

Zaslavskaya, Tatyana Ivanovna (born 1927), sociologist, Director of the All-Union Centre for Public Opinion Research 1988–92, USSR People's Deputy 1989–91.

Zhao Ziyang (born 1918), Chinese politician, Prime Minister 1980–8, General Secretary of the Communist Party of China 1987–9.

Zhirinovsky, Vladimir Volfovich (born 1946), leader of the Liberal Democratic Party of Russia from 1990, Presidential candidate 1991 and 1996.

Zhivkov, Todor (born 1911), First/General Secretary of the Communist Party of Bulgaria 1954–89, Chairman of the Council of Ministers 1962–71, Head of State 1971–89.

Zhu Rongji (born 1928), Chinese politician, elected Mayor of Shanghai 1988.

Zimyanin, Mikhail Vasilievich (born 1914), chief editor of *Pravda* 1965–76, Chairman of the USSR Union of Journalists 1966–76, secretary of the Party Central Committee 1976–87.

Zverev, Arseny Grigorievich (1900–69), USSR Finance Minister 1938–60.

Zyuganov, Gennady Andreyevich (born 1944), Secretary and full member of the RCP Politburo 1990–1, leader of the communist-nationalist movement 1992, Head of the Communist Party of the Russian Federation from 1993.

INDEX

coup of August 1991 xxi, 30, 706, 708,
749, 808–31, 839, 842–3
aftermath of 852–67, 875, 881
investigation of participators 879–80
Crimea 7, 193, 251, 314, 338, 429–30,
534, 812
Yuzhny Sanatorium 814, 818
see also Foros
cruise missiles 661
CSCE *see* Conference on Security and
Co-operation in Europe
Cuba 597, 609, 642, 661–2, 699
crisis (1962) 89
currency 508
reform (1961) 90
Cyril and Methodius, Sts 656–7
Czech Republic 894
Czechoslovakia 42, 126, 129, 196,
285, 556, 594, 599, 611, 619,
622–4, 626, 674, 804
Academy of Sciences, State and Law
Institute 103
Communist Party 104, 121, 127,
623, 626
Federal Assembly 623
occupation of 104–5

Davos 685
Decembrists 24–5
decentralization of functions 476,
758–9
Declaration of Independence of Russia
402, 420
Declaration of Sovereignty 447
Declaration on Soviet-Polish Co-
operation in Ideology, Science
and Culture 620
Decree on Power 385
defence 173–4, 277
Defence, Ministry of xvii, xviii, xx,
143, 230, 300, 301, 339, 507,
521, 522, 839
de Klerk, F. W. 801
Delhi
declaration 66, 542–4, 566
Jawaharlal Nehru museum 547

tomb of Gandhi 547
Delors, Jacques 707, 790, 792
Dementei, Nikolai Ivanovich 746, 825
Demichev, Petr Milovich 6, 145, 344,
345
De Mita, Ciriaco 565
Democratic Congress bloc 755, 762
Democratic Party 830
democratic reform 321, 897
Democratic Russia *see* DemRossiya;
Inter-Regional Deputies Group
democratization 253, 295, 322, 323,
331, 365, 476, 531, 624–5, 733,
758, 808, 891
DemRossiya (Democratic Russia) 351,
371, 447, 501, 750, 755, 757,
762, 772–3, 830, 841–2
see also Inter-Regional Deputies
Group
Deng Xiaoping 281, 631–3, 635
Denisenko, Bella Anatolievna 399
Denisov, Anatoly Alekseyevich 830
Denmark 557
Denmirtchyan, Karen Seropovich 432
Diderot, Denis 652
dissidents 196, 381, 452
Dmitriev, Sergei Afanasievich 75
Dnepropetrovsk 160, 225
Dnieper, River 244, 246
operation 41
Dobezea, N. T. 415
Dobrynin, Anatoly Fedorovich 208,
231, 306, 345, 536, 592, 598,
'Doctors' Plot' 57, 60
Dolgikh, Vladimir Ivanovich 19, 186,
187, 201, 227, 243, 282, 344, 432
domostroi 355
Don, River, rebellion 27
Donbass (Donetsk Coal Basin) 172,
400
Donetsk 14
Dortmund, Hoesch steelworks 673
Dresden 126
dual power system xx
Dubcek, Alexander 127–9, 623–4
Duberstein, Kenneth Marc 598

INDEX

HIS HOLINESS
John Paul II and the Hidden History of our Time
by Carl Bernstein and Marco Politi

From two of the world's greatest investigative journalists comes the fascinating story of the man who changed our century – Pope John Paul II.

With meticulous reporting skills and narrative excitement, Carl Bernstein and Marco Politi provide an astonishing look at Pope John Paul II and show him to be one of the foremost political figures of our time. Having gained unprecedented access to rare sources of information in Rome, Washington and Moscow, including once top-secret Soviet files and Politburo minutes, they take us inside the Soviet hierarchy to see, for the first time, key figures such as Brezhnev and Andropov heatedly discussing how to handle the Pope, whom they considered a major threat to their survival. Indeed, John Paul would come to dominate the political world, ultimately fashioning an alliance with Reagan to reverse Yalta and hasten the demise of Communism. And as it examines the controversial figure who has sent the Catholic Church on a course that has both divided and uplifted its billion members, *His Holiness* explains how an iron will and strong convictions have made John Paul II the great moral leader of our time.

'If you never read another book about the first Slav pope, then read Carl Bernstein and Marco Politi's for its lightness of touch, its human insights, its balance and – as might be expected from Bernstein's Watergate credentials – its revelations' *New Statesman*

A Bantam Paperback
0 553 40811 9

CHE GUEVARA: A REVOLUTIONARY LIFE
by Jon Lee Anderson

'Masterly and absorbing' Frank McLynn, *Sunday Times*

Che Guevara: A Revolutionary Life shuttles between the revolutionary capitals of Havana and Algiers to the battlegrounds of Bolivia and the Congo; from the halls of power in Moscow and Washington to the exile havens of Miami, Mexico and Guatemala, in a gripping tale of revolution, international intrigue and covert operations. It has an epic sweep as it evokes an era of tumultuous change, of a worldwide superpower struggle between the United States and the Soviet Union, manifesting itself in numerous 'little wars' across the globe.

Jon Lee Anderson has been given unprecedented access to the Cuban Government's archives and has had total co-operation from Che's widow, Aleida March, who has never previously spoken for publication about her late husband. He has obtained hitherto unpublished documents, including several of Che's personal diaries and, in the course of his research, broke open a twenty-eight-year-old mystery – the whereabouts of Che's body in Bolivia. There is no doubt that this monumental work will stand as the definitive portrait of one of the twentieth century's most fascinating, yet largely unexplored, historical figures.

'Absorbing and convincing . . . [Anderson] has written an indispensable work of contemporary history' Robin Blackburn, *Guardian*

A Bantam Paperback
0 553 40664 7

A SELECTION OF NON-FICTION TITLES AVAILABLE FROM BANTAM AND CORGI BOOKS

40664 7	CHE GUEVARA	Jon Lee Anderson	£12.99
40811 9	HIS HOLINESS	Carl Bernstein and Marco Politi	£7.99
50650 1	BOUND FEET AND WESTERN DRESS		
		Pang-Mei Natasha Chang	£6.99
40773 2	25 YEARS OF TERROR	Martin Dillon	£5.99
14239 5	MY FEUDAL LORD	Tehmina Durrani	£5.99
99482 0	MILLENNIUM	Felipe Fernandez-Armesto	£14.99
40929 8	THE KENNEDY WOMEN	Lawrence Leamer	£7.99
13953 X	SOME OTHER RAINBOW	John McCarthy and Jill Morrell	£5.99
03980 7	FIT TO GOVERN	Leo McKinstry	£12.99
40936 0	THE HIDDEN CHILDREN	Jane Marks	£5.99
40814 3	THE HAREM WITHIN	Fatima Mernissi	£5.99
14052 X	LORDS OF THE RIM	Sterling Seagrave	£6.99
14108 9	THE SOONG DYNASTY	Sterling Seagrave	£7.99
40551 9	IT DOESN'T TAKE A HERO	General Norman Schwarzkopf	£5.99
50387 1	TONY BLAIR: THE MODERNISER		
		Jon Sopel	£5.99
40886 0	THE RAINBOW PEOPLE OF GOD		
		Archbishop Desmond Tutu	£5.99
14114 3	THE POPE'S ARMADA	Gordon Urquhart	£6.99
50554 9	RED CHINA BLUES	Jan Wong	£7.99